THE MARITAL SACRAMENT

MARRIAGE IN THE CATHOLIC CHURCH

THE MARITAL SACRAMENT

by
Theodore Mackin, S.J.

PAULIST PRESS
New York/Mahwah, N.J.

Library of Congress Cataloging-in-Publication Data

Mackin, Theodore.
    The marital sacrament / by Theodore Mackin.
      p. cm.—(Marriage in the Catholic Church)
    Bibliography: p.
    Includes index.
    ISBN 0-8091-3055-6 : $22.95 (est.)
    1. Marriage—Religious aspects—Catholic Church—History.
    2. Catholic Church—Doctrines—History. I. Title. II. Series:
Mackin, Theodore. Marriage in the Catholic Church.
BX2250.M226 1989
234′.165′09—dc19   89-3093
                                                CIP

Published by Paulist Press
997 Macarthur Boulevard
Mahwah, N.J. 07430

Printed and bound in the United States of America

Contents

v

the Sacrament, 436. Summary, 442. Notes, 444. Bibliography, 448.

Acknowledgments

In this volume passages are quoted from the following titles with the permission of their publishers:

The passages quoted from the Old Testament are taken from *The New American Bible*, copyright © 1970 by the Confraternity of Christian Doctrine. They are used by the permission of the copyright owner. All rights reserved.

From *The Authorized Daily Prayer Book*, J. Hertz, editor, copyright © 1946 with the permission of Bloch Publishing Company. From *The Theology of Marriage*, by Joseph Kerns, copyright © 1964; from *Marriage: Human Reality and Saving Mystery*, by Edward Schillebeeckx, copyright © 1965; from *Christian Marriage*, Revised Edition, by George H. Joyce, copyright © 1948—all used with the permission of Sheed and Ward, 115 East Armour Blvd., Kansas City, Mo. From *Alexandrian Christianity*, edited by John Ernest Oulton and Henry Chadwick (Volume II: The Library of Christian Classics). Published in the U.S.A. in MCMLIV. Reprinted and used by permission of Westminster Press. From *Matrimony*, selected and arranged by the Benedictine Monks of Solesmes and translated by Michael J. Byrnes, copyright © 1963, with the permission of the Daughters of St.Paul. From *Nuptial Blessing: A Study of Christian Marriages Rites*, by Kenneth Stevenson, copyright © 1983, published by the Society for Promoting Christian Knowledge. From *Luther's Works*, volume 1, pages 68, 69, 115, 116, 117, 118, copyright © 1958; Volume 28, pages 18, 19, copyright © 1973; Volume 21, pages 86, 87, copyright © 1956; Volume 36, pages 92, 93, copyright © 1959—all published by Concordia Publishing House. Used by permission. From *Luther's Works*, Volume 44, copyright © 1966; from the Library of Christian Classics, Volume 19, *Melancthon and Bucer*, copyright © 1969, and from Volume 21, *Institutes of the Christian Religion*, copyright © 1960, with the permission of Fortress Press. From *Two Treatises of Government*, by John Locke, © 1967, reprinted with the permission of Cambridge University Press. From *Lectures on Ethics* by Immanuel Kant, translated by Louis Infield, copyright © 1930, with the permission of Methuen and Company. From *The Classics of International Law*, Volume 2, edited by James Scott Brown: *De Jure Naturae et*

Gentium, by Samuel von Pufendorf, copyright © 1964, with the permission of Oceana Publications, Inc. From *The Teachings of Pope John XXIII,* edited by Michael Chinigo, copyright © 1967 by Grosset and Dunlap, Inc. and George G. Harrap Co., Ltd. Used by permission of Grosset and Dunlap, Inc. From *On the Family: Apostolic Exhortation Familiaris Consortio,* by Pope John Paul II, copyright © 1982, with the permission of the United States Catholic Conference. From *The 1980 Synod of Bishops, "On the Role of the Family"* (*Bibliotheca Ephemeridum Theologicarum Lovaniensium* LXIV), by J. Grootaers and J. Selling, copyright © 1983, with the permission of Leuven University Press (Uitgeverij Peeters, Leuven).

to my brothers, Thomas and Edward

FOREWORD

This third volume of the trilogy, *Marriage in the Catholic Church,* is a true sibling of the first two volumes.[1] Like them it examines a history—this time the history of the Roman Catholic authorities' and theologians' teaching about the sacrament in marriage.

That last phrase, ". . . about the sacrament in marriage," should not skip past the reading eye too quickly. Its distance from the familiar formulas, for example from Jacques Leclercq's *Marriage: A Great Sacrament,*[2] suggests a difference in the way itself of understanding the sacrament in marriage. The plan is for this difference to emerge gradually and at first implicitly from chapter to chapter, then to earn explicit attention in the critical reflections making up Chapter 14.

In favoring the formulation *The Marital Sacrament* over, for example, *The Sacrament of Marriage,* I have followed St. Augustine's methodologic lead. He did not say forthrightly that marriage is a sacrament, nor even that Christian marriages are sacraments of the new law of Christ. He said that in all marriages there is a *sacramentum.* He spent many paragraphs trying to locate and to define this *sacramentum* in marriages, a task he found the more difficult because he knew that in Christian marriages it is somewhat the same as in other marriages but also somewhat different. Chapter 6 of this volume examines his effort to find and define it. There the reader may agree or not with my own judgment that Augustine never made up his mind about the definition and location, despite his conviction that it exists especially in Christian marriages—somewhere. Understanding the reasons for his final indecision will help to understand also that there was no escaping a minor struggle in selecting this volume's title.

The struggle went on despite full awareness that since the thirteenth century the dominant Catholic opinion has been that in the marriages of the baptized it is the human marital relationship itself that is the sacrament. This is also the common teaching of the Catholic Church's *magisterium.* A conclusion that the *magisterium* and most theologians have since the late seventeenth century drawn from this is that the human relationship and the sacrament, although not identical, are nevertheless inseparable. Therefore two baptized Christians can be joined only in a

1

sacramental marriage. They have not the option of a merely natural marriage even if their Christian faith is inert and their religious conduct non-existent. It is not that a non-sacramental marriage is forbidden them, but that it is impossible for them. (This is one of several points of Catholic teaching that will get critical review in this volume.)

It may seem that this study gives needlessly long and detailed attention to marriage matters that are peripheral to the sacrament. Such are, for example, the nature of marriage itself, the question of the indissolubility of marriages, and the traditional Catholic judgment on the moral character of sexual intercourse. Whether the time spent discussing these matters is excessive is a matter of judgment. But one cannot examine the Catholic teaching about the marital sacrament in the way the sacrament actually entered this teaching unless one is true to its gradual and developmental entry. No one in the Church wrote a self-contained treatise on the sacrament until Hugh of St. Victor did so at Paris in the middle of the twelfth century. Until then and for centuries afterward authorities, theologians and canonists probed the sacrament within searches and disputes about just such other marriage matters as those mentioned above. Hugh himself first addressed it in an essay, *On the Virginity of the Blessed Virgin Mary,*[3] in which he intended to demonstrate that Mary the mother of Jesus was truly married despite remaining a virgin. What is more, if one takes as a premise the common Catholic teaching already noted, that in the marriages of the baptized it is the human relationship that is the sacrament, one clearly can know little about the sacrament until one finds out the nature of the relationship. Anyone who has read the history of the sometimes bitter argument in the fourth session of the Second Vatican Council, when the bishops were formulating their statement about marriage, knows how debatable is the understanding of this nature. Like centuries of bishops before them, those at Vatican II as much decided its nature as they found it out. In doing so they decided in great measure the nature of the marital sacrament itself, despite paradoxically saying an irreducible minimum about it. Obviously one must study their determination of marriage the human relationship if one is to understand the Catholic theology of the sacrament as it has developed since that council.

As for pages spent reviewing the Catholic teachers' assessment of sexual intercourse's moral character, these are demanded by the centuries-long exclusion of Christian marriage from the number of the Church's sacraments. It is beyond denying that one of the main reasons for this exclusion was that sexual intercourse, the conduct specifically characteristic of marriage, was kept in quarantine. It was kept there because it was deemed infected with sinful concupiscence inherited from the disobedience of the first man and woman in the garden of Eden. The reconciliation of two assumed facts seemed for centuries impossible. How can an act which always climaxes in libidinous and therefore sinful pleasure have a place in a grace-giving sign of a sacred reality, which a sacrament must be?

To ignore the history of the Catholic teachers' ever-so-slow relinquishing of their fear and suspicion of sexuality would be to ignore the history of Christian marriage's release to enter the Christian sacramental life.

The review, in Chapter 10, of Catholic theology's demise into nominalism and then skepticism in the fourteenth and fifteenth centuries is needed if we are to account in part for the Protestant reformers' rejection of the marital sacrament. It is needed to account also for the unconcern with which the Catholic theology of the sacrament after the Council of Trent became mainly the theology of a juridical category. When theologians fail to see marriage as an existential relationship of persons, which is the province of both metaphysics and psychology, the temptation to treat it as such a category can prove irresistible. It did so prove.

Like its two predecessors, this volume is intended not for the expert specialists but for intelligent, curious but uninformed non-specialists. My hope is that their intelligence and curiosity will sustain them through the intricate reasoning of such theologians as John Duns Scotus in the fourteenth century, Robert Bellarmine at the end of the sixteenth, and Edward Schillebeeckx and Karl Rahner in our own century.

At this time in Catholic history, when dissent is so sensitive an issue in the Church, a word about my own dissent, especially as it is registered in the final chapter of this volume, is in order. To state my position succinctly: I disagree that the Church's teachers have argued conclusively in support of the doctrine of the indissolubility of all Christian marriages and in support of the doctrine of the inseparability of human relationship and sacrament in the marriages of all the baptized. At the same time, as I hope my attempt in Chapter 14 shows, I hold that both inseparability and indissolubility are attainable by Christian spouses.

But the point I urge most seriously is that the Church's teachers acknowledge that these and other marital matters they deem closed and beyond discussion are not closed, because they have not been resolved in ways that satisfy Christian intelligence. Finally, the understanding of the marital relationship, and therefore of the sacrament, that the bishops of Vatican II bequeathed to Catholic pondering can have come only from their experience of the marriages around them. This pondering can continue fruitfully only if the married enter it and bring their experience with them.

The bibliography appended to each chapter is limited to titles published in the English language. It does not seem reasonable to include those in European or classical languages that are mainly unavailable to the readers for whom this volume is intended. This accounts for the minimal size of the bibliographies dealing with the study of the marital sacrament from the end of the patristic age until our own century.

The reader may notice that Christ's prophetic remark about spouses recorded in the synoptic tradition changes formulation in the course of this study. In the early chapters it is ". . . two in one body." Later it becomes ". . . two in one flesh." The first of these tries to be a more exact rendering of Christ's semitic mind and speech. The latter recognizes the fact that the remark got into the Christian vocabulary of the fathers via the Greek translation, *mia sarx,* which says literally "one flesh." Thus it was taken into Latin as *una caro,* and thence into English as "one flesh."

I owe continuing debts of gratitude to the following persons for their help in producing this third volume of *Marriage in the Catholic Church:* To Rev. William Rewak, S.J., President of Santa Clara University during the time the manuscript was in preparation, for his generosity in subsidizing the leisure needed for research and writing; to Patricia Roca Hogsett, then graduate student at the University of California at Berkeley, for editing every paragraph of the manuscript and for gathering its bibliography; to Rev. Robert Dailey, S.J., professor emeritus of moral and pastoral theology in the Jesuit School of Theology at Berkeley, and to Rev. Salvatore Tassone, S.J., my colleague at Santa Clara University, for their critical reading of the manuscript; to Professors Lisa Sowle Cahill and Pheme Perkins of Boston College's Department of Religious Studies, to Prof. Bernard Cooke of the College of the Holy Cross, to Prof. William P. Roberts of the University of Dayton, and to Rev. Peter Huizing, S.J. of Nijmegen, quondam professor of canon law in the Gregorian University and in the University of Nijmegen—to all for their conversation and critical remarks that have helped in more ways than they know to develop my own thinking about the marital sacrament; to Ethel Johnston, for typing the manuscript; and finally to my mother, Theresa, whose eighty-nine years have not dimmed her acumen at proofreading.

NOTES

1. The subtitles of these first two volumes are *What Is Marriage?* (1982) and *Divorce and Remarriage* (1984).
2. New York, 1951 and 1957.
3. *De Beatae Mariae Virginis Virginitate,* in Migne, *Patrologia Latina,* Vol. 176, Cols. 857–876.

1. INTRODUCTION

That the Roman Catholic teaching about the sacrament in marriage is a child of history is evident in the succinct formulation of this teaching in the Church's revised Code of Canon Law published in 1983. There Canon 1055, paragraph 1 states, "The matrimonial covenant, by which a man and a woman establish between themselves a partnership of the whole of life, is by its nature ordered toward the good of the spouses and the procreation and education of offspring; this covenant between baptized persons has been raised by Christ the Lord to the dignity of a sacrament."[1]

The canon is singular in the formulation of law in that it claims verification of an event in history. It asserts what Christ did to all marriages in subsequent history where the partners are both baptized in the Christian religion, baptized whether before the exchange of vows that creates their marriage or after it. Since the Code is a treatise neither of history nor of theology, it does not identify the time or place of Christ's doing what this canon claims he did, nor the words in which he did it.

On July 4, 1907 Pope Pius X published, through the Church's Holy Office of the Inquisition, the decree *Lamentabili*. In it he condemned a long list of propositions from the teaching of Catholic philosophers and theologians of the time who were dubbed "Modernists." Proposition 51 in the list is this: "Marriage could not have developed as a sacrament of the New Law until later in the Church. Indeed, for marriage to be accepted as a sacrament, a full theological development of the doctrine of grace and the sacraments had to precede this acceptance."[2]

Three hundred and forty-four years earlier the bishops of the Council of Trent, in their twenty-fourth session, on November 11, 1563, anathematized the Protestant reformers' denial that Christ had made marriage a sacrament in the new law: "If anyone says that marriage is not truly and in the proper sense one of the seven sacraments of the Law of the Gospel; or says that it was not instituted by Christ but was innovated in the Church by men; or says that it does not confer grace, let him be anathema."[3]

The severity of Trent's action—"Let him be anathema" means excommunicated—does not have its warrant in an unchanged and un-

5

qualified teaching about Christian marriage's sacramentality dating from Christ and the apostles. I have already noted Augustine's search, at the beginning of the fifth century, for the *sacramentum* in Christian marriages. But his assumption that it is indeed there was still leagues short of conviction that it was put there by Christ in the sense that the bishops of Trent later intended, or that it is a source of grace in the sense they intended. I have also noted already that marriage was accepted most hesitantly of all in the canonical list of seven sacraments instituted by Christ; and that much of the hesitation came from doubt that it can grace its participants in the sense that its typical conduct can enhance their holiness. The earliest inclusion of marriage in equal status with the other sacraments was the work of the Council of Verona in 1184. Pope Lucius III presided at this council that met to counter the rigorist Catholic sects of the age, Cathars principal among them, that disdained the sacraments because of their involvement in materiality.[4]

Thus, while the condemnation of the Modernists at the dawn of our own century asserted that marriage's sacramentality is itself not the later product of theological development, that condemnation could hardly gainsay the evidence that acknowledgment of marriage's primordial sacramentality was the product of such development.

This leads to questions about the dynamics of that development-leading-to-acknowledgment. Examination of the twelfth and thirteenth century reflection on marriage shows, I believe, that acceptance then of marriage's full sacramentality was as much the product of a matured theology of sin and grace as it was of a matured theology of marriage. But the theologians who led the latter maturation surely must have looked to evidence for marriage's sacramentality in the Christian traditions at their origin. We shall see that they did so look—with varying degrees of rigor.

Those medieval theologians—Hugh of St. Victor, Peter Lombard, Albert the Great, Bonaventure, and Thomas Aquinas the most fruitful contributors among them—faced the same risk of anachronism that theologians of any age face. Even as they searched the primitive Christian evidence they already had fixed a conception of a sacrament: *Signum sacrae rei quod recipientibus confert gratiam,* "a sign of a sacred reality that confers grace on those who receive the sign." How trustworthy are the search and its findings if they both fit criteria developed before the search? How valid the evidence if the criteria help to create the evidence? (The most transparent example of this flawed method has been the use of the letter to the Ephesians, Chapter 5, verse 32. The theologians worked with the Latin Vulgate version of the Greek original, a version whose translation of the first clause of this verse is *sacramentum hoc magnum est,* "This is a great sacrament." Taking *sacramentum* in the sense accepted by the twelfth century, they found Ephesians saying that the marriage of Christians is a great sacrament. Later investigation has found that in this verse the noun *mystérion,* the Greek source of the

Latin *sacramentum,* very doubtfully refers to Christian marriage to begin with; nor does it designate a grace-conferring sign as the theologians understood this.

My own effort to avoid imposing later theological formulations anachronistically on earlier Christian belief and conduct will be to let the gradual development of belief and conduct speak for itself. It does speak in a revealing context. For we know, apart from any theology of the sacraments, what the summary Christian effort in the human race has always been. This is to rescue human beings from sinfulness; to bring them to and keep them in the friendship of God, in belief, trust and love; to bring them thereby into trust and love of one another and keep them there.

Therefore one of the questions about the developing theology of marriage will ask how Christians through succeeding ages have found their marriages contributing to this effort in its several parts. Knowing in advance that their thinking eventually brought the Christian teachers to say that marriage among them is a sacrament of the new law, we shall examine what they found in marriage's contribution to the Christian effort that makes it sacramental.

The Nature of Sacrament

Because the two sacraments acknowledged by all the traditional Christian churches, and the two most familiar to all Christians, are baptism and the Eucharist, or Holy Communion, people assume that a sacrament is a religious ceremony. This is accurate but only partly so. The reference of the word "sacrament" does include ceremony, but it reaches further to include a situation, a relationship among persons, an interaction of persons, with the interaction expressing the relationship and perhaps doing so in a designed ritual. In this fuller sense Christ is called a sacrament; so too is a community of Christians. Where a marriage is sacramental this is not because it was created in a religious ceremony, although it may have been, and the ceremony may have helped at its creation to make it sacramental.

As a situation a sacrament is a setting for interaction between God and human beings; as a relationship the substance thereof is this interaction.

God takes the initiative in this interaction. He reaches from his invisible, trans-empiric dimension of existence into the empiric, visible-tangible-audible dimension that human beings inhabit. He does so in and by means of some sign of himself. This may be a mini-drama that calls a human being to respond to his intervention. The narrative in the Book of Exodus of Yahweh's entry into Moses' life via the bush that burned but was not consumed by the burning contains such a drama. So too does Jesus' healing the blind man, Bar-Timaeus. But neither Jews nor Christians have tried to repeat these interventions in ritual and therefore repeatable form, sacramental though they may have been. Others they have ritualized, and these rituals make up a main part of their religious identity and expression.

In entering men's and women's lives thus sacramentally God does so with double and interlocking intent: to draw men and women to himself, and to draw them to one another. In drawing them to himself in faith, trust and love, he would also draw them to one another in the same believing, trusting and caring attitude.

Human freedom has set in a most tragic way the real-life context for God's intervention, and has even qualified his motive for intervening. Men and women have continually surrendered their freedom and their ability to love, to fear, anger, greed and hatred. A human atmosphere poisoned by these is approximately what the author of the fourth gospel meant by "the sin of the world" (Jn 1:30). Therefore God's effort to draw men and women to himself is an effort to draw them out of sinfulness, out of the fear and hatred that destroy belief, trust and love.

Even in a sacrament in the expanded sense of an interaction and a relationship with God, apart from any ritualized interaction in a religious ceremony, there must be a "sign" if the experience is to be sacramental. There must be some evidence that it is indeed God the creator who is present and active in the event. What exactly is needed as evidence in particular cases depends on the desire, on the need, and on the faith (the willingness to believe) of the men and women involved in the event. The Platonic current in Catholic theology has wanted this sign, this evidence of God's action, to be an image of him and his action. This image-theology has especially affected the interpretation of the sacramentality in marriage. It has insisted on locating this sacramentality in the husbands' and wives' imaging, by their love, the love of Christ and the Church.

The word "grace" (*cháris* in the New Testament Greek) refers to something in God's attitude toward human beings, to something in his interaction with them, and to something in them that is an effect of this interaction. These three referents of the term must all be understood if one is to understand the traditional statement that a sacrament is a sign of grace.

As an attitude in God the word designates his loving kindness toward human beings, his gratuitous benevolence toward them. It points to a transcendent improvement over the caprice and willfulness toward human beings that the ancient pagans thought one of the prerogatives of divinity. It also goes beyond the "give them what they deserve" attitude appropriate to a merely just God. Christ pointed to this graciousness in God when, on being asked how to pray to him, he said, "This is how you pray: 'Our Father . . .' " Centuries earlier the Hebrew prophet had put words in Yahweh's mouth to express this graciousness even more tenderly: "Can a mother forget her infant, be without tenderness for the child of her womb? Even should she forget, I will never forget you [O

Israel] (Is 49:15). The philosopher in one may prompt the addition that this paternal-maternal gratuitous love comes of God's being the creator of human beings. It is no anthropomorphism to insist about God, as about ourselves, that what we bring into existence and hold in existence we tend to love with unconditional love.

About God's interaction with human beings, grace says that simply beyond what they deserve God enters their lives to draw them into friendship with himself, into a personal relationship whose substance is faith, trust and love. This effort on God's part is all the more undeserved, but at the same time all the more needed, because of the sinfulness, the "sin of the world" noted above. But here it is not human undeservingness alone that makes God's effort at friendship gracious. Human beings' ontological distance from him, their minuscule consciousness, require that if they are to interact with God personally, they must be capacitated far beyond what is natural in their powers of awareness and of love.

Their moral distance requires the same capacitating. Sinfulness paralyzes. The fear and self-protectiveness at its core are fear of the loss of self and defense against losing the self. But accepting an invitation to trust and to love risks precisely this loss. Fear of the loss drives men and women into putting up defenses against what they most long for. This is what paralyzes, what locks men and women in loneliness. It was no small graciousness on Christ's part to make the point clearly: "One who seeks his life will lose it. But one who loses his life for my sake will find it" (Mt 16:25). The night before his death the last promise he made to the friends dearest to him was that he would ask God to send them the gift of his Spirit to make the meaning of his words clear to them and to enable them to accept and live by them.

Thus grace in the last of these three senses, as the effect of God's gracing intervention in the souls of men and women who accept it, is precisely this empowering, this capacitating. It literally enables human beings to do something that left to themselves they could never do. This takes the meaning of grace as a gift well beyond the notion of help from God—inspiration, forgiveness, justification—that a human being could never merit. It takes it into the domain of elevation, transformation, even transcendence.

Christ and the Institution of Sacraments

The Christian churches acknowledge and use only the sacraments given to them by Christ. These make up a spare selection from among many possible religious acts that could be ritualized as reenactments of significant things that Christ did. For example one thinks, although hesitantly, of his driving the sellers from the temple courtyard. But it is at this point that the Catholic and the reformation Protestant churches disagree about the number of sacraments. The latter insist that Christ gave only two to his followers. They set this limit because the gospels record his explicit institution of only two, his express command to keep and use only two, baptism and the Eucharist. (The gospel according to Matthew tells of baptism in Chapter 28, verse 19: "Go, therefore, make disciples of all peoples. Baptize them in the name of the Father and of the Son and of the Holy Spirit." Within the synoptic tradition only Luke's gospel records Christ's single mandate regarding the Eucharist at the supper with his disciples the night before his death. After consecrating the bread he said, "Do this as a commemoration of me" (22:19). Paul in 1 Corinthians records a double mandate, after Christ's consecrating the bread, "Do this as a commemoration of me" (11:24); and after his consecrating the wine, "Whenever you drink it [the cup of the new covenant] do this as a commemoration of me" (11:25). In both Luke and Paul the Greek for "commemoration" is *anámnesis*. The word designates a commemorating act, but, more than that, a reenacting of the original commemorated event. Christ's command therefore is not only to remember what he did at the supper but to reenact what he did there; to remember it in and by the reenacting.

The Catholic reply to this limiting of sacramental institution by Christ is that the Protestant criterion for it is too confining. To begin with, not all that Christ said and did is recorded in the New Testament. So it is possible that early Christian sacramental practice continued something established by Christ but not recorded in the gospels as an explicit mandate. One of the gospel authors hinted at this incomplete recording, and did so in a grand exaggeration: "There were many other things that Jesus did: if all were written down, the world itself, I suppose, would not hold all the books that would have to be written" (Jn 21:25).

More than that, it is begging the question to insist that Christ's institution could have been only by explicit command. Thus, he devoted his time and energy mainly to teaching and healing, presumably because he thought these the most seriously needed. Does it not follow logically that since he gathered followers whom he willed to continue his work, he would put them permanently to teaching and healing, both very audible and tangible works that can bring God's loving kindness, and that he would leave to his followers the matter of putting both works into a set pattern?

In any case, saying that Christ instituted sacraments in his community of followers is not to say also that he innovated either two or seven religious ceremonies, that he invented new religious rituals and commanded their repetition by Christians down through the centuries. The human substratum, the matrix of every one of the seven sacraments claimed by the Catholic churches, was in practice centuries before Christ's public ministry. His own Jewish people had blessed, broken and shared bread for centuries, had confessed their sins and asked God's forgiveness, had laid hands on in blessing to call down God's spirit on the blessed. Christ continued these, meant for his disciples to continue them, but now with their meaning and their power taken into the meaning and power of his own work in the world.

All this is true of marriage. However they have construed the marital relationship—whether as monogamous or polygamous, whether as lifelong or temporary—men and women have been marrying since before recorded history. The Catholic claim says that Christ took up marriage's meaning and its power to help in his work in the world. The intent of this volume is to find out why Catholics believe Christ did this, and what they believe this makes of marriage among themselves as Christians.

Marriage as the Matrix of the Sacrament

The matrix of a sacrament is the human conduct, conduct perhaps formed into a ritual, that is taken and made into the sacrament, or into which the sacrament is grafted and whence it draws its substance and its meaning. The matrix consists not merely of the physical ingredients of the pre-existent conduct or ritual; it is the latter, including their meaning that common use has given them to date. Thus not water alone is the matrix of baptism, nor is it alone the bathing with water prescinding from the cultural meaning of bathing. For baptism the matrix is water the source of life, the environment of new life, used in cleansing away the old and beginning the new.

Similarly in the Eucharist bread and wine reposing inertly at a food fair could not be the matrix of this sacrament. Bread blessed, broken and shared as nourishment on a journey from slavery into freedom is one part of this matrix. Wine blessed and shared from one cup by the many on this journey into freedom is the other part. Why Christ took up this sharing of bread and wine as the core conduct for his followers, the conduct that most transparently reveals and carries on what he intended to do among them, we can understand only if we first understand the kind of slavery he found men and women caught in, and the kind of freeing he wanted for them.

The marital sacrament obviously has its matrix. And here too Catholic theology is a child of history. This introductory chapter began with Canon 1055, the first statute on marriage in the revised Catholic Code of Canon Law of 1983. This canon's first words are "the matrimonial covenant . . ." The ancestor of this revised formulation, the Code promulgated in 1917, named it differently, with a difference that is verbally minimal. Its first canon concerning marriage, Canon 1012, paragraph 1, was this: "Christ our Lord raised the marital contract itself among the baptized to the dignity of a sacrament."

But the difference in meaning is most significant. This now rejected canon referred to the marital "contract," calling the marriage itself by that term. But the canon that has replaced it calls marriage instead a partnership (*consortium*). The difference in meaning of the one predication from the other comes to the surface when one goes on to compare, in the two formulas, the acts by which the partners are said to create their marriage. Canon 1081 of the replaced Code said that the partners' reciprocal consent, their acts of will, create the marriage, and that what they do in this consent is to give one another, and accept from one another, the natural right to sexual use of the body, i.e., to sexual intercourse that can lead to conception. This canon added that the exchange of this right can be only exclusive to the two partners (a polygamous marriage is impossible), as it can be only perpetual (a temporary marriage too is impossible). In the terminology of contractual law, the marital contract was said to be non-voidable. The partners' acts of will could create the marriage, and they alone could do so. But no acts of will on their part could dissolve their marriage.[5]

In the revised law it is the same canon 1055 which describes the act by which the partners create their marriage. It is an act of covenanting, not of contracting. What this act does is not to exchange rights, but to create a partnership, a most inclusive partnership—"a partnership in the whole of life."

New Canon 1057 details more exactly the nature of this act. Its first paragraph is synonymous with replaced Canon 1081, paragraph 1. But the significant difference emerges again in the second paragraph of this new canon. Here what the partners exchange by their covenanting is radically different: "Matrimonial consent is an act of the will by which a man and a woman, through an irrevocable covenant, mutually give and accept each other. . . ." Add to this the inner dynamic of the covenanting—they give over, they make offerings (not *donant* in the official text, but *tradunt*, the verb used in the Latin versions of the New Testament to designate Christ's giving of his life). Taken *ensemble* the paragraph says that in marrying a man and a woman covenant by making gifts of their persons one to the other, and by accepting this gift. And the gift-giving, the covenanting, is irrevocable. Thus the revised canon relocates the cause of the marriage's indestructibility, not in the perpetuity of the right exchanged contractually, as in replaced Canon 1081, but in the irrevocability of the act that creates their marriage.

Once this severe difference in understanding the nature of marriage is clear, it is surprising that Catholic authorities could for so long have made three interlocking claims about marriage and about Christian marriages: that any marriage is a contract in which the spouses exchange their right to reproductive sexual acts; that this contract itself becomes the sacrament, is the latter's matrix; and that a marriage of two Christians is a sacrament in that it images the love relationship of Christ and the Church. This amalgam of juridical and theological defining said in effect that the Christ-Church relationship is a contract, that Christ and the Church exchange correlated rights and duties.

It is probably more than coincidence that as long as this theological anomaly went uncontested the development of both the human understanding of marriage in Catholic teaching, as well as of the theology of marriage was locked in partial paralysis. Theological development of the sacrament as image of the Christ-Church relationship could not but undermine the contractual definition. Reciprocally this definition kept theological development stalled in infancy.

But the bishops of the Second Vatican Council, whose vision of marriage is the source of the revised definition in the 1983 Code,[6] surely saw that if marriage the human relationship is to be matrix of the sacrament, the two must be more compatible internally than a contract and a relationship of two self-giving loves can be. It is not certain that their understanding of the sacrament as an image of this love dictated their vision of marriage the human relationship. But this understanding was certainly at work in the minds of those among them who contributed the most richly to that vision. Their giving to the Church, and their sowing in the minds of its men and women the understanding of marriage as a covenant of self-giving love has freed the theology of the sacrament to develop if only because they have given the sacrament a matrix whose limits of development are not yet in sight.

This is no minor issue in the theology of the marital sacrament. In every one of the sacraments its matrix has an essential determining effect, an effect on both the sacramental action and on this action's effects. Here too baptism offers a helpful example. The first generation of Christian disciples saw the need for a ceremony of initiation of persons outside their company who wished to become followers of Christ. We know that for this they selected a ceremony of religious bathing already in long practice among their own Jewish people. These first Christians could insert, and did insert, in the ceremony a meaning it had not contained hitherto, a meaning given by Christ himself. But they could not simply void the ceremony of its extant meaning. A bathing remains a bathing even if adapted to a higher purpose. So not only the momentum of their traditional Jewish religious practice led the first Christians to appropriate this bathing as the initiation into their community. They judged that water—water with its richly accrued role in the beginning of life and the sustaining of life, with its function in washing away the debris of an unwanted past—most aptly reveals the meaning of entry among the followers of Christ.

As long as Roman Catholic teaching defined marriage as a legal bond created by a contractual exchange of rights and obligations, this contract-matrix could offer little to the understanding of the sacrament. The non-voidability of the contractual bond was perhaps the limit of its contribution, correlating as it did the indestructibility of the Christ-Church relationship that the sacrament in marriage is held to image. But the newly appropriated covenant matrix, marriage understood as a partnership of all of life created by the spouses' making gifts of their persons to one another, enriches the theology of the sacrament with a richness that, as suggested above, is as yet unmeasured.

But along with this richness the new definition has supplied the same theology with some new questions. Here I propose only three of them.

First, this covenantal self-giving bespeaks a remarkably mature capacity in a man and a woman for loving and accepting love. The required irrevocability of the covenantal exchange only increases the needed level of maturity. That much raises a serious question about how many men and women in the contemporary human population are capable of creating even marriage the human relationship. But this first question for the theology goes beyond that and asks about the commensurability of the love needed to create marriage even as a human relationship with the Christian sacrament in marriage. Are the same kind and degree of love sufficient for both? If they are, so that whichever Christian spouses can marry can also create the sacrament, what difference does the sacrament make? If not, can the spouses create a less-than-sacramental marriage? Or are they disqualified from marrying at all until they mature, if they ever do, to the point of being able to create the sacrament?

That question asks about persons' ability to create the sacrament, a question prompted by doubt about their ability to love with marital love and thus produce the sacrament's matrix. A kindred question asks about the ability to create the sacrament among men and women who have been baptized but who have abandoned the practice of the Christian religion and who believe faintly if at all in the person and the teaching of Christ.

The difficulty raised in this question is heightened by the two explanations of the Christian marital sacrament that the Church's teachers have offered over the centuries. These have sought to explain in what exact way a marriage of two baptized persons is a sacrament. One' of these is used less and less frequently because of its obvious weakness. It explains that such a marriage is a Christian sacrament in that it is a sign of the marital love relationship between Christ and the Church, in that it images this relationship. Its weakness appears when it tries to account for how the marriage of two Christians whose faith is dead, whose religious commitment is nil, can image the divine relationship.

The second and now more frequently offered explanation is that by their baptism the man and wife were taken into the mystical body of Christ, into his redemptive work in the world. The consequence of this for their marriage is that it too is taken into Christ's redemptive work and is thus made a sacrament, a manifestation of his work in the world. What this explanation does not make clear is how the marriage of two baptized persons whose faith is dead, whose religious commitment is nil, can manifest that work.

The difficulty here is exacerbated by the Catholic marriage law's insistence that where both partners have been baptized, they can marry only in a sacramental marriage. Canon 1012, paragraph 2 of the 1917 Code formulated this insistence obliquely. Since Christ has made the marriage of the baptized to be sacraments, by the fact itself of their creating the marriage, they create the sacrament: "For this reason a matrimonial contract cannot validly exist between baptized persons unless it is also a sacrament by that fact." Canon 1055, paragraph 2 of the revised Code simply repeats this claim. In doing so it goes back to calling a marriage a contract after having, in its paragraph 1, replaced the "contract" of old Canon 1012 with its "partnership" that is created by covenanting. The authorities who revised the law were apparently satisfied that the spouses' covenanting produces a contract.

Catholic canonists and theologians currently argue the issue as that of "automatic sacramentality." Is no more required to produce the sacrament in marriage than that both spouses have been baptized and that they not have expressly rejected sacramentality in their marriage?

The juridical contest that needed automatic sacramentality and forced its installation is well enough known. It was a dispute that extended through the eighteenth and nineteenth centuries between Catholic ecclesiastical authorities and Catholic civil authorities in Europe over the marriage contracts of Catholics. The civil authorities insisted on the separability as well as the distinction of contract from sacrament in these marriages. This would leave the contract within their jurisdiction, since contracts are the concern of the state. And of course, they added, the marriage is in essence the contract, while the sacrament is only a religious ornament accessory to the contract.

The ecclesiastical authorities insisted on the inseparability of the two despite their distinctness; insisted that for Christians the contract is the sacrament, that correlatively (as old Canon 1012 and new Canon 1055 imply) the sacrament is nothing other than the contract itself elevated to the status of a grace-giving instrument. This would keep the contract within ecclesiastical jurisdiction since sacraments are the concern of the Church.

Early in the dispute, when its parties were still the Catholic civil authorities on one side and ecclesiastical on the other, the latter argued their case from the premise assumed as provided by Ephesians 5:21–33, the given truth that any marriage of two Christians images the relationship of Christ and the Church. But the exceeding difficulty of explaining how the marriages even of persons who have become agnostic and atheist since being baptized can be sacraments by being such images has driven those who defend the traditional teaching, now that the dispute is among theologians and canonists, to search elsewhere for an explanation. Most have turned to the theology of incorporation in the mystical body of Christ that I sketched above. Again, according to this theology baptism incorporates persons into the body of Christ in the Pauline sense, sets them in the life-stream of the Holy Spirit in the Church. As a consequence, when they later enter and enact those life-changing moments that the Church has acknowledged and adopted as sacramental, their enacting of them is made sacramental by Christ through his Spirit working in them. That they are unaware of this, and if told of it would care nothing about it, does not block this divine work, any more than an infant's unawareness blocks the Spirit's sanctifying work in baptism.

In view of more detailed critical reflections awaiting in Chapter 14, for now only the following rejoinder to that reasoning is appropriate. The parallel with the theology of baptism does not hold, and does not because of the different human conducts incorporated in the two sacraments as the matrix of each. Since this theology of baptism confines itself to the baptism of infants, it must accept the role in this sacrament to be that of an infant. It is a wholly passive role because the sacrament enacts a symbolic second birth, a birth into the family of Christ. One needs no awareness of one's birth in order to be born; no act of one's will is required.

But the human conduct incorporated in sacramental marriage as its matrix is different. Whether as a contracting or as a covenant, it can be produced only by a decision, and by a decision that is fully free. But a decision is fully free only if it is informed, only if the person deciding is aware. Consequently as marriage the natural relationship can be created only by a person acting freely because awarely, so too the sacramental marriage can be created only in this way.

The Indissolubility of Marriage

Since the sixteenth century Catholic teaching has linked the indissolubility of marriage inextricably with its sacramentality. Here one must distinguish indissolubility from impermissibility. The latter indicates for Christians that Christ has forbidden that marriages be dissolved, and that he did so in his command recorded in the synoptic tradition, "What God has joined man must not separate" (Mk 10:9; Mt 19:6).

But Catholic teachers have interpreted these words virtually from the beginning as a command forbidding the attempt at dissolution, not as a divine declaration that dissolution is impossible. So as early as the fourth century Catholic authorities permitted and authorized dissolution, but only where the marriage was unconsummated and only for the over-riding reason that one or both spouses wished to live a life of vowed chastity in religious community life.

But the same Catholic authority has set a limit to the possibility of dissolution. This has been variously at marriages that are consummated, at marriages that are sacraments, but finally at marriages that are consummated as sacraments. In any case marriages that are not sacraments are not held to be indissoluble. This appears inconsistent with the development of Catholic marriage law, because in the 1917 Code Canon 1013, paragraph 2 stated that indissolubility is a natural property of the marital contract, therefore even of marriages that are contracts but not sacraments. But an explicit claim that unbreakable indissolubility comes only with sacramentality is in the last clause of that paragraph: ". . . [indissolubility] which in Christian marriages gains a unique firmness by reason of the sacrament." The clause is also evidence that the writers of the law did not mean that indissolubility is a trait of real-life marriages, but is a juridical category predicated of marriage conceived abstractly in the minds of the legislators as itself no more than a juridical category. It is difficult to imagine where else indissolubility so uniquely firm that it cannot be dissolved could be distinguished from indissolubility insufficiently firm, so that it can be dissolved. New Canon 1056 repeats this second paragraph of old Canon 1013 word for word.

The reason for finding radical (indissoluble) indissolubility's cause in a marriage's sacramentality is claimed to lie in the most commonly used New Testament source for the theology of the sacrament, namely Ephesians 5:21–33. We have already seen that the analogy construed there between the two love relationships, that of Christ and the Church, and that of Christian husband and wife, is the major premise of the logic that concludes that any marriage of two baptized spouses is a sacrament. But a second conclusion is drawn from the same analogy, this one about a Christian marriage's indissolubility. Because this marriage automatically images the Christ-Church relationship, and because the latter relationship is indestructible, the marriage too is indestructible—is indissoluble. In this logic the analogic similarity is accorded more than an illustrative function. It is a given a causative ontological function: it *makes* Christian marriages to be indissoluble.

This theological reasoning goes back at least as far as Augustine's essay of 419, *De coniugiis adulterinis* (On Adulterous Marriages). But the reasoning was carried one step further by Pope Gregory XIII in his apostolic constitution, *Populis ac nationibus,* of January 25, 1585. He published this decision in order to resolve benignly an added injustice brought upon victims of the slave traffic conducted by the Spanish and the Portuguese. Slaves of both sexes from African tribes, many of them married, were separated permanently by being hauled off to separate colonies in the Indies and in New Spain. There many of them accepted baptism. When those who accepted it were couples who had been married before being taken into slavery, the effect of their baptisms, according to the theology we are examining, was to elevate their marriages to sacraments—this despite their never being aware of the elevation because of permanent separation by perhaps thousands of miles. Many sought to enter second marriages, now marriages that were Christian. But they were apparently blocked from this by the indissolubility brought on by the late-arriving sacramentality of their originally nonsacramental marriages.

Pope Gregory removed this obstacle—the impediment of extant marriage—by determining that their marriages had not attained radical indissolubility. They had not, despite having subsequently become sacraments with the spouses' baptisms, because the separation had prevented their consummating their marriages specifically as sacraments. Gregory here put to use the still earlier determination of Pope Alexander III, in about 1150, that when Christ commanded "What God has joined man must not separate," the Lord referred only to consummated marriages.[7] For evidence of this limited reference Alexander adduced Christ's quoting earlier in the same passage (Mk 10:8; Mt 19:6) the author of the garden of Eden parable assessing the union of the first husband and wife, ". . . and the two of them become one flesh" (Gen 2:24). Alexander took this "becoming one flesh" to refer to the first sexual intercourse of this primeval couple, the consummation of their marriage. Thus Gregory XIII's logic: Since only a sacramental marriage is indissoluble to begin with, and since even this marriage is incompletely sacramental until consummation by sexual intercourse, it follows that finally unassailable indissolubility does not come even to a sacramental marriage until its consummation by first intercourse.

Why was an unconsummated marriage deemed incompletely sacramental? The reason was supplied by the medieval canonists and theologians, as we shall see later in finer detail. It was that until consummation by first sexual intercourse the marriage of two Christians images the relationship of Christ and the Church only imperfectly. As the same passage in Ephesians points out (5:26–28), the Church is as a wife to Christ, her husband. This marital union was fruitful in purification and sanctification. So until the source of fruitfulness in Christian marriage is activated, the marriage images the divine fruitfulness only imperfectly.

Hidden not very deeply in this logic is yet another theological anomaly. It grows out of the understanding of consummation that has been written into the Catholic marriage law. In the 1917 Code Canon 1015, paragraph 1 specified that a marriage is consummated if the spouses have completed once the sexual intercourse to which the marital contract is oriented by its nature, and (to echo Alexander III) by which the spouses become one flesh. No anomaly has appeared yet, since the nature of the consummating act specified here fits the Code's concept of marriage as a contract. According to this concept, the exchanged contractual good is each party's right to sexual acts oriented to conception. Consummation then is understood as the completing of the contract, the delivering of the promised contractual good.

The anomaly surfaces when this understanding of consummation, which is fitted aptly to a contract, is without change accepted also as the consummation of a sacramental marriage. Implicit here is the assumption that in Christian marriages the act that consummates the contract consummates the sacrament as well. But to consummate a relationship—which the sacrament certainly is—is to complete it. Therefore this juridicized theology determines that the sacrament in marriage can be completed by a single act of sexual intercourse. And this is the sacrament that is called such because the marriage images the love relationship of Christ and the

Church. In short, the human image of that love can be brought to completion within a few hours after the wedding.

The revised marriage law adds uncertainty to anomaly. By the time the Pontifical Commission for the Revision of Canon Law began its work early in 1966, serious dissatisfaction with this juridical interpretation of consummation had gathered. Bishops and canonists were aware that Catholic marriage courts had interpreted even mechanistically that the marriage and sacrament are consummated by the merest physical performance of intercourse. In one significant case appealed to the Church's Congregation of the Sacraments, the Congregation ruled that consummation had been completed even when the wife had to drug herself to unconsciousness in order to survive the ordeal of intercourse.[8]

The subcommission that drafted the proposed revision of the canons on marriage sought to correct this misinterpretation and abuse. Into the new canon defining consummation (Canon 1061, paragraph 1) it wrote a phrase qualifying the otherwise synonymous repetition of old Canon 1015: "A valid marriage between baptized persons . . . is called ratified [sacramental] and consummated if the parties have performed between themselves *in a human manner* the conjugal act. . . ."[9]

The phrase there in italics translates the Code's Latin original, *humano modo*. This did not originate in the minds of the subcommission of the Code Commission that drafted the revised canons on marriage. It is taken from the Second Vatican Council's *Gaudium et spes* (Pastoral Constitution on the Church in the Modern World) where it tells of marital love (no. 49). In a paragraph that banished finally and for good from the teaching of the Catholic Church the ancient Augustinian pessimism about sin-infected sexuality in marriage, the bishops said the following about the place of sexual expression in marital love.

> This love is uniquely expressed and perfected through the marital act. The actions within marriage by which the couple are united intimately and chastely are noble and worthy ones. Expressed in a manner which is truly human [*modo vere humano*] these actions signify and promote that mutual self-giving by which spouses enrich each other with a joyful and thankful will.[10]

It is the phrase, *modo vere humano,* minus the adverb *vere,* that is carried over into new Canon 1061. But there is a history to this carrying over, and from it comes the uncertainty about consummation of marriage. When the subcommission drafting the revised canons circulated their first formulations, this canon on consummation contained the modifying phrase borrowed from *Gaudium et spes.* But it put the phrase in parentheses, and explained thus its reason for doing so.[11]

> Although the majority of the consultors [the members of the subcommission] agree that the words *humano modo* are to be

included in the definition of the consummation of marriage, all agreed unanimously that the term should be put in parentheses so that their uncertainty in the matter may be made evident.[12]

Commentators have subsequently interpreted the phrase to mean that mere physical intercourse is insufficient to consummate, that the act must be done with the understanding and freedom needed to make it a truly moral act.[13] Others add that it must express the nature of the marital covenant; it must be done willingly and lovingly.[14]

These interpretations are accurate as far as they go. But implicit in them is the assumption inherited from the old Canon 1015, and from the replaced Code's conception of marriage as a juridical bond, namely that this bond can in fact be consummated by a single act of intercourse. The interpretations do not ask the necessary question whether marriage understood as a partnership in all of life can be consummated in the same way—a partnership created by the spouses' making gifts of their person to one another.

More than that, the interpretations do not address the question that asks whether the conduct that consummates the human partnership suffices to consummate as well the partnership become sacrament. An unhesitating "yes" to this question would imply that the sacrament makes no difference to the love that is needed to create and live a marriage that is indeed sacramental. This in turn would in effect concede that the secular-minded Catholic princes and parliaments of the eighteenth and nineteenth centuries were right after all. The sacrament is not something internal to the marriage, is not the marriage contract (now partnership) itself, but a religious ornament accessory to it.

There is this added difficulty in the law itself about the act that consummates marriage, that although in the final and published formulation of new Canon 1061 the parentheses have been removed from the phrase *humano modo,* the doubt about the meaning of this modifier that evoked the parentheses has never been removed. Neither the Commission for the Revision of the Code of Canon Law, nor the supreme Catholic legislator, Pope John Paul II, has published an interpretation of the phrase and thereby removed the doubt concerning its meaning. If the doubt is being resolved juridically and *in praxi* by the determinations coming from the Church's courts, a familiar dynamic is once again under way in the history of the Catholic treatment of marriage. Legal practice is assumed to be fashioning theology by resolving doubts that are in substance theological.

Intent and Method in Examining the History of the Sacrament

This expanded catalogue of *quaestiones et dubia* concerning the theology of the marital sacrament is, as I said at the outset, the product of history. Human needs, political-social crises, the seeds of development within the earliest Christian traditions, the liturgical celebration of marriage—all have contributed to this history. The intent of this volume is to trace the history. While bowing to the axiom that any recording of history is inevitably an interpretation of it, I hope to let as best I can the development of the Catholic understanding of the sacrament in marriage speak for itself.

Again a note about method in tracing this development and about the needed caution lest the examination fall into anachronism: one can simultaneously maintain reasonable fidelity to the development's history and avoid anachronism by setting God's saving work delineated in the scriptures as the frame of reference for the examination. Whatever else a sacrament is, it is an instrument used in this work. Indeed the very concept of sacrament is a way of understanding this work: God has broken through to human awareness, has manifested himself and his will to save. Breaking through and manifesting are the foundational vocabulary in which sacraments are discussed.

God has done this in order to save men and women, to rescue them from their sinfulness, which is their fear of and alienation from him and from one another. He seeks to draw them out of their fear and alienation and to himself. The last of these is the call to holiness, since holiness is in substance life lived in a relationship of belief, trust and love with God and with his creation.

Therefore these great categories of Christian belief, inherited from our Jewish forebears, provide the questions one asks about the development of the Catholic understanding of Christian marriage's sacramentality. The following, I believe, are the central and controlling questions:

In what ways have the Catholic teachers and scholars understood God to reveal himself and his will in marriage, and especially in the marriages of Christian spouses?

In what ways have they understood this self-revelation of God, his intervention in human affairs through marriage to be an effort at rescue from sinfulness?

In what ways have they understood him to call men and women to belief, trust and love through their marriages? The same question in other words: In what ways have they understood marriage as a setting for and an instrument of holiness?

In what ways have they understood God to use marriage as a means of reconciliation among men on one side and women on the other?

Since a treasure of belief and of custom about marriage's place in God's plan was passed down from Israel to Christianity—all but a few of the first-generation Christians identified themselves as Jews—this examination must begin with the Jewish bequest to Christian belief and practice.

NOTES

1. The canons, or statutes, on marriage in the revised Code of Canon Law are in Book 4, "The Office of Sanctifying in the Church," Part 1, "The Sacraments," Title 7, "Marriage." In this volume the canons, when quoted, are taken from *The Code of Canon Law, A Text and Commentary*, Commissioned by the Canon Law Society of America, edited by James A. Coriden, Thomas J. Green and Donald E. Heinschel, N.Y./Mahwah, 1985.

2. Denzinger-Schönmetzer, *Enchiridion Symbolorum, Definitionum et Declarationum de Rebus Fidei et Morum*. Editio XXXII, Barcinone et alibi, 1963. No. 3451, p. 673. (The translation into English of the Latin text of the *Enchiridion* is my own throughout this volume.)

3. *Op. cit.*, No. 1801, p. 416.

Earlier in the council, in 1547 during its seventh session, the bishops of Trent had set a kindred anathema. In their Decree on the Sacraments, Canon 1, they said, "If anyone says that the sacraments of the New Law have not all been instituted by Christ Our Lord, or that these are fewer or more than seven, namely baptism, confirmation, Eucharist, penance, last anointing, orders and marriage, let him be anathema" (*op. cit.*, No. 1601, p. 382).

4. Denzinger-Schönmetzer, *op. cit.*, No. 761, p. 242.

5. The full formulation of Canon 1081 was this: Paragraph 1: "A marriage is created by the legitimately expressed consent made by the parties who are capable of consenting according to the law. No human power can substitute for this consent.

Paragraph 2: "Marital consent is an act of will by which both parties give over and accept a perpetual and exclusive right to their bodies, a right ordered to those acts that are in themselves apt for the producing of offspring."

6. This vision is elaborated in their Pastoral Constitution on the Church in the Modern World (*Gaudium et spes*), Part II, Chapter 1, "Fostering the Nobility of Marriage and the Family."

7. His determination was this: "God's command that a man or woman not dismiss the spouse refers only to a consummated marriage" (recorded in the *Compilatio Prima*, Book 10, Part 32, Chapter 7).

8. This case is reported in *Canon Law Digest, Supplement* 1955–1959, "Canon 1127."

9. The italics here in the latter clause are added.

10. In *The Documents of Vatican II*, Walter M. Abbott, general editor, N.Y., 1966, p. 253.

11. This was done in the Commission's journal, *Communicationes*, Vol. 5, p. 79.

12. *Ibid.*

13. Thus Ladislas Örsy, S.J., *Marriage in Canon Law*, Wilmington, 1986, p. 68.

14. Thus Thomas P. Doyle, O.P., in *The Code of Canon Law, Text and Commentary*, p. 745.

BIBLIOGRAPHY

Boff, Leonardo: "The Sacrament of Marriage," in *Concilium* 87 (1973), pp. 22–33.

David, Jakob: "Marriage," in *Encyclopedia of Theology: The Concise Sacramentum Mundi,* Karl Rahner, S.J., editor. N.Y., Crossroad, 1982, pp. 905–937.

Haughton, Rosemary: *The Theology of Marriage.* Butler, Wis., Clergy Book Service, 1971.

Joyce, George H.: *Christian Marriage: An Historical and Doctrinal Study.* Revised Edition. London, Sheed and Ward, 1948.

Kasper, Walter: *Theology of Christian Marriage.* N.Y., The Seabury Press, 1980.

Leclercq, Jacques: *Marriage, A Great Sacrament.* London, Burns and Oates, 1951.

O'Callaghan, D.: "Marriage as Sacrament," in *Concilium* 55 (1970), pp. 101–110.

Örsy, Ladislas, S.J.: "Sacrament, Contract and Christian Marriage: Disputed Questions," in *Theological Studies* 43 (1982), pp. 379–398.

Schillebeeckx, Edward: *Marriage: Human Reality and Saving Mystery,* N.Y., Sheed and Ward, 1965.

2. THE ORIGIN OF THE SACRAMENT IN THE HEBREW SCRIPTURES

Whoever traces the origins of the Christian conception of the sacrament in marriage begins too late on the calendar of history if he or she begins only with the earliest Christian teaching. The examination must start much earlier, as far back as the earliest Hebrew traditions themselves.

Almost all the first generation of Christians, and probably the majority of the second generation, was religiously Jewish. Until excommunicated by the council of rabbis during the decade, 90–100 A.D., they held themselves organically continuous with Jewish history. But even afterward they, along with Christian converts from paganism, claimed inheritance of Israel's vocation. Although they believed that Jesus had come to put an end to the old covenant and to make all things new, they never believed that he had simply cancelled all God's prior work accomplished through the people Israel. They believed that he had continued it and meant for them to carry it on, but now given new life. This is what his promised gift of the Spirit was meant to do, not to obliterate the old, but to give it new life.

Included in this interpretation of things was the earliest Christians' understanding of marriage and its place in the Christian plan. Their sacred scriptures were the Hebrew scriptures. They did not suspect that they were producing scriptures of their own, a New Testament. What they believed about marriage was in the Hebrew scriptures. Therefore to know what they believed we must begin with those scriptures.

The Garden Parable in Genesis 2–3

We begin with a passage that is surely among the oldest of the Hebrew interpretations of the man-woman relationship. It is the story, in Genesis, Chapters 2 and 3, of the first man and woman in the garden of Eden.

24

No serious scholar today holds this to be a factual account of the beginning of the human race. It is a fiction. Yet it is more than vignette, and more and other than a legend. The latter is true because unlike the legends of Israel's patriarchs, there are no historically verifiable persons in the Genesis story who have been legendized by generations of bards and other story-tellers. And it is more than either fiction or legend because it was contrived by a teacher or group of teachers, the Yahwist and his disciples of the tenth or ninth centuries B.C., with an exact didactic purpose. This purpose shared in the larger purpose of the entire book of Genesis, which is to introduce the book of Exodus, and therein the narrative of God's forming a people chosen to be his instrument in the saving of his damaged creation. The particular purpose in Genesis is to make clear how the damage was begun, namely by the first human beings. On these grounds it is reasonable to judge the story a parable, a fiction devised, like Jesus' parables, to convey a serious religious message—fiction in the service of truth.

In the parable the setting for the forming of the first human being (Chapter 2) is a garden of pleasure. He is there not, as in the Platonic Greek tradition, a spirit in exile. The garden is his home by nature, because "man," *'adam*, is taken from the soil, *'adamah* (verse 7). The case has been made that because the name designating the first human being does not designate the male exclusively but is generic (the juxtaposition of *'adam* and *'adamah* calls for the translation "earth-creature"), the author intended that this being is an androgyne. Had he intended the male, he ought to have used the exclusive designation, *ish* ("man" or "male") employed later, in verse 23, where he plainly so intends.

A contemporary scholar explains this in more exact detail.

> The question arises . . . What is the precise force of this argument, "male and female he created them"? At first sight it looks quite irrelevant, speaking neither in favour nor against modern divorce; or perhaps in favour, seeing that God created two independent beings. Modern commentaries incline to slur over the difficulty. The true explanation lies in the fact that, for the Rabbis, this verse contains the doctrine—familiar to the readers of Plato—of the ideal, androgynous man, the doctrine that when God created the first man, he created him as both man and woman in one.
>
> The reasons why the Rabbis connected the doctrine with just this verse are two. For one thing, they had to harmonize this verse, "male and female he created them", with the narrative according to which Adam came first and Eve was only subsequently formed from one of his ribs. A plausible solution was to maintain that the original Adam was a composite being, and that this was the meaning of the verse in question. For one thing, the Hebrew text wavers between the singular and plural.

It starts by using the singular "man"—"God created man in his image"—and then goes on to the plural "them"—"male and female he created them". What sort of being might it be, the Rabbis asked themselves, of whom one could equally well speak in the singular or the plural? Again the answer was that the verse must refer to the androgynous man.

That this interpretation of the verse goes back to the New Testament times is certain. Philo has it. It occurs in many different Rabbinic sources. Moreover, the Rabbis inform us that the authors of the LXX, for the enlightenment of their gentile public, slightly altered the verse "male and female he created them": they translated "a male with his female parts he created them", or "male and female he created him"—"him" in the singular. . . .[1]

Assuming the accuracy of this interpretation it would follow that part of the human creature's pristine happiness lay in the peaceful integration of the masculine and the feminine in its soul, as it would follow also that the beginning of misery was their disintegration when the feminine element was separated out from the androgyne, became a woman, and acted with a kind of independent masculinity by asserting a disobedient independence against God.

A contrasting interpretation is offered by another contemporary scholar. It points to evidence that in the garden parable the product of God's work of forming mankind (called in Hebrew *ha'adam*) was not one human being but two. Certainly the choice of nouns there does not indicate a first and single male. The noun to designate such is *ish,* as indicated above. It was available, but was not used until later in the parable, in verse 23. Moreover, since the noun designating the product of God's work is translated literally as "the earth creature," it follows that not only was the first human being not a male from whose maleness the first female was taken. But it follows also that the rabbinic interpretation we have seen just above—God separated the two sexes out of an original androgyne—is not supported by the Genesis text.[2]

Whichever of these is the accurate interpretation, it is clear that the first human creature is essentially more and different than the other creatures. God brought it to life by breathing his own breath into it (verse 7). Here may be an alternative accounting for the later rebellion. In the human creature was the breath of the divine. No wonder it would later crave the knowledge reserved for divinity, namely knowledge of good and evil.

The older and conventional interpretation has it that the human creature was from the beginning only male, and that the first woman was formed because in God's judgment it was "not good for the man to be alone" (verse 18). Following immediately on this assessment of the man's condition comes a most significantly phrased divine decision: "I will make a suitable partner for him."

This formulation of the clause, which has become common in the English versions of Genesis, is slightly euphemistic. The Hebrew version of Genesis records God's intent to give the man not exactly a partner equal to him in every way, but a helpmate. This suggests an inch of inferiority. But the man's helpmate is to be one "alongside him," "corresponding to him."[3] She will be given to him because of his superiority. The author of the parable is aware of the eternal double asymmetry of the man-woman relationship: reciprocal dependencies within reciprocal ascendancies. The man's need for this helpmate will soon become the source of tension and of her eventual power over him.

That this helpmate is formed of flesh taken from his side (verses 21 and 22), unlike the animals formed from the earth and found unsuitable helpmates for him, tells that the woman has a substantial claim to equality with him. That she was taken from his own flesh while he was in a sleep brought on him by God hints that she will be in some degree a mystery to him and that he will not dominate her.[4]

The man's exclamation when God brings her to him and awakens him is "This one at last is bone of my bones and flesh of my flesh" (verse 23). The statement ranks in value with "suitable helpmate" for understanding the author's estimation of marriage.

> To understand [the exclamation] as no more than the man's acknowledgment that the women is of the same material stuff as himself, or even that she is derived from his own flesh and bone, is to catch the words' least meaning. "Flesh and bone" make up a word-pair appearing more than once in the Old Testament. "Flesh" by itself not only can mean one component of the body, but in a certain context it can mean bodily and even human frailty. It can mean "flesh-weakness." "Bone" can have the meaning of strength and power—"bone-strength." But when combined the two terms signify more than just the two realities in juxtaposition. Together they create a new meaning, a meaning that goes beyond physical power and weakness. Flesh-weakness and bone-strength are antitheses in combination, and the antithesis includes not only the two extremes but all degrees in between. They include the full range of a person's character traits, from his weakest to his strongest.
>
> Thus when the man says of the woman that she is "bone of my bones and flesh of my flesh," he means that she shares his strength and his weakness and all that lies between them. She is his partner in every contingency of his life. . . .[5]

After giving to the man in the parable this epigrammatic evaluation of his marriage's nature—and of the nature, of course, of every Hebrew marriage—the author makes the next evaluation his own. Its richness equals that of the evaluation he has just given the man to proclaim: "That is why a man leaves his father and mother and clings to his wife, and the two of them become one body" (verse 24).[6]

For the tenth century Hebrew audience he had in mind he could not have chosen more effective images for portraying the value of the husband-wife relationship. Would his hearers ask which is the relationship most precious to a Hebrew man? If they think it is his loving and obedient relationship to his parents, let them think again. For the sake of joining to his wife he leaves his father and mother—even them. And it is to his wife that he clings, not to them.

From the vocabulary of covenanting the author draws two key verbs in his comment. To leave, or abandon, his parents (the Hebrew is *asav*) means that the man severs a covenant with them. To cling to his wife (*davaq*) means that he creates a covenant with her.

The final flourish, ". . . and the two of them become one body," adds to the literally incomparable value of their union an invulnerability to human destruction. "One body" refers not primarily to sexual union, although this is implied. "Body" here (or its alternative, "flesh") designates somewhat the same as "flesh" in the "bone-strength and flesh-weakness" word-pair above. Designating a person's nature in its mortality and fallibility, it designates by extension his or her full human identity. In becoming "one body" the husband and wife thus become as one person before the law. Hence in every way—legally, emotionally, socially, all of which for the Hebrew included religiously—a husband and wife form the closest and most indestructible relationship conceivable.

That a covenantal notion characterizes this relationship already ten centuries before Christ is the first faint readying of it to be deemed and dealt with as sacramental.

The author's observation (in verse 25) that "The man and his wife were both naked, yet they felt no shame," is not a casual verification of life-style in a garden of pleasure. It asserts that the original condition, the divinely intended permanent condition of the human race, is one without shame. The author's psychology held that shame even at nakedness is unnatural; it is not good; it is the product of sin. It also suggests obliquely the peace in which the first married couple lived. They felt no need to cover and shield themselves. But when they later sinned even these spouses felt shame in one another's presence and covered themselves. The shame was especially severe in the presence of God. The man betrayed this when God found him doing the unaccustomed and strange thing of hiding from him in the garden: "I heard you in the garden; but I was afraid, because I was naked, so I hid myself" (Gn 3:10). From this psychology emerges the author's theology of sin. It is not only to disobey God. It is also to turn away from him in guilt and shame and try to hide from him.

That much of the parable completes the part of it now confined in

Genesis, Chapter 2. It described the setting and delineated the characters in preparation for the dramatic confrontations that carry the parable's message. But only in Chapter 3 is a key "character" introduced, albeit a sub-human character. I mean not the serpent but "the tree in the middle of the garden," the tree of the knowledge of good and evil. (Some scholars hold that the original version of the parable featured only this tree, that the other, "the tree of life" (Gn 2:8), was a later addition to the story in order to help account for the unending life available to the couple had they not sinned.)[7]

"Knowledge of good and evil" here involves more than theoretical understanding an ethician may have of the moral goodness or badness of certain kinds of conduct. It also signifies more than a prudent person's experience of which conduct is good or bad in the sense of which is harmful and which helpful. The phrase signifies a certain command of morality, a freedom about moral attitude and conduct. "Know" here has the biblical sense of "to experience." In our own lives we meet the attitude in a person who does the forbidden just because it is forbidden, because he or she "wants to see how it feels," wants to assert an autonomy in living his or her life. As the serpent tempter assures the woman (verse 5), to eat of the fruit of this tree is to become like the gods.

Thus the flaw in their moral defenses through which the tempter can get at the man and woman: as long as they remain obedient their range of experience is limited, especially their experience of autonomous freedom. This includes their sexual experience. There is nothing in the parable suggesting that their sin is their first sexual intercourse. This interpretation would contradict God's plan in making intercourse available to them by forming the two of them as sexual, and sexually correlated, creatures. But the lure of the darker side of sexuality that the author had in mind is what they have not experienced—how it feels when it is forbidden. The author had it in mind because his Hebrew people were surrounded and relentlessly tempted by the fertility cults of the ancient Near Eastern peoples. In these cults sexuality was sacred; it was sacred especially outside marriage with cultic prostitutes. While it was sought for fertility, it was not for family. It was especially not tethered to God's plan for his chosen people.

This is how it was to turn out. Once the man and woman had sinned, they felt shame—not compunction or contrition, but shame. So they covered themselves and hid from God. A new and powerful feeling was now in their emotional repertory.

Their sexuality thus became for them a source of tension and alienation. Moral and psychological ambivalence was born: it was God who had decided for and fashioned the two sexes, and obviously for the purpose of their joining, their "clinging" sexually. But because they overstepped the limits he set, their sexuality became the cause of alienation between themselves and of themselves against God. The author singles out their sexuality as a source of alienation when he later (in verses 14 through 19) details the punishments inflicted on each, the serpent, the man and the woman, for their participation in the disobedience. But now the alienation shows itself in the woman's weakness instead of in her strength over against her husband. Bringing children to birth, the fruit of her sexuality, will be agony for her: "I will intensify the pangs of your childbearing; in pain shall you bring forth your children" (verse 16). Nevertheless, and irrationally in face of the certain pain, she will go to her man sexually: "Yet your urge shall be for your husband."

The last item of her punishment is the most inclusive. Jewish husbands were never to forget this, and the fathers of the early Christian churches were never to let their husbands and especially not their wives forget it: ". . . and he shall be your master."

In a special way this climactic part of the woman's punishment tells of the historical context that later generations, both Jewish and Christian, were to assume about marriage and sexuality. In the beginning and according to God's plan the man and woman were to be most intimate physical and emotional partners. They were meant to live in a covenant of trust. Living together in this way they were to live also in the intimate friendship of God. (Gn 3:8 implies that God used to come to walk in the garden with them in the cool of the evening.) One and only one restricting condition was laid upon them, that they live in obedience, that they accept the human limitations of their experience, of their wisdom and their freedom.

The Christian fathers also never forgot that it was the woman who led the disobedient refusal to accept this limitation (they took for granted that the parable is factual history): "The woman saw that the tree was good for food, pleasing to the eyes, and desirable for gaining wisdom. So, she took some of the fruit and ate it" (verse 6); and that it was her prompting that led the man also to refuse obedience: ". . . and she also gave some to her husband who was with her, and he ate it" (ibid.).

The irony here is obvious. It was in the closest and most precious relationship imaginable that trust was first betrayed, that covenant was first broken. That the author intended this to explain a human history full of betrayed trust and broken promises, is suggested in the episode in the book of Genesis that follows immediately (in Chapter 4). As early as their children's generation this first couple's alienation bears fruit in a jealousy that drives their eldest son, Cain, to murder his brother Abel.

The Creation Poem of Genesis 1

Before going on to the creation poem of Genesis 1, a preliminary and spare summation of the seeds of sacramental theology planted in the garden parable is in order. First, that there are two sexes in the human race is reported as God's institution. Therefore sexual nature and sexual activity are good *a priori,* for the man clings to his wife and the two become one flesh.

Marriage in God's original intent belongs to a condition of happiness and is a most vital contributor to it. Here this happiness is not said to demand or include procreation; it is the happiness of men and women in "one flesh." It fills up the lack that God deemed serious when he affirmed "It is not good for the man to be alone."

There is no suggestion that the correlation of diverse sexes in the first two human beings images God's nature. That they could have so imaged is not unthinkable. Indeed this imaging is virtually declared in the creation poem of Genesis 1. And there is no hint in the parable that in their sexual intimacy the spouses participate in the sexual activity of gods and goddesses and thus draw on their power. If anything, as we have seen, there is in the parable a veiled polemic against this. The couple's try at tapping into divine power was a most grievous offense against divinity, not a cajoling of it nor a flattery-by-imitation. Their sexuality was precious but not sacred. It was creaturely with all the essential limitations of creaturehood. Its conduct was good but could not be in itself the inauguration of beatitude.

In the garden the couple lived in God's intimacy. He was accustomed to walk with them there in the cool of the evening. They were used to being in his presence with explicit sexual character but in untroubled innocence. For at first they were naked but were not ashamed. But after they had sinned they hid themselves because their sinning made them aware of their nakedness, and against God's will their sin made them ashamed of it.

The detailed description of the creation of the universe in Genesis 1 is no more a factual account than is the parable we have just seen. The creation narrative is a religious poem. It was composed by priestly authors during the Judean exiles' captivity in Babylon in the sixth century B.C. It was intended as a reaffirmation of the Hebrew monotheist belief in a single, transcendent and sovereign creator of the universe; a reaffirmation against the Babylonian polytheist creation myth in their saga, *Enuma elish*—from which, paradoxically, the Genesis authors borrowed the narrative structure of their poem.

Whereas in the garden parable the human creature was fashioned first and the other sentient creatures afterward in the effort to find for him a suitable helpmate, in this creation poem the human creatures, now plural, are created last, on the sixth day, as the climax and crown of the fashioning of the universe.

Where in verse 26 God announces his decision to create man, he uses the trans-sexual *adam*—"man" rather than "male"—to indicate his intent. That *adam* was to be essentially different from and superior to all the other creatures is clear in God's added and unique intent to make him in his own image and likeness. The last two substantives here are not pleonastic. Image (*selem*) is an exact copy or reproduction; likeness (*demût*) tempers the daring thought of cloning transcendent divinity by modifying it to resemblance and similarity.

In vivid contrast to the garden parable wherein the human creature first fashioned was the male and the female was formed afterward as a needed supplement, here the male and female are created simultaneously. More than that, in fashioning a creaturely likeness of himself the creator produces the two sexes. This intimates that not only must both be included in order to have *adam,* full humanity, but both are needed if God's likeness is to be realized. It is a realization that only a few Jewish and Christian teachers have dared to voice, that God is as much maternal as paternal.[8]

Here too, as in the garden parable, the first two human beings' sexuality is set at the core of their meaning: "God blessed them, saying, 'Be fertile and multiply; fill the earth . . .' " (verse 28). But there is a polemic nuance in this, because the couple's sexual fertility is a product of God's blessing and command. It is not rooted in their likeness to the creator, and therefore their sexuality is not a participation in the activity of mythical gods and goddesses themselves sexual, as in the Babylonian fertility cult. The real God, the God of Israel, stands above and apart from sexuality; it is a creaturely activity and nothing more. Nevertheless it is his invention; it is his will.

But where, in the garden parable, sexuality was for the couple themselves, for their realization in one flesh, here God gives it a purpose and duty beyond the couple (an *officium,* the Latin Christian scholars will call it later). By it they are to begin the human race, to populate the earth. But not only that. As a sexually joined couple they are also to master, or subdue, the earth. Both of them, as husband and wife, are to govern all its creatures as instruments of God's own power and authority.

As long as Christian teachers have taken both this creation poem and the garden parable as factual accounts, they have had ready evidence for insisting that God himself created marriage, that he did so in the very creating of the first human beings. They have also found in these accounts the two reasons for marriage we have already seen. And in them they have found a deposit from which marriage's sacramentality could also be drawn. Few Christian teachers have overlooked marriage's natural and pre-Christian sacramentality. Their claim for its Christian sacramentality is that Christ took its natural and then Jewish sacramentality, elevated them and made the marriages of his followers his own sacrament.

The following seem the elements of sacramentality available in these two passages of the Hebrew scriptures. Through the conduct of their marriage man and wife are in union with God by obeying his command, "Increase and multiply. . . ." This is a union of human wills with the divine. Therefore the more their conduct obediently keeps its creaturely place and carries out its mandated purpose, the firmer is this union—the more it recreates, however faintly, the pristine relationship during which God came to the first couple in the garden "in the cool of the evening." Thus there is available in marriage a characteristic holiness. But because marriage goes on no longer in the innocence of the garden, the obedi-ential holiness must contain repentance and reparation.

Assuming that the man and wife committed themselves to carry out God's mandate, and committed themselves as a couple, they entered a covenant with him. And since the author of the parable interpreted the union itself of the man and wife as a covenant, he had the covenanted spouses in turn covenant with God specifically as spouses, as one flesh.

The carrying out of their covenant will be evidence of God's activity in the world. Through their populating the earth and subduing it as instruments of his power and authority, these will be made evident in the human race. But most appositely of all, as the creation poem said ex-pressly, the marital pair is an image of God, or at least a resemblance of him, in creation. Whoever searches creation for a shadow of God's nature must not fail to search men and women in marriage. Especially on this point the Christian fathers were to deem marriage a sacrament from the beginning.

Sources of the Sacrament in the Prophetic Books

We have seen that one of the elements of any sacrament in the Jewish-Christian tradition is its function as a sign, as evidence of God's intervention in human experience, and conversely as a sign of human response to the intervention. Within this tradition there is a strand of interpretation that takes the sacramental sign from the generic to the specific. It says that in sacramental action, and in the sacramental situa-tion that the action originally establishes and subsequently expresses, the persons involved replicate sensately what God does supra-sensately. The sacramental action and situation act out, on the human stage, what has taken place or is taking place on the divine. Consequently a person who comes to the sacrament willing, in antecedent faith, to accept what it proposes can detect in it the design, even the scenario of God's action. Such is an image-theology of the sacraments.

Inevitably the neo-Platonic philosophy and world-view so current in the Hellenist culture of the early Christian generations would be most congenial to this theology, and would help to develop it. A way of seeing the sensate dimension of the universe as an image of the supra-sensate would have this congeniality ready and waiting. However Hellenist neo-Platonism did not create this image-theology. We have already seen the modest assertion of it in the Genesis creation poem. But it had begun two centuries earlier in the oracles of the prophet Hosea, had continued during intervening decades in the words of the prophet Jeremiah, and was made vivid in the sixth century by two contemporaries and fellow exiles of the Genesis poet, the prophet Ezekiel and the anonymous poet who has been named Deutero-Isaiah.

The religious experience, and the insight into this experience, that bred the image-theology was the following. Israel's teacher-prophets understood that her relationship as a people with God was a covenant. He had chosen and called this insignificant people to carry out his work of rescue in the human race, to be, in Isaiah's words, "a light to the nations" (49:6). The people Israel had responded to this call with the promise to carry on this work, to carry it on faithfully for all of history. This was the heart of their Sinai experience, which was in turn the reason for their liberation from slavery in the exodus experience.

But in succeeding centuries Israel did not keep faith. She repeatedly violated her covenantal commitment. The infidelity took form most frequently in apostasy from belief in and worship of the one true God, Yahweh, over into the alluring fertility cults of Israel's Gentile neighbors of the Near East, or in the attempt to transform Israel's religion of the Sinai covenant into a fertility cult. With this apostasy the morality of justice and compassion for all Israelites was abandoned, and was replaced by a morality of power, affluence and oppression of the poor, derived from the pagan cults taking its place.

It was against this infidelity that the prophet Hosea protested in the last years of Jeroboam II, ruler of the northern kingdom, Israel. As Jeremiah, Deutero-Isaiah and Ezekiel would after him, Hosea sought for an image, a story, a parable that could make clear to the people the nature of its infidelity and the grievousness of it. It had to be a story that could portray vividly Israel's covenant relationship with God, a story whose setting was a most serious commitment of fidelity, a promise on one side to protect, and on the other to obey and serve. At hand were such relationships as king and vassal, parent and child, master and servant. Hosea bypassed all these and chose the husband-wife relationship. In doing so he almost certainly accepted as essential to it the covenantal character that the author of the garden parable had seen two centuries earlier.

There is small hazard in guessing Hosea's reason for choosing the husband-wife relationship. In it commitment is felt the most keenly because in it love can be the most intense, beyond that of king and vassal or master and servant, and certainly at least the equal of parent and child. It can also be the most freely bestowed love, unlike that of parent and child. Therefore when this marital love is betrayed, the pain of betrayal is felt more acutely than in any other love.

Hosea's own married life became a living enactment of the parable he used in his effort to instruct the people Israel. His wife Gomer turned prostitute after bearing three children or perhaps during her years of bearing them. The prostitution may well have been the cultic prostitution of the Ba'al worship endemic among Israel's Canaanite neighbors. Hosea drew from this deeply felt betrayal to portray to his people how they were betraying their love promised to Yahweh. And in his planned treatment of Gomer he instructed them in the way Yahweh would treat them, and thereby interpreted to them prophetically their future history of punishment and humiliation. He would punish Gomer; he would take back the rich gifts he had given her, and would snatch away the gifts given her by her lovers. He would strip her and shame her in these lovers' eyes.

But Hosea did not intend this punishment by deprivation and humiliation to be irreversible abandonment. He intended it to be medicinal, to bring Gomer to her senses. If she would repent and return, and return to her first love commitment, he would take her back, with his own love stronger than ever. He had made his promise and would keep it. He would never abandon her.

This private saga of love and betrayal and then recovered love makes up the first three chapters of Hosea's book of prophecy. In it he blurs the line of distinction between his own marriage, the imaging parable, and the Yahweh-Israel covenant, the reality imaged in the parable.

> Since she has not known
>> that it was I who gave her
>> the grain, the wine, and the oil,
> And her abundance of silver,
>> and of gold, which they used for Baal,
> Therefore I will take back my grain in its time,
>> and my wine in its season;
> I will snatch away my wool and my flax,
>> with which she covers her nakedness.
> So now I will lay bare her shame
>> before the eyes of her lovers,
>> and no one can deliver her out of my hand.
> I will bring an end to all her joy,
>> her feasts, her new moons, her sabbaths,
>> and all her solemnities.
> I will lay waste her vines and her fig trees,
>> of which she said, "These are the hire
>> my lovers have given me";
> I will turn them into rank growth
>> and wild beasts shall devour them.
> I will punish her for the days of the Baals,
>> for whom she burnt incense
> While she decked herself out with her
>> rings and her jewels,
>> and, in going after her lovers,
>> forgot me, says the Lord (2:10–15).

That is the punishment Hosea promises Gomer, and in doing so foretells for Israel the punishment at the hands of Yahweh. But immediately thereon comes the promise not to abandon.

> If she runs after her lovers, she shall not overtake them;
>   if she looks for them she shall not find them.
> Then she shall say,
>   "I will go back to my first husband,
>   for it was better with me than now."
> So I will allure her;
>   I will lead her into the desert
>   and speak to her heart.
> From there I will give her the vineyards she had,
>   and the valley of Achor as a door of hope.
> She shall respond there as in the days of her youth,
>   when she came up from the land of Egypt.
> On that day, says the Lord,
> She shall call me "My husband,"
>   and never again "My baal" (2:8–18).

Did Jesus have in mind the significance of this last verse when, in his dispute with the Pharisees about husbands' right to dismiss their wives (Mk 10:1–9; Mt 19:1–9), he denied that husbands have such authority? Since God's forgiveness had come fully with Jesus' coming, a husband was no longer "Ba'al" to his wife as the garden parable had ordained in its punishment of history's first wife—no longer her master. Now he was her husband, her companion, and flesh with her again.

The Metaphor in the Oracles of Jeremiah and Deutero-Isaiah

The prophet Jeremiah warned and scolded his people of the surviving southern kingdom, Judah, during the last years before its destruction at the hands of the Babylonian king, Nebuchadnezzar, in 587 B.C. He used the same metaphor that Hosea had used to describe the conduct that was bringing punishment upon Judah, punishment by a pagan army acting as an unwitting instrument of God. The metaphor surfaces intermittently at the beginning of his oracles pronounced during the reign of Josiah (628–609 B.C.), but never in the systematic analogy that Hosea worked out.

But he made the comparison clearly. The people Israel (by now reduced to the kingdom of Judah) was like a girl who had been taken to wife by a noble and caring man. He had enriched her with every kind of gift, had made her his queen. But she had betrayed him by going promiscuously to every kind of lover.

> This word of the Lord came to me Jeremiah:
> Go, cry out this message for Jerusalem to hear!
>
> I remember the devotion of your youth,
> how you loved me as a bride,

Following me in the desert,
in a land unsown (2:1–2)

              *   *   *

How well you pick your way
    when seeking love!
You who, in your wickedness,
    have gone by ways unclean!

              *   *   *

If a man sends away his wife,
    and, after leaving him
    she marries another man,
Does the first husband come back to her?
Would not the land be wholly defiled?
But you have sinned with many lovers,
    and yet you would return to me!
    says the Lord (3:1).

A generation later the poet-prophet known to us only as Deutero-Isaiah was the third to use this metaphor. But his mood and his intent were very different from Jeremiah's. For Jeremiah his people's infidelity was still flagrant and unpunished. His intent was to warn of punishment soon to come in the destruction of Judah, of its holy city Jerusalem, and in the carrying off of the best of its people into slavery in Babylon. But Deutero-Isaiah had already seen the punishment. He was one of the exiles, living out that part of the punishment with his people. Therefore his voice was one of hope. It was not an empty hope, not a merely human optimism. It was grounded in God's faithfulness to Israel from his side of the covenant with her. It is most relevant to our own purpose that the poet saw this covenantal fidelity as that of a husband whose love cannot be destroyed. And his love cannot be destroyed because he is Israel's creator.

For he who has become your husband is your Maker;
    his name is the Lord of hosts;
Your redeemer is the Holy One of Israel,
    called God of all the earth.
The Lord calls you back,
    like a wife forsaken and grieved in spirit,
A wife married in youth and then cast off,
    says your God.
For a brief moment I abandoned you,
    but with great tenderness I will take you back.
In an outburst of wrath, for a moment
    I hid my face from you;
But with enduring love I take pity on you,
    says the Lord, your redeemer (54:5–8).

A half-century after Jeremiah, and contemporary with Deutero-Isaiah, Ezekiel uttered his prophetic oracles that included this same interpretative vision of Judah's history. The interpretation is encapsuled in Chapter 16 of Ezekiel's book of prophecy, in a parable remarkable for its savage accusation of his own people. The parable followed the by now familiar story line: Yahweh, a royal prince, has found Israel, an abandoned half-breed girl child. He has adopted her, brought her up in splendor, and made her his wife. But she has betrayed him, playing prostitute to every passer-by and to every pagan idol, even burning her children in service to the idol's cult. To shock her back to her senses her husband strips and shames her. But despite all he does not abandon her.

> For thus speaks the Lord God: I will deal with you according to what you have done, you who despised your oath, breaking a covenant. Yet I will remember the covenant I made with you when you were a girl, and I will set up an everlasting covenant with you. . . . For I will re-establish my covenant with you, that you may know that I am the Lord, that you may remember and be covered with confusion, and that you may be utterly silenced for shame when I pardon you for all you have done, says the Lord God (16:59–63).

That Catholic theology would draw a key element of its interpretation of marriage from these prophetic oracles is not surprising. But what is sometimes not noticed is the logical tactic that had to be adopted in order to gain this use. Searching about for a familiar human relationship that could portray vividly to their people the transcendent relationship God had formed with them, these prophets selected marriage. They thus implied an analogy, a similarity of these two relationships. They intended that the analogy be used to enlighten by leading the minds of their audience from the familiar relationship (here human marriage) as an entry to understanding the unfamiliar (Israel's marital relationship with God). In doing this the prophets implied that marriage on earth contains the potential to be a sign, even an image of the love relationship of God and his people.

We shall see that the Catholic theologians reversed roles for these two relationships. Starting with the transcendent relationship of God with his people—a relationship identified in Ephesians 5 with Christ and the Church—they used it as an avenue of enlightenment for understanding the marital relationship of Christian spouses. In this singular use of the *via inventionis,* the sensate sign, the image, is made intelligible by the invisible reality that it is said to image. This is a precarious use of analogy, and when it is done it deserves careful inspection.

The Prophet Malachi

Not until a century and a half after Ezekiel and Deutero-Isaiah does a prophet refer to Jewish marriages expressly as covenants. This is Malachi, who spoke to his people during the interim following the voluntary return of many Jews from Babylonian captivity and before the great reform set under way by Ezra and Nehemiah in about 445. Malachi's oracles too were in reproof of the people's conduct and were directed mainly at two abuses. The first was the carelessness and even deceit of priests and Levites in offering sacrifice of flawed animals, in violation of the law of Leviticus 22:17–25 and Deuteronomy 17:1.

The second abuse was not in worship. It cut deeper into the private lives of Jewish men and women and at the same time into their social coherence in a way that threatened their very character as a covenanted people. This was Jewish husbands' practice of abandoning their Jewish wives in order to take pagan wives in their place.

Malachi saw this as grievous infidelity in two ways. In the first place it violated Israel's covenant with God. But it also violated the covenants of husbands and wives. Indeed this second infidelity caused the first. And it involved a serious injustice toward the Jewish wives.

> Have we not all the one Father?
>   Has not the one God created us?
> Why then do we break faith with each other,
>   violating the covenant of our fathers? (2:10).

The prophet saw this abandonment itself, even short of taking pagan wives, as the destroyer of the people. For to put the wife out of the marriage, to put her out of the family, was to put her out of the bond of covenant. And thus breaking his own Jewish marriage the husband put himself outside the covenant. Malachi deemed such conduct by the husband worthy of excommunication.

> Judah has broken faith; an abominable thing
>   has been done in Israel and in Jerusalem.
> Judah has profaned the temple which the Lord loves,
>   and has married an idolatrous woman.
> May the Lord cut off from the man who does this
>   both witness and advocate out of the tents of Jacob,
>   and anyone to offer sacrifice to the Lord of hosts! (2:11–12).

The prophet reaches deeper into the husbands' reneging on covenant with God in violating the marital covenant. To dismiss their Jewish wives is to contradict God's will, to try to destroy his work. For it is he who creates their marriages, forms them in one flesh.

... the Lord is witness
    between you and the wife of your youth,
With whom you have broken faith
    though she is your companion,
    your betrothed wife.
Did he not make one being, with flesh and spirit;
    and what does that one require but godly offspring?
You must then safeguard life that is your own,
    and not break faith with the wife of your youth.
For I hate divorce,
    says the Lord, the God of Israel (2:14–16).

Malachi's contribution to the sacramental interpretation of marriage consists not only of his referring to his people's marriages as covenants. One can find it also in the way he relates them to Israel's collective covenant with God. He does not say that they are signs of it or that they image it. He repeats what his predecessors said, that God joined the first husband and wife in the most intimate personal union of one flesh, and that God acts in the creation of every Jewish marriage. But he adds his own thought that to keep Israel's covenant with God a husband must also keep covenant with his wife. To destroy the latter is to put himself outside Israel's covenant. This says at least that keeping the lesser personal covenant is a condition of keeping the greater collective covenant. It also comes very close to saying that the lesser covenant is a subset of the greater, even a constituent element of it. If this is true, it produces an illumining of understanding that is reciprocal: God's relationship with Israel is marital, and Jewish marriages are relationships containing a more than merely human value and firmness. Some vital ingredients of a sacrament are there.

Divine Blessing as a Sacramental Element

The religious act of one person's blessing another has been so common in the Judaeo-Christian tradition for so many centuries, and blessing is done so casually, that its meaning has all but vanished from the modern mind. Christians hardly treasure it as a central and characteristic element of their religious conduct.

But for the Jewish people of Jesus' time and of centuries earlier blessing was central and characteristic. How early in their history this was so is evident in the folk-traditions of their patriarchs. Esau begged piteously for his father Isaac's blessing after his mother Rebekah's trickery had got that blessing instead for his brother Jacob. He knew that his future was ruined without it.

It was not only that without it he lacked his father's approval. A contemporary scholar explains how much more was involved.

In O.T. Blessing is conceived as a communication of life from Yahweh. With life come vigor and strength and success, which bring one peace of mind and peace with the world. Yahweh himself is the only one who can bless: men bless by wishing and praying that Yahweh will bless. . . . The effect of blessing most frequently mentioned is for fertility, whether in men, animals or crops.[9]

To bless someone therefore is to either acknowledge a link with divinity or to create it. It is a productive link; through it a person is enlivened, empowered for a favorable and enriching conduct. It is akin to Christian ordaining in its fullest sense, which is to both authorize a person for important action in a community and to give that person the power to carry it on. (It should be clear that ordaining, when understood of the Christian sacraments, refers to more than the sacrament of orders. Baptism itself is an ordaining to a kind of life, confirmation more so, and marriage even more.)

Therefore even a modest examination of the marriage blessings in Jewish pre-Christian history seems certain to yield more understanding of the origins of the sacrament in marriage.

It will help to do a twin search here by including the place of fertility in Israel's understanding of marriage. As we have just seen, the effect of blessing most frequently mentioned in Jewish tradition is fertility. This means that fertility for the Israelite lay at the heart of his or her religion, of the covenant with God, of Israel's vocation in the world. For the Israelites fertility may not have involved near-organic participation in sexually imagined divinity, as in the fertility cults of their neighbors. But it certainly played a role in their religious fidelity to Yahweh.

The subgroups among them who urged celibacy and lived it at least temporarily, for example the Qumranite Essenes, did so either because they believed that Israel as a nation had forfeited its vocation by the infidelity that we have seen the prophets excoriate, or also because they awaited the imminent end of the world.

We have already seen in the creation poem the divine blessing that followed immediately on the forming of the first human couple. Its clearly intended effect was fertility, and with the fertility—and perhaps by means of it—both the authority and the power to manage the world: "God blessed them, saying 'Be fertile and multiply; fill the earth and subdue it.' "

The blessing for fertility appears in the oldest Hebrew traditions, those of the patriarchs. "God said further to Abraham: 'As for your wife Sarai, do not call her Sarai; her name shall be Sarah. I will bless her, and I will give you a son by her. Him also will I bless; he shall give rise to nations, and rulers of peoples shall issue from him' " (Gen 17:15–16).

Rebekah's brothers blessed her as they sent her off with Abraham's servant to become the bride of Isaac: "Sister, may you grow into thousands of myriads . . ." (Gen 24:60).

Isaac's blessing of Jacob, thanks to Rebekah's deceit, intended the son's prosperity to be gained from fertility:

> May God give to you of the dew of the heavens
>   and of the fertility of the earth
>   abundance of grain and wine (Gen 27:28).

Correlatively the consequence of Esau's being tricked out of this blessing of primogeniture was his infertility.

> . . . and Esau wept aloud. Finally Isaac spoke again and said to
>   him:
> Ah, far from the fertile earth
>   shall be your dwelling;
>   far from the dew of the heavens above (Gen 27:38).

Again, as Isaac sent Jacob off to his maternal grandfather to find a wife among his own kinsmen, he blessed him:

> Go now to Paddan-aram, to the home of your mother's father,
> Bethuel, and there choose a wife for yourself from among the
> daughters of your uncle, Laban. May God almighty bless you
> and make you fertile, multiplying you so that you may become
> an assembly of people (Gen 27:2–3).

Finally, when the aged Jacob on his deathbed blessed Joseph's sons, Ephraim and Manasseh, prolongation of family and fertility was the intent of his blessing:

> May the God in whose ways
>   my fathers Abraham and Isaac walked,
>   . . . bless these boys,
> That in them my name be recalled,
>   and the names of my fathers, Abraham and Isaac,
> And they may become teeming multitudes
>   upon the earth (Gen 48:15–16).

The Song of Songs

An examination of the sources of marital sacramentality in the Hebrew scriptures can draw on the Song of Songs in one or both of two ways. It can take from this love lyric directly in its own character as a celebration of erotic heterosexual love, as the lyric was probably sung in whole or in some of its parts at Jewish wedding feasts. Or the examination can draw from it in its adapted character as a Jewish allegory of the love relationship of Yahweh and Israel, or in the Christian adaptation of that adaptation as an allegory of the Christ-Church relationship.

In either case the examiner must face something unique, with a diversity in the uniqueness from case to case. If he or she draws directly from the poem, the most transparent erotically sexual themes and images await, as does the work of finding the place for these themes and images in the marriage sacrament. If the approach is by way of the allegories which were constructed in an attempt to denature the erotic sexuality, to exorcise it, one must still reckon with what happened to this erotic sexuality when taken into the allegories, and reckon with how to appropriate the now erotically sown allegories to the sacrament.

The authorship of the Song of Songs is traditionally attributed to Solomon, the third of Israel's kings, in the tenth century B.C.; hence its alternate title, The Song of Solomon. In reality its late vocabulary marks it as coming from after the end of Judah's exile in Babylon in 538. It is a cluster of songs composed by one or more authors. In literary form it is a lyric dialogue containing unresolved dramatic tension and movement. The personae of the dialogue are the girl, her lover, and "the daughters of Jerusalem," a dramatic chorus. The poem is obviously influenced by Egyptian erotic love poetry, since in imagery and vocabulary it is so akin to that poetry. For example, the lover calls the girl his sister, an endearing appellation characteristic of Egyptian love poetry, thanks probably to the Isis-Osiris sibling marriage.

Whether the allegoric associations mentioned above can be justified is an independent question, and does not concern us here. But in origin the poem is not an allegory. Its original and unadapted referent is a fictional but powerful, consuming, indestructible relationship of two young heterosexual lovers—not spouses but lovers. As such it was first understood and sung by the Jewish common people before being allegorized by their religious authorities. As such it may be used as a source of marriage's sacramentality.

The following are themes in the poem that seem most assimilable into the theology of the sacrament.

The lovers' passion is awakened especially in the springtime along with nature's fertile awakening, is stimulated by this awakening, is expressed in its images. Nothing of Yahweh's curse of nature as man's enemy in punishment for the first sin is here. Their love extends and affirms an innocent and fruitful nature; this nature does the same for their love (2:8–14).

The goodness and innocence of what is natural is asserted three times in the girl's plea to the young women in the chorus that they not stir up love artificially or apart from its own impulse. It has its own season, its own pace; these must be honored.

> I adjure you, daughters of Jerusalem . . .
> Do not arouse, do not stir up love
>   before its own time (2:7, 3:6; 8:4).

A theme central to erotic love everywhere and in all ages, and certainly an erotic dream scenario, is desire intensified by the lovers' separation. Their time together is rare and brief and therefore spent the more passionately. They wander, searching for the absent lover, but futilely (3:1–4; 5:2–8). Meanwhile they are sick with unfulfilled desire (1:2–4; 4:9–11). The hint is somber: it is passion's fate to go unfulfilled in this life.

The lovers' passion is locked exclusively onto one another. They willingly grant to one another possessory rights of their persons: "My lover belongs to me and I to him" (6:3). Because of this they reserve the sexual expression of their love to one another. Her lover honors this in the girl: "You are an enclosed garden, my sister, my bride, an enclosed garden, a fountain sealed" (4:12). But the garden is rich in fruits not for its own sake. They are meant to be given in love. The loved one is invited to come and make the garden his own, and partake of all the fruits. This love is self-giving.

> Let my love come to his garden
> and eat its choice fruits.
> I have come to my garden, my sister, my bride;
> I gather my myrrhs and my spices.
> I eat my honey and my sweetmeats,
> I drink my wine and my milk (4:16–5:1).

The imagery of offering and taking love—a key characteristic of the love in the poem—is sexual. And the chorus' comment in the verse immediately following once again addresses this love's innocence: "Eat, friends, drink! Drink freely of love!" (5:1).

In the song's most passionate verses the lovers express their desire for love's completion in sexual intercourse, express it in traditional images that veil thinly the sexual yearning. First the lover:

> How beautiful you are, how pleasing,
> my love, my delight!
> Your very figure is like a palm tree.
> Your breasts are like clusters.
> I said: I will climb the palm tree
> I will take hold of its branches (7:7–10).

The girl replies in the language of sexual yearning:

I belong to my love,
and for me he yearns (7:11).

The Hebrew verb that is here translated "yearns" is the same as that used in Genesis 3:6, *tešûqâ,* to express women's sexual desire for their husbands despite the agony of childbirth, as punishment for the first wife's having led her husband into sin. But here the yearning is emphatically not punishment.

Where, toward the end of the song, the lovers declare their love's power to endure, we come upon a feature unique in the treatment of love in the Judaeo-Christian tradition, a feature that has not been well integrated in the Christian theology of marriage. It is that erotic love itself wants to be permanent. The passion that impels the lovers to sexual union gives their love such strength. It is the girl who says this; the verses of the song in which she makes the claim begin with a metaphor of belonging and fidelity: "Set me as a seal on your heart, as a seal on your arm" (8:6). (In ancient times a cylindric seal containing an image or an emblem was hung like a pendant about the neck or tied to the arm.) Note well that it is the kind of love lyricized throughout the entire poem, love that lingers over and feasts on the physical beauty of the beloved, that urges this monogamous fidelity.

The girl continues, insisting that the love she shares equals in strength death and the nether world, two forces perceived by the ancients as both overpowering and beyond resisting. It is even stronger than the primeval waters, another preternatural power in the ancient cosmogony.

For stern as death is love,
  relentless as the nether world is devotion;
  its flames are a blazing fire.
Deep waters cannot quench love,
  nor floods sweep it away (8:6–7).

That the sexual passion that produces erotic love has not been well integrated into the Christian theology of marriage is most evident in Christian teachers' following the Jewish lead in interpreting the Song of Songs as an allegory of God's love for his people. The strong-as-death love, the desire that craves union, the exclusive belonging of the lovers to one another are all taken away from the possibility of human desire and resolve. They become, in the Christian allegory, traits of Christ's love for the Church and of her, metaphorized as bride, for him. We shall see that the Christian fathers do not credit faithful monogamy and lifelong devotion to eros, and certainly not to its sexual expression. They establish rather an inverse proportion: they hope for faithful monogamy and lifelong devotion the more firmly Christian spouses tether their eros, and in its place accept and live by God's gift of agapaic love.

The Story of Tobit

The Song of Songs may have been popular in post-exilic Jewish wedding feasts to help carry the mood of happy sensuality. But the Jewish scripture that got closest to the heart of the wedding ceremony of Jesus' people in his day, then during the Talmudic period and permanently thereafter, was the book of Tobit.[10]

Tobit is a religious novelette rich in Jewish folk customs of marriage and family in the post-exilic generations. Therefore, despite its character as fiction it contains much factual information about attitudes toward and conduct in marriage. Its date of composition is probably about 200 B.C.; its place is probably a Jewish community in the Mesopotamian valley where the story is set, or perhaps in Palestine itself. Its central figures are a devout, generous and even heroic Jewish father living in Nineveh among the exiles from Israel deported by the Assyrian conquerors in 721 B.C.; the man's wife, Anna; his son, Tobiah; Sarah, who in the course of the story becomes Tobiah's wife; and the angel Raphael.

Tobit, old, stripped of his wealth and blind, sends Tobiah to the city of Rages in Media to recover money held there on deposit and to find a wife among his kinsmen in the city of Ecbatana. This was to be his wife Sarah.

The great risk in the latter project lay in this, that Sarah had already been wedded to seven husbands, but every one of these had been killed in the bridal chamber on the wedding night before the marriage could be consummated—killed by the demon Asmodeus.

The pertinence of the story to this examination differs from the story's own formal intent, which is to show God's providential care for his people even in deepest adversity, and to vindicate the belief that piety and fidelity are ultimately rewarded with happiness in this life—a belief that Job did not share. Our interest centers rather in the following points. The first is that among the devout faithful a marriage is so much God's doing that he even preordains who the partners are to be. For the angel Raphael assures Tobiah against his fear to take Sarah in marriage: "But do not be afraid, for she was set apart for you before the world existed" (6:18). This faith was echoed by Sarah's father, Raguel. When giving his daughter ceremonially to Tobiah in marriage, he declares, "She is yours according to the decree of the Book of Moses. Your marriage has been decided in heaven!" (7:11)

Tobiah himself, in his prayer that night in the bridal chamber with Sarah, reaffirms the divine hand in the marriage, even in its institution at the beginning of history, and acknowledges God's benign intent in instituting it.

"Blessed are you, O God of our fathers;
    praised be your name forever and ever.

Let the heavens and all your creation
  praise you forever.
You made Adam and you gave him his wife Eve
  to be his help and support;
  and from these two the human race descended.
You said, 'It is not good for the man to be alone;
  let us make him a partner like himself' " (8:5–6).

A second matter of relevance in the story contrasts the impulse and motive for Tobiah's marrying with the passionate force that brought the lovers together in the Song of Songs. Tobiah expressly disavows desire as the motive for his wedding Sarah; by no means does he marry her out of erotic longing. For his prayer (above) continues immediately:

"Now, Lord, you know that I take this wife of mine
  not out of lust,
  but for a noble purpose" (8:7).

The noble purpose is made clear from early in the story and is a main part of its theme. It is to preserve the name, the home and the fortune of Tobit, and by doing so to glorify God who rewards religious loyalty and filial obedience with this life's happiness. For Tobiah takes Sarah out of obedience to his father's desire and command that he find a wife only among his kinsmen. In fact the reason he comes to love her is that she is a kinswoman. He falls in love with her for just this reason before ever laying eyes on her.

When Tobiah heard Raphael say that she was his kinswoman,
of his own family lineage, he fell deeply in love with her, and
his heart became set on her (6:18).

To prove the nobility of his motive in marrying Sarah, Tobiah refrains that wedding night from consummating the marriage. The verses closing the nuptial prayer in which he claims the nobler purpose, also close down abruptly the scene of the wedding night.

"Call down your mercy on me and on her,
  and allow us to live together to happy old age."
They said together, "Amen, amen," and went to bed for the
  night (8:7).

Centuries of commentators have suggested that Tobiah escaped being the demon's eighth victim, by spending his wedding night in prayer and quiet sleep rather than in indulging his lust—this in face of the plain explanation (in 8:1–3) that the demon fled to the Egyptian desert because Tobiah assaulted it with the repellant odor of burning fish giblets. Nevertheless the story makes the point clearly enough. It would be repeated centuries later and would become decisive in the Christian patristic and medieval interpretation of marriage: marriage's goodness is to be found elsewhere than in the powerful, interpenetrating, sexually pleasurable, reciprocal expression of erotic passion. Such passion is not only subservient to a higher purpose but is to be denied because of this purpose. Since later theology of the sacrament will say that the sacrament is the marriage itself made a sign and instrument of God's sanctifying action in the spouses, the place of erotic passion in the sacrament will be a dubious one.

This denial of passion would also breed a theological problem rarely noticed. Since the authoritative Christian teachers accepted the Song of Songs only on condition it be construed as an analogy of the love relationship of Christ and the Church, and since they repeated for centuries that a marriage of two Christians is a sacrament in that it images that divine love relationship, what happens to erotic passion in this analogy? Is it simply forgotten? Is it replaced by an exclusively agapaic, solely self-sacrificing love? Or is it taken up into and expressed in Christ's self-giving love, so that this self-giving is driven by Christ's very human passion? If the last is the case, two questions arise, both of them little examined by the theology of marriage. First, is Christ's redemptive love also erotic? Second, what is the role in Christian sacramental marriages of erotic passion?

The Christians' preference for Tobiah's noble purpose served also to reinforce a persuasion they would later draw from classic Greek political philosophy. It is that marriage in its own nature is a dutiful vocation (the medieval theologians would call it an *officium*). It is not for the spouses themselves. It is an instrumental good in that it exists in order to realize a good outside itself. This is the continuation and the well-being of civil society and the state.[11] Tobiah's main motive for marrying Sarah differed from this only in the size of its object. It was the continuation and well-being of his father's family.

The Jewish Marriage Blessings

That the Jewish people of the generations following Jesus did not concede exclusive first place in marriage to Tobiah's noble purpose is evident in the blessings that were a central part of their wedding ceremony. These blessings, The Seven Benedictions, in the formulas that come down to us, date from the Talmudic period, which began c. 200 A.D. But they may well have been handed down from Jesus' generation itself.

The blessings include petitionary prayers. What is petitioned in them most repeatedly and earnestly are the pleasure and the joy of the bridal couple and of the other celebrants of the wedding. The fertility of the couple is not mentioned. The only hint at the continuation of the people Israel is in the fourth benediction, wherein Zion (a metonym for Jerusalem, in turn a metonym for Israel) rejoices at finding her "children" themselves gathered happily within her. Not to go unnoticed is the creature named in the first benediction as the reason for gratitude to Yahweh.

> Blessed art thou, O Lord our God, King of the universe, who created the fruit of the vine.
>
> Blessed art thou, O Lord our God, King of the universe, who hast created all things to thy glory.
>
> Blessed art thou, O Lord our God, King of the universe, Creator of man.
>
> Blessed art thou, O Lord our God, King of the universe, who hast made man in thine image, after thy likeness, and hast prepared unto him, out of his very self, a perpetual fabric. Blessed art thou, O Lord, Creator of man.
>
> May she who was barren (Zion) be exceeding glad and exult, when her childen are gathered within her in joy. Blessed art thou, O Lord, who makest bridegroom and bride to rejoice.
>
> O make these loved companions greatly to rejoice, even as of old thou didst gladden thy creature in the garden of Eden. Blessed art thou, O Lord, who makest bridegroom and bride to rejoice.
>
> Blessed art thou, O Lord our God, King of the universe, who hast created joy and gladness, bridegroom and bride, mirth and exultation, pleasure and delight, love, brotherhood, peace and fellowship. Soon may there be heard in the cities of Judah, and in the streets of Jerusalem, the voice of joy and gladness, the voice of the bridegroom and the voice of the bride, the jubilant voice of bridegrooms from their canopies, and of youths from their feasts of song. Blessed art thou, O Lord, who makest the bridegroom to rejoice with the bride.[12]

Marriage in the Wisdom Literature

There is another kind of Hebrew religious literature that influenced Christian teaching substantially and even made its way organically into this teaching and its own literature. It is the wisdom literature, a genre that the Jews themselves borrowed from neighbors older than themselves in the Near East, most evidently from the Egyptian *Sebayit,* ancient instruction in the proprieties of life for courtiers.

The material of wisdom literature consists of instructions in attitudes and conduct, instructions that accumulated and were passed down

through the centuries. It was the custom for later purveyors of this literature to attribute it to the authorship of a single wise man in antiquity. For
the Jewish wisdom literature this was King Solomon, the wise man par
excellence. The attribution was of course pseudonymous, since this literature, despite its long accumulating, dates in its present form from after the
Jews' return from Babylonian exile in the last third of the sixth century
B.C. Like other peoples' wisdom literature, Israel's is the product of two
main and mostly anonymous sources, her own wise men (the *hakamin*),
and the people themselves, who were often the wisest of all.[13]

Although the ancient wisdom literature was in general not religious,
the Jews' literature was. For them all of life was lived under God's
scrutiny; therefore instruction in life attitudes and conduct was instruction in living that is righteous under that scrutiny. Since marriage lay at
the heart of Jewish religious life, Jewish wisdom literature had much to
say about it and about sexuality itself. What is striking to the modern eye
is that wise instruction about them is clearly formulated not only by men
alone but for them alone. Women's place in them is always literally
objective. They are the objects of passion, of admiration, of care, of
gratitude, of caution, of suspicion, of contempt. Not even fictionally is
any saying ever addressed to a woman. Husbands are warned repeatedly
against the other woman's allure. No wife is ever warned about a husband's fragile fidelity.

For a survey as brief as this it is helpful to distinguish examples of
kinds of wisdom sayings and lodge them under certain themes. There is
first the theme of good fortune of having a good wife, and of the happiness that can come of life with her. The book of Proverbs states this in its
characteristically succinct style.

> He who finds a wife finds happiness;
>   it is a favor he receives from the Lord (8:22).

Certainly the most explicit praise of women in the wisdom literature
is the portrait, in the final chapter of Proverbs, of the ideal wife. It
almost certainly found its way into the Jews' sacred writings before the
Song of Songs did. But one suspects that even if its author had read or
heard the Song of Songs he would have found it difficult to include
among the traits of his good wife that which made the shepherd girl the
object of her lover's passion. The portrait is very likely the work of a
sober-minded husband of middle years or later. In selecting for praise in
the wife the virtues that he lists, he moves in the direction of Ben
Sirach's undisguised caution about wives and women generally.

> When one finds a worthy wife,
>   her value is far beyond pearls.
> Her husband, entrusting his heart to her,
>   has an unfailing prize. . . .

She picks out a field to purchase;
  out of her earnings she plants a vineyard.
She reaches out her hands to the poor,
  and extends her arms to the needy. . . .
She makes garments and sells them,
  and stocks the merchants with belts. . . .
She opens her mouth in wisdom,
  and on her tongue is kindly counsel.
She watches the conduct of her household,
  and eats not her food in idleness.
Her children rise up and praise her;
  her husband too extols her.

The author of Ben Sirach is more copious in his favorable commentary on marriage, as we shall see he is also in his somber commentary.

Dismiss not a sensible wife;
  a gracious wife is more precious than corals (7:19).

Sheepfolds and orchards bring flourishing health,
  but better than either, a devoted wife (40:19–20).

Happy the husband of a good wife,
  twice-lengthened are his days;
A worthy wife brings joy to her husband,
  peaceful and full is his life.
A good wife is a generous gift
  bestowed upon him who fears the Lord;
Be he rich or poor, his heart is content,
  and a smile is ever on his face (26:1–4).

A gracious wife delights her husband,
  her thoughtfulness puts flesh on his bones;
A gift from the Lord is her governed speech,
  and her firm virtue is of surpassing worth.
Choicest of blessings is a modest wife,
  priceless her chaste person.
Like the sun rising in the Lord's heavens,
  the beauty of a virtuous wife is the radiance of her home.
Like the light which shines above the holy lampstand,
  are her beauty of face and graceful figure.
Golden columns on silver bases
  are her shapely limbs and steady feet (26:13–18).

A woman's beauty makes her husband's face light up,
  for it surpasses all else that charms the eye;

And if, besides, her speech is kindly,
   his lot is beyond that of mortal men.
A wife is her husband's richest treasure,
   a helpmate, a steadying column.
A vineyard with no hedge will be overrun;
   a man with no wife becomes a homeless wanderer (36:22–26).

The following passage from Qoheleth is understandable only within the author's characteristic perplexity and sadness about the elusive meaning and value of anything in life. His counsel for a man is to enjoy simply and sincerely what he has while he has it, including the companionship of a good wife.

Go, eat your bread with joy and drink your wine with a merry heart, because it is now that God favors your works. . . . Enjoy life with the wife whom you love, all the days of the fleeting life that is granted you under the sun. This is your lot in life, for the toil of your labors under the sun. Anything you can turn your hand to, do with what power you have; for there will be no work, nor reason, nor knowledge, nor wisdom in the nether world where you are going (9:7–10).

But there is the other and somber side of wisdom about marriage. It can bring as much grief as it can happiness. The cause of this, that the authors recognize, is almost always the flawed character of the wife, and only that. Again the author of Proverbs is typically succinct.

It is better to dwell in a corner of the housetop
   than in a roomy house with a quarrelsome woman (21:9).

It is better to dwell in a wilderness
   than with a quarrelsome and vexatious wife (21:19).

For a persistent leak on a rainy day
   the match is a quarrelsome woman.
He who keeps her stores up a stormwind;
   he cannot tell north from south (27:15–16).

The same author of Ben Sirach who recorded lyric praise of a beautiful and good wife had fears about the other kind.

Worst of all wounds is that of the heart,
   worst of all evils is that of a woman.

         *   *   *

No poison is worse than that of a serpent,
   no venom greater than that of a woman.

With a dragon or a lion I would rather dwell
   than live with an evil woman.
Wickedness changes a woman's looks,
   and makes her sullen as a female bear.
When her husband sits among his neighbors,
   a bitter sigh escapes him unawares.
There is scarcely any evil like that in a woman;
   may she fall to the lot of the sinner!
Like a sandy hill to aged feet
   is a railing wife to a quiet man.
Stumble not through woman's beauty,
   nor be greedy for her wealth;
The man is a slave, in disgrace and shame,
   when a wife supports her husband (25:12–21).

At the end of the passage the author goes for the religious-moral jugular, repeating the most serious charge about the origin of sin, a charge that was to be kept alive by the Christian fathers, as we shall see, including St. Paul himself.

In woman was sin's beginning,
   and because of her we all die (25:23).

But long before this author warned about the grief that may await a man in marriage he warned about the snares in association with women generally.

Give no woman power over you
   to trample upon your dignity.
Be not intimate with a strange woman,
   lest you fall into her snares.
With a singing woman be not familiar,
   lest you be caught in her wiles.
Entertain no thoughts against a virgin,
   lest you be enmeshed in damages for her.
Give not yourself to harlots,
   lest you surrender your inheritance.
Gaze not about the lanes of the city
   and wander not through its squares;
Avert your eyes from a comely woman,
   gaze not upon the beauty of another's wife—
Through woman's beauty many perish,
   for lust for it burns like fire.
With a married woman dine not,
   recline not at table to drink by her side,
Lest your heart be drawn to her
   and you go down in blood to the grave (9:2–9).

The one thought that the husband himself may be the cause of his grief is in the first verse of the passage just recorded:

> Be not jealous of the wife of your bosom,
>   lest you teach her to do evil against you (9:1).

Summary

When a Christian student searches the Jewish scriptures for the sources there of the later theology of the sacrament in marriage, he or she will inevitably search in the light of Christian hindsight, since the Christian scriptures already disclose what they have drawn from the Jewish. In one way this helps rather than hinders, because the object of inquiry is exactly the flow of nurture from the Jewish sources to the Christian use of them. Objectivity's demand is that the Christian not read his or her meanings anachronistically back into those sources.

With this caution in mind we make bold to say that at least the Catholic theology of marriage's sacrament is drawn almost entirely from the Jewish scriptures—provided one allow that adaptation in the New Testament may be included in the process of drawing. To justify this claim of entirety is the work of the chapters that follow in this volume. But note that a sacramental experience in a sacramental life-setting is one in which God draws a human being into union with himself—or into closer union—in a way that manifests the drawing and the union sensately.

In light of this it is justifiable to point out what the Jewish scriptures take for granted, that among human beings the two sexes, their need for one another and their irresistible attraction for one another, are God's invention. Because too God is by definition good, these cannot possibly be evil but must be good. So also must be the sexual acting out of men's and women's need for and attraction to one another.

Even before reading in the later creation poem of Genesis 1 that in order to fashion an "image and likeness" of himself God created both the sexes, a person of philosophic mind could reason that if one wonders what God the creator is like, if one searches in his work for traces of his nature, one can find them in his work pictured in the earlier garden parable of Genesis 2. His nature is such as to make the most precious union in the sensate universe the sexually expressed union of a man and woman—more precious than even the union of a man with his parents. God the creator is one who desires union—but only at the price of separation.

In all this the man and woman join with God because in uniting they obey his will. This is a will that has taken the initiative to join them to him, not a will merely responding to any petition on their part to take them to him. This is especially true in the sexual expression of their union because the first command recorded in the Jewish scriptures is

"Increase and multiply; fill the earth and subdue it." (The first express command in the earlier garden parable does not touch the first couple in their sexuality. It is negative: "You may eat from any of the trees of the garden except from the tree of knowledge of good and evil. From that tree you shall not eat . . ." (2:16).

The four prophets—Hosea, Jeremiah, Deutero-Isaiah and Ezekiel—who found in marriage one of the facets of an analogy to describe to the people Israel the grievousness of their episodic apostasy from the God of their fathers did not say that marriage is an image of this God's relationship with the people. They did search for and find an enlightening comparison there. But a comparison does not in itself involve an imaging—as calling King David the lion of Judah does not mean either that David's conduct images a lion's or that a lion's conduct images his. What these prophets did was to imply that a careful examination of the husband-wife relationship can reveal both how it ought to be between God and Israel, and how it in fact has been. They implied clearly that a human marriage carries the potential for disclosing both the ideal of the God-Israel relationship and its less than ideal history. But when one sees the analogic bridge spanning from the one relationship to the other, one must be careful not to think that the model from which the bridge was designed was the divine-human relationship of God with the people Israel. (Centuries later Catholic theologians would assume this and set out to draw their theology of the sacrament from it.) On the contrary, the prophets' model was the human marriage. They could imagine God as the metaphoric husband in a metaphoric marriage only after having known real husbands in real marriages. In short, the *via inventionis* they opened led from the earth upward, not from heaven earthward.

Nevertheless their opening that road also opened access to a prescriptive model of caring love that could be urged on all husbands—and a model of submissive, obedient love that could be urged on all wives. And if it could be established that a human husband and wife could sustain such love only on condition that they live in union with God, their union could, by the inquiring eyes of faith, be seen as evidence that God is active in their marriage.

That the primeval model of marriage designed by God was covenant is hinted, as we have seen, in the verbs used to describe a man's separating from his father and mother in order to go and join most intimately with his wife—to cling to her. The prophet Malachi took this interpretation from hint to express declaration. He warned and scolded the husbands of his time who abandoned their Jewish wives and married Gentiles: they were reneging on a covenantal commitment. This was the commitment not only to their wives but to the God of Israel himself. Here, perhaps unwittingly, Malachi added strength to the earlier prophets' analogy. Not only can a marriage be evidence of God's loving relationship to Israel, but Jewish husbands' fidelity is a condition of their keeping covenant with God. And since they make up the real, non-metaphoric Israel, its fidelity to God is kept only by their keeping covenant with him by keeping covenant with their wives.

The authors of the wisdom books told, from nearer to the first demise of Israel as a gathered people, of the fulfillment of both the primeval promises about marriage. It was to be a source of the most inclusive and profound happiness for men and women. It was also, and paradoxically, to provide the most lasting and bitter unhappiness. These authors did not insist on the assumed fact of primitive history that so many Christian fathers would intone repeatedly, that it was first woman who took the lead in bringing misery into marriage by going first in breaking the implied covenant of paradise. But the author of Sirach, for one, left the clear message that women generally, and wives particularly, can lead a man to misery and ruin. His warning against their power over men pointed backward to the power of the first woman—the "suitable helpmate" God gave to the first man because it was not good for him to be alone—that had led him to choose her will over God's.

The facet of man-woman love least assimilated into marriage by Israel's prophets, by her poets and her wise men, was the erotic passion of the lovers in the Song of Songs. The only relevance to marriage they permitted the Song was its allegoric reference to the metaphoric God-Israel relationship—safely out of the way of real-life marriages. Gratefully the Jewish common people kept it alive in their wedding feasts, where its passion still waits to be taken over into its place in the sacrament in marriage.

NOTES

1. David Daube, *The New Testament and Rabbinic Judaism,* Part II, Legislative and Narrative Forms, N.Y., 1973. Chapter 3, "Precept and Example," p. 72.

2. Phyllis Trible, *God and the Rhetoric of Sexuality,* Philadelphia, 1978.

3. "When the author of the parable adds that she will be a 'helpmate' to the man, he has in mind not only the daily help that she will provide him in the home. The expression 'helpmate' has a distinctly personalist meaning. The Bible uses it frequently in relationship to God: 'God is my helpmate,' that is to say 'my refuge;' 'the staff on which I lean;' 'I can trust myself totally to him;' 'in him we find safety.' The kind of enslavement of the woman to the man common in the epoch of the religious reflection that makes up the substance of Genesis 2 is here interpreted by the author as a consequence of sin, as the punishment for the disobedience in the garden (Genesis 3:16)." (Translated from Edward Schillebeeckx, *Le Mariage est un Sacrement,* Brussels, 1961, p. 24.)

4. "Genesis shows clearly that the life of the man and the woman constitutes a 'dialogue.' The man's need for the woman, and the desire that carries him to her, are explained in a still primitive way. The inspired author sees in this universal human phenomenon a mysterious disposition of the God of the Covenant. It is his gift. The words 'while the man slept' (verse 21) point to this. They

mean that all was done without his collaboration. He received his companion from the living God as the latter's gift—and as a most exceptional gift. The marital hymn that he intoned immediately afterward shows this clearly." (ibid.)

5. Taken from Volume 1 of this trilogy, *What Is Marriage?*, Chapter 2, "The Primitive Christian Understanding of Marriage," pp. 44–45. The analysis there is in turn adapted from Walter Brueggeman's essay, "Of the Same Flesh and Bone," in *The Catholic Biblical Quarterly*, Vol. 32.4 (1970), pp. 532–542.

"The mythic image of the man's sleep tells equally that the inspired author intends the taking of the woman from the man's side to be a mystery (cf. Ps. 139:13–15; Proverbs 30:18–19; Job 10:8–12; Canticle 8:6–17). Its source is God, but he has not yet revealed the secret of it. To this day the Arabs say of an intimate friend, 'he is my side.' For our part, we say 'He is a piece of my heart.' The meaning then of this image is that the woman 'is taken from the man's heart,' that God has made them for one another. The Scripture thus hints that in the divine intention marriage is to be monogamous, with the man and the woman partners fitted to one another" (Schillebeeckx, *ibid.*).

6. The English version of these Old Testament passages is taken from *The New American Bible*, N.Y.–London, 1970.

7. Thus, for example, E. A. Speiser, *The Anchor Bible:* Genesis, Garden City, 1964, p. 20.

8. See, for example, Isaiah 49:15: "Can a mother forget her infant, be without tenderness for the child of her womb? Even should she forget, I will never forget you."

9. John L. McKenzie, *Dictionary of the Bible*, Milwaukee, 1965, p. 98.

10. Tobit is not included in the Jewish canon of accepted books, and is therefore not in the Protestant versions of the Bible, which traditionally follow the Jewish canon. It was rejected by the Talmudic rabbis because it suffered from two liabilities: it was composed in Aramaic rather than in the sacred language, Hebrew, and it was thought to have been composed outside the homeland, Israel.

11. See Plato's *Republic*, Book 5; Aristotle's *Politics*, Book 7, Chapter 16, and *Nicomachean Ethics*, Book 8, Chapter 12.

12. In *The Authorized Daily Prayerbook*, edited by J. Hert, N.Y., 1946, p. 1013.

13. The Hebrew wisdom books accepted in the Catholic canon of sacred scripture are Wisdom, Job, Proverbs, Qoheleth (Ecclesiastes) and Ben Sirach (Ecclesiasticus). The modern Jewish and Protestant canons exclude Wisdom and Ben Sirach but countless pieces of Hebrew wisdom are found in others of the sacred books, both canonical and extra-canonical. The gospels contain many of Jesus' wisdom sayings, such as "What does it profit a man if he gains the whole world but suffers the loss of his soul?" (Mt 16:26), and "It is not right to take the children's food and throw it to the dogs" (Mt 15:26).

BIBLIOGRAPHY

Bird, Phyllis A.: " 'Male and Female He Created Them': Genesis 1:27b in the Context of the Priestly Account of Creation," in *Harvard Theological Review*, 74/2 (1981), pp. 129–159.

Brueggeman, Walter: "Of the Same Flesh and Bone," in *Catholic Biblical Quarterly,* 32 (1970), pp. 532–542.

DeVaux, Roland: *Ancient Israel,* Vol. 1. N.Y., McGraw-Hill, 1965. Part I, "Family Institutions."

Grelot, Pierre: *Man and Wife in Scripture.* N.Y., Herder and Herder, 1964.

Jewett, Paul K.: *Man as Male and Female.* Grand Rapids, William B. Eerdmans, 1975.

Trible, Phyllis: *God and the Rhetoric of Sexuality.* Philadelphia, Fortress Press, 1978.

3. SOURCES OF THE SACRAMENT IN THE NEW TESTAMENT

Jesus' instructions about marriage that the gospels record contribute to a theology of marriage only *virtualiter*. They serve as premises from which one must draw conclusions. They say nothing about marriage as a sign or image. They say only implicitly that it can be a source of holiness for men and women. This they do by reclaiming the marriages of Jesus' own people from human control and reasserting God's authorship of all marriages and therefore his control of them. But they show Jesus using and validating a crucial passage from the garden parable in Genesis 2, "That is why a man leaves his father and mother and clings to his wife, and the two of them become one body." They also show him adding his own moral stricture drawn as a conclusion from that high evaluation of marriages: "Therefore what God has joined man must not separate" (Mk 10:9; Mt 19:6).

We find Jesus' instructions in the synoptic gospel tradition in two passages, Mark 10:1–12 and Matthew 19:1–12. (A one-verse excerpt of the instruction is in Luke 6:8.) Both report a confrontation of Jesus with a group of Pharisees, and an argument between them about the right of Jewish husbands to dismiss their wives and thereby dissolve their marriages. Although the two gospels report one and the same argument, the questions argued in the two differ significantly, as we shall see.

According to Mark the Pharisees' challenging question to Jesus asked simply whether a husband is permitted to dismiss his wife. The question arose from no uncertainty in their own minds on this point of the law, and probably from little uncertainty about Jesus' mind on the subject. For by this time in his ministry the people had accepted him, the carpenter's son, as a rabbi, a teacher of the law, as one who, unlike the scribes or the Pharisees, taught with authority and power (Mk 1:27).[1] The Pharisees, many of them teachers of the law, took this ill. They followed Jesus about, listening to him critically. Almost certainly by this time they had hints of his mind about husbands' dismissing their wives. So now, as the passage says (10:2), they put him to an open test.

The test is whether he teaches according to the law of Moses or contradicts it. The law, in the book of Deuteronomy, simply assumed a husband's right in the matter.

> When a man, after marrying a woman and having relations with her, is later displeased with her because he finds in her something indecent, and therefore he writes out a bill of divorce and hands it to her, thus dismissing her from his house; if on leaving his house she goes and becomes the wife of another man, and the second husband, too, comes to dislike her and dismisses her from his house by handing her a written bill of divorce . . . then her former husband, who dismissed her, may not again take her as his wife after she has become defiled . . . (24:1–4).

"Something indecent," as the justification for the husband's dismissing his wife, translates the Hebrew *erwat dabar* (which is *áschēmon prâgma,* "a shameful deed" in the Greek of the Septuagint translation of Deuteronomy, but *pornéia* in Matthew's citation of the passage, as we shall see.)

This item of case law simply assumes a husband's right to dismiss his wife, because the point on which it rules is not the permissibility of his doing so, but the permissibility of his later remarrying her after she has been dismissed by yet a second husband. The law of Moses made no provision for a wife's dismissing her husband. Custom by Jesus' time only permitted her to initiate this divorce action by demanding that her husband dismiss her.

Note too that the agency that works here to dissolve the marriage is not the will of a priest or magistrate. It is the husband's own will. And the object of the act of dissolution is not immediately the marriage, as in modern Western divorce law. It is the wife. The husband dismisses her, gets rid of her. Thus the test to which the Pharisees put Jesus here in Mark is not whether the law authorizes a husband to dismiss his wife. A misreading of the challenge "Is a man permitted to dismiss his wife?" could construe it in this way. It is whether Jesus teaches in obedience to the law on this point.

In his reply we find his assertion of the holiness of marriage, its antecedent holiness. He acknowledges implicitly that the Pharisees do teach according to the law of Moses as formulated in Deuteronomy. But that is their mistake—their double mistake in fact.

> 2. Some Pharisees came up and asked him, "Is a man permitted to dismiss his wife?" They asked him this in order to put him to the test. 3. In reply he said, "What did Moses command you?" 4. They answered, "Moses permitted a man to write a writ of dismissal and to send her away." 5. But Jesus told them, "Because of your hardness of heart he wrote that command for

you. 6. But from the beginning of creation 'Male and female he
made them.' "

In the first place the Pharisees think mistakenly that Moses gave
them permission to dismiss their wives when the latter are found in some
sexual delinquency. Jesus corrects this. Moses did not give them permission; he commanded them to do so. Knowing their hardness of heart and
sure that they would get rid of their unwanted wives in any case, he gave
them "a bad law" as punishment and in order to make vivid the wrong-
ness of their conduct.[2]

The Pharisees' other mistake was to have fastened upon God's will
regarding marriage in the wrong part of the law. Moses' command mediating God's will in Deuteronomy is *post factum;* it is conditioned by the
husbands' sinful will. But that was not the way it was "from the beginning." Deuteronomy does not express God's original and unconditioned
will, a will they have set aside and mostly forgotten. It is at this point
that Jesus reaches into the law at its beginning, in the first two chapters
of Genesis, claims all it says about the meaning and value of marriage,
and sets these as the criteria of a husband's treatment of his wife—even,
by implication, when she is found in *erwat dabar.*

> 6. "But from the beginning of creation 'Male and female he
> made them.' 7. 'For this reason a man shall leave his father and
> his mother and shall cling to his wife; 8. and the two shall
> become one body.' So that they are no longer two, but one
> body."

The following are Jesus' main points of emphasis here. First, men
did not invent marriage. God did so, at the dawn of creation. Therefore
it goes on under God's authority, not under men's. Jesus makes this fact
explicit in verse 9, in his terse addition to the clauses he quotes from
Genesis: "Therefore what God has joined man must not separate."

His marriage is a man's most precious relationship. For its sake he
leaves even his father and mother and clings to his wife. By implication,
if he would not think of ridding himself of his parents, much less should
he think of getting rid of his wife.

A husband and wife are as one person before the law, for the two of
them are "one body." By implication, for a man to seek to dismiss his
wife is to try to dismiss himself.

Like Matthew in his version of the confrontation, Mark reports Jesus' second conversation on this subject, but this time with his disciples.

> 10. Back again in the house the disciples asked him about this.
> 11. He said to them, "Whoever dismisses his wife and marries
> another commits adultery against her. 12. And if she dismisses
> her husband and marries, she commits adultery."

These three verses, despite their brevity, carry a weight of meaning almost equal to that of the verses that precede them. To begin with, Mark also has Jesus forbid the wife to dismiss her husband. (This the Jewish law under which Jesus' hearers lived did not permit. Mark's having Jesus forbid it suggests that Mark interpolated these words. If he did so, he had good reason, since tradition holds that he compiled his gospel for Christians in the community at Rome, some or all of them living under Roman law, which did permit a wife to repudiate her husband. He felt justified in adapting Jesus' teaching to the question raised by this other law.) In any case, the twin prohibitions against doing what was in itself possible to do presupposes the legal and social equality of the spouses.

But more penetrating than this is the implication that can be easily ignored in Jesus' judgment on the husband's dismissing his wife: ". . . he commits adultery against her." With this clause Mark has Jesus change the meaning of adultery for his Jewish followers.[3] Until then a man committed adultery only if he had intercourse with another man's wife or fiancée. He did not commit adultery if the woman were both unmarried and unbetrothed. And if a married man thus committed adultery, it was not an offense against his wife but against the other husband or fiancé. His adultery was not infidelity to his wife but a violation of the other man's exclusive right to his wife's or his fiancée's sexual acts—a trespass on his property.

But now according to Jesus a husband's dismissing his wife and marrying another woman is adultery against the wife, infidelity to her, a violation of their covenantal commitment.

Matthew's Account of Jesus' Teaching

The significant differences in Matthew's account of this conversation are two. The first of them is in the question with which the Pharisees begin their challenge. It is not "Is a husband permitted to dismiss his wife?" but "Is a man permitted to dismiss his wife for just any cause?" The challenge here is thus not about Jesus' teaching according to the law of Moses. It is about the side he takes in a dispute begun by the rabbis Hillel and Shammai in the generation preceding their own and continuing into their day.

The dispute had two parts. First was the interpretation of *erwat dabar* that Deuteronomy 24 names as the conduct or condition in the wife justifying her dismissal. Shammai took the narrow interpretation: it referred only to adultery on the wife's part or to delinquency in marriage equally serious. Hillel interpreted the term broadly: it referred to a spectrum of conduct ranging from the wife's adultery through such trivialities as her preparing poor meals and talking too loudly in the house.[4]

The second part of the dispute was about the conjunction or disjunction in Deuteronomy 24 of grounds for dismissal that could be construed as distinct. Note again that verse 1 reads, "When a man, after marrying a woman and having relations with her, is later displeased with her because he finds in her something indecent. . . ." Is only one ground named here, the "something indecent" which displeases the husband and impels him to dismiss? Or does the passage name two grounds, the "something indecent," and, distinct from and even dissociated from it, the husband's simple displeasure with his wife? Hillel championed the second of these interpretations and thus opened the way for much easier dismissal because the husband needed allege no fault in the wife, much less prove it.

The Pharisees' challenge to Jesus to choose sides in the dispute probably had the intent of cutting him down to size. He had to date shown exasperating independence of their "traditions of men" and even contempt for them. Now he would be trapped into seeking allies and creating enemies because of a dispute about one such tradition.

Here too Jesus' reply challenges the assumption that makes possible the Pharisees' challenging him. But here the assumption differs from that in Mark's account. It is that the issue to be argued is Hillel versus Shammai. Jesus ignores this issue: On which grounds may a man dismiss his wife? He goes immediately to the issue the Pharisees are ignoring: May a man dismiss his wife at all? He goes to it by quoting immediately the words of God's law in Genesis: "He said in reply, 'Don't you understand that he who created them in the beginning "made them male and female"?' "

Jesus here uses the Genesis passage to the same purpose and effect that he had in the Marcan account. Along the way he denies to the Pharisees their justification for permitting and sponsoring the dismissing of wives: Moses did not *command* them to give wives the writ of dismissal (the *get pitturin* of rabbinic law, in Greek the *bíblion apostasíou*); he only *permitted* this, and only because of their hardness of heart. And Jesus implies a teaching credential at least equal to that of Moses: "I say to you, whoever dismisses his wife . . . and marries another commits adultery" (19:9).

Then Matthew has Jesus do in the same clause the incomprehensible thing of siding with Shammai, where he adds the phrase ". . . except for her *pornéia.*" That is, he attenuates Jesus' command in Mark, "What God has joined man must not separate," which he himself repeats in verse 6b, by now having Jesus make the exception that a man does not commit adultery if he remarries after having dismissed his wife for her *pornéia*.

Scholars agree that this exceptive clause is not from Jesus himself, but that Matthew interpolated it, just as Mark most probably interpolated Jesus' forbidding a wife to dismiss her husband. Matthew's reason too for doing this is generically akin to Mark's: the community of Christians for which he compiled his gospel needed to know Jesus' mind about a marital question particular to itself. Tradition says this was a community in Syria, probably in Antioch, comprised mainly of Jewish followers of Jesus. Their application of the law in Deuteronomy permitted husbands to dismiss wives because of *pornéia*.[5] Does Jesus' teaching end this practice or permit it to continue? Matthew judged that his teaching permits it to continue.

Evidence of Sacramentality

Catholic theologians have found in this passage evidence of Jesus' making marriage a sacrament, in his asserting marriage's indestructibility over against human will and authority. This indestructibility disposes it to be an earthly image of the indestructible covenantal commitment between God and his people. The words in question are those he quotes from Genesis against his Pharisee interlocutors, climaxing in his own prohibiting command, "What God has joined man must not separate."

Marriage among his followers images God's love that created the first human beings, who by his intention were husband and wife: "In the divine image he created him; male and female he created them."

It is also a sanctifying image, sanctifying *a priori* because in entering this humanly indestructible commitment the spouses conform themselves to God's will: "God blessed them, saying, 'Be fertile and multiply; fill the earth and subdue it.' " Their conduct within the indestructible union already established by God's prior will is itself sanctifying. It is so because within this union they become one flesh, and such intimate joining of what was at first separate is itself holy.

Before leaving the gospels we must take note of a passage in the synoptic tradition (it is in Mark 2:18–21, Matthew 9:14–17 and Luke 5:33–35) that Christian teachers have used to validate Jesus' character as a bridegroom within his community of followers. The passage reports Jesus' being asked censoriously why, when the disciples of John the Baptist and those of the Pharisees fast, his do not. He replies (in Mark's version),

> 19. . . . . Can the companions of the bridegroom fast while he is still with them? As long as they have him still with them they cannot fast. 20. But the day will come when the bridegroom will have left them. Then on that day they will fast.

Jesus' intent in saying this was to make clear that while he was present on earth the end-time, the *éschaton,* had already begun. Therefore the time for which fasting had been the preparation, but only the preparation, has come. So fasting for at least now has no purpose. If this passage is a parable, it would be unusual for Jesus to intend it as an allegory, and to insert himself in it in the person of the bridegroom. He did not treat his parables in this way. But if verses 19b and 20 are not a later addition, as many scholars contend, but Jesus' own words, he so plainly points to his death and departure in them that here he may well allegorize himself into the parable.

In any case the passage is there for Christian teachers to use later to establish Jesus as a bridegroom. And if a bridegroom, he has a bride—one whose identity the epistle to the Ephesians will say is the Church. Thus the synoptic tradition joins with the Pauline to set out the ingredients of the later theology of the sacrament in marriage.

The Sacrament in the Pauline Tradition

Christians are accustomed to reading Paul's reflections on marriage in two principal places, in 1 Corinthians 7, and in Ephesians 5:21–33. Because there is serious reason to think that Ephesians comes not immediately from Paul but from one of his disciples, while there is no doubt that 1 Corinthians is immediately Paul's, the latter tells us more exactly his own unadapted and uninterpreted mind on marriage. This uneven authenticity is regrettable because Ephesians, which contains the stuff of theology, is indeed the *locus classicus* of the theology of the sacrament in marriage, while 1 Corinthians 7, wherein Paul passes moral judgment on marriage and its conduct, must have theology teased from it by way of inference.

Sometime during the year 56 or 57, while in Ephesus on his third missionary journey, Paul wrote a letter to the Christian community in Corinth that he had founded six or seven years earlier on his second missionary journey. His main purpose in writing the letter was to answer questions and resolve problems that had come to his attention, some of them in a letter written to him earlier from this community. It will be helpful to get at chapter 7 of Paul's letter part by part.

1. Now for the matters you wrote about: "Is it better for a man to have no relations with a woman?" 2. But because of sexual immorality it is better for each man to have his own wife, and for each woman to have her own husband. 3. Let the husband fulfill his obligation to his wife, and likewise the wife her obligation to her husband. 4. A wife has no authority over her own body, rather her husband has it; just as a husband has no authority over his own body, but his wife has it. 5. Do not deny one another, except perhaps by mutual agreement for a time, so as to devote yourselves to prayer. Then return to one another so that Satan may not put you to the test through your lack of self-control. 6. I say this to you by way of counsel, not of command. 7. I would that all were as I myself am, but each has his or her own gift from God, one person one gift, another person another.

We could better interpret Paul's instructions here if we had the Corinthians' questions to which they are answers. The first difficulty their absence creates is in verse 1. My translation of it above supposes that Paul quotes back to the Corinthians their own question in preparation for answering it. If it is, on the other hand, Paul's own opening statement, as most modern versions have it, he would be asserting something inconsistent with most of what he says in the following verses. We know from evidence elsewhere in the Pauline letters that Gnostic tendencies were alive in the Corinth community. He would seem to be urging a life of celibacy for all in the community; in doing so he would be conceding to the Gnostics on a major point of dispute. It would also undermine the meaning and value of the marriage analogy in Ephesians 5:21–33, whether its formulation be Paul's immediately or that of a disciple.

The adjective that Paul uses to designate the preferability of sexual abstinence is *kalón*. To translate it as "better" (to have no relations with a woman) may be to understate its claim. In the New Testament the word is sometimes used for "the right thing" or "the necessary thing" to do. Thus in Mark 7:27 Jesus tells the Syrophoenician woman who has asked him to cure her daughter, "It is not *kalón* to take the children's food and throw it to the dogs." And in Mark 9:43 Jesus tells his hearers, "And if your hand should cause you to sin, cut it off; it is *kalón* for you to enter into life crippled. . . ." Surely entering eternal life in whatever condition is not merely the better of two commendable options.

But this does not close the case against the verse's containing Paul's own counsel, as we shall see in a moment.[6] In any case, whether the preference Paul urges is marriage or celibacy, he defends marriage's goodness. But even in this case his defense is not enthusiastic—not, at least, at this point. It is qualified, for a reason that will later among the Christian fathers and theologians become virtually a first principle for their interpretation of marriage's purposes. Paul says, in verse 7a, that he prefers that all Christians be as he is, unmarried. (It is most unlikely that he had been unmarried all his life, he, a devout Jew for whom marriage and the producing of a family were a serious obligation. Most probably he was a widower, or possibly divorced from a wife unwilling to join him among the followers of Jesus.)

But prudence tempers Paul's desire for celibacy for all. He knows that to lead this life is a gift, a *chárisma* (verse 7b), that many are not given it, but are given other gifts. To mistake one's gift and try to live this life without it is to risk moral disaster. So it is better for each man to have his own wife and each woman her own husband.

This qualified defending and commending of marriage as a refuge from sexual sin could obscure an assumption that Paul makes about marriage's holiness in this very passage. It is the *a priori* holiness that we saw in the Genesis command, "Be fertile and multiply; fill the earth and subdue it." It is the holiness of a gift from God. A man and woman who marry because of this gift accepted in faith and trust obey God's will. They obey it in more exact detail when, as Paul says in verses 3 and 4, they acknowledge each one's claim over the sexual conduct of the other, and honor the obligation arising from this claim.

But Paul turns back again to the qualified goodness of even marriage as God-given gift where, in verse 5, he counsels more specifically against abstinence forced on a spouse. The only abstinence must be mutually agreed on. It must be temporary. And its only motive must be devotion to prayer. Among the regrettable lacunae in Paul's letters is this one, the missing explanation how sexual intimacy in marriage hinders the spouses' prayer, and how their abstinence helps it. Perhaps there is a residue here in Paul's Jewish mind of the levitical purity code according to which sexual intercourse even between spouses renders them ritually unclean ("If a man lies carnally with a woman, they shall both bathe and be unclean until evening"—Lev 15:18). Even though Paul assures his readers, in verse 6, that this is not a command but only his counsel, it will not be forgotten later when Christian theologians dispute whether marriage is to be numbered among the Church's sacraments. For how can conduct that hinders prayer be a medium of grace?

Paul's advice, in verses 8 and 9, to the unmarried in the community, those widowed or those never married, applies to them the principle of preference that he has just enunciated: "8. To the unmarried and to the widows I say that it is *kalón* for them if they remain as I am." Here is a reason for thinking that the earlier verse 1 may be Paul's own advice. The key adjective, *kalón,* can here mean nothing other than "a better good." Paul would hardly tell the widowed and the unmarried that their remaining unmarried is imperative or necessary. Thus wherever used in the entire passage, *kalón* may indicate only preferability and thus be within the limits of Paul's prudence in counseling, not intended as a command.

Paul clearly indicates no more than preferability in the following verse where he implies that perhaps not all the widowed and unmarried have the gift of celibacy, and concedes that for them marriage may be the *kalón.* Again his reason for so conceding casts marriage in the role of refuge from sin: "9. But if they [the widowed and unmarried] cannot contain themselves, let them marry. For it is better to marry than to be burned" [in eternal punishment].[7]

Paul's advice to the married in the community, where both spouses are Christian, is not his own. Nor is it merely advice. He passes along what he has learned is Jesus' command. But he is just as free as Mark in interpreting and adapting the command, and just as free as Matthew in doing both to the point of making an exception to Jesus' apparent assertion that dissolving a marriage is beyond human power. Where Jesus in the synoptic tradition said a husband is not to dismiss his wife, Paul says she is not to be separated from the marriage. *Chorízein,* the verb here, used commonly in Roman law to designate divorce, is in the aorist passive infinitive form, *choristhénai.* It seems to indicate what is done to a wife when her husband dismisses her: she is "separated."

Paul most nearly repeats Jesus' own instruction when, in the same verse, he specifies that a husband is not to dismiss his wife (although he uses the verb *aphiénai* where the synoptics use *apolúein*).

He introduces his startling exception to the limits of human power declared by Jesus when he states the options available to a Christian wife who has in fact been "separated" from her marriage. She is either to reconcile with her husband, or she is to remain unmarried. Paul's adjective identifying the second option is *ágamos*. It signifies literally "unmarried." He has already used it in verse 8 to designate the widowed and those who have never married. He will use it again in verse 32 to indicate the unmarried, who are better situated to face the Christians' trying future.

Assuming that Paul means by *ágamos* here in verse 11 what it means in the other two places, he acknowledges that human will *can* separate what God has joined, however severely the divine will may forbid the separating. Though forbidden, divorce is possible. Why Paul forbids the wife to remarry though once again single, he does not explain. If she is only the victim of the separation, the reason cannot be her punishment. But in naming her first option, to return to her husband, Paul shows how far he has removed himself from the law of Moses. This return of a wife to a husband who has once dismissed her is precisely what Deuteronomy 24:1–4 forbids.

It is surprising that Paul makes his express claim to marriage's sanctifying capacity not when counseling couples both of whom are Christian, as we have just seen. He does so when he turns to those marriages in the Corinthian community wherein one of the spouses has become a Christian, while the other has not. From his assessment of their relationship it is plain that the Christian spouses there are worried that continuing in marriage with the pagan, and especially continuing with sexual intercourse, may corrupt them. This anxiety is not necessarily Gnostic. It can have come from the Jewish law which forbade marriage with Gentiles, now carried over into the Christian situation.

> 12. To the rest I say, not the Lord, if a brother has a wife who is an unbeliever, but she is willing to live with him, he is not to dismiss her. 13. And if a wife has a husband who is an unbeliever, but he is willing to live with her, she is not to dismiss him. 14. For an unbelieving husband is sanctified by his wife, and an unbelieving wife is sanctified by her husband. If it were not so, your children would be unclean. But in fact they are holy.

Now Paul makes clear that his advice is his own, not from Jesus. His verdict on the reason for the Christian spouses' suspecting that they ought to dismiss their pagan partners contradicts it exactly. Not only are the Christian spouses not corrupted by the pagan, but the latter are sanctified by the Christian.[8] As evidence of this Paul reasons in an endearingly naive way. The children of these religiously mixed marriages are not unclean; they are holy. How then could the marriages which produce them be unholy?

It is regrettable in light of our search for the earliest elements of sacramentality in marriage that Paul says no more exactly what he means here by the Christian spouses' sanctifying the pagan. It is not unlikely that the reason he has already given in the preceding chapter in urging the Corinthian Christians to avoid fornication, probably their men's going to the city's cultic prostitutes, is still working in his mind.[9]

There his religious-moral logic asserted two interlocked reasons. And it turns out that these reasons for not going to prostitutes are themselves seeds of the theology of the sacrament. The first uses one of Paul's favorite metaphors: a Christian's body is a member of Christ. The word for "body" here in Paul's Greek is *sôma*. So he means exactly that, the human body, not the entirety of a person that the *sárx*, the Septuagint's and the synoptics' "one flesh" denotes. But Paul does use the latter denotation when he reasons why it is unthinkable that a member of Christ's body would go to a prostitute: a man who does this becomes *mía sárx*, one flesh, with her. Bridging from the meaning of *sárx* to that of *sôma*, Paul reminds such Christian men that they desecrate Christ. They try to make him "one body" with a prostitute, to wed him to her.

The second of the interlocked reasons is again a Pauline metaphor. The body of a Christian, again his or her *sôma*, is a temple of the Holy Spirit. Therefore this body belongs not to the Christian but to God, and to have intercourse with a prostitute is to desecrate this temple and sin against the Holy Spirit.

But if a Christian body's being a member of Christ and a temple of the Holy Spirit is the reason for the Christian's not going to a prostitute, it is also presumably the cause of a pagan spouse's sanctification by intercourse with the Christian. From this passage itself we can find out no more about the nature of this sanctification. But we can wonder what Paul would have said about the resulting sanctification where Christian spouse has intercourse with Christian spouse. His reflections would have been no small contribution to the eventual theology of the sacrament.

The Origin of the Sacrament in Ephesians 5:21–33

Until the end of the eighteenth century the letter to the Ephesians was commonly accepted as authentic in the sense of coming immediately from Paul himself. Since that time opinion has divided, with one side acknowledging the letter's authenticity only at one remove, as coming from a disciple of Paul. Whichever the accurate judgment, verses 21 to 33 of its Chapter 5 have served as the preeminent scriptural source for the Catholic theology of the sacrament in marriage. In this passage Christ is presented under two metaphors, as head of a body which is the

Church, and as husband of a bride which is the same Church.[10] The author has been understood to propose Christian marriage as an earthly image of these two metaphoric relationships and thus as a sacrament.

To read the passage accurately we must first examine its context within the entire letter. The letter is divided quite clearly into two parts, Chapters 1–3 and Chapters 4–6. Paul's intent in the former is to announce and explain to his readers God's *mystérion,* his plan of reconciliation set from all eternity. This plan is that through his death and resurrection Christ break down the ancient barriers of hostility that divide Jews and Gentiles, and unite them instead in one community, the Church. The executing of this plan has already begun in Christ's death and resurrection and in the forming of the community.

It is essential for understanding the letter's second part to first understand that this community is quickened by Christ's love, and that this love is active in the community through the Spirit of Christ and the Father. For in this second part, beginning in Chapter 4, Paul spells out gradually the consequences of this *mystérion* for the Christians' conduct of life, the consequences of the Spirit's action in them. He instructs his readers how to live in such a way as to manifest the *mystérion.* In places the instruction elides into exhortation.

> The first such instruction-exhortation is in 4:1–6. There Paul urges his readers to acknowledge that different persons have received different gifts of the Spirit, some to be apostles, others to be prophets, others pastors, others teachers. But all gifts are from the one same Spirit. All are intended for the building up of Christ's body, the Church.
>
> From 4:17 to 5:18 the substance of the instruction is that the new Christians give up the conduct of the old life that Paul's readers have already abandoned, and that they put on a new life, even a new self. Here begin the *Haustafeln,* the inventory of the kinds of conduct to be avoided, such as lying, foul talk, drunkenness.[11]

It is at 5:18–19 that Paul moves from conduct to be avoided to the kinds of conduct that those who live by the Spirit *will* produce. His exhortation to this conduct contains a slightly veiled play on two contrasted notions of "drinking deeply": not "drunk with wine" (*mē methýskesthe*) but "filled (*plerôusthe*) with the Spirit."

> 18. And do not get drunk with wine (in which there is dissipation), but be filled with the Spirit, 19. singing to one another in psalms and hymns and spiritual canticles, singing and chanting to the Lord in your hearts, 20. giving thanks always and everywhere to our God and Father in the name of our Lord Jesus

Christ, 21. deferring to one another in the fear of Christ, 22. wives to their own husbands, as to the Lord, 23. because the husband is the head of the wife, just as Christ is the head of the Church, being himself the savior of her, his body. 24. Therefore just as the Church defers to Christ, so too must wives to their husbands in all things.

Paul closes in on the husband-wife relationship as the first of three for which he has specific instructions, the others being of fathers and children (6:1–4) and masters and slaves (6:5–9). The verbs he uses here in the early part of the instruction and exhortation are not in the imperative mode but are all participial in form, beginning with "singing to one another" in verse 19. The conceptual continuity from one participle to the other is that each urges a kind of conduct that comes of being filled with the Spirit.

When Paul gets to the kind of conduct befitting husbands and wives who are filled with the Spirit, his verbs are still participial. This makes a difference for our understanding the nature of the husband-wife relationship that he urges. Despite centuries of translations that put a verb in verse 22 in the imperative mode—or sometimes in the hortatory subjunctive, as in the Vulgate *mulieres viris subditae sint*—the verse in the original Greek does not even have its own verb.[12] There the verse is a run-on clause that continues and applies the exhortation in the preceding verse 21, ". . . deferring to one another in the fear of Christ, 22. wives to their husbands as to the Lord. . . ." (The meaning here is even clearer if the reader imagines a "for example" at the juncture of the two verses.)

Even more important for understanding the husband-wife relationship that Paul has in mind is an accurate rendering of the participle in verse 21 that determines in verse 22 the wife's attitude toward her husband. It is *hypotássesthai*—here as a present participle, *hypotassámenoi*. In the conventional translations it is rendered as either "obey" or "be subject to." But everywhere in the New Testament, including Paul's letters, the verb for "obey" is *hypakóuein*. It is what Paul urges on children (in 6:1) and on slaves (in 6:5). Presumably if he wanted wives to obey their husbands, he would use the same verb somewhere in his exhortation to them. He does not.[13]

Hypotássesthai signifies generally "to defer to." It does not necessarily imply "be subject to" because it was used to denote the attitudes of persons who are not in fact subject to one another, and in doing what the verb denotes do not subject themselves. Scholars who in debate seek the truth rather than victory may defer to one another in the way the verb signifies. Commanders in the same army who want victory rather than personal ascendency may do the same. But Paul clearly intends that in a marriage the wife be the one who defers. When he sets forth the reasons for this we come upon the several rich metaphors he built into the difficult, multifaceted analogy that has become the core of the theology of the sacrament.

He reasons that the wife ought to defer to her husband because he is to her as her head, as Christ is head of the Church, his body. Here are the first two metaphors. (Note the added third metaphor within the second one here. The Church is not, like the wife, a real person. It is a society, a fictional person.) Paul asserts a similarity of the two relationships— Christ-Church and husband-wife[14]—and thus sets the first facet of the analogy.

But one must be alert to a subtle distinction here. Paul says that the reason for the wife's deferring to her husband is the same as the reason for the Church's deferring to Christ. He asserts a similarity of the two relationships and thus a similarity of wifely obligations. But he does not say that the similarity is itself the reason demanding the wife's deference. Nowhere does he say *because* (in Greek *hóti*) the husband's headship is like the headship of Christ, the wife must defer to him. He says instead that the husband is head of the wife *just as* (*hōs*) Christ is head of the Church. Fine though it is, the distinction is necessary and important, because the later theology of the sacrament will have as one of its premises an assumed causal relationship between the two metaphoric relationships making up the analogy, i.e. *because* the Christ-Church relationship is such-and-such, it follows that the human relationship is the same. The assumption will appear most commonly in that part of the theology used to demonstrate the antecedent indissolubility of all sacramental marriages: "*Because* the Christ-Church marital relationship is indissoluble, so too *is* (not just "so too *ought to be*") the marriage of every Christian couple indissoluble."

Verse 23b, ". . . Christ is the head of the Church, being himself the savior of her, his body," determines what will be said in the following six verses. What Paul has done thus far is to set the model for the husband-wife relationship, and has begun to exhort the spouses to reproduce in their conduct the elements of the model. He has begun with the wife's deference to the husband. Now he turns to the husband's conduct, for which the model is Christ's love for the Church.

The key clause at this point is the last in verse 23. Christ is not only the head of his body, the Church, but is also her savior. In verse 24 Paul urges this fact as an added reason for wives' deferring to their husbands, because their model, the Church, defers to Christ as her savior. Here the analogy becomes fragile. If Paul followed its scenario faithfully, he would say that the husband too is savior of his wife. But he stops short of this, saying only that *just as* the Church defers to Christ her savior, so too the wife must defer to her husband.

But in verse 25 Paul moves back into the hazardous demands of the analogy as he begins to describe the kind of love the Christian husband must have because Christ's love is its model.[15] He comes very close to demanding from the husband a salvific love. For Christ's love for the Church is self-giving and sacrificial: "Husbands, love your wives just as Christ loved the Church and gave himself up for her." The verb here, *paradídomi,* signifies a relinquishing of oneself, a giving over of oneself for another. Paul obviously refers here to Christ's death by crucifixion, which he takes for granted was sacrificial.

This love had as both its intent and its effect to purify the Church and to sanctify her. Paul borrows his imagery here from the traditional bridal bath and transforms it into the Christian baptismal bathing to explain how Christ's sacrificial death does in fact purify and sanctify the Church.

> 25. Husbands, love your wives just as Christ loved the Church and gave himself up for her, 26. so that he might make her holy by cleansing her in the bath of water that is joined to the word, 27. so that he might himself present the Church to himself in her splendor, having no stain or wrinkle or anything of this kind, but so that she might be holy and blameless.

In this metaphor Paul puts Christ in a double role in the imagined wedding ceremony. He is the *prónubus,* the person who presents the bride to the groom. He is also the groom. The image reflects the divine prince of Ezekiel 16, who finds the girl child, Israel, adopts her, and takes her as his bride.

Then as Paul links this model of divine love with the human love he asks of the spouses, he borrows elements of the Genesis parable to close the links.

> 28. [Earthly] husbands must love their wives in this way, as their own bodies. In loving his wife a man is loving himself, 29. for no man has ever hated his own flesh, but he nourishes it and cares for it, just as Christ does the Church, 30. for we are members of his body. 31. "For this reason a man leaves his father and mother and clings to his wife, and the two of them become one flesh."

He has thus far used the metaphor of the Church as the body of Christ, her head, in order to form the analogy of Christian wife as body to her head, her husband. Now he goes to the source of these metaphors in Genesis 2:24. He presents husband and wife, whether metaphoric or real, as "one flesh"—not "one body," but one flesh in the Hebrew sense of one person. This gives the Christian husband an added reason for loving his wife: in loving her, he the head is loving his own body. Or in Genesis' meaning of "one flesh," in loving her he is loving himself.

Verse 32 is Paul's statement that Catholic teachers and theologians who read it in the Latin of the Vulgate welcomed for centuries as summarizing and clinching the case for Christian marriages' sacramentality: *Sacramentum hoc magnum est, ego autem dico in Christo et in Ecclesia* ("This sacrament is a great one. I say this in reference to Christ and to the Church"). But the verse's primary meaning does not do this. The Latin noun *sacramentum* translates the Greek *mystérion* (the entire clause in its original form is *tò mystérion toûto méga estín*). *Mystérion* in Ephesians does not denote the reality we now call one of the seven sacraments. It denotes, as pointed out earlier, God's plan for reconciliation, and the revelation and working out of this plan. It is the two-in-one-flesh relationship of the Genesis story, of the first man and woman, that is the *mystérion* here. Paul's saying it refers to Christ and the Church implies that it foreshadows, reveals in anticipation, is a type of the relationship of Christ and the Church. (He could have said accurately that a Christian marriage too is a *mystérion* of Christ and the Church, or, more accurately, that it can become such a *mystérion*. Although he did not say this, the spouses' heeding his exhortation could make their marriage to be such.)

We cut to the heart of Paul's contribution to the theology of the sacrament in marriage by asking whether he proposed the marriage of Christian spouses as an image of the metaphoric marriage of Christ and the Church.

To prepare for the answer it helps to recall Paul's intent in this passage as well as the literary device he uses to carry out this intent. The intent is to bring the Christian spouses to understand how they ought to love and treat one another because they are impelled by the Spirit—love and treat one another in a way that may realize the *mystérion* that is God's bringing reconciliation through Christ. Beyond wanting the spouses to understand all this, he wants them also to carry on this love and this conduct.

To prepare further for the answer, note that in describing the Christ-Church relationship Paul either uses two metaphors or constructs a single but mixed metaphor. He has Christ as head of a body that is the Church, and Christ as a husband of a bride that is the Church. He proposes the former first and keeps it dominant; he uses the second to fill out details of the first by having Christ the head treat his body as a husband treats his wife.

Thus Paul's encompassing literary device, or form, is *paraklésis*, exhortation. It is neither *kérygma* nor *didáche*, neither the proclaiming of doctrine nor the teaching of it. But at least explanation, *paranésis*, has a place in this exhortation, in order to provide both the model and the warrant for what he exhorts. Husbands and wives ought to love and treat one another the way Christ loves and treats the Church, and because he loves and treats it the way he does.

The extent to which Paul says that the marriage of Christian husband and wife is an image of the Christ-Church relationship is found in verse 23a: ". . . because the husband is the head of the wife just as

Christ is the head of the Church. . . ." The principal difficulty against admitting any more decisive imaging in the Christian marriage is that in finding this earthly image Paul does not look to real-life marriages. He looks to a metaphor. A husband can be said only metaphorically to be a head, a wife only metaphorically to be a body. Metaphors exist only in the minds of persons who conceive and express them, which is only where ideal models exist as well. To say this most exactly, the earthly image of the Christ-Church relationship exists nowhere else but in Paul's mind, and in the minds of those readers in any century who agree that his metaphor is apt. So also does the analogy from which the theology of the antecedent sacramentality of all Christian marriages has been drawn have only a metaphorically conceived marriage as one of its facets, an abstracted-from-real-life model marriage. But metaphors established only conceptually in the mind cannot be living images of real sacred realities.

A clue to his abstracting from real-life marriages is found in the fact itself that Paul exhorts the spouses of Ephesus to attain the love and the conduct befitting the Christ-Church model. Metaphoric marriages are not the object of exhortation; they can be only the models of the conduct to which the exhorter exhorts. Therefore Paul does not say to the spouses that their marriages are in fact images of the Christ-Church metaphoric marriage. (If he thought they were, why would he exhort them?) Therefore too he implies that their marriages participate in the two earlier stages of God's *mystérion*—the one-flesh foreshadowing relationship of the first man and woman, and the one-flesh relationship of Christ and the Church—only inchoately. In our own theological terms, he implies that their marriages have the potential to become images of the Christ-Church relationship. He implies that the spouses can take what is only inchoate in their marriages, and, by co-working with the Spirit who "fills" them, can bring them to richer and richer realization. They can in this way gradually bring their marriages to be images on earth of the Christ-Church relationship—can bring them gradually to be sacraments, we would say.

The gradual pace of this realization, its processual nature, is borne out by verse 27. There Paul tells of Christ's presenting his bride, the Church, to himself in her splendor, "having no wrinkle or stain," not as an accomplished fact, not as a goal attained instantly. His interpretation of this attaining is instead eschatological; he tells of what will be accomplished in a future climax of attainment. The tense and the mode of the verb he uses here suggest this: it is the aorist subjunctive following the particle that indicates intent and purpose: ". . . *hína parastēse . . . tēn ekklēsían.*" Thus since the model that Paul urges on Christian spouses is a relationship striving for a goal through time, so too their striving may be expected to go on through time. Even more exactly, since the Church's purity and splendor are a goal toward which she is striving, the substance of the Christian spouses' striving is to image the Church's striving. Thus earthly holiness in marriage consists first of all in the spouses' effort to co-work with the Spirit who is in them. The full and final imaging of the full and final splendor of the Church's relationship with Christ is the goal the spouses hope and work for.

It may well be that in this analogy the author combats an interpretation of marriage current in his time among certain Gnostic Christians, especially those of the Valentinian school. This interpretation sacralized real-life marriage among Christians, made it a sacrament in the sense of an image of an invisible sacred reality. Ephesians 5:21–33 may challenge this interpretation on two points: first, about the invisible sacred reality of which Christian marriage is an image; second, on the need to exclude sexual intercourse and procreation from marriage in order to make it this image.

The invisible sacred reality, according to the Valentinian Gnostics, was "the bridal chamber." In it the human soul, which had been lost in "prostitution" by being united with a body, is reunited with her heavenly savior.[16] (This borrows from or runs parallel with the Jewish philosopher Philo's interpretation that each human soul, or mind, has had a pre-existence in union with God, but has lost it in seeking union with a body.)

Another Christian Gnostic treatise, the Tripartite Tractate, saw a different primeval union of the human and the divine. It pictured the Church as a heavenly aeon joined to the Father and the Son in a holy embrace. It also had a savior who incarnated himself in self-giving love in order to gather out of the world and into heaven those souls predestined to complete the *pléroma,* the final and full company of spirits intended by God to live in beatitude through eternity. These souls made up the "body" of the savior, a body which was to become sound and complete when the *pléroma* was filled.

This interpretation and use of Christian marriage on earth to image one or other of the heavenly unions just indicated appears to have been acted out by some Gnostic sects in a ritual of the bridal chamber. One of these is suggested in the Gospel of Philip. The ritual was anti-sexual, freed of the defilement of passion and the flesh. The joining of the man and woman was not the work of desire but of pure will.[17]

Another Gnostic treatise preserved in fragment, the *Testimony of Truth,* attacked both orthodox Christians and the followers of the libertine Gnostic, Basilides, for allowing sexual passion into marriage, and from sexual passion the birth of more human bodies with which to ensnare and imprison spiritual souls.[18]

Whatever the Gnostic version, it meant to teach that the proper function of marriage in the Church is to image the invisible, spiritual reality in which the soul of the Gnostic saint is united with its heavenly counterpart.[19]

If Ephesians 5:21–33 is indeed written, at least in part, to gainsay this interpretation of marriage, it appears to do so in the following ways. First, it affirms that the invisible sacred reality in question is the union of

Christ and his bride, the Church, not the union of the soul with its heavenly counterpart. And the Church in Ephesians is not a heavenly aeon. Yet the author's conception of the Church shares one of the Gnostic features, and perhaps two. For his analogy he devises a meta-phoric, idealized Church, almost entirely abstracted from a this-earthly community of men and women, while at the same time implying that its members are also idealized abstractions. A second shared trait may be the idea of an incomplete, still processual condition of the Church. In the Gnostic imagination it was the company of souls predestined to fill up the *pléroma* which was thought to be still incomplete. In Ephesians it is a Church-bride not yet fully cleansed, not yet entirely spotless and without wrinkle, but still in the process of being purified.

Ephesians may gainsay the Gnostic interpretation in a second way by refusing to condemn the sexual character of marriage, by refusing to say the proper marital union is impelled by will alone without the inter-vention of desire. The passage's link with the *Haustafeln*, the household instructions immediately preceding it in the epistle, shows that children in marriage were taken for granted. Indeed their loving nurture is part of the holiness of marriage.

The ascetic Gnostic sacramentalism sought to lift marriage out of the sexuality that it regarded as darkness, corruption, a participation in cosmic sin. Ephesians' sacramentalism sought to lift it out of the ordinari-ness of life, its merely utilitarian service as provider of helpmate for each spouse and of children for state and Church. It sought to show instead its role, by the spouses' mutual love, in Christ's work of reconciliation in the world. This reconciliation, we recall, is the theme that dominates in the epistle.

For the time being we may leave moot the question whether the author of Ephesians taught that not only Christian marriage taken ab-stractly, but every Christian marriage is an image of the heavenly mar-riage of Christ and the Church. What he certainly did was to lay out in plain sight the ingredients that could be combined in a theology holding all Christian marriages to be sacraments simply because they do in fact image the heavenly marriage. The temptation to gather the ingredients into just this theology is clear and strong. At critical points in the follow-ing chapters we will try to show what Catholic authorities and scholars have done with the temptation.

We may note in anticipation that one of the things they did was to forge a link of explanation between this passage in Ephesians and Jesus' synoptic instruction on divorce and remarriage. Beginning in the middle-late patristic period, clearly with Ambrose, Jerome and Augustine at the end of the fourth century and beginning of the fifth, Catholic scholars interpreted Jesus to not only forbid the dismissing of one's wife and the taking of a second as immoral, but to declare that dissolving the marriage by such dismissal is impossible. This interpretation calls for special expla-nation. One must ask about this invulnerability to dissolution that must be internal to marriage, a trait of its nature. Here is where the link of explanation was forged. The invulnerability inherent in at least Christian marriage was identified as the image in it of the Christ-Church marital relationship. It is indestructible. So too, the logic of explanation went, must be the imaging Christian marriage on earth. Clearly this conclusion depends for its validity on the accuracy of interpretation of the two New Testament passages.

Summary

The synoptic tradition in Mark 10 and Matthew 19 reports that Jesus appropriated and affirmed Torah's teaching about marriage. It is not men's invention, but God's. Therefore marriages are created and sustained under his authority, not under men's. Therefore too men have no competence to dissolve them—at least not by the Jewish custom whereby husbands dismissed their wives.

His marriage is a man's most precious relationship, even more precious than his filial relationship with his parents. That is a covenantal relationship that he replaces with his covenantal marriage. From this Jesus drew a new definition of adultery. It is a man's infidelity to his wife (and her infidelity to her husband). It is no longer one man's invasion of another's property.

Paul asserted in 1 Corinthians 7 that marriage is a place and a source of holiness for Christian spouses. It is the holiness of accepting a gift from God—which marital life is—and the holiness of meeting the obligations inherent in the gift.

But Paul's judgment on this holiness is ambiguous. He advises the Corinthian Christians that it is better not to marry, while conceding that if the attempt at sexual abstinence is an occasion of sin, then it is better to marry. On the other hand the holiness available to a Christian spouse in marriage is such that it can over-ride the non-belief of his or her pagan spouse, and can sanctify the latter too. It may be that the Christian spouse can thus sanctify the pagan because the former's body is a member of Christ and a temple of the Holy Spirit.

In his exhortation to the Christian spouses of Ephesus to live their marriages as men and women impelled by the Holy Spirit, the author proposed as the model for their love the love relationship of Christ (metaphorized as both a head and a husband) and the Church (taken in abstract ideal and metaphorized as both a body and a bride). In this exhortation the author implied that the husbands and wives ought, specifically as spouses, to have a role in Christ's work of reconciling the human race to God—to participate, later theologians will say, in Christ's paschal mystery. In constructing his analogy the author also laid out for later theologians the elements of their claim that the real-life marriages of all Christians are in fact images—sacraments—of the Christ-Church relationship.

NOTES

1. Mark comes back again and again to Jesus' character and work as a teacher: "And he began to teach beside the sea" (4:1); "And when it was the sabbath he began to teach in the synagogue" (6:2); "And he went about the villages teaching . . ." (6:7); ". . . and he took pity on them because they were like sheep without a shepherd, and he began to teach them many things" (6:34); "And he began to teach them that the Son of Man must suffer much" (8:31); ". . . and he taught them and said, 'Is it not written, "My house will be called a house of prayer for all people"?' " (11:17); "Later, while teaching in the temple, Jesus said . . ." (12:35); "And in his teaching he said, 'Beware of the scribes' " (12:38).

2. Jesus' religious logic in this passage, though so familiar to the Jews of his own time and earlier, is strange to the Western religious mind. In his eyes the legal warrant for a man's getting rid of his wife was a command set down by Moses which obligates Jewish husbands to disobey God's law, but obligates them only because of their already fixed hardness of heart. This is a prophetic interpretation proportioned to one kind of significant moment in the history of the people Israel. They had again and again been faithless to the Lord's commands. One of the consequences of this faithlessness was that he had given them "laws that were not good"—not so much to punish them as to bring them to realize that he is still their Lord. This is Ezekiel's thought in his book of prophecy (20:25) where he speaks in the words of Yahweh who is recalling to the people their history of disobedience: "I gave them laws that were not good, commands they could not bear . . . so that they might realize that I am Yahweh." This faithlessness was at its worst when Moses, coming down from Sinai with the tablets of the law, found the people adoring the golden calf. Jesus' implication here in Mark is that the accepted practice of getting rid of unwanted wives is a continuation of this same spirit of faithlessness, and because of it the people were given "a law that was not good." Their hardness of heart drew upon them Moses' command to dismiss their wives.

3. Some intepreters question the authenticity of the words "against her" in Jesus' statement. They suggest that Mark interpolated them, since neither Matthew nor Luke has them in his version of the same logion. If this second conversation is Mark's invention, of course, the question of authenticity arises only if Mark borrowed actual words of Jesus for his invention. In any case, his reinterpretation of adultery as a spouse's violation of a personal covenantal commitment is consistent with what Jesus has already appropriated from the law in Genesis.

4. Since, as we saw above, *erwat dabar* is translated literally as "the uncleanness of a thing," in the Greek of the Septuagint as *áschēmon prâgma,* and in the New Testament as *pornéia,* a term used there to designate sexual sin generically, it is clear that in any of the three sources these terms leave ample room for contextual and discretionary interpretation.

5. What *pornéia* meant to Matthew in this context and to his readers is disputed to this day. It certainly referred to the wife's condition or conduct or both. The most common conjectures are these: the wife's adultery; her coming to the marriage not physically a virgin; her bearing a legal disability, such as Gentile parentage or a loathsome disease; marriage within a forbidden degree of kindred according to stricter Jewish interpretation of the law, such as that of the Qumran Essenes.

Whatever Matthew meant by *pornéia,* his making this exception because of it is one of dozens of points of evidence that the gospels' prescriptions for conduct are their compilers' adoptions, adaptations and interpretations of Jesus' teaching— an enterprise not only not reprehensible but unavoidable.

6. Nothing in the syntax of the verse tells the reader which is the accurate translation. And the written Greek of Paul's time was not punctuated.

7. I depart in this translation from the usual ". . . better to marry than to burn" because in Paul's Greek the latter verb, *pyrôusthai,* is a present *passive* infinitive. This suggests that he meant not the burning of lust but that of eternal punishment.

8. Part of the full-blooded Jews' case against the Samaritans was grounded in the inverse of this logic. Since the latter were offspring of one Jewish parent and one pagan, they were unclean.

9. The passage, 6:15–20, is the following: "Don't you understand that your bodies are members of Christ? How then can I make the members of Christ's body those of a prostitute? Never! 16. Don't you understand that a man who joins with a prostitute becomes one body with her? 'And the two,' it is said, 'become one flesh.' 17. But a man who joins with the Lord becomes one spirit with him. 18. So avoid fornication [*pornéia*]. Every [other] sin a man commits is apart from the body. But a man who commits fornication sins against his own body. 19. Or don't you understand that your bodies are temples of the Holy Spirit who dwells in you, the Spirit whom you have from God? Don't you understand that you are not your own property? 20. You have been bought at a [great] price. So glorify God in your bodies."

The passage is an example of *porneia*'s meaning being determined by context. Here it is the sexual sin a man commits by intercourse with a prostitute.

10. The metaphor of the Church as the bride of Christ is not exclusive to Ephesians. It is in the book of Revelation, Chapter 21: "I also saw a new Jerusalem, the holy city, coming down out of heaven from God, beautiful as a bride preparing to meet her husband" (verse 2); "Come, I will show you a woman who is the bride of the Lamb" (verse 10). An earlier use of the metaphor of Christ as the head of the body which is the Church is in Ephesians 1:22ff: "He [the Father] has put all things under his [Christ's] feet, and made him, as the ruler of everything, the head of the Church, which is his body, the fullness of him who fills the whole creation." The wealth of metaphorizing in Ephesians appears a few verses later in a new figure (2:20–22): "You are part of a building that has the apostles and the prophets for its foundations, and Christ Jesus himself for its main cornerstone. As every structure is aligned on him, all grow into one holy temple in the Lord. . . ."

The figure of Christ as head and the Church as body appears in another of the captivity epistles (Col 1:18): "Now the Church is his body, he its head." The idea itself in less explicit form Paul had introduced six or seven years earlier in 1 Corinthians, in the passage warning against fornication that we saw just above.

11. From the author's essay, "Ephesians 5:21–33 and Radical Indissolubility," in *Marriage Studies,* Vol. 3, Washington, D.C., 1985, p. 26.

12. In the Greek manuscripts that do contain the verb it is in participial form (*hypotassómenoi*), indicating that this deferring is the last in a series of conduct forms that Paul urges on his Ephesian readers since all the forms preceding it in this series are also indicated by participles. Therefore the Vulgate translation of this verb (as it is translated in turn in English) as "be subject to" or "obey" is

arbitrary—as the inclusion of it in Paul's exhortation is itself arbitrary. The ancient manuscripts do not agree about its presence as a verb in this clause. Codices Sinaiticus and Alexandrinus have it in the imperative form. Codex Vaticanus (the oldest), Ephraem and Bezae Cantabrigiensis do not have it.

13. Paul gives this same instruction to Christian spouses in Colossians 6, although there in miniature. In verse 18 he uses the same verb to explain what the wife's conduct ought to be, but there in the present imperative of the middle voice, *hypotássesthe*. The same contrast in conduct is apparent there in the verb designating the appropriate conduct of children and of slaves. Again it is *hypakoúein*.

14. The idea of a Christian community as bride of Christ appeared earlier in the Pauline letters, in 2 Corinthians 11:2: "I am jealous of you with the jealousy of God himself, since I have given you in marriage to one husband, presenting you as a chaste virgin to Christ."

15. The idea that a husband should treat his wife not as a master does a subordinate but as a soul cares for the body is not exclusively Christian. Paul's pagan contemporary, Plutarch, has it in his moral essay, "Conjugal Precepts," 142E.

16. This myth is developed in "The Exegesis on the Soul," in *The Coptic Gospel*, II, 6, 132, 23–133, 10.

17. *The Coptic Gospel*, II, 3.

18. *Op. cit.,* IX, 3.

19. For this information on the Gnostic idea of Christian marriage as an image of a heavenly union, and for the suggestion that Ephesians 5:21–33 is a veiled polemic against it, I am indebted to Professor Pheme Perkins of the Theology Department, Boston College.

BIBLIOGRAPHY

Balch, David: "I Corinthians 7:32–35 and the Stoic Debates on Marriage, Anxiety and Distraction," in *Journal of Biblical Literature,* Vol. 102 (Summer 1983) pp. 429–439.

Barth, Markus: *Commentary on Ephesians, The Anchor Bible,* Volume 34A. Garden City, Doubleday and Company, Inc., 1974. Chapter XI: "Christ's Rule in All Realms, 5:21–6:9, Part One: Husband and Wife, 5:21–33."

Byrne, Brendan: "Sinning Against One's Own Body: I Cor. 6:18," in *Catholic Biblical Quarterly,* Vol. 45 (October 1983), pp. 608–616.

Byron, Brian: "General Theology of Marriage in the New Testament and in I Cor. 7:15," in *Australasian Catholic Record,* Vol. 49 (1972), pp. 1–10.

Daube, David: *The New Testament and Rabbinic Tradition,* N.Y., Arno Press, 1973.

Fitzmyer, Joseph A.: "The Matthean Divorce Texts and Some New Palestinian Evidence," in *Theological Studies,* Vol. 37 (1976), pp. 197–226.

Furnish, Victor: *The Moral Teaching of St. Paul: Selected Issues.* Nashville, Abingdon Press, 1979.

Kardorf, W.: "Marriage in the New Testament and in the Early Church," in *Journal of Ecclesiastical History,* Vol. 20 (1969), pp. 193–210.

LaVerdière, Eugene A.: "The Witness of the New Testament," in *Dimensions of Human Sexuality,* Dennis Doherty, editor, N.Y. Doubleday and Company, 1969.

Mackin, Theodore: "Ephesians 5:21–33 and Radical Indissolubility," in *Marriage Studies,* Vol. 3, Thomas P. Doyle, editor, Washington, D.C., Canon Law Society of America, 1985.

Moiser, Jeremy: "A Reassessment of Paul's View of Marriage in I Cor. 7," in *Journal for the Study of the New Testament,* Vol. 18 (June 1983), pp. 103–122.

Murphy-O'Connor, Jerome: "Sex and Logic in I Cor. 11:2–16," in *Catholic Biblical Quarterly,* Vol. 42/4 (1980), pp. 482–500.

Perkins, Pheme: "Marriage in the New Testament and Its World," in *Commitment to Partnership: Explorations of the Theology of Marriage,* William P. Roberts, editor, N.Y./Mahwah, Paulist Press, 1987.

———: *Ministering in the Pauline Churches,* N.Y., Paulist Press, 1982.

4. MARRIAGE AND THE SACRAMENT UNTIL NICAEA

Paul's message to the Corinthians was a double one, that for most it is better to be married, but that in the ideal it is even better to live a life of virginity. He made clear too that the goodness in marriage is a double kind. It provides a refuge from sin; it also sanctifies the spouses—as he assured those Christians worried about being married to pagans and tempted to dismiss them. But to understand how these Christians understood this goodness, even this holiness available in their marriages, we must first examine marriage's place in their lives generally.

To begin with, a very high percentage of Christians during the earlier generations were adult converts. Without presuming to resolve the dispute about the earliness of infant baptism's entrance into Christian praxis, we can say that until the fourth century most of those baptized were adults. Therefore it is most probable too that of those Christians who married, most did so before conversion. This is all the more likely because of the young age at which sons and daughters were then put into marriage, from twelve to fourteen years by the Jews and other Semites, and before the end of adolescence by other ethnic groups. As the decades went by the practice grew of at least male converts' prolonging their catechumenate—the probation stretching from first request for baptism until actual baptism and reception into full communion—into their middle years. (The reason for this was an inelegantly pragmatic moral theology. Baptism was held to forgive all sins committed and guilt incurred before receiving the sacrament. Sins committed after baptism could be submitted to forgiveness in public repentance, the *exomologésis,* only once. After that a recidivist Christian was handed over to God's recondite mercy to seek forgiveness alone. Therefore it was prudent to postpone baptism until youthful passion had abated somewhat. Augustine's long put-off baptism and Monica's strategies to get him married meanwhile make up the most famous paradigm of this.)

This fact of marriage before conversion to Christian discipleship

83

produced both an assumption and a question. The assumption was that marriage is what Martin Luther was to call it centuries later, *ein weltliches Geschäft,* an affair of this world. By this neither Luther nor the earlier Christians meant that the marriages of at least Jews and Christians are non-religious, non-sacred. Both understood the Genesis accounts to say literally that marriage was immediately God's invention, and is for that reason alone sacred and therefore religious, a link with God. What they understood rather was that marriage is pre-ecclesial. It pre-dates the societal organization of God's people into synagogue and Church. It is not the invention of either. So it does not by nature come under the rule of either's authority. Christians can live maritally without the authority of the Church.

The question bred by the usual marriage before conversion asked, "What does becoming a Christian do to a marriage already constituted?" Presuming that conversion to Christian discipleship is an advance in moral and religious goodness, where does this new goodness gain place in one's marriage and what demands does it make on the marriage? These questions were vexed and complicated where only one of a pagan couple—more frequently the wife—became Christian. (We have already seen Paul address the worry about this among the Christians of Corinth.)

But before attempting to set out the early Christians' answer to this question, let us return to the assumption outlined just above, that marriage, although by nature sacred and therefore religious, is not an ecclesial affair, not a thing of the Church. To whom, then, in the minds of the earlier Christians, did it belong? Who had authority to regulate it in practice?

Marriage as Family Affair

For the Christians the answers were the same as for the Jewish communities from which so many of them came. Marriage is a thing of the family. Therefore it is ruled by the person who has natural authority in the family, the father.

This was borne out by the way the Jews of the time married. To begin with, marriage was obligatory for both sexes, so much so that a boy who had not married by his eighteenth year could be compelled by the court of elders to do so. Girls were ordinarily put into marriage as soon as they reached puberty, which was reckoned legally at twelve and a half years. The earliest at which boys could be married was thirteen years. The reason for such early marriage was a reason of family—to see to its continuation in a most serious sense. Belief in personal survival beyond death was fragile among the Jewish people. If a man died without heirs, especially without male heirs, his name died out, as did the name of his father if he himself was an only son. To marry and produce children was therefore a sacred duty, a familial duty. The duty was all the more grave because of high infant mortality and limited life expectancy among those who did live beyond childhood. These argued for as many births as possible as early as possible.

Marrying and producing children was a sacred duty for a kindred but much more comprehensive familial reason. This was the vocation of the entire people Israel. It had accepted, in covenant with God, to be a light to the nations, to bring God's mercy to all peoples on earth in all ages. If Israel were allowed to die out, this would be to renege in this covenant commitment, to abandon that divine vocation. It would be for Israel to lose her very meaning as a people. So the two reasons for marrying, though so unequal in size, interlocked in intent to keep a divine vocation alive by continuing the family in existence.

It was consistent with these interlocking intents then that Jewish fathers supervised closely the marriages of their children. In consultation with their wives the two fathers arranged their children's union. It was not the reciprocal consent of the young spouses that created their marriage, as it would in later centuries in the Christian West. The wills of the fathers held good for the children's and created their marriage. Such marital consent as the spouses exercised was more an obedient acceptance of the partners chosen for them. Yet it was an acknowledged part of paternal love not to force sons and daughters into marriage with unwanted partners.

The holiness available in this marriage was found in the spouses' obedience to God's will, an obedience carried out comprehensively in helping to fulfill Israel's vocation; but fulfilled particularly in sons' and daughters' obedience to their parents and in care for their families. Holiness here consisted also in guarding chastity in two ways, by fidelity's protecting the parental family, and by its mirroring and embodying in tangible conduct the covenant fidelity of God and Israel.

Jewish marriage's serious purpose in the divine plan along with its familially held firmness must have brought perplexity to Jews who took up Christian discipleship, and must have helped inspire the questions we have listed above. Let us rehearse them in variant form. Given the Christian conviction that Israel's vocation had now passed over to Jesus' followers, did their marriages now also take over the vocation of Jewish marriages? But how could they do so in face of the Christian expectation that the risen Christ would soon return to consummate his kingdom? What role could their marriages have in preparing for this return? In short, how could the climactic realization of the ancient blessing and promise to Israel be abetted by Christian marriages at the brink of history's end?

Marriage in the Roman Tradition

In consideration of these questions need we be surprised if we were to come upon this paradox, that the early Christians suspected that marriage as understood by their Gentile families and neighbors may have fitted more coherently into life lived in that expectation of history's imminent end?

If we found this to be true, it would be all the more paradoxical because by the advent of Christianity marriage in Roman law and Hellenistic culture was not only not ecclesial but was almost wholly nonreligious. It had come to the third and last stage of its cultural migration. There had been the thoroughly religious marriage that throve during the kingdom and the early years of the republic. But this religiousness was not that of a national cult. It was that of the hereditary family and the immediate family. It was a religion of the paternal hearth, the *focus patruus*. Each family venerated its own household gods, the *lares* and the *penates,* along with its *manes,* the spirits of departed ancestors. The father of the family was ruler of wife and children and domestic priest. Together they formed a kind of church in miniature. Therefore when a son married, his wife was incardinated in this family church and its household cult. When a daughter married, she was excardinated from it and incardinated in that of her husband. The wedding ceremony was at every step religious, was elaborate and was laden with religious symbolism.

But this paternally ruled religious marriage gradually lost its place as the patriarchal structure of Roman society broke down. Sons and daughters gradually gained freedom in marrying, although in unequal measure. The former could take the wife of his choice by *coemptio,* a fictitious purchase, or by *usus,* cohabitation with a woman for an uninterrupted year with the intention of taking her as wife. In either case he established *manus* over her in place of her father or guardian.

But even as early as the Law of the Twelve Tables, dating from 450 B.C., *matrimonium liberum,* the free marriage, was made available to women. Once she had reached the legally marriageable age of twelve years a girl could declare herself *sui juris,* a legally free woman. From that time no one had *patria potestas* over her. She could betroth herself to and marry whom she chose. And in marrying she was no longer passed from the *manus* of father or guardian to that of her husband.

Pari passu with this democratizing of marriage went its secularizing. In fact the latter helped to induce the former as the religion of household gods gave way to the impersonal religion of the imported Olympian gods and goddesses. The latter religion had not a fraction of the former's ethical grip on family and marriage. Indeed its exemplars of conduct rather inspired their disintegration. Among patrician families all or some of the ancient religious wedding ceremony survived into the second and third centuries of the empire, but by then drained of its religious meaning.

For all others in the empire by the advent of Christianity the procedure in marrying was virtually empty of the traditional ceremony and therefore of religious meaning. In the *matrimonium liberum* there was almost a formless transaction. The conjunction of three causes was required to create a marriage and sufficed for doing so. The first was *connubium* possessed by both parties, the citizen's right to marry. Then there was *maritalis affectio,* the desire and the will of the parties to be married to one another. It was this *affectio* that differentiated marriage from any other kind of relationship. Finally this *affectio* had to be manifested in some reciprocal consent that could be verified. If the bride had not declared herself *sui juris* but still lived under the authority of a *paterfamilias* or *curator,* his consent too was required. This was the wholly secular marriage, the marriage of equals *communi consensu,* by simple reciprocal consent.

The question asking how marriages created this way could gain place in Christian life and abet its striving for holiness was complicated by the fact that a significant number of the first Christians came from the empire's slave population. Their conversion did not free them; and because of their slavery they were not allowed *connubium,* the right to marry, but only *contubernium,* a legally accepted concubinage. They remained the property of their owners; they could be separated and sold (or killed) at their owners' pleasure. Children born to them also became such property and could be similarly disposed of. What were slaves converted in concubinage to do about this relationship because of their baptism? How could their sexual union be taken with meaning into their new life if it could be ended so abruptly and permanently? Or if they were baptized beforehand, would this inhibit their choice for *contubernium,* a sexual relationship denied the status of marriage by Roman law and custom?

I said above that it may have been paradoxically true that the situation of marriage among the pagans of the apostolic age was more coherent with Christian belief and practice than was Jewish marriage. For one thing, the Roman law's denial of marriage to slaves left the way open for Christian churches, if they were willing, to make marriage available to them on their own authority and on their own terms. Some were willing to do this. Despite scanty records surviving from the first centuries we know that Christian slaves did in places marry in their churches and against Roman law. Even more daringly, some churches sponsored the marriages of slaves with citizens. This was done frequently enough to draw the complaint of the Christian philosopher Hippolytus that Pope Callistus (217–222) permitted Christian citizens to marry freedmen as well as slaves in the Church at Rome against imperial law. The angry objection suggests two things, that Christians of the time ordinarily married according to civil imperial law, and that the communities in question had an independent if nascent Christian law of their own in mind.

In addition to this, the availability of the *matrimonium liberum* to women living under Roman law lodged them far more comfortably within the equal rights relationship taught by Paul in 1 Corinthians 7:3–4.

3. Let the husband fulfill his obligation to his wife, and likewise the wife her obligation to her husband. 4. A wife has no author-

ity over her own body, rather her husband has it; just as a
husband has no authority over his own body, but his wife has it.

Even if the primary intent of these verses is not to assert equality of
all rights in marriage, but to reassert the priority of the marital right to
intercourse over the sexual abstinence urged by the ascetics in the Corinthian community, Paul implies clearly that husbands and wives hold this
right equally. They hold it against either's counter-claim to abstinence.
Even where he concedes to their abstaining for the sake of prayer (verse
5), this they may do only by agreement.

To return to our earlier question asked in view of most Christians'
marrying before conversion—"What does becoming a Christian do to a
marriage already constituted?"—the most evident answer is that it puts
severe moral demands on the spouses. They must rise above the permis-
siveness of pagan sexual mores, mainly in the domain of fidelity, and
there in two ways. They must keep one another as spouses for as long as
both live. And they must reserve their sexual activity exclusively for one
another. The former they must do even if one of the spouses refuses to
convert, as Paul instructed—but this only if that spouse agrees to live in
the peace to which conversion drew the Christian (7:12–15). Some Christian writers and teachers were to put a third moral demand, a demand
strange to our modern minds. It was that Christians once widowed never
remarry. Their main reason for demanding this, that remarriage is a
capitulation to lust, makes clear the object of their ascetical concern.

Marriage and Early Christian Eschatology

A second answer to the question, one richer in religious consequences, is that married converts had to fit their marriages somehow
into the Christian eschatological view of life and history. The uprooting
of marriage from the ancient time-and-space-bound family religion unwittingly helped this fitting in. The eschatological view, described
briefly, was this. The first two ages of the history of the human race—
that of the nations and that of the law of Moses—had come to an end.
They were dominated by sin, and were in great part ruled by evil spiritual powers. It is true that God had instituted marriage before even the
first of these ages, in the brief innocence of the first couple in the
garden. But like everything else human it had been taken and wounded
by the world's sinfulness. Moses' concession to Jewish husbands' hardness of heart was evidence of this.

But now the followers of Christ, and all human beings, lived in the
last age of history, the age of God's kingdom. Christ had begun it
through his death, his resurrection and, in cooperation with his Father,
through the sending of the Spirit. The Spirit was at work in the world,
striving to make all things new. Christ would complete this renewal,
would bring it to its climax by bringing all who believe and hope in him

to the Father in triumph. He would do this in his second coming, his *parousía*. This would be the end of the human race. But during the time of waiting married Christians filled with the Spirit would find their marriages taken beyond mere restoration to the primeval situation of the garden, where the vocation was given to "Be fertile and multiply; fill the earth and subdue it." Now it had a different vocation, but one defined only very generally, to somehow help the spouses prepare for Christ's return.

How inclusively, how firmly and how long this expectation held the minds of Christians at the beginning is difficult for us to know. Paul accepted it unhesitatingly in his first letter to the Thessalonians, which dates from 51 or 52. He wrote of ". . . any of us who are still alive until the Lord's coming" (4:15), and ". . . then those of us who are still alive will be taken up in the clouds . . . to meet the Lord in the air" (4:17). Matthew's and Luke's inclusion of Jesus' eschatological discourse (in their chapters 24 and 21 respectively) suggests that this expectation was alive in the communities for which they compiled their gospels within the decade 75–85. The author of the first epistle of Peter wrote that "Everything will soon come to an end . . ." (4:7); many scholars hold that its pseudonymous composition dates from about 110. The author of the second epistle of Peter, who was certainly not the apostle, devoted a long instruction (chapter 3) to conduct of Christians appropriate to anticipation of Christ's early return to render judgment. The letter is commonly dated during the first twenty years of the second century.

It is no tour de force to interpret the various Christian attitudes toward sexuality and marriage that throve until about the end of that second century as answers to the question about their meaning and conduct during the period of waiting for Christ's return. How these attitudes congealed in moral demands and conduct tells us how the Christians thought God enters their lives via marriage (if he does), how marriage in turn leads them to God (if it can)—in a word how it may serve as a channel of God's grace and as a sign of his presence and action.

As we have seen, the synoptic authors recorded little that Jesus taught about marriage. In the confrontation narratives of Mark 10 and Matthew 19 he is recorded as reaffirming marriage's divine origin, its supreme value among all human relationships, the unity of the spouses that transcends human power to dissolve, and his demand that human authority not try to do away with this union that is created by God's power and under his authority.

But another confrontation narrative (in Matthew 22:23–33, Mark 12:18–27, and Luke 20:27–40), with Sadducees who rejected the resurrection of the dead and tried to trip Jesus up by asking him to which of her seven successive husbands a widow in the next world would be wife, brought a less supportive reply from him: "Is not the reason why you go wrong that you understand neither the scriptures nor the power of God? For when they rise from the dead, men and women do not marry; no, they are like the angels in heaven" (Mk 12:24). Clearly, to Jesus' mind marriage is an affair of this life. It seems unneeded for beatitude in the eternal kingdom, an irrelevance that must raise a question about its function in the kingdom on earth as a preparation for beatitude in eternity.

We have already examined, in part, Paul's most detailed instruction about marriage, in 1 Corinthians 7. It is helpful to return to it, to review other details of it, but now in light of this eschatologic expectation. There can be little doubt that his instruction there was conditioned in some degree by this expectation. He wrote, "About the unmarried I have no command from the Lord, but I offer my opinion as one who, thanks to the Lord's mercy, can be trusted. I think this, that it is good in this time of stress for a man to remain as he is. Are you bound to a wife? Do not seek to be freed. Are you free of a wife? Then do not seek one" (7:25–27).

Two verses later he seems to specify what he means by "this time of stress." It can have been no general persecution of the Christian communities in the year 57, when he wrote this letter. He had suffered personally. But apart from some harassment by synagogue authorities angered at losing people to Christian discipleship, these communities carried on unmolested by the authorities. Paul stated it thus: "This is what I mean, brothers: the time is growing short. For the time remaining those who have wives should live as though they had none" (7:29). Thus Paul's inclusive prudent counsel: Sit tight. This is not the time to change one's life condition. Stay as you are.

But along with this tolerant insistence he had already made his own preference clear, while making clear also that he would impose it on no one: "I wish that all men were as I am . . ." (7:7). How he was, he made clear two verses later in designating his condition as identical with that of the unmarried and the widows. But he acknowledged that whether to be married or to be single is a *chárisma* from God (7:7), an added reason for not seeking to change one's condition. Hence his advice to the unmarried and to the widows that they stay unmarried (7:8).

But Paul is a realist, not an idealistic ascetic. For he qualifies this last advice, to the unmarried and to the widows, immediately: "But if they cannot master themselves, let them marry. For it is better to marry than to be burned" (7:9). This repeats, in variant form, the advice in his first answer to the Corinthians' question put to him: "But because of [the danger of] sexual sin, let each man have his own wife and each woman her own husband" (7:2).[1]

From what we have seen in this letter, both here and earlier, we can sort out and itemize Paul's evaluation of marriage and its sexuality, at least as it appears here. Thus, in comparison with the single state, marriage is objectively the less helpful form of life in which to await Christ's return. In a life of expectation and preparation celibacy and sexual abstinence are better, while marriage and its sexual conduct are recommended mainly as a protection from sin.

Even within marriage sexual intercourse hinders prayer (7:5–6). Therefore spouses may abstain for the sake of prayer, but only by equal agreement and only temporarily lest, again, the weakness of one or both lead to sin.

In a more general and comprehensive estimation, married life limits a person's service to the Lord: "An unmarried man is concerned with the affairs of the Lord, how he will please the Lord. But a married man is concerned with the affairs of the world, how he will please his wife; and he is tugged in two directions" (7:32–33). Again the point is made: Marriage is an affair of this world; and pleasing the Lord and pleasing one's wife are enterprises at odds with one another. The odds against holiness in marriage are increased when Paul appraises the situation of women: "The unmarried woman, like a young girl, concerns herself with the Lord, so that she may be holy in body and in spirit, while the married woman is concerned with the things of the world, how to please her husband" (7:34–35).

If one could query Paul about the invisible logical links of statement with statement in this chapter, one would be tempted to ask him about the nature of the charism of marriage. Since marriage stands in the way of holiness despite being or containing God's gift, what is this gift? What does it do for a Christian spouse? Without doubt Paul himself set out the elements of an answer to this question, elements which Christian fathers and theologians would later piece together with a simple logic: it is a medicinal gift, or grace—either prophylactic or therapeutic. It does not capacitate for true holiness, for union with God. It keeps spouses from falling into sin, or it helps to heal them from sin.

Coming back to Paul himself, at the risk of taxing him for more logical coherence than he thinks needed in his instruction, if one were to ask him about the sanctification a pagan undergoes by living peacefully in marriage with a Christian (7:14), would he say that its substance is the pagan's also being protected and healed from sin?

Three times in this chapter Paul assures his readers that the advice he offers is only that, advice and not command (7:6; 7:25; 7:35). Only twice does he command, in 7:8–9, where it is rather the Lord's command that he passes along, that a husband is not to dismiss his wife and a wife is not to abandon her marriage; and in 7:17–24, where he himself rules that everyone, married or unmarried, circumcised or uncircumcised, "should stay as he was before God at the time of his call."

But not all the Christian teachers were to be as sensitive to and supportive of human weakness as Paul was.

Early Christian Asceticism, Sexuality and Marriage

Along with the eschatological expectation there was a second attitude that seriously conditioned the attitude of Christians toward marriage. Examining it will oblige us to go back again into the Pauline writings, for beginning with the apostolic age a movement of rigorist asceticism began that was to continue until at least the demise of the Manichees at the end of the fourth century and the beginning of the fifth. The principal manifestations of it meanwhile were the Gnostic ascetics, the Montanists and the eremitic solitaries who went by the thousands into the Egyptian desert. There were multiple other lesser manifestations of it, but the ascetic movement was to have a lasting effect on the Christian estimation of marriage and of its function in the effort to attain holiness or to simply remain good.

The sources whence this rigorism infiltrated Christian minds before the end of the first century were several. Here at the beginning of a brief review of them we must not pass over a simple source, one that underlay all the others and took various specific forms in them. This was a psycho-social reaction one finds in any century in any society. When a sufficient majority of its population perceives that anti-social conduct among them has run to an extreme of destructiveness no longer to be tolerated, this majority reacts against this conduct typically to the opposite extreme. The nineteenth and early twentieth centuries saw an example of this in the United States. Heavy consumption of alcohol and resultant public rowdiness were common on the Western frontier. The millions of European immigrants among whom wine and spirits were common diet flooded into the country and brought their own roistering. In reaction some indigenous Americans already nurtured on Protestant sobriety went to the extreme of condemning alcoholic drink altogether and produced the eighteenth amendment to the nation's constitution.

Add to this the ascetic folk principle which says that if one's moral superiority to others consists of being different from them in a certain way, it follows that one is as much superior as one is different in this way. And if one ambitions outright moral perfection in this ascetic goodness, what follows for one's difference in conduct is obvious.

Something of this nature went on among certain Christian groups from the beginning. What they found to react against was the emotional-moral abattoir of sexual conduct in the Roman-Hellenistic world. As an extreme example one recalls that if in a stage play the plot called for a rape, a slave girl in the cast was raped on stage. As a common example one recalls that husbands' recourse to prostitutes or to slave girls was as taken for granted as our modern business lunch. It is understandable that to this extreme of sexual license one or more reactions would be extreme.

The preparation of minds for extreme reaction to pagan sexuality came from diverse places. One of these consisted of segments of the Jewish population addicted to mythologizing the legend of the sons of heaven and daughters of men in Genesis 6—mythologizing it productively by drawing attitudes and norms of conduct from the story. It is in its place in Genesis as part of the author's attempt to explain how evil entered the world.

1. When men began to multiply on earth and daughters were born to them, 2. the sons of heaven saw how beautiful they were, so they took for their wives as many of them as they chose. 3. Then the Lord said, "My spirit shall not remain in man forever, since he is but flesh. . . ."

4. At that time the Nephilim [titans] appeared on earth (as well as later), after the sons of heaven had intercourse with the daughters of man, who bore them sons.

The Jewish interest in this passage shows up most richly in the Book of Enoch, a work of prophecy and apocalyptic vision produced by multiple authors during the century 200–100 B.C. It had extensive influence on the Christian scriptures. It was regarded by most of the earlier Christian fathers and apologists as a canonical Jewish writing, so a number of them quoted from it or paraphrased it without hesitation.[2]

The thesis of this myth as reproduced in Enoch is that evil entered the material universe and human experience thanks to angelic lust for human feminine beauty. Note that this key passage from Enoch virtually repeats Genesis 6:1:

And it came to pass when the children of men had multiplied that in those days were born unto them beautiful and comely daughters. And the angels, the children of heaven, saw and lusted after them, and said to one another, "Let us choose wives from among the children of men and beget us children" (6:1–2).[3]

This angelic lust for women opened the way for all the evil and misery known to mankind to enter.

And all the others together with them [the ten leaders, with Semjaza at their head] took unto themselves wives, and each chose for himself one, and they began to go in unto them and defile themselves with them. . . . And they became pregnant, and they bore great giants . . . who consumed all the acquisitions of men. And when men could no longer sustain them, the giants turned against them and devoured mankind (7:1–3).[4]

The angels' evil communicated itself to men. Enoch specifies the implements of war as the first evidence of this evil among human males, and bodily adornment as the first among women.

And Azazel taught men to make swords, and knives, and shields, and breastplates, and made known to them the metals (of the earth) and the art of working them, and bracelets, and ornaments, and the use of antimony, and the beautifying of the

eyelids and all kinds of costly stones, and all colouring tinc-
tures. And there was much godlessness, and they committed
fornication, and they were led astray, and became corrupt in all
their ways (8:1–3).[5]

It is significant that an element of the fallen angels' evil, along with
defiling themselves through sexual intercourse and bringing misery upon
human beings, was that they revealed heavenly secrets to them.

"Thou seest what Azazel hath done [Michael, Uriel, Gabriel
and Raphael speak to God], who hath taught all unrighteous-
ness on earth and revealed the eternal secrets which were (preserved) in heaven, which men were striving to learn" (9:6).[6]

A variant manuscript reading of the last two clauses is ". . . and
revealed to the world the things which are (preserved) in heaven. And
the children of men are practising his practises in order to know the
mysteries" (note 6).[7]

The central place of secret knowledge among the Gnostic despisers
of marriage we shall see in its place. For now it is enough to note that
human desire for this knowledge was, according to this passage in
Enoch, a consequence of angelic desire for women. Sexuality is firmly in
place and indicted as an agent introducing sin into the human race. Its
role is reinforced by Jewish apocryphal writers identifying Azazel, one
of the lust-smitten angels, as the Satan-serpent who tempted Eve in the
garden (in The Testament of Abraham, 23).

The Books of Adam and Eve, a Jewish apocryphal legend dating
from probably the first century A.D. in Alexandria, makes the point
explicit. The legend has Eve, now with Adam exiled from the garden,
explain to her son Seth how the tempter serpent brought her to sin.

And when he [Satan] had received the oath from me [to give
the forbidden fruit also to Adam], he went and poured upon
the fruit the poison of his wickedness, which is lust, the root
and beginning of every sin, and he bent the branch on the
earth, and I took and ate (xix:3).[8]

Another Jewish work of this apocryphal genre, but one more expressly Gnostic, The Apocalypse of Adam, identifies the first couple's
sin as sexual. As a variation on the paradise temptation and fall, Eve was
seduced by a lower god (one of the angels of Enoch?), who also awakened sexual desire in Adam. This created an evil generation and bound
Adam and Eve to their fate in death. Thus sexual desire, both angelic
and human, is indicated as the cause of death in addition to sin. Thus
Adam narrates:

> Then the god who created us, created a son from himself [and]
> Eve [your mother], for . . . I knew a sweet desire for your
> mother. Then the vigor of our eternal knowledge was de-
> stroyed in us, and weakness pursued us. Therefore the days of
> our life became few. For I knew I had come under the author-
> ity of death.[9]

To the case against sexual desire and conduct that it brought sin and
death upon the human race is added this last indictment, that it forfeited
the eternal knowledge with which the first man and woman were originally gifted. The thesis is characteristically Gnostic.

Philosophic Hostility to Sex and Marriage

To the extent that Jewish teachers studied the philosophies of their
times, and early Jewish-become-Christian teachers did the same, they
could find in them too hostility to sexual passion, and the judgment that
only men who suppress this desire in themselves can attain to true wisdom. The Stoic teachers said this; so too did the Cynics. Seneca's re-
nowned judgment on a husband's motives for having intercourse with
his wife we have thanks to St. Jerome's quoting it in his diatribe, Against
Jovinian (1:49).

> All love of another's wife is shameful; so, too, too much love of
> one's own wife. A wise man ought to love his wife with judg-
> ment, not affection. Let him control his impulses and not be
> borne headlong into copulating. Nothing is fouler than to love
> a wife like an adulteress. Certainly those who say that they
> unite themselves to wives to produce children for the sake of
> the state and the human race ought, at any rate, to imitate the
> beasts, and, when their wife's belly swells, not destroy the
> offspring. Let them show themselves to their wives not as lov-
> ers but as husbands.

One of the later Stoics, Ocellus Lucanus, in his Universal Nature
(4), formulated the thesis that was to become axiomatic among the
Christian fathers: "Not for the sake of pleasure do we approach one
another, but in order to create children. . . . The sexual organs are
given to man not for pleasure but for preserving the species."

Musonius Rufus, the teacher in Rome of Epictetus and Pliny the
Younger, urged implicitly a control of sexual desire by formulating the
most interpersonal understanding of marriage of all the Stoics. It is a
companionship or community of life (a *koinonía*) and of the procreating
of children. The spouses are to consider all things as shared and nothing
as private, not even their own bodies. Everything is shared, their souls,

their bodies, their goods—everything except their distinct identities as husband and wife. To express fully this sense of shared lives he used the terms *symbíosis, kedemonía* and *harmonía*. By these he meant that the partners take full care of one another in true devotion and have everything in common.[10]

He admitted that marriage is natural, that the creator intends for men and women to marry. For this he offered four points of evidence: the correlated anatomies of men and women; men and women have a natural desire for one another; the intimacy of marriage is the most inclusive and intense of all intimacies; the gods intend for men and women to marry, since Hera, Eros and Aphrodite attend and supervise marriage and procreation.

But he considered procreation the only innocent object of sexual desire and the only reason for sexual intercourse in marriage. Any other object or reason reduces the human being to the level of an animal.

> Not the least part of the life of luxury and self-indulgence lies also in sexual excess; for example those who lead such a life crave a variety of loves, not only lawful but unlawful ones as well, not women alone but also men. . . . Men who are not wanton or immoral are bound to consider sexual intercourse justified only when it occurs in marriage and for the sake of begetting children, since it is lawful but unjust when it is mere pleasure-seeking even in marriage. . . . There must be sheer wantonness in anyone yielding to the temptation of shameful pleasure and like swine rejoicing in his own vileness.[11]

It was typical of the Cynics that they called into question all human endeavors to find happiness, all human relationships entered for this purpose and all human institutions. Among these they included marriage. They held that it deludes men and women into hoping for happiness in it, and traps them in its concerns. Diogenes reasoned as follows:

> One should not wed nor raise children, since our race is weak and marriage and children burden human weakness with troubles. Therefore, those who move toward wedlock and rearing of children on account of the support these promise, later experience a change of heart when they come to know that they are characterized by even greater hardships.[12]

The way to escape the delusion and the trap is to suppress desire right from the beginning of its temptation.

> But it is posssible to escape right from the start. Now the person insensitive to passion, who considers his own posses-

sions sufficient for patient endurance, declines to marry and produce children.[13]

To the anticipated objection that if everyone followed his advice the human race would vanish, Diogenes offered the most nihilistic reply:

> But even if the human race should fail, would it not be fitting to lament this as much as one would if the procreation of flies and wasps should fail?[14]

The Pauline Communities

That Paul had to contend with this ascetic devaluation of marriage in at least some of the communities he established is evident in what we saw in the preceding chapter's examination of his first letter to the Corinthians. There he had to deal with probably an early form of Gnosticism that had already attracted the Jewish members of that community before their conversion. We have evidence of his having to contend with it in other communities and during the last years of his life, if the pastoral epistles (1 Timothy, 2 Timothy and Titus) are his. If they were written by a different Christian teacher at the end of the first century instead of by Paul c. 65–67, we have evidence of the shape this problem as ascetic depreciation of marriage had taken by that time in some of the communities in the eastern Mediterranean. Timothy was head of the community in Ephesus, Titus of that on the island of Crete. Favoring the later date is the over-arching concern of the pastoral epistles to form the Christian communities into stable, lasting, mini-societies of responsible citizens of the world. Anticipation of Christ's return is still evident in them, but the only history whose early climax is clearly expected is the personal history of Paul.

> As for me my life is already being poured away as a libation, and the time has come for me to be gone. I have fought the good fight to the end; I have run the race to the finish; I have kept the faith; all there is to come now is the crown of righteousness reserved for me, which the Lord, the judge, will give to me on that day, and not only to me but to all those who have longed for his appearing (2 Tim 4:6–8).

As in 1 Corinthians, here too Paul, or the later author, offers "household" instructions for different categories of persons in the communities addressed. We note here only the instructions that touch marriage and sexual conduct. Elders who preside over the communities must have been married only once (1 Tim 3:2). This bars widowers who have remarried and men who have divorced a wife married before conversion and have remarried after it. The same instruction holds for deacons (1 Tim 3:12); and the same instruction for presiders is repeated in the letter to Titus (1:6).

Widows formed a recognized group, or "vocation," in these communities. Paul has reasons for setting exact norms of a woman's acceptance in such a group. She must be at least sixty years of age; she must have been married only once; "she must be known for her good works and for the way in which she has brought up her children" (1 Tim 5:9–10).

With the groups of widows there has been trouble of some degree. For one thing, widows are too numerous for the communities to support. Hence Paul's instruction, which assumes that there are women of independent wealth among those to whom he writes: "If a Christian woman has widowed relatives, she should support them and not make the church bear the expense but enable it to support those who are genuinely widows" (1 Tim 5:6).

But the more serious trouble appears to have been with widows who were still young women. That these were not few is likely considering the acceptability of very young girls' marrying men much older than themselves. (We recall that in Jewish families the usual age at which girls married was from twelve to fourteen years.) Paul's instruction about them is that they not be accepted in the ranks of widows. The reasons he gives for this may be also the reason for setting the norms we have just seen. Passion is still very alive in them; they want to marry again—which is in itself not reprehensible since he advises that this is just what they should do: "I think it is best for young widows to marry again and have children and a home to look after, and not give the enemy any chance to raise a scandal about them" (2 Tim 5:14).

What is reprehensible in them comes from the fact that widowhood as a vocation in the community appears to involve a serious religious commitment. A young widow's wanting to remarry after having made this commitment is what disedifies: ". . . their natural desires get stronger than their dedication to Christ, they want to marry again, and then people condemn them for being unfaithful to their original promise" (2 Tim 5:11–12). In one sense Paul wishes to shield these young women from the painful consequences to them in the community of their own weakness.

That remarriage and childbearing are the better part for young widows echoes what Paul said earlier about the role of women in the churches, a role not only of young women. This appears in the *Haustafeln* in 1 Timothy. There he addressed an issue that had arisen either among Gentile converts with their far more liberal attitude toward women's participation in religious ministry, or among converts from Judaism seeking to interpret and apply liberation from the Jewish traditions. The issue was whether women could speak out and even teach in the Christian assemblies. Paul's instruction on this point does two significant things, one directly and the other obliquely. First and directly, it puts women's place back where it was in the synagogues, while obliquely it gainsays the importance of sexual abstinence for salvation. Along the way he justifies his instruction by a hurried exegesis of the garden parable that was to be seized on and repeated by Christian fathers in the following centuries.

> 11. . . . During instruction a woman should be quiet and respectful. 12. I am not giving permission for a woman to teach or to tell a man what to do. 13. A woman ought not to speak, because Adam was formed first and Eve afterward, 14. and it was not Adam who was led astray but the woman who was led astray and fell into sin. 15. Nevertheless she will be saved by childbearing, provided she lives a modest life and is constant in faith and love and holiness (1 Tim 2:12–15).

But the most serious trouble that Paul had to deal with was created by a group within these communities that was either genuinely Gnostic or was purveyor of the post-exilic myths and fables on which Jewish Gnosticism nourished itself. That these people were not outsiders but members themselves of the communities is suggested (though not proved) by their being able to get effectively at just the women who were already troubled for the reasons noted above. That they were Gnostic-minded is evident in their condemning marriage—". . . they will say marriage is forbidden" (1 Tim 4:3); in that they claim an elitist knowledge of God, a knowledge they appear to deem unavailable in Paul's teaching—"They claim to have a knowledge of God" (Tit 1:16); in that they traffic in "pointless speculations and those genealogies" (Tit 5:9); and in that they deny a future resurrection and glorification, claiming that these have already taken place (2 Timothy 2:17–18).

That these false teachers were Jewish is suggested by, again, their interest in genealogies; by their condemning certain foods ("they . . . lay down rules about abstaining from foods which God created to be accepted with thanksgiving by all who believe and also know the truth").

How troublesome these persons were is evident in Paul's worry about their ability to get at and pervert the minds of just those members of the churches whom he regards as the least stable.

> 6. Of the same kind, too, are those men who insinuate themselves into families in order to get influence over silly women who are obsessed with their sins, 7. and follow one craze after another in an attempt to educate themselves, but can never come to the knowledge of the truth (2 Tim 3:6–7).

This too points to Gnostic infiltrators. Worrying women about their sins hints at attacks on marriage and sexuality. Spurring them to educate themselves points to striving for the secret gnosis via learning myths and legends. Searching for the truth points out a special irony in Paul's condemnation here, as just above. For the truth is what the Gnostics purported to bring to replace what they regarded as the deceptions taught from the scriptures, which at that time were for Christians exclusively the Jewish scriptures.

It may be that Paul's condemning the false teachers who insinuated themselves into Christian families had as one of its purposes to keep women taken over by them from in turn spreading their teaching in the communities. He may also have sought to take their intended prey out of range of these teachers by reducing the number of widows—by setting the rigorous qualifications for formal widowhood, by urging families to care for their own widows, and by urging young widows to remarry.

Gnosticism and Christian Marriage

Gnostic teaching and conduct very probably infiltrated Christian communities of the first century because they had already got into some of the synagogue communities from which came so many converts to Christianity. There is no way to mark exactly the date at which the teaching and conduct first surfaced in the synagogue communities. It took form as a gradual accumulation from different sources, most probably during the last century before the common era. It was never an independent sect that lured away into conversion; it infiltrated extant communities and sought to mutate them from within. It had no singular founder figure such as Jesus, the Buddha or Mohammed. Its heroes were not noted Gnostic teachers, but Jewish heroes of antiquity and later the Christian apostles, to whom some of the best-known Gnostic writings, such as the Gospel of Thomas, were attributed. The Gnostics had no sacred cities or places, no Mount Zion, no Holy Sepulchre, no Mecca. They had no fixed dogma or fixed common ritual.

In composition Gnostic teaching was a mixture of reworked ancient Near Eastern mythologies, and a pseudo-scientific lore of astrology and medicine; of mythicized persons and events out of the post-exilic Jewish apocalyptic literature; of pseudo-scientific speculation in the hermetic esoteric wisdom, especially from its schools in Egypt, where Jewish Gnosticism appears to have thriven most; of Stoic philosophy, especially in its theory of the divine as an innate and ordering intelligence in the universe. One of its main uses of philosophy was to borrow from it a vocabulary with which to narrate its myths, while along the way depersonalizing the standard mythic figures into such abstractions as Depth, Silence, Mind, and Truth.

Within Judaism Gnosticism may have begun as a revolt, perhaps in those communities where Hellenized Jewish wisdom and Jewish apocalyptic enthusiasm were strongest. In such milieux the anthropomorphic image of the creator-God, one who walked on earth and talked with his human creatures (as in the garden parable of Genesis 2–3), was unacceptable. The movement may have offered a growing Jewish middle class outside Palestine a way of escaping Judaism's earthy peasant beginnings and of discoursing with pagan neighbors in intellectual-cultural parity. Accordingly among the Christian communities the Gnostics' intent was at bottom to free their members from the embarrassing baggage of at least the earth-bound and legalistic portion of the Jewish scriptures. We recall that for the first Christian generations the Jewish scriptures were the scriptures *tout court*. Hence the Gnostics offered a higher, spiritual interpretation of the gospels and of Paul; they posed as champions of the freedom from the law which Jesus had brought, and after him Paul.

The Gnostics held to two major points of belief that more than all others disagreed with orthodox Christian doctrine.[15] One was a predeterminism, a denial of the part played by free will in either a person's salvation or damnation. The most glaring by-product of this was the religious-anthropological categorization and distribution of the human race worked out by the Roman Gnostic, Valentinus. He saw all mankind divided into a tiny and elite group of "the spiritual," a somewhat larger group of "the psychic," and a huge majority of "the earthly," or "the animal." "The spiritual" Valentinus held to be pre-determined to salvation, and nothing in their conduct could alter this fate. "The earthly" were just as immutably pre-determined to damnation. As for "the psychic," their fate alone depended on their free decisions in belief and conduct. Predictably the cadre of "the spiritual" was made up exclusively of the true Gnostics.

The second major point of gnostic heterodoxy was their pessimistic view of the world and of the human race. This was no mere moral discouragement or psychological morosity. It was a cosmic pessimism. It saw evil not in the deprivation or perversion of goodness, but as a component of the universe equally as real as goodness. This pessimism was an ontological dualism; it fused moral evil with ontic evil, as it fused moral goodness with ontic goodness. Conveniently for the Gnostic system, the spiritual component of the universe is good, the material is evil. And this dualism-pessimism dictated a fundamental Gnostic attitude toward marriage and sexuality. These are obviously material, bodily enterprises. So radically, at their source and in their nature, they are evil. And since they are ontically evil, indulgence in them by a man or woman is morally evil.

Because the material sector of the universe was taken as evil, the Gnostics had to revise the traditional Jewish-Christian interpretation of the creator and creation. The creator of this sector cannot be the good God whom Jesus revealed to be his Father and the father of the saved. Its creator is rather an inferior deity, a demiurge, who is evil. The God Yahweh-Elohim whom the Old Testament presents is this evil deity. Indeed the entire Old Testament is an earthly document produced by earthly men who have gone to their pre-determined damnation. Therefore what it says about marriage and sexuality—whether in commendation of marriage or in condemnation of certain kinds of sexual conduct—is at best worthless and at worst misleading and corrupting. The entire law set forth in the Old Testament is fit to govern only the earthly, those men and women of animal souls. "The spiritual" have risen above this law; their perfect knowledge (their *gnosis*) has gained for them the freedom of the true sons of God that St. Paul claimed and preached.

Certain Gnostics offered variant explanations of this dualistic creation, bizarre borrowings from Eastern spiritualism. I shall review them presently and suggest how they affected the Gnostic attitude toward marriage and sexuality.

But to come at this attitude from a less crude source, one must note how orthodox Christianity itself fed the Gnostic inclination to spiritualism and thence to dualism. The Gnostics claimed to find clear support in the New Testament, in certain passages whose meaning they twisted to their own purposes.

Beginning with the assumption that Christians now live in a new age, the age of the kingdom, they interpreted Jesus' words, "But woe to those who are with child or have infants at the breast in those days" (Mt 24:19 and Lk 21:23) to mean that in the kingdom there is, by Jesus' will, to be no childbearing. They found the same meaning in his words, "The children of this world take wives and husbands, but those who are judged worthy of a place in the other world and in the resurrection from the dead do not marry . . . for they are the same as the angels" (Lk 20:35–36). And they easily turned Jesus' disapproval of the man invited to the banquet who excused himself with "I have married a wife and so cannot come" (Lk 14:20) into the conclusion that those who marry are excluded from the eschatological banquet at the end of time. They pointed out too that Jesus himself had never married, and neither had John his precursor; they noted that Paul had married but had left his wife, and had told the Corinthians (as they understood his counsel): "It is good for a man not to touch a woman" (1 Cor 7:1).

Diverse Gnostic Attitudes Toward Marriage

In Book 3, Chapter 5 of his *Stromata* Clement of Alexandria explains that the Gnostics' dualist view of creation led to two disagreeing attitudes toward marriage and sexuality. These were the extremes of a rigorous and negative asceticism on the one hand, and a licentious, all-is-innocent antinomianism on the other. (Some modern scholars have identified a compromise position lying between these two extremes.) Whether and in what degree Clement's, and also Irenaeus', descriptions of the several sub-species of Gnosticism are accurate we have no way of knowing. But their accuracy is not at issue here, nor the point. The point is their perception of the Gnostic threat whether accurate or inaccurate. For it was from this perception that the orthodox patristic defense of marriage came. It was their understanding of the Gnostic abuse of marriage and sexuality that produced their reasoned claim for the value of both.

The best-known of the ascetic Gnostics were the three, Marcion (in Rome, with his complete community having its own hierarchy and liturgy), Tatian (an Assyrian, converted probably in Rome, and a disciple there of Justin, the apologist and martyr), and Julius Cassianus (a dissenter from Valentinian Gnosticism, who taught in either Antioch or Alexandria ca. 170; he is identified with yet another Gnostic sub-group, the Encratites or "Self-Controlled").

It was Marcion especially who insisted that the Old Testament is the work of earthly, sensuous men, who in it tell of the inferior God, the evil creator of the material universe. According to Marcion it was this God, who, as the book of Genesis records, gave the command: "Increase and multiply." This was of a piece with his design to fill the earth with brutish men and women. No true Christian, no spiritual or even psychic believer in the gospel, would listen to this command; none would engage in sexual intercourse and thereby increase the number of the brutish who are in any case pre-determined to damnation. Therefore Marcion simply forbade his followers to marry or to engage in sexual conduct in any circumstance.

About Julius Cassianus we know only from Clement's reference to him in Book 3, Chapter 13 of the *Stromata*. Clement quotes there from his treatise, *Concerning Continence and Celibacy,* his condemnation of sexual intercourse, and in it gives a fair sample of the Gnostics' hermeneutic in defense of their position.

"And let no one say that because we have these parts, that the female body is shaped this way and the male that way, the one to receive, the other to give the seed, sexual intercourse is allowed by God. For if this arrangement had been made by God, to whom we seek to attain, he would not have pronounced eunuchs blessed; nor would the prophet have said that they are "not an unfruitful tree" [Isaiah 56:3], using the tree as an illustration of the man who chooses to emasculate himself of any such notion."[16]

The Gnostics whose teachings seem known in greatest detail were a group established in Alexandria, by the middle of the second century the intellectual capital of the Roman-Hellenistic world. These were the Carpocratians, a group of disciples gathered during that time and instructed by and taking their name from their master, Carpocrates. Clement lays the heaviest weight of blame upon the Carpocratians for bringing general suspicion of sexually dissolute conduct upon all Christians, even though Tacitus in his *Annals* (15:44) and Pliny in his *Epistles* (10:96) had reported this reputation in the first century. Celsus, the bitter pagan critic of Christianity (in his *On True Doctrine,* ca 177–180), may have been in part the cause of Clement's judgment of the group. Celsus considered their religious ritual as licentious as the orgies of the devotees of Antinoous, the homosexual child favorite of Hadrian, who after drowning in the Nile in 130 was made by that emperor the object of a hero cult at Antinoopolis in Egypt.

In his *Against the Heresies,* Book 1, Chapter 25, Irenaeus attempts a summary of Carpocrates' teaching. According to it the material universe has been created by the inferior angels. But Jesus, the son of Joseph of Nazareth, used in an extraordinary way his power of *anámnesis,* the Platonic recalling of what his spirit had gazed on in the divine sphere before being incarnated in birth. By dint of this he gained power from the Father, the highest and good God, by which he escaped from the control of the world-creators. Jesus gained this power by his purity and steadfastness. But those souls after Jesus who can gain the same power, now by true knowledge and by magic, can make the same escape from the world-creators. Since they have this power and have freed themselves from evil control, they can engage in any kind of conduct without danger. The moral right and wrong detailed by human law are no more than human conventions about what harms souls still vulnerable to harm. But they, the Carpocratians, are free and above this harm. They have already been saved by their faith and love, and of course by their secret knowledge. Finally, in order to avoid reincarnation after one's spirit has once departed the earthly sphere, the Gnostic must, before his departure, have every kind of experience—especially in the domain of sexuality. In this sense the Carpocratians interpreted Jesus' admonition (in Luke 12:59), "I tell you, you will not get out [of the debtors' prison] until you have paid the last farthing." Hence Irenaeus' indictment of the male Carpocratians (in *Against the Heresies,* Book 1, Chapter 25), that in their arrogance the teachers and spiritual leaders among them seduce their women followers, live with them, and—ironically—get them pregnant. It was entirely consistent with such ethical premises that the Carpocratians should make a religious ritual of sexual intercourse a means for entering the kingdom of God. In any case Clement accuses Carpocrates and his associates (in *Stromata,* Book 3, Chapter 2) of even turning the last moments of the eucharistic agape into a ritual of "holy copulation."

The morality of the antinomian Gnostics was grounded in part in their singular cosmogony, their theory of the origin of the universe. This was explained in multiple ways by the many Gnostic sub-groups, and Irenaeus has an elaborate rehearsal of it in the first five chapters of Book 1 of *Against the Heresies.* But in general the cosmogony involved a monadic self-multiplication, a kind of caricature of the generation of the divine Word explained by orthodox theologians in the developing doctrine of the trinity of persons in God. Thus, at the beginning of all and the source of all was the entity called the Monad. It—or he or she, because the entity proved indeed fertile—was alone at first. But it seemed good to its unity not to be alone. It generated the Idea, then had intercourse with it, and from this came the invisible spirits, the "powers" of the universe. These, when generated in the pre-ordained full number, will make up the *pléroma,* the fullness, of the universe.

To a fuller explanation of this notion of the *pléroma* I shall return in a moment. But two other representatives of the antinomian Gnostics deserve mention. One of these were the Nicolaitans, a group surfacing early in Christian Gnosticism. Their *Book of Apocalypse* was composed in the last few years of the first century, and in his letter to the Church in Ephesus the author mentions this group: "But you have this much in your favor: you detest the practices of the Nicolaitans, just as I do" (2:16). The others were the followers of Prodicus in Rome. They too defended their attitude and their conduct by twisting to their purpose New Testament passages on the theme of liberation. They called themselves "lords of the sabbath" and "royal sons," and deemed themselves bound by no law. Clement accused them (in *Stromata,* Book 3, Chapter 4) of committing adultery in secret, considering themselves already predestinately saved, so that nothing they did could change this blessed fate.

The notion of the *pléroma* makes its most developed appearance among the Gnostics in the teaching of Valentinus. He was an Egyptian who claimed to have studied under a certain Theodas, a personal disciple of Paul. He first taught in Alexandria, then came to Rome, and stayed and taught there until Hyginus became bishop of the city and pope, from 135 to 160. Valentinus' followers became the best known of all the Gnostics.

Valentinus approved of marriage, but his reason for doing so was most unusual. The remote source of this reason was the Platonic-Hellenistic notion that earthly structures imitate heavenly structures, and that accordingly earthly conduct ought to imitate its heavenly models. According to Valentinus the godhead, which is the *pléroma,* consists of thirty spiritual beings, the aeons. The *pléroma* began its cosmogonic history with the aeon *Bythos* (Depth or Abyss) and his consort *Sige* (Silence). Their marriage produced *Nous* (Mind) and *Aletheia* (Truth). This pair in turn produced *Anthropos* (Man) and *Ecclesia* (Church). These eight form the cosmic Ogdoad, and from it the rest of the *pléroma* evolves gradually until the full thirty aeons are attained. In this Gnostic sect the sacred marriages of the aeons served as the model for the Gnostic bride and groom on earth. The latters' experience of marriage and sexuality was a counterpart and an imitation of the very life of the godhead; the experience was a foretaste of the final happiness of the Valentinian spouses after death.

(The concept of the *pléroma* was taken into the christology of the early Church, a christology that antedated Valentinus' teaching. We find it expressed clearly in the Christus-hymn of Paul's letter to the Colossians, 1:15–20. The poet, whether Paul himself or some anonymous

Christian, says first (in verse 16) that the totality of all things, *tà pánta,* in heaven and on earth, was created in Christ. The poet gives a sampling of the hierarchy he has in mind: Thrones, Dominations, Sovereignties, Powers. All these were created through Christ and for Christ. In verse 19 he seals his thought by using the word itself: the divine plan from the beginning has been that the *pléroma,* the fullness and the fulfillment of the universe, be found in Christ. And (in verse 20) this is to be done by Christ's bringing all creatures together in peace by his death on the cross. That this faith-assertion about Christ is a reply to the Gnostic belief is hardly to be doubted.)

The Gnostic linking of the *pléroma* of aeons to their sexual conduct lay in this, that some of them thought this fullness would come only through the emission of their seed by spiritual men on earth. Apparently with each emission another of the aeons took its place in the hierarchy of celestial beings. If the orthodox teachers of the time searched for some purpose for sexual intercourse—some purpose beyond the act itself, nobler than it, one that would take it beyond mere pleasure-seeking— these Gnostics offered them a noble find. What nobler purpose could a man's and a woman's intercourse on earth have than to generate a spiritual being and thereby bring the divine history nearer its goal? This was to do the work of the godhead itself. And it was perfect without any reference to human reproduction.

The other group of Gnostics of this middle way between asceticism and sexual license were Basilides, his son Isidore and their followers. Basilides himself taught in Alexandria between 120 and 140; he claimed to have received his doctrine from a certain Glaukias, the interpreter of St. Peter. He taught that to marry is not a sin; that it is better, as St. Paul said, to marry than to burn. But, he insisted, marriage and its sexual involvement are obstacles to Christian pefection. Irenaeus had different information about Basilides. He reported in Book 1, Chapter 24 of *Against the Heresies,* Basilides' saying that marriage and the bearing of children are from Satan, but that the practice of lusts is at the same time a morally indifferent matter.

The Androgynous God of the Gnostics

Running through much of this Gnosticism, and apparently coming from rabbinic teaching of the time, was a belief in the androgynous character of the divine. An androgynous divine being was said to have played an essential role in creating the universe. (We have seen a hint of this in the Carpocratian cosmogony of the Monad, which was said to have begun creation by generating out of itself Idea.) Thus in implicit contradiction of the premise in the creation poem of Genesis 1 that the creator transcends sexuality, this cosmogony proposed a creator who is inclusively sexual. And since nature is creation in imitation of the divine, divine androgyny is the model and the ideal for human sexuality,

Logically this may lead to two main consequences in human attitude and conduct. Sexual intercourse is not for procreation but for the partners' experiencing in themselves the divine ideal, that is, the blending of the sexes instead of their fruitful interaction is the ideal. And the Gnostic, who has the true knowledge of the divine, is to locate the experience of androgynous sexuality, the full repertory of sexual experiences, at the center of his or her life. (According to Irenaeus, Carpocrates believed the latter and advocated it.) One consequence of this attitude for sexuality was to void it of any reason for situating it within marriage, and therefore of any reason for confining it to marriage. For if sexuality finds its reason in richness of experience, marriage would only constrict it and procreation would worsen the constriction.

Whether derived from these quasi-doctrinal elements or only concomitant with them, some Gnostics held that in the communities of true believers the women should be available for marriage, or at least for intercourse, with any man. Presumably this was to be both a sign and an enacting of the full freedom of those who are already saved for having attained the true knowledge.

Clement reports this in Chapter 2 of Book 3 of the *Stromata:* "But the followers of Carpocrates and Epiphanes think that wives should be common property." He explains how these Gnostics come to this as a conclusion of their theology: the universal righteousness of God intended that in creation there be no difference and separation; that as all differences are included in himself and there reconciled in non-difference (here is the androgynous trait of divine sexuality), so in creation there ought to be no difference and separation: "The righteousness of God is a kind of universal fairness and equality. There is equality in the heaven which is stretched out in all directions and contains the entire earth in its circle. . . . There is no distinction between rich and poor, people and governor, stupid and clever, female and male, free men and slaves. . . . And for birth there is no written law (for otherwise it would have been transcribed). All beings beget and give birth alike, having received by God's righteousness an innate equality. The Creator and Father of all with his own righteousness appointed this. . . . He did not make a distinction between female and male, rational and irrational, nor between anything and anything else at all. . . . God made all things for man to be common property. He brought female to be with male and in the same way united all animals. He thus showed righteousness to be a universal fairness and equality."[17]

The Orthodox Reaction to Gnostic Teaching in the Second and Third Centuries

From an observer's distance the Gnostic attacks on marriage are seen to have come from two directions, and the attacks to have indicted it for two distinct and unequal faults. The ascetics attacked it and its characteristic conduct, sexual intercourse, for being evil. The antinomians spared sexuality but condemned marriage as at best meaningless but at worst as an obstacle to sexuality's realizing its exalted vocation. It is true that we have examined Gnostic teaching only in the form found in Clement's and Irenaeus' polemics against it, the only form in which it could be studied until the discovery, in 1945 and 1946, of the forty-four Gnostic documents at Nag-Hammadi in upper Egypt.[18] For this reason our understanding of the teaching may be flawed in some degree. But as I explained earlier, this is beside the point of our examination of its attack on marriage and of the orthodox reply to the attack. It was the orthodox perception exemplified in the *Stromata* and in *Against the Heresies,* and the reply this perception inspired, that helped produce the eventually accepted Catholic doctrine concerning marriage and sexuality. What is more important than understanding the Gnostic teaching in itself, and unrefracted through Clement's and Irenaeus' anger, is to understand their and other orthodox writers' understanding of that teaching. This is what the digest above has offered.

If one were to estimate only the orthodox counter-attack on the Gnostic ascetics, one would say that their task was a simple one, provided one accepted two premises: first, that the creation poem in Genesis 1 and the garden parable in Genesis 2 and 3 are factually accurate; second, that the creator pictured there is the one creator of all the universe, spirit as well as matter, the good God, the same as the Father of Jesus told of in the gospels. The ascetics' charge was that marriage and sexuality are in themselves evil, the invention of an inferior god, a demi-urge. But this is impossible, since the Genesis passages say that they have been institutued by the one and good creator. This is proof *a priori.* Jesus confirmed marriage's goodness *a posteriori,* and by derivation approved the goodness of sexuality, in accepting the invitation to the wedding feast at Cana of Galilee. It is unthinkable that he would have participated in the celebration of something evil.

Wittingly or unwittingly this vindication of marriage's goodness against the Gnostic ascetics was needed to keep open its candidacy as a Christian sacrament. With the vindication accomplished there would remain only the need to verify wherein lay marriage's intrinsic goodness— the goodness designed into it by the Creator who can bring into existence only good things; the goodness too by which Christian marriages could be sacramental.

But against the Gnostic antinomians' attack on marriage, and against their attempt to emancipate sexuality from its enslavement to marriage, the task of refutation was not so simple. The high vocation they claimed for sexual intercourse—the experience that asserts and demonstrates freedom, that cooperates in completing the *pléroma* of the universe, that enables men and women to imitate on earth the conduct of the spirits, that gives them a foretaste of the bliss that awaits in the next life—would seem to carry marriage along with it into a supernal goodness. But we know already that these other Gnostics rejected marriage as a dead weight on sexuality's potential for beatitude. Their effort was expressly to free sexuality from this fatal constraint. Therefore the orthodox task was not only to keep sexuality within marriage, away from what it deemed adultery and fornication, but to keep it within marriage by providing an unassailable reason for its being there. To do this they would have to identify a goodness that it can realize only within marriage. To further complicate their task, this must be a goodness that demands as a moral imperative that it be kept within marriage.

Before examining the orthodox teachers' reply to the Gnostic antinomians it is helpful to ask, with the benefit of hindsight, which side's appreciation of sexuality in Christian life was more congenial to the theology of the sacrament in marriage that was to develop in the long future. We will see Clement and Irenaeus repeating the ethical conclusion of Philo and the Stoics that because sexual intercourse's only natural intention is conception, it must be kept within marriage. We will also see Origen saying that the institution of marriage was an indirect consequence of primordial sin, but a consequence nonetheless. Because preexistent human souls sin in the spiritual universe and are punished by temporary imprisonment in earthly bodies, bodies must be supplied. To supply them is the duty of sexual intercourse and marriage. That marriage gets its purpose from the history of sin in the world, though in a way different from Origen's interpretation, will be repeated in the fourth century by Gregory, bishop of Nyssa, and by John Chrysostom. Finding in this dour vision a goodness in marriage that is holiness, or at least the matrix of holiness, would be a sore challenge.

On the other hand the antinomian Gnostics had their holiness designed into the nature itself of sexual intercourse. They held to an unbroken continuation from its pleasure in this life to beatitude in the next. They taught that it imitates, and even participates in, the conduct of the divine spirits—an ingratiating claim in a Christian epoch that saw much of holiness consisting of earthly imitation of and participation in spiritual reality. How could denying these claims for marriage's most characteristic conduct, and instead tying this conduct down to life on earth and its fleeting purposes, not disqualify marriage from acceptance among the sacraments?

Among the Jewish teachers who had a lasting effect on the Christian fathers' attitude toward sexuality and marriage no one's was more lasting than that of Philo, a contemporary of Jesus and Paul. One reason for his influence was that he taught in Alexandria, successor city to Athens as intellectual capital of the world. It was there that the most active catechetical center of early Christianity was started up by the middle of the second century. What Philo taught was all the more congenial to the orthodox teachers because he was a monotheistic Jew, a man as committed as they to a pure life and to holiness—and fundamentally approving of marriage, in ironic contrast to such Gnostic Alexandrian Christians as Basilides, Valentinus and Carpocrates. Moreover his lifelong work of fusing Jewish religious belief with Greek philosophy, using the latter to explain the former reasonably and thus make it acceptable to serious-minded pagans, helped provide the orthodox Christian teachers with what they needed. This was a philosophically reasoned case against the Gnostics of both persuasions, the ascetics and the antinomians. Philo's ability to supply this case was born in his anthropology.

Deeply influenced by Platonism, he held to a sharp dualism of soul and body, of the rational and the sensate elements in the human makeup. He insisted on the moral necessity of persons' freeing themselves from the power of the sensate in themselves. The Stoic ideal showed itself in his moral teaching, in his urging that the only true good for men is virtue, and that their only virtuous relationship to their passions is apathy.

Consistently with this anthropology and the moral teaching it bred, Christians could take the following from Philo about sexuality and marriage.[19] He laid down a judgment that for later Christians was to gain the status of a first principle. Writing in Book 4, Chapter 15 of his *Special Laws,* he describes the ruinous effects of desire in those foolish enough to let themselves be enslaved by it. He warns especially against the ruin brought by desire fixed on four objects: money, reputation, office and bodily beauty. Of the last-named he says, "If the object of their desire is bodily beauty, they become seducers, adulterers, pederasts, devotees of lust and promiscuity. And they regard these vile evils as the highest blessings."[20]

Earlier, in Book 3, Chapter 2, he had undertaken to explain Moses' meaning in each of the commandments of the decalogue. When explaining the first commandment of the Second Table, "Thou shalt not commit adultery," he used the occasion to point at the ruinous effect of the desire for pleasure.

> In the Second Table the first command is "Thou shalt not commit adultery"—first, I think, because physical pleasure breathes everywhere in the civilized world so powerfully that no part of it escapes its tyranny.[21]

Lest one think that Philo here accuses enslavement to physical pleasure only outside marriage, either in fornication before or in adultery during it, he passes judgment on this slavery even within a man's marriage in otherwise permissible sexual intercourse.

> For even that pleasure which is according to nature earns a frequent and serious reproach, when one is ruled by an immoderate and insatiable desire for it. It may, for example, take the form of insatiable gluttony, even though one should eat none of the foods that are forbidden. Or we may see it in woman-lovers, who hunger constantly for sexual intercourse, who behave

shamefully with women—not necessarily with other men's wives but even with their own.[22]

What Philo considers immoral about sexual intercourse even kept faithfully within one's own marriage occurs when it is immoderate and insatiable. While in this passage he sets no norms for the moderate and the satisfied, he hints at such in an entirely different treatise, *On Joseph,* Chapter 9. By way of explaining why Joseph, a devoutly moral Jew, resisted the attempt of the pharaoh's wife to seduce him, he has him deliver to her an extraordinarily prolix rebuke even as she tries to drag him to her bed.[23]

Joseph explains that not only do men of his race and religion not lie with other men's wives, but that even "before the lawful marriage we have no intercourse with other women, but as men untouched we come in marriage to untouched virgins. And the goal we seek with them is not pleasure but the begetting of lawful children."

Philo's implied thesis that the only morally permissible intercourse is had within marriage, and even there if motivated only by the desire to conceive, appears in slightly different guise in Book 3, Chapter 6 of his *Special Laws.* There he explains the heterosexual relationships listed in Leviticus 18 within which intercourse is forbidden, and adds the reason for the prohibitions. In every instance the reason is some demand of the law of nature. Thus a man may not have intercourse with a woman during her menstrual period because his seed would be wasted. Its release could not be intended for its natural purpose, which is conception.

> Whenever a woman is having her menstrual flow, a man is not to touch her. During this time he must observe the law of nature and refrain from intercourse. He must at the same time learn not to spend his seed in an untimely and purposeless way, for the sake of mere gross pleasure. For it would be as if a farmer, while drunk or in a fit of insanity, were to sow wheat and barley in ponds and streams instead of in his fields. . . .[24]

The same reason, the evil of using his seed unnaturally by releasing it when conception is impossible, forbids a man's having intercourse with his wife when he knows her to be sterile.

> These men too must be blamed severely who plow the hard and stony land. And who are these men if not those who have intercourse with sterile wives? Driven solely by the uncontrollable desire for pleasure they deliberately waste and destroy their seed like the most lecherous of men. For what other goal can they have in approaching such women? They cannot do so in hope of children, a hope they know is doomed to failure. Their

only motive must be an incurable incontinence, a lust that they
find unbearable.[25]

Such is the long-term moral loan that the Christian fathers took
from Philo and from the Stoic philosophers. There is in it an unchallenged assumption about the psychology of male sexuality, that only one
or the other of only two motives, and these irreconcilable, could lead a
husband to intercourse with his wife. These are the desire for a child and
the satisfying of uncontrollable lust. If honorable love for the wife has
any place, it could be only within the desire for a child. This meshes well
with the advice in 1 Timothy 2:15 that Christian wives will be saved by
childbearing. It also specifies more exactly the task of later-developing
theology of marriage, to explain the role in the sacrament of the tethering of male lust, as also of the confining of male sexual desire to the one
motive of conception.

The Orthodox Reply to the Antinomian Gnostics

It is mildly ironic that Irenaeus, Clement and the other orthodox
teachers found their most effective reply to the libertine Christian Gnostics in the sexual ethic of the Jew Philo and of the pagan Stoics. This
ethic in turn was drawn from an assumed anthropology, that human
sexuality exists only for conception—or more exactly, in Philo's formulation, that the male genital anatomy, which was for him the epicenter of
sexuality, is for conception alone. From this came the ethical first principle: sexuality is used rightly only when two conditions obtain, that conception is possible and that the partners' only motive is this same conception. Assuming the accuracy of the anthropology and thence the validity
of the principle, the Gnostics who were sexually active in order to have
all the experiences, or to complete the *pléroma,* or to anticipate in this
life the rapture of heaven, stood condemned as violators of nature and
rebels against the will of the creator and designer of nature.

The Alexandrian orthodox teachers were not the only ones to use
this ethic to control and explain sexual conduct. In his *First Apology*
written in Rome between 155 and 165, Justin Martyr responded to the
popular accusations against Christians of sexual immorality. He insisted
about his community, "Either we marry with only one thought, to have
children; or if we forgo marriage, we keep ourselves continent at all
times" (1:29).

Athanagoras, like Justin a Christian apologist and his contemporary, addressed his *Supplication for the Christians* to the emperor and
the Roman people in 177. Like Justin he insisted that the Christians
marry only in order to have children. He used the popular analogy with
agriculture that we have already seen in Philo's ethic. In sexual conduct
Christians are true to nature's demands. They do not have intercourse

during the wife's pregnancy: ". . . as the farmer, throwing the seed into the ground, awaits the harvest, not sowing more upon it, so the procreation of children is the measure of our indulgence in appetite."

The African Christian rhetorician Lactantius reinforced this mind about intercourse in marriage in his *Divine Institutes,* Book 6, Chapter 23. He used the Stoics' teleological argument to undergird the norm for intercourse—the argument that structure and function of anatomy tell its natural purpose.

> God gave us eyes not to see and desire pleasure, but to see acts
> to be performed for the needs of life; so too, the genital part of
> the body, as the name itself teaches, has been received by us
> for no other purpose than the generation of offspring.

Or the same thought in Lactantius' own summation: God has implanted sexual instinct in all animals so that impelled by this burning desire they can propagate and multiply the species.

Any student of the Christian ethic of sexuality knows that Lactantius was not the last writer to assess its conduct morally after having reduced sexuality to genital anatomy and the physical urgency that activates it. Again the question forces itself: With marriage's characteristic conduct understood in this reductionist way, how could it be accepted as a Christian sacrament?

About 380 in Syria or Constantinople an Arian Christian author who has remained anonymous to us published, in eight books, the largest collection of legislative and liturgical material of earlier antiquity. It is titled the Apostolic Constitutions (*Diatágai tōn hagíōn apostólōn*). Several of its canons condemn kinds of sexual conduct as immoral: sodomy, bestiality, fornication, adultery. They include with these intercourse during pregnancy, and name as the reason for the latter's immorality that such intercourse is against nature. It is not used to beget a child but in order to have pleasure.[29]

But nowhere is singleness of motive both so claimed for the Christians and demanded of them as in the writings of the Alexandrians. Clement comes back to the principle repeatedly that a husband must have intercourse only in order to conceive a child. He turns this motive about in order to condemn any competitor to it. The husband in intercourse must exclude from his soul any other motive, any other desire. Physical pleasure especially is to be fought against and denied. Clement also proposes this as a norm that distinguishes moderate sexual activity from immoderate. It is moderate if the spouses seek in their intercourse nothing else than to conceive a child. In his *On Virginity,* Chapter 17, he hints transparently at his understanding of marital love in his supposing that if a husband goes to his wife drawn only by desire, he does not love her. He loves her only if he seeks to conceive a child by her.

> The man who has taken a wife in order to have children should also practice continence, not even seeking pleasure from his own wife, whom he ought to love, but with honorable and moderate desire, which is to beget children.[30]

He repeats virtually the same instruction in his *Stromata,* Book 3, Chapter 7: "A man who marries for the sake of begetting children must practice continence, so that it is not desire he feels for his wife, whom he ought to love, and that he may beget children with a chaste and controlled will."[31]

How thoroughly Clement had borrowed from the Stoics and from Philo is evident in still further reflections in this chapter of his *Stromata.* He accepts the Stoic rule about the place of any desire at all in a person's life. He goes beyond it, but admits that surpassing the ideal when this is applied to sexual desire is beyond unaided human strength.

> The human ideal of continence, I mean that which is set forth by the Greek philosophers, teaches that one should fight desire and not be subservient to it so as to bring it to practical effect. But *our ideal* [emphasis added] is to not experience desire at all. Our aim is not that when a man feels desire he should conquer it, but that he should be continent even respecting desire itself. This chastity cannot be attained in any other way except by God's grace.[32]

The opening this offers for the role of specifically marital sacramental grace, when this later enters the speculation on the sacrament, is obvious. From the positive point of view it will be an enabling actual grace; from the negative it will be a restraining medicinal grace.

Origen, Clement's successor at the catechetical school in Alexandria, agreed that both marital chastity and marital love demand a husband's confining his intercourse exclusively to the begetting of children. In his *Third Homily on Genesis* (6) he explains that the truly circumcised Christian not only does not commit adultery; but more than that, even with his wife he has intercourse only in order to conceive. In his *Fifth Homily on Genesis* (4) he uses Seneca's argument from the conduct of animals, pointing out that there are some women who, in contrast to the animals, "serve lust without restraint; indeed I would not liken them to dumb beasts. For beasts, when they conceive, know not to indulge their mates further with their plenty."[33] In short, once a woman is pregnant, the one motive justifying intercourse is *in suspenso* until she has delivered that child and can conceive again. It would be no help for marriage's candidacy as a sacrament that its characteristic conduct has, at one level, the same reason as copulation among the beasts; and that the reason differentiates only in the capacity of the offspring to participate rationally in human society.

As one reads through this Christian teaching about marriage during the generations from the apostolic period until Nicaea one begins to notice a formulation of the moral question about sexuality that must seem incomplete to the modern mind. The incompleteness grows out of an assumption apparently shared by everyone in these centuries, Christians and pagans alike. It was that in having sexual intercourse with his wife or with any other woman, a man is impelled by one or the other of two motives, but never by both. One of these is lust, the self-serving need to relieve the demand of genital urgency. The other is to conceive a child. Included in the first of these may be also the desire to catch and subdue a sexually alluring prey. The female counterpart of this is to complete the alluring in triumph.

Out of the assumption comes the formulation of the speculative moral question: "Which of these two motives is the acceptable one?" Since the answer leaps out at one instantly—it cannot be the unrestrained acting out of genital demand—the practical moral question becomes the following, along with its codicil: "How tether one's genitality and keep it within one's marriage?" And the codicil: "Even within one's marriage how conquer and banish the motivation that is evil because it is lust longing for satisfaction?"

Nowhere in the literature does one come upon a third motive for intercourse, a motive appropriate to what we would call lovemaking in its best sense. This is the desire and the will to show caring love for one's spouse, and to do so through giving and receiving pleasure that is both physical and emotional. The ancients not only do not approve of this motive, they all but explicitly reject it. We have seen the judgment that in having intercourse with her a man loves his wife, and loves her as a wife rather than as a whore, only if he is motivated exclusively by the desire to conceive.

It is almost certainly from this assumption about the motivation available in sexuality that the Christian teachers counseled and exhorted their people to the choice for lifelong virginity. The exhortation did not take the later and more developed form of urging the celibate life for the sake of free and mobile Christian witness, with sexual continence a taken-for-granted ingredient of the celibacy. It was aimed exactly at sexual conduct in itself as an obstacle to Christian holiness. The teachers did not think marriage evil. How could they, since the scriptures made clear that it is God's invention? But since his inventing it men and women have been wounding it unrelentingly by their sinfulness, beginning with the first man and woman by their sin in the garden of Eden. One may choose marriage without sinning, but only if control of one's sexual need is so weak as to advise against attempting the life of permanent virginity. To make the attempt in the face of this weakness is to risk damnation. But in choosing for marriage one thereby forfeits any expectation of holiness, unless and until one later converts one's marriage to a virginal relationship. In short, a Christian living normal married life can be good—but never holy.[34]

Montanist Christian Rigorism

The rigorist Gnostics were not the only Christians as a group to push this irreconcilability to the brink of condemning marriage as evil, and at times over the brink. At about the time the Gnostic teaching was drawing Clement's, Origen's and Irenaeus' bitterest criticism in the second half of the second century, another rigorist movement began to appear in the Christian East. It took its name from its founder, Montanus. He started it up shortly after his conversion in Phrygia (then a district in northwest Asia Minor, now in western Turkey). It had the characteristics of those groups appearing intermittently in the Christian population called illuminists and enthusiasts. They claim extraordinary intervention and instruction by the Holy Spirit that takes them up and beyond the morals and customs—and the governance—of ordinary Christians. They consider themselves an elite group within the Church divinely called to bring it back to its primitive simplicity. As evidence for this vocation they demonstrate the charismatic gifts that were once exercised in the fervor of the first Christian generations.

Montanism became significant for the developing place of marriage in Christianity because of its rigorist moral demands. It replaced the relatively mild fasting from food in the Church with severe fasts from both food and drink. It urged virginity as the ideal Christian life and gave it exorbitant preference over marriage. It exhorted husbands and wives to either separate or to live in sexual abstinence.

The Montanist voice that sounded most volubly and critically on the theme of marriage was that of the Carthaginian layman, Tertullian. He was born about 160, the son of a pagan captain in the Roman army. Like so many young men of his time he sought his education in Rome, and there principally in law and rhetoric, both disciplines a boding of disaster for theological learning. He lived a dissolute life in Rome, but repented, was converted to the Christian faith, and returned to Carthage about 195. There he turned his brilliant fluency in Latin to a career of writing in religion and morals. By his death in 220 he had published twenty-one treatises. He broke with authoritative Catholicism in or about 205 and went over to Montanism. His pessimism about human weakness, and his brutal impatience with it in face of the official Church's patient acceptance of repentant sinners and those who wished to return after apostasy under persecution, inspired his conversion to unforgiving Montanism. His writings on marriage are accordingly divided between his pre-Montanist and his Montanist periods.

In 203, before going over to Montanism, he wrote a kind of last will and testament to his wife in essay form. It is titled simply *Ad Uxorem* (*To [My] Wife*), and is completed in two brief books.[35] Suspecting that he was soon to die (he lived seventeen years longer), he urged her not to remarry after his death.

It is reasonable to assume that before turning Montanist Tertullian was a typical enough representative of the rigorist Christian mentality. Although the case he argues in *Ad Uxorem* is expressly against remarriage in widowhood, most of it could be brought against marriage in any circumstance. We will trace his reasons, extracted from his dense rhetorical logic, from chapter to chapter. In them we will note a mixture of argument borrowed from the Pauline New Testament writings and much of his own.

He asks his wife to not remarry not for the sake of marital fidelity to him, but to guard her *integritas carnis*. For even when the two of them are finally together again in eternity they will not resume marital intercourse, since there is no restoration of marriage there where Christians will carry on an angelic existence and holiness (Chapter 1, Col. 1276).

He does not deny that the union of husband and wife has been blessed by God. But this has been done only for propagating the human race. And the marriage God first blessed was that of Adam and Eve, a union of but one man and one woman (Chapter 2, Col. 1277).

It is true that Christ never forbade marriage. But the divinely inspired apostle Paul proposed a higher good than marriage, one more fitted to "the stress of the times." He only permitted marriage, and this because of the danger of incontinence. If, as Paul says, it is better to marry than to be burned, it is still better neither to marry nor to be burned. And the fact that he urges continence is in itself a dissuasion from marriage (Chapter 3, Cols. 1278–1279).

For the widowed marriage is needed only because of two kinds of weakness, concupiscence of the flesh and *concupiscentia saeculi,* the desire for security, comfort, affluence, reputation. Widows ought not be taken in by suitors who want to protect them from unkind rumors. They are married now to Christ and he will provide for and protect them (Chapter 4, Col. 1280).

To remarry in order to produce heirs is foolish, since in times of stress children are a burden, and Christians should be intent not on continuation of family but on eternal salvation (Chapter 5, Col. 1282).

Since Paul urged that because of the stress of the times the married should live as though not married, *a fortiori* should the widowed not remarry (Chapter 6, Col. 1283).

Since her husband will have died as an effect of God's will, his wife will be widowed by God's will. Why, then, oppose his will by remarrying? And why give up the freedom gained from being widowed? What is more, Paul commanded that for a woman's acceptance in the company of the formally acknowledged widows, she must have had only one husband. For a widow is an *ara Dei,* an altar of God, and (the clause reveals Tertullian's unstated judgment on sexual intercourse that runs just under the surface of this instruction) an altar of God must be kept clean. Indeed a widow who does not remarry is more virtuous than a virgin. A virgin does not desire what she has never had; it is easy for her to resist what she has never desired. A virgin is praised only for a gift she has been given, but a widow for the virtue she has attained (Chapter 7, Cols. 1286–1287).

Book Two of *Ad Uxorem* proceeds on the assumption that notwithstanding his urging in Book One, Tertullian's wife may indeed remarry after his death. The node of his advice in this case is that she marry a Christian. The reasons he adduces for this help to reveal at greater depth the unacknowledged assumptions underlying the entire essay. They will also display samples of theology devised by a man trained in rhetoric.

To begin with there is Paul's command, following immediately on his permission, in 1 Corinthians 7:39–40, "A wife is bound to her husband as long as he lives. But if he dies, she is free to marry whom she chooses, only it must be in the Lord" (Chapter 1, Col. 1290).

By dint of some tortured theology he rebuts the anticipated objection that it cannot be *ipso facto* harmful for a Christian to marry a pagan, since Paul himself insisted, in 1 Corinthians 7:14–15, that far from a Christian convert's being corrupted by staying married to a pagan, the latter is sanctified by marriage to the new Christian. Tertullian reasons that God graces a person in her condition at the time the grace is given to her. If she is married at the time, the grace coming through baptism sanctifies her in her marriage, even if with a pagan. But if she is unmarried, the grace—through baptism or otherwise—sanctifies her there. No holiness awaits her in marriage, especially not with a pagan (Chapter 2, Col. 1292). He returns to this thought in Chapter 6 (Cols. 1298–1299): A person who is baptized while already married to a pagan is given a special protecting grace, and can even be used by God to better the pagan's conduct.

Christians who marry pagans commit adultery, Tertullian reasons, because by baptism they become members of Christ's body, so that when they have intercourse with the pagan spouse they defile that body. What is more, the motive and manner of intercourse with a pagan is easily sinful, whereas with Christians it is carried on decently as a kind of dutiful vocation, chastely and moderately, as if under the gaze of God (. . . *officia sexus cum honore ipsius necessitatis tamquam sub oculis Dei modeste et moderate transiguntur*) (Chapter 3, Cols. 1293–1294).

In Chapters 4, 5 and 6 Tertullian sets before his wife the hazards to Christian life that marriage with a pagan would bring. She would be kept from her religious duties; acts of piety by their nature private and of recondite meaning would be found out and misunderstood. For example, how could a pagan understand the practice before the family's main meal of eating the consecrated bread brought home from the preceding Sunday's Eucharist? The Christian spouse may be compelled to take part in pagan rites and take up pagan social habits.

It is the ninth chapter of this Book Two of *Ad Uxorem* that contains the apparent description of a Christian wedding early in the third century, and along with it the ingredients of specifically Christian happiness and holiness in marriage. It will be examined later in a more opportune part of this chapter.

After Tertullian had joined the Montanists in about 205, his judgment against remarriage in widowhood became even more severe. His attacks on it appear mainly in two essays of this period. One is *De Monogamia* (On Monogamy, meaning in this case not life with but one spouse at a time, but only one marriage in one's lifetime). The other is *De Exhortatione Castitatis* (The Case for Chastity). In the latter he returned to the reason he had developed briefly in Book One, Chapter 4 of *Ad Uxorem:* The only motive for either a man's or a woman's remarrying in widowhood is concupiscence of the flesh (Chapter 1, Cols. 913–915). This amounts to adultery because concupiscence, which is a man's lusting in his heart after a woman, is what Christ condemned as adultery of the heart in his sermon on the mount (Mt 5:28). Whether a man desires another man's wife or remarries, it is concupiscence that drives him in either case.

In *De Monogamia* he takes the argument that for a Christian to marry a pagan is adultery, and applies it to a Christian remarrying in widowhood even with a Christian. This too is adultery because God said that in marriage a husband and wife become two in one flesh (or body); but to remarry is to commingle with a third flesh—which is precisely the substance of adultery (Chapter 9, Col. 941).

But it is now as a Montanist that Tertullian introduces the most theological of his reasons opposing remarriage in widowhood. He appeals to Christian marriage's function as a *sacramentum,* which in context here most probably means as an image of the Christ-Church relationship.

> The law which demands but a single spouse—"They will be two in one flesh"—Paul referred to the spiritual marriage of Christ and the Church (for there is one Christ and his one Church). But we must understand that this law has been repeated in us and reinforced here, both by the law of our nature and by the *sacramentum* of Christ.[36]

What he means by the *sacramentum* in marriage he makes clearer in rebutting with sophisticated irony the argument that since the patriarchs of Israel did not sin in taking multiple wives and even concubines, a Christian does not sin in remarrying in widowhood.

> Will we also for this reason be allowed plural marriages? Of course we will—if there still remain [or are left over], some foreshadowings [*typi*] that your marriage may image— foreshadowings that are *sacramenta* of something in the future.[37]

The logic here will later be picked up and used by other fathers to excuse the polygamy of the patriarchs. Their multiple marriages served to foreshadow the many nations which would enter the Church to make up the one bride of Christ. Tertullian apparently means that the Church itself, not the second marriages of Christian widows, is the fulfilling antitype correlated to these ancient patriarchal types. In any case the *sacramentum* here is the foreshadowing image-in-anticipation of the relationship of Christ and the Church.

The Earliest Perception of a Sacrament in Marriage

The induction of marriage into the ranks of the Christian sacraments was a long and gradual process. The evidence we have examined thus far shows how the teachers of the first two-and-a-half centuries looked on marriage's place in the Christian life. Its path toward full status among the sacraments, all of it narrow and uphill, was to stretch through the next nine hundred years. The reasons for this we have seen at length, but they can be concentrated in the following formulation. A sacrament images some invisible sacred reality and leads its participants to holiness. But marriage, although not evil in itself and indeed good because it is God's creation, has been so wounded by sinful concupiscence that it cannot be a way of holiness. Those who seriously seek holiness must choose lifelong sexual abstinence, either outside marriage or within it.[38]

But even against such odds marriage was eventually accepted in both the Catholic East and West as a way of holiness, and this in and through its sacramentality. Three causes account for this. The authorities gradually adopted the preparation for marriages and the marriages themselves into their pastoral care, and they took the wedding ceremony into the common liturgies of the regional churches. But liturgy is by definition a consorting with God and therefore leads onto the path of holiness.

The second cause was the Christian teachers' realization that in demanding that Christian spouses bring marriage back to God's original intention for it, they demanded more than weakened human nature could accomplish unaided. For men and women to be "suitable companions" to one another, ultimately one flesh in a union of love for an entire lifetime, and to be fruitful in children, they have an absolute need of God's help, of his enabling grace. Trusting that a fair and merciful God does not make demands of human beings without helping them to meet the demands, the teachers soon came to the conclusion that Christian spouses are offered this grace for their marriages, in their marriages, and perhaps even somehow through their marital conduct.

This conviction that God offers his helping grace to Christian spouses is in the first of Tertullian's essays that we have already examined.

If then such a marriage as this is affirmed by God, why should it not go on happily? Why should it not be spared wounding

from sorrows and tensions and obstacles and sins, since it goes
on in the patronage of God's grace?[39]

The third cause was the teachers' and writers' gradual extraction
from the marriage passage in Ephesians all that was implicit there. They
saw the first marriage in the garden of Eden to have a role in the
mystérion of God's saving the human race through Christ, by its foreshadowing Christ's love relationship with the Church; so too they saw
the marriages of Christians to have a correlated role in the *mystérion* by
somehow imaging the same relationship. But until the deepening of
theological insight in the fourth century the teachers and writers did
little with Ephesians 5 other than to repeat it as Paul had written it. They
hardly mined it for the wealth of meaning locked within it. For example
Clement of Alexandria, as we have seen, defended the place of marriage
in Christian life in part because it serves now, since the coming of sin, as
a refuge for human weakness. Yet it still has its own goodness and
dignity; it was blessed by God in the garden and given its good vocation.
Clement barely hints at Ephesians' enriching the understanding of this
vocation when he adds, ". . . as the Law is holy, so is marriage. This is
why the Apostle compares this mystery with Christ and the Church."[40]
    The momentum toward marriage's eventual acceptance among the
sacraments was accelerated in the West, however minutely at first, by
two writers' predicating of it the Latin noun *sacramentum*. These were
Lactantius and Tertullian, with Tertullian doing so the more frequently.[41] The effect was that because *sacramentum* was already in use
to designate the Eucharist and baptism, predicating it of marriage drew
it into the company of these acknowledged sacraments. At bottom the
reason for the noun's being called into use in the Latin Church was that
this Church needed a fixed term to translate the Greek *mystérion*. This is
the key substantive in Ephesians 5:32 (*to mystérion toûto méga éstin*)
that is one germ of the theology of the sacrament. A counter-flow of
meaning into this theology then took effect because *sacramentum* already had its own meanings in Latin society, such as a seal (including a
symbol), an oath committing to personal service, a divine secret. (We
shall see in Chapter 6 Augustine's struggle to find which of these imported meanings could be affixed accurately to Christian marriage, and
which one or two of them discloses its nature best.)
    We have already seen Tertullian's use of *sacramentum* in his essay
De Exhortatione Castitatis, Chapter 5. He used it again in his *De
Monogamia,* Chapter 6, where he continued his endless diatribe against
remarriage in widowhood.

> . . . but the more perfect Adam, Christ (more perfect because
> inviolate) has come to you as a eunuch according to the flesh.
> Or if this is not convincing, he has come monogamous in the
> spirit, having but one spouse, the Church, corresponding to the

model of Adam and Eve. This is the model that the Apostle interprets as a great *sacramentum,* through Christ and the Church, and thus applies the model to carnal marriage through spiritual marriage.[42]

What is clear in Tertullian's convoluted meaning here is that this very early use of *sacramentum* has the noun designating not Christian marriage itself, but the spiritual marriage of Christ and the Church.

In his essay *De Anima adversos philosophos* he uses *sacramentum* again to translate the idea contained in the *mystérion* of Ephesians 5:32. And the meaning is the same as that in the *De Exhortatione Castitatis:* the *sacramentum* is the marital union of Christ and the Church: "For even though Adam immediately in prophecy attributed that great *sacramentum* of Christ and the Church . . . saying 'This one at last is bone of my bones, etc. . . .' "[43] He repeats the same thought almost verbatim in Chapter 21 of this essay.[44] And in his *Liber de jejuniis* (Book on Fasting), Book 3, he mentions in passing that before eating the forbidden fruit Adam uttered the same prophecy.[45]

The final passage in which Tertullian mentions the *sacramentum* of marriage, but again adds nothing to the understanding of it, is in Book 5, Chapter 18 of his essay *Adversus Marcionem (Against Marcion).* He is contending, against the Gnostic doctrine of dual deities, that the creator of the physical universe is the one true God.

> I will strive now to show that there is one same God of both the first man as of Christ, of the first woman as of the Church, of the flesh as of the spirit. The Apostle himself quoted the Creator's words and indeed proclaimed them: "For this reason a man will leave his father and mother. . . ." And it is enough if the Creator's *sacramenta* are great for the Apostle even if minimal for the heretics. But in claiming, "I say this in regard to Christ and the Church," he meant not to deny that it is God's *sacramentum* but to interpret its reference. He showed that the reference of the *sacramentum* was preestablished by him whose *sacramentum* it was in fact.[46]

Use of the term *sacramentum* in reference to marriage shows up once more at the end of this pre-Nicaean period. The African rhetor-apologist Lactantius composed his principal work, *Divinae Institutiones* (The Divine Teachings), in seven books between the years 304 and 313. This was a defense of the Christian religion against its pagan detractors. Book 5 castigates the common immorality of the pagan populace and opposes to it the high moral ideals and conduct of the Christians. In Chapter 6 Lactantius describes, in a kind of apostrophe to his fellow Christians, how precious to them is the virtue of fidelity to promises.

Hold to it [fidelity] in all life's duties. Hold to it in marriage. It is not enough that you stay away from another's bed and from brothels. . . . The man who has a spouse must desire nothing apart from her. Let him be content with her and let him keep and protect the vows [*sacramenta*] of his chaste and inviolate bed.[47]

Here Lactantius advances the as yet inchoate theology of the sacrament a tiny step. The meaning he gives to the word *sacramentum* in reference to marriage is not Tertullian's "type" or "image," but a meaning drawn from commitment of person to person. It signifies a vow, an oath. The meaning is not uncongenial to that of Tertullian drawn from Paul, but at least two centuries will go by before only Augustine will try to fuse the two in explanation of the *sacramentum* in marriage.

The Appropriation of Marriage by the Church

The marriages of her people were taken into the life-processes of the Christian Church, and to this day keep their place there, not through the speculation of theologians nor even mainly through the teaching of the authorities. This drawing into the Church was done in two ways: through pastoral care eventually growing into juridical governance, and through inclusion in the Church's liturgical celebration.

This accounts in part for the slow pace at which Christian couples' marrying and living their marriages became an ingredient of formal Church life. For one thing, the establishing of a single and universal law in the Western Church lay almost 1,000 years beyond the period which we are here examining. During those centuries regional structures of law were created in checkerboard pattern around Italy, Lombardy, North Africa, Spain and the Frankish kingdom. These structures were built up mainly of the decrees of regional bishops meeting in council. In the Eastern Church the law was the law of the Byzantine empire, first codified by Theodosius II in the fifth century, then revised by Justinian in the sixth. More than one of the Christian writers of our period insisted that the law their people were to observe in marriage was the civil law of the state. This was part of their claim to being good citizens.

The drawing of her people's marriages into the liturgical activity of the Church by the beginning of the fourth century was minimal. To understand why this was so we must note again a difference at that time of marriage's social-juridical situation from our own. In our Western world a marriage is created within the purview of civil authority, of religious authority, or of both. With the peoples among whom Christianity was born and spent its childhood this was not the case. With them it was family authority that governed marriages, in the way explained in detail at this chapter's beginning. Consequently where the Christian bishops had to take hold of their people's marriages in order to take them away from pagan belief and custom, they had not to wrest them from imperial power and take them into their own total and protective control. A few commands were deemed sufficient to banish from family-controlled marriage those inherited pagan elements considered idolatrous or dangerously compromising.

A brief repris of the common procedure in marrying, mainly in the Latin West, will suggest which of its elements the Christians could keep, and which they could not or even would not. To begin with, the betrothal (*stipulatio*) was arranged by the fathers of the affianced, unless the bride had declared herself *sui juris*. In this case her *tutor* or *curator* would do so. This was a contract, but lacking a form of law. From the East there came the custom of both families' exchanging pre-nuptial pledges, the *arrhae*, a kind of bond given reciprocally in order to hold both sides to the marriage. These were rings or some other articles of value.

By the time of the empire the ancient and elaborate wedding ceremony of *confarreatio* had all but disappeared. *Coemptio*, a man's creating his marriage by simply living with a woman for an uninterrupted time with the intent of having her as wife, was similarly rare, thanks in part to women's acquired freedom to choose their husbands. Four elements, when verified, sufficed to create and hold a *matrimonium justum*, a marriage legitimate according to law. These were the *affectio maritalis*, the will to be married; this *affectio* manifested *mutuo consensu*, by reciprocal consent shown in a way sufficient to be verified and recorded; *domum ductio*, the taking of the bride to her husband's home; and the *individua vitae consuetudo*, the couple's stable cohabitation. The partners' (and families') signing of *tabulae nuptiales*, the permanent record of the marriage's creation, came into practice in the West for the first time under the emperors.

Some families retained an assortment of the old pagan religious elements, but with their meanings now almost entirely lost: the consulting of the auguries shortly before the wedding; the wearing of the *corona*, the garlanded crown; the animal sacrifice at a shrine; the offering to the household gods, the *lares* and the *penates*, of the bride's new home. Where these were included with some degree of understanding and religious intent, a pagan priest might participate by offering a prayer. In the East he offered the sacrifice and instructed the new spouses in their duties.

In marrying, the Christians of this time followed in part the practice of their pagan neighbors but in part rejected it emphatically. Imitation was guaranteed when the bride or groom was the only member of the family, or one of its few members, to have converted. Correlatively this made voiding the wedding of its meaningfully pagan elements all the more difficult. This may account for the Christian authorities' repeated insistence that they be omitted. An abuse attacked frequently over a long period must have vexing power of survival.

What the Christians did keep without demur was the exchange of the *consensus nuptialis,* but often with an added invocation to God the Father or to Christ. So too were kept the *dexterarum coniunctio,* the bride's and groom's joining of their right hands, the kiss, the veiling of the bride with the *flammeum* (without objection despite pagan matrons' wearing this red veil at sacrifices), and the signing of the *tabulae nuptiales.* Later, as a bishop or his presbyter was invited to the wedding, he too might sign the *tabulae.*

It goes without saying that the consulting of auguries, the animal sacrifice at a pagan shrine, and the offering to the household gods were all kept from the Christian ceremony. An unrelenting campaign was kept up by the authorities against a different pagan tradition that had little religious meaning but much moral reverberation. Where the wedding party was led in procession through the streets from the bride's home to the groom's, the festivities along the way were joined by clowns and prostitutes who led the celebrants in lewd songs and performed obscene skits at streetcorners and at the home of the bride. Where the extended family of a Christian bridal pair was pagan, suppressing this popular entertainment was not easy.

The Christians saw no need for the purification ritual, as the pagans did, especially not the traditional bridal bath of the semitic peoples. They held that purification had been completed by baptism. An especial object of assault by some Christian writers and authorities was the bridal couple's wearing of the *corona,* the garlanded crown. The reason for this was apparently that garlands were worn by pagan priests when sacrificing to their gods. Tertullian's attack against their use in his *De corona militis* (13:14–14:2) shows that some Christians were still using them at the beginning of the third century. He inveighed against their use as a consequence of a Christian's marrying a pagan, and as at least religiously redundant for the Christian: "Their marriages crown our spouses. Therefore let us not marry pagans lest they lead us to the idolatry with which these marriages begin. For you have your law from the patriarchs . . . you have the Apostle commanding you to 'marry in the Lord'."[48]

The drawing of Christian marriages within ecclesiastical authority began, however faintly, with the custom of the blessing of the bridal pair. During the centuries we are reviewing this blessing was bestowed by the parents, according to the Jewish model in the story of Tobit (7:11–12). The custom had a doctrinal and even polemic impetus. We have seen that one of the arguments against the Gnostic indictment of marriage as evil was the record, in Genesis 1:28, of God's having blessed the first husband and wife. (How could he have blessed something evil?) To perpetuate this warranty of goodness the blessing was made a fixed part of the Christian wedding ceremony. But it was reserved for those who were marrying for the first time and was denied to those marrying in widowhood. The biblical models that were cited showed a first and only marriage.

When a bishop or presbyter was present at a wedding in order to congratulate the spouses and their families, or because he was an invited guest, or because he was *tutor* of an orphan bride, he was frequently asked to bestow the blessing. The earliest textual evidence for this practice dates from the fourth century. And even then the sacerdotal blessing was not construed as an act of authority. The authority in charge was still familial; the parents officiated at the ceremony.

Early Evidence of a Marriage Liturgy?

Because it is a major piece of textual evidence from early in the third century, a passage from Tertullian's *Ad Uxorem,* Book 2, Chapter 9, calls for more detailed examination. It is a kind of peroration to all the author's earnest pleading with his wife not to remarry after his death (this in Book 1); but if she should remarry, not to do so with a pagan but with a fellow Christian (in Book 2). The passage is the climax of his argumentation for the latter plea.

> How could one describe the happiness of that marriage that the Church arranges, that the offering strengthens, that the blessing seals, that the angels witness, that the Father ratifies? For not even among the peoples do children rightly and legitimately marry without their father's consent.
>
> What manner of yoke is it for two Christians who share the same faith, the same rule of life, the same devoted service? They are members of the same community, they are fellow servants; there is no superiority in either body or spirit. For they are two in one flesh; and where the flesh is one, so is the spirit one. They pray together, they meditate together, together they keep their fasts. They teach one another, they exhort one another, they sustain one another. They share as one in God's church, as one in God's banquet, as one in sorrows, in persecutions, in repose and peace. Neither hides aught from the other, neither avoids the other, neither is dour with the other. They are free to visit the sick, to help the poor; they can offer charities without worry, sacrifices without hesitation. They can carry on their daily devotions without hindrance—with no furtive signs of the cross, no nervous salutations, no wordless blessings. The two together sing songs and hymns and inspire one another to sing the more sweetly to their God. Christ rejoices at hearing and seeing such things, and to such spouses sends his peace. Where the two of them are, there also he is. And where he is there is not the evil one.[49]

Tertullian wrote this some five years before crossing over to the Montanist sect. Its second and longest paragraph contains his vision of the ideally happy Christian marriage, a vision that he never abandoned even as a Montanist. Its context within the essay discloses much of its meaning, because the portrait of husband and wife praying and singing together, and of either or both without stealth or anxiety visiting the sick, helping the poor, crossing themselves, greeting friends with a blessing, is the exact converse of his picture in chapters 4, 5 and 6 of the furtiveness and anxiety attending a Christian wife's doing all these things when married to a pagan. In addition one ought not miss the supposition of the wife's equal status in this marriage, and equal because it is fully Christian. Where, by contrast, she is the only Christian spouse, her taking from family resources to give to the poor is fraught with anxiety because presumably an invasion of her husband's authority. But here because both spouses are Christian she apparently shares that authority.

The first and shorter paragraph attracts critical attention because it at least seems to list the ingredients of a Christian wedding at the end of the second century or the beginning of the third. If it does, it tells of a thoroughly religious ceremony, one in which many of the liturgical elements of a sacrament are in place. But even if this is so one must note cautiously that Tertullian describes a ceremony only in the Church of north Africa. Given the distance and tenuous communication among the regional churches of that time, and their consequent independence in liturgical development, it says nothing helpful about the churches in Spain, Gaul, Rome and elsewhere. But there are serious doubts that the passage does list the elements of a wedding ceremony even in the one Church of north Africa.

Tertullian's intent in the passage is to plead the rich religious advantages in a marriage both of whose partners are Christian. He matches it with the principal elements of an honorable pagan wedding to show that for each of those elements there is a corresponding Christian one—not only corresponding but, by implication, transcendently superior.

The Church's arranging the marriage (. . . *quod Ecclesia conciliat*) echoes the role of the *conciliator* in pagan marriages, the person who brings the families together, gains agreement about betrothal pledges, about dowry and wedding gifts. To say that the Church is the *conciliator* in a Christian marriage is not to say that a bishop or a presbyter performs this traditional function. He may do so in some instances, but only as a *tutor* of an orphan girl. Otherwise he would interfere with the families' prerogative set by age-old custom. That "the Church arranges" is verified sufficiently if both parties to the marriage are Christian, and if both families are. The marriage is thus created wholly by and in the Church. This much of itself would constitute obedience to Paul's command that Christians must marry "in the Lord" (1 Cor 7:39).

The marriage's being "strengthened by the offering" (*et confirmat oblatio*) correlates with the sacrifice offered by the pagan wedding couple at an altar on the morning of the wedding feast. It may point to a

Christian nuptial Eucharist, but there is no supporting evidence for this. More than two centuries later Possidius, Augustine's pupil and biographer, reported no such Eucharist in the same Church of north Africa when telling of his bishop-teacher's arrangement for marriage. It is most unlikely that such a substantial part of a Christian wedding would have been abandoned after having been once formally installed. The reference is accounted for sufficiently by the fact that since both spouses are Christian, they can participate as one in the Eucharist, as the second paragraph points out, and can thus strengthen their marriage.

"The blessing that seals the marriage" (*et obsignat benedictio*) is the Christian analogue of the seal placed on the *tabulae nuptiales* in a pagan marriage. It echoes God's blessing (in Genesis 1:28) on the first marriage in the human race. It is remotely possible that the phrase designates a blessing bestowed by a bishop or presbyter, but the evidence against this is compelling. There is no textual witness earlier than the fourth century to clerics' having a liturgical part in ordinary Christian weddings. As indicated earlier, the families officiated at their children's weddings; the fathers bestowed the blessing. By Augustine's time in north Africa the bishop came to the ceremony if invited, and blessed the young spouses. Again it is unlikely that in the same Church two hundred years earlier a clerical blessing would have been a fixed feature, only to be abandoned later. Added counter-evidence is this, that the term *benedictio* in that era's vocabulary of piety had a second meaning of "praise to God." So here it may refer to the spouses' sealing their marriage by their together praising God in prayer—a less likely interpretation because such a meaning would tangent away from Tertullian's evident intent to set Christian correlates with the elements of the pagan ceremony.

That the angels witness the Christian marriage (*angeli renuntiant*) matches the witnessing presence of the household gods in pagan marriage. This is a contrast to Tertullian's insistence that the marriage of a Christian with a pagan is surrounded by "demons and spirits of misfortune" (Book 2, Chapters 4 and 8). (We recall this passage's intent, to persuade a Christian widow away from remarriage with a pagan.)

The correlation of "that the Father ratifies" (*Pater rato habet*) is comparatively weak. It suggests the consent by the father of the bride in a pagan wedding. But the Christian meaning is clear: Because a marriage of Christian with Christian is formed within the Church, God the Father of this Christian family can bless it and does so.

If this interpretation is accurate, it has Tertullian find the Christian character of a marriage not in its beginning with a liturgy that includes a Eucharist and an episcopal blessing, but in the shared faith and Christian life described in the passage's longer second paragraph. While this may seem to rob it of even the little raw material for an eventual theology of the sacrament that it contains, it does not. It frees this theology from any lock step with historical liturgical development without tearing it away from such development. It contributes unwittingly to that theology by claiming Christian goodness for the enduring married life itself, distinctly from the religious ceremony. In short, it accelerates, although slightly, the development of the sacrament's human matrix.[50]

The Juridical Assimilation of Marriage

The assimilation of marriage into the juridical authority of the Church was helped by a point of civil law of the Roman empire that we have already seen, the denial to slaves of *connubium,* the right to marry. They could not marry one another, and they especially could not marry freedmen or citizens. They were allowed only *contubernium,* a kind of legitimized concubinage that could be dissolved by their owners, and that left any children born of the union the disposable property of their owner.

It would be gratifying to say that all Christian writers and authorities challenged this violation of human right. Not all did. But some did, in one or both of two ways. They either regarded the slaves' unions in *contubernium* as *matrimonium* and treated them as such. Or they went further and approved slaves' *matrimonia* with freedmen and citizens even in contravention of civil law. This law deemed such unions null as marriage. And a senate decree under Marcus Aurelius in the second century established that any woman of senatorial family who married a man outside her social class forfeited this rank, as did her children.[51]

The Christians' strategy for avoiding this penalty, and a worse penalty for Christian slaves, was to form such cross-cultural marriages in secret. These were called "marriages of conscience," some of them known only to authorities in the Church, but all of them hidden from civil authorities. By no means all Christians looked favorably on the practice. We have already seen that in his *Philosophoumena* (9, 12, 24), the class-conscious Christian writer Hippolytus criticized Pope Callistus (217–222) for permitting high-born Christian citizens to marry freedmen and slaves.

The marriage of conscience also gave opportunity to the suspicion that it was exploited by couples of easy conscience who claimed such marriage while actually living in true concubinage. Tertullian wrote his *De pudicitia* (On Chastity) before turning Montanist. In its Chapter 4 he writes, "Therefore among us those secret marriages, those which have not been first disclosed to the Church, run the risk of being judged adultery and fornication, and may be vulnerable to the charge of marriage by coercion."[52] Very probably in order to avoid such suspicion, and moreso any just grounds for it, the couple was held to secure from their bishop permission for such a marriage of conscience.

But a set of decrees purporting to come from popes of the second and third centuries, and ordering that the marriages of Christians be solemnized publicly in church and before a witnessing priest, are forgeries. Especially influential were two spurious letters attributed to Pope

Evaristus (c. 99–107) that prescribed the contracting and blessing of marriages in public. These decrees belong among the pseudo-Isidorian decretals because of the added fiction that they were gathered and published by Isidore, bishop of Seville, in the seventh century, whereas in fact they date from the ninth century in central Europe.

A second and tentative path for marriages' entry into clerical governance was created by the plight of orphaned boys and girls of marriageable age, bereft not only of parents but of *tutor*. A passage from the Apostolic Constitutions tells plaintively of these young people, and urges alternative forms of rescue for them.

> If there is among the Christians an orphan boy or girl, it is good for one of the brethren who has no children to adopt the boy as his child. If a girl is an orphan, let her be adopted by someone who has a son, and at the proper time he can give her to him as his wife. Thus his work in God's service will be complete. But if there are persons who do not want to do this because they want to please men, and in their wealth they despise the abandoned . . . then you, the bishops, take responsibility for them [the orphans]. Take care of them so that they lack nothing. And when she is of age, give the young woman to some man among the brethren. And teach some trade to the boy when he is grown.[53]

Note that the writer envisions bishops as *tutores* only in the event that the charity of laypersons should fail. Feeling against bishops' involving themselves in the complications and risks of arranging marriages ran strong in the first two centuries. In fact bishops' guardianship at all of the poor and of orphans was at first forbidden by law in the Church of north Africa, as Bishop Cyprian of Carthage attested in his letters written toward the middle of the third century. But the contrary custom in the Eastern Churches gradually made its way into the West and was accepted there.

A last glance at Bishop Ignatius of Antioch's letter to his fellow bishop, Polycarp of Smyrna, takes us back to the earliest non-biblical instruction on marriage coming from a bishop. In it Ignatius wrote, "It is right for men and women who marry to contract this union with the advice of their fellow bishop, so that their marriage may be made in the Lord, and not for the sake of passion."[54]

Again, the phrase "in the Lord" almost certainly repeats Paul's instruction in 1 Corinthians 7:39–40. In Ignatius' correspondence his quoting Paul on the subject of marriage is of a piece with his general advice, "Do nothing without your bishop." By far the least likely meaning of his instruction on marriage is that all Christian marriages were to be created before an episcopal witness and have his blessing, and that Ignatius is appealing to a practice already fixed in the Church of Syria (his own province) and of Asia Minor (Polycarp's province). There is no evidence of such a practice from earlier than the fourth century.

More probably Ignatius was urging that bishops be involved in their people's marriages in a pastoral way. Perhaps their permission should be asked. Perhaps they should be invited to wedding feasts where they may bless the bridal couple. And most likely they should be involved at the crucial point of their people's marrying "in the Lord," counseling and urging them against taking pagan spouses and thus hazarding loss of their faith in an increasingly hostile world.

Interpretation of this very early passage ought not overlook Ignatius' hint that marriages formed not "in the Lord" but with a pagan are suspect of motivation by passion alone. Its companion hint is that the motivation of Christians who marry Christians is, or at least ought to be, some other than passion. We have already seen that this is a theme that will be developed relentlessly by the Christian teachers during the generations after Ignatius and Polycarp.

Summary: The Epoch's Preparation for the Sacrament

The Christian interpretation and regulation of marriage from the close of the apostolic age until the early fourth century showed little express concern for its sacramental character in the sense that Augustine was to ponder this character a century later. Thanks especially to Tertullian the word *sacramentum* was inducted permanently into the Christian vocabulary of marriage, but only according to its quasi-religious meaning as a solemn oath or commitment. Ephesians 5:21–33, the Pauline instruction on spousal love that was in time to become the classic source of the theology of the sacrament, received little more than passing acknowledgment from a few of the writers we have seen. Tertullian especially could have used it but did not as an argument for his wife's remaining unmarried in her widowhood. He could have urged that a second husband would blur the image of the Christ-Church relationship that her marriage to him, Tertullian, had already established. Instead he exhorted her to remain a widow principally in order to escape suspicion of concupiscence in her later years. In his letter to Polycarp Ignatius of Antioch referred to Ephesians' analogy ever so briefly: "Tell my brothers that they are to love their wives as the Lord loves the Church." And the author of the Apostolic Constitutions appealed to the metaphor of the husband as head of his wife as passingly in Book 6, Chapter 29: "Wives, be submissive to your husbands, hold them in honor, and serve them in fear and love. . . . Likewise you husbands, love your wives as your own members, as your companions in life and helpers in the nurture of your children."[55]

What the Christian writers of the period were most concerned to verify were two facts concerning marriage generally plus one about the marriages of Christians. The first of the two was asserted against the extreme ascetics of whatever stamp, the despisers of marriage, that it is in itself good. It is good *a priori* because instituted by God himself in the garden, in the first hours of human history. The nature of its intrinsic goodness awaited fuller explanation until more philosophically sophisticated intellects pondered this nature in the fourth century. But the elements of this goodness were set out in the verification of the second fact mentioned above. This was that marriage is carried on with moral rectitude when intercourse within it is intended for conception alone, and is foregone when conception is impossible. This was the answer to the antinomian Gnostics and, with the addition of one link to its moral logic, the answer also to the promiscuity endemic in the pagan population of the time. Included in this answer to the antinomians was the denial that sexual intercourse—kept free of marriage's dead weight—is the foretaste of heavenly beatitude, an anticipatory participation in the final union of all spirits in the *pléroma*. The insistence on the essentiality of children to intercourse and marriage was meant to take the wind out of that high-blown idea. Aiding this disillusionment was the awareness, drawn from the promiscuity that the writers saw surrounding them, that men and women have been seriously wounded in their sexual self-control. But the explanation that this wounding is the effect of inherited original sin was little more than hinted at, and awaited its full development in Augustine's synthesizing mind.

The third fact, about Chrisitan marriages, was that holiness is available in them. For this too there was *a priori* evidence. It was in Paul's insistence that marriage is one of God's gifts, a *chárisma,* just as truly as a life of committed celibacy. It is a gift that a Christian can share with a non-Christian spouse even to the extent of sanctifying the latter as well as their children.

But this marital holiness is of a participated kind. It is not something uniquely marital, and certainly not something exclusive to sexual union. It is the holiness first gained in baptism, then brought into marriage and expressed there in marriage's specific way. This way is fidelity—a trait, be it noted, itself brought over from the baptismal commitment. Clement of Alexandria summed up the features of this holiness in his *Stromata* (Book 4, Chapter 20): "Marriage that is concluded according to the *logos* [the word of God] is sanctified if the marital community is subject to God and is established with a sincere heart in full fidelity by those who have purified themselves of guilt and have washed their bodies with pure water and agree in the same hope."[56]

But even this holiness is of second rank. The writers and teachers understood Paul's advice in 1 Corinthians 7 quite simply: ideally the celibate life is *kalón,* the good and even better life for a Christian; but realistically it is better for most to marry because of their vulnerability to sexual sin. Thus they passed on to succeeding generations the quasi-principle that marriage is the default vocation of the weak. Along with the principle they passed on the question asking about exactly the kind of holiness possible in such a vocation, as also (but more reconditely) the question asking how such a form of life could be a sign, even an image, of an invisible sacred reality.

NOTES

1. I translate the verb here, as above, "to be burned" rather than as the usual "to burn" because the Greek original has it as a present infinitive in the passive voice, not in the middle voice. This suggests that the burning to which Paul refers is not that of lust but of eternal punishment. The thought may echo a preference recommended by Jesus in a synoptic *logion:* "It is better for you to enter into life with one eye, than to have two eyes and be thrown into the hell of fire" (Mt 18:9).

2. A translation of this book, along with introduction and critical notes, is in R.H. Charles, editor, *The Apocrypha and Pseudepigrapha of the Old Testament in English . . . Vol. II, Pseudepigrapha.* Oxford, 1913, pp. 425–469.

3. In Charles, *op. cit.,* p. 191.

4. *Loc. cit.,* p. 192.

5. *Ibid.*

6. *Loc. cit.,* p. 193.

7. *Ibid.*

8. *Op. cit.,* p. 146. A more contemporary translation of the same passage renders it differently: ". . . he went . . . and sprinkled his evil poison on the fruit which he gave me to eat, which is his covetousness. For covetousness is the origin of every sin." (In *The Old Testament Pseudepigrapha,* Volume 2, . . . edited by James H. Charlesworth, Garden City, 1985, p. 279.) If "covetousness" is the more accurate rendering, it would designate Satan's desire for Adam's and Eve's place in the garden.

9. In Pheme Perkins, "Marriage in the New Testament and Its World," pp. 7–8.

10. Musonius Rufus, xiii:A, in C. Lutz, *Musonius Rufus,* New Haven, 1947, p. 89.

11. Musonius Rufus, xii. C. Lutz, *op. cit.,* pp. 85–89.

12. Diogenes, #47 in Malherbe, *The Cynic Epistles,* Missoula, 1977, pp. 178–179.

13. *Ibid.*

14. *Ibid.*

15. This analysis of Christian Gnosticism is taken from Volume 1 of this series, "What Is Marriage?", Chapter 4.

16. *The Library of Christian Classics,* Vol. 2, *Alexandrian Christianity: Selected Translations of Clement and Origen . . .* by J.E.L. Oulton and Henry Chadwick, Philadelphia, 1954, p. 83.

17. *Alexandrian Christianity,* pp. 42–44.

18. These are available in *The Nag Hammadi Library in English,* translated by members of the Coptic Gnostic Library Project of the Institute for Antiquity and Christianity, James M. Robinson, Director. San Francisco, Cambridge, *et alibi,* 1977.

19. This anthropology and the morality drawn from it are especially evident in Philo's treatise, On the Fashioning of the World (*De opificio mundi*), 50:144.

20. I have translated these passages from the Loeb Classical Library edition of Philo's works in ten volumes, Cambridge and London, 1939. Book 4 of the Special Laws is in Volume 8 of this edition.

21. *Op. cit.,* Vol. 7, p. 478, par. 8.

22. *Ibid.,* par. 9–10.

23. *Op. cit.,* Vol. 6, pp. 162–164, par. 40–45.

24. *Op. cit.,* Vol. 7, p. 494, par. 32.

25. *Ibid.,* p. 496, par. 34–35.

26. No. 33 in *Ancient Christian Writers,* J. Quasten and J.C. Plumpe, editors; Vol. 23, Westminster and London, 1956, p. 74.

27. In John T. Noonan, Jr., *Contraception,* N.Y., 1965, pp. 103–104.

28. One must not confuse these *Constitutions* with the *Teaching (diatáxeis) of the Twelve Apostles,* a much shorter work composed by a Jewish-Christian bishop in north Syria during the first decades of the third century. It makes up the first six books of the *Constitutions,* with some minor changes due to changed conditions; e.g. infant baptism is recommended. It contains material from other earlier Christian writings, e.g. from the *Didache* and from the *Apostolic Tradition* of Hippolytus.

29. *Apostolic Constitutions,* Book 6, Chapt. 28; PG 1:984–985.

30. CSEL, 2:45.

31. *Alexandrian Christianity,* p. 67.

32. *Op. cit.,* p. 66.

33. In Noonan, *op. cit.,* p. 102.

34. Bits and pieces of judgment on sexual conduct have survived from other writers of these early centuries. From the anonymously composed Shepherd of Hermas at the middle of the second century there is Mandate 4:1: "I order you to guard chastity. Never let the thought of another's wife enter your heart. . . . Think always of your own wife and you will not sin." In Mandate 7:8 the shepherd orders Hermas to take back his wife if she should be unfaithful but later repent, because if he does not, he himself will sin seriously.

In his letter to Polycarp, written about 110, Bishop Ignatius of Antioch praised the life of continence but warned against excessive demand: "If a Christian, in order to honor the Savior's flesh, can keep continence, let him do so, but without pride. If he becomes vain over this, he is lost" (PG 5:723–724).

Dionysius of Corinth wrote, in about 160, to Bishop Pinytos of Cnossos, advising him to not impose the heavy burden of continence on his flock as an obligation, but to have consideration for the weakness of most men and women (PG 20:387–388).

Toward the end of the second century Minucius Felix wrote in his Octavius, "We gladly adhere to the bond of marriage. . . . Most of us live in the perpetual virginity of an untouched body, but do not boast of it. Indeed we so experience no incestuous desire that for some even the chaste coming together [*conjunctio*] is a matter for shame" (PL 3:337).

Taking probable exaggeration into account in the last statement, we still find the Pauline norms expressed in these passages: Sexual continence the ideal for Christians, but marriage permitted and even advised in consideration of human weakness.

35. Book I is in PL 1:1273–1288; Book II in the same volume, cols. 1287–1304.

36. Cap. 5, PL 1:920.

37. Cap. 6, *op. cit.,* Col. 921.

38. Tertullian explained this freedom of options—and their irreconcilability—in another of his Montanist essays, *Adversus Marcionem* (Against Marcion, the Gnostic teacher at Rome): ". . . we, who know there can be holiness without our condemning marriage, pursue the holiness and prefer it, not as a good over evil but as a better good. We do not reject marriage, but we demote it; we do not forbid it, but we urge people instead to holiness; we hold to it as a good but cultivate the better according to each one's strength; in all we strenuously defend marriage against those enemies of it who call it filth in contempt of the Creator, he who blessed it as good in its right and authentic uses for the increase of the human race and for all of creation. . . . As a forest is cut down not in order to punish it, as a field is mowed not to condemn it but because it has come to harvest, so also marriage welcomes the saw and the sickle of holiness—not because it is evil but because it has come to maturity. Having been kept for the sake of holiness, it gives place to it and thereby shows that it has been attained" (Book 2, Chapter 29; PL 2:280–281).

39. *Ad Uxorem*, Book II, Chapt. 7, PL 1:1299.

40. *Stromata*, Book 3 (PG 8:1186).

Ignatius of Antioch referred in passing to these verses in Ephesians, in his Letter to Polycarp that we have already seen: "Tell my sisters that they are to love the Lord and are to be content with their husbands in body and spirit. Likewise tell my brothers that they are to love their wives as the Lord loves the Church" (PG 5:724).

41. How difficult it will be to settle on an exact signification for *sacramentum* when predicated of marriage in early Christian writing is evident in the wandering use Tertullian made of it in his writings—he who was the most effective in introducing the term into the language of the Latin Church. For him it designated variously the gospel itself, arcane or hidden teaching, the doctrine of the Trinity, a type or image of a sacred reality, a parable, an enigma, a mystery suggested in dreams by which God's will is revealed, the communion of Christians, baptism, sacred external signs given by God, Christ himself. See the full list, with *loci*, in the *Index Latinitatis Tertulliani* in PL 2:1361–1362.

42. PL 2:936.

43. PL 2:665.

44. PL 2:684.

45. PL 2:958.

46. PL 2:518.

47. PL 6:1080.

48. PL 2:96.

Clement of Alexandria voiced a complaint that was not without its amusing overtone. In his *Pedagogue* (Book 3, Chapt. 11) he complained of some brides' continuing the custom of wearing a wig: "The wearing of a wig must be absolutely forbidden. It is truly irreverent to cover one's head with a wig made of dead hair. In such a case whom does the priest lay his hands on [in blessing]? Whom does he bless? Not the woman who wears the wig, but another's hair and therefore another's head" (PG 3:657).

49. PL 1:1302–1304.

50. Edward Schillebeeckx makes the point in the following way: "It is true that Tertullian had said that the heavenly Father protected marriage with his gift of salvation . . . and that Christ was always present in any marriage made 'in the Lord' as the factor binding the two baptized parties together. . . . But Tertullian

said this not so much of marriage as such as of the fact that, in a marriage between two Christians, domestic life was able to develop into a true family liturgy. In his *Ad uxorem,* life in the Christian family is depicted very much as monastic life in microcosm. Nonetheless he did say that God himself ratified the marriage of two baptized Christians. . . . He only saw the consequences of this for the Christ-like life of the married couple and not for the married life of Christians" (*Marriage: Human Reality and Saving Mystery,* N.Y., 1965, pp. 280–281).

51. Ulpianus, in Justinian's *Digesta,* Book I, Part 9, paragraph 8.
52. PL 2:987.
53. PG 1:807.
54. PG 5:724.
55. PG 1:985.
56. PG 8:1338.

BIBLIOGRAPHY

Blenkinsopp, Joseph: *Sexuality and the Christian Tradition.* Dayton, Pflaum Press, 1969
Corbett, Percy E.: *The Roman Law of Marriage.* Aalen, Scientia, 1979
Fuchs, Eric: *Sexual Desire and Love: Origins and History of the Christian Ethic of Sexuality and Marriage.* N.Y., Seabury Press, 1983
Mackin, Theodore: *Marriage in the Catholic Church: What Is Marriage?* N.Y./ Ramsey, Paulist Press, 1982. Chapter 3: "Christian Marriage in the Roman Empire," Chapter 4: "The Church Fathers and Marriage."
Noonan, Jr., John T.: *Contraception: A History of Its Treatment by Catholic Theologians and Canonists.* Cambridge, Mass., Harvard University Press. Chapter 3: "Gnostics, Pagans and the Alexandrian Rule."
Perkins, Pheme: *The Gnostic Dialogue: The Early Church and the Crisis of Gnosticism.* N.Y. *et alibi,* Paulist Press, 1980. Chapter 10: "Salvation and the Image of Christ."
Schillebeeckx, Edward: *Marriage: Human Reality and Saving Mystery.* N.Y., Sheed and Ward, 1965. Volume II: "Marriage in the History of the Church," pp. 231–255.
Stevenson, Kenneth: *Nuptial Blessing: A Study of Christian Marriage Rites.* N.Y., Oxford University Press, 1983. 2: "Literary Evidence: The First Three Centuries," pp. 13–21.
Tertullian: *Treatises on Marriage and Remarriage; To his Wife, an Exhortation to Chastity and Monogamy.* Translated and edited by Wm. P. LeSaint, S.J. Westminster, The Newman Press, 1951. *Ancient Christian Writers: The Works of the Fathers in Translation,* edited by J. Quasten and J.C. Plumpe, Volume 13.

5. THE SACRAMENT IN THE POST-NICAEAN CHURCH

This chapter covers the period from the Council of Nicaea in 325 until the end of the patristic period—in the West until the demise of Pope Gregory I in 603, in the East until that of John Damascene in 760. It is the golden age of the fathers, an epoch of immense pedagogical and literary energy in the Church, with the energy awakened and spurred in considerable part by the doctrinal controversies of the time—the trinitarian controversy with the Arian Christians, the christological with the Adoptionists, Nestorians and Monophysites, the controversy over grace and free will with the Pelagians, over the structure of the Church and her power to forgive with the Donatists.

Any expectation we may have that marriage profited by that energy and was drawn into theological speculation and development is a wasted one. The reasons for this are evident and simple. Time and energy available for such development were taken up almost entirely in the controversies named just above. Again, marriage was not a subject new and challenging in the arena of thought and debate; it was too old, too familiar and seemingly already well understood. Christian despisers of marriage were still active, with the Manichees now the most vigorous among them. But they were never as dangerous a threat as the Gnostics because they never got into the heart of the communities as the Gnostics had, via these communities' early converts from Judaism. The Manichees remained for the most part an esoteric and marginal Christian sect. But most especially the dominant concern for marriage was not about marriage itself but about marriage's being brought, as a primeval, universally human and earthly relationship, into the Christian agenda of realizing God's kingdom in history, and into the Christian invitation to personal holiness.

Paul's legacy in 1 Corinthians 7 helped to make this the primary concern. One must keep in mind that what he wrote there was fitted to Christian life in exceptional crisis. The holiness for which he counseled the way was the holiness of heroism under persecution and in face of a cataclysmic end of the race. Therefore the question about marriage most demanding for Paul, for his Corinthian converts and for all other Christians, asked what the married ought to do in this crisis, what is the form of holiness conformed to it. We have seen that Paul's three-part reply was, in digest, that the married should stay married, but for the sake of praying well ought to abstain from intercourse at the time of prayer, but not for too long. The widowed should not remarry, unless the attempt at sexual continence proves too difficult and becomes an occasion of sin. And the unmarried should stay unmarried, unless like the widowed they find this too dangerously difficult.

But with the persecutions all but ended after Emperor Licinius' Edict of Milan in 313, and with the expectation of the human race's end and of the return of Christ for judgment deferred indefinitely, the holiness needed in marriage changed form. Now fidelity within marriage and perseverance in one's marriage came to be the most serious preoccupations. These were brought on by the gradually increasing favor shown the Christian religion, until it was in effect made the state religion of the empire in 392 by the withdrawal of all support from the ancient pagan cult. In 313, according to reasonable estimate, no more than ten percent of the empire's population was Christian, and the majority of this was non-citizen. But as imperial favor increased, and especially after 392, the opportunistic among the citizens converted in huge numbers. They had grown up, had married, had lived in a marital ethos that was almost limitlessly permissive of husbands' sexual excursioning outside their marriages, and in which divorce was easily available. As a couple could marry by simple *communis consensus,* by no more than some verifiable expression of their will to be spouses to one another, so they could dissolve their marriage *communi consensu,* by a simple withdrawal of the same will. They needed ask no civil authority to dissolve the union; they needed to allege and prove no grounds. Their only needed recourse to authority was in regard to the division of assets and recovery of dowry.

In a matter as sensitive as that of happiness and unhappiness in marriage, this centuries-old tradition of escape from unhappiness via easy divorce was not to be given up readily. The record shows that the Christian bishops and other teachers fought this tradition for centuries, and always with qualified success. In fact the contention about divorce came to be not whether it is permitted, but who has the authority to execute it, on what grounds and in what way. When the law of the Church and that of the empire now Christian became one and the same, as it did under the great Byzantine emperors of the fifth and sixth centuries, the contest inevitably centered in the holding and use of authority in the Christian imperial Church.

Our own interest in this contest centers in the question whether the bishops fought for authority over Christian marriages because they regarded them as sacraments, and whether they asserted these marriages' sacramentality as a reason for their invulnerability to divorce. It may surprise us to find faint record, if any, of their doing the first, and that only Augustine, at the end of the fourth century and the beginning of the fifth, made the second claim in a persistent and reasoned way.

At the same time two other Christian concerns for marriage came alive and call for our attention. We have already seen the hesitant beginnings of one of them, the entry of the clergy into the solemnization of marriages, or, reciprocally, the drawing of this solemnization into the Church's liturgy and under its authority. The second was the beginning of Church legislation for marriage, of decretals and statutes published by individual bishops and by bishops in council—all these distinctly from doctrinal teaching, and pastoral exhortation and management.

Continued Ambivalence About Remarriage in Widowhood

A phenomenon that must remain curious to the modern Christian is the unrelenting insistence by the writers and teachers during these centuries that it is better for the widowed to not remarry, and in a kindred way better for those not yet married that they never do so. So serious were these two concerns that their expression at least equals the number of pages devoted otherwise to divorce and remarriage in the Christian writing of the time. As one reads through these pages one comes to see that Tertullian was singular only in the severity of his hostility to remarriage in widowhood. One looks in vain for a writer who unequivocally favored such remarriage or was even neutral toward it. The common most favorable attitude was that of toleration.

The target of our interest here in this fundamentally inconsequential matter (so we would say) is not the fact that remarriage in widowhood was discouraged so universally, but the reasons that motivated the discouraging. We have examined the earlier reasons, those as early as Paul's. We have seen that later none of his contemporaries disagreed with Tertullian's extension and adaptation of Paul's reasons, namely that a person remarrying in widowhood, very probably at the end of or beyond the childbearing years, cannot claim the one honorable motive for marrying, procreation, but rightfully draws the suspicion that concupiscence dominates the motivation.

The serious question this raises for the theology of the sacrament we have already formulated in various ways. A fair formulation of it at this juncture asks whether suspicion of concupiscence as the reason for opposing remarriage in widowhood is a reason limited to remarriage in widowhood. If concupiscence lurks there why may one not suspect its presence in marriage at any time in any circumstance? Paul himself opened the door to the suspicion by first urging that the unmarried, whether young or widowed, stay unmarried, but allowing tolerantly that they go ahead and marry if they find the attempt to live continently an occasion of sin. (There is some *a fortiori* logic barely hidden here. If the struggle against temptation can prove too much for a person never married, so that honorable capitulation to weakness by marrying is advised, how much more is the same retreat from heroism advised for the widowed who have long tasted the pleasure of sexual intercourse?)

A simple formulation of the consequent doubt about the sacrament in marriage asks how this way of life can be a path to holiness when its most typical conduct is a retreat from holiness. How can an acknowledged defeat in the battle for heroic self-sacrifice be an earthly image of Christ's triumph of self-sacrificing love for his Church?

The acknowledged beginning of this resistance to remarriage was, again, Paul's urging in 1 Corinthians 7:8–9. The prolongation of the resistance never, except for Tertullian, strayed from what Paul either said or implied. Remarrying is not a sin. But the better way is to stay single and to keep sexually continent. But with Paul's two main reasons for urging this taken away—threatening persecution and expectation of the imminent *parousía*—only one reason seemed left standing starkly alone. This is the asserted inferiority of marriage in the economy of Christian holiness. It will be interesting to examine how the more influential of the fathers in this epoch used this reason in their own urging and instructing.

Basil (330–379), bishop of Caesarea in Cappadocia, imposed penance on the *dígamoi* in his flock, those who remarried in widowhood. By this he did not mean to impute sin to them, but to have them make recompense for giving in to weakness. He ranked the penances imposed according to the repetition of the weakness. For a *dígamos* he imposed one year. For a *trígamos* or a *polýgamos* he extended the penance proportionally because of their "moderate fornication" (their *pornéia kekolasméne*). He barred none of these from communion with the other faithful.[1] But in later correspondence he wrote harshly of those who married a third time and more. He called them a stain on the Church, and accepted their marriages only in preference to their sinning by fornication or adultery.[2] He spent his anger especially on persons marrying a fourth time. He described their conduct as fitted for animals rather than human beings, as worse than fornication and meriting a penance of three years.[3]

Basil's contemporary, friend and fellow bishop, Gregory of Nazianz, was just as severe toward the *polýgamoi*, but in the domain of conscience rather than in that of ecclesiastical penance. He made approximately the same distinction as did Basil between second marriages and third and fourth. His criticism of all of them went beyond moral considerations to theological by drawing from Ephesians 5: "If there are two Christs, then let there be two husbands or two wives. But there is only one Christ, only one head of the Church; so there should be only one flesh. Since taking a second wife is discouraged, what shall we say about a third? A first marriage is permitted by law; tolerance and indulgence allow a second. But a third is iniquitous. As for one who goes beyond this number, he is swinish (*choirōdēs*)."[4]

This severity of the two Cappadocian bishops was not shared by others among their noted contemporaries in the Eastern churches. Epiphanius (315–403), bishop of the island of Salamis, hewed more faithfully to Paul's instruction in 1 Corinthians 7:39. He saw no reason to limit what Paul had not limited, to deny widows a right that he had acknowledged. This held no matter how many times she remarried. She married "in the Lord" as long as she ruled her conduct within marriage by his commands and kept the virtues of her state, among which Epiphanius did not number sexual abstinence.[5]

John Chrysostom (344–407), archbishop and patriarch of Constantinople, was of a similar tolerant mind. He urged widows that in a spirit of continence and renunciation they not remarry, but put them under no obligation: "It is one thing to exhort, another to command. . . . For in this matter the Church does not command but only exhorts with good reason, since Paul permitted second marriages. . . ."[6]

He continued in this fidelity to Paul when addressing an essay to a young widow urging her not to remarry. He reasoned that one cannot condemn a widow for remarrying without being more severe than Paul. He broke out of the common preoccupation with sexual need by acknowledging that a woman may have various reasons for remarrying, among them simple unwillingness to live alone and in loneliness. He asked that his eulogy for virginity and widowhood not be misconstrued as a condemnation of remarriage.[7]

Nevertheless John did disapprove of remarriage, and he brought yet a different argument in support of his attitude. Widows and widowers, he insisted, who cannot bear the yoke of chastity have little of the Christian spirit.[8] He added non-religious reasons: Those who marry show small wisdom in taking the burdens of marriage on themselves for a second time. And in another essay he leveled the accusation that they fail in fidelity to the deceased spouse.[9]

The Latin Fathers and Remarriage

A sampling of the greatest of the Latin fathers of this period shows little or no variation in attitude toward remarriage. Only Jerome hinted at the same severity with which Tertullian had opposed it a century and a half earlier. He pointed out that Paul permitted remarriage only once, and this reluctantly; therefore plural remarriages would surely be an abuse of his permission. He did not restrain his customary sarcasm in so saying, nor was he hesitant about interpreting Paul's mind:

> Granted that Paul allowed second marriages, and by the same law allowed third and fourth marriages, as often as a woman loses a husband. But the Apostle was compelled to grant much that he did not want. I do not condemn the twice-married, nor the thrice-married, nor even—if one may use the term—the

octógamos. I add that I would also take back a penitent fornicator. Whatever is permitted equally must be weighed in the same balance.[10]

The same denigrating moral comparison appears later in the same essay:

God does indeed permit marriage; he permits a second marriage; and, if it comes to that, he prefers a third marriage to fornication and adultery. But we who ought to present our bodies as living victims holy and pleasing to God . . . ought not consider what God permits but what he wants. . . . What he permits is neither good nor pleasing nor perfect. God's will is one thing; his indulgence is another.[11]

Ambrose too, bishop of Milan and hero to the young Augustine, found a comparison with the lesser species to the disfavor of Christians who marry even a second time. He pointed out that the turtle dove, after losing its first mate to death, does not take a second one. But in all he was gentle, and distinguished clearly in stating his preference: "But what we say as a matter of counsel we do not impose as a precept. We urge rather than obligate. We do not forbid remarriage, but we do not recommend it. . . . More than this, while not recommending a second marriage, we disapprove of oft-repeated marriage. . . ."[12]

The Preference for Virginity Over Marriage

But if it is better, more holy not to remarry in widowhood even though this is not forbidden, does it not follow that it is better not to marry at all? Even with persecution and anticipation of the imminent *parousía* vanished as reasons for holding tightly to one's state of life unchanged, does not the case for sexual continence in widowhood conclude also to such abstinence from the beginning of life to its end?

The fathers' virtually unanimous answer to this question was affirmative. For a Christian man and woman the better thing is not to marry. To marry is by no means sinful, but if one seeks holiness, or at least seeks the greater holiness, one's choice must be for a life of permanent, dedicated virginity. The reasons for this judgment came from various quarters of human experience and from an implied theory of holiness that worked as a critical measure of the experience. But the all-controlling reason was taken from Paul's opinion in 1 Corinthians 7:32–34 (drawn from his own experience as a married man?):

32. An unmarried man can devote himself to the Lord's affairs; all he need worry about is pleasing the Lord. 33. But the married man has to bother about the world's affairs and devote

himself to pleasing his wife; he is torn in two ways. 34. In the same way an unmarried woman, like a young girl, can devote herself to the Lord's affairs; all she need worry about is being holy in body and spirit. The married woman, on the other hand, has to worry about the world's affairs and devote herself to pleasing her husband.

The case here against marriage seems, in brief, to be that it divides attention and divides affection; that attention given to one's spouse and one's marriage is attention taken away from God; and that affection given to one's spouse is affection taken away from God.

Such was the mind of the fathers who read Paul and applied his instruction to what they knew of marriage. Zeno, a north African who became bishop of Verona in 362, detailed in mildly dramatic fashion that what a wife may do to make herself alluring to her husband is the contrary of what pleases God; and that affection given to one's spouse is affection taken away from God.

The married woman is thinking of how to please her husband, the virgin of how to please God. The one is set off by lavish adornments, the other is far more attractive for not knowing how to be adorned. The one is fragrant with ointments and scents, the other, more pleasing than any meadow with that flower that is herself, sends the fragrance of joyful service up as high as heaven.[13]

Gregory of Nazianz pictured the division of affection in poetic form, developing implicitly a theme akin to "You cannot serve both God and mammon" (Lk 16:13).

Just as one who looks at two heads or two faces
Or words written on two pages
Does not really comprehend the whole form,
though he wants to,
But grasps one part, while the other
escapes his imperfect vision
Which must look at once in two directions,
So is weak love divided between the world and Christ. . . .
Either, having Christ as all, a man despises his wife,
Or fostering fleshly love, he forgets about Christ.[14]

Ambrose conceded a point while developing the same theme of divided affection. Reflecting on the man in the Gospel parable who could not come to the banquet because he had just married (Lk 14:20), he qualified this when applying the parable to the married. They do come to the banquet, but not as promptly as do the unmarried, because their attention is turned partly away from God.[15] He was concerned also about marriage's divided attention that leads to the divided heart.

> There are many chains in this world. The desire to live is a chain. The allurement of pleasure is a chain. There are chains of honor, chains of remarriage. . . . He does not sin who takes a wife, but he fastens himself in chains of the mind because he is anxious about how to please his wife. More fortunate would he be if his only desire were to please God.[16]

Augustine underlined single concentration of attention and affection as the reason for virginity's greater holiness by preferring even a married woman to a girl who is merely unmarried but in her desire for a husband lets mind and heart wander uncontrolledly. Therefore the superiority of the virginal life lies not in mere sexual abstinence, but in its making possible single-minded dedication to God.

> What we preach about virgins is not that they are virgins but that they are virgins dedicated to God by pious continence. I would not feel rash in saying that to me a married woman seems better off than a girl who is eventually to be married. She has what the girl is still anxiously seeking, especially if the girl is not yet even spoken for. The wife is eager to please one person to whom she has been given, the girl to please many, because she does not know to whom she is to be given. . . .
> Therefore the virgin who deserves to be ranked above a married woman is the one who neither presents herself to many to be loved, because she is seeking the love of one of those many, nor adorns herself for one she has already found, thinking about the things of the world, how to please her husband, but instead has loved the most handsome among the children of men and loved Him so deeply that, since she could not conceive Him in her flesh like Mary, she keeps her flesh intact for Him. For he has been conceived in her heart.[17]

To say that marriage holds a person back from God, or at least cripples one's movement toward him, is a mild indictment compared to that which a few fathers leveled against it thanks to a strained exegesis of a gospel passage. They interpreted it to imply that God instituted marriage expressly because he foresaw the sinfulness of human beings and because of this sin, or as an emergency measure because of sin already committed and raging in lust in the human race. Take sin out of human experience and marriage with its sexuality would never have come into existence. Gregory, bishop of Nyssa in Cappadocia and Basil's brother, proposed this as a conclusion that must be drawn from Jesus' reply to the Sadduccees' attempt to trap him in their conundrum about the woman who had had seven consecutive husbands: "You are badly misled, because you fail to understand the scriptures and the power of God. When people rise from the dead they neither marry nor are given in marriage, but live like the angels in heaven" (Mt 22:29–30).

Gregory reasoned that since the life of those restored to original innocence after the resurrection at the end of time will be like that of the angels, then the innocent life of the first parents before their sin must also have been like that of the angels. He pointed out the obvious, that there was no need for sexual intercourse in this once regnant angelic condition.

> For although there is no propagation among the angels, as we have noted, their host is still in some sense infinite in number. . . .
> Therefore if we had not fallen because of sin from the condition and rank in which we were equal to the angels, not even for us would there have been any need of marriage to increase our kind.[18]

John Chrysostom developed the same opinion but more vividly as befitted the orator. Speaking of that period in salvation history after the sin of the first parents but before the coming of Christ, he explained marriage's emergency vocation.

> The age demanded it, with human nature raging and neither standing firm against the attack of sensuality nor having any port to flee for safety in the storm.
> What was commanded? That they live in continence and virginity? Why that would have caused a greater fall and a more vehement flame. . . . That is why virginity was not given in the beginning; or rather, that is why, though virginity did not exist in the beginning—even before marriage—marriage thrust itself upon the scene and seemed necessary; whereas if Adam had remained obedient, there would have been no need of it.
> "But who", he says, "would have begotten so many thousands of men?"
> Since this anxious fear haunts you, I ask in turn where Adam came from and where Eve came from when there was no marriage?
> What then? Is that the way all men were to have been born?
> Whether in this way or some other way is not for me to say. The point is that God did not need marriage to fill the earth with men.[19]

Theodoret, an interpreter of the scriptures a half-century later than Chrysostom, explained the reason for marriage by linking sin with its consequence that is death. Because of their sin human beings must die. Therefore some way of perpetuating the species is needed. Foreseeing this sinfulness and this need, God designed the two sexes and their correlated sexuality in order to meet the need, but only for this reason.

> Foreseeing and foreknowing that Adam would be liable to death because of the violation of the command, He already fashioned a nature of this kind beforehand and formed it into a male and female body. The reason, of course, was that this is the design of bodies that are mortal and need the procreation of children to conserve the race.
> An immortal creature has no need of a female sex. This is why the Creator produced the entire number of bodiless creatures at the same time but, when it came to creatures which had bodies and could die, created two of each species, male and female, and later gave them the blessing of increase, "Be fruitful and multiply."
> Thus He also designed human nature as male and female and gave them the same blessing.[20]

The last of the Greek fathers, John Damascene, repeated the same thought as late as the eighth century: "Since God in his foreknowledge realized that he would violate the law imposed on him and fall into corruption, He fashioned a woman from him. She was like him and was a helpmate for him—a helpmate, I say, to preserve the human race by begetting one generation to take the place of another."[21]

This exegetical explanation of marriage's origin and reason was not so current among the Latin fathers of the West. But that it was known to them is evident in this passage from the writer Dionysius Exiguus (in Rome c. 510–545). That he was a student and translator of the Greek writers may account for his interest in keeping the theory in mind and passing it on.

> The grace of the resurrection promises us nothing else than that we shall be changed from our fall to the ancient state. . . .
> If therefore restored men will be like the angels as far as number and relationship to one another are concerned, it is clear that man before the fall was regarded as a kind of angel. . . .
> Logically, therefore, if no sinful excess had removed us from the angelic dignity, the means for us to multiply our race need not have been marriage but whatever that natural process is by which angels are multiplied—perfect, indeed, though it cannot be imagined by any conjecture of man's.[22]

Dionysius did not doubt that the reason for God's creating the two human sexes and their sexuality was that the first parents' sin lowered them from the original angelic condition and its mysterious a-sexual kind of reproduction. A substitute way had to be found.

> He [God] knew in His all-powerful providence that the choice of the human will would not be moved to the right things and that, as a consequence, man would withdraw from those family ties with the angels. Lest the number of human souls be diminished, since theirs was the same process by which the angels are multiplied . . . in the design of human beings, in place of the sublime power of the angels, He included the process by which beasts and irrational things receive life from one another.[23]

What divides the mind and the affections of the married and pulls them away from God, according to the writers we have just seen, has thus far been named no more exactly than concern for pleasing the spouse and managing of family life. We shall see in the next chapter how much more precise Augustine was in his judgment of the exact cause of this division and distraction. For a moment we may inspect a more concentrated but just as searching a judgment coming from a bishop who wrote and taught in the West almost two centuries later than Augustine. Pope Gregory I's mind in the question we may piece together from different parts of his writings.

We begin with his *Expositio* of the seven penitential psalms, where he comments on verse 7 of Psalm 51, "Indeed, in guilt was I born and in sin did my mother conceive me." About this he first reiterates the principle that what God has instituted cannot be sinful.

> Men are conceived in sin not because it is sinful for spouses to have intercourse. This is chaste conduct in which a spouse does not sin. For it was God who instituted sexual intercourse when in the beginning he created man and woman.[24]

But from the reading of cognate passages one finds that here above Gregory was writing of sexual intercourse understood in abstraction from real life, as an ideal coming from the divine mind. In the real-life conduct of even Christian spouses the ideal may survive in their minds and wills, but their conduct is infected by concupiscence. This is why in real life the act is always venially sinful among good Christian spouses, "not because something illicit is done, but because what is licit is not kept within moderation." An act good in itself, and provided it is kept within proper limits, becomes sinful when it, or something within it, is taken beyond these limits.[25]

From this Gregory draws a conclusion about a moral-ascetical duty incumbent on Christian spouses: "Consequently they should by frequent prayer cleanse away what they dirty in the lovely character of intercourse by the voluptuous pleasure they allow into it" (*Unde necesse est ut crebris orationibus deleant quod pulchram copulae speciem admistis voluptatibus foedant).*[26]

In a letter to Bishop Augustine of Canterbury he urged another ascetical rule of conduct for spouses. Again the culprit is sexual pleasure; and the penitential practice he prescribed is needed both because this pleasure is sinful and because it is inescapable.

> The Romans have had the custom from antiquity, that after intercourse with one's spouse, one takes a purifying bath, and out of reverence refrains for a while from entering a church. I say this not because I think the spouses are at fault. But because the marital intercourse that is in itself licit cannot be had without carnal pleasure, spouses should refrain from entering a holy place because the pleasure itself cannot possibly be had without fault.[27]

Gregory was not at all clear about what is blameworthy in intercourse and what is not. Intercourse itself is not; therefore spouses are not forbidden it. Carnal pleasure is at fault; and he seems to say that because this pleasure is inescapable, the spouses, being victims of it when carrying on otherwise licit conduct, are not at fault because of it. But then he turns about and names its *culpa* as the reason for spouses' avoiding holy places for a while. And two points of fact about which Gregory is also less than clear are the exact nature of carnal pleasure, and the exact reason why it is sinful even within one's own marriage.

A student of the scriptures may recall that the levitical code of the Hebrews rules that men and women incur ritual uncleanness by having sexual intercourse: "If a man lies carnally with a woman, they shall both bathe in water and be unclean until evening" (Lev 15:18). But there is a substantial difference between this uncleanness and the reason Gregory assigned for the Christian couple's not entering holy places. The levitical code does not call the "carnal pleasure" in intercourse a *culpa*. It is not the cause of the ensuing uncleanness; it is not so much as mentioned. But for Gregory it is precisely this pleasure that brings on the *culpa* barring the church door to the spouses.

Neither did Paul, when he recommended in 1 Corinthians 7:5 that spouses abstain from intercourse for the sake of prayer, explain that the same *culpa* is the reason for the abstention. But in the fourth century Jerome did not hesitate to lay a specific blame on sexual intercourse, although for something less than a moral fault. He blamed it for hindering prayer. To warrant this he drew an exaggerated conclusion from 1 Corinthians 7:5: "If we must always pray, it follows that we must never use marriage, because as often as a man renders the debt to his wife he is unable to pray."[28] To strengthen his case he then did a twisted exegesis of his own paraphrase of 1 Peter 3:7:

Peter the apostle has experience of the chains of marriage. See how he instructs the Church and what he teaches Christians: "Similarly, you husbands, under the guidance of wisdom lead the common life with your wives, the weaker sex, and honor them as joint heirs of the blessing the Christian life imparts, so that nothing may diminish the efficacy of your prayers." Notice how in the same sense, because also in the same spirit, he says prayers are hindered by the marriage debt.[29]

Later in the same essay, he completes a summary indictment of the heterosexual love that brings men and women together to begin with: "The love of a woman is always insatiable. After abundance it is needy again. It makes a manly spirit effeminate, and will not allow it to think of anything but the passion it bears."[30]

Three more brief quotations exemplify this groping and confused ascetical psychology of sex proposed by the fathers: "Through continence prayer is made more earnest" (John Chrysostom).[31] "Marriage is pure, but a person should still abstain even from what is permitted so that his prayer may more easily lead to results. . . . When he does not touch even the things he is allowed, he shows that he wishes to receive what he prays for" (Ambrosiaster).[32] ". . . they will give their prayers more appeal by this abstinence just as by fasting" (Augustine).[33]

The Developing Liturgy of Marriage

A student pondering these great Christian teachers' discouraging assessment of sexual intercourse, the conduct most specific to marriage, must wonder how the latter ever came to be accepted by the Catholic Church among its sacraments. To phrase the apparent disqualification yet again and succinctly: a relationship whose physical union is dominated by sinful carnal desire can hardly be an instrument of holiness and a sign of an invisible divine reality.

But even while on one side the doctrinal door to the house of the sacraments was closing against marriage, on the other the door of ritual was beginning to inch open. Despite the fathers' pessimism the Christian people continued to marry. They sought for the most part to marry Christianly, "in the Lord," and their bishops exhorted them to do so. What this demanded was at first not clear. But it seemed self-evident that it called for making Christian in some degree the ceremony that creates a marriage. What this Christianizing would be was to be found in practice as time went on.

It may surprise us to find that even when the Christian authorities were freed in 313 to do so, and implicitly authorized in 392 to do so, they did not Christianize their people's marriages by immediately seizing the wedding ceremony and making it distinctively Christian. The reasons for not doing this we have already noticed. Perhaps most importantly, the creating of a marriage was a family affair in every society of the time touched by the Christian religion. Almost everywhere parents arranged marriages and managed the weddings; and where these did not, the spouses were conceded the freedom to do so themselves. On this count alone clerical intervention would have been deemed an invasion.

A second reason lay close to that one. In our modern Western religious view of things, when dividing life rather sharply into the two domains of secular and sacred we assume that the latter is also ecclesial. We take for granted that all things religious are also churchly; we take it as a matter of course that churchmen tell us our obligations to God and how we ought to pray. The ancients, the people who became Christian during the epoch we are examining, did not at all take this for granted. The Jews for one acknowledged no merely secular domain. They lived all of life under God's will. Roman citizens become Christian did distinguish the two domains; their empire's system of law, which was secular, assured this. But within the religious domain they staked off territory that was not ecclesial, territory that belonged to the people, not to the priests (as in the ancient household religion of the *lares* and *penates*). Marriage stood in this territory. It was religious but belonged first to the family. The simple truth is that Christian marriage eventually became ecclesial mainly because the families first invited the churchmen to take part in their weddings, and eventually the churchmen took over.

And since the churchmen took over not by replacing the family weddings with ceremonies innovated by themselves, we must survey briefly the more widely used ceremonies already in place as the Christian people of the fourth century began to invite bishops and priests to these ceremonies.[34]

The Byzantine Greeks had a betrothal ceremony whose main element was the man's giving of the *arrabōn,* the pledge to marry, to his fiancée. Her accepting it constituted her pledge. The *arrabōn* could be money, but was more frequently a ring. If the man broke his pledge, his fiancée kept the *arrabōn.* If she broke her pledge, she must return the *arrabōn* to him, and with interest. Supplementing this exchange was the betrothal kiss and the joining of hands. The two families might participate in the last of these gestures.

From Constantine's reign onward this betrothal gained consideration in the imperial law. In the Justinian legislation of the sixth century two kinds of betrothal were legally accepted. There was the ancient classic betrothal dating from before Constantine; it had no formality and the affianced were free under the law to break it. The other was the formal betrothal described just above. It was legally sanctioned, and authorities in the Church favored it for the obvious reason that it taught the seriousness of commitments and strengthened fidelity in honoring them. There is no evidence from earlier than the eighth century that a priest's blessing was included in the betrothal ceremony.

In John Chrysostom's Constantinople and its environs the wedding ceremony began at the elaborately decorated home of the bride. There the guests feasted at noon and in the evening. After the evening meal the bride's parents and close relatives, joined by a contingent of friends and accompanied by musicians, went to fetch the groom at his family home. They brought him to the bride's home, where the heart of the ceremony, the *ékdosis,* took place. In this the bride's father "gave her away" to the groom. He then placed wedding crowns on the heads of both.

By this time night had fallen, and the procession to the newly married couple's home got under way, a procession made up of family, guests, dancers, and musicians, with bride and groom riding in a gaily decorated and enclosed vehicle. As the procession wended its way through the streets, the city's clowns and prostitutes often joined it to continue the ancient pagan custom of singing bawdy songs and, at street corners, halting the procession to act skits just as bawdy. Church authorities tried to temper the latter pagan elements, and we shall see later the decrees that either forbade clergy to join this after-dark parade or obliged them to leave it as soon as the clowns and prostitutes arrived.

Bishops' and priests' induction into a permanent role in the ceremony began with the families' inviting them to come and offer a blessing at the home of the bride. This was a significant move toward the ecclesial because the blessing was inserted in the ceremony at the moment when the father of the bride crowned the couple. This crowning was one of the most ancient elements brought over from the pre-Christian, pagan ceremony. Its importance was therefore rooted in family tradition. But now it acquired a new and Christian meaning, drawn from one of Paul's favorite metaphors, that of the Christian as victor in the combat or the race (e.g. Phil 3:13–14). Chrysostom himself, in his Ninth Homily on 1 Timothy, interpreted the crowning to mean that the spouses had arrived at their wedding as victors in the battle with lust. In fact the blessing that came to accompany the crowning was denied to a widow remarrying, and to women otherwise not virgins, as well as to men who could not give evidence of an exemplary life before the wedding.

Bishops and priests blessed according to no set formulas, but were free to extemporize their own. (No blessings are to be found among documents that survive from the era.) Psalm 127 became a favorite: "Happy are you who fear the Lord."[35] But the wedding was drawn slowly but surely into the Church's ceremonial, and how it was drawn is evident in various ways. Chrysostom tells of prayers and blessings, *euchâi* and *eulógai,* as common elements in the Byzantine ceremony at the end of the fourth century and the beginning of the fifth. To his blessing the priest or bishop came to add special prayers for the future happiness of the bridal couple, and for God's grace on them.

There in Constantinople the wedding was drawn further into the liturgy by Chrysostom's and his fellow bishops' insisting that priests not take part in the hold-over pagan parts of the celebration. To put distance between these parts and themselves clerics began to give their blessing on the eve of the wedding proper, in the home of the bride. It is clear how the separation of this blessing from the family celebration would help to develop a separate religious ceremony. Yet a bishop's or priest's blessing was never obligatory at this time or for centuries afterward. Families were only exhorted to invite one or the other to come and bless the bridal couple. As the custom took hold and spread, other parts of the ceremony came into the hands of the invited clergy. For example, by the end of the sixth century the crowning, the *stephanōma,* was customarily done by the cleric.

Chrysostom's most detailed passage witnessing to the priest's role may also describe a wedding ceremony of his time in Constantinople. He notes that marriages are conducted by the priests, who "through prayers and blessings bind [the couple] together in the same will and the same home," in order that the groom's love may increase, and the maiden-hood (*sophrysýne*) of the bride may be broken. In the passage he speaks of the spouses' new works of virtue in their home, of their triumph over the wiles of the devil, and of their happy life together under God's protection.[36]

Half a generation earlier Basil's Cappadocian priests were assisting at the ceremony with prayers and psalms, but were also beginning to do the crowning of the bridal pair and the joining of hands. The centrality of the blessing, and its character as the element of the ceremony at which the latter could best be drawn into Church ritual, is evident in Basil's canonical instruction to one of his suffragan bishops, Amphilocus of Iconium. In his Canon 27 Basil condemns the innovation of private weddings performed by priests, since these cheapen the blessing. That he thinks the blessing is meant for communal ceremony, is for the good of all concerned, is a measure of its importance to him. While he nowhere tells the contents of nuptial blessings, he perhaps unwittingly moves the theology of marriage forward an inch where, in his *Hexaemeron,* he ponders Ephesians 5:25 and says of marriage that it is "the bond of nature, the yoke [fashioned] by the blessing, the uniting of those who are separate." If the blessing creates the marriage, and the priest bestows the blessing, this comes to the logical conclusion that it is the clerical representative of the Church who creates the marriage. But it is not clear that Basil intended all and precisely this much.

His brother bishop, Gregory of Nazianz, reported that in his part of Cappadocia priests were already being asked to do the crowning of the bride and the groom; but in his own opinion it was more appropriate that their fathers do this. He was inclined to favor the new way of performing the *ékdosis,* the handing over of the bride, by the priest's joining the couple's hands. To this he added the interpretation that this was to join their hands in God's hand.[37]

By this time the priest's thus guiding the *ékdosis* was already routine in the patriarchate of Alexandria, under the archbishop Timothy.

In a baptismal homily Gregory borrowed from Ephesians 5:25 to liken the Church to the bride in marriage. Had he thought to reverse the comparison and liken the bride to the Church, he would have touched what was to be later the core of the theology of the sacrament.[38]

To summarize what has been said to this point, from the fourth century onward the custom grew in the Christian East to invite a bishop or priest to the family ceremony at which the fathers officiated. One or other cleric was invited in order to bless the bridal couple and to offer prayers for them—but only in a marriage that was the first for both. Of a nuptial Mass as the setting for these Christian weddings there is scant evidence. At the time Mass was celebrated frequently enough in private homes, and its association with weddings is hinted at, but never as the context of the wedding itself. From this beginning of clerical presence a liturgy of marriage developed because bishops and priest gradually took over certain family functions in the ceremony. This began with the *ékdosis* and the crowning.

But how minor a role clergy played even at the end of the fourth century is suggested by the concerns that occupied the bishops' minds about marriage in the Council of Laodicea in Asia Minor. They published five canons concerning marriage. Canon 1 ruled that the twice-married could return to Communion after a short time; Canon 31, that Christians must marry only Christians; Canon 52, that weddings were not to be solemnized during Lent; Canon 53, that Christians were not to dance at wedding feasts, but were to dine temperately and sing modestly; Canon 54, that where the feast included the traditional plays, or skits, the clergy were to leave when these began.

Marriage Liturgy in the Church of Rome

Betrothal among the Romans and in Italy was in this post-Nicaean period substantially unchanged from what it had been earlier. Especially among patrician and senatorial families daughters could be affianced while still children. Their fathers could arrange this through an intermediary, a courtier who negotiated marriages as a profession. From the time of classic Roman law in the third century betrothal was a contract without form. But even before the Constantinian era the custom of the *arrabōn* had been brought from the East into Italy. Here too it was not only a pledge in good faith but a kind of bond subject to forfeit if one party or the other violated the pledge. This pledge in the form of a ring was favored especially by Christian families because the willingness to wear it was seen as a visible test of fidelity and a sign of it. Other elements of a betrothal ceremony common to Christian families were the kiss and the joining of hands. And among high-born families there was sometimes a betrothal banquet.

Like the Christians of the East, those in Rome and Italy managed their weddings in a way substantially the same as that of their pagan relatives and neighbors. We recall that the ancient ceremony of the *confarreatio* had long since disappeared from Roman wedding custom. A couple could, with the freedom granted them by law and custom, wed with no more ceremony than simple expressions of consent in the presence of witnesses, who were usually members of the two families. But the more common elements of the Roman wedding by the middle of the fourth century included, first, the crowning with garlands, a practice originally repugnant to Christians because of its link with pagan sacrifices. But by the end of the third century it had lost that meaning and was accepted by Christians, and, as we have seen, even came to be interpreted in the Pauline sense as a crown of victory over sin and temptation. There was the *junctio dexterarum,* the spouses' joining of their right hands, and the signing of the *tabulae matrimoniales,* the written agreement to marry and the conditions of the marriage. By the end of the fourth century the custom had grown that if a bishop were present at the wedding, he signed the *tabulae*—a beginning of clerical witness.[39] In all, the church in Italy, like that in the East, simply took over the civil family ceremony, professing thereby the goodness and holiness of marriage as a natural relationship. The Christian authorities strove only to subdue the distinctly pagan parts of the celebration, as we have seen them do in the East.

From the evidence available it appears that the central element of the Western wedding, and here too the point at which it was most amenable to induction into the Christian liturgy, was the nuptial blessing joined with prayers for the bridal couple. The earliest witness to this practice comes from the second half of the fourth century, in the writing of the Ambrosiaster. (The identity of this author has always remained uncertain. It is known that he lived and wrote in Rome during the papacy of Damasus, 366 to 384. His work was identified as that of Ambrose until the fifteenth century. Hence his pseudonym and hence too the inordinate influence he has had on Western Catholic thought in particular areas, among them the theology of marriage.) He claimed this blessing's continuity with God's blessing on the first married couple told of in Genesis 1:28. He reported that the blessing was used in the synagogue and was likewise given in the Church.[40] Because God's blessing was given only to a first marriage, the Ambrosiaster insisted that its repetition among God's people should likewise be confined to first marriages. For while celebrated on earth, it is also celebrated *sublimiter,* in heaven: "*Primae nuptiae sub benedictione Dei celebrantur.*"[41]

Within this blessing as a key part of the ceremony was one of its constituent parts, the *velatio,* the veiling of the bride and groom. Pope Siricius (384–399) wrote instructions for the veiling to Bishop Himerius in Spain, who had asked Siricius' predecessor for the same but had had no reply from him. Siricius counseled that it was the bride who was to be veiled; her veiling was to be joined to the priest's blessing; and the blessing was not to be given in religiously mixed marriages.[42]

It was Paulinus, the poet-bishop of Nola (353–431), who, among all the surviving hints and fragments, has left the most detailed portrait of the Christian wedding ceremony in Italy of his time. His *Carmen 25* is an epithalamion, a hymn for the bridal chamber, written for the wedding of Julian, son of the bishop of Benevento, with the daughter of the bishop of Capua.[42] In his account the wedding took place in a church. The groom's father acted as paranymph, escorting the bride and the groom to the altar. There the bishop laid his hands briefly in blessing on both, meanwhile extemporizing a prayer and bringing to them the grace of Christ, "Who gives them reverent hearts through the chaste hands of the bishop." Then he covered the heads of both with the wedding veil. In all this there is no mention of a nuptial Mass; nor is it evident that the ceremony as Paulinus described it was typical of the time. The bride and groom were both children of prelates.

A significant point in the thought of the Ambrosiaster, one that seems to have been unique to him, is that the groom was not to receive the nuptial blessing. It was his reason for this denial that is most significant. The groom was not to be blessed because he stood in the marriage in God's image, whereas the bride was only the image of him, and only through him the image of God. As it was unthinkable that anyone should bless God, so it was out of the question that anyone should bless the groom. The source of this logic-via-metaphor was 1 Corinthians 11:3, 7–10, a passage in which Paul struggled to justify his instruction that during divine services men's heads should be uncovered but women's covered—and in the attempt wrote a manifesto for male dominance in the Church.

> 3. However, what I want you to understand is that Christ is the head of every man, man is the head of woman, and God is the head of Christ. . . . 7. A man should certainly not cover his head, since he is the image of God and reflects God's glory; but woman is the reflection of man's glory. 8. For man did not come from woman; 9. woman came from man, and man was not created for the sake of woman, but woman was created for the sake of man. 10. That is the argument for women's covering their heads with a symbol of authority over them, out of respect for the angels.

It was the practical consequence of this reasoning that the Ambrosiaster insisted that during the nuptial blessing the bride's head be completely covered while the groom's be uncovered, and that he not be blessed at all. This was to urge production of almost a mini-tableau of the analogy in Ephesians 5:22–25: "22. Wives should regard their husbands as they regard the Lord, 23. since as Christ is head of the Church and saves the whole body, so is a husband the head of his wife, 24. and as the Church submits to Christ, so should wives to their husbands in everything."

To Paul's weight of authority in declaring husbands alone the immediate images of God and therefore the masters of their wives, add the fact that for the following twelve centuries the Ambrosiaster was thought to be Ambrose, one of the great teachers of the Latin Church, and one sees why this patriarchal Church would find in Paul's analogy a compelling source for its theology of the sacrament in marriage.

The Ambrosiaster worked again and again, in his commentaries on St. Paul, at the theme of the husband's supremacy in marriage as the immediate image of God in Christ, and because he is this image. He did so in his *In Epistolam I ad Corinthios* 11:3–25.[43] And in his *Commentarium in Colossenses* 3:8–11 he wrote the following about the passage we have read just above from 1 Corinthians 11.

> But it is incongruous that having been created subject to the man, [the woman] should be thought an image of God. For Genesis says, "And God made man; in the image of God he made him" (Gen. 1:27), so that since there is one God, there should come from him only one man; and as all things come from one God, so from one man the entire race should spread over the face of the earth. Thus one person created one person who would bear the image of his oneness. And the likeness itself of Father and Son would be borne in the man and in the woman.[44]

In his *Commentarium in I Timotheum* 2:13–15 the Ambrosiaster reminded the reader that "Adam was the first to be created (Gen. 2:7), and only afterward Eve (Gen. 2:21); and that it was not Adam who was seduced by the serpent, but it was the woman who was seduced by the serpent's lie (Gen. 3:36). . . . [God] set the man over the woman, and for this reason created him first; whereas because she was created after the man and from him, she was made subject to him; and [Paul] added this, that the devil seduced not the man but the woman, while he was deceived by the woman."[45]

Given the widespread reading during the ensuing centuries of the Ambrosiaster's interpretation of Paul within the assumption that it came from Ambrose, we have part of the explanation for the eventual fixing of the analogy from Ephesians 5:21–33 at the center of the theology of the sacrament. That the interpretation gained currency as much through liturgical use as through theological reflection (the nuptial blessing containing the Ambrosiaster's interpretation lodged itself in two of the three major sacramentaries in the Latin Church, the Gelasian and the Gregorian) only helped to fix the analogy in the theology securely and everywhere.

Marriage Elsewhere in the Latin West

We do well at this point to survey briefly the marriage customs of other peoples in the Latin West. As the influence and authority of Rome spread northward and westward into Europe, its customs came into conflict with those of the Lombards and the Franks. These peoples controlled the marriages of their sons and daughters firmly. For their daughters to marry was to be handed from the authority of the father into that of the husband, with little choice of the person of the latter or of the time of the handing over. The simple Roman taking of a spouse of one's choice *communi consensu* was unacceptable to the European peoples.

Along with this parental control went a multi-step process in marrying. And with such a process went uncertainty about which step created the marriage, or at least disagreement from one ethnic group to another about which step did so. For example, a question that was long in the answering asked what part first intercourse has in creating a marriage. If it has an essential part, so that there is no marriage until it is completed, two other questions must be answered. The first asks: Since even after the earlier steps the marriage does not exist until intercourse creates it, can intercourse do so after only the betrothal promise, with marital consent itself bypassed—the consent that was essential in Roman marriage?

Again, assuming the eventual Catholic doctrine that the marriage of two Christians is a sacrament—or that there is a sacrament in the marriage of two Christians—an inevitable second question attends that one: If the marriage comes into existence only with first intercourse, is that also when the sacrament comes into existence? And does the intercourse help to produce it? If so, it follows that the Church fathers' centuries-long pessimism about intercourse was ill-advised. For how could an act which, as they said, is inescapably dominated by sinful passion create a sacrament? Or perhaps does the act not create the sacrament if it is thus dominated?

But explore the other possibility, that some earlier step in the process creates the marriage. Does it create the sacrament too? If it does, how does it? And if it does, what role has subsequent intercourse in the sacrament?

We know how the Catholic authorities eventually answered these questions. In the twelfth century they fashioned a compromise of the Roman and the European positions. They determined that it is the spouses' consent that creates their marriage. No other act can substitute for it and none other is needed; nor can betrothal followed by intercourse do so. There is the Roman share of the compromise. But the European portion was that the marriage created by the marital consent alone is incomplete, only inchoate. It can be completed only by full sexual intercourse.

The student of the sacrament may ask at this point whether the sacrament too is created by the marital consent alone, but only incompletely; and whether it too is completed by the intercourse. If the answers to these last questions are affirmative, the next question asks about the character of the intercourse that can complete the sacrament. What must this character be, given the assumption taking root from Augustine onward, that a marriage's sacramentality consists of its imaging the love-relationship of Christ and the Church? Can a concupiscence-infected act really do this imaging?

Whether these questions would have been drawn to the surface without the conflict between the simple Roman process in marrying and the multi-step European process, it is impossible to know. But that conflict did in fact produce the questions. Hence the usefulness of looking at least briefly at the European traditions.

Following their invasion of the Italian peninsula in 568 the Lombards were, by 680, all converted to Catholicism from either paganism or their Arian Christianity. Being a Germanic people they held to a multi-step process in marrying. Their law that governed this and other facets of marriage was the most integral example of Germanic legislation. It distinguished between a true, permanent marriage and a *Friedelehe*, a "free marriage."[46] In the former the bride's father or her tutor handed her *mundium* over to the groom. This was the authority to govern her, to protect her, and to represent her before the law. This handing over, accomplished earlier in a single act, had divided into two by the time in which we are interested, into the betrothal (*desponsatio*) and the marriage proper, the handing over of the bride herself (*traditio puellae*). The father or tutor betrothed a girl under his authority by handing over to her fiancé certain symbolic items, earlier a cloak, a sword or a banner, but later a ring. This gave to the groom provisory possession of his bride-to-be. But he returned the items or the ring to the tutor in order to put the girl under his governance—in escrow, we would say—until the wedding.

The marriage itself was created by the submitting of the *cartae*, the documents by which the groom determined the dowry and the *Malschatz*, the latter a kind of fee to the tutor for his transferring governance of the bride (her *mundium*) to the groom. Finally the tutor handed her over to the groom by joining her right hand to his. The groom paid him the *Malschatz*, and he in turn remitted to the groom full authority over his new wife and over all her possessions.

The *Friedelehe* resembled in some degree the Roman wedding *communi consensu*. It involved no dowry. Although it was considered a true marriage, it involved no tutelage over the girl and was meant to be only temporary.

One must suppose that even if this Lombard tradition had not conflicted with the Roman, it surely must have fit ill with the Christian concept of marriage and the slowly growing awareness that it is or contains a sacrament. The Lombard wedding was a conveyance; the bride was passed from one male authority to another virtually as a chattel. But on second thought, how ill did it really fit? What would have to be changed in that tradition, or subtracted from it, to fit it to the image of 1 Corinthians 11, especially in the Ambrosiaster's interpretation of the passage? Or to borrow from Ephesians 5, would not a Lombard bride given into the governance of a man better image the Church-bride of Christ than would a Roman bride making her own choice of a husband and creating their marriage with him by her free and equal consent?

Marriage Among the Franks

Among the Germanic tribes, to create a genuine marriage demanded more than did the permissive Roman law, as we have already seen. Each tribe had its own laws and customs which bound its people securely. Among the Franks these included both betrothal and wedding, in which the partners' freedom was reined in by parental as well as by tribal authority. The wedding consisted, again unlike the Roman by *communi consensu,* of juridically specified acts which had to be executed before witnesses. These were climaxed by the *cursus nuptialis,* the leading of the bride to her new home.

The custom of a cleric's blessing the marriage was already alive in the churches of Gaul by the fourth century. But this was a blessing not in church or parental home, but in the bridal chamber. The earliest evidence of this comes from the *Vita Sancti Amatoris de Auxerre,* composed by Stephanus Afer and Avitus of Vienne, who likened the blessing of the bride in the bridal chamber to the consecration of a virgin at the altar. (It is a comparison that was to help lead Western Catholic theology to the conclusion that a marriage too can image a sacred reality and is therefore sacramental.)

Unlikely as it may seem, the practice of blessing the bridal chamber made its way into the Western Church, and even as far as Gaul, thanks to the apocryphal Gnostic document, The Acts of Thomas. This continued the legend telling how the apostle Thomas, en route to India, was constrained during a stopover at Andrapolis to assist at the wedding there of the king's daughter. At the king's request he pronounced a prayer and blessing over the bridal couple who had already entered their chamber. The legend spread from Syria westward, and in one of its many mutations contained a prayer-blessing which made its way, in turn, into the liturgical books of France, England, Germany, Scandinavia and Spain. It is highly probable that this widely popular legend from a Gnostic document accounted for the *benedictio thalami* in the Frankish Church.

But the Gallic wedding liturgy with this blessing of the chamber began to be over-run and replaced by the Roman liturgy as early as the sixth century. Cyprian of Toulon reports in his biography of Caesarius, archbishop of Arles (502–542), that the latter ruled that the nuptial blessing was to be given in a church, and, out of respect for the blessing, given three days before the spouses came together and consummated their marriage. How widely beyond Arles the change to the Roman way of blessing spread in the sixth century it is impossible to know. Caesarius conformed to Rome also in restricting the blessing to those who came to their wedding still virgins. Beyond the notice in the biography of Caesarius there is almost no evidence for the practice or the manner of blessing in the Gallic Church during the Roman and Merovingian periods. Only the *Statuta ecclesiae antiquae,* a set of canons produced probably by a reform-minded cleric in Italy, which got to the Gallic Church by the begining of the sixth century, prescribed in their Canon 101: "When the bride and groom are blessed by the priest, they are to be presented by their parents or the paranymph. After being blessed they are to keep their virginity during the night following, out of respect for the blessing."[47]

The marriage liturgy of Spain was, in the law of the Visigoths and after the conversion of this Arian people to Catholicism by 589, partly like that of the Gallic Church and partly unlike it.[48] It contained a betrothal in which the *arrha* was the engagement ring. After this was blessed the groom handed it over to the bride and kissed her. In the wedding itself a deacon bound the bride and groom together with a cloth (there was no veiling as in the Gallic ceremony). The main element of the ceremony as early as the fourth century was the blessing of the bridal chamber by a priest or bishop.

In the British Isles during the Celtic and Anglo-Saxon periods the marriage seems to have been quite similar to the Gallican. While no evidence survives from that period itself, later liturgical books tell of a customary entry of the couple into the bridal chamber, a ceremony which must have been of long standing. As among the Franks, the Roman ritual eventually replaced the ceremony indigenous to the early Celtic Church in Britain.

Rules for Marriage in the Western Church

Sparse though it was, the governance of marriage in the Latin West began early in the fourth century to draw it slowly toward unity and coherence. A brief review of the statutes and decrees dating from that time will help also for unity and coherence in this examination, and for this reason justify the repeating of things already noted.

We recall that Christian lay people were not obligated to have the nuptial blessing. The "Decretal of Pope Hormisdas" (514–523) that made the blessing obligatory for every Christian who married was inauthentic, even though Burchard of Worms included it in his *Decretum,* his collection of canonical decrees, compiled and published in 1000–1025.[49] The Catholic authorities accepted the traditional regional ceremonies as valid for creating marriages without religious addition or modification. Families and bridal couples were no more than encouraged to invite a bishop or priest to the ceremony and to ask his prayer and blessing. This held for the first ten centuries in the Christian West until the pseudo-Isidorian decretals (whose origin and influence will be explained in a later chapter) were used to impose an obligatory religious ceremony.

Those for whom the priestly blessing was made obligatory were the lower clergy who married. As we have seen, Pope Siricius decreed this in his letter of 385 to Bishop Himerius of Tarragona.[50] Pope Innocent I repeated this demand, in 404, in his letter to Bishop Victricius of Rouen.[51] A second obligation imposed on this clergy was that they marry only virgins. Only on this condition could they receive the nuptial blessing, since a widow who remarried or a woman who had intercourse before marrying was not given the blessing. Innocent I attested to this custom in the same letter to Victricius.[52] The reason given for the denial was that marriage to such a woman could not image perfectly the Christ-Church relationship. In his letter to Himerius, Pope Siricius ordered that a woman who violated her betrothal to one man in order to marry another was to be denied the blessing.[53] But in no case was the denial of the blessing a denial of either the validity or the legitimacy of the marriage. It was thus far a denial only of a privilege of honor.

But though elective in the process of creating a marriage, the blessing was put to both moral and juridical use. Reversing the moral logic that only those whose premarital conduct deserved it could receive the blessing, the receiving of it was in turn taken as evidence of the deserving good conduct. Juridical use appeared in the taking of the blessing and other elements of the wedding liturgy as evidence of the spouses' *affectio maritalis,* their intention to wed one another. Pope Leo I specified in his letter to Bishop Rusticus of Narbonne that the giving of the dowry joined with other steps in marrying helped to distinguish true marriage from concubinage.[54] Pope Gelasius I (492–496) instructed Hostilius that the veiling of the bride was acceptable as evidence of true marital consent.[55]

The Nuptial Mass

It may come as a surprise to the modern Catholic accustomed to the solemnizing of his or her Church's marriages within a nuptial Mass to find little or no mention of this until late in the period we are reviewing here, and then almost exclusively in the official sacramentaries, or books of ceremonies, coming from Rome. Paulinus of Nola does not mention the Mass in his *Carmen 25,* the most detailed description of a wedding in this period. The earliest from whom we do have evidence is the anonymous author of the essay *Praedestinatus,* in its Chapter 3. We know of him only that he wrote the essay in Rome during the papacy of Sixtus III (432–440).

Surmising the reason for the hesitant and relatively late introduction of the nuptial Mass is not hazardous. Recall that the authorities in both East and West accepted that their Christian marriages were literally family affairs, and that the ancient family customs in marrying, once purged of their pagan ingredients, were good and holy. Had not pre-Christian marriage been instituted by God himself in paradise? And had not he himself begun it with the most obvious religious sign, his blessing on the first couple recorded in Genesis 1:28? Was it not enough then for Christians to simply continue this blessing? To introduce the nuptial Mass into various Catholic peoples' already satisfactory solemnizations of marriage would have entailed replacing them all. This did eventually happen, but again only slowly, as the wedding customs of Rome replaced those of the European peoples, thanks to their rulers' appropriating the sacramentaries produced and authorized by Rome.

These were, first, the Leonine sacramentary, taking its name from Pope Leo I (440–461), which embodied the liturgy of Rome but was produced in Verona (whence its other name, the *Veronense*). It contains the nuptial Mass in its Rubric 31, *Incipit velatio nuptialis* ("The nuptial veiling begins"). It contains a collect, a secret prayer and a post-Communion prayer specific to the wedding. At the end of the eucharistic prayer, or canon, and very probably just after the Lord's prayer, there is inserted the nuptial blessing that at the beginning of the Christian era had coincided with the veiling of the spouses. The blessing here is in reality two prayers, first a short one that later made its way into the Roman Missal that remained in use until 1969; the second a much longer prayer that recapitulated awkwardly the theology of marriage reigning at the time. As a prayer it was aimed exclusively at the bride in consideration of her moral frailty.

The Gelasian sacramentary was named for Pope Gelasius (492–496) despite its composition in the second half of the seventh century for the presbyteral liturgy in Rome. Its Book 3, Chapter 52, contains the nuptial Mass under the rubric, *Incipit actio nuptialis*. It borrows generously from the Leonine sacramentary; it has the two-part prayer-blessing after the Lord's prayer at the end of the canon (the second part repeated the longer prayer from the Leonine). But it departs from the Leonine in adding a blessing after the Communion, a blessing invoked not on the bride alone but on both spouses.

The third of these sacramentaries, the Gregorian, takes its name from Pope Gregory I (590–604), but survives in a form produced about 735 and sent by Pope Adrian I (772–795) to Charlemagne in 785 or 786. The latter established it as the rule of liturgical action in the Frankish empire. Its use eventually became universal in the Latin Church. Its nuptial Mass, under the rubric *Oratio ad sponsas velandas* ("A prayer for the veiling of the spouses"), survived, except for its preface and part of the canon (the *hanc igitur*), in the Roman Missal until 1969. The longer form of the earlier nuptial blessing also survived in the Roman Missal, but with revisions that improved its use of the scriptures, its theological coherence, as well as its latinity. What did not change from its origin in the Leonine sacramentary was the invocation of its blessing almost exclusively on the bride, and the attention of its supplicatory prayer to her emotional and moral frailty.

This is the blessing in its shorter first part and its longer second part:

Let us pray.

Listen with favor, O Lord, to our prayers; and in Thy goodness maintain the ways which Thou hast established for the continuation of the human race, so that the union which has been founded by Thy authority may be preserved by Thy aid. Through our Lord Jesus Christ, Thy Son, Who lives and reigns with Thee in the unity of the Holy Spirit, God, world without end.

Amen.

Let us pray.

O God, Who by Thy mighty power hast made all things where before there was nothing; Who, having put in order the beginnings of the universe, didst form for man, made to Thy image, an inseparable helpmate, woman, so that Thou didst give woman's body its origin from man's flesh and teach that it is never right to separate her from the one being whence it has pleased Thee to take her:

O God, Who hast consecrated the union of marriage making it a sign so profound as to prefigure in the marriage covenant the mystery of Christ and the Church:

O God, Who dost join woman to man, and give to that society, the first to be established, the blessing which alone was not taken away in punishment for original sin nor in the doom of the Flood:

Look with kindness on this Thy servant who is now to be joined to her husband in the companionship of marriage and who seeks to be made secure by Thy protection.

Make this yoke that she is taking on herself to be one of love and peace. May she be faithful and chaste, marrying in Christ, and may she always imitate the holy women. May she be the beloved of her husband, as was Rachel; wise, as was Rebecca; long-lived and loyal, as was Sarah.

May the author of sin have no mastery over her because of her acts. May she hold firm to the Faith and the commandments. Faithful to one embrace, may she flee from unlawful companionship. By firm discipline may she fortify herself against her weakness. May she be brave in her modesty, honorable in her chastity, learned in the teachings of heaven.

May she be rich in children, prove worthy and blameless, and may she attain in the end to the peace of the blessed, the Kingdom of heaven.

May she and her husband together see their children's children to the third and fourth generation and enjoy the long life they desire. Through our Lord Jesus Christ, Thy Son, Who lives and reigns with Thee in the unity of the Holy Spirit, God, for ever and ever.
Amen.

The Sacrament in Patristic Theology

Near the beginning of this chapter we took note of the problem posed for Christian authorities in the domain of divorce and remarriage when the Roman persecutions ended, when Christianity gained favor and became the religion of the empire, when opportunistic citizens converted to this religion by the thousands and brought with them their permissive sexual habits and their tradition of easy divorce. Our questions about the problem asked whether the bishops sought authority over their Christian people's marriages because they considered them to be sacraments, and whether they claimed these marriages' invulnerability to divorce also because they considered them to be sacraments.

But these are not apt formulations of the questions. They presuppose that the bishops considered their people's marriages sacraments to begin with at a time when this idea was no more than gestating, and in the minds of only a few. It was only Augustine who brought it to birth after the turn of the fifth century, as we shall see. A formulation better fitted to the facts would void the first question because we know now that the Catholic authorities left marriages under family authority until after the end of the patristic period. For the second question, it is more realistic to ask whether, in their combat against divorce, the bishops and other teachers used as weapons those few parts of the New Testament from which the Catholic teaching about the sacramentality of marriage was later drawn.

The evidence provides a divided answer. The Christian teachers did go immediately to these passages in the synoptic gospels (Lk 16:18; Mt 5:31–32 and 19:1–12; Mk 10:1–12) containing the accepted (and adapted) record of Christ's mind on divorce and remarriage; and to Paul's mind on the subject in 1 Corinthians 7:10–16, and 39. A few of them took note of the theology of the marital sacrament latent in these passages and offered a quick sketch of its potential development. But no one labored at this development until Augustine, and his labor was anything but systematic. The fathers used these passages mainly for a kind of moral catechesis, as forthright statements of God's will about fidelity and about permanence in marriage.

They put Ephesians 5:21–32, the eventual *locus classicus* for the theology of the sacrament, to a kindred use. They glanced at, and offered a glimpse of, its rich theological resources. But again no one—not even Augustine—tried to mine and develop these in a serious and persevering way. Again it was pastoral concern that dominated, and profited from the idealized husband-wife relationship pictured in these verses.

Some samples of the use of these passages are enlightening, as are instances of the bypassed opportunities to use them. We begin with a few Eastern Fathers. Basil, bishop of Ancyra in Galatia from about 336, in his *True Integrity of Virginity,* explained why a consecrated virgin cannot be freed from her commitment. Christ, the spouse to whom she is wedded, is immortal; and his immortality causes the indestructibility of their relationship. To explain this mystical marriage, its demand and its effect, Basil claimed its analogy with marriage in real life.

> Do you not understand that he who marries a wife who has been dismissed commits adultery? Even if she has been dismissed with just cause, the Scriptures say, her husband is still alive. Then why do you trouble a dismissed wife? Why do you not allow time, to her on the one side to correct the faults that were the reason for her dismissal; and on the other, time to him who dismissed her, so that in his mercy on her in her repentance, he may recover her who is a member of his own body?[56]

In the last clause here Basil has used one-half the analogy that will later be used to demonstrate the indestructibility of sacramental marriages. That logic will say that since the Church as the body of Christ is inseparable from its head, so is the Christian wife as body inseparable from the head who is her husband. Basil claims only that the wife as body is inseparable from her husband as head, even though she has sinned seriously enough to justify his dismissing her. This reasoning ventures hardly an inch toward calling the marriage a sacrament because an image of the Christ-Church relationship, and toward claiming the marriage's indestructibility because of this sacrament.

As bishop of Caesarea in Cappadocia, the other and better known Basil had to rule repeatedly in the matter of one spouse's dismissing the other, and the subsequent remarriage of one or both. His judgments are recorded in the *Moralia,* an essay he composed before 365 while still an anchorite in Pontus,[57] and in three letters written in 374 and 375 to Bishop Amphilochius of Iconium (letters numbered 188, 199 and 217).[58] In these works he ruled on such cases as one spouse's abandoning the other in order to take up monastic life, on one's dismissing the other for adultery, on one's abandoning the other for no punishable reason, on one's keeping the other despite the other's adultery. In all cases he drew his judgment from the New Testament synoptic passages and from the unwritten penitential customs of the churches in Cappadocia. Nowhere did he draw from the scriptural elements that were later to serve as the sources of the theology of the sacrament.

But Gregory of Nazianz used these elements expressly and indeed poetically in his Sermon 37 on Matthew. There he pleaded with the husbands in his community to maintain a marital fidelity exactly equal to that which they demanded of their wives. It is one of Gregory's reasons for demanding this equality that anticipates the later theology of the sacrament.

> The two of them, say the Scriptures, shall be one flesh. Then let this one flesh be accorded the one same honor. And it is by this example that Paul promulgates the law of chastity. How and in what way? "This is a great mystery; I refer to Christ and the Church." It is a beautiful thing for the wife to honor Christ through her husband; it is a beautiful thing also for the husband to not denigrate the Church through his wife. "Let the wife," says the Apostle, "honor her husband"—for this has to do with Christ. But the husband too, let him keep his wife in his care, for so does Christ with the Church.[59]

There are possibly three ways in which Gregory reasons here, two of them quite evident, the third less so. Certainly he holds up the relationship of Christ and the Church as a normative model for Christian husbands and wives. Almost as certainly he employs the image-theology so dear to the Eastern Christian thinkers: *because* Christian husband and wife image on earth the Christ-Church relationship they must live out this imaging in their conduct. The husband must do so by loving his wife faithfully, and thus he will honor the Church. The wife must do so by loving her husband faithfully, and thus she will honor Christ.

But does Gregory mean that in loving her husband she does in fact love Christ, that her husband and her love for him are intermediaries, instruments of her love for Christ? Does he mean that in loving his wife the husband loves the Church? It does not appear that this is the meaning. The metaphysics of instrumental causality were hardly as developed among the fourth century fathers as they would be among the thirteenth century scholastics of the Western Aristotelian mentality.

In all his homilies excoriating divorce or asserting the impermissibility of remarriage even after dismissal of a spouse for adultery John Chrysostom did not argue from the elements of Christian marriage that constitute its sacramentality.[60]

But he did so briefly and tentatively in his early *Treatise on Virginity* of 382. In it he argued for the husband's fidelity by insisting that spouses hold equal rights in marriage, that according to 1 Corinthians 7:3 a wife has a right over her husband's conduct equal to his right over hers. He went on to warn wives that even if their marriages become slavery for them, they ought to bear this. In any case they have only two options in a marriage they find unbearable. They may reform the husband, if this is possible. It it is not, they must, as he has already said, bear their living martyrdom patiently. But then he relents and acknowledges that Paul gave a kind of *post factum* permission to wives who have fled their marriages. They are not obliged to return to their husbands, but neither can they remarry as long as the latter still live.[61]

It is in explaining why these wives cannot remarry that John uses the elements of the sacrament. He reasons that just as a consecrated virgin can never marry because her spouse, Christ, lives eternally, so a wife cannot remarry while her husband still lives.[62]

Note first of all that John does not set a causal link between the two relationships making up his analogy; he does not say that the permanence of the consecrated virgin's relationship *causes* a wife's relationship to her husband to be permanent. Once again, as we have seen Basil of Ancyra fashion it, the link is comparative-illustrative: the latter relationship is as permanent as the former. Both relationships are not only permanent but are indestructible (John says not that wives must not remarry but that they cannot). The reason for this indestructibility is the same in both cases: the other spouse still lives.

John does not take the one last step into a theology of the sacrament by saying that the husband-wife relationship is an image of the former relationship. For he has deflected the analogy of Ephesians 5:21–33. He has Christ's bride not an idealized and abstract Church, but a real-life but idealized consecrated virgin. But even if John has only laid out some of the elements of the later theology without trying to reduce them to order, he has anticipated a logic that will later be vital to the asserting of marriage's sacramentality: since the consecrated virgin stands in the role of the bride-Church in its relationship to Christ, so too does the Christian wife.

Hints of the Sacrament in the Western Fathers

Except for Ambrose and Augustine (who together merit a chapter of their own in this study) the Western fathers used the key sacramental sources in the New Testament in the same way, in their campaign against infidelity and divorce, as did the Eastern fathers. Rarely did they develop from them the sacramental reasons for fidelity and permanence. They used them instead as bearers of divinely revealed rules of conduct.

But there were exceptions. One of these was Bishop Zeno of Verona, in Homily 4 of his *First Book of Homilies,* completed in about 365. He combined the logion of Genesis 2:24 with that of Ephesians 5:32 to claim a reason for marital fidelity.

> Thus, since they [husband and wife] are a single flesh, a single *sacramentum* of the divine creation, because the woman has been made from her husband and therefore, juridically speaking, they are of the same lineage, there is no doubt that whichever of the two deceives will receive a terrible punishment.[63]

The use that Zeno makes here of the Genesis logion is almost but not quite identical with the use Ephesians makes of it. He says that the two-in-one-fleshness of a Christian husband and wife is a *sacramentum*, a revelation of God's creative plan, where the author of Ephesians said this of the marriage of the first man and woman in the garden of Eden. But Zeno draws a justified conclusion: for one spouse to deceive the other by infidelity is to violate the two-in-one-flesh union and therefore God's revelation. Hence the seriousness of the punishment in eternity. Though so brief a statement, it is a striking advance in understanding the evil of adultery beyond that of a violation of another man's exclusive right to his wife's body. It also goes off on a tangent from Christ's interpretation of it, in Mark 10:11, as an offense against the spouse. While not expressly denying that it is the latter offense, he centers adultery's malice in the damage done to the marital union itself, and to its work of revealing God's action in human relationships.

The Ambrosiaster appears to be the writer of the generation prior to Augustine's who most nearly detected in Ephesians 5:21–33 the same elements for a theology of permanence in marriage that Augustine himself would develop. But instead of using the passage to argue that because the union of Christ and the Church is unbreakable, so too is that of husband and wife, he seems to have sent the logic in the opposite direction: from seeing the unity of husband and wife we can come to see the mysterious union of Christ and the Church.

In his commentary on Ephesians 5:21–33 the author explains why Paul quoted Genesis 2:24 in this passage ("For that reason a man will leave father and mother and cling to his wife, and the two will become one flesh"): "In order to urge unity [in the Church?] he gave an example of unity; that just as husband and wife are one through nature, so Christ and the Church are understood to be one through faith."[64]

Then he moves to his logical development by first pointing out that the unity of a husband and wife is a *sacramentum* of the "great mystery" named in Ephesians 5:32, which is itself to be found in the unity of Christ and the Church. (Note that Ambrosiaster keeps the word *mysterium* to designate the Christ-Church relationship; that of husband and wife he calls the *sacramentum*.) He says that verse 32 declares the unity of husband and wife itself to be a great *sacramentum* of the unity of Christ and the Church (i.e. of the *mysterium*).[65]

But he insists that to say this much is not enough. He points out that Paul demanded that another cause of unity be identified, one that does not disagree with the *mysterium* just named, one that works for the good of the human race. This cause is the Church's replicating what a man does in leaving his father and mother and clinging to his wife. It does so by leaving behind all error and clinging to and subjecting itself to its head, who is Christ.

As suggested just above, the Ambrosiaster's *expositio* here of Ephesians 5:32 is not the familiar one. Indeed it does not join and develop the theology of the sacrament of marriage, but the theology of the Church as a sacrament. But like others among the fathers' brief uses of the classic passages from the scriptures, it helps to lay out the elements of the future theology of the sacrament. In this passage the Ambrosiaster helps to root firmly in the Christian mind what Tertullian planted there over a century and a half earlier, that there is a reason in the marriage of a Christian couple to call it a *sacramentum*. And since he grounds this predication in the marriage's relationship to the union of Christ and the Church, he invites his theological heirs to find out if there is some causal link between the divine union and the human marriage.

Pope Leo I (440–461) had posed to him by Rusticus, bishop of Narbonne in France, a difficulty that must have been common enough in a European society arranged strictly in social strata, and in which sons and daughters of nobility had their spouses chosen for them by parents, with the choice ruled frequently by political and economic considerations and rarely by the preference of the sons and the daughters. Young male reaction to this constraint—a constraint that must at times have included parental selection of undersirable wives—was the sometimes taking of concubines from the lower classes and even from among slaves. These could provide for crude genital needs before marriage and often during it.

Hence Rusticus' question to Leo: A Christian man in his jurisdiction has had a slave concubine, but now he is on the verge of marriage to a more honorable woman. Can he marry the latter? Is not concubinage really a form of marriage that blocks any other attempt at marriage?

Leo's reply became a most active precedent in Western Catholic marriage jurisprudence. It must have simultaneously strengthened the distinction of class from class among the Europeans and made their young males feel freer about taking concubines. For Leo insisted that a free person can marry only a free person. So, for the man in Rusticus' question, his concubinage falls short of a marriage on the strength of that principle alone. He is free to marry the woman to whom he is affianced.

But Leo did not leave his judgment at that. He added a second and conjoined reason for the man's not being married to his concubine. This reason is that such a marriage has no *sacramentum* in it. Inspection of the entire passage may show what he means and how his two reasons are joined.

> Not every woman joined to a man is that man's wife, just as not every son is his father's heir. Now the covenant of marriage between freedmen is legitimate, as it is between equals. The Lord himself determined this long before even the earliest Roman law came into existence.
>
> Therefore a wife is one thing, a concubine another, just as a handmaid is one thing, a free woman another. For this reason the Apostle himself, in order to clarify the distinction between two such persons, drew his evidence from Genesis, where the

order is given to Abraham, "Expel the handmaid and her son; for the son of a handmaid will never be the heir along with my son Isaac."

Therefore since from the beginning the marital union has been so designed that in addition to the joining of the sexes it should have in it also the *sacramentum* of Christ and the Church, there is no doubt that that woman is not a wife in whose person it is evident that there is no nuptial *mysterium*. Therefore too a cleric of whatever place, if he gives his daughter in marriage to a man who has a concubine, is not judged to have given her to a married man—unless perchance his consort has been emancipated from slavery, has been provided with the dowry required by law, and has had her union legitimized publicly as a marriage.[66]

In passing this judgment—in supplying reasons for it—Leo forgets and exaggerates on at least one point. The exaggeration is measured by the later Christian theology of marriage. He seems to claim that any and every marriage is designed to be a *sacramentum* of the Christ-Church relationship, whereas that theology claims this for the marriages of Christians alone. What some proponents will say about one pre-Christian marriage, the marriage of the first couple in the garden, is that it is a kind of *sacramentum* of the Christ-Church relationship. They will say that that is why that first marriage is to be called a "great mystery," as Paul called it.

But to get to the pertinent clauses here, what, in Pope Leo's mind, is the *sacramentum* that is not found in concubinage even among Christians? And why is it not found there?

What it is, is easily inferred; why it is not in concubinage even among Christians, less easily. What it is seems to be the heterosexual union's imaging the Christ-Church relationship. Leo could easily have had this confirmed by his reading of his predecessors, Augustine principal among them.

Why this imaging is not found in Christian concubinage may, in his mind, have had the following reasons. First, the union of a slave with a citizen or freedman cannot so image because it is a union of unequals. They are presumed to be unequal in personal quality and unequal in social status, because even though the concubine of a freedman or citizen, the concubine in question is still a slave. Leo may hint at this in his last clause where he says that the nuptial *mysterium* is absent not from the concubinate union but from the woman herself.

Or the concubinage may lack the *sacramentum* because it has been created and is sustained by no lifelong, irreversible commitment. If this is Leo's reason, two meanings of *sacramentum* converge in it, namely the image of the invisible sacred reality, and the sworn commitment. So what in this case would Leo imply? That the absence of the commitment accounts for the absence of the image? Or that the impossibility of such a union's imaging the Christ-Church relationship blocks the possibility of the sworn commitment? Even though the former seems more probably his reason, we cannot know for sure. As so often in the history of urgent pastoral questions in the Church, Leo's answer to this one has produced more, and more searching, questions. But it has made its contribution to fixing the imaging role of a Christian marriage at the heart of its sacramentality.

Other Elements of a Sacramental Theology

To this point in the present chapter we have inspected the elements that the post-Nicaean writers supplied for the eventual theology of marriage while dealing with the major problems vexing Christian marriage in their time. (Ambrose's and Augustine's contributions to these elements we reserve for a separate chapter, because the two of them contributed more to this theology than all the other writers combined, and because Augustine seems to have first heard from Ambrose the ideas that he later worked at in his major essays on marriage, *The Good of Marriage* [*De Bono Conjugali*], *On Marriage and Concupiscence* [*De Nuptiis et Concupiscentia*], and *On Adulterous Marriages* [*De Adulterinis Conjugiis*]).

We have found that the writers supplied the elements of the theology almost inadvertently while dealing with the problems of infidelity in marriage, of dissolution and remarriage, of remarriage in widowhood, of the comparative merits of marriage and a life of consecrated virginity. While finding that a virtually unanimous judgment for virginity and a common suspicion of sinfulness in sexual intercourse threatened to block marriage's eventual acceptance among the sacraments, we found also that at the same time marriage began to be drawn into the economy of Christian holiness via the wedding liturgy. We found finally that the New Testament statement about marriage that we, with the benefit of hindsight, would expect these fathers to have used the most diligently in speaking to the marital issues mentioned above—this is Ephesians 5:21–33—was in fact used seldom, by only a few of them, and always cursorily.

But suppose we measure these fathers' contribution, somewhat arbitrarily and in retrospect, by the definition of a Christian sacrament worked out by the scholastic theologians. Did they not meet the measure at any point, even if unwittingly?

We have seen examples of the few who claimed that the marriage of two Christians is a replication, an image, of the metaphorically marital relationship of Christ and the Church. In saying this they implied that it is a sign of an invisible sacred reality.

No one said expressly that Christ established marriage's character as such a sacred sign. The more common assertion was that marriage—marriage taken universally as well as concretely in any time and place—

is God's invention for providing children and thus continuing the human race. Because this is God's plan it must be a good plan; therefore marriage is good. Two or three examples of this reasoning used against the despisers of marriage suffice here.

John Chrysostom claimed simply that marriage must be pure because it is God's creation.

> If marriage is impure, the living beings begotten from it are all just as impure; and therefore you too, not to mention human nature. . . .
> Where shall we put you? With the Jews? They will not put up with you. They honor marriage and accept the creation of God.
> With us? But you are not willing to listen to Christ, when he tells us through Paul, "Let marriage be held in the fullest honor."[67]

The Apostolic Constitutions of the late fourth century drew on the cosmic optimism of Genesis 1:31–"God looked at everything he had made, and found it very good"—to apply this expressly to marriage and indeed to all things physical.

> If any bishop, priest or deacon or other members of the clergy abstains from marriage, flesh meat and wine, not from a motive of asceticism, but because he detests these things, forgetting that "all things were very good," that God made human beings male and female, and blasphemously finding fault with creation, let him be corrected or deposed and ejected from the Church. The same applies to a layman.[68]

The Ambrosiaster explained, in commenting on Paul's instruction to the Corinthian Christians, why the apostle admitted he had received no command from Christ about the unmarried who ponder a choice between marriage and a life of virginity (verse 25).

> He says he has not received a command from the Lord, because the originator of marriage could not impose any command against marriage without criticizing his deed of long ago.[69]

And Pope Gregory I took the claim for goodness coming from divine invention beyond marriage itself to its specific conduct, sexual intercourse.

> It is not as though men are conceived in sin because it is sinful for married people to have intercourse. That chaste activity involves no fault in one who is married. It is God who designed

that there would be marital intercourse when he first created men and women.[70]

Even insight as modestly offered as this was the germ of the later theology. For if God invented marriage, designed the two sexes, gave them sexual intercourse as their conduct, and this in order to continue his own primeval goodness in creating the human race, it both is a sign of his goodness and contains his goodness. Add the belief expressed in the early marriage liturgy that the blessing he gave the first couple, in Genesis 1:28, God repeats in at least every Christian marriage in history. The result is that the argument for his sanctifying presence is advanced even more, as is the argument for such marriages' being signs of his presence.

That Christ acts in and by the selected human conduct to sanctify its participants is essential to the later and developed Catholic theology of the sacraments. The assertion that Christ did this and continues to do it in the marriages of Christians is scarce in the writings of the fathers. One of their preferred entries into this consideration was their explanation for his accepting the invitation to the wedding feast at Cana of Galilee (Jn 2:1–11). Cyril of Alexandria's explanation contained a barely disguised dig at the frequently rowdy wedding festivities of his time.

> Because the wedding was celebrated in all honor and modesty, the mother of the Savior was present. He too came with his disciples, not so much to take part in the feast as to work a miracle and sanctify the source of the bodily generation of man. It was indeed appropriate that he who was to renew human nature and elevate it to a more perfect state, should not only give his blessing to those who were already there alive, but to also prepare his grace for those who would be later born and to sanctify their birth beforehand.[71]

If Cyril had said that Christ was to renew and elevate not only human nature but marriage itself, he would have anticipated explicitly one of the essential parts of the scholastic theology of the sacrament. While he did not do that, he did suggest that Christ's gracing of Christians involves marriage somehow as its instrument. But he was hardly exact about the way in which it functions as this instrument.

Epiphanius accounted for Christ's coming to the wedding with reasons that hint at this gracing, but a gracing that was later to be called medicinal, a gracing that diminishes and even inhibits threatening sin. A last clause points also to an enabling grace, that which makes possible the spouses' bearing the trials of marriage. His formulation carelessly assigns the motive to the wedding hosts rather than to Christ himself.

> It seems to me that Christ was invited for two reasons: first, to surround with chastity and dignity the marriage in which hu-

man passions are unleashed like a raging fire, and also to lessen
the future trials of marriage by the sweetness of the wine that
lightens disappointment, and by his grace.[72]

John Chrysostom explained not the motive for Christ's presence at
a wedding but a means of his being there.

Let what was done by the citizens of Cana in Galilee be done
today as well by those who now take wives. Let them have
Christ sitting in their midst.
"How can this be?" you ask? By having the priests there.
"For he who receives you receives me."[73]

That Chrysostom meant the attending priest is a sacramental instrument of Christ's presence at the wedding, a sign of his presence that
makes him to be really there, suggest a metaphysics of causality that was
unlikely in the explanation. More probably the thought here belongs to
the image-theology current at Chrysostom's time: The priest is an *eikón*
of the invisible Christ (as, in 1 Corinthians 15, Christ is "the *eikón* of the
invisible God"). In having Christ's image present the spouses and celebrants somehow have Christ present. Here as elsewhere this early and
inchoate theorizing on Christian marriage lays out the elements of the
later theology of the sacrament.

The Leonine sacramentary produced in the Roman Church carried
the insight into Christ's sacramental presence one small but significant
step further in the succinct formula of its prayer for the veiling of the
bride. It points clearly to Christ's gracing action in the marriage, first in
his joining the spouses, then in his preserving their union.

In your kindness be present at this institution of yours by which
you have arranged for the propagation of the human race, so
that what is joined at your initiative may be preserved by your
help.

In another sacramentary, the Gregorian, Christ's gracing action was
requested for the tangible blessing of children. This was in the canon of
its nuptial Mass.

As you have granted that she [the bride] arrive at the age of
marriage, complete your work by seeing that she, who by your
gift is joined in the marriage union, may rejoice in the children
she desires.

Despite their unanimous judgment for the superiority of the life of
consecrated virginity, did the fathers nevertheless deem Christian
spouses capable of holiness? If some did, they accepted for marriage

yet another ingredient of the sacrament, implicit though the acceptance may have been. But this must depend on the avenue to holiness. If it was the spouses' marital conduct itself, the ingredient of the sacrament was accepted. If it was in and by conduct peripheral and non-specific to marriage, the acceptance was either minimal or denied. The Ambrosiaster took note of the conduct of some of the candidates for holiness whom he knew, and found the conduct to gainsay the accepted theory.

> If virgins have their minds on God and women with husbands have theirs on the world, what hope in the things of God is left to those who marry? If this is how things are, there is doubt about their salvation.
>
> No; we see virgins with their minds on the world and married persons eager for the works of the Lord. To those virgins sainthood will never be granted by God, and for these married there will be a reward from God, because though they were bound by earthly and fleshly bonds, they took care to merit an imperishable reward of some kind in eternity.[74]

This reluctance to concede holiness to the married in life on earth is evident here, even when they are superior in conduct to consecrated virgins. Their prize is reserved for the afterlife. The Ambrosiaster does not hide the reason for his reluctance: The married are "bound by earthly and fleshly bonds." They remain so bound; so their goodness consists of being good *despite* being sexually active. Clearly he does not think that whatever holiness is possible for the married is gained in and by their marital conduct. (Here again, in succinct formulation, is the obstacle that will block marriage's inclusion among the sacraments for six and even seven centuries after the Ambrosiaster.)

The Eastern fathers of the fifth century had abandoned most of the earlier reserve toward marriage shown by Origen and Clement. Cyril of Alexandria (380–451) touched on the internal holiness of marriage by reflecting on the external cause of this holiness, Christ's presence to it and his blessing of it. The key to this reasoning was the Pauline axiom that Christ is the instrument of God's renewal of all creation following the damage done to it by sin. Marriage especially has benefited from this renewal.

> Since the wedding is celebrated chastely and honorably, the mother of the Savior is indeed there; and He Himself, invited along with His disciples, comes not so much to dine as to perform a miracle and also to sanctify the source of man's bodily generation.
>
> For it was fitting that He who was to renew the very nature of man and recall the whole of it to a better state, should not only impart a blessing on those who had already been brought

to birth but also prepare grace for those to be born later and make their birth holy.

Honorable marriage is made holy and the curse against women removed. They will no longer bear children in sorrow now that Christ has blessed the very starting point of our generation.[75]

Augustine's pupil in the Church of north Africa, Fulgentius of Ruspe, brought to bear the same reasoning from divine causation. Since Christ blesses a marriage and acts in it, holiness must be available in it.

The Lord Himself has bound them together with the bond of fidelity, favored them with the gift of His blessing, multiplied them by the addition of children. . . . For we confess that the fidelity of marriage is from God, and the love of the spouses and their fecundity. "Each has his own gift from God, etc.," we too recognize the distinctive rank of each gift and do not deny that each has been given to the faithful by God.[76]

Pope Gregory I suggested a social categorization of holiness in the Christian communities that was to be explained by medieval writers as the different "orders" in the Church, each called to its kind and degree of holiness. Gregory included marriage among these, and the married among the participants in holiness.

The three daughters can also symbolize three classes of the faithful . . . shepherds, virgins and married people. . . .[77]

Even before the coming of the Savior there were preachers and virgins and good married people who stood ready for His coming and, with the great thirst of desire, yearned to see Him. Also after His coming, as we see, there are preachers and virgins and good married people who no longer yearn for Our Savior to take flesh but long to see Him in the glory of His majesty.[78]

Pope Innocent I (401–416) continued the biblical theme set by the Old Testament stories of the finding of wives for the holy men of Israel (Rebeccah for Isaac, Rachel for Jacob, Sarah for Tobit), that a good wife is found and given to a man by God himself as a blessing for him. Because she is God's gift, holiness in a life spent with her is assumed to be possible.

When a wife is taken strictly in accord with the precept of the law, as in Paradise when the parents of the human race were joined, they are blessed by God Himself. And Solomon says, "A wife shall be prepared for a man by God."[79]

Jerome and the Holiness in Marriage

Jerome deserves special consideration in this examination of the post-Nicaean fathers because in the forming of the medieval mind on marriage his influence was second only to that of Augustine. But what he wrote is to be examined apart from Augustine because neither was mentor or pupil to the other. Although they were contemporaries (Jerome 340?–420; Augustine 354–430) and exchanged correspondence from their respective residences in Palestine and north Africa, their relationship was a chilly one. For one thing the literal-minded Jerome, whose special competence was the translating and interpreting of the scriptures, found his patience strained by Augustine's interpretation of some of the passages in the sacred books.

Like so many of the fathers and more than most, Jerome contributed to the germinating theology of marriage in an indirect way. He insisted on marriage's fundamental goodness while at the same time warning that it could cripple a Christian's efforts toward holiness.

> [Paul said] "I wish that all men be as I am, so that being as I am they may become like Christ, since I am as he. 'For whoever believes in Christ, he ought to walk as Christ walked' (1 Jn. 1:6). But each one has his own gift from God; one one gift, another another" (1 Cor. 7:7). What he wants in saying this is obvious. For since there are diverse gifts in the Church, I grant that marriage is among them, lest I seem to condemn what is of nature.
>
> Consider at the same time that the gift of virginity is one thing, the gift of marriage another. For if the reward of the married and the virginal were the same, he would never have followed his rule of continence with the words, "But each one has his own gift from God; one person one gift, another person another." (Where individuals are unique there is a ranking of their differences.) And I grant that marriage is a gift of God, but between gift and gift there is a great difference.[80]

Jerome contributed to the common rigorous judgment on sexual intercourse even in marriage that claimed an almost unchallenged place in Western Catholic teaching until at least the thirteenth century, namely that intercourse is free from sin only when the spouses have procreation and no other goal as their motive. The language of his judgment was seldom gentle: "The activities of marriage itself, if they are not modest and do not take place under the eyes of God, as it were, so that the only intention is children, are filth and lust."[81]

He also helped to root a derivative idea in the Western mind, that since conception is so rarely the only motive in sexual intercourse even among good Christians, and intercourse is therefore almost always sinful in some degree, it should keep its distance from the Eucharist. His most succinct statement on the point seems not even to exempt the rare sinless intercourse: "Near the cleanness of the body of Christ all intercourse is unclean."[82]

He made the same point much more copiously in a letter to his Roman patrician friend, Pamachius, written near the end of the year 393.

> And in another place he [Paul] said "You have been bought at a price. So do not become slaves to men." (1 Cor. 7) You see then how clear is the definition of marital slavery. . . . If therefore a good marriage is slavery, what is a bad one, when the spouses are unable to sanctify, but rather to bring one another to ruin? Everything I have said in so many places about marriage Paul has captured here in a few words. . . .
>
> Let husbands fume at me for asking, "Please tell me, what kind of good is it that keeps you from praying, that forbids you to receive the body of Christ?" . . . The same Paul commands in another passage that we pray always. (1 Thess. 5) "But if we are to pray always," I said, "then we are never to serve the demands of marriage, since as often as we render the debt to our wives we cannot pray." Why I said this is obvious; I was interpreting Paul's words, "Do not deny one another, except perhaps for a time and by agreement, so that you may give yourselves to prayer" (1 Cor. 7:5). Paul the Apostle said that when we have intercourse with our wives we cannot pray. So if intercourse impedes the less holy thing, which is to pray, much more does it impede the more holy, which is to receive the body of Christ. . . .
>
> I know that it is the custom in Rome for the Christian faithful to receive Christ regularly (*semper*). Of this I neither approve nor disapprove. "Each one is free to hold his own opinion" (Rom. 14). But I do appeal to the consciences of those who take communion on the same day [on which they have intercourse], even though, in the words of Persius, they "cleanse off the night in a stream." Why then do they not dare to visit the martyrs' shrines? Why do they not visit the churches? Is Christ one thing in public but another at home? What is forbidden in church is forbidden at home. [This alludes to the Roman practice at the time of keeping the consecrated eucharistic bread at home and consuming it there.] But nothing is hidden from God. Darkness is bright light in his presence. Let each one examine himself and only then approach the body of Christ.

It is not that delaying communion one or two days makes a Christian holier, so that what he doesn't merit today he will merit tomorrow or the day after; but so that while he grieves for not having communicated of the body of Christ, he may abstain for a while from his wife's embrace and learn to prefer the love of Christ to her love.[83]

There is bitterness here, and perhaps it is this that drove Jerome into his specious logic that makes Paul set either prayer or sexual intercourse as iron-clad alternatives for Christian spouses. A person peering into the future as he read Jerome insisting, in 393, "You must choose one or the other, either intercourse in your marriages or the Eucharist," could guess well which way the general choice would go. He could also guess well that marriage would not soon be included among the Christian sacraments.

The most effective thing that Jerome did to fix his norm for sexual intercourse in the Western mind—it is sinless even within marriage if its only motive is conception—he did unintentionally. At the request of bishops Chromatius and Heliodorus, he translated the Hebrew book of Tobit into Latin. He knew that the Jews did not include this book in the canon of their scriptures despite its popularity among them. He also worked from an Aramaic version of it; and distrusting his command of this language, he engaged a Jewish friend to translate it orally into Hebrew, from which he wrote his Latin translation. Working in this awkward way and hurriedly, he completed the translation in one day. The product of that day's work was accepted by the Western Church as a translation of a divinely inspired book of the Old Testament. The passage so telling about intercourse in marriage is in no other version of Tobit than in Jerome's Latin Vulgate.[84] In it the angel Raphael instructs the young Tobiah how he is to escape the fate of his seven predecessors who had married Sarah, only to be killed by a demon during the first night in the bridal chamber before consummating the marriage.

Listen, I am going to show you those whom the demon can conquer. Those who at the time of their marriage banish God from their thoughts and give themselves over so completely to their instincts that they have no more intelligence than a horse or a mule, the demon is stronger than they. But you, when you marry her, spend three days in continence, having no concern but praying with her. . . . After the third night, in the fear of the Lord take the maiden, prompted not so much by inner instinct as by the love of children (Tob 6:16–22).

Jerome's translation makes the point clearly enough: Sexual intercourse even within marriage that is the indulging of lustful passion deserves the severest penalty. The escape from the penalty even within marriage is intercourse motivated only by the desire for a child. Jerome's putting this passage in his translation of Tobit is also the main source of the later Christian custom of the *trinoctium,* the newlyweds' abstaining from intercourse for three days after the wedding—out of respect for the nuptial blessing, as some medieval teachers were to explain.

Since Jerome was a monk-scholar his experience of married life was only that of an observer. But probably from his own earlier pre-marital experience he felt informed enough about marriage to explain in which ways it distracts from the things of God.

> Do you think the same way of life can combine spending days and nights in prayer and fasting with freshening up at the arrival of your husband, mincing your step, devising flatteries? . . .
>
> The cook with sleeves rolled up is grinding meat. The girls are chattering at their weaving.
>
> Meanwhile word arrives that the husband has come with some friends. She flies like a swallow through every room of the house. Is everything in order? Have they swept the floors? Is the table set? Is dinner ready?
>
> Now tell me, among all these things where is there any thought of God?[85]

To this dramatic case against marriage as the enemy of attention to the things of God Jerome added his own recommendation, one that drew a further conclusion from Paul's recommendation in 1 Corinthians 7:5 that husbands and wives abstain from sexual intercourse at times and briefly for the sake of prayer. Jerome suggested that by doing this they would develop a taste for continence, which he assumed they must have if they are to grow in holiness.[86]

He drew another and more demanding conclusion from the same passage in Corinthians, but joined to Christ's admonition to pray always ("Stay awake, praying at all times for the strength to survive all that is going to happen . . ."—Lk 21:36). Given this admonition, and given too Paul's advice that couples should abstain from intercourse in order to pray, it follows logically that they should abstain permanently.

> If we must always pray, it follows that we must never use marriage, because as often as a man renders the debt to his wife he is unable to pray.
>
> Peter the apostle has experience of the chains of marriage. See how he instructs the Church and what he teaches Christians: 'Similarly, you husbands, under the guidance of wisdom lead the common life with your wives, the weaker sex, and honor them as joint heirs of the blessing the Christian life imparts, so that nothing may diminish the efficacy of your

prayers.' Notice how in the same sense, because also in the same spirit, he says prayers are hindered by the marriage debt.[87]

Jerome adds a cutting judgment on the effects on husbands of sexually expressed love.

> The love of a woman is always insatiable. . . . After abundance it is needy again. It makes a manly spirit effeminate and will not allow it to think of anything but the passion it bears.[88]

But he does find a commendable role for women in marriage. He borrows the thought from the counsel to women in 1 Timothy 2:15. Against the background of his conviction that virginity is the Christian's way to holiness, but this only for those who have been given the gift of it by God, he says, "A wife will be saved if she begets children who are to remain virgins, if what she herself has lost she gains in her offspring, and the loss and corruption of the root are compensated for by the blossom and the fruit."

Jerome on Ephesians 5:21–33

Jerome went at his *Commentarium in Epistolam ad Ephesios* with no less haste than he had at his translation of the book of Tobit. He completed it at the rate of one thousand lines a day. (Reckoning each printed line in the Migne *Patres Latini* edition of the commentary as the equivalent of one of Jerome's manuscript lines, one finds the entire work to consist of 5,750 lines. Thus Jerome completed it within about a week's work.)[90]

Before examining his commentary on the crucial verse, Ephesians 5:32, it will help to note his reflections on the earlier verses in the same chapter, those that deal with the relationship and the conduct of husbands and wives. This will bring further into light Jerome's understanding of the sacrament's matrix, marriage the human relationship and institution.

He begins by acknowledging that in verse 22 the command to wives that they be subject, or obedient to their husbands, is not in the Greek manuscripts but has been added in the Latin versions.[91] But he insists that this interpolation is justified by the logic of the passage, which begins (in verse 21) with "deferring to one another in the fear of Christ," and continues (in the Greek of verse 22) with "wives to their husbands as to the Lord." He adds that the analogy is clearer in Greek than in Latin: As the Church is subject to Christ and Christ therefore rules the Church, so is the order to which husband and wife are bound (*huic enim ordini maritus et uxor astringitur—sic*). She is subject to him and he is to rule her. He goes on to reason that the more willing is this spontaneous subjection in marriage, the more it leads to equality of persons. Indeed it leads the ruling husband into a kind of servitude.[92]

He turns to the Christ-Church, husband-wife analogy to draw from it a moral-ascetical conclusion. Where the wife is truly subject to the husband, but subject to him in the way that the Church is subject to Christ, their union will be the more holy and they will never subject themselves to bodily passion (*numquam corporis servient passionibus*). If one opposes to this Paul's advice in 1 Corinthians 7 that husbands and wives must render the marital debt to one another, one ought to note that there Paul was advising very immature and flawed Christians. But he had lived with the Ephesians for three years and instructed them to religious maturity. In any case, Jerome concludes, Christian spouses are free to choose salvation the Corinthian way or the Ephesian way, by sexual servitude or by sexual freedom. But he adds the warning-by-analogy: When the flood comes, let Christians not be caught buying and selling, marrying and joined in marriage. But let them be ready with loins girt and lanterns in hand.

Continuing with verses 25 and following—"Husbands, love your wives just as Christ has loved the Church and has given himself up for her"—Jerome urges that still no wise man would ever compare a husband's love with Christ's love for the Church. Even so a husband's love for his wife should be like Isaac's love for Rebecca, because "in his love for her Isaac found solace after the death of his mother, Sarah" (Gen 24:67). Whether Jerome means that a man should love his wife with the same love that he had given his mother, or because his wife can console him for the loss of his mother, he does not explain.[93] Indeed sexual intercourse is no more than permitted spouses so that they may produce children. To go beyond that and have intercourse for pleasure is sinful. Once a child is conceived the spouses should give themselves to a life of prayer.

Paul's command that husbands love their wives as their own bodies draws on Adam's exclamation, "This one at last is bone of my bones and flesh of my flesh," and on Christ's reaffirmation that husband and wife become two in one flesh. Jerome interprets this to mean for the husband that since he loves his own body not for the sake of copulation but as the vessel of his soul, so should he love his wife as the body to his soul. This she is as long as she is pregnant and nurturing his children. But when she chooses rather to serve the Lord, she passes into "manhood," into true discipline of spirit.[94]

The great analogy of verse 32—"This is a great *sacramentum*, I say this in reference to Christ and the Church" (*Sacramentum hoc magnum est, ego autem dico, in Christo et in Ecclesia*)—Jerome explains in the following steps.

To exhort husbands and wives to mutual love Paul used Adam and Eve as examples. Eve was built up from one of Adam's ribs to be given to him as wife; but once his wife, she became again one flesh with him. Thus a man who loves his wife loves himself.

Jerome then says that Paul applied this to Christ and the Church in allegory. Adam prefigured Christ, the new Adam; Eve prefigured the Church. Just as the entire human race is drawn from Adam and Eve, so the entire multitude of the faithful is drawn from Christ and the Church. Once the faithful are joined in the one body of the Church, they are reinserted in the side of Christ, replacing the extracted rib and becoming his one body, as Christ himself prayed, "Father, grant that they may be one just as you and I are one" (Jn 17:21).[95]

Jerome identifies clearly the referent of Paul's "This is a great sacrament." It is found in Adam and Eve. Not that everything narrated about them in Genesis can be referred readily to Christ and the Church. Here Paul intended that only three key phrases link the husband-wife relationship in Genesis with the Christ-Church relationship in such wise that the former relationship be a *sacramentum* of the latter. These are the consecutive phrases, "For this reason a man will leave his father and his mother," "will cleave to his wife," and "they shall be two in one flesh." He explains that Adam, the first human being and the first prophet, referred these phrases in prophecy to Christ and the Church. That is, Adam meant to foretell that Christ would leave God, his Father; would leave his mother, the heavenly Jerusalem; and would come to earth for the sake of his body, the Church. He would form her from his own side; on her account the Word would become flesh. And because some sacraments are great and others small, Paul made clear that "this is a great sacrament." But at the same time he indicated his own modesty as an interpreter of the *sacramentum*. He ventured no more than "I say this in reference to Christ and the Church."[96]

Nowhere in his commentary on Ephesians is Jerome's hasty composition more evident. He has garbled the analogy. He himself admits in the succeeding paragraph to a kind of despair in digging out the passage's meaning. He claims to join Paul in uncertainty, for he confesses that when discussing the passage with Bishop Gregory of Nazianz, a man thoroughly educated in the scriptures, the latter was wont to say to him, "See how great is the 'sacrament' in this brief passage, that when Paul interprets its reference to Christ and the Church, he does not claim to state it with the dignity that its witness deserves. But Paul says 'I know that this passage [in Genesis] is filled with inexpressible mysteries (*ineffabilibus sacramentis*), and needs an interpreter gifted with divine understanding. In my feeble understanding I interpet it for now to refer to Christ and the Church.' I do not mean to say that there is any mystery greater than Christ and the Church, but only that it is difficult to interpret as referable to Christ and the Church everything said of Adam and Eve."[97]

Jerome ends his consideration of these crucial verses in bathos. He notes that on reading Paul's admonition to Christian husbands, "Let each of you love his wife as he loves himself," some men may conclude that they need love their wives with no different or no greater love than that with which they must love their neighbor, since the law of Moses commands "You shall love your neighbor as yourself" (Lev 19:18), and Christ has said that any and every man is one's neighbor. Therefore it seems that the same love is owed to every human being as to one's wife, or vice versa.

This is absurd, Jerome insists, and he adds that the misinterpretation of meaning comes from misinterpretation of an adverb. "As" in the second phrase—"You shall love your neighbor *as* yourself" (*hōs* in Greek, *sicut* in Latin)—is not an adverb expressing similarity, but one expressing approbation and confirmation—with emphasis.[98]

With an eye to the interpretation that future generations of canonists and theologians will give this passage in Ephesians and thereby establish it as the pivot of the theology of the sacrament, we note the following obvious points in Jerome's interpretation of it.

The *sacramentum* to which Paul refers is found in the words of Genesis that Jerome attributes to Adam. More exactly, this *sacramentum* is these words' reference to the relationship of Christ and the Church.

Nowhere does Jerome hint that any clauses in the two passages, Genesis 2:23–24 and Ephesians 5:32, refer to the marriages of Christian spouses. He does not understand Paul to say that Christian spouses' being "two in one flesh" is this *sacramentum*. Therefore he does not understand him to say that the relationships of Christian spouses are earthly images, or signs, of the relationship of Christ and the Church.

He is of the opinion that Adam's words refer, as *sacramentum,* to Christ's leaving his "home" in eternity in order to form from his own body a "wife" for himself that is the Church, an allegoric marital union that would produce the multitude of the Christian faithful.

Of this interpretation Jerome confesses that he is much less than certain. Paul called the Genesis passage a *sacramentum magnum* with good reason: it is filled with unfathomable meaning.

Summary

This chapter has examined a sampling of the minds that during the three hundred years following the apostolic age shaped the Christian appreciation of marriage that was to last into the nineteenth century, and in a few themes in the Roman Catholic Church into the twentieth century. As the following chapter will show, Ambrose and Augustine contributed to that appreciation in a measure equal to all their predecessors. But their contribution was not to change it, but to clarify and emphasize it. The following observations about the men who during these first three centuries produced this appreciation are not irrelevant to the product of the shaping.

The first observation is that the shaping was done exclusively by men.

Secondly, all these men lived in a freely chosen celibacy—all except Tertullian, whose experience of marriage left him less than enthusiastic for it. For all their adult lives, or for at least a part thereof, most of these men were monks. Therefore they had no personal experience of marriage. They instructed about this way of life they had rejected because they thought it an obstacle to holiness—an obstacle at least for themselves, but in most cases for any and every Christian.

The setting in which they saw and assessed marriage was first the promiscuity and cruelty of the pagan society of the Mediterranean basin and of the Near East, and later the frequent compromising of marriage vows and therefore baptismal vows by the opportunistic who converted to Christianity because it had been made the religion of the empire. As teachers these men had as one of their purposes to put an end to the lifestyle of the pagan empire that accepted genital activity as a major commercial enterprise, and later to hold converts to the vows they had made so easily. Their own experience of sexuality was its impulsive and vagrant form in youth and/or the effort to live continent lives once they had taken up celibacy.

Insofar as they thought holiness possible in marriage, this was the holiness appropriate to a monk. Apparently they saw the essence of this monastic holiness not in *charitas,* in self-giving love, but in contemplative union with God, in a condition of mental attention whose lead the intention of will and emotions was to follow. This was the key to their distrust of marriage: its undeniably distracting, this-earth busy-ness keeps the mind from centering itself in God, and derivatively keeps will and affections earthbound.

In their judgment sexual passion even at its best is earth-bound. There is no evidence that any of them thought bodily tenderness could be self-giving, an expression of *charitas.* They thought it innately self-seeking, if not of its nature, then because infected by inherited sinfulness. Paul's psychology of sexuality they conceded the credential of a divine instruction: "It is good for a man not to touch a woman." It is good (*kalón,* the better thing) that he put sexuality out of his life entirely. They admitted it on the one ground that the attempt at a life of continence is probably too difficult for most and an occasion of sin.

Active in this assessment of marriage was the Stoic assumption that the immoral component of sexual activity where it is in fact immoral is lust swamping mind and will. They wed it to Paul's psychology of inherited sin in Romans 7 where he admitted to a "law," a power in his members that he was helpless to control.

Yet they held marriage in honor. They did so *a priori* because it is God's invention, because Christ blessed it, and because it can provide citizens for the kingdom of God. They honored it from experience because it provides opportunity for the courageous virtues; and a marriage showing these virtues can image the love of Christ and the Church.

Their understanding of sexuality was almost exclusively of its male variety. Even this was narrow and primitive. It appears to have included little more than genital urgency, with the little more a foolish vulnerability to women. Consequently the problem they saw in sexual conduct—the problem both psychological and moral—was not how to employ it in loving a partner, but how to restrain it. This left scant place for it in the marital sacrament, no place at all for it in that element of the sacrament that is the imaging of the Christ-Church relationship. In the element that is the conferring of grace, they saw sexuality's role to be the beneficiary of the grace of temperance—to keep it within one's marriage and there to reserve it for procreation.

NOTES

1. Epistle 188, no. 4, PG 32:673–674.
2. Epistle 199, no. 50, PG 32:731–732.
3. Epistle 217, no. 80, PG 32:805–806.
4. Oratio 37, no. 8, PG 36:291–292.
5. *Haereses*, 49, no. 6, PG 41:1027–1028.
6. Oratio on "Let a widow be chosen. . .", Ch. 5, no. 6, PG 51:325–326.
7. *On Not Reentering Marriage*, 1, PG 48:610–611.
8. *Ibid.*, 612.
9. *On Virginity*, no. 37, PG 48:559–560.
10. *Adversus Jovinianum*, Book I, no. 15, PL 23:234.
11. *Op. cit.*, I, no. 37, Col. 262.

Jerome also suggested that an oblique argument against remarriage is found in the combination of animals Noah took into the ark: "There is other evidence [*sacramentum*] of a single pair, that digamy was not found even among the beasts or the unclean birds" (*op. cit.*).

12. *Hexaemeron*, Book 5, nos. 62,63, PL 14:232–233.
13. *Tractatus V:* De Continentia, PL 11:302–303.
14. *Carmina*, Book 1, sec. 2,11, PG 37:563.
15. Epistola 1, Ch 10, PL 65:309.
16. Expositio in Psalmum 118, no. 20, PL 15:1300.
17. *De Sancta Virginitate*. Ch. 11, PL 40:401.
18. *De Opificio Hominis*, Ch. 17, PG 44:87.
19. *On Virginity*, Ch. 17, PG 48:546.
20. *Questions on Genesis*, Ch. 3, qu. 37, PG 80:135.
21. *On the Orthodox Faith*, Book 2, Ch. 30, PG 94:975.

A hint of the psychological source of these fathers' animus against sexuality may be seen in Theodoret's assmption that the angels are male in species and in Damascene's assumption that the one sex originally intended by God for the human race was the male.

22. *An Interpretation of the Book of Creation*, Ch. 18, PL 67:376–377.
23. *Ibid.*
24. PL 79:86.
25. *Pastoral Rule*, III, 27, PL 77:102.
26. *Loc. cit.*
27. Epistola 1, 19, 64, PL 77:1196.

28. *Adversus Jovinianum,* Book 1, no. 7, PL 23:230.
29. *Ibid.*
In its original form the passage in 1 Peter reads as follows: "In the same way husbands must always treat their wives with consideration in their life together, respecting a woman as one who, though she may be the weaker partner, is equally an heir to the life of grace. This will stop anything from coming in the way of your prayers."
30. *Op. cit.,* no. 28, PL 23:261.
31. Homily 19 in I Cor., no. 2, PG 61:153.
32. *In I Corinthios* 7:5, PL 17:228.
33. *De Bono Conjugali,* Ch. 10, PL 40:382.
34. A fuller description of these early Christian wedding ceremonies is in Kenneth Stevenson's *Nuptial Blessings* (New York, 1983). I have borrowed copiously from it in providing this sketch of the ceremonies.
35. In Catholic editions of the Hebrew scriptures this is Psalm 128. Its reference to marriage begins in verse 3: "Your wife shall be like a fruitful vine in the recesses of your home; your children like olive plants around your table." This survived in the Roman Catholic wedding liturgy until 1969 as the final blessing in the nuptial Mass. In the revised ritual it is one of the recommended responsorial psalms.
36. Homily on Genesis, 48, 6, PG 54:442–443.
37. Letter 231, PG 37:374.
38. Oratio 40, on Holy Baptism, 18, PG 36:382.
39. Augustine reported this in his Sermo 332,4 (PL 38:1463), Sermo 9,11,18 (PL 38:88) and in his Sermo 51,13,22 (PL 38:345).
40. *Liber quaestionum novi et veteris Testamenti,* CSEL 50,400,11–14.
41. *In I Corinthios* 7:40, PL 17:238.
42. CSEL 30:238–245.
43. PL 17:252.
44. PL 17:436.
45. PL 17:252.
That this religious anthropology did not die with the Ambrosiaster is evident in some clauses that survived in the nuptial blessing of the Roman Catholic wedding ceremony until its reform in 1969: "O God . . . who, having put in order the beginnings of the universe, didst form for man, made to thy image, a helpmate, woman, so that Thou didst give woman's body its origin from man's flesh. . . . May the author of sin have no mastery over her because of her acts. . . ."
How far the reform has gone is suggested by some crucial changes in the revised formulation of the blessing: "Father . . . in the beginning you created the universe and made *mankind* in your own likeness. . . . May her husband put his trust in her and *recognize that she is his equal*" (*Rites,* p. 564, no. 33, italics added).
That is in the nuptial blessing of first choice; its direct aim is at the bride alone (in the spirit of the Ambrosiaster?). But an alternative blessing is plainly directed to both bride and groom: "Father, stretch out your hand, and bless N. and N." (*op. cit.,* p. 587, no. 120).
Note that reform or not, the assumption remains that it is a *paternal* blessing that comes from God.
46. Cf K. Ritzer, *Le Mariage dans les Églises chrétiennes du Ier au XIe siècle.* Paris, 1970, pp. 220–222.

47. Ritzer, *op. cit.*, p. 279.
48. *Ibid.*
49. In PL 140:816.
50. PL 13:1411.
51. PL 20:473–477.
52. *Ibid.*, 473–475.
53. *Loc. cit.*
54. Epistola 167, PL 54:1204–1205.
55. Ritzer, *op. cit.*, p. 236.
56. PG 30:751.
57. PG 31:700–870.
58. PG 32:663–684; 715–752; 793–810.
59. PG 36:290–291.
60. These were the main themes of a series of homilies he delivered in Antioch in 390, especially in Homily 17 on Matthew 5:31–32 (PG 57:259ff.) and in Homily 62 on Matthew 19:3–12 (PG 58:595–604); in Homily 19 on Corinthians 7:1–40 in 392 (PG 61:151–160); in Homily 19 on 1 Corinthians 7:2–4 (PG 51:151–160); in Homilies 26 and 29 on the same passage (PG 51:218–219 and 225–242)—these last three in 398.
61. PG 48:562–563.
62. *Ibid.*
63. PL 11:299
64. This is in his *Commentaria in XIII Epistolas Beati Pauli Apostoli,* PL 17:45–510. The commentary on Ephesians 5:21–33 is in Cols. 398–399.
65. *Ibid.*, Col. 399.
66. Epistola 167, Inquisitio 4, PL 54:1204–1205.
67. *On Virginity,* Chapter 8, PG 48:538.
68. Book VIII, Chapter 51, quoted in Kerns, *The Theology of Marriage,* p. 25.
69. *In I Corinthios* 7:25, PL 20:351.
The Leonine Sacramentary repeated this thought in its prayer for the veiling of the bride: "Receive, Lord, we beg, this gift that is offered here in accord with the sacred law of marriage, and be the director of this work of which you are the author."
70. *Homiliae in Evangelia,* Book 2, 36,5, PL 76:1269.
71. *On John* 2, 1,2, PG 73:223–224.
72. *On the Heresies,* 51, 30, PG 41:942.
73. *25 Homilies on Select New Testament Passages,* on "Because of fornication", PG 51:210.
74. *In I Corinthios* 7:35, PL 17:236.
75. *On John* 2, 11, PG 73:227.
76. Epistolae 3, Ch. 9, PL 65:329.
77. *Moralia,* Book 1, Ch. 14, PL 75:535–536.
78. *Homilia in Ezechielem* 2,4, PL 76:976.
79. Epistola 2, Ch. 6, PL 20:175.
80. *Adversus Jovinianum,* Book 1, No. 8, PL 23:221–222.
This is edited also as Epistola 48, in PL 22:493–511. It is called a *liber apologeticus,* written to Pamachius to defend himself against Jovinian's charge that he was excessively favorable to virginity and excessively hostile to marriage.
81. *Ibid.*, Col. 223.

82. *Ibid.*
83. *Op. cit.,* Cols. 405–406.
84. There are other versions of this part of the book of Tobit, the most common of them in Greek in three different recensions. In 1955 fragments of the book in Aramaic were recovered from Cave 4 at Qumran. Those fragments agree substantially with the Greek recensions, so it is possible to compare Jerome's versions with them.

What is striking is that none of the Greek recensions nor the Qumran fragments even contain the verses 16 through 22 that Jerome has in his Vulgate. In fact, his translation is the only one in the history of the Jewish and Christian scriptures that contains them.

85. *De Perpetua Virginitate Beatae Virginis Mariae,* 20, PL 23:214.
86. *Adversus Jovinianum,* Book 1, No. 12, PL 23:238.
87. *Op. cit.,* No. 7, PL 23:230.
88. *Op. cit.,* No. 28, PL 23:250.
89. *Ibid.,* No. 27, PL 23:260.
90. Pierre de Labriolle reports this in his *Latin Christianity: The History and Literature of Christianity from Tertullian to Boethius,* London and New York, 1924, p. 361.
91. PL 26:530.
92. *Ibid.,* Col. 531.
93. *Ibid.,* Col. 532.
94. *Ibid.*
95. *Loc. cit.,* Col. 535.
96. *Ibid.*
97. *Ibid.*
Since there are no quotation marks in the Latin text of this passage, I have had to guess at which clauses come from Jerome, which from Gregory, and which from Paul.
98. *Ibid.,* Col. 536.

BIBLIOGRAPHY

Mackin, Theodore: *Marriage in the Catholic Church: Divorce and Remarriage.* N.Y./Ramsey, Paulist Press, 1984. Chapter 7: "Christian Teaching and Discipline in the Fourth Century."

Schillebeeckx, Edward: *op. cit.* "Christian Marriage from the Fourth to the Eleventh Centuries," pp. 256–266.

Stevenson, Kenneth: *op. cit.* 3. "Literary Evidence: The Fourth to the Sixth Centuries."

6. AMBROSE, AUGUSTINE AND THE SACRAMENT IN MARRIAGE

A student who inspects the Roman Catholic legislation for and the theology of marriage written during the one thousand years from Augustine's death in 430 until the Renaissance finds all the major jurists and all but two of the theologians in a mildly tortured posture. They strain toward the future, intent on holding the words of Christ and Paul and the teachings of the fathers in control over vagrant and fragile marriage during a chaotic millennium. At the same time they peer intently into the past, anxious to teach nothing but what they learned from Christ, Paul and the fathers, while struggling to understand what they said. Only two theologians dare to venture on their own and say unconventional things about the marriage sacrament. These are Hugh of St. Victor in the middle of the twelfth century, the morning of the medieval day, and John Duns Scotus at its dusk in the fourteenth century. All the others labor to repeat and to preserve what was said before them, and, in a method characteristic of the time, to comment on what was said—not to examine critically, but "to say what it means," to illustrate by example and analogy, to draw inferences, to make practical applications.

None of the fathers appears in the medieval commentaries on marriage more frequently than Ambrose and Augustine. It is no exaggeration to say that their thought, with lesser help from Tertullian, Jerome, the Ambrosiaster and Gregory, rules Western speculation on marriage during the ensuing one thousand years. This is all the more striking because neither Ambrose nor Augustine ever attempted a theology of marriage. Ambrose's main concerns were to argue for the superiority of consecrated virginity over marriage and to sustain the permanence of marriage against the Roman tradition of divorce. Augustine got briefly and inconclusively at the *sacramentum* of marriage *passim* in his writings. His hurried speculation on it is concentrated mainly in two of his three essays on marriage, *On the Good of Marriage* (*De bono conjugali*) of 401, and in *On Adulterous Marriages* (*De adulterinis conjugiis*) of 418.

(The third essay is *On Marriage and Concupiscence—De nuptiis et concupiscentia—*of 418–419.)

In examining Ambrose and Augustine we face the same problems of interpretation as with the other fathers we have already seen. Among those in the West the term *sacramentum* was in common use. But there was no fixed definition of the word that could be used as a norm for judging whether marriage belonged among those things of which it was predicable. Certainly the marriages of Christian spouses were not thought of as either *mysteria* or *sacramenta* in the same sense as baptism and the Eucharist. The word *sacramentum* was occasionally predicated of marriage, mainly because the Latin translations of Ephesians 5:32 rendered Paul's "great mystery" as *sacramentum magnum*. But the predication was almost always oblique, as "the *sacramentum* of marriage" or "the *sacramentum* in marriage." Its reference varied from writer to writer within a limited homogeneity of meaning. It frequently varied within the same writer from essay to essay. So we must be alert to the same variation and the same elusiveness in Ambrose and Augustine.

Taking baptism and the Eucharist as normative models we may search to find if Ambrose and Augustine say that marriage does for Christian goodness what baptism and the Eucharist do for it—does it by at least generic similarity. Do they say it brings or restores or intensifies friendship with God? That is, does marriage grace the spouses in some way? Do they say it produces in them some enduring effect, one that lasts beyond whatever gesture or ceremony creates the marriage—an effect analogous to the baptismal character that keeps a person a Christian after the Christianizing ceremony has ended, thus an effect that keeps the spouses Christianly married after their act or ceremony of consent has ended? Do they verify some words or deeds of Christ in which he installed marriage as a substantial religious element of life among his followers? Do they say that the marriage of two Christians is a sign, an image, of some invisible sacred reality that transcends life on earth?

It is neither realistic nor fair to expect Ambrose and Augustine to have stated their minds on every one of these four elements. Again, neither of them wrote a theological treatise on the marriage sacrament. But they are the elements found, even generations before Ambrose and Augustine, to be essential in making the baptism and the Eucharist what they are. If marriage is to be found sibling to them, it must have in it all or most of them. So we shall search to find how many of them Ambrose and Augustine acknowledged in marriage.

We know already that both men came to the study of marriage with a bias against acknowledging that it can be a source of holiness. The causes of this bias are somewhat the same for both and somewhat different. There was for Augustine the sexual irresponsibility of his adolescence and early manhood with its lifelong residue of remorse. Both read Tertullian's brilliant bitterness against marriage and sexuality. Both were discouraged by the promiscuity and infidelity brought into the Christian communities on the fourth century's flood of politically motivated conversions. Both meditated on St. Paul's pessimism concerning holiness in marriage and on his preference for the life of sexual abstinence even within marriage.

Add to these Augustine's brief years as a Manichee and then as a neo-Platonist. They may have reinforced his animus against sexuality, but he initially courted these two sexually abstemious life-forms in part because he was struggling at the time against his own imperious passion. And for Augustine too there were the sermons of Ambrose to which he listened so vulnerably during the years in Milan before and after his baptism.

As we shall see, this bias produced a strange rift within their estimation of marriage. They could not deny its primeval and fundamental goodness. It is God's invention, and God is one and good. There are not two deities, one of them evil and the inventor of all things physical including marriage, as the Manichees said of the deity Darkness.

But on the other hand the goodness that the one and good God intended for marriage, a goodness which reigned only briefly in Eden in the marriage of the first couple, was wounded by this couple's sin. After that sin and as an effect of it the couples passed down this wound to their children. They did so by their sexual intercourse, which was dominated by a lust called concupiscence because it inevitably swamped reason and will in them during the act of conceiving. Every generation in the history of the race has done this to its children, and every generation will do it until the end of time. So marriage, which was initially good and is still fundamentally good if only because it produces children and gives men and women the opportunity to practice both fidelity and perseverance, is nevertheless the nursery of sin.

Ambrose and the Qualified Goodness of Marriage

Ambrose, bishop of Milan from 374 until his death in 397, father of the church, teacher and scolder of emperors, hero of the youthful Augustine, shared the qualified judgment on marriage of his predecessors and contemporaries among the Christian teachers, as he also shared their specific qualifications. First and most fundamentally, he deemed marriage good, and good for two reasons. It is God's invention, and he has declared it good: "We have exalted virginity, but in such a way that widows are not spurned. We honor widows, but in such a way that honor is kept for marriage. It is not our authority which teaches these precepts. It is God's."[1]

He noted Christ's own approval of marriage by repeating, and adding to, the inspired logion in the book of Genesis: "Nor do I deny that marriage has been sanctified by Christ, according to the divine utterance, 'They will be two in one flesh and in one spirit.' "[2]

It is good also because it produces children, so that anyone who despises marriage and sexual intercourse within it despises children.

Someone will ask, "Therefore you dissuade people from marriage?" No, I persuade people to it, and I condemn those who have made a practice of dissuading people from it. . . . For he who speaks ill of marital relations also speaks ill of children.[3]

These statements claim God's approval of marriage in general. But Ambrose insisted that the same approval touches individual marriages, even to the extent of God's bringing spouses together in real life.

There is also another motive for chastity if you believe that the marriage which you have drawn as your destiny has been given to you by God. This is why Solomon says "A wife is prepared for a man by God."[4]

We have already seen that a century later than Ambrose Pope Leo I was to decide that not every union of a man and woman humanly considered a marriage is really such in the eyes of God. He said this of presumed marriages wherein the *sacramentum* could not be found in a woman because of her inferior social status. Ambrose made the same kind of distinction, but in the case of a Christian presumably married with a pagan. He sought to explain how Paul could advise the Christian spouses of Corinth who had pagan spouses to let the latter, when unwilling to live in peace, dissolve their marriages by departure. Ambrose explained this by pointing out first that Christ's command was "What God has joined man must not separate," thus hinting that not every marriage is joined by God. Only where both spouses are Christians does he do so. Consequently Christ's command does not hold marriages where one or both spouses are not Christian. (Ambrose passed over the fact that Christ addressed his remark to an exclusively Jewish audience.)

I must first, I think, speak of the law of marriage so as to treat afterward the prohibition of divorce. Certain persons think, in fact, that every marriage is of God, especially since it is written, "What God has joined man must not separate." So then, if every marriage is of God, it is not permitted to dissolve any marriage. Why then has the Apostle said, "If the unbelieving spouse departs, let him depart?" His discernment here is admirable. He wanted no motive for divorce to remain available to Christians, but showed that not every marriage is of God. For it is not by God's authority that Christians marry pagans, since the law forbids this.[5]

In his wonderful way, he did not want the cause of a divorce to lie with Christians; and at the same time he showed that not every marriage is from God. Christian women are not joined to pagans by the judgment of God, since the law forbids it. . . .

Harmony is when the pipes of the organ, blended in a certain combination, keep the beauty of a true melody, or when an apt order preserves the concord of the lute strings. Marriage, therefore, does not have its harmony when a pagan wife, in violation of the law, is joined to a Christian husband.

Thus, where there is marriage, there is harmony. Where there is harmony, God has joined them.[6]

While the latter part of the statement, at least, fails in exactness, Ambrose appears to conclude that it is because the marriage, or the presumed marriage, of a Christian and a pagan lacks harmony that it can be dissolved. And perhaps this keeps it from being a marriage at all. But where in a marriage there is harmony (and this can be found only in the marriage of two Christians?) one knows that it is God who has brought the spouses together and has created their marriage. Perhaps too the harmony is his work.

For Ambrose marriage has its honored place in the Church along with consecrated virginity and widowhood: ". . . this field of the Church is fertile indeed, now bright with flowers of virginity, now rich and ripe with the gravity of widowhood, now abounding in the fruits of marriage. For though different, they are the produce of one field."[7]

With these favorable judgments in place it is possible to introduce the qualifications. For one thing Ambrose shared the antipathy common among Christian teachers of the time toward remarriage in widowhood. In this he was far gentler than Tertullian had been, even while suggesting a comparison with a lesser species to the disfavor of Christians who remarry even once. He pointed out that the turtle dove, after losing its mate in death, does not take a second one. But he limits carefully the valence of his judgment against remarriage:

What we say as a matter of counsel we do not impose as a precept. We urge rather than obligate. We do not forbid remarriage, but we do not recommend it. . . . More than this, while not recommending a second marriage, we disapprove of oft-repeated marriage. . . .[8]

While he included the marriages of Christian spouses among the good fruits of fertility in the Church along with consecrated virginity and widowhood, Ambrose ranked it as the least valuable among the three. He was convinced that it puts limits to holiness because it catches and holds the married from a free and complete response to God's call. Reflecting on the man in the gospel parable who could not come to the banquet because he had just married (Lk 14:20), he qualified this when applying the parable to the Christian married. They do come to the banquet, but not as promptly as do the unmarried because their attention is turned partly away from God.[9]

More than once he used the metaphor of fetters to describe marriage's inhibiting effect on spouses' efforts to respond to God.

> There are many chains in this world. The desire to live is a chain. The allurements of pleasure are a chain. There are chains of honor, chains of marriage. . . . He does not sin who takes a wife, but he fastens himself in chains of the mind because he is anxious about how to please his wife. More fortunate would he be if his only desire was to please God.[10]

This image of chains belongs to the more inclusive image of slavery. Ambrose did not omit the opportunity to use the latter too in making his point.

> The chain of love is indeed good, but it is still a chain. A wife cannot release herself from it when she likes. She cannot have free disposal of herself. . . .
> If the one who is stronger does not have power over himself, how much less the weaker? The wife is not exempted from this mutual slavery. In fact, she is the one more closely bound.[11]

If one wonders what it is in the reality of marriage that inspires Ambrose's metaphor of chains and slavery, we already have his indictment of diminished freedom to dispose of one's own life, with its consequent inability to respond either quickly or fully to God's prompting. But there is another reason for thinking in the image of slavery, one about which Augustine will pass judgments that will, in turn, command the minds and emotions of Latin Catholicism for centuries. This reason is *libido,* or concupiscence, in the sexual activity native to marriage. Again Ambrose makes the necessary distinction, one demanded by the fact of God's authorship of marriage and its sexuality. The latter was just as good as marriage when both came from God's creating hand. But sin—sin as early as the first sin of the first married couple—wounded and sickened even married sexuality.

> Show him that Adam who existed before sin, that Eve who existed before she drew in the serpent's deceptive poison, before they were brought to ruin by his wiles, in the days when they still had nothing to be ashamed of. For now, although marriage is good, it includes something that even married people blush at themselves.[12]

Ambrose agreed too with the principle that the Christian teachers had borrowed so willingly from the Stoic and neo-Platonic philosophers that the one justifiable motive for sexual intercourse even within marriage is conception. He affirmed this in a roundabout and even quaint way. In his *Exposition of the Gospel According to Luke* he explained why Elizabeth, the wife of Zachary, was embarrassed at conceiving a child in her old age. She understood, Ambrose explained, what every good Christian must know, that intercourse is to be reserved for conception, so that the elderly, who cannot conceive, are suspect of sinful desire if they exercise their marital right. She was vindicated, of course, by the miraculous conception of John the precursor, and thereby provided evidence that her intercourse with Zachary had been divinely impelled.[13]

Ambrose and the *Sacramentum* in Marriage

In his essay *De Abraham* Ambrose made passing mention of the *sacramentum* when attacking the infidelity of husbands to which his converts had become so accustomed in the society in which they had been reared. He insisted that fornication, a husband's intercourse with a prostitute or with a slave girl—which in that society was not considered adulterous infidelity—is in fact just that.

> Every fornication is adultery; and it is not permitted to a man to do that which is forbidden to a woman. The same chastity is demanded of a man as of a woman. Everything committed with her who is not the legitimate spouse is condemned as the crime of adultery. You have taken note then of what you must avoid lest you show yourselves unworthy of the sacrament.[14]

The last clause here is tantalizing. To which *sacramentum* does Ambrose refer? Since he is writing for the instruction of the catechumens, his reference is less probably to any *sacramentum* in marriage and more probably to the *sacramentum* in baptism. If this is the case, he means baptism as a *mysterium,* as the neo-Christian's reenacting of, a participation in, the death and resurrection of Christ, according to Paul's analogy in Romans 6:3–4: "You have been taught that when we were baptized in Christ Jesus we were baptized in his death . . . so that as Christ was raised from the dead by the Father's glory, we too might live a new life." The message to Ambrose's catechumens is that infidelity in marriage makes a person unworthy of this participation.

Returning to Book 8 of Ambrose's exposition of Luke, in its Paragraph 9, we come upon perhaps his most explicit contribution to the nascent theology of the sacrament. Since Augustine learned so much from Ambrose's sermons during his Milan sojourn, one may imagine his pondering the following passage and drawing much from it for his own thinking on the sacrament in marriage. In the passage Ambrose insists again on the uniqueness of the marriage of two Christians. But now he gives his reason for the uniqueness.

> . . . because Jesus had said that not even the least part of the law is to be abandoned, he added "Anyone who dismisses his wife and marries another commits adultery." So the Apostle writes wisely when he says that this is a great sacrament of Christ and the Church. Here therefore you will find a marriage that is undoubtedly joined by God, since Jesus himself said "No one comes to me unless the Father who has sent me draws him." For the Father alone could join this marriage. Therefore Solomon said in a spiritual sense [*mystice*] "God shall prepare a wife for a man" (Proverbs 19:14). Christ is the husband; the Church is the wife—by her love [*caritate*] a wife and by her integrity a virgin.[15]

The logic of the passage is loose-jointed. One must take care not to draw from it more than Ambrose put into it. But he does seem to lodge the sacrament in the marriages of Christian spouses rather than in the Genesis marriage of the first couple.[16] In the Christian marriages, in turn, he lodges it in the impermissibility of dissolution, in its permanence, because in this it images the Christ-Church relationship. He accounts too for the source and the strength of the Christian marriage's performance in that God himself joins its spouses. Indeed only God could fashion such a marriage, and reciprocally such a marriage reveals God's work in the world. The last clause forms a kind of apostrophe. But it tells which work of God the Christian spouses reveal by their fidelity and perseverance in marriage. Although Ambrose does not put all these elements of the later theology of marriage in order, he does set them out in full view of Augustine and of all who would later read this theological heir of his.

Augustine and Marriage

A useful and even necessary entry into Augustine's thought on the marriage sacrament is a brief examination of the referents in his writing of the two key terms, *sacramentum* and *mysterium*. He took little care to predicate the two of them distinctly of distinct referents. On the contrary, he gathered a family of cognate terms and used them diffusely and often interchangeably: *figura, allegoria, prophetia, velamen* (veil, screen), *symbolum, mysterium, sacramentum.*[17]

Among all the meanings Augustine intended in predicating these terms, three generic classes can be identified. These are: the rituals told of in the Old Testament; symbols or contrived images of someone or something sacred; a revealed "mystery" or dogma of the Christian religion. In addition to these three generic classes we shall find a meaning used especially if not uniquely about marriage. This is *sacramentum* as pledge, as sworn commitment—of the spouses to one another, of each singly to God, or of the two jointly to God. Whether this meaning can be subsumed under one or more of the three generic classes remains to be found out in our later examination of Augustine's texts dealing with the marriage sacrament.

How diffuse is Augustine's use of the term *sacramentum* is evident in his predicating it of the following rituals and things in Old Testament Judaism: the sabbath day, circumcision, animal sacrifice, the sacrificial victim itself, Passover, religious ceremonies generally, the temple, altars, the Passover unleavened bread, feast days, the priesthood, anointing, dietary observances. What seems the element common to each of these is an observable manifestation or enactment of a sacred reality.

New Testament elements that Augustine calls *sacramenta* are baptism, the Eucharist, Passover again, ordination to the priesthood, anointing, the chi-rho abbreviation for the name "Christ," the imposition of hands, religious profession, the credal profession of faith, sacred scripture, the Lord's prayer, feast days, the words "Amen" and "Alleluia."

He uses *sacramentum* in a secondary sense to designate sensately observable things and actions as symbols or figures or images of invisible sacred realities. One finds this use everywhere in his allegoric exegesis of the scriptures. There he finds such an image in virtually every significant person, thing or event.

We must give particular consideration to Augustine's interpretation of the sacrament in baptism. This is because he reasons about the sacrament in marriage in close analogy with that in baptism, as we shall see. An earlier effort to understand the former may lead to clarity about the latter.

The spur to his interpreting the sacrament in baptism was the argument with his Donatist Christian neighbors that engaged him from the beginning of his episcopate in Hippo. They argued that baptism's working its effect depends on the moral rectitude of the person who baptizes, that a priest or deacon who has apostatized, or fallen into heresy, or has sinned seriously and not yet repented, not only ought not baptize but cannot in the sense that his baptism has no effect.

Augustine retorted that the ritual of baptism works the same effect in a person rightly disposed to receive it whether it be administered by a saint, by a sinful person or by a heretic. This is so because it is not human power that is at work in baptism; it is divine power, and this cannot be corrupted by human sinfulness.

> But the baptism of Christ, consecrated by the words of the Gospel, is holy even though administered by adulterers to adulterers, even though they be unclean and unchaste; and the divine power accompanies [*assistit*] its *sacramentum* either for

the salvation of those who receive it worthily or for the ruin of those who receive it unworthily.[18]

This reply necessarily bred, in its turn, two questions: Why is it that even an apostate, a heretic and a sinner can administer the sacrament of baptism? If an unworthily disposed person receives baptism to his or her ruin, but nevertheless receives it, what is the effect that he or she receives in it?

Augustine's answer to these questions unfolds as follows. The right or power to baptize, which is conferred in ordination, is a sacrament, just as the effect produced in the person baptized is a sacrament. In other words the ceremonies of both ordination and baptism produce a lasting effect in the recipient, an effect that is not voided or destroyed by the subsequent sin of the person ordained or baptized. In each case this is the sacrament.

> For what some of them [the Donatists] are saying after being defeated by the truth is this, 'That one who abandons the Church does not lose his baptism but does lose the power to baptize.' This is on several counts a futile and empty argument. For both of these are *sacramenta,* and both are given to a person by a certain consecration, the one when he is baptized, the other when he is ordained. Hence the Catholic Church permits neither to be repeated. For even when their clergy return and . . . are accepted back, and when there is need that they perform the same office that they had earlier, they are not ordained again. For their ordination has remained undisturbed in them, as has their baptism. Their schism is where the damage was done. But this has been repaired by their reunion in peace. No harm was done to their *sacramenta,* which are the same wherever they be.[19]

In the following paragraph Augustine sets forth the analogy that was his favorite in his dispute with the Donatists. In it we get a yet more emphatic claim for the presence and function of the abiding sacrament of both baptism and ordination. To be sure, the analogy proves nothing. But it must have been an effective rhetorical gambit among disputants enamored of rhetoric. We will recognize the analogy when it reappears in Augustine's attempt to explain how it is that spouses remain married even though they go their separate ways and take on second partners.

> Or let us say some person, a deserter or one who has never served in the army, should brand a private citizen with the military seal. When the man just branded is caught, won't he be punished as a deserter himself, and all the more severely if it can be proved that he has never actually served in the military?

And won't the one who branded him so boldly then turned him in be also punished? Or say the man bearing the brand should refuse to fight but instead flees in terror. If he later begs clemency of the Emperor, and after gaining forgiveness returns to battle, will he be branded again? Won't he simply be accepted as already branded?

Now do the *sacramenta* inhere any less firmly than does this physical seal, when we see that apostates do not lose their baptism? that when they repent and return we do not restore it to them since we acknowledge that they could not lose it to begin with?[20]

In a quite different passage Augustine develops his interpretation of the baptismal sacrament when he explains why the Christians' solemn Easter celebration is either called a sacrament itself, or a sacrament is said to take place in it, while the celebration of Christ's birth is not a sacrament but only the calling to memory of a past event.

The reason for finding the sacrament in the Easter celebration is this, that not only is it a commemoration of an event, but, in the celebration the participants receive of, they share in the holiness that is commemorated.

For we so celebrate the passover that we not only recall to mind what was done—that Christ died and rose again—but we include in the signing of this *sacramentum* the other things that we believe he did. For as the Apostle said, "He has died because of our sins but has risen for the sake of our purification." Thus a certain passing from death to life is solemnized in the passion and resurrection of the Lord. . . . This passing we carry on now in faith which brings forgiveness of sin, in the hope of eternal life for those who love God and their neighbor. . . .[21]

Here is one of the richest perceptions of the Christian sacrament, that in and by it Christians participate in the saving action of Christ and gain from it the beginning of eternal life.

Augustine sets out a cause-effect correlation when he accounts for what cause in baptism produces the observable evidence of the grace given the recipient, and what cause produces the gift itself of the grace: "So it is that water signs exteriorly the *sacramentum* of grace, while the Spirit operates interiorly to produce the gift of grace. . . ."[22]

This linking of causes and their specific effects he repeats in his argument with the Donatists: "How can it be that the *sacramentum* can be holy in a murderer while his heart is not? . . . because God gives the *sacramentum* of grace even through evil men; but grace he gives only himself or through his saints. . . ."[23]

Let me point out again that these passages detailing Augustine's understanding of the sacrament in baptism are helpful for understanding his identification of the sacrament in marriage because when he tried most carefully to do that identifying he worked out an analogy of the marriage sacrament with that in baptism. We shall look carefully to see how willing he was to find in the former all that he claimed for the sacrament in baptism.

Augustine and the Matrix of the Marital Sacrament

As with Ambrose so with Augustine, if we are to understand what he said about the sacrament in marriage, we must first understand what he said about marriage the human relationship and institution. A first reason for this we have already seen. It is that every one of the sacraments in its ceremonial stage is composed of a determinable element and a determining element. The former is matrix to the latter. For example in baptism the heart of the determinable matrix is the bathing with water—not the water alone, but the bathing with it. Bathing is an ordinary experience. But in baptism it is transformed into a second birth into friendship with God in the Christian community—it is determined to this birth—by the power of God channeled through the person who baptizes. In the Eucharist the matrix is the blessing, sharing and consuming of bread and wine. These too are ordinary experiences, but they too are in the Eucharist determined to a reenacting of Christ's death and resurrection and thereby to an enriching of the participants' union with God in Christ.

A person wholly ignorant of bathing or of communal blessing, sharing and consuming of food and drink could not understand baptism and the Eucharist. The same holds for marriage. If we assume that among Christians it is a sacrament, we cannot understand it as such unless we first understand it as a human relationship. In turn we equally cannot understand the relationship as Christianized unless we also examine it "from above," from God's revelation of his mind about marriage. But I am convinced that in the sequence of investigation understanding the human matrix must come first. As I have already suggested, this sequence is demanded by the fact that the human expression itself of God's revelation about marriage has drawn its images and vocabulary from human matrices, from cultural versions of the marital relationship.

We have already reviewed briefly in Augustine's writing his principal referents of the word *sacramentum*. Now we survey with like brevity what he said of marriage the human relationship. We shall look for two kinds of statements, those about the relationship itself taken statically, and those about the relationship in action, taken functionally, producing effects and having consequences.

But understanding what Augustine said of marriage calls for first understanding the context in which he said it. It was a context that affected in varying degrees all the Christian communities contemporary with him, and affected him seriously. His thinking and writing on marriage were in great part a reaction to challenges aimed at him from two sources that were almost polar opposites. On the one side there was the Manichee condemnation of marriage, or at least of procreation, as essentially evil. On the other there was the charge against him personally coming from certain Pelagian Christians who insisted that his refutation of the Manichees was so qualified as to leave him in fundamental agreement with them.

The attack from this other quarter came mainly from Pelagius' disciple, Julian of Eclanum. Again it was that Augustine's defense of marriage against the Manichees was a half-hearted one. In truth Augustine was caught in a tangle of twisted meanings. He insisted against the Manichees that marriages since the fall of the first parents—therefore since the dawn of creation—are not fundamentally evil. He based this insistence on evidence available to all. For even if the great majority of marriages are lived sinfully by Christian spouses themselves, the cause of this cannot be marriage itself. Marriage can yield verifiable goods, and in fact does so among many Christian spouses.

But the Pelagians charged him with conceding too much to and even siding with the Manichees in acknowledging this sinfulness in almost all marriages. They acknowledged no real historical fall of mankind from original grace, and could thus see no fundamental difference between the human condition vis-à vis sinfulness after the first sin and before it. Consequently by conceding the general sinfulness of marital conduct since a supposed but fictitious fall, Augustine had, they thought, acknowledged the fundamental sinfulness of marriage.

What Augustine did to counter both attacks was first to defend the fundamental goodness of marriage against the Manichees, and this at two moments, or epochs, in marriage's history. The first of these was the all too brief moment of marriage in the garden of Eden, when there existed only the one original pair of spouses, before their sin. The second period is that of the human race ever since that sin, the period that will last until the final destruction of the race and of this world. About two points of history here Augustine had no doubt. Since he read the first three chapters of Genesis as factual narratives, he took for granted that the first human beings were one man and one woman fashioned immediately by God and given to one another as husband and wife, both of whom soon disobeyed him by eating fruit from the tree of good and evil that had been forbidden them. The second point of fact is that the human race, and probably the planet earth, will be destroyed as a single event.

For marriage in the two periods—before and after the first sin—Augustine claimed two different kinds of goodness. For its goodness in the first period he laid less emphasis than his predecessors had on its goodness *ab extrinseco,* its being instituted by a good God who by definition can create no evil. He appealed to the goodness of the purposes in marriage, the goods it is meant by nature to produce. About its apparently obvious purpose, to continue the human race by providing succeeding generations to replace the preceding that disappears in death, he made a distinction that his adversary, Julian, should have thought of. Random sexual activity could produce the children for the succeeding generation. Marriage, supposing sexual activity is kept within it, has an added purpose, namely that fathers and sons may identify one another and thus form friendship.

> You are entirely mistaken when you think that marriage was instituted so that the passing of the dead would be compensated for by the succession of those who were born. Marriage was instituted so that the chastity of women would make sons known to their fathers and fathers to their sons.
>
> True, it was possible that men be born of promiscuous and random intercourse with any women at all, but there could not have been a bond of kinship between fathers and sons.[24]

From another historical-religious assumption that Julius' Pelagianism would not accept Augustine drew a conclusion that should have been equally obvious, namely that if the first parents had not sinned, death would not have entered human experience. Thus there would never be perishing parental generations needing to be replaced. Asserting this as a past-potential matter of fact demanded that Augustine explain at least three more things: why men and women in a sinless world would have had intercourse at all; why the first man and woman had no intercourse in the brief time they lived in such a world; what would have happened to the human race had no one ever died. His answers to these questions were: (1) to bring the human population up to its divinely predetermined number; (2) because the sinless period of the human race was too brief, and because during that period the first man and woman were not driven by uncontrollable passion; (3) all would have lived until the predetermined number was reached and would then have been transformed into spiritual and therefore immortal bodies.

> We read that they were already expelled from paradise when they had relations and conceived children. Still I do not see what could prevent their having honorable marriage and an immaculate marriage bed even in paradise. When they were living faithfully and justly, serving Him with obedience and holiness, God could have arranged that, without any restless ardor of sensual desire, without any labor or childbirth pain, children would be born of their seed.
>
> The idea would not be that the children take the place of their parents when they had died. The parents would remain in some bodily state and draw bodily strength from the tree of life

which had been planted there. The children too would be brought to the same state, until the predetermined number was complete.

Then, granted that all lived justly and obediently, the final stage would come. Without any death, animal bodies would be transformed into another kind in the sense that they would bow to every wish, even the slightest, of the spirit that ruled them, would live merely because of the lifegiving spirit without nourishment from bodily food, and would be called spiritual. . . .

'Why then did they not have relations until they had left paradise?' We can answer at once. Because that sin took place soon after the woman was created, before they had had relations. . . . It can also be argued that God had not yet commanded them to have relations. For why would they not await His authorization for this when there was no concupiscence like the goad of disobedient flesh to keep prodding them? God had not given this command because He was arranging everything according to His providence, and by this He knew in advance beyond all doubt that they would fall and that the human race would already be mortal when it was propagated.[25]

Bringing the divine foreknowledge of human conduct into play, Augustine found another reason for God's instituting marriage. Foreseeing that because of its sinfulness the human race would need a redeemer, he instituted marriage in order to provide this redeemer by providing a select people who would in time produce him. It was for this purpose that the saintly patriarchs of Israel married and produced children.[26]

This implies that holiness is possible in marriage, even in the present age of sinfulness, the age of which the patriarchs were citizens. For the holiness of their marital conduct lay in their having intercourse out of obedience to God and to the vocation he gave them to produce the people who would produce the savior. The same possibility of holiness is by implication available to Christians if they would just confine and dedicate their intercourse to a kindred purpose.

Obedience compelled them to marry, so that the people of God . . . would be propagated, since those people . . . were nothing less than a prophet of Christ and from them would even be born the flesh of Christ. . . . Thus even holy women were inflamed, not with the desire of intercourse but with a faithful concern to have children. Indeed, it is by no means incorrect to suppose that they would not have sought intercourse if they could have had children in some other way.[27]

Just as that wise and just man [St. Paul] who yearned to be dissolved and be with Christ . . . took nourishment in order to remain in the flesh, since it was necessary for the sake of others, so the holy men of those days regarded intercourse with women as an obligation of the marriage law.[28]

To say this is to imply also that even this antecedent goodness of marriage is instrumental. Marriage is not, and has not, a goodness-in-itself; it is not and has not a self-warranting good like wisdom or friendship. It exists rather to serve the need and advantage of goods apart from and more valuable than itself. For example, marriage's relationship to friendship is this, that it provides children who may grow up to be friends from family to family, as it also, as said earlier, makes possible the friendship of fathers and their sons. As for the friendship of the spouses themselves, a potential good-in-itself within marriage, Augustine preferred to claim for marriage that it provides a companionship that is natural to the two sexes. This is a natural good in the domain of charity. The companionship is especially available to the elderly who cannot have intercourse, and among spouses who have not had children.[29]

One may notice that Augustine's reasons for the goodness of marriage in its condition before the entry of sin should lead to the conclusion that marriage is now no longer needed since that entry. Indeed Augustine himself drew this conclusion. Enough human beings have been produced to fulfill the purpose of the race's existence, the bringing of the city of God. So there is no further need of sexual intercourse even within marriage. But even as he asserted this he added the one reason why marriage should continue.

> But I know some will complain, 'What if all men wished to abstain from sexual relations? How would the human race survive?'
>
> If only all men would have such a wish! . . . The City of God would be filled much more quickly and the end of the world made to come sooner.
>
> What else does the Apostle seem to urge when he says on this point, 'I would wish that all were like myself,' or in that passage, 'I say this however, brethren: the time is short. It remains that those who have wives be as though they did not have them . . . ?' From all this it seems to me that in this present age only those who lack self control should marry.[30]

To put it succinctly and somewhat crudely, God instituted marriage originally, when offspring were needed, to make friendship possible between parents and children and among the children themselves. But now that this purpose has been realized sufficiently, only one reason remains, namely to provide men and women with a sexual outlet as sinless as possible.

Why this outlet is needed, and needed grievously, calls for the explanation telling of the other reasons that marriage is good—the reasons that persist in the history of the race following the first sin. To understand these we must outline Augustine's theory of the first sin, original sin, and of its effects in human beings since that sin.

Augustine's Interpretation of Original Sin

Again, he took for granted that the narrative in Genesis 3 of the first man's and woman's sin in the garden of Eden is a factual account of an event that transpired at the dawn of history. He also took for granted that in species their sin was disobedience to God's forbidding command. From these two assumptions he developed a kind of psychology of sinfulness. Thus because the first couple's reason and will disobeyed God *ad extra*, it followed that within them their lower powers, their emotions and bodily urges, broke loose from the control of reason and will and rebelled against it. That reason and will should control them is the natural order designed by God in human beings. Consequently their rebellion is disorder, is against their nature as designed by God, and is therefore disobedience against him as well. As disobedience it is sinful, sinful not only as an evil act when the lower powers actually erupt in rebellion against reason and will, but also as an abiding condition of the human person. It is sinful permanent disorder.

The name for this disorder, this relentless inclination of the lower powers to rebel, is concupiscence. For Augustine the term's reference went beyond the modern bias that limits it to lust. He referred it to all the rebellious emotions and feelings. But he no doubt meant it to describe mainly vagrant sexual urge and conduct; and in this description the term took on cognates, so that as virtual synonyms for *concupiscentia* he used *libido* and *voluptas*. He used them interchangeably in his three essays devoted expressly to marriage, On the Good of Marriage, On Marriage and Concupiscence, and On Adulterous Marriages. These terms designate at one and the same time: (1) the residual effect in men and women of Adam's sin; (2) the punishment in all of Adam's heirs for his sin; (3) this inherited sin itself; (4) the evidence of the presence of this sin; (5) a wound in every human being's nature; (6) a sickness or infection carried in this nature; (7) the cause within persons of the sinfulness in their sexual acts.

In Augustine's estimation concupiscence manifests itself most frequently and most vividly in men's and women's sexual condition and conduct. Here the reference to it is enlivened by its synonyms, *libido* and *voluptas*. In explaining the conduct of concupiscence he explained also the way in which it is an inherited punishment for the first parents' sin. Had they not sinned, they would indeed have had intercourse in Eden, and their offspring down through the centuries would have had it too until the predetermined number of human beings had been reached.

But their intercourse would have been procured in an ordered, reasonable way. Reason and will would have commanded the genital organs to prepare for and execute the act. This would have proceeded calmly, with no obscuring of reason and no swamping of will.

> 'Increase and multiply and fill the earth.' Although it seems that this could not happen without the intercourse of man and woman . . . still we may say that in immortal bodies there could have been another process in which, by the mere emotion of pious charity, with no concupiscence, that sign of corruption, children would be born.[31]

> For who denies that there would have been intercourse even if no sin had gone before? But it would have taken place with the generative organs moved by the will like other members, not excited by the sex instinct—or if you insist, by the sex instinct itself, not as it is now but subject to the direction of the will.[32]

> No turbulent heat would stir those parts of the body. A free control would make use of them when there was need. . . . Just as it is not the cry of pain but the impulse of a completed process which releases the female organs to bring forth a child, so it would not be the cravings of *libido* but an act of the will which would bring the sexes together to conceive one.[33]

Concupiscence as punishment lies in this, that since the first sin men and women come to intercourse not at the dictate of reason, but driven by *libido*. And during intercourse their conduct is controlled not by reasonable will, but is driven out of control by the same *libido*. Augustine deemed this degrading for men and women. It is to act like animals. An earthy phenomenon that he reports more than once is this, that whereas a man's reason and will can command the performance of his hands, his feet, his tongue, his lips, even of his bladder, when it comes to the performance of conceiving a child—a good and holy duty—he loses command of the member created specifically for this task. He must wait patiently as it obeys its own law. Sometimes it refuses to stir when he wills it to; at other times it stirs when he wills it not. He laments, "Must not the freedom of human choice blush on finding that for having despised the commanding will of God it has now lost command over members that are its own possession?"

Because Augustine describes this as the condition of every man and woman since the first parents' sin, he must explain how this has indeed become the condition of all. His explanation is his historical theology of *peccatum originale originatum,* inherited original sin.[34]

Adam's sinful disobedience produced in him this effect, that his sexuality, both emotions and anatomy, were infected with sinful *libido*.

He could have sexual intercourse only under its impulse and its control. Thus the act itself was sin-infected. By an inescapable cause-effect linkage the sin-infected act produced a child conceived as a carrier of the same infection, the *vitium* of sin. Augustine assured his readers that the semen itself carries the infection.[35] (The metaphor of a psycho-moral venereal disease is therefore not inept.) The longer consequence of this is that when the child matures physically and becomes sexually capable, his intercourse too is already infected, so that it passes the same infection on to his offspring. In this way the entire human race has been infected with this element of inherited original sin that is concupiscence. This has been in and will be in every human being, with Christ the only exception, even though he or she were never to sin personally, because all are linked by flesh (we would say genetically) with Adam's sinful flesh.[36] Augustine explains this in his graphic way.

> But when spouses come to the dutiful work of conceiving, the very licit and good act of intercourse, which ought to be the effect of reason in them, cannot take place without the heat of concupiscence (*ardor libidinis*). And certainly this heat, whether it follow upon one's choice or precede it, stirs one's members only by a command of its own, and shows itself to be stirred not by a free choice but by a licentious stimulus. . . . From this concupiscence of the flesh as from the daughter of sin—which is also the mother of sin when surrendered to in shameful acts—any child that is born is itself bound by original sin.[37]

What effect does the sacrament of baptism, which is administered by Christians expressly to get rid of original sin, have on this sin's effect that is concupiscence? First of all baptism as a conveying medium brings to the person baptized the grace that Christ, by his death and resurrection, merited from God the Father. To understand the effects of this grace in the inherited original sin, one must, with Augustine, distinguish two forms of this inherited sinfulness. One of these persists before baptism; it is *reatus*, guilt which merits God's punishment. It is because of this *reatus* that a person who dies without the grace of Christ brought by baptism deserves damnation. It is precisely this *reatus* that baptism removes.

The second form of the inherited residual sinfulness is *supplicium*. It is an inherited punishment for Adam's sin. It is either identical with concupiscence, or concupiscence is a principal part of it. It is not guilt. Its presence in a person brings not God's punishing wrath but his pity. And as a punishment it is an inescapable inheritance: "That sickness . . . is the punishment of sin; and human nature cannot exist without it, since it is not yet entirely restored to health."[38] An element of this punishment is shame, the shame that even devout spouses feel at their feeble self-control. Augustine insists again on the appropriateness of the punishment's striking the organ which reproduces the human nature wounded by the first sin.

> Human nature is beyond all doubt ashamed of this *libido*, and deservedly ashamed. For in its disobedience, which has subjected the genital organs of the body to its impulses alone and snatched them from the power of the will, it is all too evident what man's punishment is for that first disobedience. It was most important that it appear in the part which generates the nature which was changed for the worse by that first and terrible sin.[39]

What the grace of Christ mediated by baptism does in regard to the *supplicium* is to lend the baptized person strength to control and conquer concupiscence in himself or herself. Rarely is it extirpated entirely from a person's soul and body, as everyone's experience shows. It is always there as a source of potential sinful conduct. But lifelong, persistent prayer and self-denial can tether it with near-total success. It is concupiscence understood as this *supplicium* that either drives even the baptized to their sexual acts, or invades these acts en route. Obviously a sexually dormant life would lend mightily to the final victory over this *supplicium*.

Does a person then sin inescapably when he or she has sexual intercourse even within marriage, even after baptism and where married to a Christian spouse? This question is almost a disguised form of the question—or more accurately the accusation—leveled at Augustine by his Manichee adversaries. If intercourse is inescapably sinful, can there be any excuse that justifies engaging in it? Or if such an excuse is available, does it reach so far as to rid the intercourse of its sinfulness? The Manichees' answers to the questions were uncompromisingly negative. Augustine's were more nuanced.

He did offer a broad, inclusive and unnuanced answer that proves a basis for his subsequent nuances. It is that at least for Christians there exists a justification for engaging in intercourse that qualifies as an excuse for risking the sin so easily committed therein. (The reservation that the justification is available to Christians is here because to survive the risk persons need the grace of Christ.) This justification consists of the intent to realize three goods that are available in marriage, and that can be secured mainly by sexual intercourse. These are the *bona matrimonii*, the goods available in marriage. They are the best-known features of Augustine's philosophy and theology of marriage. They are *fides, proles* and *sacramentum*—fidelity, offspring and the sacrament.

The explanation of the first two of these we can intertwine with the qualifications Augustine sets for intercourse that he holds to justify risking the sin lurking in the act.

Intercourse outside one's marriage he judged to be the grievous sin of adultery. By definition this act can be excused by no motive. Within one's marriage one sins grievously if one goes to the spouse in the manner of an adulterer or fornicator, which is to say as one disregarding the fact that the partner is one's spouse, and seeking only the selfish satisfaction of *libido.* Augustine calls such a husband "a too ardent lover of his wife": "Too ardent a lover of his wife is an adulterer, if pleasure in his wife is sought for its own sake."[40] And one's sin within marriage is even worse than adultery or fornication if one has intercourse with one's spouse in such a way as to avoid conception.

Intercourse within one's marriage is venially sinful if one goes to it impelled by *libido* even while accepting the possibility of conception, or if, though impelled at the outset only by the desire to conceive, one subsequently consents to the libidinous pleasure accompanying the act.

Intercourse is without sin within one's marriage if it is motivated by one or both of two goals. One of these is the more excellent goal of conceiving a child for the kingdom of God. In this case the act's sinlessness depends on the exclusivity of this motivation in two ways: It must be the only initial motive; any intent to take pleasure in the satisfying of *libido* must be excluded from the beginning.[41] And no consent must be given subsequently to such pleasure that may accompany the act. The only pleasure affording sinlessness is that which comes from the hope of conceiving a child.[42] Augustine judged that the realization that they may become parents may suppress *libido* in the spouses even as they have intercourse.[43] It is the rare instances in which motivation is so confined and pleasure so carefully focused that produced his lasting judgment that intercourse even of devout Christians is almost never without sin.

The other motivation that keeps marital intercourse sinless is the intent to keep one's libido-driven spouse from going outside the marriage to fornication or adultery.[44] But even here one may not request intercourse from the spouse thus driven, but may only accede to his or her demand. Nor may one share his or her libidinous pleasure. One's sole motivation here must be to keep the spouse from sinning grievously by keeping his or her intercourse within the marriage, and there to keep it as venial as possible. Its being kept venial depends too on both spouses' accepting the possibility of conceiving.

The Ways in Which Marriage Is Good

Implicit in this, Augustine's ethic of sexual conduct, is his claim for the goodness of marriage even in the epoch of the human race's sinful condition and despite this condition. Again, he says that three goods are available in marriage; and the spouses' will to realize them justifies their marrying and excuses their having intercourse therein despite the near certainty of their sinning at least venially. We have seen that the first of these is *fides,* fidelity. It is a virtue that is both a value in itself and instrumentally serves the further values of enabling parents and children to know and care for one another, and enabling siblings to know and love one another.

The second good is *proles,* offspring, a good that deserves realization because of God's command to the first parents in Genesis 1:28, "Increase and multiply," and until the number predestined for the city of God is filled up.

The third good available is the *sacramentum.* Its explanation will occupy the last part of this chapter.

Augustine's briefest formulation of these goods is in the earliest of his essays on marriage, *De bono conjugali:* "These are all the goods on account of which marriage [itself] is good: offspring, fidelity and the sacrament."[45]

He offered two other formulations of the goods. In his Commentary on the Literal Meaning of Genesis (*De Genesi ad litteram*) he explains as follows:

This [good] is three-fold: fidelity, offspring, sacrament. Fidelity means that one avoids all sexual activity apart from one's marriage. Offspring means that a child is accepted in love, is nurtured in affection, is brought up in religion. Sacrament means that the marriage is not severed nor the spouse abandoned, not even so that the abandoner or the abandoned may remarry for the sake of children. This is a kind of rule by which nature's fruitfulness is honored and vicious sexual vagrancy is restrained.[46]

Yet a third formulation is in his treatise On Original Sin (*De peccato originali*).

Marriage is therefore good in all those elements that belong to marriage. And these are three: The orientation to procreation, the fidelity in chastity, and the sacrament of marriage. Because of the orientation it is written, "I want that young widows should marry, bear children, become mothers of families." Because of fidelity in chastity a wife has not authority over her own body but her husband has it; as likewise a husband has not authority over his own body but his wife has it. Because of the sacrament of marriage what God has joined man must not separate.[47]

Because of these goods available in marriage the evil inherited via sexual intercourse from Adam can be partly healed by putting the sexual anatomy that carries and passes on the evil to the good work of keeping fidelity, producing children and maintaining the sacrament.[48]

It was crucial for Augustine to insist against the Manichees that marriage is not inherently evil. Although sinful concupiscence lurks in it always, the married can use this concupiscence for a good purpose. For this reason the act of intercourse is itself good. A person sins only in the degree that he or she allows concupiscence to enter this inherently good act.

> Incontinence is evil, but it does not follow that marriage is too, or that the act by which the incontinent have intercourse is not something good. No, this good is not to be blamed because of that evil. Rather, because of this good, that evil is rendered harmless. For the good that marriage has, and that makes marriage good, can never be a sin.[49]

Augustine and Holiness in Marriage

Thus Augustine acknowledges that sexual intercourse free from sin is possible in marriage, however rare its realization. But to ask a question that is central to the theology of the sacrament in marriage, does he think holiness that goes beyond this difficult innocence is also possible for the married? Yes, he thinks it available. But the part that sexuality plays in the holiness—an issue equally central to this theology—gets an unusual interpretation in his essays.

To begin with, one spouse can show a charitable compassion toward the other, as we have already found, and when needed even an extraordinary mercy. If the other will not or cannot maintain sexual continence, the one can rise to holiness by never asking for the payment of the marriage debt, but only granting it at the other's request.[50] By having intercourse with the other he or she saves the weaker one from mortal sin and reduces the sin to venial.[51] And where one concupiscence-driven spouse has been unfaithful but has repented, the other can act as an instrument of God's mercy by taking the repentant sinner back.[52] And Christians married to non-Christians can sanctify the latter, as Paul made clear in 1 Corinthians 7:14.[53]

Within marriage a Christian wife's holiness consists in part of obeying her husband, as his consists in part of ruling her with love, since he is head to her as Christ is the head of his body that is the Church.[54] This status and ruling vocation as head takes the husband's obligation to fidelity beyond one of equality with his wife's obligation. His is the more seriously binding. But the bodies of both spouses who remain faithful to one another and to the Lord are holy too.[55] These bodies are temples of the Holy Spirit.[56]

But there is a holiness in marriage even more excellent than that of fidelity, of compassion and forgiveness, of ruling with love and obeying with love. This is the holiness of sexual abstinence. Marital chastity, Augustine insists, is the more excellent the more it is tested by abstinence and the more passion in one's marriage is subdued;[57] for continence within one's marriage is even nobler than keeping fidelity.[58] Moreover, by this abstinence within marriage, Christian spouses can witness to the true condition of the human race. Marriage exists only to serve its earthly and temporary condition, a condition that will be destroyed at the end of history. The final, eternal and true human condition will be one of angelic continence. Therefore this continence is the ideal way even now for men and women in this life: ". . . this mortal generation, which is the purpose of marriage, will be destroyed, but freedom from all sexual intercourse is both an angelic ideal here, and remains forever."[59]

It is because of this freedom from marriage, Augustine says, that the unmarried woman has the better opportunity for holiness. How does this freedom provide the better opportunity? Including but going beyond the reason already made clear, that the unmarried life shuts off the way for concupiscence, one also gains what Paul pointed out to the Corinthians, tranquility of mind and sufficient time for prayer and for the other things of God.[60] For although offspring are a good of marriage, yet to not seek them is to maintain a perpetual freedom while being subject to only one man, Christ. This is especially true if women use the freedom thus gained in the way that Paul urged, "to think of the things of the Lord, how one may please God."[61]

Augustine has a warning for men both similar and dissimilar to that one, one apparently drawn from his own experience in heterosexual passionate involvement. There is nothing Christian about the warning, including as it does a bleak assessment of this involvement that could have been offered by any Cynic commentator on the human condition.

> Make her as attractive as you will. Heap every good quality upon her. I have still determined that for me nothing is to be shunned so completely as sexual relations. I feel that there is nothing which so plunges the soul of a man down from the heights as a woman's blandishments and that bodily intercourse which is implied in having a wife.[62]

But in the face of this serious preference for the life of sexual abstinence, and this preferably in the vocation of consecrated virginity outside marriage, Augustine chose to report from experience on this front as well. The experience was not that of his own person, but one gained no doubt as pastor of a Christian community. The first of his comments we quote here makes clear that it is not the mere abstinence from sexual intercourse that constitutes holiness. A life ruled by orthodox faith within the Christian community is the matrix of holiness in this as in any state of life.

> How can it reasonably be asserted that a body is chaste when the soul itself is fornicating by yielding itself to another than the true God? . . . Therefore the only thing that should be called true chastity, either married, widowed or virginal, is what is bound to

the true faith. Although sacred virginity is with good reason preferred to marriage, what Christian with sense does not put even Catholic women married to one husband ahead of vestals and even of the virgins among the heretics?[63]

Even within orthodox belief within the Christian community failure to mature in the virtues common to any human goodness can undermine in real life the ideal preferability of the life of virginity.

> If I were to consider each of your good qualities separately, you, the man who has renounced marriage, are better than your father, and you, the woman who has renounced marriage, are better than your mother. For virginal holiness is better than married chastity. . . .
> But which is better, pride or humility? . . . If you hold fast to pride and your mother to humility, the mother will be better than the daughter.[64]

Even beyond the grounding in right faith that gives elected virginity its fundamental meaning in the Christian life, that election must aim its motive beyond the social-psychological state itself if it is to gain its full meaning and value. The election must be an election for a very personal human love relationship with the human Christ. If a virgin does not have this, she is inferior to a Christian wife who loves even her husband with such a love. I offer again Augustine's preferential judgment.

> What we preach about virgins is not that they are virgin but that they are virgins dedicated to God by pious continence. I would not feel rash in saying that to me a married woman seems better off than a girl who is eventually to be married. She has what the girl is still anxiously seeking, especially if the girl is not yet even spoken for. The wife is eager to please one person to whom she has been given, the girl to please many, because she does not know to whom she is to be given. . . .
> Therefore the virgin who deserves to be ranked above a married woman is the one who neither presents herself to many to be loved, because she is seeking the love of one of those many, nor adorns herself for one she has already found, thinking about the things of the world, how to please her husband, but instead has loved the most handsome among the children of men and loved Him so deeply that, since she could not conceive Him in her flesh like Mary, she keeps her flesh intact for Him. For he has been conceived in her heart.[65]

But when all else is said, whatever the state of life one elects, this ought to accord with God's gift, as Paul himself taught. Which gift a person has been offered is not easily found out. God acts in hidden ways. Therefore one must be patient perhaps for a long time, and must submit to testing in order to discern one's gift. One of these tests—the most severe of them, the test of martyrdom—may bring to light a further and startling fact. It is that a married woman, because of her gift, has reached a holiness far more excellent than the still timid and untested virgin.

> The gifts of God are secret. Only putting them to the test, even within oneself, brings them to light. For, not to mention other cases, a virgin may be anxious about the things of the Lord, how to please the Lord; and yet for all she knows, it may be that, because of some weakness of soul unknown to her, she is not yet ripe for martyrdom, while that wife to whom she used to be so happy to prefer herself can already drink the chalice of the Lord's humility, which he once offered to disciples eager for high places.[66]

> It is one thing not to consent to persuasion and blandishments for the sake of truth and a holy ideal, but another not to yield to torture and blows. These things lie hidden in the powers and strength of souls. Temptation spreads them out for display. Experience makes them public knowledge.[67]

This is a rich accolade for the possibility of holiness in marriage. But is it a specifically marital holiness, of a kind not available to the unmarried? Does the conduct most typical of marriage, sexual intercourse contribute to it? If it does, what is this contribution? If the act is virtually always sinful, do the married encounter this paradox, that in order to join the virgin in the courage for martyrdom, they must first join him or her in the courage for sexual abstinence? must live as though not married?

Or is specifically marital holiness available in the thrid of the goods whose hope of realization Augustine deemed sufficient reason for risking marriage's resident sinfulness? This is marriage's *sacramentum*. It will be useful to trace his understanding of it successively through the three essays on marriage that we have already listed and borrowed from.

The Sacrament in *De Bono Conjugali*

The term *sacramentum* appears for the first time in this essay in its Chapter 7.[68] In a curious *non sequitur* Augustine cautions individual spouses who wish to live in sexual abstinence out of desire for greater holiness, that they not drive the other spouse to damnation by driving him or her to sexual release outside their marriage. To reinforce his warning he quotes the synoptic instruction on marriage, which is not about sexual denial resulting in the other spouse's going outside the marriage, but about the Jewish dismissal of wives. The warning is that a man who dismisses his wife, except for her unchastity, causes her to commit adultery. Augustine then completes the thought: "To such a degree is the marital covenant the product (the *res*) of a certain *sacramentum* that it is not cancelled even by the separation itself, since as long as the husband who has abandoned the wife is still alive, she commits adultery if she marries another. And the husband who has abandoned her is the cause of her sin."[69]

Augustine does not say that the marital covenant itself is the *sacramentum*. Rather the covenant is the *res*, the effect or product, of a certain *sacramentum* in marriage. Whether it is premature to find here the cause–effect alignment so dear to Augustine remains to be seen, i.e. whether he is here designating the marital covenant as the product of the *sacramentum* understood as observable ceremonial sign.

He returns quickly to the function of the marital *sacramentum* in holding spouses within their marriage. He asks whether a man who has dismissed an adulterous wife may marry another after the dismissal. He admits that the New Testament does not provide an exact answer to this question. He admits too that even a person who marries in order to have children, but finds the spouse sterile, may not divorce and remarry in order to have the desired children. But he then asks what may be the meaning of such tenacity of the marital bond (*quid sibi velit tanta firmitas vinculi conjugalis*). His own answer is: "I do not think this bond could possibly be so strong unless some *sacramentum* of a much greater reality were at work in this fragile human mortality, a *sacramentum* which remains unbroken for the punishment of those who desert their marriages and wish to dissolve them."[70]

He adds that, despite the divorce, the marital covenant (this time the *confoederatio*) is not destroyed, and the spouses remain spouses to one another even though they live the rest of their lives apart.

Neither in this passage does he identify the *sacramentum* exactly. In the previous passage it is the cause which produces the marital covenant. Here its function is added to and apparently even changed: it is something which remains between the spouses despite their separating by divorce and keeps them married to one another despite the separation. It does this in virtue of being (here is the unclarity) a *sacramentum* of some reality greater than itself or the marital covenant itself. Whatever the *sacramentum* is, and one may guess it is a sign or image, it is the causal bridge from that higher reality to the marriage that makes the latter invulnerable to divorce.

Quite in passing in Chapter 13 Augustine uses the term *sacramentum* to designate the foreshadowing role of the Old Testament patriarchs and their conduct. He praises them for seeking marriage and intercourse only for the sake of propagating the people of God. "In their day the mysteries of our salvation were still veiled in prophetic signs" (*Illis vero temporibus, cum adhuc propheticis sacramentis salutis nostri mysterium velabatur*).[71] Note that here the word *sacramentum* is not the Latin translation of the Greek *mystérion*. Augustine in this passage renders the latter as *mysterium* to designate the hidden divine reality-plan, which was in turn manifested in the *sacramentum* which was the conduct of the Old Testament saints.

In Chapter 15 he returns again to the *sacramentum* of marriage taken as the reason for, or cause of, marriage's indestructibility—but now specifically of marriage in the City of God, among those who believe in and obey the true God. "Once marriage is entered in the City of God—wherein beginning with that of the first human beings, our unions bear a certain *sacramentum* of marriage—it can be dissolved no other way than by the death of one or other spouse."[72] Again the identity of the *sacramentum* is not stated. It is something that the union of the spouses, their covenant, "bears." Again it is the cause of their union's indestructibility as long as both spouses live.

The most dense and the most fruitful consideration of the *sacramentum*'s function in marriage appears in Chapter 18, where Augustine explains in what way it demands that among Christians marriage be monogamous. He explains the demand rather by a reverse logic: Among Christians the *sacramentum* of marriage is found only in first and monogamous unions. The reason for this is that in and by the *sacramentum* these marriages signify, or image, the one society of the blessed souls in eternity. A consequence of this imaging is that a Christian man is not ordained to the ministry if as a widower he has remarried. This is not because a second marriage in widowhood is sinful but because of the demand of the *sacramentum* of marriage, or rather of the holiness of the *sacramentum*.

If a man were ordained after having had more than one wife, he would fail the *sacramentum* of marriage because in marriage a Christian spouse is to image the future uniting, in eternity, of all peoples in subjection to Christ—just as the Old Testament patriarchs in union with their multiple wives imaged the future joining on earth in our churches of many peoples in submission to the one man Christ.[73]

From that point Augustine jumps immediately to a second but unlinked conclusion about Christian marriages. Because of the demand of marriage's *sacramentum,* a woman cannot go from one husband to another while the first still lives.

What can we wring by inference from this logic? We still do not find Augustine saying exactly what the *sacramentum* of marriage is. Nor, after having earlier called marriage both a bond and a covenant, does he here say what the relationship of the *sacramentum* is to either of these.

What we do find him stating clearly enough is a characteristic or demand of marriage's *sacramentum.* This is that among Christians marriage be monogamous. The reason for this he also states clearly: either the *sacramentum* itself, or perhaps the marriage itself in and by its *sacramentum,* is to image the monogamous and future union in eternity of all peoples joined in loving obedience to the one Christ. By force of metaphor Augustine turns "all peoples" into a monogamous spouse of Christ.

Not to be ignored is his insisting that monogamous Christian marriage images, by reason of its *sacramentum,* not a union of Christian peoples with Christ in the Church in this life on earth. Likewise not to be ignored is his failure, or reluctance, or refusal to use the classic metaphor of Ephesians 5:32 of the Church as the bride of Christ just where, in his logic, its use seems most appropriate. Indeed, could one have asked Augustine where he had found out that the demand of the *sacramentum* fixes monogamy in Christian marriages, he could have appealed to no other New Testament passage than Ephesians 5:32.

The theological dynamic that will in ensuing centuries be repeated endlessly is here set in motion for the first time: the demand of the *sacramentum's* imaging fixes a characteristic in the Christian marriage. That is, because what it images is a monogamous union, the image itself must be a monogamous union. And as I have pointed out, almost as an afterthought here Augustine adds that the demands of the same imaging fixes in marriage also its characteristic that is invulnerability to dissolution by any cause except death.

In Chapter 25 of this essay, the third from its last, Augustine summarizes what he has said only disjointedly to that point. He abbreviates and concentrates the case for marriage's goodness, making at the same time a significant distinction. For all peoples and all times marriage has these two good traits: its goal which is children, and its safeguard, which is the marital chastity of fidelity to the spouse. But among Christians marriage has these goods plus one more. This is the holiness coming from its *sacramentum.* An effect of this holiness is that not only may one spouse not desert the other, but no desertion by either for whatever motive has the power to dissolve the marriage. Because of the *sacramentum,* or of its holiness, Christian spouses are married to one another until at least one of them dies.[74]

He adds to this summary the logic of an analogy. Despite spouses' separating, their marriage remains because its *sacramentum* remains, just as a man's *sacramentum* of orders remains even though, despite his being ordained to minister to a congregation, no congregation gathers, or just as a man's *sacramentum* of orders remains even though he be removed from the ministry and clerical office because of some fault.

Although Augustine has not yet explained exactly the inner, abiding relationship of the *sacramentum* to the marital bond or marital covenant, he is certain of one effect that it works on them. It makes them invulnerable to dissolution by any cause short of death. He does not explain how it causes this invulnerability. His earlier analogy using the relationship of all peoples gathered in the Church obedient to one master, Christ, was used to explain how the *sacramentum* demands not indissolubility in Christian marriages, but monogamy.

The Sacrament in *De Conjugiis Adulterinis*

Late in the year 419 Augustine composed an essay in two books in order to reply to some questions and opinions about divorce and remarriage written to him by his friend, Pollentius.[75] While he was busy answering Pollentius' original queries the latter wrote asking further questions. But before Augustine could include the answers to these in his first reply, his friends had laid hands on and published this reply. Consequently he was constrained to produce a second essay, now Book II, and therein to track again over the territory of his first answers.

But both books make up one logical web, in places inordinately intricate and convoluted, explaining why remarriage attempted by a Christian for any motive, after divorce for any reason, inescapably becomes adultery. Whether a spouse is dismissed because of infidelity, or because of sterility, or because of illness or deformity, or because of apostasy from the Christian religion, or because of refusing to become a Christian while harassing the spouse who has converted—in any case it is adultery if either spouse, the dismissing or the dismissed, remarries. So too does a person who marries either of them commit adultery. The reason for the sin is identified simply, and we are by now familiar with it: the marriage of a Christian can be ended in no other way than by the death of one of the spouses. A divorced Christian is still married to the original spouse despite the divorce.

Throughout the forty-eight chapters of the two books Augustine's argument is drawn almost but not quite entirely from the New Testament passages dealing expressly with divorce and remarriage, i.e. from the synoptic *logia* and from Paul's instruction in 1 Corinthians 7. In only one brief passage, in Book II, Chapter 5, does he name the marital *sacramentum* as the reason for the perdurance of the Christian's marriage despite divorce.[76] What he says of it there repeats what he said years earlier in his *De Bono Conjugali,* but with one significant change and one significant though unsatisfying expansion of the thought.

Again he reasons by analogy. Even though a Christian is excommunicated for some serious sin, the *sacramentum* of his baptism remains in him, and will remain even though he never be reconciled with God. In the same way even though a man justifiably dismisses his wife for her adultery, there will always remain between them the bond of the marital covenant, and it will remain even though she never be reconciled with him. Her bond with him will vanish only when he dies.[77] At this point comes the significant change: whereas in *De Bono Conjugali* Augustine said it is the *sacramentum* of marriage that remains despite the dismissal, here it is the marital bond that remains. Does he mean by this to identify the bond and the *sacramentum?* Since he himself does not explain, the reader is left to guess at the answer.

The significant expansion lies in Augustine's terse accounting for the imperishability of the baptismal *sacramentum* in the soul of the excommunicated sinner. The reason for this is that God never dies. It is not the character in itself of the *sacramentum* that it be imperishable, but the relationship of the *sacramentum* to God that makes it so. Does Augustine, in virtue of his analogic reasoning, mean that it is likewise the imperishability of some other agency that makes the marital bond (or perhaps the *sacramentum*) imperishable? He does not say. Perhaps he espied that symmetry in his analogic reasoning would demand his identifying this agency as the imperishability of either the husband himself or of the husband's marital pledge. Since the first of these imperishabilities is contrary to fact, and since naming the second would invite perishability in order to get rid of an unwanted wife, he may have just decided to move on quickly and leave his readers to guess again at this meaning.

The Marital Sacrament in *De Nuptiis et Concupiscentia*

That the *sacramentum* in Christian marriages draws its meaning from Ephesians 5 Augustine suggests for the first time only in Book I, Chapter 10 of his essay, *De Nuptiis et Concupiscentia* (On Marriage and Concupiscence).[78] He wrote this essay in 419 and 420 as a kind of letter in essay form addressed to his friend, Count Valerius. As we have already noted, it was intended as a denial and refutation of the charge made to Valerius by anonymous Pelagians of Hippo that Augustine condemned marriage as evil. (After he had completed Book I, this came into the hands of Julian of Eclanum, the Pelagian bishop, who in reaction wrote and sent to Valerius an essay in four books. Valerius sent excerpts of this to Augustine, who in turn replied to this in writing Book II of *De Nuptiis et Concupiscentia*.)[79]

The issue of marriage's *sacramentum* breaks in abruptly and out of context in Book I, Chapter 10 where Augustine repeats, now in variant form, his earlier threefold claim for the goodness of marriage among Christians: "Fertility makes marriage good; its fruit is offspring. Chastity (*pudicitia*) makes it good; it bond is fidelity. And a certain *sacramentum* also makes it good where the marriage is of Christians. On its account Paul said, 'Husbands, love your wives just as Christ has loved the Church' (Ephes. 5:25)."[80]

Then he names exactly not the inclusive *sacramentum* itself, but the *res*, the abiding fruit of it: "Without a doubt this is the abiding fruit of the *sacramentum*, that as long as they live husband and wife stay joined inseparably in marriage; nor is spouse permitted to separate from spouse unless because of adultery (*excepta fornicationis causa*). . . ."[81]

Augustine's next clause contains an extraordinary claim, very probably the product of his usual hasty dictation: "This is what we hold to in Christ and in the Church, that for all eternity no divorce will separate living spouse from living spouse." If he means that the Christian spouses' marriage survives even the death of one or both, he contradicts what he has already said repeatedly and will say again shortly, that it is the death alone of at least one of them that ends a marriage. If he means that this principle of invulnerability to divorce in Christian marriage survives into eternity, his way of saying so is misleading. We may have a hint at what impelled this extraordinary claim where he says, in a clause immediately following, that the Christian spouses whose marriages are indestructible *in aeternum* are members of the body of Christ (*qui sine dubio sunt membra Christi* . . .). Does he mean that because they are members of the Christ who survives in eternity, their marriages likewise survive? He does not explain.

He falls again immediately into unclarity as he goes on to confirm his assertion. Just above he said that the invulnerability of Christian marriage to dissolution is the *res sacramenti* in it, the abiding fruit of its sacramental state. But here he says that so firm is the adherence to this *sacramentum* itself of marriage among Christians, and among them alone, that neither Christian men nor women abandon their first spouses and take over others, even though they have married expressly in order to have children, but find the first spouse sterile. The laws of pagan peoples and even the law of Moses permit divorce and remarriage on this ground. But the law of the gospel forbids such dismissal, and declares the ensuing remarriage adultery. Even though the original spouses separate and take other partners, they remain married to one another as long as both live. Only with the death of one of them can the surviving second and adulterous union become a marriage.

He rounds off his thought, and ends the chapter, by turning again to the analogy that has become his favorite for this issue. He also becomes even more indecisive in identifying the nature and function of the marital *sacramentum:* "So firmly does a certain conjugal something (*quiddam conjugale*) remain between the spouses while they both live, that neither separation nor union with another can remove it . . . just as the soul of an apostate, deserting as it were its marriage with Christ, even though it loses its faith it does not lose the *sacramentum* of faith that it received in baptism. If he lost the *sacramentum*, it would without doubt be restored to him provided he returned. But in fact he keeps it, unto the increase of his punishment, not for the earning of his reward."[82]

Let us assume that Augustine intends this analogy not for mere illustration but in order to explain his meaning here and to prove his case. He says that the "certain conjugal something" in Christian marriages remains as immovably in the souls of the spouses as does the baptismal *sacramentum* in the soul of a person who has been baptized. What is more, just as the presence of the baptismal *sacramentum* keeps the person "wedded" to Christ even despite apostasy, so the presence of the "conjugal something" keeps the spouses wedded to one another even though they separate and enter second unions. Whether Augustine means to identify this "certain conjugal something" as the marital *sacramentum* itself, or only as the *res* of this *sacramentum,* one can only guess.

But one may justifiably query Augustine about the method in his logic at this point. How does he *know* that there is in Christian marriages a certain conjugal something (a *sacramentum,* or a *res sacramenti*) having the same effects in these marriages that the baptismal *sacramentum* has in the souls of the baptized? From what source does he have it that the analogy explains rather than merely illustrates attractively? A reasonable guess at the answer is this, that he is trying to supply a theology that will give the internal reasons for the New Testament teaching about divorce and remarriage as he understands these. He has an earlier assumption about these teachings, that where Christ said in the Matthean version that a man may dismiss his wife if she commits adultery, Christ meant not the dismissal that dissolves a marriage, but a dismissal that only separates the spouses while leaving them still married to one another. Augustine wanted to explain the internal possibility of this survival of the marriage despite the ending of the spouses' union—a survival unheard of in history until he and Jerome thought it up. If the union ends for good but the marriage remains, what else is it that remains?

Augustine's assumption that this is what Christ's words in the Matthean passage meant seems compelled by two prior assumptions on his part. The first is that the key New Testament passage about divorce and remarriage, the one passage in whose clear light all other uncertain and apparently contradictory passages are to be interpreted, must be Romans 7:2: "A wife is bound to her husband as long as he lives." The second assumption is that Paul and Matthew—or Christ interpreted by Matthew—would not contradict one another, that all apparent contradictions are only that—apparent.

About the first assumption again, Augustine seems to want to explain what none of his predecessors in Christian teaching tried to explain, namely how and why it is that the bond of wife and husband remains for life despite the death of their union, and, even more exactly, what it is that remains between them and is their marriage despite their separating and entering second unions. Here, where he could have called this the *sacramentum,* the most that he ventures is the "certain conjugal something."

He returns to the function of the marital *sacramentum* in his Chapter 17, and states it in yet another way.[83] He cites again the three goods by reason of which marriage itself is good. He develops the meaning of *proles* to include not only the conceiving and bearing of children, but their rearing as Christians, beginning with their baptism. Fidelity (*fides*) too he develops by suggesting how marital fidelity among Christians differs from the same among pagans: "And fidelity, not such as pagans who hunger for the flesh have with one another. For what husband, however unfaithful himself, wants an unfaithful wife? Or what unfaithful wife wants an unfaithful husband? This desire for a spouse's fidelity is a good that is natural to marriage. But it is only carnal."[84]

But for a Christian, because espoused to Christ and a member of his body, the concern about fidelity is different: "However, a member of Christ the spouse ought to fear adultery not out of concern for the self but for his or her spouse; and ought to hope to be rewarded by Christ for the fidelity he or she shows to the spouse."[85]

Then he points out in what way the *sacramentum* is a good specifically Christian that helps make Christian marriages good in their specific way: "And [our] spouses may preserve and guard the *sacramentum* peacefully and chastely, the *sacramentum* that remains even in the separated and the adulterous."[86]

Again uncertainty enters. In light of Augustine's insistence that despite adultery and separation the marital *sacramentum* remains in the spouses' souls, one would expect him to say not that the spouses preserve and guard the *sacramentum*, but that it does so to them. He has insisted that its perdurance in their souls, once they are married, transcends their wills to reject or to keep it.

But his inchoate theology does begin to congeal in another quarter. This marital imperishability guaranteed by the imperishable *sacramentum* despite infidelity and desertion grows out of the Christian spouses' being "members of Christ," and members in a relationship Augustine has suggested is itself conjugal.

In Chapter 21 he comes back for a second and last time in this Book I to *sacramentum* as the Latin translation of *mystérion* in the Greek of Ephesians 5:32 ("This is a great *mysterion* . . ."). He does so in a fanciful dramatic recitation in which each of the three goods of marriage, in personification, exonerates itself from infecting newborns with the sinfulness Augustine believed every human beings contracts at conception and by conception.

> If we could in some way question those marital goods, to ask them how sin could be communicated from them to infants, the act of conceiving would reply, "I would have been much happier in Paradise, had sin not been admitted there. For to me was given God's blessing, 'Increase and multiply. . . .' For this worthy task the different organs of the two sexes were designed, and they existed before the sin, but were then not a cause of shame."
>
> Chaste fidelity would reply, "If they had not sinned, nothing in Paradise could have been more secure than myself. I would not have been tantalized by my own desire nor tempted by another's."
>
> The *sacramentum* of marriage would reply, "Before the sin it was said of me in Paradise, 'A man will leave his father and mother and will cleave to his wife, and they will become two in

one flesh. . . .' The Apostle called this . . . a great *sacramentum* in Christ and in the Church (Ephes. v:32)."

Therefore that which is great in Christ and in the Church, but small in each and every husband and wife, is yet the *sacramentum* of inseparable union. Which of these could be the source in marriage whence the bond of sin would pass to the next generation? None of them!. . . .[87]

Despite Augustine's entering here into greater detail about the marital *sacramentum* than hitherto, his referents seem no more exactly identified. The identity of the *sacramentum* emerges no more clearly. Apparently he reverses his earlier opinion that it is found only where the marriage is of two Christians. The declaration in Genesis 2, "For this reason a man will leave his father and his mother . . ." refers to all marriages of all peoples throughout history. Yet he insists that it was said there of marriage's *sacramentum*.

This opens the way to asking what exactly the substance of the *sacramentum* is, since that prophetic declaration was predicated of it. Is it the first man's cleaving to his wife so that they become two in one flesh? Within this is it the man's and woman's will to establish and keep this union? Or is it the union itself?

Whatever it is, it is a great *sacramentum* "in Christ and in the Chruch," i.e. in the form and stature in which it is found in them. This suggests that it is indeed the union of the spouses; in Christ and in the Church the union of metaphoric spouses, while in the real-life marriage of every man and woman (again not only in the marriage of every two Christians) it is a very small union, but there a union of real spouses. In either case, however, it is a *sacramentum* of indestructible union. If, in Augustine's Latin—*conjunctionis inseparabilis Sacramentum*—the third word is simply in apposition with the first two, he is saying finally that the *sacramentum* is the indestructible union itself. But if he intends the possessive case of the first two words to have its formal value, then the *sacramentum* is not the indestructible union itself but a property or sign of it. Again, I believe, Augustine dictating in haste leaves his readers to finish his thought.

He calls Ephesians 5 back into consideration only once in Book II of this essay. In its Chapter 4 he explains how God can speak through a human being's prophetic utterance.[88] For example, in Adam's calling his wife *Vita* (life), and thus mother of all the living (Gen 3:20), he is asserting a great *sacramentum* of the Church. Here *sacramentum* appears to signify a pre-figure, a type. That is, Eve, as mother of all the living, prefigures the Church, which is mother of all those who live in the grace of Christ. Augustine cites immediately an example of two men's speaking the mind of God at vastly separate times, with the declaration of the first serving as a type of the second. Thus Adam's declaration, "For this reason a man will leave his father and his mother, and will cling to his wife, and they will become two in one flesh," prefigured what Paul was to write in Ephesians 5:31–32. But what Adam's words prefigured Paul called the *sacramentum magnum*. Again this suggests that in Augustine's mind in the year 420, the last year in which he discoursed on marriage, marriage's *sacramentum* in the indestructible union of the spouses. From the evidence he provides we can interpret no more confidently than this.

We may note in closing this chapter that Augustine stated the function of the marital *sacramentum* in two other essays within a formulation that belonged to his stock in trade. In Book 9, Chapter 7 of his *De Genesi ad Litteram* (On the Literal Meaning of Genesis, a commentary worked at across a span of thirteen years, from 401 to 414) he wrote, "This good of marriage is threefold: fidelity, offspring, *sacramentum*. Fidelity means that one avoids all sexual activity apart from one's marriage. Offspring means that a child is accepted in love, nurtured in affection, and brought up in religion. *Sacramentum* means that the marriage is not severed nor the spouses abandoned, not even so that the one abandoning or the one abandoned may remarry in order to have children. This is a kind of rule set for marriage, by which nature's fruitfulness is honored and vicious sexual vagrancy restrained."[89]

Finally, in Book II, Chapter 39 of his *De Peccato Originali* (On Original Sin, composed in 418), he repeats the formula, but with variations: "Marriage is therefore a good in all those elements that are its own. And these are three: the orientation to procreation, the fidelity in chastity, and the *sacramentum* of marriage. Because of the orientation to procreation it is written, 'I want that young widows should marry, bear children and become mothers of families' (1 Timothy 5:14). Because of the fidelity of chastity a wife has not authority over her own body, but her husband has it; as likewise a husband has not authority over his own body, but his wife has it. Because of the *sacramentum* of marriage what God has joined no man must separate."[90]

It is obvious that Augustine made no attempt in these essays to compose a systematic treatise on Christian marriage. They are polemic treatises. His strategy in them was dictated by the form of the Pelagian attacks to which for the most part they were replies. It was also dictated by something over which Augustine himself could have set more control, namely the busied and hurried condition of his life. When one looks at the diary of his literary production during these years, one finds him, along with his multiple other duties as a bishop and as a quasi-abbot of a community of clerics, always at work on at least three and sometimes five essays simultaneously. He could not, perhaps would not settle down and develop an orderly and exact explanation of the Christian religion's demands on marriage. He fastened on the idea that a main reason for every and any marriage's goodness is that in it there is a *sacramentum*, as also that this sacramentum is the reason for Christian marriages' superiority over all others; that it is the reason why Christian marriages must be monogamous; but most of all that it is the reason for Christian marriages' lifelong indestructibility despite even the lifelong separation and alienation of the spouses.

He did not say, as Catholic authorities and teachers were to say later, that the *sacramentum* is the marriage itself. That is, he did not predicate the term *sacramentum* of the marital union *in recto*, but *in obliquo*. He said that Christian marriages *have* the *sacramentum*, or alternately that all marriages have it. Nowhere did he set himself the task of isolating the *sacramentum*, of identifying it exactly.

Summary

Ambrose joined the fathers who defended marriage against its detractors. He insisted it is good because it was instituted by God who can cause only good. And it is God himself who brings devout spouses together in marriage. Marriage is good also because it produces children.

He urged that marriages which lack the *sacramentum* because one spouse is not Christian are not really marriages at all.

He opposed remarriage in widowhood. He also ranked marriage below virginity and widowhood because it keeps the married from a free response to God's call to holiness. It is sexual concupiscence, inordinate since the sin of the first couple, that keeps the married from this freedom.

The marital sacrament in the unions of Christian spouses he apparently found in their permanence, in their resistance to dissolution.

Augustine's earliest and indirect contribution to the theology of marriage was to insist that certain Christian rituals, such as baptism and ordination, and marriage too, produce in the souls of the recipients an effect distinct from grace. This is the *sacramentum*.

He insisted, against the Manichees, on the goodness of marriage, both before the fall and after it because its reason is to produce children, and it enables parents and children to identify one another; after the fall for the added reasons to propagate the race that would produce the redeemer, and to provide a relatively sinless refuge for concupiscence. His memorable summary apologia for marriage is that even after the fall it enables spouses to realize three goods, namely fidelity, offspring and the sacrament.

He acknowledged that holiness is available in marriage in these ways: Out of compassion one spouse may accede to the other's need for intercourse and thus keep him or her at least from sinning mortally outside the marriage. Out of mercy one can take back the other even after the latter's infidelity. But the finest holiness in marriage is a life of sexual abstinence. This not only conquers concupiscence but frees the spouses to attend to the things of God. But the truly superior holiness is that of the virginal unmarried life, provided this is animated by orthodox faith and Christian charity.

Augustine identified the *sacramentum* in marriage variously. The marital covenant is the product (*res*) of the *sacramentum*, with the latter apparently the observable ceremonial sign; it is a quality or trait of the marital bond that prevents its dissolution; as such a trait it is found in all marriages, or alternately it is found only in Christian marriages; it is that in the marriages of Christian spouses whereby these image the Christ-Church relationship—or is perhaps the image itself; as such it is the source of the demand that Christian marriages be monogamous; it is analogous to the effect of his ordination in a priest that keeps him a priest all his life, as it is analogous to that effect of a Christian's baptism that keeps him a Christian even despite his permanent apostasy; it may be identical with the *quiddam conjugale*, the "certain conjugal something," that remains in the souls of separated Christian spouses and keeps them married until one of them dies; it remains in their souls because both are members of the metaphoric body of Christ. The sacramentum was in Adam's and Eve's marriage as a foreshadowing of the union of Christ and the Church.

What Augustine certainly provided were the ingredients of a theology of the marital sacrament that invited ensuing centuries' theologians to work them into a coherent teaching. Our task is to find out how they did so, and with what success.

NOTES

1. *De Viduis*, Chapt. 4, PL 16:242.
2. Epistola 42, ad Siricium, PL 16:1124.
3. *De Virginibus*, Book 1, Chapt. 7, PL 16:198.
4. *De Abraham*, Book 1, Chapt. 9, PL 14:473.
5. *Expositio Sancti Evangelii Secundum Lucam*, Book 8, no. 1470, PL 15:1765.
6. *Op. cit.*, Book 8, Chapt. 9, PL 15:1855–1856.
7. *De Viduis*, Chapt. 14, PL 16:273.
8. *Hexaemeron*, Book 5, no. 6, PL 14:232–233.
9. *Expositio Sancti Evangelii Secundum Lucam*, Book 7, no. 1458, PL 15:1752.
10. *Expositio in Psalmum 118*, no. 20, PL 15:1300.
11. *Exhortatio Virginitatis*, Chapt. 4, PL 16:342.
12. *Op. cit.*, Chapt. 6, PL 16:316.
13. Book 1, nos. 1281–1282, PL 15:1551–1552.
14. Book 1, Chapt. 4, PL 14:431.
In Chapter 7 of the same book he returned to the thought. But he is no clearer about which sacrament a married man loses if he commits adultery:

> We know that God is present as presider and custodian of marriage, one who does not allow another's bed to be defiled. One who does defile it sins against God whose law he violates, and he loses grace. Therefore too, because he sins against God he loses the companionship of the heavenly sacrament.

That the sin of adultery entails the loss of grace suggests that the sacrament in question is baptism.

15. No. 1472, PL 15:1767–1768.

Ambrose found another way in which a Christian husband and wife may act out the *sacramentum,* and reciprocally a demand that the *sacramentum* puts on the wife. She ought not seek out the man for her husband, but must let him find her. This is because the Church did not seek out Christ as a spouse, but he found her. (*De Abraham, loc. cit.,* Col. 454)

16. But Ambrose's indecision about the locus of the sacrament shows up in his essay, *De Paradiso.* He explains why, in the Pauline metaphor, the wife has the husband as her head. It is because the first wife was the spouse who first succumbed to the tempter in Eden. Worse still, she led her husband into sin. That is why she is put under his rule, his headship. Yet their relationship was the *magnum sacramentum,* as Paul said (Chapt. 4 PL 14:284).

Ambrose uses the first wife's alleged initiative in sinning to account for the wife's being the only spouse who is veiled during the wedding ceremony. In doing so he also adds a mite to the theology of sacramental imagery in marriage. The wife's sinfulness calls for her to keep her head covered in the presence of the bishop, who represents Christ in the Church: "The woman should have her head veiled because she is not the image of God. The veiling will show her subjection (I Cor. 11). And because it was through her that sin was started up, she ought to maintain this sign of subjection in the Church. Out of reverence for the bishop she ought not be bareheaded, because he represents the person of Christ. So because of the primeval guilt she should be seen in subjection before the bishop who is the vicar of Christ the judge." (*In Epistolam ad Corinthios,* Chapt. 11, PL 16:1292)

17. I have drawn from W. van Roo, *De Sacramentis in Genere,* Romae, 1957, pp. 21–35, as a partial source of this information.

18. *De Baptismo contra Donatistas Libri Septem,* Book 3, Chapt. 10, PL 43:

19. *Contra Epistolam Parmeniani Libri Tres,* Chapt. 13, no. 28, PL :70–71.

20. *Ibid.*

It is most significant for Augustine's later and developed theology of the sacraments that he here calls the permanently effective military brand a "character": ". . . numquid homine liberato atque correcto character ille repetitur, ac non potius agnitus approbatur!" Yet nowhere will he call a character the analogue in a married person to the character in a person baptized or ordained—the analogue that keeps spouses married to one another despite their permanent separation.

21. Epistola 55, PL 33:204–205.

22. Epistola 98, PL 33:359–360.

23. *De Baptismo contra Donatistas* . . . , Book 5, Chapt. 21, PL 43:191.

24. *Opus imperfectum contra Julianum,* Book 6, Chapt. 30, PL 45:1582.

25. *Loc. cit.*

26. *De Bono Conjugali,* Chapt. 9, PL 40:380.

27. *De Bono Viduitatis,* Chapt. 6, PL 40:435–436.

28. *De Bono Conjugali,* Chapt. 15, PL 40:385.

29. *Op. cit.,* Chapt. 3, PL 40:375.

30. *Op. cit.,* Chapt. 10, PL 40:381.

31. *De Genesi ad Litteram,* Book 3, Chapt. 21, PL 44:555.

32. *Opus imperfectum contra Julianum,* Book 4, Chapt. 11, PL 44:765.

33. *De Civitate Dei,* Book 14, Chapt. 26, PL 41:428.

34. Cf *De Nuptiis et Concupiscentia,* Book 1, Chapt. 20–26, PL 44:426–431.

35. *Ibid.*

36. *De Peccato Originali,* Book 2, Chapt. 37, PL 44:406.

37. *De Nuptiis et Concupiscentia,* Book 1, Chapt. 24, PL 44:429.

38. . . . *contra Julianum,* Book 4, Chapt. 10, PL 44:765.

39. *De Nuptiis et Concupiscentia,* Book 1, Chapt. 5, PL 44:416–417.

40. . . . *contra Julianum,* Book 2, Chapt. 7, PL 44:687. See also *De Bono Conjugali,* Chapt. 6, PL 40:378.

41. *De Peccato Originali,* Book 2, Chapt. 38, PL 44:406–407.

42. *De Bono Conjugali,* Chapt. 10, PL 40:381.

43. *Op. cit.,* Chapt. 3, PL 40:375.

44. *Op. cit.,* Chapt. 6, PL 40:377.

45. Chapt. 24, PL 40:394.

46. Book 9, Chapt. 7, PL 34:397.

47. Book 2, Chapt. 39, PL 44:404.

48. *De Bono Conjugali,* Chapt. 3, PL 40:375.

49. *De Genesi ad Litteram,* Book 9, Chapt. 7, PL 34:397.

Toward the end of his life, when writing his *Retractationes,* Augustine deemed it useful to reiterate this disclaimer: "I also wrote two books to the illustrious Count Valerius after hearing that the Pelagians had written something or other to him about my claiming that I condemned marriage by relating it to original sin.

"The title of these books is *Marriage and Concupiscence.* I defended the goodness of marriage lest it be thought that concupiscence of the flesh and that law in the members rebelling against the law of the mind was a vice inherent in it, when, really, married chastity puts the evil sex appetite to good use in order to have children." (Book 2, Chapt. 53, PL 32:651)

50. *De Bono Conjugali,* Chapt. 17, PL 40:386.

51. *De Conjugiis Adulterinis ad Pollentium Libri Duo,* Book I, Chapt. 4, PL 40:453.

52. *Op. cit.,* Book 1, Chapt. 6, PL 40:474.

53. *Op. cit.,* Book 1, Chapt. 13, PL 40:459.

54. *De Bono Conjugali,* Chapt. 12, PL 40:383

55. *De Conjugiis Adulterinis,* Book 2, Chapt. 8, PL 40:475.

56. *De Bono Conjugali,* Chapt. 11, PL 40:382.

57. *Op. cit.,* Chapt. 3, PL 40:375.

58. *Op. cit.,* Chapt. 6, PL 40:378.

59. *Op. cit.,* Chapt. 8, PL 40:379.

60. *Op. cit.,* Chapt. 11. PL 40:382.

61. *Op. cit.,* Chapt. 24, PL 40:394–395.

62. *Soliloquia,* Book 1, Chapt. 10, PL 32:878.

63. *De Nuptiis et Concupiscentia,* Book 1, Chapt. 5, PL 44:416.

64. *Sermo* 354, no. 9, PL 39:1567–1568.

65. *De Sancta Virginitate,* Chapt. 11, PL 40:401.

66. *Op. cit.,* Chapt. 44, PL 40:422.

67. *Ibid.,* Col. 424.

68. PL 40:378.

69. *Ibid.*

70. *Ibid.*

71. *Loc. cit.*, Col. 384

The same use reappears in Chapter 17 where Augustine says that the intercourse of the patriarchs was in accord with the *sacramentum* of their time, i.e. with the foreshadowing role of the old law's holy men (Col. 587). A few lines later he calls this foreshadowing work the *nuntia futurorum*, the announcing of what was to come.

72. *Loc. cit.*, Col. 385.

73. *Loc. cit.*, Cols. 387–388.

74. *Loc. cit.*, Col. 394.

75. *De Conjugiis Adulterinis*, Book 1, PL 40:451–470; Book 2, PL 40:471–486.

76. *Op. cit.*, Col. 473.

77. *Loc. cit.*

78. *De Nuptiis et Concupiscentia ad Valerium Comitem Libri Duo* (Book 1, PL 44:413–438; Book 2, PL 44:437–474).

79. Augustine tells of this in his *Retractationes*, Book 2, Chapt. 53, PL 32:651.

80. PL 44:420.

81. *Ibid.*

82. *Ibid.*

The Latin text here is "Ita manet inter viventes quiddam conjugale, quod nec separatio, nec cum altero copulatio possit auferre." Some manuscript editors' apparent dissatisfaction with the vagueness of *quiddam conjugale* ("a certain marital something") prompted them to insert a clarifying substantive that makes the first clause read "Ita manet inter viventes quoddam vinculum conjugale. . . ." In reference to marriage *vinculum* meant then, as it still does, "the marital bond." Thus changed, the clause claims "a certain marital bond. . . ." Augustine repeats the thought with only minimal added exactness in his *Contra Julianum*, Book 5: "I have pointed out that there ought to be in marriage, in addition to the fidelity the spouses owe one another, and offspring, a third good. It is found especially among the people of God. It is a certain sacrament (*aliquod sacramentum*). It forbids divorce even to that spouse who cannot obey." (Chapter 12, PL 44:810)

83. *Op. cit.*, Cols. 424–428.

84. *Ibid.*, Col. 424.

85. *Ibid.*

86. *Ibid.*

87. *Op. cit.*, Col. 427.

88. *Op. cit.*, Col. 443.

89. PL 34:397.

90. PL 44:404.

BIBLIOGRAPHY

Saint Augustine: *Treatises on Marriage and Other Subjects.* edited by Roy J. Deferrari, N.Y., 1955; *The Fathers of the Church in New Translation.* Washington, The Catholic University of America, Volume 15.

Børresen, Kari E.: *Subordination and Equivalence: The Nature and Role of Women in Augustine and Thomas Aquinas.* Translated from the Revised French Original by Charles H. Talbot. Washington, University Press of America, 1981.

Brown, Peter: "Sexuality and Society in the Fifth Century A.D.: Augustine and Julian of Eclanum," in *Tria Cordia: Scritti in onore di Arnaldo Momigliano,* Biblioteca di Athanaeum 1. Como, Edizione New Press, 1983.

Evans, Gilliam: *Augustine on Evil.* Cambridge and N.Y., Cambridge University Press, 1987.

Mackin, Theodore: *Marriage in the Catholic Church: Divorce and Remarriage.* N.Y./Ramsey, Paulist Press, 1984. Chapter 9: "Jerome and Augustine."

Miles, Margaret Ruth: *Augustine on the Body.* Missoula, Scholars' Press, 1979.

7. THE SACRAMENT IN AN AGE OF TRANSITION

It is only a seeming paradox that during the epoch to be examined in this chapter we find the most far-reaching changes in the socio-political condition of the Roman Catholic Church but simultaneously the slightest development in its theology and discipline of marriage. A society in turmoil is not the setting for the patient meditation and discussion needed to extend in an institution the theological understanding that in turn produces the innovative legislation in its regard. Legislation in such a society seeks to hold fast, to brace established structures and conduct against collapse. Thus it was that the five and a half centuries from the end of the patristic age until the mid-morning of scholasticism at the start of the thirteenth century saw little development in the understanding of marriage. Legislation for it there was aplenty during these centuries. But it was legislation fitted to a theology about where Augustine left it when he completed *De Nuptiis et Concupiscentia* in 421. More than that, it was a legislation needed for a Catholic society trying to assimilate a huge new population clinging stubbornly to old tribal ways.

The forces that destroyed the Hellenic-Roman civilization that nested the first Christian theology of marriage are well known: genocide from within because the lettered leisure class, addicted to pleasure, refused to reproduce its own in sufficient numbers; the migration of the great tribes across the western empire—Visigoths, Ostrogoths, Vandals, Huns, Teutons—seeking the amenities of the higher civilization but changing it as they came and returning it to a primitive form of itself; crusading Islam that in the seventh and eighth centuries destroyed the Catholic civilizations of Syria, Palestine, Egypt, north Africa and most of Spain, and in the destruction included the most prolific centers of Christian thought, Alexandria and Antioch.

Italy too shared abundantly the turmoil of these centuries, as the peninsula took the shock of successive invasions, the Arian Ostrogoths at the beginning of the fifth century, the pagan Huns in the middle of it. Justinian's imperial army from the eastern empire invaded the peninsula in 535 to take it back from the Ostrogoths. In the process he established a Byzantine semi-control that was to harass the popes and to war for two centuries with the Lombards from the north only to lose that control to them in the end. The papacy meanwhile produced very few great men, with Gregory I (590–604) and Nicholas I (858–867) the only two who live in memory. The rest were mediocre men caught up in the peninsula's political struggles, and struggling themselves to free the office from interference by Italian factions, from domination by Byzantine emperors and exarchs, by Lombard Catholic kings and by Carolingian emperors.

When Pope Stephen II in 751 approved Pepin's palace revolt and overthrow of the last of the Merovingian kings of the Franks, and then in 754 invited him to bring his army to free Italy from Lombard control, he moved decisively, and perhaps unwittingly, in two directions. The papal rule of Rome and central Italy was solidified (but thanks only to its Frankish protector) and started on its long ambition to establish an empire of all the Catholic world. And Catholic power and planning took a decisive step northward across the Alps. For all the ensuing centuries until our own the Church that had been culturally first Palestinian-Jewish, then Hellenic-Roman successively through Syria, Asia Minor, Egypt, Greece, Italy, North Africa and Spain, became equally European—and often more than equally.

It was not that the Church had to start over in Europe. Across the English channel there was already a Celtic church three and a half centuries in existence and energetic enough to send its missionaries across Scotland, down through Europe and into Italy as far south as Bobbio. The Anglo-Saxon invasion had already destroyed a Roman church among the Britons; but with the arrival of the Benedictine Augustine and forty monks in 597 the conversion of England had begun again. But not until a century later did Willibrord and his eleven companions begin the conversion of the Frisians in northwest Europe. And not until then did Boniface begin to bring order to the scattered German communities converted earlier by Irish missionaries.

Out of this massive moving and incessant fragmenting came a condition of the Church that in turn conditioned the Catholic teaching and legislation for marriage. Communication with any one magisterial and legislative center was made slow and uncertain. In its place regional authorities legislated for marriage independently and often idiosyncratically, as we shall see presently that Frankish and German councils of bishops did. Where a central authority did legislate effectively, it was frequently in the person of a layman ruling monarchically in his territory and taking for granted that the care of religious and moral matters therein was his. Charlemagne was the arch-example of this.

To whatever thinness the flood of untested converts in the fourth and fifth centuries had diluted the once-stringent sexual-marital morality of the earliest Christianity, at least its ideals were still in place where Roman law ruled, and were with a few exceptions defended by the authorities. Slavery had been suppressed as an institution in the fifth century. With it went the disenfranchisement of the empire's huge slave population from marriage. Their institutionalized concubinage—the *contubernium* to which they were limited by law—was abolished. All could now marry, bear children, and keep and nurture them. Thanks to the custom of marriage *communi consensu* men and women could choose their own spouses. Wives were granted equal rights with their husbands, even if the equality was often honored in the breach. Divorce was controlled by authority. And divorce by one spouse's repudiating the other could be executed only after the spouse's proving against the other one of a set of causes listed in Chapter 15 of Justianian's *Novella 22*. Meanwhile bishops and other teachers in the Church railed against this heavy residue of pagan divorce legislation in a supposedly Christian society, as they did against the long taken-for-granted infidelity of husbands and punished it with severe penances.

But north of the Alps moral habits were of a kind that inspired Gregory of Tours, in his *History of the Franks,* to refer to these people as monsters. The habits he had in mind that were grafted in marriage were, no doubt, incestuous relationships begun before marriage, continued despite it and sometimes turned into presumed marriages; children put into marriage with no choice of their own, with the nearly inevitable consequence of concubinage later accompanying the marriage; easy divorce by dismissal of the wife for no more than suspicion of her adultery; wives forced into adultery and even prostitution in order to gain cause for dismissal; girls forced into marriage by kidnap and rape.

Among the Germanic tribes divorce was fitted to their conception of marriage. This was the conveyance of a woman (of her *mundium*) from the authority of her father to that of her husband. By this transfer the latter gained absolute authority over her. For her adultery he could kill her or have her killed. He could dismiss her without cause provided he paid her family a compensatory fine. Among these tribes the Burgundian Code, the *Lex Gundalati* of c. 517, allowed the husband to dismiss the wife without compensation if he could prove against her adultery, poisoning or the violation of sepulchres. The same law prescribed that a wife who tried to dismiss or abandon her husband could be punished by drowning.

The conduct most difficult to eradicate and therefore the longest persisting was in great part a reaction of young people to parentally arranged marriages. This was the clandestine marriage, couples' creating their marriages apart from and against the wills of their fathers, without witnesses and therefore with no possible verification. They could marry in this way despite bypassing the prescribed ceremonies of betrothal and wedding, first by exploiting the provision of Roman law, if they lived under its jurisdiction, that couples could marry *communi consensu,* by no more than marital consent expressed to one another. They could do this in the presence of no other persons. Or they could marry clandestinely even in the presence of others if these were not authorized witnesses. In any case, the marriage, although valid, was not legitimate.

Or they could exploit a custom among the Germanic peoples that held a man and woman to be married if they had intercourse after having promised to marry. A young man and woman intent on not being forced into a marriage of the parents' choosing and on keeping their freedom to marry whom they wished could falsify a confession of intercourse after promising to marry, and could later recant the confession. It was a strategy for keeping freedom sometimes hazardous enough to bring on parental punishment by death.

In listing such an inventory of sexual-marital conduct as we have here we are not pointing at and accusing peoples still pagan. We are taking note of the conduct of at least nominal Christians, conduct persisting among them still one and two centuries after taking on the name of Christian. The over-arching reason for its persistence was the practice of tribal conversion. In earlier centuries, in the churches of the Mediterranean basin, when becoming a Christian put one at great risk, conversion had been a long and testing process. And where a man judged himself still unable to live the demanding Christian sexual morality, he did what the young Augustine did; he delayed full enrollment in the Church by prolonging his catechumenate for years.

But when Clovis, king of the Franks, accepted baptism from Bishop Remigius in 496 for the sake of political advantage, his people accepted it with him after little or no preparation. Some three centuries later Charlemagne converted the still-pagan Saxons east of the Rhine at the point of the sword, offering them the simple choice of baptism or death.

Mixed with these primitive abuses was a disagreement both theoretical and practical that we have already noticed. According to Roman custom and law a couple needed do no more to create their marriage than to manifest their reciprocal *affectus maritalis,* their will to be married to one another, by a reciprocal expression of consent. They could lodge this expression in a multi-step ceremony if they wished, but the ceremony was in no sense needed for creating the marriage. The European peoples, on the other hand, had long-established ceremonies mandatory for creating a marriage. Since salient parts of this were executed by two sets of parents, as the exchange of dowry and wedding gifts had to be, the ceremony served as an instrument for parental control of their children's marriages.

The European peoples were adamantly opposed to accepting the Roman way of marrying and thereby losing that control. The Mediterranean peoples living the Roman tradition were equally unyielding to the European tradition. This was the issue, the dispute, that was to drag on the longest in the western Catholic Church without resolution. How it tangled with the abuse of clandestine marriages is evident. The European multi-step creation of marriage closed down the possibility of clandestinity except for the one crucial gap we have already seen. The Roman way opened unhindered access to clandestinity.

The Teachers of the European Peoples

The work of civilizing and Christianizing the baptized barbarians of Europe was taken up by the zealous among their own bishops, by the monks of St. Benedict, and by the masters in the schools started up by both. Some of the early masters wrote in order to teach, and we have multiple examples of what they wrote. The most notable among them were Alcuin (735–804), whom Charlemagne invited from Northumbria to open his palace school at Aix-la-Chapelle; Rabanus Maurus (776–856), abbot of the great monastery at Fulda and later archbishop of Mainz; Walafrid Strabo (c. 808–849), Rabanus' student, tutor of Charles the Bald, then abbot of Reichenau; Paschase Radbert (785–860) of the monastery at Corbie; and Hincmar (806?–882), archbishop of Rheims and consultor-critic of Frankish kings. Given the people whom they taught and the abuses they fought to remove, some of the issues that had exercised Tertullian, Ambrose and Jerome—remarriage in widowhood and the superiority of consecrated virginity over marriage—got little of their attention. The work of such teachers was broken off and even destroyed by the Norse and Danish invasions in the ninth century and by the Magyars in the tenth; it was hampered continually by princes and lesser nobles who preferred their own permissive Christianity, and by the clergy whom they appointed and controlled.

Eventually the work of civilizing and Christianizing succeeded to a reasonable degree. The long, quiet work of the episcopal and monastic schools was the principal agent of this success until the universities grew out of them and took up the work on a larger scale. The greatest of them, Oxford and Bologna, started early in the twelfth century. Paris grew from the school of Notre Dame Cathedral at the turn of that century. Cambridge came a century later, Salamanca in 1227. The same work of education and correction was concentrated and accelerated in three general reforms of the European church: the Carolingian at the end of the eighth century and beginning of the ninth, the Cluniac in the middle of the tenth, and the Gregorian at the end of the eleventh.

We will divide the examination of this epoch into two parts, marked off by significant junctures in the treatment of marriage during the five and a half centuries in question: Part one, in this chapter, from the end of the patristic period until the Gregorian reform; part two, in the following chapter, from that reform until just before the apogee of scholastic theology in the middle of the thirteenth century.

Our curiosity will bear on a number of elements or a process through time that was in its first part a correction of a primitive and mistaken estimation of marriage and a reform of the conduct flowing from it, and in its second part the early scholastics' reawakening and development of the fathers' theory of marriage and the sacrament therein after its five-century dormancy.

Fundamental among these elements was the understanding of marriage itself, the matrix of the sacrament. Did this change from where Ambrose, Augustine and the others had left it? The answer to this question we shall find almost exclusively outside any specific treatment of marriage. Only one such treatise was composed, and only at the end of the period in question, by Hugh of St. Victor at Paris. We must search elsewhere, in the period's answers to the questions handed down to it by the fathers.

Thus is marriage itself good? If so, only in the ideal set by divine intention, although no longer in actual life? Or despite sin endemic in the human race is goodness still found somewhere in lived marriages? If so, of what does it consist? Is even holiness available in marriage itself? If it is, does this holiness include the sexual conduct that is specific to marriage? Or is this conduct an enemy of holiness that must be subdued? What freedom, if any, do couples have for ending their marriages, especially where these are sterile or simply a misery? Accepting the fathers' bequest that there is a *sacramentum* in Christian marriage, what is this? Does it have a place in the Christian spouses' gaining holiness? a role holding them in their marriages and faithful therein to one another? In their long work of correcting the grave abuses of marriage and marital sexuality we listed above, did the teachers and legislators of this period appeal to the demands of its sacrament and use them as norms of correction?

The Understanding of Marriage

We look first at the understanding of marriage in the minds of the period's writers, before going on to examine what the authorities did to carry through the reform of attitude and conduct. We shall see that what the latter did was to take control of marriage by bringing it under ecclesiastical legislation and jurisdiction and by folding it gradually into the Church's liturgy. But it is helpful to know first what they thought they were appropriating under legislation and jurisdiction and into liturgy.

This contains no surprises. The writer-teachers do hardly more than repeat the opinions they read in the fathers. This is so because their standard method of teaching was to explain the pertinent biblical passages, to write a *commentarium,* an *enarratio* or *expositio* on this or that book. In doing so they mainly repeated what the fathers had said before them. Or they later gathered the sayings of the fathers themselves, formed anthologies of their *sententiae,* and still later arranged and commented on them.

But it is useful to retreat a few years, to return to the last of the Western fathers, because what he wrote about marriage, however briefly, both served as a bridge to the early medieval mind and exemplified that mind's intent to repeat the fathers faithfully but do little more. Isidore of Seville was born c. 560 in a Spain that was a Visigothic kingdom by then securely converted from Arian to orthodox Catholic Christianity. He succeeded his brother Leander as archbishop of Seville in the year 600, and held that office until his death in 636.[1] His essay that provides the most relevant passage concerning marriage is *De Ecclesiasticis Officiis.* The title designates not exclusively "ecclesiastical offices" in our sense of archbishop, canon, pastor, et al., but "dutiful functions." It thus includes not only those just mentioned, but marriage as well. Isidore completed the essay in two books: on the Mass, liturgical prayers, festivals and feast days in Book I; on duties and states in the Church in Book II.

Chapter 20 in this Book II is *De conjugatis,* "Concerning the Married." Like his predecessors Isidore was pessimistic about marriage within and despite an inclusive doctrinal optimism. His optimisms and pessimisms were the familiar ones. He took for granted that God had invented marriage in the garden of Eden when he gave Eve to Adam as a helpmate, and said to them, "Increase and multiply, and fill the earth." Thus marriage was born in the time of happiness, before the trials and sorrows that followed on the banishment from the garden. And at first Eve was rather a comforting companion to Adam (a *solatium*) than a wife, since it was not until after the two had been expelled from the garden that they had their first intercourse.

> 1. The law of nature for the married dates from the beginning. For God formed Adam and gave Eve to him as a helper, with the command to procreate, saying "Increase and multiply, and fill the earth" (Genesis 1). But the woman was at first formed more for companionship than for marriage, until their disobedience should drive them both from the paradise wherein obedience had kept them. It was after their departure from that blessed home that the man was driven to know his wife, as the Book of Genesis says, "And Adam knew his wife, and she conceived, and bore a son" (Genesis 4).[2]

Isidore is thus clear that what marriage is for is offspring, and that the intercourse that produces this is not lodged within that part of marriage that is its *solatium*. But even though the producing of offspring belongs to the time of marriage's trials and tribulations, honorable intercourse has its fruits in holy offspring. Thus marriage is good in itself. It is sinful not in itself but only circumstantially. Even so, its goodness does not equal that of either widowhood or vowed continence, since both of these do without intercourse.

> 2. Therefore marriage preceded the labor that was inflicted on them; the tribulations and pains they were to suffer lay still in

the future when they formed their covenant. Their burden awaited them later in procreation; the sentence was pronounced on one who was to give birth in the future. "In pain," he said, "and in grief will you bear children" (Genesis 3). And we know well how many and different tragedies and sorrows came upon them who were created in this way. Hence in his preaching the Apostle said, "But they will have troubles in married life" (I Cor. 7). But the undefiled bedroom and its honored marriage bed are not without their fruit (Hebr. 13). For the heritage of holiness and honored virginity come from marriage. Therefore we neither deem marriage sinful nor do we hold it equally as good as the continence of virginity and of widowhood.[3]

A first and preliminary consideration of the sacrament enters when Isidore argues for monogamy in marriage. He says that the evidence that God intends marriage's monogamy is found in two places. The first is in his making only one man and one woman the partners in the first and permanently exemplary marriage. The second is in the *sacramentum Christi*, which is the spiritual marriage of Christ and the Church. Here too there are but one husband and one bride. He assumes that the spiritual marriage is, in form, normative for all marriages. And it is probable that in calling this marriage a *sacramentum* he intends on one hand a predication akin to that in his calling the marriage of Adam and Eve an *exemplum* (an example), and the other an assertion of the one-to-one commitment of the spouses, in the sense that Augustine intended for the *sacramentum*.

> 3. Marriage is good only in itself. It becomes evil through what is accessory to it, through those things that the Apostle pointed out, "But he who has a wife is preoccupied with the things of the world," and "Because of the sin of fornication let each man have his own wife" (I Cor. 7). That a man is not joined with many women but each with one, this we have from the example of the first and divinely established union. For when God formed the man and saw that he needed a suitable companion, he took one of his ribs and made it into one woman. Thus Adam and Eve, made one by marriage, validated its form according to this first and primal will of God. So too in accord with the spiritual marriage of one Christ and one Church, there is to be but one husband and one wife, and this according to both the record of their origin and the *sacramentum* of Christ.[4]

This interpretation of Isidore's understanding of the *sacramentum* in marriage is supported by his answer to the question asking why men cannot now have multiple wives, since the patriarchs of Israel had them.

He repeats Jerome's answer, that this would still be permitted if there were still men who were types of a future sacrament involving this multiplicity, men who would pre-image a marriage of one man and multiple spouses. Although it is not exactly clear to what Isidore refers as this future sacrament, it is apparently the Christ-Church "marriage" that involves Christ's union with the multitude of the faithful.

> Polygamous marriages began only with the curse on man. Lamech was the first to marry two women and thus to bring about three in one flesh. If you say, however, that the patriarchs had several wives simultaneously, therefore we should be allowed several; I reply that surely this should follow if there still remain among us any types of some *sacramentum* yet to come in the future, a foreshadowing which might image multiple marriages. But the Apostle advises second marriages [only] because of unchastity (I Cor. 7); for it is better to then marry one man than to fornicate with many in order to satisfy lust. All too often the reason for marrying is not religious but sinful.[5]

The Earliest Medieval Writers

We will return later to this passage in order to draw from it a reliable picture of the wedding ceremony in seventh-century Spain, as well as an estimation there and at that time of the place of the sacrament in marriage. But what we have read thus far contains in concentrate just about all that will be said by the writers of the next few centuries— except for the one man already mentioned, Hugh of St. Victor. Let us see now the themes from the fathers that these writers repeated, supplying in each case one or two of the better examples of their repetition.

> *Marriage as instituted by God, in its ideal state, is good.*
>
> We must realize that marriage is clean and holy. It is celebrated at God's command and involves nothing base, nothing dishonorable. If married persons admit something shameful, dishonorable, indecent, the fault is not in marriage but with men.[6]
>
> It is not as though men are conceived in sin because it is sinful for married persons to have intercourse. That chaste activity involves no fault in one who is married. It is God who designed that there would be marital intercourse when He first created man and woman.[7]
>
> "And he blessed them and said, 'Increase and multiply and fill the earth and subdue it.' " This multiplication of human beings and filling of the earth was to be accomplished only by the union of man and woman. So if it is by God's gift that the human race grows and is multiplied, how worthy of condemna-

tion are those who forbid marriage and despise the divine plan as though it were devised by the devil. So marriage, which the gift of heavenly blessing has instituted for propagating the human race and filling the earth, is not to be condemned.[8]

The life of consecrated virginity is preferable to marriage; the latter is the intrinsically inferior state of life.

But more to be honored, more worthy of the divine blessing is virginity which, after the earth is full, desires with pure soul and body to follow the Lamb wherever he goes and to sing the new song that no one else can sing. . . .

For God and Our Lord, who in the first age of the newborn world formed a woman from the side of the man to teach us that the earth was to be filled by their union with each other, has Himself in the last age of history taken manhood from the flesh of the Virgin . . . to prove that He loves the glory of virginity more than marriage.[9]

The conviction about the superiority of virginity over marriage was carried through this age and emphasized by the legend of St. John the apostle. It told that he was the bridegroom at the wedding feast in Cana of Galilee (Jn 2:1–12). On meeting Jesus and witnessing his miraculous changing of water into wine, he left his bride before consummating their marriage, thus preserving his virginity, and followed Jesus as his beloved disciple. Or according to an alternative version, he left his bride as a fiancée, before concluding the marriage with her—but keeping his virginity, of course, in this case as well.

But marriage too, despite its lesser rank, is God's gift; a Christian who elects it does so as called by God.

To lend his approval to the choice of every rank and yet show the different merit of each, He deigns to be born of the stainless womb of Mary the Virgin, is blessed soon after His birth by the prophetic voice of Anna the widow, as a young man now is invited by those who are celebrating a wedding and honors them with the presence of His power.[10]

By a comparison with the body he shows, not the nature of the members but that the functions are different, and that no one ought to be anxious about the function he has since all are quickened by the same spirit.[11]

Each one who comes to the faith should remain in the state in which he has been called and realize that this state is a call from God.[12]

We have put virginity over all but in such a way that we still recognize the order of marriage.[13]

Christian couples ought to abstain from sexual intercourse for the sake of prayer; and after intercourse they should abstain a while from the Eucharist and not enter the church.

[The married who have recently had sexual intercourse], coming irreverently into church are not only so indiscreet as to come up as far as the holy altar, but even think nothing of receiving the body and blood of Christ. Let them understand that they should enter Christ's church and receive His body and blood only with a clean body and a pure heart.[14]

Therefore when the bride and groom have received the nuptial blessing they ought not have intercourse immediately. But they should honor the sacrament and spend the first night watching and praying with lighted candles in a church. For we read that Sara, the daughter of Raguel, married seven husbands, who, seeking to approach her with lust immediately on the first night, were suffocated by demons.[15]

"This will keep anything from hindering you in prayer": And Paul says, "Do not deny one another except perhaps by agreement and for a time, in order to devote yourselves to prayer" (I Cor. 7). He reminds us that prayer is hindered by the marital duty, because as often as one renders the debt to his wife he is unable to pray. One ought therefore never concede to marriage's demands lest any hour of one's life be closed to the prayer to which I am urged to devote myself always.[16]

Sexual intercourse is unclean and degrades a person.

With what intention marriage is to be celebrated is indicated when there is added "There was a wedding in Cana of Galilee." For Cana means "zeal", and Galilee means "transmigration". With this zeal ought we to take wives, not so that we may abide with them in carnal pleasure [*luxuria*], but in order with them to escape that pleasure and migrate to chastity. Let us flee vice and pass over to virtue. Let us spurn earthly things and pass over to the heavenly. Hence the Apostle says, "But because of fornication—understand 'in order to avoid'—let each man have his own wife" (I Cor. 7). For marriage has its chastity. But those sin, my brothers, who marry not with right intention, but because of lust, because of beauty, because of wealth.[17]

There would be no carnal pleasure in intercourse were it not for original sin.

A heart that has been conquered by carnal pleasure is accustomed to reason thus: "Why do you not linger for a bit in your sensual pleasure, since you know not what the future holds? You ought not waste this your desire, since you know not how quickly it may pass away. For if God did not want us to enjoy the pleasure of intercourse, he would not have created men and women from the very beginning of the human race."

But as divine authority attests, God did not create men and women so that they might enjoy carnal desire or live in the delights of the flesh. He created them so that they might with the divine blessing come together to produce children. And if there had been no transgression of God's command, no one would experience carnal pleasure in the intercourse of the married. Carnal pleasure is an uncleanness of the body which comes from uncontrolled lust and the weakness of the soul which gives in to the sin of the flesh. For a sin may be committed in three ways: by suggestion, by delectation and by consent.[18]

If man had not sinned, he would never be driven on by the ardor of pleasure. Just as we turn the eyes here and there . . . so would we use the genital organs not for pleasure but for begetting children.[19]

Sexual intercourse is without sin only if it is motivated exclusively by the desire for begetting children.

9. Among the ancients, when women sought husbands, they looked for four qualities in them: virtue, family, comeliness, piety. When husbands sought wives they looked for three qualities in them: fertility, good morals, beauty. But now not family nor good habits but rather riches are what women seek. Nor does it matter how modest a woman is, but how beautiful—the kind who stirs up lustful desire and elicits the sighs of many. The beautiful woman (as a certain wise man once said) is very quickly loved but very feebly controlled, because so many desire her.

The true marriages are those wherein couples seek not pleasure but offspring. For marriage has been instituted not to serve the pleasures of the flesh but only in order to secure the fruit of offspring.

10. Indeed the marital stipulations themselves [*dotales tabulae*] show that a wife is taken in order to have children. Therefore when a person is more sexually active than needed for their procreation, he sins. Those who defile the chastity of the marital bed frequently by their incontinence have great need for daily prayer and almsgiving.[20]

A wife is a grievous burden, and marriage itself is such a burden.

A wife is a grievous burden, since husbands are not allowed to dismiss them nor may women dismiss their husbands, no matter how they may treat one another. . . . Each then must realize the risk he or she takes.[21]

The contract is of itself difficult to keep faithfully, because of the many miseries of the contracting parties and the infirmities, physical and moral, of two persons who are bound to come to each other's aid until death.[22]

Marriage can be a way to eternal salvation and to holiness.

A wife can gain salvation if she has begotten sons and raised them in the belief and service of Almighty God and led them on to the perfection of a good life. If she has been negligent in anything, she shall be saved in consideration of the work she constantly strove to do for them.[23]

Married life is not far from the world, but neither is it estranged from the joy of salvation.[24]

It does not follow that, if there is greater toil in one case than in another, there will thus be greater glory. Virginity is a greater good in itself than marriage, and yet some married people are of no less merit than some virgins.[25]

As His apostles He chose some married men, some continent, some virgins. And yet he placed St. Peter, a married man, over all the orders so that virgins would not grow proud or married persons despair of being able to arrive at that perfection which virgins achieve.[26]

Explicit Consideration of the Sacrament

When examining Augustine's speculation about the sacrament in marriage, we found that even within his indecision about identifying it, he thought it to be most probably the spouses' sworn commitments to one another—or their commitments singly to God, or even as a couple to God. What he noted only tentatively, that the sacrament lies perhaps in the Christian marriage's imaging the Christ-Church relationship, the medieval writers installed gradually at the heart of their theology of marriage. Our attention at this point turns to the earliest of these writers' contribution to the installing. Our curiosity asks what they thought the sacrament to be when they pondered it explicitly and formally.

Isidore of Seville, the earliest of them—too early in fact to belong properly among the medievals—took Augustine's thought barely an inch beyond where he found it. He explained, as we have already seen, that although men and women in his day married less often for the honorable motive of procreation and more frequently for the sinful motive of carnal pleasure, yet the reason for the priestly blessing of those marriages is the same as for God's blessing the first marriage before the fall. He blessed it for the double reason that he had created it to be an image of himself, and that he had given it the vocation to populate the earth.

5. That in the wedding itself the marriage is blessed by a priest, this was done by God too in the first condition of man. Thus it is written: "God made man; in the image of God he made him; male and female he created them, saying, 'Increase and multiply' " (Genesis 1). By this likeness there is now done in the Church what was then done in Paradise.[27]

When he closes in on an exact identification of the sacrament he cites the three *bona* of marriage canonized by Augustine. Again, they are *fides*, the sexual fidelity of the spouses; *proles*, the procreation that includes the loving acceptance and pious nurture of children; *sacramentum*, the inseparability of spouse from spouse, so that not even for the sake of *proles* can a man leave an infertile wife in order to take a second and fertile one.

Isidore acknowledges that a Christian marriage's sacrament lies in its resembling the relationship of Christ and the Church. But he does not say that this sacrament-resemblance constitutes the earthly marriage an image of the heavenly. He says rather that the resemblance lies in this, that just as Christ and the Church cannot be separated, neither can Christian husband and wife. Thus the inseparability found in the Christ-Church relationship that is found also in the Christian spouses' relationship is the latter's sacrament. It was for this reason that Paul, in 1 Corinthians 7, forbade wives to leave their husbands, and that Christ, in Matthew 19, forbade husbands to dismiss their wives except for their *fornicatio*, which is their adultery.

But when the wife commits adultery her husband may dismiss her. Indeed he must do so, as Jerome counseled, lest he cooperate in her sin. Isidore adds the startling mandate that she must be dismissed even if she is merely suspected of adultery. While he does not say expressly that this dismissal dissolves the marriage, he apparently thinks it does. The wife's adultery destroys her *affectus*, her will to be married; it sunders the two-in-one-flesh relationship with her husband.

There is said to be a *sacramentum* between the spouses because just as the Church cannot be separated from Christ neither can a wife from her husband (Ephesians 5). So what is found in Christ and the Church is found also in the union of each and every husband and wife—the inseparable *sacramentum*. . . . It is only adultery (as Jerome says) that destroys the wife's will to be married. Moreover, because she has torn the one flesh into two, and separated herself by her fornication, her husband must not keep her lest he too come under her curse; as the Scripture says "He who keeps an adulterous wife is stupid and irreligious" (Proverbs 18). So whenever a wife has been unfaithful, or may be suspected of infidelity, her husband may freely dismiss her.[28]

Thus for Isidore the earthly marriage is not created a sacrament by these commands that the spouses not separate, but the commands to not separate were given because marriage is already a sacrament. And he affirmed this sacramentality of all marriages, not only of Christian marriages.

We go now from Isidore to four writer-teachers whom we have already seen, selecting them as adequate representatives of the theologizing on marriage from the eighth through the eleventh centuries. These are Bede, Alcuin, Paschase Radbert and Rabanus Maurus. Theirs were not the most emphatic and memorable statements on marriage coming from these centuries. We will see those when we come to certain disciplinary decisions about the marrying, divorcing and remarrying of wanton Christian nobility. For now our interest is still fixed on the independent speculation of this time about the sacrament in marriage. When we examine select passages from the four named above, we will find out to what they referred when using the word "sacrament." This reference showed various meanings. To trace them we must venture a short distance here and there outside their statements about marriage.

Like a few of his contemporaries Bede wrote a book of reflections on the Old Testament's Song of Songs, his Allegoric Exposition on the Canticle of Canticles (*In Cantica Canticorum allegorica expositio*).[29] He shared their talent for linking imaginative, daring and even bizarre associations from the canticle's details to persons and things in the Church. But to be noted first are a few of his referents of the term *sacramentum*.

In his *Expositio* he joins his peers in taking for granted that the canticle's shepherd bridegroom is Christ and the peasant girl is the Church. He himself says that in the canticle Solomon set forth allegorically the *mysteria,* the hidden meanings, of Christ and the Church.[30] While setting an equivalency of the entire girl with the entire Church, he nevertheless makes discrete parts of the girl refer to discrete parts of the Church. Her eyes are allegorically the appointed teachers in the Church because the latter can peer into the hidden things of the Church's *sacramenta*.[31] It is reasonable to interpret the latter as the mysteries of the Christian faith. This is confirmed by his saying earlier in this Book 2 that believing Jews and Christians had and still have *disparia sacramenta,* disagreeing religious beliefs.

Shortly after making the allegoric identification of the Church's teachers with the girl's eyes he does the same with her breasts: ". . . in saying this he [Solomon] explains the *sacramentum* of the Church's breasts"—which are its teachers because they nourish her children with the milk of Christian doctrine.[32]

In Chapter 2 of Book 2 *sacramentum* designates the human signs of Jesus' divine nature: ". . . because when he was born into the world the Lord seemed, to those who believed in him, a sublime man. But with the passing of time he was revealed as true God. And now all the elect are, through the acknowledged *sacramentum* of his humanity, drawn to the contemplation of his divine glory."[33] In Book 3 he calls Jesus' death such a *sacramentum*.

Bede brings his *expositio* of the canticle only as close to marriage as to find a *sacramentum* in the metaphoric marriage of Christ and the Church. This reluctance to acknowledge in the canticle any reference to actual human marriage one finds among all the writers of the age who produced commentaries on the canticle. Despite its being in semitic origin a dramatic hymn extolling the sensual happiness of marriage, they refuse to let it interpret this happiness. Thus Bede says in Book 4, ". . . by these words the union of Christ and the Church is praised richly. He is the head of the body that is the Church; she is body to his head. Hence the Apostle said 'They shall be two in one flesh. This is a great mystery. And I refer here to Christ and the Church.' "[34] Not to be ignored here are Bede's identifying the "great mystery" with the Christ-Church union rather than with the marriage of a Christian husband and wife, and his preferring to keep the Greak *mystérion* in the clause rather than replace it with the Latin *sacramentum*.

Alcuin

We find a variety of referents of the word *sacramentum* in the writings of Alcuin. In his Epistola 36, to Arno in the year 769, he wrote: "There are in baptism three visible *sacramenta* and three invisible. The visible are the priest, the body and the water; the three invisible are the spirit, the soul and faith."[35]

He repeats the commonplace that the Church is the bride of Christ: "For the Church is the bride of Christ. And whoever seeks to violate her, to steal what belongs to her, will feel the vengeance of her spouse, Christ who is God."[36]

His metaphoric interpretation of the guests at the wedding feast of Cana, in his *Commentary on the Gospel of John,* Book 1, veers toward saying that the marriage of two believers is an image of the Christ-Church relationship. But he stops short and limits the affirmation to this marriage at Cana. And he sees the marital *sacramentum* not in that real-life marriage but in the metaphoric marriage of Christ and the Church.

> [The passage] describes accurately three orders of guests at this wedding which imaged the *sacramenta* of Christ and the Church. These orders are separated one from the other in dignity. For there are three orders of faithful making up the Church: the married, the continent and the teachers. The lowest order of guests rejoicing at this wedding of the heavenly spouse—living, that is, in the Church in faith and good works—are the faithful married.[37]

What a wandering career the word *sacramentum* enjoyed at this time is even more evident in the capitularies (the decrees) of Alcuin's royal pupil, Charlemagne. In his *Codex Diplomaticus* the *Capitulare Aquisgranense* of 805 (par. 9) says that an oath of allegience to himself is a *sacramentum,* as is a sworn commitment of his nobles one to another. In the *Capitula Presbyterorum* of 806 the Mass is a *sacramentum.* (Charlemagne there prescribes that water is always to be mixed in the chalice with the wine. He the emperor prescribes this!)[38]

Paschase Radbert predicated the term *sacramentum* in the same diverse ways. He interpreted Adam's encomium for marriage as prophecy, as God's revealing through him the *sacramentum* of marriage, in the words "For this reason a man leaves his father and mother and clings to his wife, etc. . . ."[39] He also interpreted Paul to have said, in Ephesians 5:32, "Hoc sacramentum magnum est . . ." because Christ is the head of his body the Church. It is his body with its members; and Christ and Church become two in one flesh. He goes on to explain this *sacramentum* in fuller and more unfocused detail. It consists of Christ's leaving the eternal Father, emptying himself, accepting the form of a slave (leaving also his mother, the synagogue), and clinging to his wife, the Church, which was formed from his side and is built up day by day into a wife, just as every newborn is formed from husband and wife.[40]

He does not think Ephesians refers the *sacramentum magnum* to Christian marriages. The only relevance to such marriages he sees in the phrase is that because the Christ-Church union is inseparable, no one must try to separate human marriages on earth. Indeed it is not clear what Paschase thinks the *sacramentum* to be, whether Adam's prophetic utterance, or his and Eve's relationship that foreshadowed the Christ-Church relationship, or the latter relationship itself, or perhaps the concatenation of all these. But plainly not included is the marriage of Christian husband and wife.

Rabanus Maurus

In his commentaries on the New Testament passages that deal with marriage Rabanus Maurus (776–856) broke from his contemporaries in places to offer singular interpretations of these passages. In his *Commentarium in Genesis* he does agree that God created the two sexes for the sake of procreation. He enriches the interpretation of the first couple as a primeval sacrament by suggesting that God produced the first woman in the way he did, by drawing her from Adam's side, in order to prefigure the birth of the Church and its sacraments from Christ's side as he died on the cross.[41]

His innovativeness appears earlier in this same commentary when he says that God's creating the first man and woman in his own image and likeness consisted not in creating both the male and the female. It consisted rather in designing rational intelligence into them. Because she has this intelligence the woman is as much this image and likeness as is the man. The same can be said of every woman who has ever lived.[42]

In his *Expositio in Epistolam ad Ephesios*[43] Rabanus presents a logic of equivalency that in the history of the theology of the sacrament has been the point of departure toward the conclusion that every marriage of two Christians is a sacrament. Rabanus is not the first nor the only one to set out this logic. But he does so with the innocent ambiguity that has made possible the eventual arrival at that conclusion. His own is the logic of "just as" that is later to be turned into a logic of "because." He reasons that a wife should be subject to her husband who is her head *just as* the Church is subject to her husband, Christ, who is her head. His statement of this contains a curious theory of natural law.

> Women are bound by the natural law to be subject to men because the man is the source [*auctor*] of the woman. . . . For *just as* [italics added] Christ is the head of the Church, so the husband is head of his wife. The Church took its origin from Christ and hence is subject to him, *just as* [italics added] the wife ought to be subject to her husband.[44]

The elision from a logic of equivalency—*just as*—to a logic of causation has occurred when theologians have reasoned that Christ's being the metaphoric head of his wife, the Church, *causes* the real husband to be head, or ruler, of his real wife. Rabanus does not here yield to the temptation, presuming he felt it at all, to shift from the logic of equivalency to this logic of causation.

His grip on reality is evident at two other points in this commentary. He notes that there is this difference between the Christ-Church relationship and that of a husband and wife, that in the latter the wife is of the same nature (*consubstantiva*) with her husband, whereas the Church can participate in Christ's existence not by nature but only by attribution (. . . *Ecclesia autem in nomine patet non in natura participari Christo*).

In the second point he shows an honest attention to the facts of Christian life that the otherwise Platonic mentality of his age did not when thinking and writing of a purely conceptual and idealized Church. He does this when he comments on verses 25–28 of Ephesians 5, and asks exactly when Christ will present his Church-bride to himself "glorious, with no stain or wrinkle." His answer is this:

> For when Paul says that Christ will present to himself not only a Church having no stain or wrinkle but also one that is glorious, he indicated clearly enough when it will in fact be "without stain or wrinkle or anything like that," namely when it is also glorious. Because it cannot now be called glorious when it is afflicted by so many evils, by so many scandals, by such a traffic of evil men, by the persecutions of the irreligious. And the fact

that kings minister to her makes her all the more tempting and her condition all the more perilous. But then she will be glorious when there happens what Paul said, "But when Christ is revealed—and he is your life—you too will be revealed in all your glory with him" (Colossians 3:4).[45]

Rabanus' originality appears again in his interpretation of Ephesians' *sacramentum hoc magnum est* (as he read it in the Latin Vulgate translation). He says first of all that the *sacramentum* is found in the imaging function of the monogamous union of husband and wife, in its imaging the mystery of Christ and the Church. But he adds immediately that this affords little help; it does not advance understanding very much. So he essays another interpretation that he trusts does not contradict that one, an interpretation that includes the growth of the entire human race in its relationship to God. He says that what Paul urges in his analogy is that just as a man leaves father and mother and clings to his wife, so the Church must abandon all error and cling to, and be subject to, its head who is Christ.[46]

With this Rabanus makes a startling shift of roles in the analogy. Now it is not the wife who images the Church, but it is the husband who has left father and mother. Consequently there is a crossover from one gender to the other. For whereas in the Genesis source it is a male who leaves father and mother and clings to his wife, here it is a presumably female Church (or is it now male in Rabanus' mind?) who clings to the male Christ.[47]

But still apparently dissatisfied with that second try at interpretation Rabanus immediately suggests a third. The "great mystery" declared in Ephesians is Christ's leaving the eternal Father (and his mother synagogue, or perhaps the maternal heavenly Jerusalem) to become man, to suffer and die, and in his death to give birth to the Church from his own body, and then to adhere to her as his bride. This is the *mysterium* proposed in Ephesians 5:32. Whether there is also a *sacramentum* indicated there, distinct from the *mysterium* and functioning as a sign and image of it, he does not say at this point. If he nevertheless has such a *sacramentum* in mind, it is most probably the Genesis declaration that a man "leaves his father and mother and clings to his wife, and the two become one flesh."

Rabanus' attempts at interpreting Ephesians 5:32 are admittedly undeveloped, as was characteristic of the medieval commentaries on scripture, and tentative. Nevertheless they offer a compelling suggestion, even if only implicitly. It is that the Church that is included in the interpretation ought not be an ideal model, a Church merely conceptualized and having all the immunity from human failings that conceptualizations enjoy. Another and more inclusive way of interpreting his suggestion is that conceptualization ought not be forced on and force reality, but reality should shape conceptualization.[48]

The Church's Appropriation of Marriage

What we have just surveyed are samples of the understanding of marriage that throve in the minds of the ecclesiastical writers of this period. We noted minimal development beyond what the fathers said of marriage by the end of the sixth century. These writers echoed faithfully the two patristic themes that worked against one another with such tension, namely that marriage in its hypothetical and ideal condition is good, but in its actual historical condition is wounded and sick. And the sexual conduct typical of it is, except in rare instances, at least venially sinful. Such they held to be the condition of the sacrament's matrix, when we appraise their judgment from the vantage point of our later and developed sacramental theology.

We examined also, and just as briefly, this period's understanding of the sacrament in marriage—and found this also undeveloped beyond the fathers. Now it is time to see how the authorities gradually took control of the marriages of the Catholic people of Europe. To do this we examine samples of the decrees coming from the regional councils of the time, and of the instructions coming from bishops (including the popes) to answer questions, resolve doubts and decide disputed marriage cases. The examination will look most attentively at the place of the sacrament in these decrees and councils. We recall two kinds of abuses that needed attention most urgently. These were divorce (bad enough in husbands' dismissing their wives on poorly sustained allegations of adultery, but at its worst in their forcing them into adultery in order to establish grounds for dismissal), and marriages formed in clandestinity. Documents from this age show relentless concern too for the problem of incestuous marriages. But this seems not to have involved marriage among close relatives, but rather among cousins, nieces and nephews in the fourth degree and beyond. The issue was violation of Roman law, a trouble idiosyncratic for the culture of the time. In trying to end these abuses did the authorities appeal to marriage's sacrament as a principle of correction, as a norm of conduct? or to the New Testament mandates alone on divorce and remarriage? or to the two in combination?

Before we set about examining samples of decrees and instructions we must note in a general way how it came about that Church authorities gained control of Europe's marriages between the seventh and twelfth centuries. The occasions and causes were multiple and mutually reinforcing. To begin with, the abuses named above themselves invited intervention. The structure of Germanic society was patriarchal. It could not tolerate the uncontrolled independence of its sons' and daughters' clandestine marriages. As for husbands' asserting independence after the arranged weddings by dismissing wives chosen for them so that they could marry their own choice, this contravened exactly what Christ's words in the synoptic gospels forbid. The flagrancy could not be ignored by the bishops acting either singly or in council. The obvious measure for blocking clandestine marriages was to mandate authoritative witness of the contracting of marriage as a condition of the latter's legitimacy. (Even more effective would be to mandate the same witness as a condition of validity itself. But this would have to wait seven and eight centuries until the Council of Trent's decree, *Tametsi,* in 1563.)

The obvious measure for restraining the dismissing and remarrying was a kindred one. This was to reserve to ecclesiastical authorities the competence to decide grounds for dissolution, as well as the competence to dissolve—in effect to shut down the traditional dismissal of spouse by spouse and to replace it with juridical dissolution by civil and/or Church authority.

The erecting of stable and centralized political rule worked in a more fundamental and comprehensive way to put a control on marrying and divorcing. Unlike our own society of the twentieth century wherein this or that marriage or divorce is of incidental interest to our civil authorities, the authorities of the patriarchal and newly feudal society of these centuries had a keen interest in marital conduct, expecially in that of its nobles. The stability of this society, its alliances, its enmities, depended seriously on who married whom and on how long they stayed married. This interest was the more insistent and powerful the more the persons in authority were religiously animated and saw themselves as custodians of morals in their portion of the society. Charlemagne was the arch-example of this.

Ultimately of course the installing of a single and universally effective regulation of marriage was identical with the popes' gradually more effective assertion of their own governance. This became more possible as the barbarian incursions of the fifth and sixth centuries dwindled, as communication across the reaches of Europe was reestablished, as bishops could be summoned to Rome or be examined by papal visitors. We must keep always in mind that medieval Europe, although not exactly a theocratic society, worked out no clear division of civil and ecclesiastical territories of governance. This was both the opportunity for a single, homogeneous regulation of marriage and the invitation to ceaseless feuding between popes on the one side and kings on the other about who was to rule which facets of life in this huge Catholic *polis.*

Our concern, again, in peering at the measures taken by bishops individually and in council, by kings and by popes to regulate marriage, is to find how they employed the sacrament to do so, if indeed they did this at all. We begin by retreating to a few of the earlier councils in the years spanning from the old Roman empire to the neo-Europe of the eighth and ninth centuries.

The earliest is the Eleventh Council of Carthage, held in June of 407 as one of a series of synods of the north African churches that began in 393 under the presidency of Aurelius, bishop of Carthage. Its Canon 8 was to be quoted again and again in succeeding centuries throughout the western Church.

We decree that according to the evangelic and apostolic discipline neither a husband dismissed by his wife nor a wife dismissed by her husband may marry another; but they are to
remain as they are or to be reconciled to one another. If they
despise [this law] they are to be subjected to penance. And on
this subject an imperial law ought to be promulgated.[49]

The first clause of the canon incorporates, in digest and in sequence, the New Testament synoptic instruction (the evangelical discipline) and the Pauline instruction in 1 Corinthians 7 (the apostolic discipline). No use is made of Ephesians and its marital *mystérion*. One
probably ought not expect such use in a conciliar decree. But this one
proposes as a norm of conduct an unnuanced repetition of prescriptions
that in their biblical sources were nuanced indeed. For one thing it omits
the exceptive clause of Matthew's version of the synoptic instruction
regarding dismissal of a wife.

A century later, in 506, a council of Frankish bishops met at Agde
in Narbonne to attack the abuse of husbands' dismissing their wives in
order to enter second marriages. Its Canon 25 was formulated in the
following awkward way.

Those laymen who with grave fault dare to abandon the marital
union or have even done so, and in order to take up an illicit or
adulterous union desert their marriage without alleging a cause
therefor in a fitting manner, if they do this before alleging the
cause of their departure before the bishops of their province,
and dismiss their wives before these have been condemned by
judicial sentence—they are to be excluded from communion in
the Church and from the holy company of the people because
they defile their trust and their marriages.[50]

The last clause of this canon offers the opportunity to say that
arbitrary dismissal of a wife violates the *sacramentum* in a Christian
marriage, or at least that it offends against the love that, according to
Ephesians 5:28–31, a husband ought to have even for a wife suspected of
infidelity. It veers in this last direction in its final phrase but stops short
of naming explicitly the demands of a love within the *mystérion* of Christ
and the Church.

To enrich this sampling we cite, but with little or no commentary,
regional councils in succeeding centuries. What appears characteristic
and common among them is that in trying to end the abuse of divorce by
dismissal, they appeal consistently to the New Testament synoptic instruction, not to the demands of marital love in Ephesians. A consequence of this was that the Matthean exceptive clause that permitted
dismissal of wives for their *pornéia* was kept alive and active in judicial

processes, and that accordingly the derivative abuse of forcing or luring wives into adultery was prolonged.

Under the presidency of the archbishop of Canterbury, Theodore of Tarsus, an assembly of English bishops met at Hertford in 673 to legislate on moral matters for the Catholics of their country. Their Canon 10 was intended to regulate conduct concerning marriage.

> Regarding marriages: no one is to have any but a legally recognized marriage [*legitimum connubium*]. No one is to commit incest. No one is to abandon his own spouse unless, as the holy Gospel teaches, he does so because of fornication. But if anyone dismisses a spouse joined to him legitimately in marriage, if he wishes truly to be a Christian, he is to be united to no one else, but is either to remain as he is or to be reconciled with his own spouse.[51]

In two letters written a decade apart Pope Gregory II provided an example of how a judgment seemingly absolute in an earlier declaration could be qualified when later confronting a grievous human difficulty. When he sent his legates to Bavaria in 716 to help the local bishops restore religious discipline there, he sent with them a letter of instruction that contained the following:

> This, then, the Apostle said: "You are bound to a wife? Do not seek to be loosed. As long as your wife lives do not seek to pass over to carnal relations with another woman."[52]

But on November 22, 726 he wrote to Boniface, apostle of the Saxons, to answer his questions asking what a husband ought to do if his wife can no longer have intercourse with him because of a permanently disabling illness. Gregory replied as follows in his *Epistola 3:*

> It would be good if he could remain as he is and live a life of continence. But this requires great virtue. So if he cannot live chastely, it is better that he remarry. But let him not cease to support her [his first and incapacitated wife].[53]

Both instructions draw their substance from 1 Corinthians 7. Neither draws from the marital *sacramentum* in Ephesians, not the first in order to secure an unassailable reason for the apparently unexceptionable command, nor the second to confront a reason why a wife actually and physically "stained and wrinkled" should be kept in marital love.

The Council of Friuli met in northeast Italy under the presidency of Paulinus of Aquileia in 791. It was the first synod in Catholic history to rule explicitly, in its Canon 10, that despite the wife's dismissal because of her adultery, the marriage remains in existence, and remarriage is therefore impossible for the husband. This was to decide also that the exceptive clause in Matthew 19 does not intend a dismissal that annihilates the marriage, but one that only separates the spouses from common life. How the bishops came to this interpretation is evident in their explanation of their use of Jerome's Commentary on Matthew.

> But because there is set at its heart [i.e. of the synoptic instruction on divorce and remarriage] an ambiguous clause, "except in the case of her fornication," we must ask whether this refers only to permission to dismiss the wife (". . . he who dismisses his wife, except in the case of her fornication . . ."); or whether it refers to both parts of this passage. That is, does the permission apply also to the husband's taking another wife while the first wife still lives; as though it were saying "a man who dismisses his wife and marries another commits adultery, except in the case of his wife's fornication?"
>
> Therefore we ordered that the book of commentaries of that most expert and blessed man, Jerome, be inspected carefully, hurrying eagerly to find out how this most renowned teacher would use his subtle genius to clarify the meaning of these words of the Lord.[54]

The bishops found Jerome saying that Jesus meant that the husband could do no more than dismiss his adulterous wife, but that he could not remarry afterward. Neither these bishops nor the Jerome to whom they appealed alleged as the reason for forbidding the husband's taking a second wife that the *sacramentum* of his marriage demands this. The bishops forbade it because thanks to Jerome's interpretation they thought Christ had forbidden it. Jerome said Christ had forbidden it because if he had not, he would have left the way open to husbands' slandering faithful wives, or even to forcing them into adultery.

Measures Against Clandestine Marriages

This sampling of pre-Carolingian disciplinary decrees designed to put a control on Catholic European husbands' dismissing their wives shows no evidence that the sacrament was commonly summoned as the reason for lasting fidelity or used as a regulating instrument. But as we have already seen, this sundering of marriages by unilateral dismissal was not the only abuse that came under reforming attack. Clandestinely formed marriages were another, as were marriages considered incestuous according to Roman law. The clandestinity was sometimes a companion and a sequel to another and more brutal abuse, the kidnaping of women to force them into marriage. Kidnaper and kidnaped could hardly enter marriage in a publicly approved way.

Our query about the efforts at ending clandestinity asks whether these in their turn work to awaken the minds of the authorities and scholars of the time to the centrality of the sacrament in Christian marriages, or, to phrase it another way, whether their efforts led to the setting of the sacrament at the center of these marriages, and to its use as an instrument or reform of at least this abuse.

We see that this did not happen. The grand strategy for ending clandestinity was to force the creating of marriages, the concluding of marital contracts, to be done publicly. But there is no hint that this was done as a conclusion drawn from the principle that sacraments belong to the public life of the Church. In his Frankish kingdom in the middle of the eighth century Pepin the Short forbade incestuous marriages and the clandestine forming of marriages, and punished violators of his decrees. The national synod of Verneuil decreed that marriages must be contracted in public and according to the traditional formalities. Charlemagne, in a capitulary of 802, made such control measures obligatory for all in his empire.

But all these tactics were destined to fail because even though sometimes reinforced by threat of excommunication, they never went beyond simply forbidding clandestine marriages. Those willing to challenge the law knew that its punishments, even excommunication, were always temporary and therefore worth risking. The one effective measure was delayed, as we have seen, until near the end of the Council of Trent in 1563. This was to set authorized witness of the marital vows as a condition for their validity, so that the attempt at clandestine marriage would be null and void.

Disciplinary Efforts in Post-Carolingian Europe

This effort to establish control over marriage continued beyond Charlemagne into the division of his empire among his three sons and into its ninth-century crumbling under their separate rules. The effort was aided greatly by a set of ecclesiastical decrees that came to be known as "The False Decretals" and "The Pseudo-Isidorian Decretals." Their origin is not known with certainty. They were assembled between 844 and 852 at Rheims or at LeMans or at the royal chapel of Charles the Bald, ruler of the western third of the divided empire. The collection's denigrating titles fit its character. Among authentic letters of earlier popes its author or authors mingled about ninety apocryphal letters— mingled them there in order to forge for them a pseudo-authenticity. Sixty of them dated from the period of Clement I (88–97) to Melchiades (311–314), thirty or more of them from the period of Sylvester I (314–335 A.D.) to Gregory II (715–731 A.D.). They carry the second title because part of their forgery was to attribute the entire collection to the authorship of Archbishop Isidore of Seville in the seventh century. The motive for the forgery was to consolidate a central authority in the European church, specifically that of the pope against the regional bishops, against the latters' national councils, and against princes convinced they were the anointed caretakers of the church in their territories. The false decretals, along with the genuine that formed their context, were taken undetected into the most influential collections of ecclesiastical legislation until the middle of the twelfth century.

An example of the anonymous authors' tactic for gaining control is found in a decretal letter attributed to Pope Evaristus (97–105) to the bishops of North Africa.

> A marriage is not legitimate unless she [the bride] is asked for as a wife from those who have authority over her; unless she is sponsored by her parents and relatives; unless she is dowered according to law; unless she is blessed by a priest according to custom and at the proper time with prayers and offerings; unless she is brought by her friends at the appropriate time, accompanied and guarded by the paranymphs; unless she is solemnly received, and unless they [she and the groom] devote themselves in chastity to prayer for two or three days.[55]

Despite its being a forgery the letter almost certainly gives an accurate sketch of a wedding ceremony in the western Frankish empire in the middle of the ninth century. Its success as a forgery depended on such accuracy. The sketch indicates how much the wedding was still a family affair, and at the same time how far it had been drawn into an established church liturgy.

Benedict the Levite, a deacon of the church of Mainz, compiled his *Collectio Capitularium* between 847 and 850, a work of pretended scholarship which nevertheless had considerable influence because he was able to give the impression that his work was the product of collaboration between civil and Church authorities. In his Book 3, no. 179 he matched the False Decretals' proscriptions against marriage following abduction, against marriage within certain degrees of relationship, and against clandestine marriages. In Book 3, no. 436 he set down requirements for the legitimacy of a marriage that approximated those of the apocryphal letter of Pope Evaristus. They were the following: the marriage must be contracted in the presence of the bride's father or guardian, who must consent to the marriage; the contracting must be done at the bride's petition; the dowry must be given; the priest must give his blessing; the bride must be handed over to the groom according to local custom. For Benedict the legality of the marriage depended primarily on the consent of the bride's parents. Their giving the dowry was taken as conclusive evidence of their consent.[56]

Hincmar, archbishop of Rheims from 845 until his death in 882, worked as effectively as any king or council to draw marriages in central Europe into Church control. His great concern was that marriages take place publicly according to the formalities of civil law and the customs of the Church set out in the False Decretals, which he took to be authentic. To this end he insisted that for the legitimate contracting of marriage a formal betrothal must precede, the dowry must be arranged and delivered, and the bride must be handed over into the authority of the groom.[57] In some of his instructions he added to these required elements the priest's blessing for marriage generally, and his liturgical blessing of the bride. He specified that these are for the mediating of God's graces to the bridal couple for their sanctification—a reason hinting at the sacramentality of both the blessing and the spouses' married life.[58]

The Case of Lothair and Teutberga

But Hincmar's most valuable contribution to the expanding place of the sacrament in the Western Church's pondering and regulation of marriage is in his analysis of a disciplinary case most notorious in its time and best known to us because of the full documentation that has survived. The case was that of Charlemagne's grandson, Lothair II, king since 855 of Lotharingia (Lorraine), the middlemost of the three subdivisions of Charlemagne's empire. In the year of his accession, at seventeen years of age, he was put into marriage with Teutberga, daughter of the Duke of Burgundy. But within three years he sought to divorce her by dismissal in order to marry Waldrada, his mistress from before his marriage.

But he could dismiss Teutberga legitimately only if he could prove against her some crime against marriage that Frankish law recognized as a justifying cause. So he accused her of incest, consummated from before the wedding, with her brother Hubert, abbot of St. Maurice in Vallais. According to Frankish law this was a crime that invalidated any subsequent attempt at marriage.

At a council of bishops and nobles that Lothair assembled at Aachen in 860 Teutberga was forced to confess to the incest. The council convicted her of the crime and declared her marriage to Lothair null and void. But she escaped the monastic imprisonment planned for her and found refuge with her uncle, Charles the Bald. From there she appealed to Pope Nicholas I.

In answer to her plea Nicholas sent two delegates to complete a new investigation and process, in a council held at Metz. But his legates, Rodoald de Porto and John of Fiacla, accepted bribes from the court of Lorraine, and with the other prelates and nobles at Metz confirmed the decision handed down earlier at Aachen.

Then Nicholas took personal action. He suspended the bishops who had concurred in the fraudulent judgment against Teutberga, and rejected both of Lothair's claims. He excommunicated Waldrada, and compelled Lothair under threat of excommunication to get rid of her and to take Teutberga back. Lothair did this, but only briefly before dismissing her again. In her weariness and discouragement Teutberga asked Nicholas to declare her marriage to Lothair null. But his reply to this request was that this was impossible. Nicholas died in 867, Lothair two years later at the age of thirty-one.

Before the assembly at Aachen in 860 Lothair's partisans had asked Hincmar to declare in favor of the king and his charges against Teutberga. He was asked also to take part in that assembly, but pleaded poor health in order to escape participating in the travesty. The party of Lothair tried to represent his refusal as tacit approval of the assembly's judgment. But this drew from Hincmar a document in which he offered a most detailed judgment of the case. It is titled "Concerning the Divorce of King Lothair and Queen Teutberga" (*De divortio Lotharii regis et Teutbergae reginae*).[59]

In character the document is a not very expert amalgam of philosophy, scripture, theology and law concerning divorce and remarriage. Even so it deals mainly with points of law, and especially with procedures because of the seriously unjust process to which Teutberga was subjected. In it Hincmar devised a plan of twenty-three *interrogationes* to himself by which he meant to cut to the heart of Lothair's case against Teutberga. His *responsiones* to the *interrogationes* make up the amalgam mentioned just above. Perhaps the most valuable trait of the whole is that it is the earliest attempt in Christian history at a comprehensive gathering and ordering of the judgments, or *sententiae*, of synods, prelates and scholars on the question of divorce and remarriage. Hincmar used each of his *responsiones* as the occasion for reviewing the history of Christian judgments on the question it was meant to answer.

Our interest in the compilation centers in Hincmar's own judgment on divorce and remarriage, specifically in the sources and principles from which he drew his judgment. Is the sacrament in marriage, and its demands, among them? If they are, how does he apply them?

It helps to know beforehand his understanding of sacrament generally in the Christian religion. This appears in the epistolary essay, "On the Marriage of Stephen and the Daughter of Count Regimund" (*De nuptiis Stephani et filiae Regimundi comitis*, in *Epistola 22*).[60] The matter in question was this, that Regimund had given his daughter in marriage to Stephen, but Stephen refused to have intercourse with her because, as he confessed, he had had it earlier with a female relative of his bride. According to the tradition of the time this created the impediment of affinity (*affinitas superveniens*) with the bride. He protested that in conscience he must represent his case to the Church authorities. Hincmar's judgment on it is the following.

> One must understand about such a union as this that there is no marriage where there is no joining of the sexes, no hope of offspring and no pledge of permanent commitment [*sacramentum fidei*]—the pledge that has its place in all conduct having to do with salvation, in such conduct as this wherein a man and a wife are made one by the marital mystery. But this

pledge functions especially in baptism. By it not only does the entire Church become in general the body of Christ, as the Apostle says, but every one of the faithful taken singly is incorporated in Christ and made a member of him.[61]

Hincmar here assumes as a principle a most comprehensive referent of the term *sacramentum,* the pledged commitment that Augustine preferred as its meaning. He holds this commitment to be essential for creating a marriage. We shall see below how he uses it to pass judgment on the possibility of dissolving a marriage.

In the same letter Hincmar states, "A husband and wife separating [*discedentes*] from one another because of adultery must, because of the *sacramentum* of their marital union, either remain unmarried until one or the other dies, or try to reconcile with one another." The judgment is unequivocal. Hincmar skirts the synoptic instruction on divorce by dismissal and thus avoids reckoning with the Matthean exceptive clause. He goes directly to the heart of Ephesians 5 and names the reason why the spouses must not attempt remarriage until one or the other dies. This is their marital *sacramentum.* That he means that their marriage remains despite the separation is evident first of all in his rare choice of the verb *discedere* at the point where far more commonly authors wrote of the wife's being dismissed (*dimissa*). *Discedere* is an apt choice for designating a separation that is less than a dissolution. But he erases any trace of doubt by continuing immediately in the same passage: "Hence St. Augustine in his Book 2 of *De adulterinis conjugiis* says: 'Consequently a spouse may be dismissed licitly on the ground of adultery. But their bond of chastity [*vinculum pudoris*] remains. That is why a man is guilty of adultery if he marries a woman even if she has been dismissed for her infidelity.' "[62] Hincmar then goes on to complete his thought by repeating Augustine's analogy: Just as a man who receives the *sacramentum* of baptism never loses it even though he may turn apostate for the rest of his life, so a woman who is dismissed does not lose the *sacramentum* of marriage until her husband dies.

To return to Hincmar's analysis and judgment of Lothair's attempt to dismiss Teutberga, he offers his most succinct judgment in his response to *Interrogatio 1:* "Here we recall briefly . . . that sacred authority does not permit that a wife leave her husband."[63] In his response to *Interrogatio 2* he lays down the principle that Christians live by a different law than does the rest of the human race. He insists, with Paul in 1 Corinthians 7:27, that a wife is bound to her husband as long as he lives, and that she is free to marry again only after his death.[63] He adds that a man may dismiss his wife, not for just any reason, but only for her infidelity. Then comes the assertion of his own mind regarding the crucial next question: Even if a husband dismisses his wife after proving her infidelity, he may not remarry as long as she lives, nor may she as long as he lives. But here the reason Hincmar offers differs from that he offered in judging the case of Stephen and the daughter of the Duke of Burgundy. Here it is not the *sacramentum* surviving in the souls of both spouses. It is rather God's command given through Christ: "What God has joined man must not separate." And just because the command is God's own, he and he alone can separate marriages. With this Hincmar implies that marriages are not by nature indissoluble. But even God separates marriages not by dissolving them, but by inspiring the husband to forgo sexual intercourse for the sake of better serving God.[65] He refers to the practice, honored since the age of the fathers, wherein unconsummated marriages were dissolved by one or both spouses' entering monastic life.

He brings the *sacramentum* into this judgment when he quotes Pope Leo I's letter to Bishop Rusticus of Narbonne (his *Epistola* 95) that distinguished two kinds of unions:

> Not every woman . . . joined to a man is his wife, just as not every son is his father's heir. The covenant of marriage between freedmen and between equals is legitimate—as God himself determined long before Roman law came into existence. Therefore a wife is one thing, a concubine another. . . . Because from the beginning the marital union has been designed so that in addition to the joining of the sexes it contains a *sacramentum* of Christ and the Church, there is no doubt that that woman is not married in whom this marital *mysterium* is lacking.[66]

We recall that this reply from Leo to Rusticus was to the latter's query whether a father can wed his daughter to a man who has a concubine. Is the man already married? Leo's reply was that the concubinage lacks the *sacramentum* that must be found in a sexually joined relationship if it is to be a marriage. The nature of the *sacramentum* Leo (and Hincmar) hint at by calling it the *sacramentum* of Christ and the Church. But Hincmar says no more about it in this response.

He returns to the function and the demands of this marital *sacramentum* in his response to *Interrogatio 5*. Since in all this he is passing judgment on Lothair's attempt by now to rid himself of Teutberga by dismissing her for her alleged adultery, one would expect Hincmar to draw from the *sacramentum* the conclusion that because of it such dismissal is not only forbidden but impossible. But he does not do so—yet. He first draws a conclusion about the love that ought to thrive in a Christian marriage. Here he uses the *sacramentum-mysterium* of Christ and the Church as model and norm for this love.

> If therefore in the home of any Christian such justice and kindness are to be maintained even toward one of such servile condition, between a master and a servant, how much greater, richer

and more inclusive ought they be between a husband and wife . . . between head and body! For, as the Apostle teaches, (Ephesians 5:22) the husband is head of the wife as Christ is head of the Church, he the savior of the body. Thus husbands should love their wives as their own bodies. . . . Surely the apostles so praise the love between husband and wife, a love so special and so surpassing—saving always the husband's rule in marriage and the wife's obedience—that there can be no greater love than in this union first instituted by God and now rightly concluded. For what is more to be esteemed than that marriage be the mystery of Christ and the Church? What more holy than that husbands love their wives as Christ loved the Church, giving himself up for her so as to cleanse and sanctify her? What more dear and intimate than that a husband be head of his wife as Christ is head of the Church and savior of her, his body? . . . Thus if husbands ought not be harsh toward their wives, how much less should they be savage, cruel, violent, respecting no law, no reason, no restraint such as the Christian religion demands one show even to servants. . . .[67]

Hincmar finally comes to the judgment about the question posed in this *Interrogatio 5,* and draws it from the presence of the *sacramentum* in marriage. Note that he does this by quoting from Augustine's *De bono conjugali.* He apparently agrees with Augustine that the *sacramentum* that makes dissolving a marriage impossible except by death is found in every marriage. By this tacit agreement he doubles back on his earlier statement that designates the *sacramentum* as the sacrament, the mystery, of Christ and the Church. But it is not likely that he thinks that this is found even in the marriages of pagans. Or perhaps he thinks that because pagan unions do not contain the *sacramentum,* they are not marriages. He leaves the matter just as undecided as Augustine had left it four hundred years earlier.

> For the holy Fathers teach about the good of marriage. Marriage does have goods, and having these is not sinful. . . . In it are *fides, proles, sacramentum. Fides* means that a spouse lies with no one apart from his or her marriage bond. *Proles* means that children are accepted with love, nurtured with kindness and brought up religiously. *Sacramentum* means that the marriage be not separated and that spouses once dismissed not marry again for the sake of children.[68]

A Moratorium of Theology and Law

The rebirth of Catholic theology in the Carolingian renaissance was interrupted cruelly through the second half of the ninth century, all of the tenth and approximately the first half of the eleventh. Consequently the minimal development in the understanding of marriage and its sacrament during the seventh, eighth and early ninth centuries—Hincmar's contribution was the best of the lean period—was followed by two centuries of virtually nothing. Two worthy collections of Church legislation appeared, including legislation for marriage. But our brief notice of them in a moment will show that their essentially retrospective and conservatory character added nothing to what had already been said.

Three causes combined in unequal proportions to produce the interruption. The first and least was the civil warring among the heirs of Charlemagne following his son Louis the Pious' parcelling out of his empire among three of the grandsons, Charles the Bald, Lothair I and Louis the German, in the Treaty of Verdun in 843. Not only they and their children but the bishops they installed spent their efforts struggling for dominance over the disintegrated population of Franks, Saxons, Lombards et al. Hincmar of Rheims himself was a long and active supporter of Charles the Bald. His attention to the affair of Lothair II and Teutberga was a minor expenditure of his energy.

A second and far more grievous cause was the second series of invasions that struck Christian Europe. These came from three quarters and three very different peoples, but in combination swept over the entire continent and the Italian peninsula. The Moslems came from the south and from Spain in the west. They came up the Rhone valley in 842. Fifty years later they ravaged the Mediterranean coast of France. In 940 they raided as far as the monastery of St. Gall in Switzerland. In 972 they ambushed and captured the abbot of Cluny in an Alpine pass. After attacking Rome in 846 they continued to raid in Italy and gained strongholds in Calabria and in Sicily.

From the east came the Magyars. They crossed over the Hungarian plain in 896 and for a half-century raided in northern Italy and Germany and in the western Frankish kingdom as far as Rheims and Utrecht. The worst were the Norsemen who, beginning about 830, raided in their long-boats up every navigable river in Europe to loot and destroy. London, Paris, Cologne, Bordeaux, and Nantes were some of the major cities they plundered and burned. Favorite targets of the invaders' plundering were churches and monasteries because of their wealth in sacred vessels and vestments. Clergy and monks were slaughtered or taken into slavery. The libraries were simply burned.

A third cause was a characteristic element of the feudal society that emerged from the chaos of the earlier and then these later barbarian invasions. This was the division of Europe into dynastically related domains ruled in descending hierarchy by kings, princes, dukes and counts—with huge territories deeded to bishops who ruled too as feudal lords. The lay lords controlled the bishoprics of their fiefs. They created parishes and appointed their pastors, often from among their illegitimate sons. Most of these—lay lords, bishops and pastors—had only the faintest interest in Christian goodness, and even less in the advance or even preservation of learning. The knowledge that did interest them was that of law. Accordingly this is, as mentioned above, where the sterile age produced the little that it did.

Regino, abbot of Prüm in Lorraine from 892 until his expulsion from that office in 899, continued the collecting of canons, decrees and patristic *sententiae* that had been started earlier in his century by Halitgar and the deacon Benedict. The passages on marriage are found in Book 2 of his *De ecclesiasticis disciplinis.*[69] His main concern there was to assemble those articles that would help to control the dismissing of wives. Attention to the sacrament as a cause of permanence in marriage was consequently absent from his collection. Burchard, who held the bishopric of Worms from 1000 to 1025, compiled his *Liber decretorum* (Book of Decrees) between 1008 and 1012.[70] It was a rich collection of synodal and papal decrees and scholarly judgments on Church government. Of its twenty "books" (1,785 chapters in the *Patrologia Latina*) he devoted Book 9 to "non-consecrated women."[71] His principal concern too was to end the abuse that was the dismissal of unwanted wives.

It was in the latter half of the eleventh century that the control of bishops and parishes by the lay lords of Europe began to be broken. The reform started up by the Benedictines of Cluny spread throughout the continent and Italy and the British Isles. It gained success first and fundamentally because the Cluniac charter came not from any prince or king but immediately from the pope. Thus monasteries reformed in this movement were taken out of the control of local lay nobility. A series of strong popes took the papacy out of the hands of both the Roman families and away from installation by the German emperors. A Lateran synod in 1059 determined that for all the future only the cardinals of the Church could choose and install a pope, with no more than a vague right of confirmation left to the emperor. That much was mainly the work of Pope Leo IX (1049–1054), Victor II (1055–1057) and Nicholas II (1059–1061). But it was the monk Hildebrand who, as Gregory VII (1073–1085), made the most decisive moves. Drawing from the biblically recorded giving of "the power of the keys" to Peter (Mt 16:18) he claimed as successor to that apostle uncontestable authority over all Christian institutions, authority that included the crowning and removing of kings of Christian peoples. A fortiori this authority was exclusive in installing and removing bishops and abbots. The conflict over this with Emperor Henry IV and until Gregory's death in semi-exile at Salerno is well known, including the latter's twice-over excommunication of Henry, and reciprocally Henry's letter deposing and cursing Gregory, and his installation of the anti-pope, Clement III.

The main thrust of Gregory's reform, to end imperial control of the Church and lay investiture with it, had limited success within his lifetime. But combined with the Cluniac reform and the rebirth of monastic learning, the ending of the Moslem, Magyar and Norse invasions, the rise of the cathedral schools soon to become the great universities, the reform set under way by Gregory and his immediate predecessors brought back to life a common interest in theological inquiry. This included a renewed study of the sacraments in the Church, with now among them, and for the first time with conviction, the sacrament in marriage.

Before turning to this renewed inquiry in the following chapter we must look briefly at the last significant canonical collection in the period that ended with the Gregorian reform, and then in more inclusive detail at the solemnization of marriage, the Christian wedding celebration of the time. It was in the latter that the drawing of marriage into the formal and regulated life of the Church took place most effectively.

This last collection was the work of Yves (or Ivo) of Chartres, born c. 1040, a student first at the cathedral school of Paris, then at the abbey of Bec in Normandy. He was consecrated bishop of Chartres in 1090, and governed there until his death on December 23, 1115. As a theologian he helped in fixing the number of Christian sacraments at seven. But it is his canonical collection that merits our interest—or rather his collections. For he completed three, first the sparse *Tripartita;* then the *Decretum* in 1095, a huge and jumbled anthology of texts from the past; and finally his *Panormia* shortly afterward.

As a juridical writer Yves was a conciliator. While accepting the Gregorian reform in principle and substance, he insisted on preserving among the ancient disciplinary norms taken into his compilation those of his own Frankish tradition. He sought to fuse the strict juridical principles of the Roman-Gregorian law and the particular legislation of his Frankish tradition. What this produced was an amalgam, an evolved Roman rigorism gentled by local custom. The material for the *Decretum* he drew from Burchard of Worms' *Decretum* (he took over virtually all of it), from his own *Tripartita,* from an anonymous collection of papal decrees, from the text of Justinian's Roman law, from the texts of Carolingian civil law, and from historical texts in the *Liber Pontificalis.*

Yves worked his influence on later generations through his *Panormia,* which not only drew the major part of its material from his own *Decretum,* but reduced its confusion to a usable system.

The *Panormia's* value for our inquiry is this, that in this most inclusive and expert encyclopedia of Catholic regulation in Christianity's first ten centuries—for us, half its lifetime—we see the role of the marital sacrament in the regulation of marriages. In naming this value we must trust Yves' judgment that in his collection he selected the questions and problems about marriage that most needed answering and resolving by his time. We must also trust his diligence in ferreting out the *sententiae* of the fathers, the canons of councils, and the decrees of popes that worked most immediately in the answering and the resolving.

Marriage matters are treated in the *Panormia* in its Books 6 and 7 through their two hundred and eighteen chapters (some of these as brief as a single sentence, others as long as a minor essay).[72] What will be noted here are two kinds of passages in the collection. They are those that refer to the marital sacrament in order to answer and resolve, and the chapter subjects wherein one could reasonably expect to find such reference in order to answer and resolve. But there is none to find. The omissions here carry a message of their own.

Book 1, Chapter 30 includes the briefest mention of the *sacramentum* from Augustine's *De Nuptiis et Concupiscentia*, Book 2, Chapter 2: "Therefore every one of the goods of marriage was fulfilled in Christ's parents, *fides, proles, sacramentum* . . . the *sacramentum* because there was no divorce."[73]

Chapters 35 through 42 deal with Christian slaves' right to marry, and of the right of slaves, freedmen and citizens to inter-marry. No passage containing the *sacramentum* is enlisted to support the Christian teaching in this matter.

Chapter 65 quotes from Augustine's *De Bono Conjugali*, Chapter 28, declaring that married clergy must be married no more than once: "In our time the *sacramentum* of marriage has been so identified with one husband and one wife that a man may not be ordained a minister of the Church unless he has been married only once."[74]

The following chapter quotes from Chapter 18 of *De Bono Conjugali* to explain further why it is that a man may be ordained only if he has been married but once: "Just as because of the holiness of the *sacramentum* a woman who has had sexual intercourse while yet a catechumen cannot be accepted among the consecrated virgins after her baptism, so it seems not absurd to say that a man who has been married more than once, although he has not sinned, yet in a certain way fails the demands of the *sacramentum*—not the demands of a good life but those of a seal [or sign—*signaculum*] needed for ordination in the Church."[75]

In Chapter 74 Yves quotes predictably the passage from Augustine's *De Bono Conjugali* containing the analogy that just as the *sacramentum* of baptism remains in the soul of an apostate Christian, so that of marriage remains in the soul of a dismissed wife as long as her husband still lives.[76]

No passage referring to the sacrament is quoted to resolve questions about spouses who seek dissolution of their marriage in order to enter monastic life (Chapters 75–85), about the possibility and permissibility of remarriage for those whose spouses have been kidnaped or taken into captivity (Chapters 86–93), about the impermissibility of dissolving marriages (Chapters 102–106), about not forcing sons and daughters into marriage (Chapters 108–109), and about dissolving marriages because of sexual impotence (Chapters 112–119).

When dealing in Book 2, Chapters 18–26 with the legitimate recourse spouses may take in a marriage damaged by adultery, Yves cites no passage containing the sacrament. The same is true in Chapters 39–42 about the spouses' oath of reconciliation when reintegrating their marriage after adultery. Coincidentally in these chapters it is the oath itself that is called a *sacramentum*.

In chapters 43–51, about the necessity for wives' submission to their husbands, the only hint of sacramentality is found in Chapter 44, which quotes Augustine's *Quaestiones in Vetus Testamentum,* that the husband should rule in the marriage because he is the image of God in the sense of Genesis 1:26, but the wife is not. This argument is repeated in a kindred way in Chapter 51 wherein Ambrose is quoted from his *Commentarium in Epistolam ad Corinthios,* Chapter 11, to explain that a wife wears a veil because in the marriage she is not the image of God.

Finally there is no reference to the sacrament in the passages solicited to rule on attempted marriage of blood relatives (Chapters 52–62) and of persons related in law (Chapters 76–90).

Summary

This era, from the end of the patristic age until the Gregorian reform, was perforce conservative. For churchmen and religious teachers it was a struggle to hold values appropriated at the birth of Christianity and even inherited from centuries earlier.

The struggle was not only to survive a disintegrated civilization and the cruelty of foreign marauders, but to survive the diluting effects of the fusing of two cultures, the Hellenic-Roman and the Germanic. Such fusing always demands compromise. We have seen one example of this in the application, by the regional councils of Europe's bishops, of the New Testament teaching concerning divorce and remarriage. The uncertainty of the teaching in the face of stubborn local tradition resulted in a legislation almost incomprehensible to a modern Catholic.

The effort to discipline the convert peoples of European tribes into marital fidelity might have spurred development of the theology of marriage. But the schools that could have provided the scholars had been destroyed. The abuses themselves were too gross and too much in need of immediate action. They could not abide the long and patient debate indispensable for theological growth. More urgently needed was clear and emphatic regulation of conduct.

One wonders too whether a theology of the sacrament would have developed even if there had been the needed tranquility. The opportunity had been there from at least the middle of the third century until the end of the fifth. But the most competent minds were then busy with issues more exalted in character and more challenging to speculative talent—the trinitarian and christological controversies, the dispute over divine grace and human initiative. Marriage did not loom large in religious consciousness. Since it was such a familiar institution—in both senses of the term—it seemed the proper child of pastoral exhortation and of civil as well as ecclesial regulation.

And was the Platonic mentality dominant in the Church equipped to work out a theology of the sacrament? It was retrospective, concerned with ideal models, inattentive to the this-world, concrete realities for which the ideas are models. It sought for truth in contemplation, in the divinely illumined intuitive gaze, not in hard dialectic analysis. It is not clear that speculation concentrated on "marriage" could produce a theology helpful for marriages.

It is striking that through the one thousand years we have reviewed not a single scholar attempted a painstaking analysis of Ephesians 5:21–32, the passage which almost everyone knew is the wellspring of knowledge about the sacrament in marriage. Even the best minds seemed content to do a brief *commentarium* on it, to say superficially what it means, to draw the apparently obvious conclusions from it, and to use it according to its author's original intent as an analogy in the service of exhortation. No one, for example, asked what could be learned about marriages as experienced in daily life from a model made up of a metaphoric body and a metaphoric marriage. Only Rabanus Maurus, as we have seen, thought to challenge the dubious realism of referring this model to countless Christian marriages that do not correspond to it.

But during the twelfth century the needed analytic tool was found for the scholars, at the very time when the new universities began to make tranquil dialogic learning possible. The metaphysics of Aristotle was found in both Greek manuscripts and in Arabic translations of the Moslem scholars in Spain. With this available there was no longer any excuse for failing to "reduce" the metaphors making up the scriptural sources about the sacrament—to resolve the metaphoric figures, the divine marriage and the divine body, into conditions and relationships of existence. A project implicit in the following chapters is to find out how well the tool was used.

NOTES

1. "Isidore, who was an extraordinarily industrious author, is one of the great teachers of the Middle Ages. His learned works, mostly only mosaic-like compilations from other authors, did not only serve his own time but preserved many treasures of antiquity for the future. Their lack of originality together with their clarity of expression and their encyclopedic character made them widely popular; thus his *Etymologies,* for example, are extant even today in about 950 manuscripts." (B. Altaner, *Patrology,* N.Y., 1960, pp. 594–595)

2. PL 83:809.

3. *Ibid.,* Cols. 809–810.

4. *Ibid.,* Col. 810.

5. *Ibid.*

6. Hatto of Vercelli, *Expositio in Epistolas Pauli, I Cor.* (in J. Kerns, *The Theology of Marriage,* p. 27).

7. Gregory, *Homiliae in Evangelia,* Book 2, 36, 5, PL 76:269 (in Kerns, *op. cit.,* p. 27).

8. Rabanus Maurus, *Commentariorum in Genesim Libri Quattuor* (819 A.D.), Book 1, Chapt. 7, PL 107:461–462.

9. Venerable Bede, *Hexaemeron*, Book 1, PL 91:31 (in Kerns, p. 104).

10. Venerable Bede, Homilia 1, no. 14, PL 94:68 (in Kerns, p. 208).

11. Sedulius Scotus, *In I Cor. 12*, PL 102:153 (in Kerns, *ibid.*).

12. Bruno Astiensis, *In I Cor. 3*, PL 111:159 (in Kerns, *ibid.*).

13. Abbo Fleurens, *Apologeticus*, PL 139:463 (in Kerns, *ibid.*).

14. Jonas of Orleans, *De Institutione Laicorum*, Book 2, Chapt. 11, PL 106:188 (in Kerns, p. 123).

15. Radulfus Ardens, *In Epistolas et Evangelia Dominicalia Homiliae*, Homily 21, PL 155:1743–1744.

16. Venerable Bede, *Super Epistolas Catholicas Expositio: in Primam Epistolam Petri*, PL 93:55.

17. Radulfus Ardens, *ibid.*

18. Halitgar, *De Vitiis et Virtutibus et De Ordine Poenitentiarum Libri Quinque*, Chapt. 16, "De Vitio Luxuriae," PL 105:668.

19. Remigius of Auxerre, *Commentarium in Genesim* 2:25, PL 131:63 (in Kerns, p. 52).

20. Isidore of Seville, *De Officiis Ecclesiasticis*, Book 2, Chapt. 20, PL 83:812.

21. Paschase Radbert, *In Matthaeum*, Book 10, Chapt. 19, PL 120:651 (in Kerns, p. 148).

22. *Reportorium*, Book 4, Dist. 28, Quest. 1, Schol. 2 (in Kerns, p. 145).

23. Haymo of Halberstadt, *In I Timotheum 2*, PL 117:791 (in Kerns, p. 246).

24. Rabanus Maurus, *Enarratio in Epistolas Pauli*, Book 10, Chapt. 7, PL 112: 64 (in Kerns, p. 18).

25. Unknown author, *Quaestiones in Epistolas S. Pauli*, in I Cor., Quest. 64, PL 175:526 (in Kerns p. 237).

26. Christian Druthmar of Corbie, *In Matthaeum 19*, PL 106:1414 (in Kerns, p. 239).

27. Isidore of Seville, *op. cit.*, Cols. 810–811.

28. *Loc. cit.*, Cols. 812–813.

29. In PL 91:
This dramatic poem, a canonically received book of the sacred scriptures, the one that tells most expressly of the kind of love that lures men and women into marriage, was almost entirely neglected by the Christian writers and teachers of the first five centuries. Why they did so is not obscure. They could not on the one hand distrust and condemn sexual passion even in marriage, and on the other praise it in lovers as yet unmarried—or, far short of praising it, even alert Christian readers that this love is dramatized in their sacred writings. Origen produced two homilies on it, and Jerome two—both allegorizing it in the way familiar to us: the girl as the bride-Church and Christ as the husband. One Italian author, Aponius, produced a voluminous allegorical exposition of the Cancticle c. 405–415. The layman-abbot Cassiodorus' supposed commentary on it from the middle of the fifth century is spurious. Isidore's supposed commentary is, in turn, an excerpt from the Cassiodorian forgery. (On this cf Altaner, *op. cit.*, pp. 554, 586.)

30. Book 2, Introduction, PL 91:1083–1084.

31. Book 4, Col. 1133.

32. *Ibid.*, Col. 1134.

33. *Op. cit.,* Col. 1102.
34. *Op. cit.,* Col. 1141.
35. PL 100:194.
36. Epístola 11, to Aedilred, king of Northumbria, and to his princes, PL 100:159.
37. *Commentarium in Joannem,* Book 1, Chapt. 2, Verse 8, PL 100:771–772.
Alcuin was a rarity among the teachers and writers of his age. He was not a cleric or a monk, but a married layman and parent. But he apparently found no difficulty in accepting the ranking of his "order" reported in the last sentence of this passage.
38. PL 97:281–282.
39. *Expositio in Matthaeum,* Book 9, Chapt. 18, PL 120:647.
40. *Ibid.*
41. Book 1, Chapt. 14, PL 107:484.
42. Book 1, Chapt. 7, PL 107:461.
43. This is Book 17 of his *Enarratio in Epistolas Pauli,* PL 112:381–478.
44. *Loc. cit.,* Col. 456.
45. *Ibid.*
This honestly realistic assessment of the Church's condition and its relationship to Christ has consequences for the image-theology of the sacrament in marriage. These consequences will be examined more detailedly in the final chapter, but they are worth suggesting at this point. Assuming what later theologians will take for granted, that Christian marriages' sacramentality lies in their imaging the Christ-Church relationship, what may one expect in these marriages when this relationship is so troubled? Since the relationship of the actual Church to Christ is a process slow, painful and wavering in its growth in trust and love, ought one not take for granted that Christian marriages will involve the same process? Does one conclude from this that these marriages' being sacraments is not a simply given characteristic but is one to be acquired in painful process? And does the gaining of the sacramental status occur somewhere along the process?
46. *Ibid.*
47. *Ibid.*
48. Rabanus' insistence on dealing with marriage as it is lived by spouses instead of as idealized by religious writers appears in this same *Expositio in Epistolam ad Ephesios,* Book 18. Despite its length it deserves quotation at length.

"That the wife fear her husband" (Ambrose). Because a man and woman have the same nature a husband is advised that in loving his wife he is loving himself. But because the wife is a person inferior by condition although not in nature, she is commanded to be subject to her husband and to fear him (Jerome). Note that while a husband is commanded to love his wife but she to fear him (for love is appropriate to a husband but fear to a wife), a servant is commanded not only to fear but to tremble. Hence Paul says later, "Servants, obey your human masters with fear and trembling. But let a wife (he says) fear her husband."

If the fear of God that arises from fear of punishment keeps the one who fears from being perfect, how much more imperfect will a wife be who fears not only God but her husband. Hence we must ask whether the wife and her fear in this case are to be understood physically (*carnaliter*). For frequently wives are found to be much better than their husbands. They rule them. They manage their homes. They bring up the children and hold the family together while husbands go on their sexual adventures and frolick with prostitutes. Whether these women are to govern their husbands or to fear them I leave to the reader to decide.

But if in allegory (as I said above) the wife is to be understood as the body and the husband as the soul, there is nothing incongruous in the man's fearing her as his handmaid (*ancilla*) lodged in inferior rank and of less worthy substance. . . . But if one understands husband and wife in the literal sense, one can see two meanings in the word "fear." One is that about which John says "To fear is to be punished," and "One who fears is not yet perfect" (1 John 4). According to this servants have the spirit of servitude in fear. . . . Another meaning is that which philosophers call *eulathéia,* and which we call reverence, although the meanings of the two are not exactly the same. And the prophet understood the fear of those who are perfect as he said in Psalm 30 about those who though perfect still fear, "There is nothing wanting to those who fear him." Therefore a wife understood literally can be commanded to fear her husband in the sense of showing him reverence (*ut revereatur virum suum*). (*loc. cit.,* Cols 462–463)

49. In H.T. Bruns, *Canones Apostolorum et Conciliorum Saeculorum IV, V, VI, VII.* Berolini, 1839. Vol. 2, p. 143.

50. *Op. cit.,* Vol. 2, p. 151.

51. *Op. cit.,* Vol. 2, p. 310.

52. Epistola 26, ad Probum (in A. Bevilacqua, "The History of the Indissolubility of Marriage," *Proceedings of the Twenty-Second Annual Convention of the Catholic Theological Society of America,* Vol. 22, p. 284).

53. *Ibid.*

54. PL 99:299.

55. In Gratian's *Decretum,* Case 30, Question 5, PL 187:1447–1448. Gratian includes the passage under the heading, "That clandestine marriages must not be formed, according to the authority of Pope Evaristus in his Epistola I to the bishops of North Africa."

56. In his *Capitularium Collectio* Benedict provided a summation of Carolingian legislation on marriage—in the awkward Latin so typical of his age.

In the work of our council we agreed also on some other issues pertaining to the obedience and the well-being of the lay faithful. We here pass over detailed explanation and do no more than mention them. They [the lay married] must understand that marriage was instituted by God, not for the sake of carnal pleasure but rather in order to have children; in order to preserve virginity until marriage, as our authorities have taught; so that those who have wives must not also have lovers and concubines; that they ought to love their wives chastely and show them honor as the more fragile vessel; that sexual intercourse with their wives must be for the sake of offspring, not for pleasure; that husbands should abstain from intercourse with their wives when the latter are pregnant; that they should abstain during their wives' menstrual period; that, as the Lord teaches, a man commits adultery if he dismisses his wife and takes another, except in the case of adultery; that Christians must avoid incest. . . . (PL 97:867–868)

57. Epistola 21, PL 126:148
58. *De Divortio Lotharii Regis et Tetbergae Reginae,* Interrogatio 3, PL 125:653.
59. The document is in PL 125:619–772.
60. This is in PL 126:132–153.
61. PL 126:145.
62. *Ibid.*
63. PL 125:639.
64. *Loc. cit.,* Col. 642.
65. *Ibid.*
66. *Loc. cit.,* Cols. 649–650.
67. *Ibid.*

The context of this statement affords a singular meaning to this ninth-century exhortation to marital love. Just before it Hincmar pointed out that if a master kills his servant he is excommunicated for two years if he killed without a judge's approval. If a house-mistress flogs her servant, he adds, and the latter dies under the flogging, the mistress is to be denied Communion for seven years if she killed the servant deliberately, five years if unintentionally, saving always her right to viaticum, "which is never to be denied one at point of death." Hincmar's *a fortiori* argument for marital love here has as its point of departure this Christian norm of kindness toward a servant—about whose chances for viaticum he says nothing.

68. *Op. cit.,* Col. 736.
69. The collection is in PL 132:184–400.
70. This is in PL 140:537–1058.
71. *Op cit.,* Cols. 815–830.
72. Book 6 is in PL 161:1243–1278, Book 7 in the same volume, Cols. 1279–1304.

Variations and contrasts in Yves' selection of titles betrays the status of marriage in the Church of his age. Book 1 of his *Panormia* treats *De sacramento baptismatis* in Chapters 8 to 112 (Cols. 1049–1070), *De sacramento confirmationis* in Chapters 113 to 122 (Cols. 1069–1072), and *De sacramento Eucharistiae et celebratione missarum* in Chapters 123 to 162 (Cols. 1071–1084). It has no *De sacramento matrimonii.* And not until Book 6 is there *De nuptiis et matrimonio* Cols. 1243–1278. In all of Books 6 and 7 of the *Panormia* the sacrament of marriage appears only when Yves quotes Augustine about the perpetuity of the marital bond in analogy with the perpetuity of the baptismal character. His independent use of the word *sacramentum* is only in the subtitle, *De sacramento et juramento reconciliationis,* where it refers to a commitment under oath to take back a spouse who has been unjustly accused and dismissed (in PL 161:1289–1290).

73. PL 161:1249.
74. PL 161:1257.
75. *Ibid.*

76. PL 161:1258.
Yves quotes this again in Book 2, Chapter 5, when he deals with the separation of spouses because of infidelity. The point there is to argue that the separation does not end the marriage.

BIBLIOGRAPHY

Joyce, George H.: *Christian Marriage.* Second Edition. London, Sheed and Ward, 1948. Chapter 2: "The Formation of Christian Marriage."
Kelly, William: *Pope Gregory II on Divorce and Remarriage.* Roma, Pontificia Università Gregoriana, 1976.
Mackin, Theodore: *Marriage in the Catholic Church: Divorce and Remarriage.* Chapter 10: "From Augustine to the Canonists of the Twelfth Century."
Schillebeeckx, Edward: *Marriage: Human Reality and Saving Mystery.* N.Y., Sheed and Ward, 1965. Volume 2: *Marriage in the History of the Church:* Christian Marriage from the Fourth to the Eleventh Centuries.

8. THE SACRAMENT IN THE EARLY SCHOLASTICS

We move now from a substantially completed Gregorian reform early in the twelfth century into the thirteenth, and there into the scholastic theology and study of law at their richest. It is in examining these one hundred and fifty years that we find the answer to the question that asks how the Catholic Church came finally to grant marriage a place among its sacraments, with a claim thereto seemingly as worthy as that of baptism and the Eucharist.

We have seen the reasons for the delay in granting this place to marriage: the closing down of the theological investigation of marriage for nearly seven centuries while energy was spent almost exclusively on the reform and regulation of marital conduct among the newly Christian peoples of Europe. Within the long moratorium there was the hobbled condition of the few who did try to reason speculatively about marriage, such as Lanfranc at Bec in Normandy until 1070, later at Canterbury until 1089,[1] and the two Anselms, the Piedmontese who followed Lanfranc from Bec to the archbishopric of Canterbury (1093–1109), and Anselm of Laon in France (d. 1117). Working in isolation they were starved of the stimulus that comes of discussion and dispute with peers as acute as themselves. And lacking the keenly analytic metaphysics of Aristotle they had not the intellectual tool needed indispensably for doing a theology of the sacrament in marriage. Scholarship in the subject was still dominated by the *sententiarii,* the collectors and arrangers of anthologies of patristic, papal and conciliar statements about marriage. There was, always, the legacy of fear and suspicion of sexuality in marriage passed down by both the Eastern and Western Fathers, and kept alive by the writers of the transition into early medieval Christendom. Again the statement of their near-dilemma: we are told that there is a sacrament in marriage, as there is in baptism, that brings God's grace; that in it is a *mystérion,* an image of some sacred, invisible reality. But how can a man-woman relationship whose typical conduct is the carrier of hereditary sin, and in practice almost inevitably sinful, be an

image of something sacred and an avenue of the divine grace that produces holiness?

We know in large outline the moves that led to and stimulated the
serious intellectual work whence came the definitive locating of the
sacrament in marriage, and the accepting of marriage among the
Church's sacraments. We have already seen that the Gregorian reform
included a thorough inventory of conciliar legislation in the Western
Church, including the legislation for marriage. We have glimpsed samples of this in the work of Burchard of Worms and of Yves of Chartres.
It had the effect of bringing to light the discordance and indecisiveness
of much of the legislation to date. The rediscovery of Roman law in its
fullness in Justinian's sixth-century emendation of the Theodosian Code
conspired with the improving talent of critical analysis in the universities
to produce the science of canon law at the end of the eleventh century
and early in the twelfth. With this the law of the Church became both
systematic and self-critical—twin growths in character that produced, as
one valuable product among others, Gratian's *Decretum* in the middle of
the twelfth century. His name for it tells its character: *Concordantia
discordantium canonum* (A Concordance of Discordant Canons). The
renaissance of philosophy, spurred especially by the translation into
Latin of the rest of Aristotle's works beyond the *Organon,* and especially of his *Metaphysics,* provided scholars with the analytic tool they
had lacked. With it they moved beyond the gathering and arranging of
texts from the past, and beyond the succinct and fragmentary glossating
of them in the margins of manuscripts. The fruit of this by the last
quarter of the twelfth century, valuable beyond compare and destined to
become the work-book of theologians for the next century and a half,
was Peter Lombard's anthology, *Libri IV Sententiarum* (The Four
Books of Sayings). It included a feature that its ancestor collections had
lacked, a feature born of the newly matured critical method. This was
the juxtaposing of conflicting statements from the fathers and authorities not merely to show their disagreement as Abelard did in his *Sic et
non,* but to try to resolve the disagreement into accurate knowledge.

Finally, the Cathars and Albigensians renewed in the twelfth century, in southern France and in Italy, the ancient dualistic assault on the
material component of human nature, and therefore on marriage and
sexuality. This drove scholars again to their defense. As Augustine had
done seven centuries earlier, they included in this defense the presence
in marriage of the sacrament. But they lingered over it and sought to
explain how its presence renders marriage good and even holy, where
Augustine had only reported his rich intuition rhetorically and moved
on.

We take up the examination of this final inclusion of Christian marriage among the sacraments—and simultaneously bridge over into the
high middle ages—by first accounting for the role in this inclusion of the

gradually enriching wedding liturgy in the Western Church. Edward Schillebeeckx's summary thesis about this role is that the ecclesiastical authorities' taking the public, familial, traditional solemnization of marriage gradually under their jurisdiction brought the wedding and the marriage to be more and more a visible religious reality.[2] This in turn spurred the authorities and simultaneously the scholars to finally identify and explain the *sacramentum* that had been acknowledged in Christian marriages for centuries. A salient element of his thesis is that the authorities took juridical control of marriages not because they acknowledged finally that among Christians they are sacraments—acknowledging this as the fruit of a matured theology of marriage. The converse happened: their taking over of marriages for pastoral–canonical reasons—their bringing them into the mainstream of juridical and liturgical life in the Church—heightened awareness of their kinship with baptism, with the Eucharist, and somewhat paradoxically, with the ceremonial veiling and blessing of women in the vocation of consecrated virginity. This in turn inspired more careful theological examination of the *sacramentum*.

The Appropriation of Marriage by Church Authorities

We note again how the regulation of marriages came, by the year 1000, quite completely into the hands of churchmen. The centralized authority of the Roman empire had fragmented in the fifth century and given place to a multitude of regional authorities. These were in character civil and ecclesiastical authorities fused into one, so that life in newly Christian Europe was ruled by kings as presumed heads of their local churches, or more often by nobles and bishops having equal status in councils. But the centralization that Charlemagne had effected briefly in the ninth century was recreated permanently in the last decades of the tenth with the reestablishment of the Holy Roman Empire under the Ottos in Germany, with the coming of the Capetian dynasty in France, and with the new Norman monarchy in England. Accordingly local princes lost ecclesiastical advantage to kings and emperors and to the bishops whom these installed, or to the bishops installed independently by the popes. The latter bishops were especially powerful where they held not only ecclesiastical authority but civil authority as well—or at least claimed, or were conceded, authority over the civil effects of marriage such as the setting of incest barriers and the determining of rules of inheritance.

Another brief consideration of the False Decretals will remind how they were used to strengthen the authorities' regulation of marriages. Recall that these were produced in the Frankish church near the middle of the ninth century to reassert the authority of the bishops and therefore their right to discipline marriages, especially regarding the worst abuses of the time—incestuous marriages, kidnap and forced marriages, clandestine marriages, and dismissal of wives joined with adultery. The decretals, the authentic among them and the inauthentic, made demands that both brought the concluding of marriages under public surveillance and worked toward setting a fixed form for this concluding. These demands included that the intended bride be asked for in marriage from those holding authority over her, whether her parents, others of her family, or a guardian. A dowry had to be agreed on before the wedding as convincing evidence of parental consent. A pre-nuptial examination must go before betrothal and the setting of the dowry in order to verify that the intended spouses were not related within forbidden degrees, that the marriage would not be the denouement of a concubinage, and that the wedding would proceed with the consent of those whose consent was required. A false decretal attributed to Pope Evaristus (99–107) demanded that unless the bride be presented in marriage by her parents and/or relatives, and at the proper time, her presumed marriage would be held invalid and the union to be either concubinage or adultery.

Included in the collection was this ruling from the Fourth Council of Carthage that indicated the function of the priest late in the history of the north African church: when the bride and groom were to be blessed by the priest, they were to be presented to him in the church by the parents or the paranymphs. Once they had received the blessing they were to keep their virginity that night out of reverence for the blessing.[3] An almost identical decree was attributed to Pope Soter (166–175): "Let the bride and groom be blessed with prayers and offerings; let them be betrothed and dowered according to the law; let them be accompanied by paranymphs and publicly and solemnly accepted [as husband and wife]. Let them also abstain for two or three days."[4]

We recall that a synod of Bavarian bishops organized by Boniface c. 743 had already required that no one marry before the pre-nuptial inquiry had been completed by both parents and priest. A capitulary issued by Charlemagne in the Frankish church in 802 had required this. And canons on marriage included in the collection sent to Charlemagne by Pope Hadrian in 774 had demanded the same.

A byproduct of such demands as these, when and where they were heeded, was to open a defined and permanent place for the priest in the concluding of a marriage. We recall that from as early as the fourth century it had been the custom in the Mediterranean churches to invite a bishop or priest to the wedding to bless the marriage. Now the elective and invitational status of this blessing began to migrate toward the obligatory.

The ways in which marriages were concluded by the turn of the eleventh century indicate how much marriage had been taken under Church authority and the clergy had gained a fixed function in the ceremony. Two parts of a letter of instruction, *Ad consulta vestra,* sent by Pope Nicholas I in November of 866 to the legation of Bogor, king of the Bulgars, who shortly before had accepted Christianity along with his people, offer evidence of how far these had gone by the middle of that century. The first part instructed concerning the details of the wedding ceremony.

> When they form the marital covenant [*nuptialia foedera*] our men and women do not wear on their heads bands of gold or silver or of any other metal. But after the betrothal, which is a promise of the marriage-to-be, we solemnize the covenant [*foedera*] by the act of consent of those who are marrying as well as of those in whose authority they live. After the bridegroom has taken his chosen bride to himself by placing a ring on her finger, and has in the presence of invited guests given to her the dotal gift agreed on by both and stated in writing (and has done these things promptly, although not before the time set by law), both he and she are led forth to the marital covenant [*ambo ad nuptialia foedera producuntur*]. They are first made to take their place in the Lord's church, where they make the required offering through the service of the priest, and finally receive the blessing and the heavenly veil.[5]

Despite its awkward attempt at semi-poetic description, and despite the assigning of at least two meanings to the word *foedera* in its three uses, and thus making impossible a verification of the exact moment that creates the marriage, the passage does make clear that the marriage is to be concluded publicly, with the permission of the parental authorities, in their presence and in that of other witnesses, and is to include the priest's blessing, the veiling of the bride and groom, and possibly their participation in a nuptial Mass.

But earlier, in Chapter 3 of this same letter, Nicholas had already undermined the intended effect of his urging this public ceremony on the newly converted Bulgars. Adhering to the Roman principle of freedom in choosing a spouse and in the manner of creating a marriage, he insisted, "According to the laws the consent of the parties concerned is sufficient to create their marriage. But if consent is perchance the only element omitted from the wedding, all the others, even including copula itself, are rendered null and void [*frustrantur*]. The great doctor John Chrysostom attests to this in his words, 'It is not coitus that creates a marriage, but consent [*voluntas*].' "[6]

The place of the clergy in concluding marriages in the Frankish kingdom and then in the France of the Capetian dynasty was assured by the adoption there of the Roman ceremony of marriage contained in the Gregorian sacramentary. The adoption was assured in turn by the suppression of the earlier Gallic liturgy. This survived only in fragments thereof taken into the Roman liturgical books. Caesarius of Arles (470–543) had already during the Merovingian period introduced the Roman form of nuptial blessing into his diocese. Pepin installed the Roman ceremony in his nascent Carolingian monarchy in the middle of the eighth century. Until Pope Hadrian's gift to Charlemagne of "the sacramentary of Gregory the Great" this was the ceremony contained in the Gelasian sacramentary.

Marriage According to the Sacramentaries

Despite its origin in the north of France at the beginning of the eighth century the Gelasian sacramentary carried forward the substance of its predecessor, the Leonine. It is helpful to recall some of the salient features of the latter. It contained a Mass quasi-nuptial in character and offered *pro famula tua illa*—for the bride.[7] This specific reference was in its canon in the *Hanc igitur*. At the end of the Mass, before the dismissal, were interposed a fourth oration and a long blessing, both exclusively bridal. In the scriptural elements of the Mass the Old Testament predominated, with creation themes and the model wives of the patriarchs given particular attention. In this blessing there is no sacramental reference nor any reference to Christ. The Pauline analogy of Ephesians 5 does not appear. An implicit theory of marriage is also present in the blessing, in its saying that God instituted marriage for children, but also for the spouses' love, mutual help and fidelity. Even though the entire ceremony has the title indicator, *incipit relatio nuptialis,* a veiling does not appear in it.[8]

The marriage ritual in the Gelasian sacramentary is the Leonine-Roman carried forward, but because of its origin in northern France it contains Gallic elements. It continues the "bride alone" attitude of the Leonine in its long blessing, a revision of the Leonine, to be read at the end of the canon. A distinct Gallic feature is the inclusion of the groom as a recipient of the long blessing just before the dismissal. The Mass has also a long preface to the canon which refers to marriage as a yoke of concord, an indissoluble chain of peace, and meant for children, who are in turn for the increase of the Church.

The Gregorian sacramentary's marriage ritual takes a distinct turn into the New Testament.[9] In its long nuptial blessing at the end of the canon there is a reference to Christ's command that a marriage not be sundered, and reference to Ephesians' metaphor of Christ as bridegroom-head of the Church. This leads in turn to a reflection on the new husband and wife as companions despite the sin of the first husband and wife and the universal destruction at the deluge. Those elements are in the deprecatory part of the blessing; its benediction part counsels that the bride remain chaste and faithful in Christ and replicate the virtues of the holy women of the Old Testament.

In a few early ninth-century versions of this sacramentary, before Charlemagne's enthusiastic Romanization of his empire, the verbs in this blessing are in the plural number in order to include the husband and also to align it with the plural reference of the Mass orations. But the later and imposed versions restored the blessing for the bride alone. The reason for this reaches far back into Roman tradition, beyond the beginning of Christianity to the pagan veiling of the bride. Stevenson explains the bridal exclusivity of the blessing in conjunction with the introduction in it of the Ephesians metaphor.

> The question really centers around the *use* of the Ephesians passage, and I would venture to suggest that it was inserted as a relatively new idea by the author of the Gregorian prayer (it is not a favourite image of marriage among the Fathers) in order to explain the already-existing and long-standing custom at Rome which went right back to pagan times.[10]

But despite this entry of Ephesians into the Gregorian nuptial blessing, the passage hardly came into enthusiastic use. Through the twelfth century it is found among the scriptural readings in only one liturgy, that of the Troyes missal of that century. Other New Testament passages were preferred, among them 1 Corinthians 6:15–20 (a warning against fornication), 1 Corinthians 7:32–37 (a commendation of the celibate life), John 2:1–11 (the narrative of the wedding feast at Cana of Galilee) and Matthew 19:1–6 (Christ's assertion against the Pharisees of marriage's permanence).

What emerges from this nearly exclusive installation of the Gregorian Roman liturgy in the churches of Europe by the end of the ninth century at the latest is that marriage was being drawn irreversibly into the religious experience of the Church as a whole, and that the clergy were being accorded and were taking an increasingly important place in the concluding of marriages. But this was accomplished not principally by substituting the Gregorian liturgy for the various European peoples' traditional procedures in marrying. It was done for a long while by inducting the priest into those procedures and having him take over what had hitherto been done by parents, by guardians or by the *mundoaldus*. The folding of the entire procedure into the wedding Mass was to come later, in the late twelfth and the thirteenth centuries, after the triumph of the *consensus* theory of the creation of the marriage.

Regional Wedding Ceremonies

Sketches of the German and Frankish wedding ceremonies, and glimpses of the Spanish and English, will show how and where the priest could be given a role in the traditional ceremonies.[11]

From the end of the fifth century through the eleventh the German procedure in marrying included the following steps. The bride was requested from her parents for the husband-to-be by his parents or by an intermediary, the *mundoaldus*. The dowry was arranged by the two families and the couple was betrothed by the giving of the ring. This seemingly coercive management of the bride's life was qualified, at least in Bavaria from the eleventh century onward, by the emergence of the *Friedelehe*, the granting to the bride of the right to determine whom she would marry and when, as shown in the legend of Gudrun, in the *Nibelungenlied* and in other sources.

The second step in the process was the dialogue of consent carried on in the presence of blood relatives of both parties. Bride and groom were asked their consent—this by a third party who was traditionally the *mundoaldus*. This suggested even more clearly the bride's right of self-determination and her juridical equality with the groom. And it was here that the priest could and did enter the ceremony as he replaced the *mundoaldus*. But the husband's authority might be reasserted in two ways: first and most frequently, where the bride did not claim the *Friedelehe*, by her being handed over into the *mundium* of the groom by the *mundoaldus* or by the priest taking his place; less frequently by the groom's drawing his sword whereon both he and the bride swore fidelity to one another.

The process was concluded in a third step, the *domum ductio,* wherein the groom led his bride to their new home. After these steps— sometimes even several days after them—came the properly religious elements, perhaps the full nuptial Mass with the blessing of the bride according to the Gregorian sacramentary and then her veiling, or the blessing and veiling as a ceremony done outside a Mass.

Where in the sequence of these several steps the bride and groom became spouses to one another, by which gesture or catena of gestures their marriage was created, remained a matter of dispute, as I have already suggested, until after the middle of the twelfth century and the triumph-cum-compromise of the *consensus* theory of the Paris canonists. This is not to gainsay Nicholas I's declaration that the expression of consent is the one essential element in creating a marriage. It is rather to point to the indecision about which step in the process was to be taken as the expression of consent that creates a marriage—not a betrothal but a marriage—and which creates a marriage that is invulnerable to dissolution.

The manner of concluding marriage among the Franks passed through two main stages during the centuries that interest us, first through those before the Carolingian Romanization, then through those following it and regulated by the Pseudo-Isidorian decretals. In both periods the authorities, both civil and ecclesiastical, kept the traditional secular and familial ceremony along with their accrued Christian religious elements. When Caesarius of Arles urged in the sixth century that marriages be concluded *secundum morem Romanum*—according to Roman custom—it was to the latter elements that he referred.

The process began with the parents of the groom asking those in authority over the bride-to-be for her hand in marriage for their son. At this point, at the urging of the False Decretals, the authorities examined the proposed union for its legitimacy, with special concern that it not be incestuous and that it not be the continuation of concubinage. It was at this point, from the time of Charlemagne onward, that a priest might enter the process, as he joined family and civil authorities in the examining.

If legitimacy were verified, a dowry and gifts were agreed on and exchanged. On the wedding day the bride was brought by the paranymphs to the door of the church. Here her parents or guardian presented her to the groom. Here too as time went on the priest intervened to present the bride to the groom, or later to present the spouses to one another. He then blessed them, in a modification of the early Gallic blessing *in thalamo*—in the nuptial chamber. When Roman custom had gained place the bride was veiled there at the church door, a gesture continuous with the blessing and deemed an element of it. There followed the nuptial Mass, during which the bride and groom offered gifts for its celebration. Then came the wedding feast and the leading of the new husband and wife to their bridal chamber. Hincmar wanted that the first intercourse be a part of the process of marrying, a judgment that was to stay and ferment until the resolution of the *consensus* dispute.

The earliest evidence coming down to us of wedding customs in the British Isles dates from the late Anglo-Saxon period in the tenth and eleventh centuries, after the controlling influence of the Gregorian sacramentary had already entered. An element kept over from the earliest Gallic-Celtic epoch was the *benedictio in thalamo*. This was preceded by the leading of the bride to the new home and into her bridal chamber; it was followed by the blessing of the bridal pair themselves, and of the wedding ring. The point of entry for the priest in this process is obvious, but all the more so where the *domum ductio* was either preceded or followed by a nuptial Mass. In some dioceses this was celebrated in the morning, with the blessing of the home and the thalamus put off until evening. In this case the wedding ring too might be blessed during the morning Mass.

The Spanish tradition deserves at least brief mention because in it the veiling of the bride and the binding together of the wedding pair had exceptional importance. In Book 2, Chapter 19 of his *De Ecclesiasticis Officiis,* Isidore of Seville explained the symbolic reference of these.[12] The veiling of the bride signified her submission to her husband's authority. The binding together of the bridal pair by a single ribbon signified the invulnerability of their marriage to dissolution. That the ribbon was both white and violet signified respectively the purity of life expected of the spouses and the continuation of the blood lines, i.e. that they would both keep continence at the right times and render the marriage debt at the right times according to the counsel of Paul in 1 Corinthians 7.

What we have reviewed here briefly of the wedding ceremonies that were common in Europe through the twelfth century can only begin to explain why the marriages were finally, in that same century, accorded full status among the other sacraments. That the bridal couple, or the bridal chamber, or the bride alone was blessed tells that marriage was thought to retain the goodness that was designed into it in the beginning, in the garden. This goodness was there verified by God's first blessing of the marriage and his giving it its *intentio* by this blessing: "Increase and multiply and fill the earth." Implicit in the blessing was that the spouses would live obedient to God's will, would be good and even holy, if they lived out this vocation. The added blessing of the bridal chamber and even of the nuptial bed in these European traditions clarified and emphasized this vocation and its potentiality.

That the creating of the marriage was associated with the Eucharist in increasing proximity grew from and verified the understanding that in their marrying the Christian spouses were simultaneously drawn into the interior life of the Church and meeting with the redeeming Christ in doing so. That redemption was somehow available in their marriage was the clear suggestion in this.

Ephesians 5:21–33 in the Developing Theology of the Sacrament

But through all this adolesence of the theology of marriage we find with some surprise that an element that was later to be central in it developed very slowly. This was the interpretation drawn from Ephesians 5:21–33, that the marriage of a Christian couple images the love relationship, the metaphoric marriage, of Christ and the Church.

How the passage and its relevance to marriage contributed to the developing conviction that the marriages of Christians are among the Church's sacraments Schillebeeckx explains in his *Marriage: Human Reality and Saving Mystery*.[13] He maintains that the idea that the marriage of two Christians is a sacrament did not enter Christian minds, say from the fourth century onward, from an analysis of the Ephesians passage, nor by inference from the "two in one flesh" declaration of Genesis 2:24. It entered via a gradual assimilation of the wedding ceremony (of the lower clergy and of exceptionally devout Christians) to the veiling ceremony of consecrated virgins. He notes what is obvious about Ephesians, that one of its two key metaphors has the Church as the bride of Christ (and that this became central to the Gregorian sacramentary's implicit understanding of Christian marriage). But as early as Tertullian in the third century the vocation in which this celestial marriage was understood to be reenacted on earth was not Christian marriage but a woman's living a life of virginity consecrated to God. And the liturgical practice that dramatized this relationship of the Church to Christ was not the Christian wedding, but the ceremony of veiling the virgin with the traditional Roman *flammeum nuptiale*—the red nuptial veil. This was done to signify that in her consecration the woman became a bride of Christ. Thus this ceremony, and the woman's consecrated life, were deemed to enact, to image publicly and officially, the essential relationship of the Church to Christ.

But to defend marriage against its denigrators, the Manichees principal among them, this function of imaging the Christ-Church relationship began to be attributed to it as well, attributed to it in a way both like and unlike the way it was attributed to the veiling and the life of the consecrated virgin. Whereas she is related maritally to Christ immediately, through no human medium, the Christian bride is related to him in and by her marriage, through the medium of her husband. In marriage the Church's submissive love for Christ is acted out symbolically in the wife's loving and obedient service of her husband, analogically as the virgin acts out the same obedient love of the Church not symbolically but directly. (A cloistered nun in adoration before the eucharistic sacrament would exemplify this.)

This interpretation demanded that the husband be accepted *in figura Christi,* as taking the role of Christ in the imaging to correlate with the wife's role as the Church. For this reason the husband was never blessed alone, and the earlier blessing of the bridal couple elided into the blessing of the bride alone. For to bless is to sanctify; but Christ needs no sanctifying, while the Church does and so too does the wife, the weaker member of the marriage. Again because in the metaphor Christ has and will have only one wife, the nuptial blessing and veiling were denied to a widow entering a second marriage. But that they were also denied to a bride who had earlier lost her virginity as an unmarried woman implied a foreclosed judgment on Ephesians 5:27. There Christ is portrayed as bathing his bride-Church in the (baptismal) water joined to the word so as to present her to himself "not having stain or wrinkle or anything like that." The denial of the blessing and veiling to the non-virginal bride implied not that the bride-Church was cleansed by Christ's bathing her, but that she came to it already without stain or wrinkle—and lacking any reason for being bathed.

Why then was the Christian marriage accepted among the sacraments while the veiling and life of the virgin were not, and this despite their having gained candidacy for inclusion long before marriage did? Schillebeeckx's answer draws again from the immediacy of the consecrated virgin's love relationship with Christ. She experiences the *mystérion,* the Christ-Church love, directly and not through any intermediary—most especially not through a conventional human relationship whose form and essential conduct can be taken as a *signum,* an imaging, a sensate acting out of the Christ-Church relationship. The real bride, on the contrary, lives in just such a relationship and conduct. She experiences the *mystérion* in them. Her marriage is a conventional human relationship-institution that has been taken up by the Church into its work of imaging God's action in human lives, and of carrying on this action. This taking up of the conventional is essential to the character of a sacrament, as conventional washing with water is essential to baptism, as nourishing with bread and wine is essential to the Eucharist. That is, a familiar and reasonably universal human institution or relationship or conduct (or a congeries of all three) must be taken up and engaged in imaging God's action in the world and in the carrying on of it if there is to be a sacrament.

Hence the acknowledgment of marriage's qualification for a place among the sacraments, an acknowledgment produced by detecting the dissimilar similarity of the bride's blessing and veiling to those of the consecrated virgin. As Schillebeeckx writes, "It was in the light of the veiling of virgins that the Church became explicitly aware of the separately religious 'sacramental' nature of marriage—the discovery of marriage as a sacrament was made in the Church in the light of 'virginity for the sake of the kingdom of God'."[14]

(Without referring to Schillebeeckx's interpretation expressly Stevenson disagrees with it, perhaps even unwittingly. He writes: "Metz's study has shown that the blessing of virgins with a special veil during their mass of consecration is borrowed from the more ancient blessing of the bride which we see in the sacramentaries, not vice versa."[15] I suggest a plausible, though of course unverified, resolution of the disagreement. It is that as a kind of religious event in the Church of the fathers the veiling of the bride antedated that of the consecrated virgin, since the former is acknowledged to come from pagan antiquity. This practice was borrowed for the consecrated virgin precisely because she too was understood to be a bride, but of Christ. But then the richer meaning of the virgin's veiling was reflected off her veiling back onto that of the bride— the meaning that in the bridal veiling the mystery of the Christ-church relationship is imaged and acted out.)

The Marital Problematic for the Medieval Church

Even if Schillebeeckx's interpretation is correct—that marriage was drawn into the company of the sacraments in the late eleventh century and the twelfth because of the assimilation of the wedding ceremony to the veiling of the consecrated virgin—substantial questions remain. In our century we are accustomed to speak of "the sacrament of marriage" in the sense that the marriage itself is the sacrament. This is current Roman Catholic doctrine. But it was not always so. As we have seen, in the fifth century Augustine wrote of the *sacramentum* in marriage, referring to it now as the spouses' inviolable pledge to one another, or to God (singly or jointly); then to their marriage's character as an image of an invisible sacred reality; then to a kind of seal that remains in the spouses' souls even if they separate permanently. He did not decide finally for any one of these as the sacrament in marriage. He left all of them as his legacy for the ensuing centuries' students of marriage. It was for them to find out which of these interpretations is the accurate one, or whether each may in its way have a part in marriages' sacramentality. We know that some were to suggest a fourth interpretation, namely that the sacrament is the priest's blessing of the couple or the bride, a gesture extrinsic to the marriage itself and fleeting in its existence.

In addition Augustine's speculation implied that the sacrament, if not something extrinsic to the marriage, at least accrues to it. If it is a pledge to God as known and worshiped by Jews and Christians, or an image of an invisible sacred reality (we know that in Augustine's mind this reality was the metaphoric marriage of Christ and the Church), these cannot be found in the marriages of non-believers who are polytheist or atheist. Yet no one denies that these can by their commitment create marriages which are not sacraments. Therefore either one must say that the marriages of Christians are totally different from those of such non-believers (which the Church of these centuries never said because it never required that converts from non-belief recreate their marriages), or one must say that the sacrament is something that accrues to the natural human relationship that non-believers can create. If this is true, where does it accrue in marriages? And which action by the spouses or by other agents puts it there?

But no answer to these questions about the sacrament's identity and about the agent or agents that create it could be worked out until two other and more fundamental questions were answered. These remained unanswered surprisingly far into the twelfth century. They asked precisely about these issues: which agency creates the marriage, and what a marriage is when it has been brought into existence. The first of these was the more urgent question of the two for the obvious reason that it touched every marriage at its creation in a most practical way. In a painful way it was at the heart of the abusive practice of clandestine marriages. For if the reciprocal consent of the parties is accepted as sufficient to create the marriage, no obstacle could be put effectively in the way of their making this consent non-ceremonially, without authorized witnesses.

Lurking in the shadow of these two issues was a third that was an ancient one now in a new guise and context. The denigration of marriage by the Gnostic rigorists through the first century and a half of Christian history, and by the Manichees in the fourth and fifth centuries, came back to life at the end of the eleventh among the Cathars. This was an ascetic movement grounded in a cosmic dualism; it started up among the Bulgars, then spread throughout the Christian part of the Mediterranean basin. It became especially strong in northern Italy and in southern France, where it took the name Albigensianism because of its stronghold there in Albi.

Because the Cathari ("the pure ones") believed physical reality to be essentially evil they condemned marriage; but like Gnostic libertines their conviction that they were free of all human law led some of them paradoxically to sexual promiscuity. To refute them scholars and councils had to verify the goodness in marriage. Augustine's argument against the Manichees that there are three goods in marriage was ready at hand. But using it brought with it the question about the place of intercourse in marriage and in the conduct that creates marriages. For if the procreation of children helps to make marriage essentially good, must not intercourse have an essential place in marriage? Therefore must not the agency that creates a marriage intend intercourse or even include it? If a marriage—indeed any marriage—is good because of the sacrament in it, must this not be found in the essence of marriage? And must it not be intended and put there by the agency that creates the marriage?

Tracing from the end of the eleventh century until the middle of the thirteenth through the work of answering these questions leads into the richest development thus far of the theology of marriage. This development is complex, in places illogical, and at certain points constrained by the demands of discipline and Catholic belief related to this theology only where consequences converge. The dominant example of the latter was the problem of explaining how one can say that Joseph and Mary, the mother of Jesus, were truly married while one yet holds to the tradition of Mary's permanent virginity. This conditioned seriously any judgment about the essentiality of sexual intercourse in marriage.

Canonists and Theologians of the Twelfth Century

In his *Panormia* Yves of Chartres favored the theory that a marriage is created by the consent of the parties. In support of it he quoted Pope Leo I's imprecise dictum in his *Epistola 167 ad Rusticum:* "No woman has entered a marriage unless a man has celebrated with her the nuptial ceremony."[16] Anselm of Laon (d. 1117) was more precise in his *Tractatus de Matrimonio,* affirming that the immediate agency creating a marriage is the parties' mutual consent.[17] However until the first intercourse their marriage is incomplete and can be dissolved. He added that because it is the parties' consent and not any Church minister that creates their marriage the unbaptized can marry. He said that the latters' marriages too are sacraments since they too are signs of the God who instituted marriage. But they lack the grace of charity that unites the spouses with God.

The debate about the agency that creates the marriage continued through the first half of the twelfth century. It was intricate, and was confused by the debaters' tardiness in agreeing on an exact and restricted set of terms for designating the acts thought essential in this agency. We can glance here at only a sampling of the terms and their elusive reference. *Desponsatio* and its cognate, *sponsalia,* were used with the most damaging ambiguity. At times they appear to have designated what we call betrothal, at other times the wedding ceremony. But they were not the only elusive terms. William of Champeaux (d. 1122) distinguished the *fides pactionis* (the pledge of agreement or covenant) and the *fides conjugii* (the pledge of marriage), affirming that only the latter creates a marriage, while the first is a man's promise that he will take the woman as his wife sometime in the future.[18] He enriched the vocabulary of the dispute even more by referring to the two steps as the *sponsalia de futuro* (the espousal for the future) and the *sponsalia de praesenti* (the espousal for here and now).

Peter Abelard made the same distinction in slightly different terms, the *foederatio de conjugio contrahendo* (the covenanting for the marriage to be contracted) and the *foederatio conjugii* (the covenanting of the marriage).[19] He and his disciples continued the thought begun by Anselm of Laon, that intending intercourse as the object of the marital consent is essential for creating a marriage.

Gratian's *Decretum*

But by the middle of the twelfth century the distinction between the two consents—*consensus de futuro* and *consensus de praesenti*—had been decided. The debaters had agreed too that by itself the first of these does not create a marriage, but only promises marriage in the future, and that it is the latter that creates the marriage. The debate then turned on more refined disagreements. Granted the *consensus de futuro* by itself cannot create a marriage. But when made under oath and followed by intercourse, although not a *consensus de praesenti,* may they not in combination create the marriage, especially since the combination may be interpreted as consent to marry here and now?

About the *consensus de praesenti*—even if, as many insisted, it is by itself sufficient to create the marriage, can it alone make the marriage to be indissoluble? If it can, and if, as Augustine and many following him had said, the sacrament is the cause and seal of indissolubility, does it not follow that the *consensus de praesenti* produces the sacrament and the indissolubility? But what then is left for the first intercourse to produce? And why has the Church for centuries allowed spouses to dissolve their marriages by entry into monastic life provided their marriages are unconsummated by first intercourse?

By the middle of the twelfth century the debate between the Roman and the European traditions had been taken over and championed, respectively, by the theologians of the University of Paris and the canonists of the University of Bologna. The master at Bologna was Gratian. We have already taken note of his *Concordance of Discordant Canons,* composed by 1140 or 1141, known commonly through the centuries as his *Decretum.*

To Gratian's mind the debate came to a point in this question: Are a man and a woman who have consented to marriage—whether by *consensus de futuro* or *consensus de praesenti*—truly married before their first intercourse? He acknowledged the consequences of the two possible contradictory answers. If a man and woman who have thus consented are not truly married before their first intercourse, Mary and Joseph were never truly married. But if they are, then a brother and sister, or a father and daughter, or a mother and son can marry, and do so innocently provided they never have intercourse.

In his Case 27, Question 2, Chapt. 34[20] he made use of a distinction that had already been made by the theologians at Paris, between a *matrimonium initiatum* and a *matrimonium ratum*—between an inchoate marriage and a completed marriage. It is the *matrimonium initiatum* that is created by the *desponsatio;* it is made *ratum* by first intercourse. With this distinction Mary and Joseph could be said to have been truly married. As to how their marriage was completed, Gratian suggested that a different and richer completion was there in the three goods of marriage: fidelity, offspring and the *sacramentum*. From this one may conclude that he did not think intercourse needed for producing the *sacramentum*.

But he failed at providing a resolution of the debate between the two schools because of his ambiguous use of the term *desponsatio*. He made it synonymous with the consent *de praesenti*, which was generally agreed to produce the inchoate marriage. But *desponsatio* was commonly used to designate betrothal; and elsewhere in this same passage he said that the *desponsatio* by itself is insufficient to create the marriage. At this point he advanced to his uniquely recommended solution: while the *desponsatio*—obviously synonymous in his mind with the *consensus de praesenti*—is by itself insufficient to create the marriage, nevertheless it has this effect, that with the ensuing intercourse the marriage does come into existence. In other words, for creating a marriage the consent and the subsequent intercourse act as co-causes, each insufficient without the other, but in cooperative tandem producing their effect. Gratian made this clear in commenting on the ancient axiom, "It is not intercourse that creates a marriage, but consent that does so."

> . . this is to be understood in the following way: intercourse without the intent to contract a marriage, and the deflowering of a virgin without the exchange of consent, do not create a marriage. But an antecedent intent to contract marriage and the exchange of consent have this effect, that in the losing of her virginity, or in her intercourse, a woman is said to marry her husband, or "to celebrate her marriage."[21]

Peter Lombard

Peter Lombard's masterwork followed Gratian's by a decade and a half. He composed his four *Libri Sententiarum*, his four-volume anthology of theological and philosophical statements, at the University of Paris during the years 1155–1158. It became a source-book and a kind of work-book for subsequent generations of scholars. A compiler of *senten-*

tiae had the prerogative of setting forth his own interpretations of the passages he had gathered, of criticizing them and drawing conclusions from them. Lombard used this prerogative generously, as is evident in his teaching on marriage that occupies Distinctions 26 through 42 of Book 4 of his compilation.

About the issue disputed by Bologna and Paris he was simple and clear. In Distinction 26, Chapter 6 he wrote that what creates a marriage is the mutual consent of the parties, expressed either in words or in equivalent signs.[22] His judgment about the essence of marriage he expressed obliquely in Distinction 28, Chapter 4.[23] There he faced the problem of all analysts of marriage, that of establishing a specific difference within the object of marital consent, some element of it that would make the consent distinctly marital, would make of it a cause whose effect is a marriage and nothing else, yet not so lodge intercourse as the specific element within that object as to define the virginal marriage out of possibility and thus deny the marriage of Joseph and Mary.

He acknowledged that procreation is among the *fines principales,* the principal ends, of marriage. Nevertheless he did not want procreation or even intercourse within the object of marital consent—and this for the reason mentioned just above. Apparently for this reason he named life in a marital society as the object of the consent that creates a marriage. This left intercourse and procreation as optional ingredients of this life.

In saying that the act that creates a marriage is the parties' mutual consent, he made the careful distinction that Gratian did not, between the *consensus de futuro* and the *consensus de praesenti.* Both are consents to marriage, but the first establishes only the betrothal. By itself, without the subsequent *consensus de praesenti,* it never creates the marriage, even when made under oath and followed by intercourse. It is only the *consensus de praesenti* that creates the marriage, and creates it before and separately from intercourse.

Both Lombard's and Gratian's answers to the question about the act or acts needed to create a marriage helped, each in its own way, to prepare the way for the later defining of marriage as a contract. Since both the consents, *de futuro* and *de praesenti,* bind the spouses in obligations of justice to exchange some good in the future, in obligations having lasting effects that can be verified and sanctioned forensically, the consents have the properties of contracting. For Gratian the consent *de praesenti* obligates the spouses to intercourse. For Lombard it obligates them to a life in marital union, with its rights and duties yet to be itemized. Marriage was to wait another century and a half until Duns Scotus called it a contract explicitly. When he did, he would take his two predecessors' thinking along the trajectory on which they had launched it. And for all who would after him ponder the sacrament in marriage, there awaited the task of showing where this could be found in a contract and its rights and obligations.

The Resolution of the Conflict

The disagreement between the canonists of Bologna and the theologians of Paris did not come to an end because the two bodies resolved it, or because one conceded victory to the other. They were no more likely to do that in the twelfth or thirteenth century than two proud university faculties are today. Indeed where the dispute came to an end was only in the larger and comprehensive institution, the Church, and there not by resolution or concession but by authoritative decree.

This went in favor of the theologians, but in steps and only with compromise. Alexander III (1159–1181), while still Cardinal Rolando Bandinelli, in his *Summa Rolandi* sided with Gratian. Later, in his *Sententiae*, compiled between 1150 and 1158, he went over to Lombard's opinion, agreeing that the mutual consent of the parties is sufficient to create their marriage provided it is expressed in proper formulation.[24] But before consummation by first intercourse it is incomplete and thus can be dissolved. The mind of the judge is evident in his qualifying his opinion with the proviso that in order to create the marriage the consent *de praesenti* must be expressed legitimately, in proper formulation. He accepted another practical qualification in ruling that when betrothal is followed by intercourse this creates a marriage even without the consent *de praesenti*. For this he offered two reasons, one of them the practical consideration that among some European peoples this had been the custom so long that the effort to suppress it would destroy peace among them. The other reason was that sworn betrothal followed by intercourse can be interpreted as here-and-now consent to marriage.

But Alexander's most effective and lasting contribution was his affirmation that until a marriage is consummated by intercourse—until it gains the biblical *unitas carnis,* the two-in-one-flesh condition—it remains incomplete and can be dissolved. In his *Compilatio Prima* he wrote, "God's command that a man or woman not dismiss the spouse refers only to a consummated marriage."[25]

An earlier and singular judgment by Alexander about a case presented to him by the archbishop of Genoa had, or at least could have had, serious consequences for not only the Catholic marriage law but for the theology of the sacrament as well. The case grew out of the Roman tradition's vulnerability to the clandestine marriage, a vulnerability that persisted because this tradition demanded no ceremony, no authorized witnesses in the creating of a marriage. In this case the parties had lived together publicly, but the man had later abandoned the union, claiming that it was no more than concubinage. The woman claimed it was a marriage. The question to Alexander asked how to determine which it had been.

His instruction to the archbishop was that he have his ecclesiastical judges inquire among the relatives and friends of the couple for evidence that could be adjudicated on an essential point. That is, did the man evidently *consider* the woman to be his wife? or to be his concubine? This consideration, this intent in the man's mind, was crucial since—and here the definition of marriage in Justinian's *Institutes* was put to use— ". . . a marriage is the union of a man and a woman that perseveres as an undivided sharing of life."

How the use of the definition could help in examining and judging the case is not at first apparent. In all outward, judicially verifiable traits marriage and concubinage look alike. Both relationships can intend and include cohabitation, intercourse, procreation and nurture, sexual exclusivity, and even the sacrament if this is taken as a pledge to stay together until death. That is, both can intend and include what are deemed the substance of marriage and the goals of marriage. They can be copies of one another. Yet one partner can claim that the relationship is a marriage, the other that it is only concubinage. An expression of marital consent could not be adduced as the distinguishing element, because if one party claimed it had been made, but clandestinely, while the other denied this, forensic examination could not verify which was telling the truth. The only means then of determination was to verify the parties' intent, with this to be inferred from their conduct while together.

Implicit in Alexander's instruction was his assumption that the *Institutes'* definition of marriage is an adequate one. Hence whether he intended to say it or not, he put the specific difference of marriage from concubinage in the man's and woman's intentions, but not their intentions to realize the Augustinian goods of marriage, whether conceived of as goals or not. For man and concubine can intend these while rejecting marriage, even while intending expressly and persisting in a relationship sinful in the eyes of the Church. This cannot but seem to identify as the finally decisive cause of marriage what pre-Christian Roman tradition had identified, the parties' reciprocal *affectio maritalis,* namely their will to be married to one another.

This question and Alexander's proposed tactic for answering it had a logical link with an issue lying at the time far down the path of marriage's history in the Catholic Church, an issue at least as weighty as the question itself. By the middle of the sixteenth century the majority opinion in the Church was that they are the spouses themselves who "administer" the sacrament of marriage to one another, as the authorities in the twelfth and thirteenth centuries had determined that it is their marital consent that creates their marriage. But since, according to Alexander's implication, it is ultimately their intent to be married to one another, their *affectio maritalis,* that causes their marriage to come into existence, does it not follow that the sacrament in marriage is produced in the same way—that their intention, their will to administer the sacrament to one another, is the necessary agent for putting it in their marriage, so that without their intention and will it is not put there? (The relevance of this question will surface more clearly toward the end of this study when we probe the issue of "the automatic sacramentality" of

Christian marriages, and the current denial by Catholic authorities that Christian spouses must want and intend the sacrament in order to have it in their marriages.)

They were Popes Innocent III (1189–1216) and Gregory IX (1227–1241) who most effectively and finally established the Catholic teaching about the creation of a marriage. In cases of *sponsa duorum*, wherein a woman has exchanged marital consent with two men successively through any of various combinations of betrothal promise followed by intercourse, or of marital consent without intercourse, Innocent ruled that the first marital consent by itself creates the marriage. This consent prevails against any other promise to marry followed by intercourse, whether the former be the betrothal promise or the promise *de praesenti*.[26]

The principle, "It is consent that creates the marriage, not intercourse," dominated all of Book 4 of Gregory's *Liber Decretalium*, which appeared in 1234.[27] With his rich contribution to and sponsorship of decretal law in the first half of the thirteenth century, the Roman (and Parisian) consensual theory of the agency that creates a marriage triumphed conclusively.

Hugh of St. Victor

During the first half of the twelfth century Hugh of St. Victor worked out the elements of an anthropology and of a theology of marriage that in combination were a striking innovation in his time. These elements appeared first in his *libellus epistolaris*, an essay in letter form, titled *De Beatae Mariae Virginis Virginitate* (On the Virginity of the Blessed Virgin Mary).[28] There he set forth his understanding of marriage's nature. He did this not in a formal attempt at defining, but as a needed tactic in a quite different task, one with which we are already familiar. It was a task which faced any Catholic scholar who set out to examine marriage in its nature and its sacrament. This was to justify two points of belief about Mary, the mother of Jesus. At first hearing the two seem contradictory, impossible of simultaneous affirmation. They are that Mary kept, and intended to keep, her physical virginity for the duration of her life. The other is that she was truly married to Joseph.

We know the causes of the apparent irreconcilability here that seems even a dilemma. This grew out of the Parisian interpretation, by Hugh's time gaining ground toward final authoritative acceptance, that the act creating a marriage is the spouses' consent; and that this consent is to a marital union that includes the right to and use of sexual intercourse. The conflict was obvious. Even if one says that Mary remained a virgin in fact, one could also say, in virtue of the definition just above, that if she and Joseph were truly married, she must have given up her virginity in intent. Or, if she kept her virginity in intent, she could not have intended marriage with Joseph, and thus was never married to him.

Hugh's device for breaking the dilemma was the first move of his innovative thinking. This is his definition of marriage, which begins conventionally enough:

> For what is marriage but a legitimate partnership of a man and a woman, a partnership in which each owes the self to the other by reciprocal and equal consent? But this owing may be understood in two ways: in one way that the spouses reserve themselves to one another; in a second way that they not deny themselves to one another. They reserve themselves in that after once consenting, they not go off to another partnership. They do not deny themselves in that they not hold back from those things that belong to their partnership. And this it is that creates a marriage, the free consent made legitimately between a man and a woman in which each pledges the self as debtor to the other.[29]

Hugh rounded off this definition by stating what a marriage itself is, the effect produced by the causal consent that he has just explained.

> And the marriage itself is the partnership created by such consent, a partnership which holds each spouse to what is owed as long as the other lives.[30]

He begins to break the dilemma concerning Mary's marital consent and her virginity by making immediately a distinction between that consent and a second consent. This second consent does not have a part in creating the marriage; it is only a companion or auxiliary to the consent that does. It is the consent to grant intercourse to the spouse on demand, or to demand it oneself. The obligation it sets binds the spouses equally.

This consent, because it does not have as its effect to create the marriage, produces not a bond but an *officium,* a duty. In this case the duty binds each spouse in two ways, that neither have intercourse with a third person and that neither deny intercourse to the other.

Hugh then adds a further qualification, which he believes opens the way for saying finally that Mary and Joseph were truly married despite never having intercourse and intending never to have it. The qualification is this, that the obligation to have intercourse does not bind spouses who have not made the second kind of consent explained above, even though they are married for having made the first consent.

That qualification made, Hugh must now deal with a substantial difficulty that it creates when read in consort with the conventional definition of marriage that he had accepted. This definition states that in marrying a man and woman exchange an obligation; they commit themselves to both render to one another something owed, and to refuse this something to any third party. But if what is owed is not sexual intercourse, what else is it? In both Hugh's asking and answering this question there is a hint of the next difficulty in series that he must deal with. For whatever the good that spouses exchange, the exchange must be unique enough—unique whether in the good exchanged or in the manner of exchanging, or in both—to mark marriage off from any other kind of human relationship which is created and maintained by an exchange of goods.

The exchange is not of sexual intercourse nor of the right to it. This Hugh has already stated clearly. Then his answer to the question takes the reader into the heart of his anthropology of marriage. It also, and almost without notice, enriches considerably the theology of the sacrament by enriching its human matrix.

Hugh says that the unique exchange a man and woman make to create their marriage is of a unique love. He calls this love by the familiar name *caritas*—agapaic love, or charity. The exchange of it creates a *vinculum caritatis,* a bond of self-giving love. He insists immediately that even marital relationships from which intercourse is absent are no less marriages for this absence. On the contrary, the reality as well as the holiness of a marriage is all the more present where intercourse is absent because this absence leaves more room for the kind of love Hugh here has in mind. In this marriage the commitment is rooted not in lust nor in the heat of passion but in the bond of love.[31]

He does not leave his explanation in this generality. By way of anticipating the next difficulty in series hinted at above, he lists some of the qualities of this marital love. They are qualities one may demand of a man and woman living in a union of souls, but qualities one need not expect of a couple convinced that their marriage is no more than a union of bodies.

A couple living in a marriage that is a love union of souls commit themselves to a lifelong exchange of trust, of sincere affection, of unfailing care, of loyal support, of strong comforting, of devoted fidelity. They can share all these—the joys of life along with the sorrows—because each regards the other as his or her self.

As for the physical expression of this love, one spouse can give this if the other needs it and because he or she needs it. This outward expression can spring from interior love, love so making the spouses already one that in the expression each is cherishing his or her own body and possessing his or her own soul in peace. That is, since each spouse thus lives for the other and not for the self, the consequence is that each will live for the self more happily and holily.[32]

Because all this has consequences for the sacramental marriages of Christian spouses, we may use this juncture in the examination of Hugh's interpretation to move finally from this epoch's effort to define marriage into its effort to understand the sacrament in Christian marriages. The two efforts were in places intimately intertwined, so that considering them discretely has done some violence to their history. Hugh himself was aware of the consequences for the sacrament flowing from his interpretation of marriage. He attended to them by turning to the scriptures with *a fortiori* logic. He reminded that in his letter to the Ephesians Paul had called marriage a *sacramentum magnum*. Paul did this because, as the book of Genesis first said, and as Christ repeated, the husband and wife become two in one flesh. But if their marriage is a great sacrament for that reason, *a fortiori* it is an even greater sacrament where the union is of their souls in God.

He sees immediately the consequence of saying this after having earlier said that a man and woman can be truly married despite permanently forgoing intercourse, and despite intending from the beginning never to have it. The consequence is this, that since Paul said that a marriage of two Christians is a great sacrament because of their union in one flesh, then one must accept the possibility of two kinds of sacraments in Christian marriage. Different Christian couples may create either of the two in their marriages, or they may create both. One they may create by a sexual union of bodies, the other through a love union of souls that omits the sexual and thereby transcends it.[33]

But now he must acknowledge and must reply to another difficulty in the way of his interpretation of marriage's nature, a difficulty the more formidable because it is drawn from God's command to the first man and woman as this is recorded in Genesis 2.

The difficulty is this, that God created the first woman and gave her to the man precisely in order to help him [*in adjutorium*]. But that with which she was to help God states quite explicitly. This was with the production of offspring. To make this his purpose clear God added an express command to this first married couple: "Increase and multiply, and fill the earth." Adam himself acknowledged this reason for which the woman was given to him when he commented, "This one . . . is bone of my bones and flesh of my flesh. For this reason a man will leave his father and mother and cling to his wife, and the two become one flesh."[34]

That would seem to clinch the case against Hugh's thesis that a woman could maintain her virginity but yet be married. Since a woman cannot help a man to propagate except by intercourse, and since Eve was given to Adam in such a way that they became two in one flesh, one must conclude that the essence of marriage is known from its purpose. This is sexual intercourse for the sake of propagation.

Hugh's response to this logical trap is a minor masterpiece of adroit and intricate logic worthy of his intellectual idol, Augustine. He points out that it is only after Adam commented that his woman is bone of his bone and flesh of his flesh that the scripture added *propter hoc*—"for this reason" of being already one in flesh and bone—that a man does three things. He leaves his father and mother; he clings to his wife; he becomes two in one flesh with her. But of the four things named here, the first three, including the woman's being flesh of the man's flesh and bone of his bone, suffice to create a marriage. (For Hugh's logic the woman's being thus flesh of the man's flesh and bone of his bone is distinct from their later becoming two in one flesh. It is only the last that bespeaks sexual intercourse.) Surely to be of one flesh and bone with a woman, and to cling to her, make a man to be married to her. The couple do not need to have intercourse or intend it in order to be married to one another. Indeed, becoming two in one flesh with her is not the only way in which a man may cling to his wife.

Moreover it is after he leaves his father and mother, and on condition that he leave them in order to go to her, that a man is said to cling to his wife. But what is it that he can have in the union with his wife only if he removes it from his union with his parents? Hugh's logic here is that if this can be identified, once again the core of marriage's nature will be found.

This is not cohabitation or love, since a man can have these simultaneously with both his parents and his wife. He can love both them and her, and he and his wife can live with his parents. And it is decidedly not sexual intercourse, since he never had this with his parents.

What the man must take from his parents and give only to his wife, Hugh claims, is a singular reach and intensity of love, and the inclusiveness of the partnership to which he commits himself. This is what "cling to his wife" means. It is the *affectio cordis*—the love that comes from the heart—and the bond of sharing. It is not sexual intercourse.

But if this is what "cling to his wife" means, this uniquely intense and inclusive love that can go on without intercourse and without the commitment to it, yet another obvious difficulty arises. Why need marriage be confined to the partnership of a man and woman unrelated by blood? Why can a man not marry his mother, or his sister, or for that matter his brother? Each of these he could love with a uniquely intense and inclusive love that is unexpressed sexually.[35]

To reply here Hugh takes the discussion entirely over into the territory of the sacrament. And there he reveals his most inclusive thinking about the sacrament.

But first he short-circuits the issue. He points again to the classic passage in Genesis and reminds his interlocutors of the trajectory of the divinely inspired comment on marriage: ". . . a man shall leave his father and mother and cling to his *wife*"—not to his sister, nor to his brother, nor again to the mother and father whom he has once left.

Then his theological argument; it is subtle and more than slightly forced. It is also unique in Catholic speculation on the sacrament. He claims that in a Christian marriage there is not one sacrament, but that there are two. And it is clear that by *sacramentum* in this context he means "image." There is the sacrament of marriage (*sacramentum conjugii*) and the sacrament of marital duty (*sacramentum officii*). The sacrament of marriage is an image found in a covenant of love (*in foedere dilectionis*); the sacrament of marital duty is an image found in the generation of offspring (*in generatione prolis*).

Indeed the first of these, the sacrament of marriage, is the marital love itself. Sexual intercourse is related to this love as a second sacrament within the love.

Since each of these sacraments is an image, it is in the difference of the imaging that the difference between the two sacraments is found. By reason of marital love the sacrament of marriage is an image of that love in the spirit by which God loves the human soul and the soul loves him in return (this is why this sacrament can exist without sexual intercourse). The sacrament of marital duty is an image of the love between Christ and the Church, which takes place in the flesh (this is why the sacrament of marital duty is expressed in sexual intercourse).

Hugh uses the opportunity of distinguishing and defining the two sacraments in marriage to enlarge, from the human level upward, on the aptness of marital love to be an image of God's love for the human soul. The enlarging is thoroughly conditioned by the cultural attitude of his time toward women and marriage.

He points out first that marital love can never be between equals because that which it images, the love thriving between God and the human soul, is not between equals. God has here arranged a marvelous concordance of the image with the imaged. For, as Hugh is convinced, a husband loves his wife as her ruler, her guide, her protector. He takes a free initiative in loving her, and loves her gratuitously—in the way God loves a soul. The wife, in turn, loves her husband as a soul loves God, out of its need and only because God has first attracted it to love him—but freely and willingly. These two reciprocal and aptly fitted loves make up the singular *charitas* that is married love.

These characteristics of the sacrament of marriage—this reciprocal, chaste love of one graciously dominant person and one freely submissive—are found also in the sacrament of faith (*sacramentum fidei*). This sacrament is the reciprocal love of Christ and the Church. (The same sacrament and its love are found also in the incarnation—in the love, within the person of Christ, between the eternal word of God and the human nature.)

Now nothing in human nature, Hugh insists, is more perfectly an image of these three relationships than the marital love of a man and woman. This is so because of the commitment they make to one another. It is a commitment both indestructible and exclusive.

But Hugh has not yet explained why this love, with its indestructibility and exclusivity, must be of a man for a woman. He closes his epistolary essay by offering precisely this explanation—or rather by offering a reason which, in turn, begs for development into an explanation.

As he has already said, he believes that in the sacrament of marriage it is the marital love itself that is the sacrament. This is so because in marriage they are God's love and Christ's love for their respective partner-spouses, the human soul and the Church, that the human spouses' love images. That the human spouses' love images such love demands that there be diversity in it. But the diversity in this human love is found, Hugh claims, not in the diversity of physical sex in men and women. It is found rather in the diverse natures in them, in the diversity of masculine nature and feminine nature. This is why marital love cannot be found outside the union of a man and a woman, because only in such a union is there the joining of the diverse natures. Therefore only in this union can there be the sacrament of marriage, and only in it a marriage at all.[36]

Hugh of St. Victor's *De Sacramentis Christianae Fidei*

Hugh developed elements of his anthropology and his theology of marriage also in his master work, *On the Sacraments of the Christian Faith*.[37] Despite its title the work is not a treatise on the Christian sacraments. The word *sacramentum* in Hugh's vocabulary refers here to the sacred matters of Christian belief, the "mysteries" of the Christian religion. His treatment of the sacraments, as we understand the term, is only a small part of the whole. Part 9 of Book I, *De Institutione Sacramentorum*, is a brief consideration of the nature of the Christian sacraments generally. His consideration of marriage is Part 11 of Book II, *De Sacramento Conjugii*.[38] Only the first of its three chapters is properly either anthropology or theology of marriage. The others deal with points of marriage law.

Worth noting from the former of these passages is his interpretation of a sacrament, an interpretation spelled out not quite carefully enough to be a definition, caught as it is in Hugh's need to write theology with poetic symmetry and balance.

But if anyone wishes to define more fully and precisely what a sacrament is, he can define that it is a bodily or material element set forth externally and sensately; which because of its likeness reveals and because of its institution images; and by reason of its sanctification contains an invisible and spiritual grace.[39]

Every sacrament has a certain likeness to that of which it is a sacrament, a likeness making it able to image that thing. It must also be instituted so that it be put to the work of imaging. Finally it must have sanctification so that it may contain that which it images and be effective in conferring this sanctification.[40]

Hugh here cites the use of water as an example. In its nature given by God's creation it has a natural likeness to the grace of the Holy Spirit that will be at work in baptism. But it was Christ's instituting the sacrament of baptism that made washing with water a positive image of his gracing, in that the baptismal washing images the interior cleansing of the soul. Yet this is not enough. The actual cleansing by grace is done when the minister of the sacrament adds "the word of sanctification." Only when the last is joined with the material element, the washing with water, is there the sacrament. Through this joining the invisible interior effect is worked, namely the cleansing of the soul by grace.[41]

Regrettably Hugh does not examine expressly the way in which the sacrament of marriage too is structured and carried out according to this threefold schema that he has applied to baptism. Had he done so, we would have found in the applied schema (1) marriage the natural joining of man and woman already in itself an apt image of a sacred reality, (2) Christ's formally installing or instituting the man-woman union as such an image, and (3) his making such unions in real life instruments of sanctification by joining to them his "word of sanctification." The examination is done only implicitly and piecemeal in what follows in Book 2, Part 11, *De Sacramento Conjugii* (On the Sacrament of Marriage).

He continues there the patristic idea that marriage even as a natural institution is a sacrament. This he does in asserting that marriage is the one sacrament that was instituted before the fall of the first man and woman; that it was not merely created, as this creation is explained above, but was instituted. He means to say quite exactly that even from marriage's beginning in the relationship of the first man and woman it has been an image of an invisible sacred reality. To explain this he distinguishes between marriage's origin and its institution as a sacrament.

God brought marriage into existence when he created the first woman to cooperate with the first man in the propagation of the human race. This was marriage's origin.

Marriage thus already created God then instituted as a sacrament in two instances, so that one may speak of its double institution. (This is in fact the title of Chapter 3 of this Part 11: *De duplici institutione conjugii, et de causa institutionis duplici:* On the Double Institution of Marriage, and the Double Reason for Its Institution.)

Within the double institution of the sacrament Hugh found the conventional double purpose for God's instituting marriage itself. Where the reason for the first institution was an *officium,* a dutiful vocation, for the second it was *ad remedium,* to bring about a healing—to recover damaged human nature and to restrain sin. God did this by installing the *remedium* itself in sexual intercourse. In this way he enabled it to image the relationship that was to exist in the future between Christ and the Church. For this too was to be a rescuing and healing relationship.

Comparing the first and second institutions of the sacrament more detailedly, Hugh added that in the first of these God permitted (*concessit*) that it be installed in the duty of intercourse so that in it, in addition to procreation, the weakness of the couple might be strengthened. St. Paul hinted at this first institution in 1 Corinthians 11:7 where he wrote that the husband is the image of God, implying therefore that the wife is the image of the human soul. But in the second institution God consecrated (*sanctivit*) marriage in a covenant of love so that in and by this love the weakness and sin inhering in intercourse since the fall might be pardoned.

Hugh concluded this chapter with a kind of summation that seems also an attempt to recover for his explanation the now bent and lop-sided symmetry of the two institutions. (It also appears to glance again at the difficulty about Mary's virginal marriage that prompted his *De Beatae Mariae Virginis Virginitate.*) The concentrated explanation is the following.

What the duty of marriage that is intercourse images is the union of Christ and the Church that was created by Christ's incarnation. Consequently where in a marriage there is no intercourse the marriage cannot be this sacrament of Christ and the Church.

But even without intercourse the union can be not only a true marriage but a true sacrament. Indeed it is a marital sacrament that is both more real and more holy in the degree that chastity is not diminished but charity is increased for the spouses' having forgone intercourse, because the marriage itself, apart from intercourse, is a sacrament, but is such as an image of the relationship of God the creator and the human soul.

The dutiful intercourse made a natural component of marriage in its creation has part only in the second sacrament installed by the second institution. It has this part in that it images the relationship of Christ and the Church—the sacrament to which Paul referred in Ephesians 5. Hence a virginal wife cannot have this sacrament, but she can have the first.

Even though Hugh completed his two studies of marriage well before scholastic theology's age of maturity, he was a man ahead of his time. No one was to think as independently and innovatively as he until Matthias Scheeben in the middle of the nineteenth century. Thus to account for the growth in the medieval understanding of the marital sacrament we must retrace some steps that begin near the end of the eleventh century. Here the artificiality of our strategy of examination will appear more clearly, its separation into first the scholastics' defining of marriage the human relationship, and only now their effort to identify and understand the sacrament in marriage.

The Medieval Determination of the Sacred Sign in Marriage

Much earlier we saw the Church's induction of the Catholic wedding into its liturgy, and the assimilation of this liturgy to the blessing and veiling of the consecrated virgin, as compelling reasons for both acknowledging the sacrament in marriage and as an indication of its nature. Now we look to another feature of a Christian sacrament, that of the *sacrae rei signum*—a sign, even an image, of an invisible sacred reality—as a marker of its sacramentality. We know that the search to identify this sign in Christian marriage was not a medieval innovation. The sign was in Augustine's thought, and was in Ephesians 5 as the correlate to the author's urging Christ's love for his spousal church as the model of the Christian husband's love for his wife.

But the proximate cause of the scholastics' beginning a serious search for this sign or image was the Cathars' attack on marriage that began in Europe toward the end of the eleventh century. Identifying and asserting a sacredness in marriage that lies in its drawing a divine mystery out of hiddenness into human ken was a head-on contradiction of the Cathers' contempt for marriage. But this brought with it the question we have intoned time and again in this essay. It asks: What is this sacredness in marriage, this *sacramentum?* And there is its inescapable companion question: Who puts it there? And by which action do he or they put it there?

The earliest answer to both questions came simultaneously from the first Italian scholastics. They said that the sacrament in Catholic marriages is the priest's blessing of the bridal couple (or of the bride alone) and his veiling of the bride. It is most fitting, they added, that this blessing both makes a marriage sacred and manifests God's secret plan for it, because the blessing reenacts God's blessing in Genesis that first made marriage holy.[42]

This explanation never gained acceptance. It was weakened by a fact of history—that for centuries the priestly blessing had not been required for the creating of Christian marriages. But would one say that from the beginning until the twelfth century so many millions of Christian marriages lacked the sacrament? Nevertheless even as late as the early thirteenth century William of Auvergne wanted that if not the sacrament itself, at least its saving power come from the priest's blessing.[43]

Anselm of Laon

Anselm of Laon, as we have already seen, was one of the early scholastics who said that the marriage itself as a human relationship, apart from any accrual to it and anything done to it religiously, is a sacrament in the sense of a sacred sign of a relationship of God to human beings. He acknowledged that even the marriages of the unbaptized are such a sign, as the marriage of the first couple in paradise had been. But these lack the *res sacramenti*, the sacrament's substantive effect. This is the spouses' gracing involvement in the mystery of the Church, which is, in turn, its spousal relationship with Christ.

In the *Liber Pancrisis* (the Book of Universal Opinion), a collection of *sententiae* attributed to Anselm, there is a novel theological *tour de force* that seeks to show the image of the triune God in marriage. Thus it claims three institutions of marriage: in the garden of Eden, in 1 Corinthians 7, and in the rules of the holy fathers of the Church. Marriage has three ends: to procreate, to avoid fornication, and to increase love. It also contains three goods: offspring, the bond of sworn fidelity, and the image of the union of Christ and the Church (with the last Anselm identifies the sacrament). Finally, three causes create a marriage: the consent *de praesenti,* the desire for children, and the will to be faithful.[44]

In his *Tractatus de matrimonio* Anselm recurred to the claim about marriage's institution noted just above, that unlike the other sacraments it was instituted before the first sin. God did this in creating the woman and inspiring Adam to exclaim, "This one at last is bone of my bones and flesh of my flesh." Christ did not institute it in the sense of innovating it, but in consecrating it by his presence and miracle at the wedding in Cana of Galilee. Marriage's first institution, in the garden of Eden, was an *officium,* to be a dutiful vocation for the perpetuation of the human race, which was meant to be realized by intercourse without concupiscence. Its second institution was *ad remedium,* to provide an acceptable outlet for sexual urgency and thus to avoid adultery and fornication—which always threaten because now the dutiful vocation is pursued only with concupiscence. This is why one must distinguish in sacramental marriages the sacrament itself, the image of a sacred reality, and the *res sacramenti,* the effect of the sacrament which is the grace that sanctifies. All, the sinful as well as the innocent, receive the sacrament because their unions, provided they are consummated by intercourse, image the indissoluble union of Christ and the Church and are themselves made indissoluble by the consummation. But only the innocent receive the *res sacramenti,* and specifically as married become members of Christ.[45]

Peter Abelard

In his *Sic et non,* Chapter 125, Peter Abelard presented the arguments for and against the proposition that pagans can marry. In its favor he hardly did more than quote Augustine's opinion in his *De Bono Conjugali,* but with this proviso, that in pagan marriages only two of the three *bona* are found. The sacrament is missing from them. Since it is found only in Christian marriages, only they are indissoluble except by the death of one of the spouses.[46]

In his *Sermo de annuntiatione Beatae Virginis Mariae* Peter saw the marital sacrament in the spouses' union in spirit, in their *consensus animorum.*[47] This he apparently reserved for Christian spouses because it is this conjoining that images Christ's union with the Church. In his *Epitome theologiae Christianae* Peter accepted five sacraments: baptism, confirmation, the Eucharist, last anointing and marriage.[48] About marriage he sounded the caution and set the limitation on its sacramentality that were done so commonly by his contemporaries. In this Epitome's Chapter 31, under the heading *De sacramento matrimonii,* he said that the marriage itself is the sacrament, but that it confers no gift, as the other sacraments do. He clearly meant that this gift that is absent from marriage is the sanctifying grace by which persons are joined personally to God and made holy. He said rather that the gift it gives is a remedy for concupiscence. When used properly it keeps intercourse from being sinful: "This sacrament, as I have said, is a remedy for sin, even though it does not confer a gift. Hence 'He who can, let him accept this' (Mt. 19:12); that is, he who can keep continence, let him do so. He who cannot, let him take a wife. And as the Apostle said, 'Let each man have his own wife in order to avoid fornication (1 Cor. 7:2)'."[49]

In Chapter 28 of his *Epitome* Abelard had said that marriage is to be included among the spiritual sacraments, despite its not bringing the gift of grace, because it helps to salvation. In saying this he profited by a helpful distinction among the sacraments that Durandus of Troan had made as early as the middle of the eleventh century (in his *Libri de corpore et sanguine Domini,* 5, 11).[50] It was between the *signum,* the imaging of a sacred reality, and the sanctifying power of this imaging. Anselm of Laon had made the same distinction and had detected its usefulness in explaining how Christian marriage could image a sacred reality despite being, in its sexual intercourse, a vessel of sin.

In his *Contra haereticos,* a kind of sententiary of apologetical passages, Hugh of Amiens put a further restriction on the presence of the sacrament in marriages. It is not found in second and later marriages, even though they are good and permitted: "But in remarriage . . . there is no *signum,* nor is there the sacrament of the one and unique heavenly marriage by which Christ is joined to the Church in perpetual fidelity. Therefore whoever by remarrying passes from oneness to plurality no longer images in himself the holy marriage of Christ and the Church, which remains one and unique into eternity."[51]

By the middle of the twelfth century the theologians had come finally and fully to grips with the difficulty created by the three-way convergence, that a Christian marriage is a sign, and even an image, of an invisible sacred reality; that it is a source of goodness and an opportunity for union with God; but that its most characteristic conduct (some said its essential conduct because procreation is marriage's main purpose) seldom escapes sin and is the conveyor of inherited sinfulness.

We have already seen some of the efforts at reconciling the third of these data with the first two. More examples will show varying levels of pessimism or optimism about succeeding at the reconciliation.

In his *Summa,* completed in 1158, Rufinus offered this as his judgment on the matter:

> We know that each of the Church's sacraments contains its specific grace in its own way. This each does by its imaging, and it gives the grace by virtue of the power in it. . . . Only marriage, even though it is most important [*praecipuum*] among the sacraments, images a sacred reality in such a way that it brings grace only minimally, because the law of concupiscence [in it] cripples this gracing (*quod eam lege turpitudinis impediente minime operatur*).[52]

Gandulph of Bologna, in Book 4, Distinction 1 of his *Sententiarum Libri IV*, written during the decade 1160–1170, divided the Christian sacraments among three categories. There are those, he said, whose purpose is to provide a remedy against sin and to give helping grace, as baptism does. Others, such as the Eucharist and sacred orders, give grace and strengthen the recipient by their power. Others provide only a remedy against sin. Of this last he proposed only marriage as an example.[53]

William of Auxerre (d. 1231) in his *Summa Aurea*, t. 285, suggested a different distinction. It was between those sacraments that confer grace and those, such as marriage, that only conserve, or protect, grace once conferred: "For it is like a maintaining medicine [*medicina praeservativa*] that protects the married from sin."[54]

Alain of Lille (d. 1202) said much the same but in greater detail in his *Theologicae regulae*. In *Regula 114* he explained that while certain sacraments—for example baptism and the Eucharist—are needed for salvation, and others, such as sacred orders, confer the dignity of office, marriage is an elective sacrament that ought to be chosen by prudent judgment of one's need for protection against concupiscence. Marriage is deemed a sacrament for two reasons: because of the spouses' union of spirits (*consensus animorum*) that images the spiritual union of Christ and the Church, and because of its sexual intercourse that images the union of the divine and human natures in Christ. He deemed these two imaging functions sufficient to qualify Christian marriage as a sacrament. But the question of the conferring of grace in marriage he left untouched.

Alain saw a second reason for the merely elective status of marriage. Before Adam's sin it was a dutiful and mandated vocation in order "to fill the earth." But in the centuries since that sin, after married chastity has in fact filled the earth, now virginal chastity takes its place in order to fill the heavenly homeland. For marriage the primeval mandated duty has now been changed to an available and permitted remedy.[55]

He got obliquely at the question of marriage's conveying grace in Book 1, Chapter 64 of his *Contra haereticos libri IV*, when replying to the Cathar indictment of marriage that it is a sinful state because it can be consummated, brought to its fullness, only by a sinful act.

> We grant that marriage cannot be consummated without intercourse. But this is not always a sin. For by means of the sacrament intercourse can be kept to venial sinfulness, or to no sin at all. How many indeed would fall into fornication if they were not married? But by the goodness of marriage they are saved from it. This is what Paul meant when advising, "But because of fornication let every man have his own wife. . . ." He counseled the unmarried and the widows to remain unmarried not because marriage is evil but because virginity is better.[56]

Regrettably Alain here refers marriage's remedial function only to the sin of fornication. He appears to have ducked away from the point of the Cathars' challenge that even within marriage intercourse is sinful. Or does he answer this challenge by implying a distinction, that marriage protects sinlessness not only by providing an alternative to fornication but also by offering the opportunity for continence within the alternative, while a marriage that includes intercourse protects from the serious sin of fornication otherwise committed outside itself—but at the cost of venial sin within it? Alain does not explain.

Alexander of Hales

The English Franciscan, Alexander of Hales (d. 1245) completed his reflections on marriage just at about the time the most accomplished scholastics—Albert, Thomas and Bonaventure—were beginning theirs.

Pars II-IIae, Tomus III of his *Summa Theologica*, Inquiry 3, Treatise 5, Section 2, Question 1 has for its Title 3, "On the Sins of the Married" [*De peccatis conjugum*]. Chapter 1 of this title asks what causes marital intercourse to be sinful [*Quibus ex causis actus conjugalis sit peccatum*]. Whether it asks what causes intercourse to be always sinful, or what causes it to be sinful when it is so, is not clear. One must infer the answer from Alexander's explanation, which gives a singular role to the sacrament in marriage.

> We say that there is sometimes venial sin and sometimes mortal sin in a man's inordinate intercourse with his wife. If the pleasure that he takes is subordinated to God [*si . . . illa delectatio sit sub Deo*], there is venial sin, for it is excused on account of the sacrament of marriage. Hence Augustine says in his book *De bono conjugali,* "If in their intercourse they seek more what is proper to it [*honestum*] than what is improper [*inhonestum*]; that is, more of what belongs to the married than what does not, this, according to the Apostle's authority, is allowed by way of concession [*eis secundum veniam conceditur*]." But if it [intercourse, or the pleasure of it] is sought equally with God or in preference to him, it is mortally sinful.[57]

But Alexander's most detailed accounting for the sacrament's function and effects in marriage is found in Volume 4 of his *Summa*, Part 2, Inquiry 2, Question 4, "Those who are subject to the natural law" [*Quorum sit lex naturalis*], in Member 2, Chapter 1, "Marriage in the Natural Law" [*De matrimonio in lege naturali*]. There he replies to the difficulty that a marriage cannot be both an entity [*res*] and a sign. He insists that it can be seen as both, just as one person can see a circle as a figure, another person as a sign. For a sign bespeaks a relationship of a thing to something else.

The union of husband and wife is natural. But that it is a sign of inseparability or of the union of Christ and the Church and of the graced soul, this it is by divine institution.

Or one can say that in every sacrament there are these three, likeness [*similitudo*], signing [or imaging—*significatio*], and sanctification [*sanctificatio*]. Marriage has the likeness from its beginning, its institution. It has its signing from God's putting it there [*ex informatione*]. It has its sanctification from Christ's redeeming. For from the moment that both the man and the woman were created, it was natural that they be united. But that their union signify the union of the soul with God, or of Christ with the Church, or of the humanity and divinity of Christ—this comes from divine institution. And that there be sanctification, or grace, in marriage, or in the spouses through their marriage, this is done through Christ's passion. For it sanctifies all the sacraments, and through it all the sacraments have their power to sanctify.[58]

Possibly no other juxtaposition of passages than that of these two from Alexander of Hales (artificial though the juxtaposing may be) would show more clearly the elements of the marital sacrament that these medieval scholars are trying to bring together despite the elements' obvious discomfort with one another. Alexander does not doubt that marriage's signing-imaging is of one or of all of the three holy unions that he lists. Presumably he means that it is mainly in this signing that one finds marriage's sacrament. But he has already said that what the sacrament does to marital intercourse is to excuse its inescapable sinfulness, provided this is only venial. And he says that the sanctifying in marriage, as in all the sacraments, is done by Christ's passion.

What does he think this sanctifying in marriage is? The confining of its intercourse to venial sin, and the excusing of this sin? If this is it, by doing it does the marriage of two Christians image one or all of the three unions named above? By doing something sinful, but because it is excused? Alexander's answers here are the kind that produce more, and more difficult, questions.

In his reply to the second objection in this chapter Alexander makes a distinction and out of it draws a conclusion that began with Augustine but by this time is on the way to becoming the accepted theology of indissolubility in marriage. But the path his logic takes is the reverse of what one would expect. He begins with the assumption that the marriages of the unbaptized, the *infideles,* are dissoluble. From there he goes on to ask what it is in the marriages of the baptized that makes them, by contrast, to be indissoluble—as he assumes they are.

We say that as entity, and in similitude, marriage is the same among all, because the union of husband and wife is the same

among all. But it is not so in its character as a sign and in its
signing. It signifies different things among the baptized as opposed to marriage among the unbaptized. Among the baptized
it signifies the inseparable unions of God with human nature
and of Christ with the Church. And because the [latter?] union
is inseparable, by reason of it [*propter hoc*] the marriages of the
baptized are inseparable.[59]

Alexander does not here say what the marriages of the unbaptized
signify, although he leaves the impression that he thinks they do signify
something other than do those of the baptized. He simply denies that
they signify an inseparable union—which is why they can be dissolved.

But one is left wondering what he means by the crucial *propter hoc*
in the logic of his reply. Does he mean that *because* the imaged divine
relationship is indissoluble, its human marital image, in order to be in
fact the image Christ has made it to be, is also indissoluble? Or does he
mean that the imaged divine relationship somehow *causes* its human
image to be indissoluble? He does not explain. Indeed these questions
seem not to have occurred to him.

Peter Lombard (continued)

It will help to finish this examination of the early scholastics by
returning to Peter Lombard despite his having completed his four books
of *sententiae* in about 1150, three-quarters of a century before Alexander
of Hales' *Summa Theologica*. To begin with, the plan of his Distinction 26
was to become the plan for the examination of the sacrament in marriage
for two centuries after him.[60] (His own examination of it continued
through Distinctions 27–31; and all these became a kind of source- and
work-book for the speculations of later theologians in their *Commentaria
in IV Libros Sententiarum Petri Lombardi.*) Of all the anthologies of
ancient and recent passages on marriage compiled by the medieval
sententiarii, his was, if not the most inclusive (that honor goes to Gratian's
Decretum), the most judicious in selecting salient passages and the most
diligent in trying to draw conclusive knowledge from them. As one reads
through the *quaestiones* making up the aforementioned *distinctiones* one
recapitulates the theology of marriage developed until his time, and at the
same time scans the pre-notes of the theology that will follow from that
time.

A second advantage of ending with Lombard is that with him we may
end also the artificiality of examining the scholastics' study of marriage
the natural relationship distinctly from their study of the sacrament in
marriage. For even where Lombard writes about the former he does so
within a consideration of marriage the Christian sacrament. He has no
merely anthropological or philosophic interest in marriage. Once he has
accounted for Christian marriage's sacramentality, for him the issues are,

save one, Catholic juridical issues, such as the act or acts which create a marriage, the kinds of errors that make marital consent null and void, and the impediments to marriage established by that time in Roman Catholic law. The one non-juridical issue is in *Distinctio* 31, *De tribus bonis conjugii* ("On the three goods of marriage"). There he examines the function of the sacrament in creating marriage's indissolubility. We shall inspect it, and inspect too the issues in *Distinctiones* 26 and 27 leading to it, but only those among them pertinent to the sacrament.

In accounting for the institution of marriage Lombard accounts for the institution of the sacrament itself. He implies that the natural relationship has never been less than a sacrament. Within this assumption he repeats the conventional distinction between the two institutions of the sacrament. The first took place before the sin of the first parents, which he takes for granted was an event in history, whereas all the other sacraments were instituted after that sin and because of it.

Since the sin of the first parents was not the reason for the marriage sacrament's first institution, it had a prior reason. This was the reason *in officium*, the dutiful vocation that is the procreation of the race. This was made evident in Adam's prophetic pronouncement about his being joined to Eve, "This one at last is bone of my bones and flesh of my flesh. . . . That is why a man leaves his father and mother and clings to his wife, and the two of them become one flesh."

The second institution of the sacrament took place after the sin of the first parents. Then the institution had a different reason, this time *in remedium*—in order to put control on sin by blocking the sinful movements (*illicitos motus*) of the flesh. He admitted that the sacrament does not in fact block such concupiscent stirrings, but it keeps them from being sinful because the goods of marriage provide an excuse for them.[61]

This may be a variation of the Augustinian tradition that had come down to Lombard's time. It said that the sinfulness that is otherwise unavoidable in marital intercourse is excused in marriage—or perhaps only in Christian marriage—because of all three goods that can be realized in it. But Lombard seems to say that it is marriage's second institution as a sacrament that provides this excusing cause, or perhaps that it is the presence in Christian marriage of the sacrament that provides it. It is difficult to know what he means. But if he does mean that it is the sacrament that excuses—or is at least the principal cause of the excusing—a second difficulty arises. We will come upon it presently when we see what he thought the sacrament in marriage to be.

He goes on to explain that the first institution of marriage, before the fall, was by command (*praeceptus*), as is evident in the words of Genesis, "Increase and multiply and fill the earth." The same command was repeated after the fall and the flood, after the race had in fact multiplied. But that second time it was given as a concession (*indulgentia*) in order to prevent the sin of *fornicatio* (more probably adultery than fornication in the modern sense of the term). As a concession it had the nature of a *remedium*.[62]

When, in paragraph 6 of this *Distinctio* 26, Lombard asks and answers the question, "Of which reality is marriage a sacrament?" nowhere does he distinguish between the sacrament before the sin of the first parents and the sacrament after this sin. His answer to the question is the conventional one. As a sacrament marriage is a sacred sign of a sacred reality (*sacrae rei*). The sacred reality of which it is a sign is the union of Christ and the Church. A marriage is such a sign in that the husband "clings to his wife," and thus the two become one flesh. It is of the spouses' thus becoming one flesh that Paul wrote in Ephesians 5 that it is a *sacramentum magnum*. (Linking this with what we saw him saying just above, we find him implying without hesitation that an image of the love of Christ and the Church has as its reason, or main reason for existing, to excuse concupiscent stirrings in men and women—to render these sinless.)

The conjoining (*conjunctio*) of the spouses is done in two ways, in the concordance of their spirits (*consensus animorum*) and in the commingling of their bodies (*permixtio corporum*). This double conjoining images the double conjoining of Christ and the Church, the spiritual and the corporal. For the Church is joined to Christ spiritually through its charity, through the love for him by which it wills what he wills. It is also joined to him corporally in that he took his nature from the human nature that makes up the Church. Said most detailedly, the Christian spouses' marriage images this double Christ-Church relationship—first the spiritual spiritually by their marital consent motivated by the love that is *charitas*, then the corporal corporally by their sexual intercourse.[63]

At the end of this *Distinctio* 26 Lombard takes up the question that had festered for centuries in the Catholic anthropology of marriage. It asked whether presumed spouses who have never had intercourse are truly married.

In replying Lombard shows again his identification of marriage and sacrament, although seeming to deflect the answer to fit a different question. He argues that spouses who have never had intercourse are indeed united in the sacrament, but there incompletely. Their union does not image the union of Christ and the Church explicitly and fully, since they are joined only in charity, whereby they image the love of Christ and the Church for one another. But they are not joined corporally, and thus do not image Christ's conformity of nature with the Church.

Having affirmed that marriage has been a sacrament from its beginning, and having explained in what way it is an image of the love of Christ and the Church, Lombard next, in *Distinctio* 27, reaches without hesitation into Roman law for its definition of marriage as a natural relationship.[64] Thus "marriage is the marital union of a man and a woman who are capable according to the law of marrying, a union that possesses an undivided sharing of life." That this union is undivided (*individua*) means that neither spouse may without the other's consent take up a life of continence or abstain sexually for the sake of prayer. It means also that as long as both spouses live, the marital bond remains, so that neither may take another spouse. Finally it means that each must grant to the other what is his or hers by right.[65]

After reviewing, in *Distinctiones* 28, 29 and 30, the argument between the Bolognese and Parisian canonists over the nature of the act or acts that create a marriage, Lombard returns, in *Distinctio* 31, to the consideration of marriage's nature and properties, and in doing so returns also to his interpretation of the sacrament. He cites the three traditional *bona* of marriage (from Augustine's *super Genesim*, lib. 9). The good that is found in the *sacramentum* is this, that the marriage not be dissolved (*non separetur*), and that if a spouse be dismissed, he or she is not to remarry even for the sake of having children.[66]

It is when Lombard distinguishes two kinds of "separation" of a marriage that he apparently names exactly what the *sacramentum* of a marriage is. The two kinds of separation are corporal and sacramental. The former is possible and available to spouses because of adultery by the partner (*fornicatio*), or by mutual consent for religious reasons (*causa religionis*). This separation may be either temporary or permanent.

But even given this corporal separation, it is impossible that the spouses separate sacramentally as long as both live. As Lombard names the cause of this inseparability, he begins to identify the sacrament: "For their marital bond (*vinculum conjugale*) remains even if after separating they attempt marriage with another."[67]

By way of sustaining and explaining this he quotes Augustine's *De Nuptiis et Concupiscentia, Lib. I, cap. 10* on the point and its analogy: "For there remains in the spouses, as long as they live, a certain conjugal bond, a bond that neither separation nor union with another can destroy; just as the soul of an apostate does not lose the *sacramentum* of faith it received in baptism even if it loses the faith itself and, in a sense, abandons its marriage to Christ."

With this he comes down exactly on the identity of the sacrament in relation to the marriage itself: "And note that this third *bonum* of marriage is called the *sacramentum* not because it is the marriage itself, but because it is an image [*signum*] of a sacred reality, namely of the spiritual and inseparable union of Christ and the Church."

Here we have the elements of the marriage sacrament laid out clearly enough. There is the marriage itself (*conjugium*). This is, if we carry forward the definition offered earlier in *Distinctio 27*, the union (*conjunctio*) of the spouses. Then there is the bond (*vinculum*), which is the *sacramentum*, or which is called the *sacramentum* because it (not the marriage itself) is an image of the indestructible union of Christ and the Church.

Whether Lombard has here added clarity where Augustine left obscurity is not evident. For in light of his distinction one may point out that even though Lombard earlier insisted that every marriage has been a sacrament from its beginning, the marriage (*conjugium*) is distinct from the *vinculum*, which he identifies as the *sacramentum*. One may then ask whether, since it is the *vinculum-sacramentum* that is the cause of inseparability, the *conjugium* itself is separable. Or if it is not (as Lombard would surely insist), how does the inseparable *vinculum* keep the *conjugium* also inseparable? And finally for now, how does the indestructibility of the imaged Christ-Church relationship cause automatically the indestructibility of the imaging *sacramentum-vinculum* of the Christian spouses' marriage? Lombard's theology of marital inseparability inspires the same question that Alexander of Hales' did. Must Christian marriages be deemed inseparable because their sacrament's being an image of the inseparable Christ-Church union demands inseparability—otherwise they would not be sacraments in this way, as they surely are? Or does the imaged inseparability in the Christ-Church union somehow *cause* the inseparability in the imaging Christian marriages? As they did not to Alexander these questions seem not to have occurred to Lombard.

The Juridical Use of the Marital Sacrament

Before moving on to the major scholastic theologians in the thirteenth and early fourteenth centuries we will inspect briefly the part that the marital sacrament played in the canonical legislation and the judicial rulings from about the end of the patristic period until almost the middle of the thirteenth century.

We recall that the authorities strove long and seriously during this epoch to end certain abuses of marriage. We recall which they were: clandestine marriages, kidnap and subsequent attempt at forced marriage, marriage attempted within forbidden degrees of consanguinity or affinity, divorce and attempted remarriage. Against each of them the presence of the sacrament in Christian marriages could have been used as a weapon. Thanks to a more developed theology this is now clearer to us. But it was clear enough to the authorities of the time, since Augustine had already, in his *De Conjugiis Adulterinis* of 419–420, appealed to the sacrament to argue against the habit of divorce that his century's thinly-motivated converts had brought with them.

Our question asks whether and how the sacrament was enlisted by the authorities in legislating and ruling against these abuses. Two sources offer evidence for this, sources whose origins are separated on the calendar of history by about a century. The first is already familiar to us. It is Gratian's *Decretum,* completed at Bologna about 1140–1141. The other is Pope Gregory IX's *Liber Decretalium* (The Book of Decretals) compiled by the canonist Raymond of Peñafort in 1234. The full title of Gratian's *Decretum,* as we have already seen, suggests its contents, although not inclusively. This Concordance of Discordant Canons contains more than the canons and decrees of the Church's councils until his time. It shares the nature of his contemporaries' books of *sententiae* in that it includes also passages from the fathers. Predictably Augustine is the most frequently quoted where Gratian deals with marriage. This is in *Causae* (cases) 27 through 33.[68]

As a pre-note, we find that Gratian followed the word "sacrament's" wandering path of meaning at his time. In *Causa 31*, Question 1, for example, the term designates a type, a foreshadowing, of a future person or event.[69] Thus the ancient Hebrew sacrifices were *sacramenta* of the New Testament sacrifice. So also was Abraham's remarrying after Sarah's death a *sacramentum* for later Christian widows' remarrying.[70]

A major portion of the 345 *capitula* (quotations or citations from councils, popes and fathers) making up *Causa* 27 through 33 has to do with the possibility of Christians' divorcing their Christian spouses and subsequently remarrying. As we shall soon see, Gratian thought of quoting only one passage from the fathers which proposes the sacrament as a cause of a first marriage's permanence and the obstacle to a second marriage.

In *Causa 27* he gets immediately at divorce and remarriage under the two questions "Can a person marry who has already vowed virginity?" and "Can a woman betrothed to one man marry another?"[71] Only in Chapter 10 of the second question does he mention the sacrament, and there only as one of the three goods of marriage. His appeal against divorce is always on the strength of the "two in one flesh" character of marriage proposed in Genesis 2, or of the synoptic *logion,* "What God has joined man must not separate."

In *Causa 28* he asks, in Question 1, whether pagan couples can marry, and in Question 2, whether after baptism a married neo-Christian can leave the pagan spouse and marry a fellow Christian.[72] In Chapters 8 and 9 of this second question he agrees that the neo-Christian can do just this. But he cites or quotes no text proposing as the warrant for it that the first marriage lacked the sacrament—which is the warrant that the Pauline privilege in current Catholic marriage law offers.

Causa 29 does not mention the sacrament in its Question 1, which asks whether a woman deceived about a man's identity is nevertheless married to him for having exchanged wedding vows with him.[73]

Causa 30 reports judgments against clandestine marriage. But in all the passages quoted and cited to condemn it, none does so because of the demands of the sacrament in marriage.[74]

In Question 7 of *Causa 32*, where Gratian quotes Augustine's *De Conjugiis Adulterinis* against remarriage even after divorce because of adultery, he does not touch the passages in that essay that appeal to the sacrament.[75]

It is in *Causa 33*, Question 7, Chapter 28 that we find the one passage quoting the sacrament as the reason why a person cannot remarry after dismissing even a sterile spouse.[76] This is the *locus classicus* in Chapter 10 of Augustine's *De Nuptiis et Concupiscentia,* wherein he explains why it is that despite their divorce and separation, two Christian spouses remain married to one another until one of them dies. Immediately after the passage that Gratian quotes, Augustine went on to say that Christian spouses who divorce do not thereby lose their marital *sacramentum,* ". . . just as the soul of an apostate Christian, in a sense abandoning his marriage with Christ, even though he loses his faith, does not lose the *sacramentum* of faith that he received in baptism." But leading into that passage Augustine had spoken of the *sacramentum* in this guise: "For as long as they [the Christian spouses] live there remains a certain conjugal something" (*manet quiddam conjugale*) which neither separation nor union with another can remove." It seems clear that at least in this passage the "certain conjugal something" is the sacrament.

This is the only passage using the sacrament against divorce and remarriage that Gratian quotes among all the passages he assembled on this score. Even so he either changed three crucial words in it or used a version of the passage different from that in Migne's *Patrologia Latina,* Volume 44, that supplies the text here. We have already seen the variant version. Instead of "there remains a certain conjugal something" (*manet quiddam conjugale*), Gratian has "there remains a certain conjugal bond" (*manet quoddam vinculum conjugale*). With this he unwittingly has Augustine identify the marital sacrament with the marital bond. Given Gratian's juridical mind, he may indeed have thought of the sacrament as a juridical bond. If so, he was not the last Catholic jurist to think this.[77]

The Sacrament in the Decretals

Decretals in Catholic government differ from decrees in that the latter are rules or mandates produced usually by councils, whether general or territorial, whereas the former are letters—decretal letters—written by popes to render judgment in particular questions of government and/or discipline. Gregory IX's *Liber Decretalium*—actually completed in five "books"—is therefore a collection of such judgments published in letter form, while containing a few conciliar decrees.[78] It deals with marriage questions in its Book 4. The titles in this book wherein one may rightly expect to find decretals appealing to the sacrament in rendering judgment are Title 8, "The Marriage of Lepers," Title 9, "The Marriage of Slaves," title 11, "On Spiritual Kinship," Title 15, "On Frigidity, the Maledicted [persons cursed by a witch] and Impotence," Title 16, "On Marriage Contracted in Defiance of Church Interdict," and Title 19, "On Divorce."

Of the forty-two chapters under these titles only five mention the sacrament. One of these does so only indirectly, two duplicate one and the same statement, while the other two make truly significant statements about the sacrament in marriage.

The first of the four is in Chapter 1 of Title 9, an excerpt of a decretal letter of Pope Adrian IV (1154–1159) to the archbishop of Salzburg. The latter had asked what to do about slaves who had married in defiance of their masters. Adrian's reply was that because none of the sacraments is to be denied to any Christian, whether slave or free, marriage is not to be denied to slaves.[79]

The second two letters are Chapters 8 and 9 of Title 19, "On Divorce."[80] Their one reference to the sacrament interprets 1 Corinthians 7:13 in such a way as to identify any marriage as a sacrament. The letters are of Pope Innocent III (1198–1216) to the bishop of Tiberias in the Latin kingdom of Jerusalem (in 1201) and to the bishop of Livorno. The first resolved the question asking whether spouses married as pagans but in a degree of consanguinity forbidden by Catholic law are to be separated if both are converted. The second asked whether a man may marry a woman who is his brother's abandoned wife. In both letters Innocent affirmed that ". . . since the sacrament of marriage is found among both Christians and non-Christians, as the Apostle has shown. . . ." At this point he cited 1 Corinthians 7:13, wherein Paul advised a spouse become Christian not to dismiss the spouse who has remained unbaptized provided the latter is willing to live in peace. The implication seems to be that the reason for the converted spouse's not dismissing the unbaptized is that their marriage is a sacrament. (One wonders what Innocent would have said about the marriage Paul turned to next, one about which he advised the converted spouse to let the unbaptized abandon the marriage if the latter wished to do so.)

The fourth decretal letter is also from Innocent III; it was addressed to the bishop of Ferrara on May 1, 1199, in answer to the following question from the latter: May a Christian spouse remarry if his or her spouse, also Christian, falls into heresy and abandons the marriage?[81] Apparently the first of the spouses in question was arguing his or her case as a parallel to the Pauline privilege. This frees a convert to Christianity to enter a second marriage if, after the conversion, the spouse who remained non-Christian abandons the marriage, blasphemes God or seeks to draw the convert into serious sin.

Innocent replied that in the case presented to him the petitioning spouse may not remarry because the other's lapse into heresy did not dissolve the marriage. The parallel with the use of the Pauline privilege did not hold. The reason Innocent offered for this at least seems to contradict his earlier opinion that even the marriages of non-Christians are sacraments. The coherence of his reasoning depends on the meaning of its term, *matrimonium ratum*—which appears to be a marriage in which there is the sacrament because in both spouses there is the *sacramentum* of baptism.

> For even though a true marriage exist between non-Christians, yet it is not *ratum*. But between Christians it is both true and

ratum, since once the *sacramentum* of faith [baptism] is received, it is never lost. But the *ratum* has this effect in the sacrament of marriage, that it remains as long as both spouses live.

Innocent added that the case for remarriage is not made by the de facto frequency of such lapses into heresy (probably into that of the Cathar despisers of marriage), nor by the unjust deprivation of the surviving Catholic's marital rights. What is more, Innocent added, his judgment is needed to end the abuse whereby some spouses feign a lapse into heresy in order to get out of their unwanted marriages.

In this judgment Innocent clearly assumes two things: that the presence of the baptismal *sacramentum* in both spouses (later theology calls it the baptismal character) puts the sacrament in their marriage, and that it is the presence of the sacrament in such a marriage that makes it indissoluble even despite a lapse into heresy. But as we shall see presently, this theology of marriage's indissolubility by virtue of the sacrament was, in Innocent's mind, still incomplete.

A decretal making up Chapter 5 of Book 1, Title 21 constructed a précis of the theology of marriage that was in place by the beginning of the thirteenth century. It answered the question asking whether a man who marries a virgin already betrothed to another man is to be considered a *bigamus* and thus impeded from sacred orders. (Recall that in early and medieval terminology a *bigamus* was not a man married simultaneously to two women, but one who married twice successively. But here its meaning extends to include a woman's second husband.) The excerpt from this letter of Innocent III to a bishop of Albano of Sept. 6, 1206 speaks for itself. It is a model of convoluted judicial prose.

We reply to Your Fraternity that, since there are two things in a marriage, namely the concordance [*consensus*] of spirits and the commingling of bodies—the former of which signifies the charity consisting in the spirit of union of God and the just soul, to which the Apostle referred in I Corinthians 6:17 "He who cleaves to the one God is one spirit with him"; while the latter signifies the conformity in the flesh between Christ and the Church, to which the Evangelist witnesses by his words "And the Word was made flesh and dwelt among us"; therefore a marriage which is not consummated by the commingling of bodies does not signify that marriage which has been contracted by Christ and the Church through the mystery of the incarnation. It was in reference to this that Paul, when explaining what Adam said—"This one at last is bone of my bones and flesh of my flesh; for this reason a man will leave his father and mother and will cling to his wife, and they shall become two in one flesh"—added immediately, "I say this is a great sacrament, in Christ and in the Church." Therefore it is for lack of this sacrament [*propter sacramenti defectum*] that a *bigamus* or the husband of a widow may not be raised to sacred orders, since the latter is not the one wife of a man married but once, nor the former man the one husband of a woman married but once. However, even where the commingling of bodies has not taken place between spouses of this kind, there is nevertheless the seal of the sacrament in their marriage. Therefore it follows that a man who takes as his wife a woman who was earlier betrothed to another man but who has not had intercourse with him, is not impeded from sacred orders because neither he nor she has divided his or her flesh among plural persons.[82]

Innocent's judgment at the end presumes that the woman was not only betrothed to the first man but was married to him. A theologian's digest-analysis of the decretal is this, that the second man did not become a *bigamus* by marrying the woman provided she was still a virgin, because although her first marriage was a sacrament, it was incompletely so in that, being virginal, it imaged only the union of God with human souls (which is a dissoluble union), but because virginal it did not image the union of Christ and the Church (which is an indissoluble union).

Innocent's completed theology of marriage's indissolubility appears in his letter to King Philip II of France, dated December 18, 1208.[83] Philip had asked for the dissolution of his marriage to Queen Ingeborg. She had left him to enter monastic life, and had taken an oath that the two of them had never had intercourse with one another and thus not consummated their marriage. Philip was well informed about the juridicized theology of divorce and remarriage. He adduced in his favor Pope Alexander III's exegesis of Christ's command, "What God has joined man must not separate," that this refers only to consummated marriages.[84]

Innocent agreed and granted Philip's request, reasoning in the following now familiar way. Sexual intercourse in a marriage of two Christians images the union of the eternal word of God and the human nature in Christ, whereas such spouses' marital consent images only the bond of charity between God and a graced soul. But because the union of the two natures in Christ cannot be dissolved, neither can its image, the union of Christian spouses in a consummated marriage, be dissolved as long as both spouses live. On the other hand, because the union of charity between God and a human soul is often dissolved by the latter's sin, so too can its image be dissolved, namely a marriage of two Christians where it has been joined by no more than the marital consent.

With this letter Innocent helped to produce the following effects: to fix in the Catholic discipline of divorce and remarriage that only a consummated marriage—and a consummated marriage of two Christians— is held to indissolubility by Christ's command. It helped to generate the theology warranting this discipline, namely that the consummation of a Christian marriage produces in it the complete sacrament (which implies that an unconsummated Christian marriage, although it contains the sacrament, does so incompletely); and that the sacrament in such a marriage is its imaging one or both of two sacred realities—first, the union of God and a graced soul where there has been only the union of the spouses' souls in their marital consent (this is the incomplete sacrament); then the union of the two natures in Christ where the Christian spouses have consummated their union by intercourse (this is the completed sacrament). (The object of the second image claimed here is a variant that has not survived in the theology of the sacrament. Its alternate from the beginning, the union of Christ and the Church, is now almost universally said to be the object of a consummated Christian marriage's imaging.)

Final Acceptance of Marriage Among the Sacraments

The Catholic authorities may have accepted marriage among the Church's sacraments formally and definitively as early as the Second Lateran Council in 1139, during the pontificate of Innocent II. This council condemned the errors of the Petrobrusians (the followers of the neo-Manichean Peter de Bruys) and of Arnold of Brescia. These had rejected the Christian sacraments. In defending them the council included marriage among them, but only implicitly: "We expel from the Church and condemn those who, in putting on an appearance of religion, condemn the sacrament of the Lord's body and blood, the baptism of children, the priesthood and other ecclesiastical orders, and covenants of legitimate marriage. . . ."[85]

But implication passed over into explicitation in the Council of Verona in 1184. There Pope Lucius III published a long decree anathematizing the Cathars and their condemnation of the sacraments: "We bind under permanent anathema all those who think and teach otherwise than does the Holy Roman Church about the sacrament of the body and blood of Our Lord Jesus Christ, or about baptism, or about the confession of sins, marriage and the rest of the Church's sacraments."[86]

On December 18, 1208 Pope Innocent III sent a letter to the archbishop of Tarragona setting forth a profession of faith to which the Waldensians must subscribe as a condition of return to orthodox Catholicism. They were required to accept all the Church's sacraments, marriage the last-named among them.[87]

Finally, the Second Council of Lyon (1274), under Gregory X, proposed in its sixth session a formula of faith for the Byzantine emperor, Michael Paleologas, as a condition of reunion with Rome. As with the Waldensians acceptance of the seven sacraments was made a part of this condition. Marriage was again named as the seventh and last of the sacraments.[88]

Summary

This is the period, from the Gregorian reform at the end of the eleventh century until the apogee of scholastic theology in the thirteenth, during which Christian marriage was finally accepted among the Church's sacraments. The period saw no serious development of the theology of the sacrament. The acceptance was therefore not the consequence of any such development. It was the effect rather of the Church's appropriation of the familial marriages of both the Roman and the Germanic traditions. It appropriated them in two domains, the juridical and the liturgical. It was in the liturgical celebration that the most compelling reason for acknowledging Christian marriages' sacramentality was found, namely the similarity of the bride's relationship to Christ with the consecrated virgin's relationship to him, but with the former's relationship established in the visible, humanly expressed relationship with her husband. This convinced the authorities and the scholars that the marriages in the Church must be sacred signs in the Church, human images of an invisible divine reality. The conviction was both fed by the imagery proposed in the long-neglected Pauline exhortation in Ephesians 5:21–32, and spurred theologians to examine and use this imagery more insistently. The record shows that the use ran well ahead of their critical examination.

The period's enterprises of mixed social rebuilding and religious conversion encountered and produced its own peculiar questions and conflicts. Dominant among the latter were these two: how to seal the victory over the Roman and German traditions of divorce, seal it by locking in place a theology of marriage's immunity to divorce, and how to put a control on the damaging freedom asserted in clandestine marriages.

To fashion this control the authorities had to answer the prior question that asks what is the agency that creates a marriage. The victory of the Roman-Parisian thesis that the parties' consent by itself creates it had two effects. One was to put an effective control apparently out of reach. The other was to raise the question about the minister or ministers of the sacrament. And the victory of this thesis combined with its compromise that consent creates only an inchoate marriage needing completion by consummation in first sexual intercourse, raised two more complicating questions. One asked at which step in the creation of a marriage Jesus' command that it not be "separated" takes hold. The long-standing and approved custom of dissolving unconsummated marriages provided a ready answer to this question. The renewed study of the fathers, especially of Augustine, helped spur the second question: Assuming it is the sacrament in (Christian) marriages that renders them immune to dissolution, but only consummated marriages have this immunity, how do the sacrament and consummation by sexual intercourse work together to produce this immunity? The early scholastics' answer, epitomized in Alexander of Hales' *Summa,* said that the marriages of Christians are immune to dissolution because they are images of the marital relationship of Christ and the Church, which is indestructible (or are images of the union of the two natures in Christ, which is preeminently indestructible); but these marriages are perfected in their sacramental imaging only by the Christian spouses' sexual intercourse (whereas the sacramentality of unconsummated marriages lies in their imaging only the union of human souls with Christ in charity, which is a relationship vulnerable to destruction by sin).

As to how the marital sacrament can meet the generic requirement that it be grace-giving despite the almost inevitable sinfulness of sexual intercourse because of concupiscence in it, the early scholastics reckoned that marital grace is not the kind that brings holiness. It is rather a medicinal grace, prophylactic in that it enables spouses to resist the temptation to adultery, and to temper lust within their marriages.

The scholarly energy early in this epoch was expended on a project propaedeutic to a theology of marriage. This was the gathering and arranging in anthologies of significant statements on marriage drawn from the scriptures, from the fathers, from the decrees of councils and popes, and from the decretal letters of the popes. Notable among all these were Yves of Chartres' *Decretum* and *Panormia*, Gratian's *Decretum*, Gregory IX's *Liber Decretalium*, and Peter Lombard's *Libri Quattuor Sententiarum.* The last-named especially laid out the components of a theology of marriage which were to be assembled a half-century later when the thirteenth-century scholastics had, through the study of Aristotle's *Metaphysics,* acquired the needed critical tools.

The single richest contribution to this period's nascent theology of the sacrament was Hugh of St. Victor's in the middle of the twelfth century. Laboring to explain how Mary the mother of Jesus could have been both truly married and perpetually a virgin, he posited two sacraments in Christian marriages. One is the sacrament of marriage (*sacramentum conjugii*). It is a man's and a woman's covenantal union of souls, uniquely marital because it is a love union growing out of their correlated masculine and feminine natures. This sacrament is an image of God's love for human souls and their love for him. Its love may be expressed in sexual intercourse or it may not. If it is not, the marriage is not for this reason less a sacrament. If it is expressed in sexual intercourse, the marriage has the second sacrament, the sacrament of dutiful vocation (*sacramentum officii*). It is located within the sacrament of marriage. It is an image of the mutual love of Christ and the Church, which takes place in the flesh.

NOTES

1. In his *Commentary on All the Epistles of Paul* Lanfranc took only brief notice of the two passages in these epistles that are the traditional sources of the theology of the marital sacrament. Commenting on 1 Corinthians 7:5 he quoted

Augustine's *On the Lord's Sermon on the Mount*, I, 16, that the pagan spouse's being sanctified by the Christian is the former's conversion to Christianity. But he continued, drawing from Augustine's *To Marcellus, on the Merits and the Forgiveness of Sinners*, Chapter 12, claiming that this sanctification, which consists of forgiveness of sins and becoming Christian, can be accomplished only by institutional means, by the sacraments of the Church. Otherwise the pagan spouse remains outside the kingdom of God and is doomed to damnation. Cohabitation itself with the Christian spouse does not suffice even for the minimal sanctification that is escape from damnation. (PL 150:175)

Commenting on Ephesians 5, he interprets the use of *sacramentum* in verse 22 as follows: "Paul says this of the husband and the wife. Taking it literally it is to be understood according to both secular custom and in a spiritual way of Christ and the Church. Christ it was who left father and mother when he emptied himself and took the form of a servant. He left the synagogue, the mother from whom he was born. When she persisted in her infidelity, he sent his apostles to preach to the gentiles. From the latter's conversion he gathered the Church and clung to her as to a spouse, with whom is the one-born in her flesh. This is so because in her Mass and liturgies the Church daily consumes the flesh that he received from the Virgin." (*Op. cit.*, Col. 304.)

Without committing himself expressly, Lanfranc nevertheless joined the ranks of those scholars who refer the *sacramentum magnum* to the union of Christ and the Church.

2. This thesis is in Schillebeeckx's *Marriage: Human Reality and Saving Mystery*, Vol. 2, pp. 260–280.

3. In Yves of Chartres' *Decretum*, Book 6, Chapt. 143, PL 161:616.

4. *Ibid.*, Chapt. 145.

5. In Yves of Chartres' *Panormia*, Book 6, Chap. 9, PL 161:1246.

6. *Op. cit.*, Col. 1245.

7. In K. Stevenson, *op. cit.*, pp. 35–37.

8. *Ibid.*, pp. 37–40.

9. *Ibid.*, pp. 40–47.

10. *Ibid.*, p. 47.

11. Allowance must be made for regional variations in this procedure, and for the entry of particular elements at various times during these six centuries. This sketch is comprehensive. It most nearly describes the procedure at the end of the period in question, at about the year 1200.

12. In Yves of Chartres' *Panormia*, Book 6, Chapt. 8, PL 161:1245.

13. Pp. 303–312.

14. *Loc. cit.*, p. 312.

15. *Op. cit.*, p. 47.

16. *Panormia*, Book 6, Chapt. 23, PL 161:1248.

17. In his *Sententiae*, quoted in *Dictionnaire de Théologie Catholique*, Cols. 2141–2142.

18. In Joyce, *op. cit.*, p. 63, note 1.

19. In his *Epitome Theologiae Christianae*, Chapt. 31, PL 178: 1745.

20. PL 187:1406.

21. *Loc. cit.*, Chapt. 43, Col. 1410.

22. In the Second Revised Edition of the *Sententiae*, Florence, 1916, Chapt. 6, p. 914.

23. *Op. cit.*, Chapts. 3 and 4, pp. 927–928.

24. In Joyce, *op. cit.*, p. 64.
25. Book 10, Part 32, Chapt. 7
26. *Prima Collectio Decretalium Innocentii III*, Titulus 40, PL 216:1263.
27. *Dictionnaire de Théologie Catholique*, Col. 2161.
28. The essay is in PL 176:857–876.
29. *Op. cit.*, Col. 859.
30. *Ibid.*
31. *Ibid.*, Col. 860.
32. *Ibid.*
33. PL 176:860.
34. *Ibid.*, Col. 861.
35. *Ibid.*, Cols. 862–863.
36. *Ibid.*, Col. 876.
37. For the publication of this work there is no fixed date, since its composition occupied most of Hugh's years at the College of St. Victor. It is in two books, Book 1 in PL 176:183–364, Book 2 in the same volume, Cols. 371–618.
38. *Op. cit.*, Cols. 479–520.
39. *Op. cit.*, Col. 317
40. *Ibid.*, Col. 318.
41. *Ibid.*, Col. 319.
42. Pseudo-Hilbert: *De ordinatione clericorum*, 7, PL 171:928.
43. *Tractatus de Sacramento Matrimonii*, VI, 9
44. In *Dictionnaire de Théologie Catholique*, Col. 2141.
45. PL 162:1298.
46. PL 178:1549.
47. PL 178:381–382.
48. PL 178:1745.
49. *Ibid.*
50. PL 149:1392.
51. PL 192:1289.
52. In G.H. Joyce, *op. cit.*, p. 174, note 3.
53. *Ibid.*, p. 172, note 3.
54. *Ibid.*, note 4.
55. PL 210:681.
56. PL 210:366.
The *Glossa ordinaria* on Gratian's *Decretum* compiled by Joannes Teutonicus shortly after 1215 and revised by Bartholomew of Brescia in 1238–1245, raised the question whether the exchange of money and saleable assets in the dowry affects marriage's ability as a sacrament to give grace. Joyce interpreted the gloss on Chapter 101, c. 1,1 to say that if one were to admit that this sacrament does give grace, one would admit simony, the selling of sacred things, since marriages are concluded only on condition that the dowry is given. But an alternative explanation of the gloss seems more accurate. It admits that marriage is a sacrament because it is a *signum sacrae rei*. But because it is not one of the sacraments that give grace, the dowry can be given without the danger of simony.
57. From Alexandri de Hales, *Summa Theologia, Tomus III, Secunda Pars Secundi Libri*, Florentiae, 1930, p. 635.
58. *Op. cit.*, p. 359
59. *Ibid.*
60. This is in PL 192:908–910.

61. *Op. cit.*, Col. 908.
62. *Ibid.*, Col. 909
63. *Ibid.*, Col. 910
64. Loc. cit., Cols. 910–919.
65. *Ibid.*, Col. 910
66. *Loc. cit.*, Col. 918
67. *Ibid.*
68. In PL 187:1371–1520.
69. *Op. cit.*, Col. 1455.
70. *Causa* 32, *Quaest.* 4, Col. 1476.
71. *Op. cit.*, Cols. 1371–1414.
72. *Op. cit.*, Cols. 1413–1430.
73. *Op. cit.*, Cols. 1429–1436.
74. *Op. cit.*, Col. 1435.
75. *Op. cit.*, Col. 1494.
76. *Op. cit.*, Col. 1505.
77. To this day there are canonists and others in the Catholic Church who distinguish between marriage the relationship of persons and the juridical bond of marriage. In a discourse on February 9, 1976 to the judges of the Roman Rota Pope Paul VI declared the juridical bond rather than the personal relationship to be the essence of a marriage. He added that this is what continues in existence even after civil divorce and permanent separation of the spouses. Nevertheless it is accepted Catholic doctrine that it is the sacrament that causes permanence and even indissolubility in Christian marriages. Do we therefore conclude, as Gratian apparently does, that this sacrament is a juridical bond? (The discourse is published in *Acta Apostolicae Sedis*, Vol. 68, pp. 204–208.)
78. For the examination of the most pertinent of the decretals on the marital sacrament I have used *Corpus Iuris Canonici, Editio Lipsiensis Secunda*, the Leipzig edition edited by Emile Friedberg, 1881. The *Liber Decretalium* is in *Pars Secunda: Decretalium Collectiones.*
79. *Op. cit.*, Cols. 691–692.
80. *Op. cit.*, Cols. 723–725.
81. In Title 19, "On Divorce," Chapter 7, *op. cit.*, Cols. 722–724.
82. *Op. cit.*, Cols. 147–148.
83. In *Registrarum Pontificum Liber XI*, Caput 182, in PL 214: *Saeculum XIII, Innocentii III . . . Opera Omnia*, Tomus I, *Regista sive Epistolae*, Cols. 1494–1495.
84. The absence of consummation by intercourse was deemed to leave a Christian marriage open to dissolution with other consequences. In a letter to the archbishop of Salerno Pope Alexander III ruled as follows: "Subsequent to legitimate consent *de praesenti* one of the spouses is permitted, even against the will of the other, to take up monastic life . . . provided they have not had intercourse. The other, if he or she is unable to observe . . . continence, may remarry; for, since they never became one flesh, one may join with God and the other may remain in the world." (In Denzinger-Schönmetzer, no. 755, p. 241)
85. Denzinger-Schönmetzer, no. 718, p. 235.
86. In *Liber Decretalium*, Book 5, Title 7, Chapter 9.
87. Denzinger-Schönmetzer, no. 794, pp. 256–257.
88. *Op. cit.*, no. 860, p. 277.

BIBLIOGRAPHY

Coriden, J.: *The Indissolubility Added to Christian Marriage: An Historical Study of the Period from the End of the Patristic Age to the Death of Innocent III.* Romae, Officium Libri Catholici, 1961.

Deferrari, Roy J., editor: *Hugh of St. Victor: On the Sacraments of the Christian Faith (De Sacramentis).* Cambridge, The Medieval Academy of America, 1951.

Delhaye, Philippe: "The Development of the Medieval Church's Teaching on Marriage," in *Concilium, 55.* N.Y., Herder and Herder, 1970

Duby, Georges: *Medieval Marriage: Two Models from Twelfth-Century France.* Baltimore, Johns Hopkins Press, 1978.

———: *The Knight, The Lady and the Priest: The Making of Modern Marriage in Medieval France.* N.Y., Pantheon Books, 1983.

Gies, Frances and Joseph: *Marriage and the Family in the Middle Ages.* N.Y. et al., Harper and Row, 1987.

Hillman, Eugene: "The Development of Christian Marriage Structures," in *Concilium, 55.* N.Y., Herder and Herder, 1970.

Joyce, George H.: *Christian Marriage,* Second Edition. London, Sheed and Ward, 1948. Chapter 2: "The Formation of Christian Marriage: The Essential Factor, Consent."

Mackin, Theodore: *Marriage in the Catholic Church: What Is Marriage?* N.Y./ Ramsey, Paulist Press, 1982. Chapter 6: "Marriage in Europe and the Medieval Canonists."

Schillebeeckx, Edward: *op. cit.,* Vol. 2, Chapter 1: "The Formation of Church Marriage." "The Sacramental Nature of Marriage: The Eleventh to the Thirteenth Centuries," pp. 312–325.

9. MARRIAGE AND THE MAJOR MEDIEVAL THEOLOGIANS, 1230–1330

The scholars of the high middle ages—Albert the Great, Bonaventure, Thomas Aquinas and Duns Scotus the greatest among them—inherited from the canonists of the generation before their own the opinion that in essence a marriage is a contract, or that it is a social bond created by contracting. From the canonists as well as the theologians they inherited the belief, on its way to becoming doctrine, that for Christian spouses their marriages are sacraments of the new law, or that in their marriages there is such a sacrament.

This convergence of contract and sacrament produced a new generation of questions and difficulties. These too were part of the inheritance that came to Bonaventure, Thomas and the others. The pondering they devoted to marriage was spent mainly on this inheritance; and despite the length and complexity of the pondering, neither the questions nor the difficulties were laid to rest. Along with Thomas' and the others' efforts at answers and resolutions they became in turn the inheritance of the age that saw the Protestant reformation, then the Catholic reformation that climaxed in the Council of Trent.

Duns Scotus was the scholar of the epoch who supplied the lasting formulation of the thesis that when a man and woman marry they contract with one another. Two of these formulations are in Book 4, Distinction 26 of his Commentary on Peter Lombard's *Libri Sententiarum*. There in Article 8 of the Distinction's *Quaestio Unica* (Single Question) he played on a Latin noun in order to make clear what he meant: "Marriage is called a contract as a kind of simultaneous drawing together of two wills" (*Matrimonium dicitur contractus quasi simul contractus duarum voluntatum*).[1]

In this same Distinction he added detail by naming the object of the couple's contracting: "This contract can be of no other kind than a reciprocal donation or exchange [*mutuae donationis vel permutationis*],

325

which are the same thing, of authority over their bodies for the perpetual use according to that end."[2]

But in a much fuller formulation in *Distinction 30, Quaestion 2* he supplied what was lacking thus far in the definition. He made clear that by "contract" he referred to the act that creates the marriage, and that distinct from the act is its effect, the marriage itself, which he called a bond.

> Marriage is an indissoluble bond between a man and a woman arising from the reciprocal exchange of authority over one another's bodies for the procreation and proper nurture of children.[3]

In the generation before Scotus, Albert and Thomas had been much more hesitant about referring to marriage as a contract. In one of his rare references to contracting in marriage (*In IV Sent., Book 4, Distinction 27,* Article 6) Albert asked why, in contrast to the other sacraments, the recipients' consent is needed in marriage. His reply took for granted the Roman victory in the dispute about which kind of act creates a marriage: ". . . this sacrament, as has already been said, consists of a certain exchange [*commutatio*], or contract, by the persons themselves who make the contract. But such an exchange cannot be made without the consent of the persons exchanging, or contracting."

Thomas referred to marriage as a contract only tentatively, and by analogy: "The marital joining is done in the manner of a commitment [*obligatio*] in material contracts" (*In IV Sent., Distinction 27, Quaestion 1, Article 1, Quaestiuncula 4, Solution 2*). He admitted in a vague way that a marriage is a kind of contract: "In a marriage, because it is a kind of contract, it is a certain promise by which a specific man is joined with a specific woman" (In *IV Sent., Distinction 31, Quaestion 1, Article 2, ad 2m*).

That in creating their marriage a man and woman contract with one another is an interpretation that grew up gradually through the early middle ages. The Romans had not called marriage a contract, nor sought to govern it by the law of contracts. But the expression *contrahere matrimonium* is found in the juridical vocabulary of their classical period in the second century. Their jurists noted that, like consensual contracts, marriages are created *nudo consensu*, "by consent alone" (*Digesta* XX, 1, 4 and XXII, 4).

From even before the renaissance of Roman law at the University of Bologna in the early twelfth century commentators on this law referred to marriage as a contract, and in their examples likened it to consensual contracts and to conveyances of goods. But the conception of marriage as a contract, as an agreement of wills intended to produce legal effects, arose just as much from the customs of ancient and medieval European peoples in creating their marriages. The multi-step ceremonies of the Germanic peoples and the simple expression of consent acceptable among those living by Roman law neither demanded nor excluded the contract. But both laid the way open to accepting it. Especially with its victory in Peter Lombard's theory Roman tradition did so because its creation of the marriage by the parties' consent could be construed as an agreement of wills. The Germanic tradition did so because it involved conveyances, the most notable of them the dowry and the dotal gifts. We have seen too how important the betrothal was among the Europeans, and how central these conveyances were in sealing it. Since this commitment and its sealing were so easily taken as contractual, it was logical that the concluding of marriage itself would be so taken as well, especially since betrothal had been long considered a first step in the continuum of concluding the marriage.

But the contractual interpretation took root mainly because it helped in the regulation of marriages, and thereby in the diminishing of abuses against marriage and against women and girls entering marriage. To begin with this interpretation placed marriages within a familiar and manageable social-legal category. It provided it with a legal armor and its civil and ecclesiastical defenders with weapons for this defense. The contractual interpretation made possible the specifying of the act necessary for contracting marriage generally and for verifying it in particular cases. The object and goals of the contracting could be specified and then used as criteria by which to measure sufficiency and sincerity of intent in the contractants. The conception of contract could be opened to later elaboration, as it in fact was when the permanence of marriage demanded by the New Testament teaching was written into the contractual bond and translated there as its indissolubility.

By the end of the twelfth century, then, civil law in Europe treated marriages as contracts. And the Decretalists, the commentators on the Church's own governing of marriage—especially as this appeared in Gregory IX's *Liber Decretalium*—were also treating them as such. As for the theologians, we have seen just above the hesitation with which those in the middle of the thirteenth century accepted this treatment. But eventually, and by the end of that century, the contractually formed bond was fixed firmly in the theology of marriage as well. Scotus' definitions quoted at the beginning of this chapter witness to this.

This fixing produced in turn its own inevitable questions. The easiest of all these to answer asked which kind of the several contractual acts creates a marriage—solemn, real, verbal, consensual? It was the easiest because it had already been answered in part. The contracting could not be by necessity solemn in the sense that it must be concluded by a specific and even ceremonial set of acts. We recall that Pope Nicholas I had determined this as early as the ninth century in his letter to the newly converted Bulgars. The determination had been strengthened in the twelfth and thirteenth centuries by the decretal letters that repeated Nicholas' ruling and sealed the victory of the Roman-Parisian tradition of marrying over the European-Bolognese.

That marriages must be concluded by a verbal contract had its proponents among Italian canonists until the middle of the thirteenth century, Peter Lombard among them. Their reason for urging the verbal contract grew apparently from Italian popular law, which demanded a public stipulation of intent by bride and groom themselves instead of, or in addition to, public witness and verification of their intent. But such a stipulation could be made only verbally. And since the contractual exchange has the sexual rights of the contracting parties as its object, the stipulation must be made by these persons themselves. Until the middle of the thirteenth century some canonists insisted that this must be done literally by word of mouth unless one or both parties were mute.

But this demand could not hold. Since it was by then decided that it is the parties' consent that creates their marriage, verifiable expression of this consent could be limited to no one form. Hence the conclusion that stood until the Second Vatican Council, that the marital bond is created by a consensual contracting. And if one calls the bond itself by the same name, it is a consensual contract.

For the same reason—that the marriage is created by the parties' consent alone—its creating could not be by a real contract. That is, it is not created by an exchange of services or of consumable goods. This follows from the excluding from the contracting act of all the elements of the European tradition which were in fact considered such exchanges— the dowry, the ring, the wedding gift, the handing over of the bride, the first intercourse.

This necessarily raised the next question, which asked to what the marital consent in fact consents. Despite early defenders of the thesis that it consents to the exchange that is sexual intercourse itself, a qualified version of this gained permanent acceptance. It said that the consent has as its object the exchange of the right to sexual intercourse and to all sexual acts pertinent to it. The spouses come to the marital consenting already possessing this right; by their consent they give this right over to one another. But the exchanging of the rights and reciprocal holding of them, though oriented to the use of them, are distinct from this use. In this way was virginal marriage—including that of Mary and Joseph—sustained as possible. At the same time that a man and woman give over to one another his and her right to sexual acts, and thereby create their marriage, they can agree never to exercise these rights.

The difficult questions came from the convergence, in this interpretation, of the contract and the sacrament. The simplest of these asked about the relationship of the two to one another. Are they one and the same entity? Are they different entities? Or do they fall somewhere between these two extremes? (The Catholic Code of Canon Law that was first promulgated in 1917 then revised in 1983 says, in Canon 1055, Paragraph 1, that Christ raised the marriages of Christians to the status of sacraments. This suggests something between the extremes, that is, contract and sacrament are not different entities, but they are distinct within the one entity that is the marriage. The facts of life demand this distinction within oneness. For one thing, married persons have, from the beginning of Christianity, married while still unbaptized and have later accepted Christian baptism. To make their marriages sacraments they have never been required to remarry, to repeat their marital consent so that by renewing their contract they could raise their marriages to sacramental status. The mainline Catholic theology has, since first identifying Christian marriages as sacraments, always said that with the converts' baptism their one and same marriage becomes a sacrament—by virtue of their baptism; that their baptism *makes* their marriages sacraments, so that these now cannot not be sacraments. The last is what Paragraph 2 of Canon 1055 says: "Therefore between baptized persons there can exist no valid contract that is not, by its very existence, a sacrament." In this theory it is quite accurate to see the natural marital relationship—according to the canonists the bond created by the spouses' contractual consent—as the matrix of the sacrament.

But this settled interpretation was not arrived at quickly and peacefully. The counter-thesis that in Christian marriages contractual bond and sacrament are so distinct as to be different entities kept currency among some Catholic scholars until the nineteenth century. Duns Scotus helped mightily in sustaining the thesis. We will examine his teaching later and in detail. We will find him saying that Christ *annexed* the sacrament to the contract in order to provide spouses with the graces needed to live the demands of the contract. But since the sacrament has only been annexed, it is separable from the contract. What is more, he reasoned in a complex way that we shall also examine later, no exact verbal formulation has ever been set for creating the sacrament. Consequently many men and women by their contractual consent create their marriages with no thought of the sacrament, and therefore without its coming into existence at that moment.

A variant form of this thesis, that marriage as human relationship and the sacrament are separable, is still urged by many canonists and theologians. They argue that where a marriage is in fact a sacrament, it is the human bond-relationship that is or has the sacrament; but even where both spouses are baptized, they can be in this bond-relationship without its being or having the sacrament.

From such questions and their attempted answers more questions sprang into the minds of medieval canonists and theologians. Thus, assuming that where both spouses are Christian their marriage is or becomes the sacrament, what is done to it to make it such? This is closely akin to the question that engaged and agitated Catholic theologians until the Council of Trent and after, asking: Who are the ministers of the sacrament? Who create it? The spouses themselves? The witnessing priest or bishop? Only God himself? If the spouses do, is it enough that they do no more than make a contractual exchange? To ask the same in another way, in consideration of the object of the spouses' contractual consent, can no more than the exchange of their rights to sexual acts make their relationship to be a sacrament—a sacrament whose nature is to image the love relationship of Christ and the Church? Or if they must do more, what is this more?

Abundant and complex as these questions may be, they do not exhaust the thirteenth-century list. This was made even more complex by marriage practices long since thriving among the European peoples. One of these was the contracting of marriage through the agency of proxies, frequently enough before the young spouses had even met one another. The difficulty would have been of minor juridical importance, and the theological problem non-existent, if the marrying by proxy had involved nothing more than the exchange of sexual rights. Provided the stranger-spouses had consented, and this were verified in letters of authorization, their proxies could execute the contractual exchange. But where the same exchange was held to be the creating of the sacrament— the creating, again, of an earthly image of Christ's and the Church's love union—how could this imaging be done by two proxies coming together with letters of authorization from strangers?

But before searching out how these questions were answered we must attend to one that is prior to them for reasons both logical and historical. It is the question, a question of Christian history, on which the Protestant reformers lodged one of their most serious challenges. It asks when and where the marriages of Christians were instituted as sacraments. And since the Catholic claim has been that Christ made these marriages sacraments of his new covenant, it asks also by which words and gestures he did this.

The Institution of the Sacrament

From their earliest teaching on the subject Catholic authorities and scholars have insisted that it is God who is the author of the marital sacrament.[4] This has had diverse but interrelated meanings. It means that in a concretely universal way he has determined that whichever cause or causes make marriages to be sacraments, these will act to produce this effect in every Christian marriage, and, some authorities have said, in every marriage, non-Christian as well as Christian. It means also that it is God himself who acts in the creating of individual marriages, along with the human agents, to make this creating the production of a sacrament in every case. The axiomatic way of stating this was that the human agents are the *causae proximae* of the sacrament's creation, while God is its *prima causa*.

Finally, because Christ is acknowledged as author of the new covenant of God with human beings, he is acknowledged also as the author of the sacraments of this covenant. This means that it is through Christ's humanity that God has instituted the sacraments in the universal way noted just above, as it is through this humanity that he works with the other human agents to make individual marriages to be sacraments. (This hints at a concept of authoring, or institution, of sacraments that is far more inclusive than the kind of institution by gospel mandate that many Protestant theologians have demanded for a sacrament if it is to be accepted as instituted by Christ—as they have pointed out his doing in regard to baptism ("Go, therefore, make disciples of all nations; baptize them in the name of the Father, etc."—Mt 28:19), and in regard to the Eucharist ("Then he took some bread, and when he had given thanks, he broke it and gave it to them, saying 'This is my body which will be given up for you. Do this as a commemoration of me' "—Lk 22:19).

Disagreement among scholars about the exact moment of God's instituting the sacrament, and about his words or gesture of institution, was for long as constant as the belief that he was in fact its institutor. The earlier medieval consensus held that he instituted it in the marriage of the first human couple in the garden of paradise. Peter of Poitiers called marriage the earliest of the sacraments precisely because of its institution there.[5] Alexander of Hales said expressly that it was instituted in the garden, maintaining that it was instituted there not only as a dutiful vocation (*in officium*) but also as a sacrament.[6] Rolando Bandinelli, later Pope Alexander III, held the same opinion.[7] Peter Lombard agreed, and identified the institution more precisely in Adam's words, in Genesis 2:23, "This one at last is bone of my bones and flesh of my flesh."[8] (Until our own century Catholic scholars took as one of their assumptions, when searching for the moment of marriage's divine institution, that in the creation poem of Genesis 1 and in the fall narrative of Genesis 2 and 3 they were reading historically factual accounts. Catholic authorities held to this assumption as recently as 1930, as Pope Pius XI's encyclical letter of that year, *Casti connubii*, shows.)[9] These words of Adam were taken as evidence of divine institution because it was God who inspired him to pronounce them.

Not all of Peter Lombard's contemporaries or near-contemporaries in the middle of the twelfth century agreed. Some thought the words of institution were in God's command to the first couple, in Genesis 1:28: "Increase and multiply. . . ." Hugh of St. Cher argued that this command could not have instituted the sacrament since it was directed at all the animals God had created.[10] And Godfrey of Trani considered them words of blessing rather than of institution.[11]

Albert and the Institution of the Sacrament

Albert the Great first identified the institution of marriage not when attempting to explain expressly when that was done and by which words or gestures, but when explaining simply "What Marriage Is." This is the title of Article 1, *Quid sit matrimonium* (What Is Marriage?), of Question 1, "On the Elements Essential to Marriage," of his treatise on this sacrament.[12] The reason for this is quickly evident: He believed that

God instituted marriage by creating the first man and woman in the garden and bringing them together. In his bringing them together he also made their marriage a sacrament.

Albert turned explicitly to the institution of the sacrament in Article 6 of this first question. Its title too is brief: *De institutione sacramenti.* Here he asks not when and how marriage was instituted, but when and how it was made a sacrament. As we shall see, in answering the second of these questions he also answers the first.[13]

Again he explains that in both its essential characters—as an *officium* (a dutiful vocation) and as a sacrament—marriage was instituted in the garden of paradise in the bringing together of the first man and woman. This was expressed and verified in Adam's encomium of the woman whom God gave to him, "This one at last is bone of my bones and flesh of my flesh." These words verified the sacrament because they imply that the union of this man and woman was indestructible. For indestructibility is one of the essential elements of a marriage's sacramentality. Thus by putting this element in marriage at its beginning God made it a sacrament at its beginning. Christ later confirmed this with his own words, "What God has joined man must not separate."

Albert then takes account of three aspects of the marital sacrament, and finds three distinct institutions of the sacrament, one for each of these aspects. Thus the sacrament can be considered as an image, as a cause, and as both. If considered only as an image, it was instituted in the garden of paradise; there it imaged in anticipation the union of Christ and the Church. But it was not there instituted as a cause in the sense of a *remedium* because in that state before the first sin no remedy was needed.

If considered only as a cause, the sacrament was instituted after the sin of the first man and woman, in the epoch of natural law before the law of Moses, because only then by its moral rightness (*honestate sua*) did it mitigate the damage done by concupiscence. It did not thus mitigate by producing grace in the souls of the spouses, an interior grace. But by its moral rightness it made what was evil in sexual intercourse and infected by concupiscence after the first sin to be not evil.

If one considers the sacrament as both image and cause, one can consider it in two ways, as imaging and causing one and the same effect, or diverse effects. If diverse effects, the sacrament was instituted during the Mosaic law, where it imaged grace that was to be given in the future, in the new law of Christ. In that epoch it caused as it had caused in the preceding epoch of natural law, not by producing grace in the souls of the spouses, but by mitigating their concupiscence.

But if one considers the sacrament as both imaging and causing one and the same effect, it was instituted in the new law of Christ, where it both images and causes grace in the spouses' souls. For from the abiding union of the two natures in Christ grace is caused in the sacrament of marriage, grace which helps (*promovet*) to the goods of marriage and to the mitigating of concupiscence.

This dividing and correlating shows again how for the medieval scholastics the concept of institution went beyond innovation by mandate. We see it here including appropriation, adaptation and extension.

Bonaventure and the Institution of the Sacrament

When Bonaventure, in his commentary on the fourth book of Lombard's *Sententiae,* asked about the time of marriage's institution, it was not at first clear whether he was asking about the natural human relationship or about this relationship as a sacrament. We shall see in a moment, from the evidence in Question 2 of this first article under Distinction 26, that he was even here in Question 1 asking about the institution of the relationship as a sacrament.[14] Here his acceptance of the Augustinian axiom that marital conduct needs a *remedium* impelled him to ask it as a question conditioned by that axiom: "Was marriage instituted before the fall?" His concern to ask it in this way is understandable. If marriage was instituted as a sacrament before the sin of the first man and woman in the garden—before the first sin whose inheritance has been the sinfulness of the entire human race from its beginning—how can one hold to the traditional thesis that it has indeed been instituted as a *remedium?*

He resolved the difficulty by making the distinction, common in his time, between two kinds of institution, and between two moments in history when marriage was instituted according to the respective kinds.

About the distinct moments, before the fall marriage was instituted *in officium,* as a dutiful vocation. After the fall it was instituted *in remedium,* while not, of course, relinquishing its original *officium.*

He made a second set of distinctions, each placed symmetrically under each of the first two distinctions made just above. As an *officium* marriage was instituted for the sake of two functions. The first of these is cognitive. Under this purpose marriage's function is to bring the spouses to see and enjoy exteriorly the corporeal union that they know interiorly is theirs. The second is the generative function wherein the man, who could not by himself continue the human species, is given the helpmate needed for doing so.

As a *remedium* marriage has been given the task of healing two kinds of illness. One of these is the illness of ignorance, which marriage heals by functioning as a sign that instructs the spouses about the will of God for their union. The other is the illness of concupiscence, which marriage heals by diminishing it.

As stated above, Bonaventure explained even more detailedly the distinct kinds of institution in the Question immediately following.[15] There he pointed out that while some of the Christian sacraments are exclusively religious in nature, two of them, penance and marriage, exist in answer to the demands of nature in men and women. This is in reply to the question asking whether marriage not only as a human relationship, but now too as a sacrament, has God as its author.

The question is bred by a demand of Christian history. For plainly the Eucharist, baptism, confirmation, etc. were not instituted until after the fall. For this reason their divine institution in service of the work of salvation is all the more verifiable. But since marriage as the human relationship was instituted before the fall, the same verification seems unavailable. And because it seems unavailable, it seems impossible to maintain that God instituted marriage as a sacrament.

Bonaventure's answer is another distinction, this time between two kinds of institution. The exclusively religious sacraments God instituted by mandate. But penance and marriage he instituted by illumining interiorly the mind of the first man. He did not command Adam in any observable way to take Eve as his wife. But he illumined his mind interiorly to understand that she was given to him as his wife, and that all his descendants were likewise to accept wives by free choice.

Thomas Aquinas and the Institution

A student who searches out Thomas Aquinas' thought on the sacrament in marriage is constrained within limitations set by the sequence of Thomas' writings. His earliest words on the subject are in the first comprehensive product of his twenty years of teaching and writing. This is his Commentary on the Four Books of Peter Lombard's *Sententiae*.[16]

Lecturing in commentary on this compilation was Thomas' main work during his first tenure, at about thirty years of age, at the University of Paris. This was the task of any young master in theology, to teach as a *Sententiarius*. What we read now is in part the fruit of his student auditors' faithful recording.

Therefore what we read in this commentary are also Thomas' first thoughts on the subject. We have almost nothing from his later consideration of it. He ceased writing, as we know, after celebrating Mass on the feast of St. Nicholas, December 6, 1273, protesting that what he had already written was chaff. Among the works he left unfinished was the treatise on the sacraments in Part III of his *Summa Theologica*. The marital sacrament was among the casualties of his decision to write no more. What we have on marriage in the *Supplementum* to the *Summa* is Reynaldo of Piperno's rearrangement, in the literary structure of the *Summa*, of what Thomas had taught in his *Commentary on the Sentences* seventeen years before his decision to stop writing.

His first substantial question on the sacrament is in Book 4, Distinction 26, Question 2, Article 1: "Whether Marriage Is a Sacrament" (*Utrum matrimonium sit sacramentum*).[17] We shall return to it later, after examining his passage that is more immediately pertinent to our inquiry. This is Article 2 of the same Question: "Whether Marriage Ought To Have Been Instituted Before the [First] Sin" (*Utrum matrimonium debuit institui ante peccatum*).[18] He asks the question as a derivative of the assumption that we have already seen, that marriage was instituted after the fall as a safe place within which to contain the concupiscence passed down from that sin of the first couple. The counter-logic seems convincing: Before the sin no concupiscence, therefore no need for marriage.

Thomas answers by distinguishing the institution of marriage at three different moments in history to meet human needs arising distinctly in these moments. For the sake of marriage's natural orientation to procreation, which is a need regardless of sin, it was instituted before the sinful fall of the first couple. In its capacity as a healing of the inherited wound of their sin, it was instituted after their fall by the law of Moses during the epoch of the law of nature.

But for marriage's imaging the mystery of the union of Christ and the Church it was instituted in the new law. It is in virtue of this imaging that it is a sacrament of this law. As for the other useful effects produced by marriage (its *utilitates*), such as friendship of the spouses and their mutual help, this institution it has from civil law.

Three points here, passing from the less to the more important among them, call for attention. The first is that in Thomas' mind "institution" does not designate the inventing of marriage, either as a human relationship or as a sacrament. It designates its establishment in a specific function or functions in society—although Thomas takes for granted as a fact of history that the first of the listed institutions was also its invention.

The second point contains both surprise and disappointment. Marriage's Christian institution, whereby it was made an image of the love union of Christ and the Church, seems not to be the institution that includes the spouses' mutual help and love-of-friendship, which Thomas calls *utilitates* of marriage. (This leaves the student to wonder which among the spouses' several kinds of conduct, in Thomas' mind, do image the Christ-Church relationship.)

The final point, the most significant for the theology of the sacraments, is that marriage's institution as a *remedium* for sinfulness antedated its institution as a sacrament. So for Thomas it is not precisely marriage's function as this *remedium* that makes it a Christian sacrament. Its imaging the union of Christ and the Church does this. But the earlier institution as a *remedium* seems carried forward into the later; marriage's function as a *remedium* for concupiscence seems included in its imaging the Christ-Church love union. We may expect, then, that Thomas will explain how the imaging does this healing when, as he implies, the spouses' mutual help and love-of-friendship are separable from and unessential to the imaging.

Duns Scotus and the Sacrament's Institution

Duns Scotus began his consideration of marriage where his predecessors and peers had begun it according to the medieval convention, with a commentary on Distinction 26 of Lombard's Book of Sentences, "Concerning Marriage in Its Final Cause" (*De matrimonio secundum causam finalem*). He opened his commentary with the question, "Whether marriage was instituted immediately by God?" (*Utrum matrimonium fuerit immediate institutum a Deo?*)[19] He began to develop his complex answer by moving on a tangent away from the question as he himself had posed it. In his Scholion I[20] he set out five conclusions that he was to develop immediately afterward: (1) In order to give proper nurture to offspring it is right that a man and woman be joined obligatorily in a reciprocal and indissoluble bond. (2) It is right that for procreation and nurture of offspring a man and woman grant to one another authority over their own bodies for permanent use thereof. (3) It is fitting that God have instituted and approved this reciprocal exchange (here is the answer to his own question). (4) It is fitting that some sacrament be annexed to this contract for mutual exchange, and such has in fact been done. (5) In marriage multiple distinct elements must come together. Which are they?

In a much later and independent scholion Scotus[21] will return briefly to marriage's institution. There he will say simply that marriage as a contract was instituted by God himself in the garden of paradise before the fall and after it. In both instances the institution took the form of an affirmative command. Scotus mixed clauses from Genesis 1 and Genesis 2 and 3 in order to identify the institution before the fall. Thus, after Adam's declaring "This one at last is bone of my bones and flesh of my flesh" (in Gen 2), God commanded the first couple "Increase and multiply and fill the earth" (Gen 1), and later promised the woman her punishment, "I will intensify the pangs of your child-bearing; in pain shall you bring forth children" (Gen 3:16). And still later God repeated to Noah and his sons the primeval command, "Increase and multiply and fill the earth" (Gen 9:7). Thus marriage is a permanent command for human beings, although its obligation is not continual (*obligat semper sed non pro semper*). It also arises as an obligation from the law of nature, although not in the first order of this law as an obligation that is self-evident, but as an obligation in the second order.

Our interest fastens on the fourth of the conclusions that Scotus lists above. What comes immediately to attention is his statement of the relationship between marriage the natural contract and the marital sacrament. The latter has been annexed, or joined, to the former. And we have already seen that he holds the two to be not only distinguishable, not only separately intelligible, but separate in fact.[22]

The reasons he assigns for the sacrament's being no more than annexed to the contract is unique among the reasons assigned in his generation for marriage's being a sacrament in any way. At no point does he hint that this reason is the imaging of a sacred, invisible reality. His reason is pragmatic. It is opportune that the sacrament be joined to the contract because the latter is severely demanding, and because, in turn, the obligations that the contract produces, though it be a right and just contract, are severely demanding. But to that which is severely demanding while right and just, it is opportune that the help of grace be brought.

Scotus explained more fully. Once granted that grace is needed for fulfilling the demands of the contract, it is fitting and helpful that for such a state as marriage the needed graces be brought in an ordered way (*regulariter*), i.e. by a sensate sign established by God. What is more, it is helpful that the bringing of grace to this contractual state by a sensate sign be done through a sacrament properly so called (*proprie dictum*). The reason for this is that the needed graces need to be brought by an efficacious sign thereof.

Scotus offers no more detailed explanation for these reasons. One may suspect that the need for a specifically efficacious sign of graces is found in the severity of the difficulties native to married life. They call for convincingly tangible and visible evidence of God's help.[23]

At this point Scotus moves to another point of fact about which he disagrees with a multitude of his peers. He insists that it cannot be said that the sacrament was instituted and joined to the marriage contract in the garden of Eden, in mankind's time of innocence, as this condition is reported in Genesis 2. For every one of the sacraments has its efficacy from the passion of Christ, from his passion already completed or from his passion in anticipation. But if the state of innocence had survived, if the first man and woman had not sinned, Christ's passion would have been neither completed nor anticipated. He adds that there is no evidence that the sacrament was instituted during the law of Moses.

Some may say, Scotus continues, that Ephesians 5:32—*Sacramentum hoc magnum est*—refers to marriage as a sacrament in the extended sense, as a sign of a sacred reality but not as a cause of this reality nor as an efficacious sign of it—not a sign that is an imaging which somehow replicates the reality imaged. For marriage is surely not an efficacious sign vis-à-vis the union of Christ and the Church. Moreover if there is any efficacious sign of this union, it is vowed virginity that images the union of Christ with the virgin Church.[24]

But in his second scholion Scotus acknowledges that nevertheless we know with certainty that marriage is a sacrament properly so called, an efficacious sign of grace. We know this because the Church teaches it to be so. Therefore we must acknowledge that to the marriage contract God has annexed the sacrament at least for the faithful in the new law. Otherwise marriage would not be a sacrament of this law. From this we must conclude also that the sacrament was instituted by Christ, the institutor of the new law.

That this institution has taken place is found nowhere more clearly than in Matthew 19. But since what he is recorded as doing there to the contract was to approve it, what Christ instituted was only the sacrament. That is, the words "What God has joined" in Christ's statement, "What God has joined man must not separate," are not synonymous with "God has instituted specifically the marital contract." What this key phrase tells us is that from the moment he said that, Christ joins all Christian spouses by the sacrament that is annexed to the already conjoining marital contract.[25]

The Sacrament in Non-Christian Marriages

Their pondering on the moment and the manner of the marital sacrament's institution shows that these medieval scholars formulated the question quite differently from the way with which we are familiar. In its most naive form we ask: "When did Christ institute the sacrament of marriage?" They on the other hand began with the conviction that God himself invented marriage in a definite place on earth, at a definite time, between an historically verifiable man and woman. They were convinced that he gave marriage its purpose, to populate the earth in an orderly way, but that because of the first couple's damaging the relationship and its purpose by their sin, and damaging it for all their descendants until the end of time, he gave it added emergency purposes. One of these is to restrain lust and its ruinous effects. Another is to be a sign and an avenue of his mercy—a sign of it pointing in two directions. It points first to the future, to God's climactic act of mercy in the death and resurrection of Christ. After that act it points not backward, but in a sense upward to this act's continuation in Christ's love for all men and women gathered in his following, the Church.

This interpretation of the sacrament and its institution brings one unavoidably to the question that we have already seen addressed in some decretals coming from popes of the late twelfth and early thirteenth centuries. Do unbaptized spouses, non-Christians such as Jews and Muslims, and even pagans, receive and participate in the sacrament? One cannot say immediately that they do not because they reject Christ's gospel. To begin with, very few if any of them are Jews, Muslims or pagans as a consequence of rejecting Christ. On the contrary, to be a Jew or Muslim is to accept God in a specific way. But more than this, the scholastics' claim that God began interpolating the sacrament into marriage from its beginning, or at least from the moment after the first sin, implies that this was done to marriages centuries before the coming of Christ, for the good of persons who were not baptized Christians.

Even more, pagans and then Jews could experience the effects of the sacrament as the Christian fathers and now the scholastics understood it. Their concupiscence could be restrained, their lust diminished and controlled. Especially, as we have seen some of the fathers say about the marriages of Israel's patriarchs and prophets, these could foreshadow, could image in advance, the unions of Christian husbands and wives, and even the union of Christ and his Church.

In this regard it is helpful to return to the decretal letter of Innocent III written at the beginning of the thirteenth century, and to that of

Boniface VIII written at its end. In his letter of 1206 to the bishop of Ferrara Innocent wrote, "It seems possible that the sacrament of marriage and the sacrament of the Eucharist can be received by the unbaptized." His express reason for this opinion is that although unbaptized, such persons may nevertheless have a simple belief in Christ. His implied reason is that in these sacraments God takes the initiative to act in the soul of the unbaptized persons. Provided they put no obstacle of contrary, sinful will to God's action, but instead receive it in an act of faith, this action can affect such persons. The divine action, its human reception and its working its effect—provided all are accomplished in a sensate way—make up the receiving of the sacrament.

Boniface explained it by reasoning from one of the characteristics fixed in marriage from its beginning that makes it a sacrament, and therefore a sacrament for those entering marriage from the beginning of its history. This is its indissolubility. The fact that it has been put there by the founder and head of the Church contributes to the sacramentality of marriages generally.

> But the bond of marriage received its indissoluble union from the head of the Church himself, and creator of all things, when he instituted it in paradise in the state of human innocence.[26]

As a consequence when men and women, Christian or not, enter marriage as God has designed it, they enter a union that already contains one of the main elements of the sacrament. Boniface does not say so in this decretal letter, but he could have added that because non-Christian spouses participate in this marital indissolubility, they foreshadow the indissoluble union of Christ and the Church.

The scholastic theologians expressed diverse opinions on the matter but nevertheless agreed in principle that persons can participate in the marital sacrament in degrees, in fractional ways. Thus Bonaventure, in his Commentary on the Fourth Book of the Sentences, reckoned that the marriages of the unbaptized have the elements of true marriage in only limited portions, namely the dutiful vocation, the *remedium* and the *sacramentum*.

In his commentary on the same book of Lombard's Sentences, Distinction 6, Article 6, Albert said about marriages generally, and thereby passed judgment on those of the unbaptized implicitly, that they have complete (*perfectam*) indissolubility only insofar as they are grounded in baptism and in the (Christian) faith.

Thomas phrased his qualification of non-Christian marriages' sacramentality in a still different way (in his commentary on the same Book 4 of the Sentences, Distinction 39, Question 1, Article 2, ad 1m): "Such marriages are in some way sacraments *habitualiter*, although not *actualiter*, because they are not contracted in the faith of the Church." The qualifying adverb *habitualiter* here means that the marriages of the unbaptized have the sacrament in a fundamental, abiding but inert way. "Not *actualiter*" means that this sacrament is for the spouses not a source of graced conduct, of active union with God.

Although this question about the sacramentality of unbaptized marriages may at first glance seem of secondary concern, even a theological curiosity piece, it is not. It helps to ground the entire matter in real-life experience. It also helps to make clear the meaning of an issue currently vexing the Catholic authorities. What if two unbaptized persons have almost all the Christian virtues in exceptional degree, have accepted Christ in faith as their savior, yet for some reason have never been baptized? They think they were baptized in infancy but were not? Why is prior baptism needed to make their marriage a Christian sacrament? Or granting that it is needed, what does it do to make their marriage a sacrament? Or turning the question upside down, how does their baptism make their marriage a Christian sacrament where both spouses have later become religiously inactive and live thoroughly secular lives—as Catholic authorities currently insist is the case? In short, how has this second marriage the Christian sacrament while the first does not?

The Minister of the Sacrament

The question that asks who is or are the ministers of a Christian sacrament can be easily misunderstood. This would be to ask it while assuming that in the completing of the sacrament there is one person who is the one active agent, while any others are passive recipients, that the former confers the sacrament while the latter receive it. This may still be a common misunderstanding of the Eucharist, that the sacrament in it is the "distribution" of Communion, in which the priest or other ministers give the sacrament and the communicants receive it. The same misunderstanding of penance abounds. The priest-confessor is thought to confer the sacrament in granting absolution; the penitent receives it in being absolved. That the Church is thought of as a kind of dispensary of graces is thus not surprising.

One begins to correct the misunderstanding by replacing the verbs "give" (or "confer") and "receive" with "participate in." About the Eucharist, its entire liturgy is a sacrament from beginning to end. It moves through stages to a sacramental climax—which is not the consecration of the bread and the wine, but their breaking and pouring out, and their shared eating and drinking. In all this there are multiple participants taking different functions. So if one asks about the Eucharist the traditional question concerning the minister of the sacrament, the inquiry should be about the *principal* agent or agents in the carrying on of this sacramental mini-drama. Asked in this way the question assumes that the answer may claim multiple ministers, with one or more the most active and significant among them.

It seems clear that in the European wedding tradition this was the implicit assumption about the ministers of marriage. Multiple persons had parts in it, not only the bride and groom but the two sets of parents, a *mundoaldus* (to act out the conveying of the bride), perhaps an *orator* (to inquire about impediments and to ask the parents' and/or the bride's and groom's consent), a priest (to offer a prayer and a blessing, and later to take the function of at least the *orator*).

The question that the medieval canonists and theologians asked about the minister of the sacrament in marriage was not, however, prompted by such multiple participation. It did not search for the respective functions of all these persons in creating the sacrament. Their question was prompted rather by the gradual identification in Christian marriages of sacrament and contractual bond, along with the twelfth-century victory of the Roman-Parisian interpretation that the spouses themselves do the contracting by their reciprocal consent. From this the conclusion seems logically unassailable: Since the spouses are the contractors of the marital bond, they must also be the creators of the sacrament—its ministers. What is more, they must be the only ministers of the sacrament. The assessment of clandestine marriages argued for this because all whose opinions counted in the matter—Church authorities, canonists, theologians—accepted that even though they sinned in doing so, the spouses alone and without witnesses could exchange marital consent, thereby creating their contractual marital bond—and thus their sacrament.

Few texts from this period assert conclusively that the spouses, or spouses alone, are the ministers of the sacrament, as few assert conclusively the major competing opinion from the eleventh through the eighteenth centuries, that the priest is its minister. (In both opinions "minister" designated the person or persons who confer the sacrament.)

The all-inclusive reason for thinking that the priest is the minister of the marital sacrament came out of his progressively dominant role in the solemnizing of marriages in Europe at the time. The seemingly improbable supporting reason for this ascendancy was the victory of the *consensus* interpretation of the creating of marriages. It led to the irrelevance of the old traditional ways of marrying, with their multiple "ministers," and to their gradual abandonment.

With consent by both spouses acknowledged as the fashioning of the marriage the bride gained status as a person before the law. Creating the marriage was now an effect as much of her action as of the groom's. She crowded out as irrelevant the *mundoaldus* who, among other things, used to supervise the gestures of exchange and conveyance. Indeed since in order to give consent the bride had, as we have said, to be *sui juris,* a person free for and capable of legal acts, the transfer of *mundium* over her lost its meaning. For this reason, from the twelfth century onward the *datio parentum,* the parents' *giving* their daughter to the groom-husband, began to lose its meaning—even though it survived as a ceremonial gesture.

Simultaneously and correlatively the function of the priest in the wedding ceremony began to grow by way of filling these roles that were being emptied. He began to replace the *orator* of the European tradition, the man who verified that all the conditions for legitimate marriage had been met and asked the bride's and groom's consent. From the eleventh century, when the *traditio* of the bride, or of *mundium* over her, still held place, she began to be "handed over" first to the priest, who then handed her over to the groom. Or the priest might take the place of the parents in this handing over, especially where the bride was an orphan. Or he might assume the role of the *orator* in asking both parties for their consent, or in reciting the formula of consent with them, or in holding their hands while they recited it, and, after they had recited it, in handing the bride over to the groom. Other rituals show him giving the bride and groom to one another, others joining with the groom in placing the wedding ring on the bride's finger.

By the middle of the thirteenth century, then, the solemnization of a marriage most commonly included the following elements: the spouses presented themselves at the portal of the church; the priest questioned them about possible impediments and about their intention to marry; the families exchanged dowry and wedding gifts; the bride and groom expressed their marital consent; together and led by the priest they entered the church for the blessing and for the wedding Mass, unless this were planned for a later date.

Thus a simple logic argued for the priest as the minister of the sacrament. In syllogism it reasoned that the sacrament must be the most religious element of both the Christian marriage itself and of the ceremony that creates it. But the priest's blessing is the most religious element of both. Therefore the blessing is the sacrament, and the priest who bestows it is the minister of the sacrament.

If this opinion were to be accepted as accurate, the consequences for the theology of marriage and derivatively for the law regulating marriage would be severe. Since a blessing is only a transitory act and affects the persons only extrinsically and temporarily, the sacrament would be temporary and extrinsic to the marriage. It could not be a source of grace for the spouses, not in the richer sense of a personal union with God, nor even as a help to fulfill the duties of married life. The Church's blessing from the hands of the priest could with good reason be seen as ecclesiastical intrusion in the marriage, at best benign but also a first grip of what could become an exclusive hold on Christian marriages. This is exactly the line of reasoning that Martin Luther and the other reformers were to take in the sixteenth century. Luther's verdict expressed its premise well: *Die Ehe ist ein weltliches Geschäft*— "Marriage is a secular affair." Assuming that it is, priestly participation in it must be literally an intrusion.

But the opinion that the sacrament is the blessing never gained acceptance. The competing opinion that it is the marital bond itself, and that this is created by the spouses' consent, was argued too well by the best of the scholars of the thirteenth and fourteenth centuries. Albert saw a kind of matter-form correlation in the act that produces the sacrament. He divided the agency producing the act according to these two aspects. As an *officium naturae,* and as a good of the Christian community, the Church, the marriage can be produced by the spouses' consent. But as a *remedium* it exists and functions under the *claves* of the Church, under its power and authority, and therefore under the ministry of its priests. Within the latter aspect the priestly ministry takes what is sacramental in the marriage itself and gives it a determinate form *in facie ecclesiae,* in the Church's ceremony and authority. By thus making the sacrament-in-itself a sacrament of the Church, the priest's blessing makes it a *medicina* coming from the Church's power to forgive.[27]

Bonaventure offered an explanation that used a similar metaphoric model. He said that a marriage gains its aspect (*ratio*) of spirituality and grace when the spouses' consent and the priest's blessing combine. This joining makes explicit the sacramental signing in the marriage. From the blessing comes the grace that strengthens and sanctifies the spouses.[28]

Thomas' answer to the question hewed firmly to the assumption that where the marriage is a sacrament it is the bond itself that is this. He did not enlist a hylemorphic model for this explanation. He deemed the priest essentially unneeded for creating the sacrament. After explaining that whereas the priest's absolution is indispensable for forgiving sins in the sacrament of penance, he added, "But in marriage [the spouses'] acts are the sufficient cause for producing the proximate effect, which is the bond (*obligatio*), because whoever is *sui juris* can bind himself to another. Hence the priest's blessing is not needed in marriage for the essence of the sacrament."[29]

In a later work, his *Summa Contra Gentes,* Book 4, Chapter 78, he again affirmed the non-essentiality for the sacrament of the priest's blessing. A marriage is a sacrament in itself from causes logically and temporally prior to the blessing. Where a marriage is a union of a man and a woman who intend to bear and educate children for the worship of God, it is in itself a sacrament of the Church. For this reason already established as a sacrament, the marriage gains the Church's blessing through its priest.

Duns Scotus at first, in his *Opus Oxoniense,* took a middle position that could be allied with either opinion.[30] He identified the human agents of the sacrament with whoever creates the contract—who may be persons other than the spouses themselves. If in a particular instance these are the parents, they are the ministers of the sacrament. But when commenting on the same passage in his *Reportatio Parisiensis* he thought better of this because, as he said, parents cannot confer the gift of grace. But some of his disciples persisted in the opinion that whoever can conclude the marital contract can administer the sacrament. Thus at the end of the fourteenth century Guy de Briançon reported, "It is said that the minister of the sacrament is indifferently whoever can conclude the contract of marriage. In practice this is sometimes a priest, sometimes the bride and groom (as in clandestine marriages); sometimes a cleric, sometimes a layperson. But in a well-regulated marriage only a priest is minister because such a marriage is formed only under the authority of the Church (*in facie Ecclesiae*)."[31]

The Sowing of Doubt About the Sacrament

These scholastics of the thirteenth century anticipated a difficulty that the Christian positivists of the fifteenth and sixteenth centuries were to raise with far more serious consequences. Martin Luther and other reformers were among these positivists. Their inability to resolve the difficulty reinforced their conviction that marriage cannot be a Christian sacrament.

It arose from the conclusion, now functioning as a premise in the thirteenth century, that they are the spouses themselves who create the marriage, whether one thinks of it as a bond, a contract or a social relationship. But if, as so many of the scholastics insisted, the marital sacrament is the bond, or contract, or relationship itself, one must accept that the spouses also create the sacrament.

But there is this difficulty: a sacrament is a sacred visible reality in that it images a sacred invisible reality. And a serious claim for every Christian sacrament is that it is a cause, a medium, of grace—of the sanctifying grace of personal union with God, and/or of the actual graces which help spouses to fulfill the duties of marriage. But how can mere creatures, men and women, be causes of such a sacred reality? To claim that they are seems to arrogate to them a power that belongs to God alone. Hence the positivist conclusion: either there is no sacrament in marriage at all, or it is at most what some of the scholastics themselves say it is, the priest's blessing. This is a realistically modest claim because it does not presume to attribute God's gracing power to human beings. The blessing does no more than manifest the Church's approval of the new marriage contract, and correlatively shows the spouses' religious faith in concluding their marriage *in facie Ecclesiae*—within the visibly exercised jurisdiction of the Church.

Both Albert and Thomas got at this difficulty by making distinctions in the causation that creates sacraments, but different distinctions. Albert distributed the Christian sacraments into two categories, into those purely divine and into those partly human and partly divine. Baptism and the Eucharist are among the former, penance and marriage among the latter. For these sacraments human causation is both needed and possible—possible because it produces only what is human in them.[32]

Thomas' was the distinction that he used so richly throughout his theology of the sacraments, one which though proper to a metaphysics of being is eminently common-sensible, and in fact is drawn from common sensate experience. It is between principal cause and its instrumental cause. The former's power and action use the power and action of the latter to produce the effect, an effect that transcends the causal power of the instrument left to itself. But as an instrument of the principal power and action, the latter does contribute to the effect. It does so by in-forming, specifying the action of the principal cause. For example, a brush could not by itself paint a portrait. But used by the principal cause, the painter, picked up and joined to his power and action, the brush co-works in producing the painting by in-forming and specifying the painter's action. The contributions of each of the causes are discernible in the portrait. That it exists at all, that it has its specific design and colors, are the effects in it proportioned to the principal cause, the painter in action. But that it is perceptibly brushed design and colors are effects proportioned to the instrument he has used.

God's use of human minds and wills and bodies in the sacraments works in a way analogous to this. That, for example, the sacrament exists and functions at all in a marriage is the effect proportioned to God's transcendent causation, as do its ability to grace the spouses, and to image an invisible divine reality. But that the imaging and gracing are done through human consent, wills, and bodies comes of their being taken up by the divine action and used as his instruments. An obvious difference among kinds of instruments is that some, like the painter's brush, are inert of themselves and entirely submissive to the intent and action of the principal agent, while others—like human minds, wills and senses—are active in themselves, and can co-work with the divine action only by free decision.[33]

The Matter and Form of the Sacrament

The scholastic scholars' appropriation, in the thirteenth century, of Aristotle's philosophy of nature (he himself called it his physics) brought a singular question to their analysis of the sacraments. In this philosophy every item of physical reality is composed of two fundamental elements, one of them wholly determinable, the other its determination. Aristotle called the former a physical being's *hýlē*, the latter its *morphē;* hence the term "hylemorphic" composition of physical things. The terms in Latin translation are *materia* and *forma;* in English "matter" and "form"—where "form" does not mean figure but form-of-existence. These are not each separate entities that combine; they are the determinable-determining elements of the one being or action—as, for example, the soul is the form of existence that matter has in human beings; and pitch, rhythm, timbre, melody, volume and tempo are forms of action that sound has in a song.

Because each sacrament is physical in composition, the scholastics included in their analysis the identification of the matter and the form in each of them. In baptism they found the washing with water to be its matter (not the water alone, because baptism is an action), and the baptismal formula—"I baptize you in the name of the Father, of the Son, and of the Holy Spirit"—to be the form. Without the speaking of the formula the washing would be at most a natural human cleansing; without the washing the formula would be only a prayer. But in their determinable-determining union they are the sacrament.

The search for and identification of the matter and the form in the sacrament of marriage occasioned a rewording of the question that asked who is or are the ministers of this sacrament. This was to ask who unite its matter and its form. If in a careless way the spouses' exchange of consent were taken as matter, its determinable element, and the priestly blessing as its determining element, its form, the answer to this phrasing of the question would be easy. It would be the priest who, by his blessing, joins the form to the matter of the marital sacrament. He would be its minister.

But the best of the scholastics were not so naive as this. Their insistence that the sacrament is found both in the spouses' consents and in the union that is the effect of these consents, left them the task, given their insistence also on hylemorphic analysis, of finding the matter and the form in both the consents and in the union. To be true to history on this point, not all the scholastic theologians thought it necessary to identify this matter and form. Alexander of Hales doubted the need to do so (in his *Summa Theologica,* Part 4, Question 5, numbers 1 and 2). Duns Scotus (in his *Reportatio Parisiensis,* Distinction 28, no. 23) simply denied that there is a *materia* in the sacrament of marriage.

Despite some early and minor disagreements the scholastics found that identifying this *materia* was the easier half of the task. Peter de Pallu and Antoninus of Florence thought that this is the spouses' bodies. They drew this as a conclusion from the premise that in marrying the spouses contract with one another, and that in their contractual exchange each gives to the other the right over their bodies to sexual acts. De Pallu reasoned that as in a real contract the things exchanged by agreement are the *materia* of the contract, so the bodies that are exchanged as objects of the spouses' rights are the *materia* in the sacrament of marriage.[34]

Richard of Mediavilla thought the *materia* to be the first in sequence of the words of consent expressed by one of the spouses. His reason for this was that until the second expression of consent the first is there but remains indeterminate, capable potentially of creating the marriage, but doing so only when determined and actuated by the other spouse's consent.[35]

For Capreolus the *materia* was each party's interior consent, because it remains indeterminate until expressed in some external and perceptible formula, or *forma*.[36]

Both Albert and Thomas stood by their conviction that they are the spouses who create the sacrament by making their reciprocal consents.

They drew from this that whichever acts the spouses use to express their consents are the *materia* of the sacrament. They said this also of the permanent, enduring sacrament in marriage. Its *materia* consists of the acts that are specifically marital. These are determinable, and are determined permanently by the *forma* of the sacrament—whose identity, as they conceived it, we shall see in a moment. They reasoned by analogy with the sacrament of penance. There the material element of the sacrament is the acts in which the penitent confesses, manifests contrition and resolves not to sin again, acts that are indeterminate and insufficient for sacramental forgiveness until the priest's absolution determines them. So too in marriage. Each spouse's expression of consent is the needed *materia* of the sacrament, but is insufficient by itself for creating the sacrament until it is in-formed, not by any words or actions of the priest, as in baptism, but by the reciprocal consent of the other spouse.[37]

Thus the question asking about the *forma* in the sacrament got multiple and disagreeing answers only from those scholastics who insisted that a marriage is a contractual bond created by the spouses' consents, and who insisted also that the marriage and the sacraments are separable. Albert, Thomas and Bonaventure did not say the latter. For them the sacrament is intrinsic to the marriage. Therefore its *forma* is not to be sought in something coming to the marriage from outside it, as Scotus would say later. For Thomas it is simply each spouse's marital consent—this consent both in its momentary expression at the creating of the marriage, as well as in its enduring valence in the spouses' continuing intent to be married to one another.

Bonaventure's identification of the *forma* was in the sacrament's *vis,* in its capacity for working its effects. He wrote, "In some sacraments this capacity comes not from external words, but from within, as in penance in the experience of confessing, and in marriage. In such sacraments any expression suffices whether verbal, written, or in any other gesture [on the part of the penitent or the spouse]."[38]

But for Duns Scotus, who did hold that contract and sacrament are separable, that marriage was instituted as a pre-Christian contract to which Christ later annexed the sacrament, identifying the *forma* in this sacrament proved most difficult. His intricate formulation of the difficulty demonstrates how he earned the sobriquet, *Doctor subtilis.* He pointed out that neither Christ nor the Church had decided exactly the *forma* of the sacrament. This stands against the fact that in any of the Christian sacraments its *forma* must be an observable sign instituted by God in order to signify efficaciously that grace is given in the sacrament.

About the marital sacrament Scotus reasoned either that God has decided for it no more than an indeterminate sign to be its efficacious sign of grace—just as no more than an indeterminate form of consent is needed for the spouses' creating the contract—or that in order to provide the efficacious sign God has determined this sign more exactly than human institution has determined the form of consent needed in the contract. If he has done the latter, he has either specified some exact words, such as "I accept you as my own" (*Accipio te in meam/meum*), or he has determined indifferently that the form may be any words that express such consent.[39]

But there is a great difference in the consequences coming from one or the other alternative in the last pair here. If Christ took the first alternative—if he specified exactly the words in the sacramental sign—it follows that frequently the contract is created without the sacrament even among Christians, for it is often created by different words in different places. Or even if Christ took the second alternative and determined indifferently whatever words may express consent in the sacrament, the same conclusion follows, since marriage is sometimes contracted simply without words by the mute.

Or if one takes the former set of alternatives—if one says that God has determined the sacramental sign in marriage no more exactly than human convention has determined the sign needed to create the contract—one can then say that a sacrament is annexed to any contract in the new law. This follows because by divine institution the contract may also be the sacramental sign.[40]

From this it follows, said Scotus, that the unity of the sacramental *forma* in marriage is a unity of integrity—the unity found in having one rather than plural forms. It is not the unity of indivisibility—the unity of a single and exclusive formulation. The words that express marital consent may vary from place to place and from time to time, just as the formula of consecration in the Eucharist has taken various forms.[41]

Scotus continued relentlessly this sundering of the inseparability of contract and sacrament in marriage. Here it was that he stated his judgment about the indeterminancy—even the open *indifferentia*—of the minister of the marital sacrament. In most cases these are the contractants themselves, who minister the sacrament either to one another, or each to himself or herself. But if the sacrament is annexed to every marital contract, there may be multiple and diverse ministers of the sacrament. For sometimes fathers contract marriage for their sons and daughters even in the latter's presence. (It was Catholic law in Scotus' time that if the children did not disagree with marriages contracted for them by their fathers, they were presumed to agree and consent.) Hence if in these cases the contract is created, one must conclude that the minister of the sacrament can be indifferently anyone who can minister in the contracting. But he ended his reflection skeptically with the question, "Do we really wish to say this?" (Whether Scotus himself wished to say this, he nevertheless sowed a doubt in Catholic minds that would three and four centuries later produce a bitter harvest for Church authorities as Catholic civil authorities battled to take control over their people's marriage contracts—because, as they insisted, these contracts are not in themselves sacraments.)

The Identity of the Sacrament

Our examination gets finally to the heart of the matter when it asks what these medieval scholars thought the sacrament in Christian marriage to be. Like so many of our questions this one's answering is complicated by the web of presuppositions that awaits it as it is asked about minds at work at the end of the twelfth century and through most of the thirteenth.

One complicating presupposition was created by those, like Albert, Thomas, and Bonaventure, who insisted that in Christian marriages the contract and the sacrament are one and the same reality. But how to reconcile this with that part of the Augustinian inheritance that had for centuries said that the *sacramentum* is one of the goods of marriage, one of the *properties* of it that excuses and justifies men's and women's marrying despite the inescapable activity of concupiscence in marriage? A property of a contract cannot be identical with the contract itself. So does one say that at least in Christian marriages there are plural contracts because in them there are plural sacraments, namely the contract itself plus one of its properties?

Some early scholastics—Raoul Ardent, Paucapalea, Hugh of St. Victor among them—laid out the path to a plausible answer to this question by doing what Augustine himself had not done. They identified the primary aspect of his third good of marriage, its *sacramentum*, as the *signum sacrae rei*, the sign, or image, of an invisible sacred reality. This in turn led to differing opinions about the number of *sacramenta* in a Christian marriage. As we have seen, Hugh of St. Victor proposed that there are two because such a marriage images two sacred realities. One is the love of spirit by which God loves the human soul and it loves him in return; the other is the union of love between Christ and the Church.

The most generous estimate was that in the *Glossa Ordinaria* on Gratian's *Decretum* (Case 27, Chapter 2, Distinction 26; Case 10, Chapter 1, Distinction 21). It said that in a Christian marriage there are three *sacramenta* because the one marriage images three sacred realities. The union of the two consents *de praesenti* images the union of Christ and the graced soul; the *commixtio carnis*, sexual intercourse, images the union of Christ and the Church; the joining of the spouses' bodies images the union of God and humanity.

The canonist Huguccio (Hugh of Pisa) saw the multiple imaging in Christian marriages but denied that this requires multiple sacraments. He said rather that the multiple imaging can go on in one sacrament. He specified which sacred realities are imaged, namely the union of the human soul with God in charity, and Christ's union with the Church through his human nature.[42]

Peter of Poitiers drew the sacramental unity within marriage even tighter. He named exactly what the sacrament is; he named the double imaging in it, both the two sacred realities that are imaged and the two conducts within the marriage that image them.

> The sacrament is this consent [or union] of souls and the sexual intercourse [*carnalis copula*]. Nor are there two sacraments, but one sacrament of the union of Christ and the Church, which is maintained through love [*quae fit per charitatem*]; and of his bodily union with it that is found in the conformity with it in [human] nature. The image of the latter is found in sexual intercourse, while the image of the spiritual union [of Christ and the Church] is found in the spouses' union of souls.[43]

When we come to the major scholastics to find out their judgments about the exact identity of the sacrament, we encounter this difficulty, that not all of them provide their answer in an attempt to render precisely that judgment. Since some do not ask exactly the nature of the sacrament, whatever answer they offer can be only implicit, and can be found only as part of the explanation of some other matter. Consequently one's interpretation of their answers can be no more than inference.

This appears to be the case with Albert the Great. His judgment on the identity of the sacrament is found in his answers to two other questions. One of them asks how indissolubility (*individuitas*) can be claimed for marriage when in Catholic tradition marriages have for centuries been dissolved by spouses' entry into religious life and their pronouncing of its vows.[44] We shall return to this passage later, when we consider Albert's difficulty independently.

The second passage is Question 1, Article 3 of this same distinction wherein Albert asks, "In marriage which is the principal image and which the principal reality imaged?" We shall examine his answer to this question first, but after taking note of a rare wise caution that Albert volunteers at the outset of Article 1 of Question 1 of this distinction. He offers it when setting forth succinctly his definition of marriage in itself. He accepts the definitions coming down from Justinian's *Institutes,* and even from Modestinus and Ulpianus in the classical age of Roman law: "Marriage is the marital union of a man and a woman who are capable under the law of marrying; it is a union that holds to an undivided sharing of life"; and "Marriage is a partnership of life in common, a participation in divine and human law."

It is at this point that he volunteers his wise caution. He is the only scholar of his time who thought it needed, so far as I know. If remembered today it would be useful in our own arguments about the indissolubility of marriage. The second objection in this first article has it that marriage should be defined as a bond (*vinculum*) rather than as a union or joining (*coniunctio*); and this because of what Paul wrote in 1 Corinthians 7:39, "A wife is bound to the rule of her husband as long as she lives" (*Mulier, dum vivit, alligata est legi viri*).[45]

Albert's reply to the objection is that *vinculum* is predicated only metaphorically of marriage, and therefore should not be included in its definition (. . . *dicendum, quod vinculum metaphorice praedicatur de matrimonio et ideo non debuit poni in diffinitione*). He adds the kindly warning that Aristotle first voiced: "One errs if he predicates specific meanings of things other than those specified" (*Peccant transferentes positam nominationem*).[46]

To get now at Albert's question about which is the principal image in the sacrament and which the principal reality imaged, note that he assumes that a Christian marriage's sacramentality is found principally in its imaging. That understood, it soon becomes clear that for Albert the competitors for principal image are the spouses' consents and their sexual intercourse. Albert's answer to his own question is an intricate weave of distinctions and cause-effects links.[47]

Marriage as a sacrament is related to a one reality (*res*) both by causing it and by imaging it. It is related to another reality only by imaging it. But it does the second in two ways, by imaging the union of the Church with Christ in love, and by imaging its union with him in nature.

Now just as these unions can be compared and ranked in two ways, so can the ways of imaging be compared and ranked in two ways. First, if the unions themselves are compared as goods, the union in nature of Christ and the Church is more excellent than their union in love if one considers the substance of these goods. For nothing created can be compared with the union of the two natures in Christ.

But if one bases the comparison of these goods to one another not on their substances but on each one's relationship to the goal to which they are oriented, then the prior and more excellent union is that of Christ and the Church in love. For such a union in love is the ultimate good intended for all creation. Indeed the union of the two natures in Christ was effected so as to bring about their union in love.

It is the same with the sacramental imaging of these realities, these two relationships involving Christ and the Church. First they can be compared and ranked according to the nature, or substance, of each imaging. In this case that is the more excellent which is richer as an image. This is sexual intercourse in marriage, about which Jerome said that it brings a marriage to completion not in causation nor in sanctification but in imaging.[48]

But if the two imagings be compared and ranked as each is a cause of marriage, a double comparison is in order. If one looks to causation simply, the marital consent is the more excellent cause because it causes by itself, apart from intercourse. But if one looks to causation which produces not its effect alone, but brings on everything for which this effect is intended, then intercourse is the more excellent cause. (Very probably Albert means by this last that intercourse produces not only the child but also the tranquility and stability between the spouses needed for the rearing, the full procreation of the child.)

Bonaventure on the Identity of the Sacrament

Bonaventure too took for granted that the sacramentality in Christian marriages lies mainly in their function of imaging. Like Albert he set for himself a task derived from this understanding, namely to sort out the correlations of the signings in these marriages and their *signata*, between the images and the invisible realities they image. In Question 1, Article 2 of Distinction 26 he prepares for the correlations by distinguishing elements within the sacrament itself.[49] There is the element which is only an image but not an effect (the *signum tantum*); that which is both image and effect (*signum et res*), and that which is only an effect (*res tantum*). He repeats here a difficulty he reported in the preceding question. It was that the image and the reality imaged in the other sacraments seem so readily known, but in marriage this is not so. The reason that accounts for this is that the other sacraments, for example baptism and the Eucharist, were produced solely by religious faith. Consequently their imaging has been determined clearly by mandated institution. Thus it was possible to fit their imaging more exactly to their work as sacraments, making their signing as a consequence more evident and verifiable.

But marriage was instituted long before the age of Christian faith. Its signing function began long before the coming of Christ. Moreover marriage was instituted a second time by Christ in the new law, and this second institution has added a dimension of meaning to intercourse in marriage, intercourse which of its nature signifies (or images) only the spouses' interior consent and joining of wills. What intercourse adds to this joining of wills since the second and Christian institution of marriage is to make it image also the joining of Christ and the Church, or the joining of the human soul and God.

Of its nature marriage is available (*habile*) for this added signing because one partner is male and can aptly image Christ, while the other is female and can aptly image the Church. But that husband and wife in fact image Christ and the Church respectively in the sacrament is the effect of positive divine institution.

That which is the principal *signatum* in the sacrament is the union of Christ and the Church. Because this union is twofold, through self-giving love (*charitas*) and through homogeneity of nature (*conformitas naturae*), the sacrament images said union in two ways. The spouses' consent of wills images the union effected between Christ and the Church through their self-giving love, while the spouses' sexual intercourse images this union effected through homogeneity of natures.[50] (Bonaventure is a faithful son of both his medieval culture and his Augustinian heritage in not acknowledging that the Christian spouses' intercourse too may image the union of Christ and the Church in love.)

Thomas Aquinas on the Identity of the Marital Sacrament

What Thomas said about the main sacramental element in Christian marriages is most reasonably drawn from one of his works that is seldom examined. More's the pity, because the later composition of his *Commentary on St. Paul's Letter to the Ephesians* tells us that it is much more likely his own matured and independent thought on the subject than what he said at thirty years of age in his commentary on the Sentences of Peter Lombard.[51] At that age a young *sententiarius* at the University of Paris did not wander daringly astray from the conventional thinking of his day.

At the beginning of his commentary on Ephesians 5:21–33 Thomas points out what is obvious about this classic passage, that it is parenetic; it contains an exhortation from Paul to the Christian husbands and wives of Ephesus.

Reading the Latin of Jerome's Vulgate translation, *Mulieres viris suis subditae sint, sicut domino,* he interpreted the last two words to mean not "to the Lord" but a submission, an obedience to her husband ". . . as to a lord." He apparently forgot what he had written about friendship in freedom in the *Summa Contra Gentes,* and presumed that the wife is a kind of vassal to her husband—but with this difference, that her service is for the good of the entire family, not for that of the master himself, as is the case with a mere domestic servant.[52]

With this interpretation Thomas avoids hinting at the first facet of the traditional analogy. That is, he does not hint that the husband-wife relationship is an image of the Christ-Church relationship.

But Thomas does, in commenting on verse 23, attend immediately to the ingredients of this analogy, "For the husband is head of the wife, as Christ is the head of the Church." He points out first what this means about husband and wife. He is to govern her, just as in the human body the head governs all else, because it is in the head that the eyes are located.

When he interprets "as Christ is the head of the Church," again he does not propose the traditional analogy. He does not say that the husband-wife relationship images the Christ-Church relationship. What he does say is that here Paul offers an *exemplum,* a model to be imitated.

He adds that Paul's use of this model intends two effects. One is pedagogical, to make clear and emphatic that the husband is to the wife as the governing head is to the body. Thomas hints here at the analogy. He says that just as Christ is head of the Church *suo modo,* in his specific way, so is the husband the head of the wife—also, by implication, *suo modo.* The qualification, *suo modo,* suggests that though the two relationships are similar—the Christ-Church and the husband-wife relationships— there is dissimilarity within their similarity. It will be well to remember this if and when one thinks of the husband-wife relationship as an earthly image of the Christ-Church relationship. The qualification suggests that not every ingredient in either relationship need be found in the other.[53]

The second effect that Thomas sees Paul intending in this model is deontological, the stating of a moral obligation: Just as it is disruptive (*inconveniens*) that the body disobey the head, so is it disruptive that the wife disobey the husband. Here he injects the example, ". . . just as the Church is *subiecta* to Christ."

Thomas then turns immediately to the husbands' part in this relationship. He says that in this passage Paul is counseling them (*monet*) that they love their wives—and that he offers three reasons for their doing so. Paul takes the first reason from the example that Christ has given— "*Primam rationem sumit ex exemplo Christi. . . .*" Again Thomas has Paul use the Christ-Church facet of the later traditional analogy as an example within exhortation. He does not here have him assert the analogy. Nor does he here have him say that the husband's love for his wife is an image of Christ's love for the Church.[54]

Thomas goes on to develop this exemplification on Christ's part: the evidence (*signum*) of his love for the Church was his giving himself over to death for her. When he goes on to explain Christ's motive for giving himself over, he touches a fine point of explanation that will be subsequently ignored by commentators until it is rediscovered in our own day. He points out that Christ's motive was to cleanse for himself a bride-Church that would be immaculate. Thomas divides and distinguishes two stages in this cleansing: the first stage on earth through Christ's grace; the second in after-life, at the end of history, through glory. He adds that when Paul says Christ's sanctifying death will produce a bride-Church without wrinkle (*sine ruga*), this means a Church that transcends *passibilitas,* a Church that has been taken beyond mortality, beyond fallibility. To illustrate his meaning he quotes Revelation 7:16, "They will not hunger again, nor will they thirst. . . ." He makes his point clear that this transcendent state will be attained only beyond death.

Thus Thomas does not see Paul claiming this perfect bride-Church for life this side of death. Therefore he does not see him preparing the way for the presumed ontological valence of the traditional analogy, namely that the relationship of Christian husband and wife is already perfect because it is an earthly image of an already perfect Christ-Church relationship. For the latter is not yet perfect. In the language of sacramentality, Thomas does not at this point see Paul saying that every Christian marriage is a sacrament because already proportioned perfectly to a perfect Church. So if Thomas does at some point say of Christian marriages that they are sacraments by imaging the Christ-Church relationship, he will not conclude about them that this makes them perfect as marriages.[55]

There is, of course, an appropriate place for him to say that Christian marriages are sacraments. This is in his reflection on verse 32,

Sacramentum hoc magnum est. Ego autem dico in Christo et in ecclesia.
But he does not say exactly that, that "Christian marriages" are sacraments. He steps back from the concrete universal, "Christian marriages," to the abstract universal, simply "Christian marriage."

More exactly, Thomas says that in verse 32 Paul appeals to the
authority of holy scripture for his exhortation, namely to Genesis 2:24:
"That is why a man leaves his father and mother and clings to his wife,
and the two of them become one flesh." Thomas adds immediately that
Paul calls this a *sacramentum magnum.* The "this" in question is the
man's leaving his parents, clinging to his wife and becoming one flesh
with her. But Paul predicates the *magnum sacramentum* of this, the
man's conduct, *mystice;* that is, said conduct images sensately on earth
the supra-sensate conduct of Christ. Thomas names exactly the conduct
of Christ that Paul has in mind. And he intends a fairly exact analogical
correspondence between the two conducts, the human sensate that images and the divine supra-sensate that is imaged. For he says that Christ
too left his Father—left him in becoming incarnate (here he quotes Jesus
in John 16:28: "I have come forth from the Father, and come into this
world . . ."). Christ too left his mother, namely the Jewish synagogue
(he quotes in support Jeremiah 12:7: "I have left my home and given up
my inheritance . . ."). And Christ too clings to his wife, the Church (he
quotes in support Matthew 28:20: "I will be with you all days, even to
the end of the world").

Summarily and simply, in claiming that Paul's "This is a great sacrament, etc." is predicated *mystice,* Thomas means that in Christian marriage taken universally the husband's conduct images that of Christ.

The consequence of this imaging for real-life marriages Thomas
explains in the closing paragraphs of this Chapter 5. He says that Paul
reasons *consequenter* from that imaging, but now not according to its
mystical meaning, but according to its literal meaning. That is, Paul now
draws from the mystical meaning conclusions that are applicable to marriage as it is actually lived.[56]

It is significant that this conclusion is not a statement about these
marriages' status as sacraments. It claims nothing antecedently given
and immutable about all of them. The conclusion is rather in the domain
of exhortation. But in drawing this hortatory conclusion Thomas links
exhortation with imaging: it is *because* the husband images Christ that *he
ought* to love his wife in a special way. That is, Thomas claims that the
link, the "because," in Paul's reasoning is deontological. He does not
hint that Paul makes it ontological. Thus, in Thomas' own words:

> For there are some things in the sacred writings of the Old
> Testament which are said of Christ alone, as in Psalm 21:17,
> "They have pierced my hands and my feet, etc." . . . However
> there are some things which can be explained both of Christ
> and of others; but of Christ mainly, while of others as images of

Christ, as in the preceding example [i.e., a man's leaving his father and mother, etc.].

Therefore it [the example] is to be explained first of Christ and afterwards of others. Thus it is that he [Paul] says, "However you too, let each of you love his wife [as he loves himself]", as though he were saying, "This is said mainly about Christ, but not about him exclusively, because what it says is to be expressed and fulfilled in other men as images of Christ." Paul says ". . . as he loves himself" because just as each man loves himself in his relationship to God, in this way too ought he to love his wife, not in her ability to draw him into sin. . . .

What place for the wife does Thomas see in all this? In the three last and casual lines of this chapter that he devotes to her he again clearly draws a hortatory conclusion from her place in this sacramental imaging.

But what of the wife? Paul says, "Let the wife fear her husband", that is, with reverential and obedient fear, because she should be subject to him.[57]

Duns Scotus and the Sacrament

Duns Scotus' effort to identify the essence of the marital sacrament appears in a context different from those we have just seen in the efforts of Albert, Bonaventure and Thomas. But his context is one that is already familiar to us. It is his question and answer about the creation of the marriage contract and the ministers of the sacrament. We have seen that he argued for the separability of contract and sacrament because of the uncertain identification of the form and the minister of the sacrament. But he would have been compelled in any case to argue for this separability by his near-nominalist dividing and distinguishing of the ingredients of a sacramental Christian marriage. He was the thorough philosophic-theological taxonomist. He said that the marriage itself is one *thing,* the contract another *thing,* and the sacrament yet another.[58]

The marriage itself is a bond or obligation. The contract is the spouses' act of will that creates the obligation; it is the reciprocal exchange of rights named earlier. The sacrament is the efficacious sign of grace that accompanies (*concomitans*) that act.

The marriage itself is something permanent in the souls of the contractants. Among the categories of being it may be identified as either a real relationship coming to the souls from outside them, or more probably no more than an attributed relationship (*relatio rationis*), since it puts nothing in the souls of the spouses except a new command and a new subservience created by this new exchange (*nihil est ibi, nisi dominium novum et nova servitus per novam commutationem*).[59] But none of these puts anything real in the soul of the one commanding or of the one serving. Scotus' ontology plainly does not let him see that what a marriage may be is a lasting real relationship of mind to mind, of will to will, or even of passion to passion in the spouses.

The contract exists only in passing and causatively (*tantum in fieri*). It consists of the reciprocal interior and exterior acts of the contractants. It is related to the marriage as a transitory cause, in the way that his act of impregnating is related to a man's ensuing and lasting paternity. Or the relationship is more akin to that between the baptismal ceremony and the character abiding in the soul after being produced there by the ceremony.

The third reality here, the sacrament, is likewise something transitory (*in fieri*) in its causation. It can be annexed or not to the marriage itself. Hence it need not always accompany the contract. In reality it is the spouses' acts of contractual exchange where, by God's institution, these acts are words (if indeed words are required) that produce grace.

It seems no exaggeration to say that by this point in his argumentation—adding now his ontological dissecting to his earlier dialectic raising of difficulties—Scotus has provided sufficient ammunition for the Catholic philosophers and jurists of later generations who will affirm that for Christians the sacrament in the marriage is distinct and separable from the contract, and who will affirm this in support of Catholic civil rulers wanting to control by civil law the annulling and divorcing of marriages in their realms. If it was Scotus' junior colleague at Oxford, William of Ockham, who was the more immediate theoretical leader of their cause, Scotus may justifiably be called the remote if unwitting supplier of their weapons.

This dismantling of his peers' and his predecessors' theology of the sacrament Scotus continues where still later he defines marriage according to the Aristotelian categories of causation and locates the sacrament among these categories.

According to Chapter 5 of Aristotle's *Metaphysics,* the good and the perfect, or complete, are one and the same. But there may be two perfections of a thing, one intrinsic, which is its form, the other extrinsic, which is its end. There can also be twofold ends, the proximate and the remote. The remote is ordinarily the principal end because the proximate is oriented to it.

Assuming that the marriage is the bond produced by the spouses' initial contracting, the internal *forma* of this bond—that which gives its nature, its intelligibility—is its indissolubility. The indissolubility bespeaks (*dicit*) the sacrament in that it images the indissoluble union of Christ and the Church.[60]

But this perfection, this indissolubility, is itself oriented to the mutual rendering of the sexual marriage debt. This rendering is in turn a realizing of the justice which springs from the already established reciprocal obligation. Thus this obligation to render the marriage debt—it is to be understood also as the reciprocal marital fidelity holding the spouses—is something extrinsic to the marriage, the bond. It is its proximate end. But the marital act itself which fulfills the obligation in justice is oriented ultimately to the legitimate procreation and religious nurture of offspring. This religious nurture too is a good extrinsic to marriage, the bond. It is its ultimate end.

But because of difficulties raised against this interpretation Scotus acknowledges that he must explain more exactly how the three traditional goods of marriage—sacrament, fidelity and offspring—are related among themselves.[61] It is not clear that his explanation adds intelligibility.

The sacrament understood here as one of the Augustinian goods of marriage is not the sacrament of Christ's new law. This sacrament is one of the internal goods of any marriage, its indissolubility. This in turn only bespeaks (*dicit*) the indissoluble union of Christ and the Church. It does not image it. This is consistent with what we have already found and will again find him saying, that the Christian sacrament is in the ceremony, the spouses' act of committing themselves to one another in sexual obligation. He adds that the internal good of marriage that is its indissolubility cannot be the Christian sacrament because the latter must be an observable sign (*signum sensibile*). But indissolubility is something invisible residing in the minds of the spouses. What is more, the Christian sacrament passes away immediately because it is a transitory reality (*est in fieri*), while the indissolubility abides. The sacrament is also a disposition for receiving grace worthily, while indissolubility is not.

Scotus continues this dividing and sundering as he replies to objections. Fidelity, offspring and sacrament, though goods of marriage, are not goods of the Christian sacrament. For again, the latter is only a sign accompanying the act of contracting. Rather they are three goods of marriage supplied by the indissoluble bond that abides after the contracting is completed. Hence if one asks whether the marriages of Christians are indissoluble because of the Christian sacrament, the reply is that marriage has always been indissoluble by reason of the law of nature. During the epoch of this law, before the law of Moses and before Christ, the sacrament was not annexed to the marital contract. And once Christ came he could have commanded indissolubility for marriage even if he had annexed no sacrament to the contract.

He could also have annexed the sacrament to the contract even if he had not willed the indissolubility of the latter but had approved the dismissal of wives permitted by the Mosaic law. Therefore we must conclude that indissolubility is in marriage only because Christ has willed it to be there permanently, while we allow also that Christ dispenses from this indissolubility in certain cases—as he does for Christian spouses who have not consummated their marriage and wish to take up religious life.

I believe the principal elements to be drawn from this, Scotus' examination of the sacrament in marriage, are, first, the double reference of the term "sacrament." As a *bonum matrimonii* it is formally the indissolubility of the marriage bond, the perpetuity of the obligation to render the marriage debt to the spouse, and to the spouse exclusively. As such it can be dispensed by divine authority. By its reference to the Christian sacrament, *sacramentum* refers to the ceremony, the observable sign of the grace given to those who contract marriage worthily, a grace given in order to make of their bond a graced union.

A second element, one most pertinent to this essay, is that the Christian sacrament, though it images the union of Christ and the Church, is not the source of the Christian marriage's indissolubility. Its function is to bring to the spouses the graces needed to fulfill marriage's severely demanding obligations.

The sacrament in the first sense above is inseparable from marriage because it is its formal cause. Yet God can dispense from it. But the sacrament in the second sense, the Christian sacrament, is simply separable from marriage. It is separable not only from the indissoluble bond, which Christians can create without the sacramental ceremony. It is separable also from the contractual exchange which creates the bond, since experience shows that marriages have been created apart from the Christian ceremony-sacrament for centuries before the coming of Christ.

The Role of Sexual Intercourse in the Sacrament

There are two other issues in the theology of the marital sacrament that are so tightly interwoven, that so condition one another, that deciding which to address first is most difficult. For whichever of the two a student decides, he does so with some inescapable arbitrariness. In interrogative form the issues are the following. Assuming that the sacrament is a medium for the gracing of the spouses, in what way does it grace them? The question has two meanings: First, how does the sacrament work at the gracing? And, what is the effect in the spouses of this gracing action?

The second issue, also in interrogative form, asks about the role in the sacrament of the spouses' sexual intercourse. Again assuming that the sacrament is a medium for the gracing of the spouses, does their intercourse function in this? If it does, in what way does it—in both senses of "what way"—i.e. how does it work at their gracing? and, what effect does it produce in them by this work?

A further complication, an enriching one, grows out of yet another conclusion by this time become assumption. This is that the sacrament in marriage is found mainly in its imaging the love relationship of Christ and the Church. Weave this into the two issues just broached, and one must ask about the role of this imaging in the sacrament's gracing work. Assuming it works there, how does it do so? and what is it in the gracing effect that comes precisely from this imaging? One must ask also about the function of sexual intercourse in this imaging. Does it have one? Can it have one when it seems so inescapably affected—even infected—by concupiscence? If it does, what does it do to image the relationship of Christ and the Church? And finally the question that may draw all this complication together: If we find that the imaging and the gracing are done by one and the same conduct, what function does the spouses' intercourse have in this conjoined imaging-gracing?

Regrettably but understandably the theologians whom we are consulting did not address these issues exactly in these forms. In places they touched them, and attempted answers to their interrogative forms, in dealing with and answering other and cognate questions. Consequently a student who thinks this web of questions demands answering, and searches for the thirteenth-century answers to them, must search in the cognate territories. Our own search now moves into the issue of sexual intercourse's function in the sacrament. Searching first of all for Albert's answer to the question, and finding it, is to discover anew the inextricability from one another of all the questions posed just above.

When explaining the essential elements of marriage (in his *Tractatus de Matrimonio,* Quaestio 1, Articulus 1) Albert offered his explanation for that element of marriage that is its *individuitas,* its claimed invulnerability to dissolution short of the death of at least one of the spouses. In explaining it he ran upon the obvious difficulty awaiting a Catholic theologian. How can one claim *individuitas* for marriage in face of the ancient Catholic tradition that accepts the dissolution of unconsummated Christian marriages by one spouse's entering monastic life and pronouncing its vows, even against the will of the other? He takes up the question in his reply to Objection 4 of this first article, an objection which complains, ". . . how can the definition [the classic definition of marriage from Roman law] include the adjective *individua?* For we see that one spouse can enter religious life even against the other's will provided this is done before they have sexual intercourse."[62]

Albert explains how dissolution in this case is possible. He draws on a kind of philosophy of religion, not yet on the theology of the sacrament. That is, although marriage has within itself a cause of its indissolubility (*causa individuitatis*), yet it can be dissolved by a bond stronger than itself where this bond compels a person to conduct contrary to marriage (*fortius vinculum stringens ad actum oppositum*). Such is the bond created by a spouse's vow of continence.[63]

This reply generates the next and inescapable question: If the vow of continence in religious life, being the stronger bond, can dissolve the bond of an unconsummated marriage, why can it not dissolve also the bond of a consummated marriage? After all, a bond takes its moral strength from the good to which it binds. But the good of vowed continence is greater than the good of even a consummated marriage.

It is at this point that Albert turns to the sacrament in marriage as an image, to the effect of this imaging, and to the role of consummating intercourse in producing the effect. Where invulnerability to dissolution (*individuitas*) is in a marriage, it is there insofar as the marriage is an image (*signum*), which is to say insofar as it is sacramental. And the strength of its invulnerability is determined by the value, the excellence, of the reality that it images.

This calls for a distinction, a distinction in what the two stages of a marriage, unconsummated and consummated, image respectively. A marriage unconsummated by intercourse images the union of Christ and the Church in love (*charitas*), a union which is in the domain of merit. But in this domain continence is of greater value than marriage. Therefore too in this domain the vow is stronger than the marriage and can dissolve it.

But a consummated marriage images the union of Christ and the Church not in meritorious love but in their natures, in the human nature of both. Because the consummated marriage is related to the union of natures in the relationship of image, the marriage cannot be dissolved by a subsequent vow. For even if both spouses were later to vow continence, there would remain the indissoluble bond of marriage. This would happen not because marriage is among the greater goods, but because there is no cause more powerful than the Christ-Church union imaged by the consummated marriage. (Here Albert sets out a quasi-principle of his theology. Because the human relationship images a transcendently valuable reality, the reality reciprocally works effects in the relationship that supersede the latter's natural power.)[64]

Albert comes back to this principle in even more plentiful detail later, in Question 2, On the Goods of Marriage (*De bonis matrimonii*), Article 5, Concerning Each of These Goods (*De unoquoque eorum bonorum*), in his reply to Objection 7. This asks whence indissolubility comes to a marriage. If from the marriage itself, it should be found in all marriages in the same way. But this is not so, since (as acknowledged above) an unconsummated marriage can be dissolved by a spouse's entering religious life and pronouncing its vows.

The objection has its force from a prior reason, a reason proposed in Objection 5. It said that since marriage and sacrament are one and the same, the sacrament ought not be called "a good of marriage." Since the good of marriage that is the sacarament is indissolubility, and since (as insisted in that Objection 5) sacrament and marriage are one and the same, it should follow that every marriage is indissoluble, and therefore that unconsummated marriages cannot be dissolved by the vows of religious life.

Albert's reply to this is that when one speaks of the good of marriage that is the sacrament, one speaks of marriage's capacity for, or orientation to, imaging, not to causing. But even its capacity for and orientation to causing comes not from the marriage itself, but from the power of the reality imaged.

Then he carries forward the substance of the earlier reply: what a consummated marriage images is the union of the two natures in the one person of Christ. This is a union that is unqualifiedly (*simpliciter*) indestructible. Therefore its image in the sacrament is also unqualifiedly indestructible as long as both spouses live. That the image is dissolved by the death of one of them happens because of the mortality, the dissolubility of their nature.[65]

Bonaventure on the Place of Intercourse in the Sacrament

Bonaventure takes up this question of the function of sexual intercourse in the sacrament in Article 2, Question 3 of Distinction 26 in his commentary on Lombard's *Sentences*. In Question 2, which we have passed over thus far, he has just asked whether grace is conferred in the sacrament. His answer was both positive and complex, as we shall see. But now his Question 3 asks whether for the sacrament in marriage to be complete intercourse is required (*An carnalis commixtio sit de integritate matrimonii*). What he wrote in response to Question 2 makes the issue an especially vexing one, for it contains an apparent contradiction. How can marriage be a sacrament by remedying concupiscence when it prolongs and even foments it?[66]

He begins his answer to Question 3 by making yet another distinction, this time between two kinds of completeness (*integritas*). There is the completeness of essential properties (of a thing's *esse necessitatis*), and the completeness of development (of a thing's *esse plenitudinis*). He contends that intercourse is needed for the latter completeness in marriage, but not for the former.

In explanation he points out that one must consider the sacrament of marriage as a sign (*signum*), as a dutiful vocation (*officium*) and as a *remedium*.

Under the first of these, the sacrament is a twofold image of Christ and the Church—of their love for one another (their *charitas*) and of the homogeneity of their natures (*per naturae conformitatem*).

Likewise there is in the sacrament a twofold dutiful vocation, that of mutual support and that of procreation.

Finally there is in it a twofold remedying. One controls the promiscuity (*defluxio*) of concupiscence by keeping it from going after any and every woman, while the second controls its inordinate character by leading and enabling a man to have intercourse with his wife not out of urgency for pleasure (*libido*) but solely for love of offspring—and (as an afterthought) not without marital affection.

Bonaventure then brings all these traits and their functions together. Marriage's first imaging (of the union of Christ and the Church in their love), its first dutiful vocation (mutual support) and its first remedying (the tethering of promiscuity) are in the sacrament through the joining of the spouses' souls. The second imaging (the union of Christ and the Church in the homogeneity of their natures), the second dutiful vocation (offspring) and the second remedying (the diminshing even within marriage of concupiscence's inordinacy) are in the sacrament through the spouses' joining of their bodies.

From all this he draws his answer to the question at hand. The first imaging, dutiful vocation and remedying must be in the sacrament if it is to be complete in essence (in its *esse necessitatis*); the second of them need be in it to be complete in its development (in its *esse plenitudinis*).

As to the age-old and persistent objection that the sacrament's gracing cannot be accomplished in marriage's most typical conduct, intercourse, because this is infected with concupiscence, and therefore one cannot say that the sacrament remedies concupiscence, Bonaventure answers again by distinguishing.

The remedying of sin can be done in two ways. It may be done by freeing a person from sin already committed. This is accomplished by the grace itself that is brought by the remedy. Marriage does not remedy in this way. Or it may be done by freeing from sin not yet committed but which would be committed were it not for the remedy. It is in this second way that marriage remedies concupiscence. For countless men would in their moral illness burn with concupiscence unless they could have intercourse with their wives. For this use of the sacrament there is no need that grace be given, nor is grace derived from this use, although from it a man can gain merit.

Bonaventure closes his consideration under this *Quaestio* with an equally delicate consideration. He explains that the use of intercourse can be a *remedium* in marriage, and thus qualify for sacramentality, provided a man uses it properly (*debite*). He does this if in it he intends not to have concupiscent pleasure but to produce a child. In this way he does not seek pleasure but merely permits concupiscence to burn off. But if he does have intercourse in order to gain pleasure, the intercourse is not truly marital. In this case it is not a remedy for but a fomenting of concupiscence.

This remedial service of the sacrament comes back for consideration in Distinction 31, Article 2, Question 1, where Bonaventure asks "Whether intercourse for the sake of offspring can be completely free of sin" (*Utrum coitus propter prolem possit esse sine omni culpa*). He replies, in brief, "The marital act is rendered sinless through the sacrament, as a sickness healed by its remedy; and it can be freed of all sin, whether mortal or venial."[67]

Thomas Aquinas on Intercourse in the Sacrament

Thomas' reflections on the function of intercourse in the marital sacrament we defer for a moment because he finds little of this function in the sacrament qua image. In his commentary on the fourth book of the Sentences he reserves it mainly to the sacrament's work of restraining and healing concupiscence in Christian spouses.

It is more helpful to get now finally to an issue in the theology of the sacrament equally as serious as its imaging function, and to finish our examination of Thomas' thought by pondering his judgments on this second and equally serious issue. This is the marital sacrament as a cause or medium of grace for the spouses. It will be helpful also to come up to Thomas after beginning with his predecessors' judgments in the matter, some of them dating from a century earlier than his own.

We have already noted that theologians and canonists in the twelfth century—but especially canonists—denied that grace comes through this sacrament at all. We have noted also the juridical reason for their denial. It was the role of money in the concluding of marriages in their societies, and their wish to keep the crime of simony out of these marriages. This crime is the selling of religious offices and services. The opinion at their time that the marital sacrament is in the priest's blessing, joined with the custom that the priest received a stipend for coming to the wedding and blessing the spouses, certainly seemed to combine into simony. Or if one held the other opinion, that the sacrament is in the spouses' consents, but that these were commonly given only on condition that dowry and wedding gifts were first exchanged, one seemed not to escape simony there either. The creating of the sacrament seemed conditioned by monetary exchanges.

Rather than challenge the practices of stipend and dowry and thereby remove the obstacle, the canonists asked if both could not be legitimized and thus the crime of simony avoided. The Decretists—for example the author of the *Summa Parisiensis,* Simon of Bisamano, and John of Faenza—found a way to avoid simony, as this is recorded in their comment on the decree *Honorantur* (Case 32, Question 11). They said that marriage does not confer grace. Therefore there is no danger of presuming to mediate it through the sacrament for a price. The Decretalists for the most part agreed with them.[68]

Stephen of Tournai returned to the ancient Pauline advice to find a reason for denying that the marital sacrament gives grace: Marriage distances men and women from God, "For he who takes a wife is forced into preoccupation with the things of this world, how he may please his wife. He is torn two ways."[69]

The reason against the sacrament we have repeated so often appears here once more, but now in somewhat refined form. Marriage abets concupiscence by its sinful pleasure-taking, and this it does in the conduct that is common and characteristic of marriage. How then can this conduct and this union be a medium of grace when all grace comes from the suffering and death of Christ, and any gracing acts must be in some way animated by his passion and death and reenact them?

The canonist Rufinus answered the question by reasoning that marriage among Christians may indeed have in it the sacrament. But this is no more than a significative sacrament. That is, among all the sacraments marriage alone signifies a sacred reality in such a way—and does this by intercourse—that because of lust in the act the sacrament barely (*minime*) produces in the spouses the reality it signifies. It is not an *effective* sign of the union of Christ and the Church, but only a representative sign—just as the Old Testament sacrifices imaged (*figurabant*) the justification of sinners but did not produce it.[70]

The theologians of the twelfth and early thirteenth centuries offered no unanimous judgment on the subject. Peter Cantor, for example, in his *Verbum abbreviatum*, Chapter 37, said, "There are spiritual means by which the grace of the Holy Spirit is conferred or is increased in someone. Such, for example, are the sacraments of the Church—except for marriage, orders and ecclesiastical offices."[71]

In order to save the grace-giving function for marriage Jacques de Vitry turned for his answer to another qualification, one that was to become the most commonly accepted throughout the middle ages. He said that the sacraments have been instituted to be both signs of sanctification and means of it. But the sacrament in marriage has not the power to produce grace in the soul, because its function is purely medicinal. It is permitted as a remedial alternative to fornication, in a way analogously as a monk is permitted to eat meat occasionally, or a sick person is permitted to bathe occasionally.[72] In his commentary on 1 Corinthians 7 Hugh of St. Cher appealed to the same reason that Rufinus used to deny that the sacrament in marriage is a cause of grace: "When it is said that a sacrament produces what it images, this is to be understood only of the sacraments instituted in the Gospel. But marriage was instituted even before the Law [of Moses]."[73] However in his commentary on Peter Lombard's Sentences he conceded that although grace is not given to the married through their sacrament, it is nevertheless given to them: "In the other sacraments grace is given by the power of the sacrament itself. But in marriage it is conferred not by the power of the sacrament, but is given sometimes by the power of the priestly blessing, or [to suggest a kind of occasionalism] God gives it because of the good intention of the contracting parties."[74]

Other theologians admitted that the sacrament is a cause of grace but in a yet differently limited way. It conserves grace by preventing the sin that most commonly destroys it. Thus William of Auxerre in his *Summa:* "We have explained the teaching about the sacraments which confer grace. Now we must take up that one which conserves grace, namely marriage. It is a preserver of grace in that it is a kind of preventive medicine that shields against fornication."[75] William of Auvergne, in his *De sacramento matrimonii*, said that spouses who marry in order to realize the goods essential to marriage do a good thing. God graces them in the sense that he aids them to realize these goals. However William remained uncertain about exactly what it is in the marriage that works in the gracing, whether this is the contract itself or the priestly blessing. His preference was to see the sacramental power (the *vis sacramenti*) only in sacraments that are truly and fully such. These are the sacraments which include the priestly blessing. But if he was uncertain about this agent immediately active in gracing, he was certain that the gracing does take place, and that it produces the effect that was so commonly claimed for it: "To spouses who receive this sacrament worthily and devoutly, who will keep it reverently, much relief from the ardor of carnal concupiscence is brought by the power itself of the sacrament."[76]

Bonaventure on the Grace of the Sacrament

Bonaventure began his consideration of the sacrament as a cause of grace by rejecting three of the answers we have just seen offered to this question, namely that this sacrament confers no grace because only those sacraments instituted in the new law do so; that it graces by diminishing concupiscence in the spouses, and this by indulging it legitimately—gracing thus only in the sense intended by Paul's words, "It is better to marry than to burn"; finally that it graces spouses who contract marriage religiously, through the priest's blessing.[77]

Bonaventure preferred an explanation that divides along the time boundary not between the old law and the new, but between the age of the fall and that of the new law. This explanation contends that immediately following the fall marriage had only this element of sacrament in it, that it brought a healing (*remedium*) to the spouses by providing an excuse for their intercourse and by keeping it only venially sinful, or even sinless altogether—whereas outside marriage it would have been inescapably sinful and seriously so.

But now in the new law, he continues, marriage provides not only that *remedium,* but its own characteristic grace—provides it for those who receive the sacrament worthily (*digne suscipientibus*). Those who receive it worthily he defines exactly as those men and women who join in marriage by a consent motivated by charity (*consensu charitatis*) in order to provide children for the eventual worship of God.

Now comes the intricate linking of imaging and gracing and their effects. The spouses' marital consent, joined with the Church's blessing, has two effects. First, in each spouse the soul is raised above corrupting inordinate concupiscence (the *remedium* continued from pre-Christian times). Second, grace is given the spouses enabling them to maintain a union that is monogamous (*copulam singularem*), that is fruitful (*copulam utilem*), and that is inseparable (*copulam inseparabilem*).

Schematization pushes on to yet finer complexity within more inclusive limits. Bonaventure explains that this threefold grace remedies the threefold disorder in concupiscence simultaneously, and in doing so it produces the traditional threefold goods of marriage.

Thus the grace enabling a man to maintain a monogamous union by helping him to desire only his wife remedies in him concupiscence's promiscuous urge. It thereby produces a marriage's *bonum fidei,* the good that is fidelity.

The grace enabling a man to desire intercourse even with his wife exclusively for the motive of procreation remedies in him concupiscence's urge to selfish pleasure. It thereby produces marriage's *bonum prolis,* offspring.

Finally, the grace enabling a man to maintain a permanent union by enabling him to stay with his wife remedies in him that byproduct of concupiscence that is a man's disdain for his latest partner in intercourse after using her for his satisfaction, the disdain that sends him looking for a new and different satisfier. This grace thereby produces marriage's *bonus sacramenti,* its inseparability.

The brief passage that could be Bonaventure's most valuable and lasting contribution to the theology of the sacrament, were it noticed, is his reply to the first difficulty under Question 2 of Distinction 26, Article 2.[78] The difficulty is this, that if a sacrament produces anything, it produces what it images. Now the marriages of two Christians images the union of Christ and the Church. But this marriage can hardly be said to produce that union. Therefore it produces nothing at all.

He replies that what marriage images first of all is the spouses' union of souls. (Here the term "marriage" must refer to the exterior, observable conduct, or to both.) But in and by this imaging the marriage produces the union of souls in the sense not of creating it, but of intensifying it.

He adds that the intensifying of this union also somehow produces the spouses' union of souls with God. This is so because where one member of the union is brought into closer union with the other, both are as a consequence more closely united with Christ. This is akin to what happens in the Eucharist. Because in it Christians are more closely joined with Christ, they are consequently brought into closer union with one another. And from this union with one another they are incorporated in Christ.

Bonaventure comes back to almost this same solution in his reply to the third difficulty. This is that baptism and the Eucharist produce the graces that are claimed for marriage. For if marriage is claimed to image what it produces, baptism and the Eucharist already espouse and join the soul to God, or join the members of Christ's body with one another. Thus the claim for marriage must be redundant.[79]

His reply is that it is not the espousal itself of partners' souls to God that takes place in their sacrament. Rather their sacrament images this espousal. But the espousal that their sacrament does both image and produce is that of husband and wife. In this espousal they gain as a consequence some grace that strengthens their espousal and union with God.

The theology of the mystical body of Christ is here, the theology that theologians of the late nineteenth and early twentieth centuries will use to account for Christian marriage's sacramentality. Bonaventure's assumption in his reply is that Christian spouses are members of the body of Christ which is the Church. Consequently their union with one another intensifies their union with Christ, and this intensifies the union of Christ with the Church. Hence his reply as a conclusion: The Christian spouses' marriage images first of all their union with one another, and "produces it" (*efficit*) by intensifying it. But in doing this they intensify the union of the Church with Christ, which second union their own union images by one remove. Consequently both the imaging and the producing of one same effect that are required for a sacrament are found in the marriages of Christian spouses.

Thomas on the Grace of the Sacrament

We recall that Thomas' answer to the question asking whether the sacrament in marriage is a cause of grace was contained very succinctly in his answer to the more fundamental question he posed in Question 2, Article 1 of this Distinction 26: "Is marriage a sacrament?"[80] He reasoned deductively to answer this question and used the gracing work of marriage as an implied premise in so reasoning: A sacrament is a sign, an image (*signum*) of a sacred reality. But marriage is such a sign. Therefore . . . His claim for the marital sacrament's gracing (in answer to the first question above) is in his explanation how marriage is a sign of a sacred reality. For a sacrament brings graced healing (*remedium sanctitatis*) to the sinfulness in human beings, a healing that is manifested in observable signs. But such a healing is found in marriage. Therefore . . .

It is in Article 3 of this Question 2 that we find Thomas' more explicit and developed explanation of the way in which the sacrament in marriage causes grace in the spouses. Here he asks the question in its most vulnerable form, "Whether marriage confers grace" (*Utrum matrimonium conferat gratiam*). The question is most vulnerable in this form for the reason already cited so frequently. How can a relationship whose typical conduct carries and abets concupiscence be a gracing source of holiness?[81]

In his *Solutio* here Thomas resumés and rejects the counter-arguments traditional in his time. He rejects the compromising reply that marriage, though not a cause of grace, is yet a Christian sacrament because a sign of grace. He rejects it because marriage was such a sign even under the law of Moses, before it was made a sacrament among Christians.

He rejects also the conventional reply that Christian marriage's gracing consists of this, that it withdraws the spouses from sin by providing their intercourse with an excuse, the excuse that it procreates, and by mitigating the spouses' concupiscence by confining it within their marital intercourse—but does not grace them by helping them to virtue. His reason for this rejection is the same as for his rejection just above: All this was true in the law of Moses before the institution of marriage among Christians as a sacrament.

Finally he lays out the interpretation he deems more probably accurate. Marriage that is contracted in Christian faith brings a helping grace, a grace that aids the spouses in fulfilling marriage's obligations. He reasons to this conclusion from a premise apparently philosophic. For when God gives persons a capacity (*facultas*) for some conduct, he also gives the help enabling them to engage readily (*convenienter*) in this conduct. Applied to marriage this refers to the husband's capacity to make use of his wife for procreation (the phrase here is *uti uxore suo*). God gives the grace to the Christian couple without which the husband could not do this readily (again the adverb is *convenienter*).

The reasoning is banal. It is also conventional for Thomas' age. It is a compromise with the Augustinian difficulty about concupiscence. It carefully avoids saying that marriage's gracing augments the goodness in the spouses, that it enriches their relationship with God and with one another.

But some reasoning more independently Thomas' own emerges in his replies to the objections in this article. The first of these objections says that a sacrament confers invisible grace by virtue of its own holiness (*sanctificatio*). But marriage has no such holiness essential to itself.

To this Thomas replies that just as the water of baptism touches physically the body but spiritually washes the heart by the touch of Christ's flesh, so too marriage can touch the body while sanctifying the heart because Christ has prefigured this touching in his suffering.

This narrows the focus and raises a question in light of what Thomas has just said in the *solutio* of this article. Does he really mean that the sacrament's gracing that enables a husband to procreate readily comes from Christ's suffering? It was in this suffering that Christ gave himself in love most unreservedly. So is this love's effect in a man's marriage only his ability to procreate readily? Thomas does not notice this consequence.

In his reply to the second objection, that the spouses' observable words of consent do not cause grace (since no creaturely cause can produce it), he replies that while these words do not directly cause grace, they do directly cause the union of the spouses (their *nexus*). This union is itself the sacrament; it in turn disposes the spouses for God's gracing them. In this answer Thomas draws from his interpretation of causality in the sacrament generally. It is that the immediate and proportioned effect of the sacraments' ritual action is not grace itself but a disposition in the person for receiving God's gracing.

It is in his reply to the fourth objection that he confronts the difficulty brought by the Augustinian notion of concupiscence and its crippling effect on marriage's sacramentality.

> [I reply] that a remedy for concupiscence can be applied in two ways. One way touches the concupiscence itself by repressing it at its source. This is the way that marriage applies its remedy to it through the grace given to it [the marriage].
>
> In a second way the remedy is applied to concupiscence in its activity, and this, in turn, in two ways. One way is that the act

to which concupiscence impels a man is deprived exteriorly of its immorality. This is done through the goods of marriage which legitimize [*honestant*] carnal concupiscence. The other way is that the act infected by concupiscence is itself blocked. This is done by the nature itself of the act, since in satisfying concupiscence by and within the marital act it does not incite to other acts which are corrupt—as the Apostle said in I Cor. 7–9: "It is better to marry than to burn." Thus though the acts native to concupiscence tend of their nature to increase it, yet when these are subjected to reason, they repress it. For from homogeneous acts there are produced homogeneous habits and dispositions.[82]

By way of interpreting this response note what Thomas said earlier, in the first part of the *Responsio* of this article: Assuming that the sacrament graces the spouses by repressing concupiscence in them, he there denied that it does so simply by confining it within marriage and thus mitigating it. Taking for granted too that concupiscence accompanies sexual intercourse into marriage, he now says rather that marriage represses this concupiscence at its root, and does so through the sacrament's gracing. This is how it represses concupiscence in the spouses (although he does not explain how the gracing does this).

I believe we have here in different words what Thomas implied above in the *Solutio,* that the sacrament graces a marriage by way of helping it; that it does this by helping the spouses to fulfill their marital obligations; that principal among these obligations are those involved in procreation; and it is by thus helping in procreation that the sacrament represses concupiscence in the spouses. It is not clear that Thomas intends the congealing of all his implications into this multifaceted conclusion. But I believe the conclusion is there virtually in all he implies.

It is in his reply to the third objection that he confronts the difficulty about concupiscence in marriage posed in a special way by his age's accepted theology of the sacraments in general. This was that all the sacraments work their effects by drawing on the sufferings of Christ. These sufferings were not only painful but expiatory; Christ endured them as a vicarious punishment for the sins of the race. But marriage's sexual conduct involves keen pleasure. So it seems impossible that marriage could conform spouses to the sufferings of Christ, impossible that its conduct could image this suffering and thus heal sinfulness, as a sacrament must.[83]

Thomas' reply to this is brief and avoids the heart of the difficulty. He says that it is not by its sensate pleasure that marriage conforms the spouses to Christ's suffering and enables them to draw from it. It is by their charity, their self-giving love, that they do so. He supplies the obvious model for this love: It was out of love for the Church that Christ suffered for her; it was by this suffering impelled by love that he joined the Church to himself as bride. Thomas implies, therefore, that if the spouses love one another with such a self-giving love, they can indeed be conformed to and draw from Christ's suffering. He does not say that the sensate pleasures of their marital acts can be included in this self-giving love. Therefore he leaves unexplained here how their concupiscence-infected acts can be healed by conduct specifically marital, by the *marital* sacramental signing in marriage.

Scotus on the Grace of the Sacrament

Scotus' insistence on the separability of the contract and the sacrament in Christian marriages had consequences for the latter's contribution to the gracing of the spouses. He said that provided the spouses do not place the obstacle to grace that is mortal sin, they are graced in two ways. Neither of these is a "first gracing"; that is, neither conveys a person from the state of sin to the state of grace as baptism and penance do this. But the first effect of marriage's gracing is that the spouses' contractual union is made a union of their souls. The second and more inclusive effect is that this union and the conduct flowing from it become grace-animated.[84]

From demanding, in his hylemorphic model, a specific sign for a sacramental marriage *forma,* and from demanding specific ministers, he was compelled to say that not all those who contract marriage under the law receive the gracing named just above. Yet he could say that even Christian spouses in a non-sacramental marriage receive some grace provided they place no obstacle to it. Because of the severe demands of the marriage contract God helps them, but not with graces as abundant as those received from the sacrament, especially not if the spouses could have married in the sacrament but chose not to.

Hervaeus Natalis (d. 1323) was Duns Scotus' contemporary in the last generation of high medieval scholasticism. He deserves notice not because he wrote at length on marriage but because, like Scotus, he disagreed at a pivotal point about the theology of the sacrament. It was not, like Scotus, about the separability of contract and sacrament, but about the interpretation of Ephesians 5:32 that had by his time become the accepted interpretation in the schools and among the authorities. This said that *sacramentum hoc magnum est,* as it was read in the Latin of the Vulgate New Testament, refers to Christian marriage taken universally.

Hervaeus' disagreement appears in his *Commentarium in Epistolam Pauli ad Ephesios.*[85] There he took for granted that the passage is Paul's exhortation to Christian spouses concerning the love that they should have for one another. But he held that Paul also used it as a kind of apostrophe to Christ and the Church and their love relationship. Within this he worked out a simple and inchoate theology of this relationship. And as he worked through the passage he correlated this Christ-Church relationship point-for-point with that of Christian husband and wife. He detached both relationships from their reality in life and dealt instead with two thoroughly idealized abstractions of them. Predictably he put the wife in childlike obedience to and dependence on the husband, while he gave the husband the role of flawless and loving supervisor of the wife, one who loves her even to the point of giving his life for her—a sacrificial love that is not expected of her.

He came back to reality at the end of the correlation where he acknowledged that the ideal bride of Christ, holy and spotless, without stain or wrinkle, does not and will not exist on earth, but will be found only in eternity.

His dissent is in his express denial, when he comes to verse 32, "This is a great sacrament," that it refers to Christian marriage, whether in idealized abstraction or in earthly reality.

> "This is a great sacrament" is said about the union of Christ and the Church. And lest anyone think that such greatness of the sacrament is found in each and every man who has a wife, Paul says, "I say this about Christ and the Church." For myself, I interpret the words of Genesis allegorically about Christ and the Church. But you must understand them literally and morally [*moraliter*]: "And let each of you love his wife as his own self." And the wife I exhort that "she fear her husband"—that is, let her love him with chaste fear, obey him in everything that is good, and revere him.[86]

Summary

The philosopher-theologians of the late twelfth century and the thirteenth used the critical method developed in their schools to analyze marriage and the marital sacrament with a painstaking thoroughness unequaled since their time. But it was a lopsided thoroughness. Two of the essential components of a theology of marriage—the biblical passages and the experience of marriage by the married—were examined only minimally. These scholastics' main effort was put to defining marriage in its ontological category, to identifying the causes that create and sustain marriage as such a category, to find the sacrament and explain it as a cause.

By Duns Scotus' generation in the first half of the fourteenth century they regarded marriage as a consensual contract, affirming in theory what Church and civil law had done with marriage in practice since the eleventh century. As to what the parties exchange in their marital contracting, this was deemed to be their rights to sexual acts.

This raised the question concerning the relationship of contract and sacrament in Christian marriages. Are they wholly identical? Or if they are distinct, are they also separable, so that two Christians can marry in a non-sacramental, merely human contractual relationship? A second question, growing out of the opinion that the sacrament and the relationship are distinct, asked who is or are the ministers of the sacrament. The witnessing bishop or priest? The parties themselves? God? In any case, what is done to the natural relationship to make it a sacrament? The long-established practice of concluding marriages through proxies—proxies often acting for parties still strangers to one another—raised the accessory question whether sacramental marriages could be created in this impersonal way.

But there was a question logically prior to all these. Since by the thirteenth century bishops and scholars assumed that Christ had made the marriages of Christians to be sacraments, when did he do this? By which recorded words and gestures? Their most common opinion was that God himself instituted marriage when, as recorded in Genesis 2, he inspired the first man to say of the first woman, "This one at last is bone of my bones and flesh of my flesh." An accessory opinion as common as this held that in this first institution of marriage God also made it a sacrament. This he did by making marriage indestructible, and thereby making it a type, an anticipatory image of the indestructible future relationship of Christ and the Church. But this instituting of the sacrament was a progressive work on God's part, continuing through pre-Mosaic history, through the Mosaic law, and climaxing in Christ's confirming and completing these earlier institutions. The earlier instituting of the sacrament was in consideration of all the human race's inheriting, for all time, the ruinous effects of the first man's and woman's sin. Whereas before that sin marriage had been instituted as a dutiful vocation (*in officium*), since the sin it has been instituted in the effort to heal its effects (*in remedium*). Scotus disagreed in part. He insisted that Christ no more than annexed the sacrament to the contract in the new law, and this in order to provide the spouses with the graces needed to meet the severe demands of married life.

All the better theologians of this period seem to have agreed that some of the elements of the sacrament can be found in the marriages of non-Christians who have faith in God. The principal element is the natural indissolubility of their marriages.

In the effort to identify the minister or ministers of the sacrament two theories competed. One held that the spouses themselves are the ministers of their sacrament. This followed from two linked premises, that the sacrament is inseparable from the contract in marriage, and that the spouses themselves create their contract. The other theory proposed that the officiating clergyman is the minister, because the sacrament is the most religious element of a Christian marriage, and a priest or bishop is the minister of religious acts and their effects.

The thirteenth-century theologians responded with different solutions to the difficulty springing from the premise that a sacrament graces the participating spouses. The difficulty was an apparent dilemma: either one must say that of themselves the spouses can no more than create the contract but cannot be ministers of the sacrament, because only God can be a cause of grace, or one must say that since the human creators of the contract cannot cause grace, Christian marriages are not sacraments. Albert responded with the distinction that the spouses co-work with God in ministering the sacrament by supplying the human element in it, but nothing more. Thomas' response was that the spouses cause the sacrament acting as instruments in the power of God. For Scotus the minister of the sacrament, which is in any case only annexed to the contract, is anyone who creates the latter. This may be the spouses, or their parents, or the priest.

Under the impetus of their curiosity to identify the hylemorphic elements in every physical and sensate reality, some of these scholastics sought to find them in the sensate experience that is the marital sacrament, both in the sacramental act that creates the marriage and in the perduring sacrament itself. For Thomas the *materia* is each spouse's contractual consent as indeterminate and open to determination by the other's consent, while its *forma* is each spouse's consent as determining the other's.

About the exact identity of the marital sacrament, the most thorough of these theologians found this in the marriage's imaging of some invisible and transcendent sacred reality. Where they disagreed was about the sacred reality imaged and about the elements in a Christian marriage that do the imaging, as also about the correlations of imaging and reality imaged. Thomas' interpretation was the most realistically grounded. In his *Commentary on St. Paul's Letter to the Ephesians* he said that the phrase "This is a great sacrament" refers to the Christian husband's relationship to his wife. The model for this relationship is Christ's relationship with the Church, a relationship in which he sanctifies her (his metaphoric bride) until the end of history. The consequence of this model-image correlation is deontological: it says how Christian husbands and wives ought to love one another. For Scotus the sacrament is the wedding ceremony, the spouses' committing of themselves to one another, but only where this is done in words determined by the Church and thereby made grace-giving.

From the beginning of their era the scholastics debated about the kind of grace the marital sacrament confers and how it does so. Some found such severe difficulties that they denied that it graces effectively, but only manifests God's blessing. Others denied it a sanctifying function and limited its gracing to a medicinal function, to empowering the spouses to keep fidelity with one another and to restrain their lust within fidelity.

For Bonaventure the grace of the sacrament has the multiple effects of enabling the spouses to realize in their marriage the three goods proposed by Augustine—fidelity, offspring and (Bonaventure's interpretation of the *sacramentum*) inseparability. It is especially in realizing the last-named good that the marital sacrament both images and causes. For the union that their marriage makes visible is their own love union, which is itself an image of the love of Christ and the Church for one another. Since their love union is joined to Christ by his gracing, their sacrament enriches the bond between him and the Church.

In his *Commentary on the Sentences* Thomas saw the graces of the sacrament coming from Christ's suffering and death. These are enabling graces; they capacitate especially the husband to love his wife in all the duties of marriage. The spouses' role in the gracing is that by their sacramental words that create the marriage, and by their marital conduct afterward, they dispose themselves for Christ's gracing. As for how pleasure-laden sexual intercourse can conform the spouses to Christ's suffering and death which was painful and expiatory, Thomas explained that by their intercourse the spouses are conformed to them not insofar as they were painful and expiatory but insofar as they were Christ's act of love for the Church.

NOTES

1. *Joannis Duns Scoti . . . Opera Omnia. Editio Nova, Juxta Editionem Waddingi. Tomus Decimus Nonus: Quaestiones in Quartum Librum Sententiarum,* Parisiis, apud Ludovicum Vives, 1894, p. 159.

2. *Ibid.*

3. *Op. cit.,* p. 186.

4. This has been especially clear and emphatic when the Christian despisers of the physical world have condemned marriage as evil because it is so physical. The rigorist Gnostics did this during Christianity's infancy. The Manichees did it again two centuries later. The Cathars repeated it in the twelfth and thirteenth centuries. The first reply of the orthodox Christians was in each case, "How can marriage be evil when God has instituted it?" The attendant task then was to verify this claim as an event in history.

5. *In IV Sententiarum,* Chapter 14, PL 211:1257.

6. *Summa,* Pars IV, Quaestio 2, Membrum 2, Articulus 1.

7. In *Dictionnaire de Théologie Catholique,* Col. 2215.

8. PL 192:908.

9. In *Acta Apostolicae Sedis,* Vol. 20, pp. 24–25.

10. In *Dictionnaire de Théologie Catholique, ibid.*

11. *Ibid.*

12. In *Opera Omnia, Ad Fidem Codicum Manuscriptorum Edenda . . . Curavit Institutum Alberti Magni Coloniense . . . ; Tomus XXVI: De Sacramentis, etc. . . . ,* 1958. *Tractatus Nonus, De Matrimonio,* Quaestio I, Articulus 1, p. 154, par. 236.

13. *Op. cit.,* pp. 158–159, par. 243.

14. In *Opera Omnia . . . Editio accurate recognita . . . cura et studio A.C. Peltier.* Tomus Sextus, Parisiis, 1866. *In Librum Quartum Sententiarum, Distinctio XXVI, Articulus 1,* Quaestio 1, "An matrimonium fuit institutum ante lapsum", pp. 210–211.

15. *Loc. cit., Quaestio 2,* "An matrimonii sacramentum fuit a Deo institutum," pp. 214–215.

16. In *Sancti Thomae Aquinatis Opera Omnia, Tomus VII: Commentarium in Quattuor Libros Sententiarum Magistri Petri Lombardi . . . Volumen Secundum.* Parmae, 1873 (N.Y., 1948). *Liber IV, Distinctio 26, Quaestio 2.*

17. *Op. cit.,* pp. 920–921.

18. *Ibid.,* p. 921.

19. *Op. cit.,* p. 574.

20. *Ibid.,* pp. 574–575.

21. *Op. cit.,* p. 599.

22. *Op. cit.,* p. 586.

23. *Ibid.*

24. *Ibid.*

25. *Loc. cit.,* p. 587.

26. In *Liber Sextus Decretalium,* II, 15, Caput unicum.

27. *Op. cit., De Matrimonio,* Quaestio 1, Articulus 5, p. 158.

28. *In IV Sententiarum,* Distinctio 26, Articulus 2, Quaestio 2, ad 4m.

29. *In IV Sententiarum,* Distinctio 28, Quaestio 1, Articulus 3, ad 2m.

30. *In IV Sententiarum,* Distinctio 26, Quaestio unica, no. 15.

31. *Dictionnaire de Théologie Catholique,* Col. 2207.

32. *In IV Sententiarum,* Distinctio 27, Articulus 4.

33. In this regard see especially *Summa Theologica,* III, Quaestio 62, Articulus 1.

34. *In IV Sententiarum,* Distinctio 27, Articulus 4.

35. *Super IV Sententiarum,* Distinctio 26, Quaestio 2, ad 1m.

36. *Defensiones . . .* In *Dictionnaire de Théologie Catholique,* Col. 2203.

37. Thomas, *In IV Sententiarum,* Distinctio 26, Quaestio 2, Articulus 1, ad 2m.

38. *In IV Sententiarum,* Distinctio 28, Articulus Unicus, Quaestio 4.

39. Distinctio 26, Quaestio Unica, Articuli 13, 14, 15 (*op. cit.,* pp. 168–169).

40. *Ibid.,* par. 14

41. *Ibid.,* p. 588, par. 15

42. In *Dictionnaire de Théologie Catholique,* Col. 2199.

43. *In IV Sententiarum,* Liber, 5, Caput. 14, PL 211:1257.

44. *In IV Sententiarum,* Distinctio 26, Quaestio 1, Articulus 1.

45. *Ibid.*
Albert here has his sources crossed. The Greek of 1 Corinthians 7:39 reads, "A wife is bound to her husband as long as he lives." It is in Romans 7:2 that Paul writes that she is bound to the rule of her husband.

46. From Aristotle's *De Sophisticis Elementis,* Chapt. 17
A book could be written about what has happened to Christian doctrine as a consequence of theologians' using metaphors to explain the reality, then installing the metaphoric explanation as the reality. One thinks immediately of the theology of the Church as the mystical body of Christ.

47. *De Sacramentis,* p. 157, par. 240.

48. This is attributed to Jerome with source unidentified, as recorded in Gratian's *Decretum,* Causa 27, Quaestio 2, Caput 37.

49. *Op. cit.,* pp. 214–215

50. *Ibid.,* ad 1m.

51. *Super Epistolas S. Pauli Lectura . . .* Editio VIII Revisa, Vol. 2, Taurini/ Romae, 1953.

52. Par. 317, p. 74.

53. *Ibid.*, Par. 318.
54. *Ibid.*, Par. 323.
55. Par. 331, p. 75.
56. Par. 335, p. 77.
57. *Ibid.*
58. *Op. cit.*, p. 597, Par. 16.
59. *Ibid.*
60. *Op. cit.*, p. 670, Par. 4.
61. *Ibid.*, p. 671, Par. 5.
62. *Op. cit.*, p. 155, Par. 238.
63. *Ibid.*, Par. 237 and 238.
64. *Ibid.*, Par. 238.
65. *Loc. cit.*, p. 162, Par. 248.
66. *Op. cit.*, pp. 218–219.
67. *Op. cit.*, p. 276.
68. In Joyce, *op. cit.*, p. 173.
69. In *Dictionnaire de Théologie Catholique*, Col. 2208.
70. *Summa Decretorum*, Causa 32, Quaestio 2 (in Schillebeeckx, *op. cit.*, p. 332).
71. PL 205:126.
72. *Historia Occidentalis*, Caput 36 (in *Dictionnaire de Théologie Catholique*, Col. 2209.
73. *In Epistolam I ad Corinthios*, Caput 7 (in *op. cit.*, Col. 2209)
74. In *Dictionnaire de Théologie Catholique*, Col. 2210
75. In *Summa Aurea* (in Schillebeeckx, *op. cit.*, p. 334)
76. *De Sacramento Matrimonii*, Caput 6 (in *Dictionnaire de Théologie Catholique*, Col. 220).
77. *In IV Sententiarum*, Distinctio 26, Articulus 2, Quaestio 2: "An in sacramento matrimonii conferatur gratia," *op. cit.*, pp. 217–218.
78. *Op. cit.*, p. 216.
79. *Ibid.*, p. 217.
80. *Op. cit.*, pp. 920–921.
81. *Ibid.*, p. 922.
82. *Ibid.*
83. *Ibid.*, p. 921.
84. Distinctio 26, Quaestio Unica, Articulus 15 (*op. cit.*, p. 168).
85. In PL 181:1266–1269.
86. *Ibid.*, Col. 1269.

BIBLIOGRAPHY

Aquinas, St. Thomas: *Summa Theologica*. First Complete American Edition, in Three Volumes. . . . Volume 3, Containing Supplement, QQ. 1–99, etc. N.Y. et al., Benziger Brothers, Inc., 1948. Questions 41 to 49, pp. 2711–2742.

Delhaye, Philippe: "The Development of the Medieval Church's Teaching on Marriage," in *Concilium*, 55, N.Y., Herder and Herder, 1970, pp. 83–88.

Hillman, Eugene: "The Development of Christian Marriage Structures," in *Concilium*, 55, N.Y. Herder and Herder, 1970, pp. 25–38.

Mackin, Theodore: *Marriage in the Catholic Church: What Is Marriage?* N.Y./ Ramsey, Paulist Press, 1982. Chapter 7: "The Theologians and the Nature of Marriage."

Parmisano, F.: "Love and Marriage in the Middle Ages," in *New Blackfriars,* Vol. 50 (August 1969), pp. 599–608; 649–660.

Quinn, J.: "St. Bonaventure and the Sacrament of Matrimony," in *Franciscan Studies,* Vol. 34 (1974) pp. 101–143.

Schillebeeckx, Edward: *Marriage: Human Reality and Saving Mystery.* N.Y., Sheed and Ward, 1965. Volume 2, Chapter 1, "The Formation of Church Marriage," "The Sacramental Nature of Marriage: The Eleventh to the Thirteenth Centuries," pp. 326–343.

10. REFORMATION CHALLENGE AND CATHOLIC REACTION

By 1350 almost all Catholic authorities and scholars agreed on the thesis, which was to become doctrine a little less than a century later, that Christian marriage is a sacrament of the new law, that it is a sign of grace and a cause of it in the souls of those who receive the sacrament rightly disposed. I formulate the thesis in this abstract and general way—"Christian marriage"—because, as we shall see, not all agreed that every marriage of two Christians is a sacrament, did not agree that the only marriage two Christians can create is a sacramental marriage. The difference and disagreement here point up a philosophic dispute that ran deeply and seriously through the Western Church from about the middle of the fourteenth century on into the sixteenth, where it helped to produce the religious revolution that was the Protestant reform. I mention here only one side of the dispute because it is exemplified in the formulation just above. The formulation is symptomatic of the philosopher (and of the theologian and jurist) for whom the end object of his speculation is the idea of the thing or relationship in question rather than the thing or relationship itself. The formulation points the way also to another symptom of this mind-set: it can affirm essential properties of the idea, and at the same time exempt from these properties this or that thing or relationship that embodies the idea. We see this in regard to the property of marriage called indissolubility. To this day in Catholic marriage law it is called an essential property of marriage considered abstractly and ideally, while at the same time the same law authorizes the dissolution of real-life marriages. So too in the fourteenth century there were theologians and jurists who held to the thesis that Christian marriage is a sacrament of the new law while holding also that Christian couples can create marriages that are not sacraments. Nowhere have I found the interpretation that because such marriages are not sacraments they are not Christian. Such interpretations as were offered said simply that they are not sacraments—more exactly that they are contracts not only distinct from the sacrament but also separate from it.

But beyond agreement in the fundamental thesis that Christian marriage in the abstract is a grace-giving sacramental sign, disagreement reigned in other and multiple sectors of the theology of the sacrament. Theologians and jurists in the lately planted Scotist tradition, consistent with an imperative of this tradition that screened universality out of the sensate domain whenever possible and insisted on a singularity there, insisted that the sacrament in marriage depends for its creation on a specific verbal formula of contractual consent. This they demanded because each sacrament, being a unique grace-giving sign, must have its own *forma-signum*. As we saw in the preceding chapter, this led to the judgment that not all marriages of Christians are sacraments because not all are created by the required formula.

A different reason accounted for a second insistence that some Christian marriages are not sacraments—in this case second marriages in widowhood. The reason alleged was that a marriage of two Christians is a sacrament in that it images the relationship of Christ and the Church. But this is a relationship of one to one. Therefore a man or woman taking a second spouse cannot image the strict monogamy of the divine relationship. It follows too that his or her spouse also falls short of the sacrament, since it includes both spouses or neither spouse. On the other hand, among those convinced that the marital sacrament is the priestly blessing the case against the sacramentality of second marriages was reinforced by the long-standing refusal in both the Eastern and the Western Church to grant the blessing on these marriages. Finally there was the claim that in the scriptures there is no evidence of the divine institution of second marriages.

The counter-position appeared generally in the theologians' commentaries on the fourth book of Lombard's Sentences, Question 32, and included the following elements. The reason for denying the iteration of those sacraments that cannot be repeated—baptism, confirmation and orders—is that these produce a "character" in the soul that is permanent and works its effect permanently. But no one has ever claimed that marriage leaves such a character. About the denial of the blessing in second marriages, it is only the solemn nuptial blessing that is denied; the authorized priest's blessing at the door of the church (*in facie ecclesiae*) is granted any second marriage, or even a third or a fourth. As for God's instituting the sacrament in second marriages, there is no need that he have done so, because by the one divine decree he instituted marriage in general to be sacramental.

What was conceded was that in second marriages the sacramental image is less clear and less complete, although it is indeed there since the Church as the bride of Christ is in fact a society of many persons. But the diminished sacramentality is acknowledged in this, that there is reason to suspect that concupiscence motivates the contracting of subsequent marriages, especially where the motive that is the realizing of the marital good of offspring has been fulfilled in a first marriage. But even when the suspicion was well-founded the second marriage was not denied sacramentality. Rather a penance was imposed on the remarrying spouse or spouses *ex defectu sacramenti*, for their crippling the sacrament.[1]

But a few scholars still resisted the fundamental claim for the sacrament in Christian marriage or in any marriage. Stuck in their minds was the fact acknowledged by even the champions of the sacrament, that concupiscence infests marriage's characteristic sexual conduct. The French Dominican, Durandus of Saint Pourçain, who was successively bishop of Limaux (1317), LePuy (1318–1326) and Meaux (from 1326 until his death in 1337), had his own detailed case against the sacrament. All the true sacraments in the Church have been instituted by revealed supernatural reason in the authority of Christ, and from their institution have been regulated by such reason in the authority of the Church. But from its beginning in natural reason before the law of Christ marriage was, until the institution of the Church, also regulated by natural reason. This is all the more evident in that everything about marriage, whether before the law of Christ or within it, is the same except for an accrued supernatural sign. And even this comes not from a divine source outside the marriage but from the spouses themselves in their contractual consent. What is more, Durandus pointed out, a marriage can be created through proxies by parties who are absent from one another, who have never yet met, and who can therefore hardly be said to effect a sign of the love of Christ and the Church. And contractants absent or present, if not in the state of grace when contracting, they receive no grace—as everyone admits. Hence Durandus' summary judgment: Marriage even among Christians belongs to the natural domain and is rightly regulated by civil law. It does not belong among the means of sanctification established in his Church by Christ. Thus two centuries before Martin Luther Durandus anticipated his position almost exactly.

The Council of Florence

As far as the authoritative mind of the Church was concerned, the issue was settled a little less than a century later, in the Council of Florence, on November 22, 1439. This is listed as the seventeenth ecumenical council of the universal Church; it was in fact a series of conciliar meetings that began in Basel on July 23, 1431. Pope Eugene IV dissolved the council on December 18 of that year because of the strong conciliarist move in it guided by the French bishops, and convoked it again in Bologna. But when the majority of the bishops remained in Basel he approved the decrees of the first twenty-five sessions, which were held in that city on the Rhine.

One of the principal items among the council's agenda was to reconstitute union with the many Eastern Catholics who were by now regarded by the Roman Catholic authorities as schismatics, and this mainly because they rejected the primacy in authority of the pope. To locate the council in a city more acceptable to the Eastern representatives, Eugene moved it to Ferrara on January 8, 1438, then to Florence on February 26, 1439, while the dissident bishops, the conciliarists, remained in Basel until 1448, where they elected an anti-pope.

Along with papal primacy the council's main matters of discussion and debate were the Roman addition of the *filioque* to the Latin version of the Nicene Creed (to indicate that in the trinity of persons in God the Holy Spirit proceeds from the Son as well as from the Father); the eucharistic bread (whether this is to be leavened or unleavened), and the three possible fates of souls after death (immediate beatitude for those in grace and owing no temporal punishment for their sins; immediate damnation for those still in serious sin; purgatorial and temporary suffering for those in venial sin and/or those who have not paid their debt of temporal punishment).

A statement of union after long and difficult debate was signed by the principal representatives of the two churches at the beginning of July 1439. But the union collapsed soon afterward, partly because the Western nations failed to send to the Greeks sufficient military help against the Turks.

Despite the severely differing disciplines of divorce and remarriage in the two churches—the Greeks' *eoconomia* of mercy permitted spouses to remarry after dissolution because of adultery or other serious delinquency, and for the guilty party only after the completing of a formal penance—this disagreement was not so much as mentioned in the *Decretum Unionis Graecorum*, The Decree of Union with the Greeks, published by the council on July 6.

The council produced a second significant decree three months later. Just as the Greek representatives were leaving Florence on August 2, representatives of the Armenian Orthodox Church arrived in that city. On November 22 a decree of union of the Roman Church and the Armenian was signed. Its Part 5 is a compact but complete statement of the Roman Catholic doctrine of the sacraments at this time. The paragraph concerning marriage is the last in this Part 5. It is taken in substance from a work reputed, but not without challenge, to be one of Thomas Aquinas' *opuscula* (minor treatises), *De articulis fidei et Ecclesiae sacramentis* (On the Articles of Faith and the Sacraments of the Church).

> The seventh sacrament is the sacrament of marriage, which is a sign of the union of Christ and the Church, according to the words of the Apostle, "This is a great sacrament; in this I refer to Christ and the Church." The efficient cause of a marriage is ordinarily the reciprocal consent expressed through the words *de praesenti.*
>
> A threefold good of marriage is acknowledged. The first is offspring to be procreated and nurtured for the worship of

God. The second is fidelity, which each spouse owes to the other. The third is the indissolubility of the marriage deriving from the fact that it images the indissoluble union of Christ and the Church. And although because of adultery a separation from sexual union is allowed, it is not allowed that this be followed by a second marriage, since the bond of a legitimately contracted marriage is permanent.[3]

The second sentence in this paragraph says that the efficient cause of marriage, the agency that creates it, is by law ordinarily (*regulariter*) the consent of the parties themselves expressed through words. The qualifier is in the text in order to allow that consent can be given in other ways than verbally (and perhaps to rebuff the position of Durandus of Saint Pourçain and others that consent must be expressed in a specified verbal formula if the marriage is to be a sacrament). But what the sentence does mainly is to determine exactly the ministers of the sacrament—not the witnessing and blessing priest but the spouses themselves.

The decree identifies the sacrament in marriage exactly. It is the sign, or image, in it of the union of Christ and the Church. The decree is also unhesitating in naming the marriage as the referent of Ephesians 5:32, "This is a great sacrament"—which it is, as just said, because it images the Christ-Church union.

In claiming Augustine's three *bona* for marriage the decree deflects the original meaning of the *sacramentum*. Augustine said this is the cause of a marriage's invulnerability to dissolution. The decree says it is this invulnerability, or indissolubility, itself. It also seems to claim a causative relationship between the indissoluble Christ-Church union and that of the spouses, that the former's indissolubility is the cause of the same in the latter. But that the decree says this is not certain. It may advance only the argument that *because* the Christ-Church union is indissoluble, its image on earth too must be indissoluble in order to be the image it is known to be.

But earlier in the decree the council set out other fundamental elements of the theology of the sacraments.[4] First there was the formal listing of the seven sacraments, with marriage named last after baptism, confirmation, Eucharist, penance, last anointing and orders. All seven differ significantly from the sacraments of the old law in that the latter no more than prefigured the grace that was to be given in the future through Christ's passion and death, but did not confer this grace. But the seven sacraments of the new law both "contain" this grace and confer it on those who receive them worthily. The inept verb "contain" no doubt means that the sacraments truly participate as causes in the gracing of the recipients. Whether the bishops and theologians at Florence had in mind the Ockhamism of many Western theologians when they inserted this clause, we have no way of knowing. But that philosophic system had as one of its centerpieces the denial that the human mind can know causation in the physical domain for what it is. We shall review this system presently.

The last part of the decree is one with which a modern Catholic would hardly agree, namely that the first five of the sacraments—baptism, confirmation, Eucharist, penance and last anointing—are for the spiritual perfection of each person in his or her self, while orders and marriage are for the well-being and growth of the Church as a whole.[5] It is perplexing that the bishops of both churches would interpret the Eucharist, for example, in such a privatized way.

The Decline of Theology

One does not account for the feeble state of the theology of marriage on the eve of the Protestant reformation unless one traces the discouraging history of all of theology during the fourteenth and fifteenth centuries. The latter is simultaneously the history of philosophy during these centuries—inevitably so, since philosophy is to theology what the calculus is to physics. It provides a language and a medium of interpretation of the metaphors in which virtually all divine revelation is proposed. A simple example shows this. What does it mean to say of the creator that he is "our Father"? If we predicate the noun of him univocally with the way it is predicated of human fathers, we say the creator is a creature, male, sexual, who has a female sexual consort. Among other difficulties with this, it contradicts the possibility of his being creator, because to create is to produce existence absolutely—which no creature can do.

What meaning then can be saved in this most common Christian address to the creator? If one asks the philosophic, indeed the metaphysical question about paternity and childhood, one asks about relationships in existence of father and child, since existence as such is the object of metaphysical inquiry. It is obvious that the existence of the child is contingent on the action of the father, not only for initial coming into existence but also for continuing existence that needs continued nurture (which indicates that there is as much and even more reason for predicating of the creator "our Mother"). Consequently we can conclude that Jesus meant to say, at least, that in a most fundamental way human beings depend on God's gifting them with existence, which is a fundamental act of love. We know he meant more than that. But having been able, thanks to metaphysical reasoning, to understand at least that existential dependency, we can learn the more without having to suspect it is all myth. In short, the ability to theologize stands or falls with one's command of metaphysics.

Therefore it is not difficult to estimate the fate of theology when theologians lose, or worse still willingly give up, their ability to examine metaphysically—or, even worse still, confuse metaphysics with logical analysis. All three or a selection of these came to be the attitude and the experience of many teachers in the universities of Catholic Europe by about the mid-point of the fifteenth century. At the risk of grand over-simplification in the explaining, the attitude took over for the following reasons in the following way.

An intellectual battle that Thomas Aquinas fought, and mainly lost, was to get the Augustinian-Platonist minds of the European schools, beginning at Paris, to see two things whose truths are inter-dependent. One is that in creatures essence is distinct from existence, that is, that the *kind* of existence they carry on is not identical with their existence. The other is that a human being gains knowledge, knows the reality of things—which is their truth—by observing them, by finding, through sensate experience of them, the properties and conditions of their exis-tence, and affirming these in judging about their real existence. If it seems strange to our modern minds that a man should have to argue for the second of these theses, understand that the Platonic mind sought to find the truth of things, their real natures, in the ideas of them in the mind, freed from the changeability and temporariness of their existence.

Under the rubric *parvus error in initio* (a tiny error at the outset), see what happens if one denies, or even ignores, that in creatures es-sence is distinct from existence. Take a human person as an example. Her existence, as existence, is singular and unique, induplicable. She is she and no one else. If one says that her essence, her humanness, is identical with her existence, then it too must be singular, unique, induplicable. Like it or not, one must say she is literally one of a kind; humanness is found in her and her alone.

The paths that philosophers have taken to avoid this absurd conse-quence are well enough known to the students of their discipline. The reason for pointing these out briefly at this juncture in our study is that philosophers and theologians of the fourteenth and fifteenth century took paths that dragged the Catholic intellectual enterprise down into the fatigue, discouragement and eventual cynicism hinted at above.

If one insists that all that constitutes a person is her singular and unique existence, one is tempted to say that essence, or nature, in her that seems the same as that in other persons is really only a pattern of phenomena that appears similar to others. If one insists on explaining the hundreds of millions of similar appearances not as a homogeneous multiplication of natures, then one can hypothesize that God sees to this worldwide and historical sameness. Or one can suggest that it is God who causes human senses to see them as essentially similar, despite there being no essence in them to account internally for the similarity, and also causes the human intellect to conceive of them according to a universal sameness of essence. If one is a doctrinaire Christian Platonist one could even urge that what one's sense perception of individuals in the physical world does is to trigger recognition-recollection of ideas originating in the divine mind and infused into the human mind by God.

But severe consequences would follow from this for the nature of knowledge itself. To know is to understand the natures of things, the conditions of their existence, their relationships in existence. Certainly scientific knowledge consists of this. But if the world apart from the mind is devoid of natures and consists of only appearances, it follows that knowledge cannot consist of such understanding of things apart from the mind. If one insists nonetheless that knowledge is possible, one's only alternative is to say that it consists of penetration of ideas in the mind. And this knowledge becomes scientific when one subjects the ideas to the rules of ideas, which are the rules of logic and grammar—when one knows, for example, which ideas can be subjects in propositions, which predicates, which objects, which can be combined in predications to produce necessary conclusions. As for knowledge of things in their supposed natures apart from the mind, this can be no more than the recognizing and comparing of appearances, the measuring of them for number, pattern, frequency, velocity, direction, weight, etc.

Statements about natures that are constant statements, universally applicable and therefore predicable without fear of error, are really statements about ideas in the mind. The ideas' relationship to phenomena outside the mind is not one of homogeneity between nature out there and conception of it in the mind. It is rather one of culturally agreed-on names for consistently appearing phenomena—in short, nominalism.

There is another and still more serious consequence for religious persons coming from the inability to know natures apart from the mind. A thing's nature is its essence; its essence is its way of existing. If one cannot know its way of existing, one can also not know its existing *as existing*. Again one knows only structured appearances, and only as appearing. But conditions of existence which philosophy and theology by *their* natures search out are causation and its effects, which are coming into existence, changing in existence and passing out of existence. Theology is especially concerned with the relationships between causes and effects because the specifying object of theological knowledge, the creator and his relationship with creatures, is possible only by a knowledge of the cause-effect relationships between them.

But such relationships do not "appear." Indeed even between sensately observable creatures they do not appear. For what is the mass or weight or velocity of causation? All that "appear" are the successively modified states of phenomena in time and place. Consequently if one insists that perception gathers in nothing more than appearance, one cannot know that one being is cause to another being, or correlatively that one is affected by the other's causing. As in the arch-paradigm of the billiard balls, one's movement *causing* the other's movement does not appear. All that appear are one ball's continuous relocation, its contact with the other, and the other's subsequent continuous relocation.

Again, if a person is convinced he lives in a world as vacant of known causation as this, but is nevertheless pious, he may well leave all in the hands of God. His is the only causation we can be sure of. But if we can be sure of it only because the scriptures tell of it, this is both impulse and temptation to think his is the only causation in the universe. Add to this his absolute freedom, his immunity from conditioning by creature actions and creature thoughts, and all the universe is his to do with as he chooses—and this includes the domain of sensate appearance. Then the work of theology becomes no more than a noble logic, the aligning and realigning within the mind of the revealed ideas about God and his dealing with human beings.

It is no task to imagine what this attitude can do to a theology of the sacraments. Despite centuries-long disagreement about the exact way in which the sacramental participants, human and sub-human, are used by God to communicate grace, there was little doubt before the late four-teenth century that these participants really do participate, that they carry on causation, albeit as instruments of the divine causation, that they really work effects on one another. But take away from men and women the possibility of knowing causation in the physical world, while they in their Christian faith insist on keeping sacraments, then the latter are left a very different role in the divine-human interaction. We shall see what Luther and Calvin thought their role to be. Central to their teaching and most emphatic was their insistence that the Christian sacra-ments they did acknowledge, baptism and the Eucharist, do not enter into the causing of justifying grace in the soul. At most they are signs— signs of God's gracing the soul, or signs that the Christian has accepted God's gracing with faith. It would be unfair to Luther and Calvin, espe-cially to the latter, to ascribe to them the philosophic skepticism whose nature I have delineated above. But they were certainly heirs to its distrust of theological interpretation, and heirs to the by-product pietism that attributed to God all that sin-darkened human intelligence could not explain.

The Descent to Philosophic Skepticism

Again at the risk of over-simplification let us trace the steps to the philosophic skepticism in which so many European scholars shared by about the midpoint of the fifteenth century, a skepticism that no one wanted but which seems to have been the inescapable consequence of antecedents discernible at least two centuries earlier.

The heirs and defenders of Augustinianism in the universities, the Franciscans principal among them, defended three theses concerning hu-man intellection that provided territory for dispute. One was that of divine illumination of the human intellect in its work of philosophic under-standing. In its extreme form this proposed God as the "agent intellect" for human understanding. Since essences of physical things in their natu-ral condition are not intellectually intelligible, the theory had it, they have to be made so. After being perceived by the senses and recorded there in images, they are taken into intellectual consciousness where they are given a higher form of existence, intelligible now because free of matter. The extreme form of the theory held that it is God who does this, acting within the human mind by his divine illumination. The effect of this is to make essences knowable in their purity, and especially to enable the human mind to understand them clearly and to make affirmations about them with certainty. In this process the external physical object, captured in the sense image and now in the concept, is related to its eternal exemplar in the divine mind. The divine light active in the human mind enables this mind thus to attain truth, which is to see the physically embodied essence, now in the concept abstracted from its physicality, in its correlation to the eternal and changeless idea-exemplar thereof. Matthew of Aquasparta (1240–1300) was an enthusiastic proponent of this theory of the human appropriation of truth.

Duns Scotus was the especial champion of a second thesis that worked congenially with the one just outlined. He set it against Thomas Aquinas' explanation how a person comes to intellectual understanding of the natures of things. For Thomas, a person's immediate perception of individual existences in their various essences is only through the senses. It is by them alone that he makes conscious perceptual contact with individual existence, whether physical or spiritual. By intellect he has no immediate perception of them, but by the mediation of sensation a person can with intellect abstract from the individuality of sensately perceived essences. (This was consistent within Thomas' interpretation, because to begin with he held to the real distinction in creatures of essence and existence. One could ponder the former abstractly in the intellect without denying that its real state is to be the essence of the latter.) In this way a person can know and examine essences for what they are. And this is to know scientifically, to know natures in their universality. He can also make an intellectual separation of existence from any specific form thereof, and thus appropriate the subject matter of metaphysics.

Yet, to have true knowledge—and this is essential to Thomas' theory of knowledge, and indeed central to medieval philosophy's migration toward skepticism—a person must refer his abstract conceptions of extramental things back to sense experience for verification. A semi-poetic way of pointing up the contrast is to say that where the Franciscan-Augustinian school had the human mind look to heaven to gain truth, Thomas had it return to earth. He insisted that *veritas sequitur esse rerum,* "truth is found in the existence of [sensate] things." Knowledge is gained in judgment of things that returns to the sensate experience of them.

Scotus challenged this, and we see the centrality to his challenge of his more fundamental denial of the real distinction in creatures of their essence and existence. He insisted that by intellect persons have immediate perception of physical things in their individuality. He insisted also that the human senses perceive no more than the individual *as* individual, not the individual existence in a nature potentially universal. Therefore intellect intuits immediately individual essences apprehended in sense images—which it must because, as Scotus insisted, in physical things essence is indistinct from existence. He insisted too that the human intellect has no antecedent, innate ideas—and in this departed from the Augustinian origins of his tradition.

According to Scotus the intellect's second act in understanding is to abstract conceptually the essences of sensate objects—to abstract them from all existence. And while these essences may have been collected by sensation, true knowledge of them is completed in their wholly abstracted condition in the intellect. There the mind can make formal distinctions among all the multiple facets of the abstracted essences, which are not real distinctions nor yet purely mental, but between the two.

Here is another serious point of difference between Thomas and Scotus. For the former the concept, gained from sense experience, is a medium of knowledge. Knowledge for him terminates in the exterior being whence it was derived. But for Scotus the concept was not a medium of knowledge but its terminus-object, even though the concept was, as with Thomas, gained by sensation. Here Scotus was most Platonist: Truth is in the knowledge of pure essences abstracted from perishable individuality in the physical world. And to get this truth Scotus had to acknowledge that universal essences have an existence of their own apart from really existing things. This they have as ideas in the intellect. There too the intellect within itself can establish the object of metaphysics—not, as with Thomas, existence in its reference to the physical world, but the *concept* of being, being as the highest and most universal essence.

William of Ockham

If one detects here that Scotus' theory of knowledge tended, whether he wished it to or not, to locate scientifically certain knowledge within the mind, one detects why a Franciscan of the following generation sought to undo his work. This was William of Ockham, born probably in Surrey, England, between 1290 and 1300, student later at Oxford where he began the study of theology in about 1310. Assuming the accuracy of these dates, he would have lectured there on the scriptures from 1315 to 1317, then on Lombard's *Sentences* from 1317 to 1319, and then have spent the five years following, until 1324, in study, writing and disputation at Oxford. The novelty and daring of some of his teaching blocked his appointment as a master in the university. In fact in 1324 he traveled to Avignon to defend himself before Pope John XXII against accusations of heresy and erroneous teaching brought against him by John Lutterell, the former chancellor of Oxford.

One of his main points against Scotus was Ockham's insistence that universal natures do not exist, either in the extra-mental world or in the mind itself. If his mission can be summed up succinctly, it was to show that all reality, all existence and conditions of existence are individual, absolutely singular. Consequently he insisted that sense perception brings to intellect not essences, but only empirical data—figure, color, relative position, movement, etc. Intellect can thus not discern essences in things; it can no more than accept empirical data from the senses, recognize them, compare them, assign them to categories for subsequent recognition, and conceive ideas about them. Propositions produced by intellect are therefore propositions about ideas within itself, which are in turn control categories for the empirical data. They are not propositions about existence in specific natures in extra-mental reality. This follows from Ockham's fundamental assumption noted above, that all reality, all real existence is individual and therefore induplicable. Hence universal ideas in the mind cannot correspond to anything in reality, whence it follows also that it is not the nature of these ideas to be images or representations of any real or conceivable things.

A point of this, Ockham's theory of knowledge, that conditioned his theology radically was a facet of his empiricism. It was his insistence that the human mind contacts reality outside itself only by the senses. Since their territory of acquisition is only empirical data, but existence, conditions of existence, causation of existence and relationships of cause and effect are not empirically perceptible, a person can gain no knowledge of these in the extra-mental domain. These are only categories of the intellect by which it organizes empirical data referred to it by the senses.

Since the work of a philosophy that seeks to examine reality apart from thought is mainly the discovery and analysis of existences in their cause-effect relationships, Ockham simply gave up the possibility of accurate philosophic knowledge of the world. But not for this was he a professed skeptic. Whether he ought logically to have been one along with others of his time and mentality, his religious piety kept him from that extreme stance.

Thus he judged that although one cannot know with certitude that, for example, a transcendent creator exists, because such knowledge would be the conclusion of a proof involving the principle of causation, one can nevertheless believe that such a creator exists because he has revealed his existence. Philosophic arguments can reinforce this belief; they can conclude there must be a conservor of the world that transcends it, since it goes on despite its inherent perishability. But these arguments cannot prove that there is a single divine creator. This can be known only by what is revealed in the scriptures.

Into this belief Ockham brought his campaign against the existence of universal natures, thereby rejecting one of the essential points of Augustinian theology. That is, in order to defend God's freedom and omnipotence he denied that his divine mind holds the eternal and immutable ideas of created natures by which he is supposed to have created them in the world apart from himself. Therefore no law of nature can be inducted from what is wrongly assumed to be "natural" and naturally good for creatures. For God to put such a restriction on his freedom in dealing with creatures would be to contradict his own nature. The moral law for human beings is therefore whatever God wills for them. This law is eternal and immutable, but immutably free; and like God's existence itself, it can be known only by revelation.

This divine voluntarism was by no means Ockham's innovation in the Franciscan-Augustinian tradition. A generation earlier Duns Scotus had reasoned about the indissolubility of marriage—its *natural* indissolubility—in the *Supplementum* to his *Summa Theologica*.[6] In Question 67, Article 1, he asked whether the "inseparability of a wife" derives from the law of nature. In Article 2 of the same question he asked whether it could have been licit that a wife be dismissed by dispensation.[7]

What is to our point in Scotus' answers to these two questions is his understanding of the law of nature and therefore of the word "nature" itself. For the formulation of the question we have just seen in Article 2 suggests that the law of nature may be relaxed by dispensation.

In his Response, in Article 1, he makes a crucial distinction, one whose first facet is the following:

> . . . the inseparability of the wife—that is, that marriage is an indissoluble bond of husband and wife—does not belong to the law of nature where this law is a principle of conduct whose truth is known by an analysis of its terms, nor is it a principle clearly deduced from these terms. . . .[8]

Then the other facet follows:

> . . . But it is quite true that it [the indissolubility, the insepara-bility] is concordant with the law of nature.[9]

Then from the gospels Scotus brings supporting evidence for this distinction and for the truth of both its facets. This evidence is Christ's statement containing the positive command from God. And here begins to emerge Scotus' interpretation of what makes the law of nature natural. For this command it is that makes marriage to have what indissolubility it has by the law of nature.

> That marriage is indissoluble comes from Christ's statement coming in turn from the command of God in Matthew 19, where the Savior, after abrogating the dismissal that the Law of Moses permitted, brought marriage back to what it had been at its institution, saying, "But what God has joined man must not separate."[10]

To this point Scotus has committed himself only as far as saying that marriage's indissolubility is concordant with the law of nature; it is not in marriage as a self-evident principle nor even as a conclusion drawn necessarily from such a principle. But he sees that his task is not ended there. He must still account for how indissolubility is related to marriage itself. For he had already, in his earlier commentary on Book Four of Lombard's *Sentences,* said that indissolubility belongs to the nature of marriage, that one can no more conceive of marriage without indissolubility than one can conceive of a being without its formal nature. And in his later commentary on the same passage in his *Reportatio Parisiensis* he had said that if one understands marriage as the marital bond, indissolubility belongs to it *ex se formaliter,* formally and of its very nature. He repeated there his clinching rhetorical clause: "One can no more conceive of a marriage that is not indissoluble than one can conceive of a being that has no nature, no form of being."[11] The thought is repeated in the *Supplementum:* "Therefore this indissolubility belongs to marriage formally and of its nature, and by the nature of the marital contract that marriage is."[12]

Such is indissolubility in marriage conceived of ideally in the mind. But in the practical experience of and legislation for marriage—in divine legislation as well as human—"indissoluble by nature" had a different meaning for Scotus.

> . . . although as far as it itself is concerned the contract could be an exchange consisting of a single act or be meant to hold for only a limited time. However, from the divine author the indissolubility has gained this, that once the marriage is consummated it becomes permanent and perpetual and admits of no exception because this is highly concordant with the law of nature because of the good of offspring and of the family, and of civil society.[13]

The shift is obvious: The indissolubility without which marriage is unintelligible is now said to be separable from it, and is there only because of its consummation (where it is in fact consummated), and because of offspring coming from the consummation.

Scotus' answer to the question he posed in Article 2 of this Question 67 of the *Supplementum* makes even clearer the meaning of marriage's indissolubility "according to the law of nature." The reply here is borrowed from the earlier *Opus Oxoniense* in its commentary on Lombard's *Sentences,* Book 4, Distinction 26, numbers 1–4.

> It could have been licit that the husband dismiss his wife by means of the [divine] Legislator's dispensation—from him who has determined precisely that the marital contract brings upon the contracting parties the perpetual obligation that nei-

ther leave the other. For those [obligations] which do not derive from the law of nature taken in its primary and strictest sense because they are not principles of conduct known self-evidently, and where those obligations are not conclusions drawn self-evidently from such principles, but are said to belong to the law of nature only insofar as they are concordant with its self-evident principles or are conclusions from them—those obligations admit of exceptions made by the legislator who established them.

But that marriage brings upon the contracting parties the obligation of perpetuity is the law of nature understood in that secondary sense, insofar as this perpetuity is concordant with the law of nature taken strictly.

Therefore that which is now illicit—namely to dismiss one's wife—could be licit by the intervention of the authority of the legislator dispensing from marriage's indissolubility.

In his reply to Objection 3 under this article Scotus brings to light another facet of his theory of the law of nature. The objection has it that the obligation to not dismiss a wife derives from the Second Table of the Decalogue, from those commands, beginning with the command to honor one's father and mother, that rule conduct involving other human beings. But those acts forbidden by divine command are forbidden because they are in themselves evil. They are not evil because they are forbidden by the divine command. Therefore, the objection concludes, since dismissing a wife is forbidden by God because it is evil, not even he can dispense a man to dismiss his wife licitly.

Scotus' reply to this is to insist that conduct ruled by the law of nature in its secondary sense is either good where and because God wills this conduct to be executed, or evil where and because he forbids it. Hence the same conduct which is forbidden at one time as evil could at another time be good if God then allowed it by dispensation. What is more—and here we see Scotus' concern to defend God's absolute freedom—if the commands of the Second Table of the Decalogue had their rectitude necessarily and prior to the divine will, this will would have to conform to them in order to have its own rectitude. Thus God's knowledge concerning human conduct would be determined from outside himself by conduct subject to human will. But to claim this is false and even blasphemous. Consequently one must admit that any time God thought it prudently advisable, he could dispense a man to dismiss his wife with moral goodness, although ordinarily it is evil for the man to do so because God's decree is in fact that such dismissal is evil.

To return to Ockham, the farthest reach of his philosophic-skepticism-rescued-by-trust-in-God's-freedom was probably this, that God can cause in a person the intuition of a thing not really present. This Ockham derived from a quasi-principle of his metaphysics, that every

effect God causes through the medium of secondary causes, he can produce immediately by himself. Thus God can cause a person to intuit the
here-and-now existence of another person even in the absence of any
other person. (The word "intuit" he chose carefully. "Perceive" would
imply that another person is there.) Would this be a false intuition? No,
because God, who is divine truth, has caused the intuition.

Skepticism in the Late Medieval Universities

Ockham himself hardly started up the movement in the universities
of the middle fourteenth century that took his name. Following his
appearance at Avignon he fell into serious papal disfavor and took
refuge in the empire under the protection of Emperor Ludwig of
Bavaria. He joined there with Marsilius of Padua in supporting the
emperor's campaign against papal monarchic governance of ecclesiastical matters. He died in Munich in 1349, apparently a victim of the Black
Death. But a current of thought, a philosophic attitude did start up in his
wake that has borne the name "Ockhamism." It was an element of the
new mindset, the *via moderna*. In the large view of things it was a
rebellion against the Platonist realism that had dominated Western
Christianity via Augustine. This was the persuasion that ideas in their
universal character do exist in reality, eternal and immutable in the mind
of God, immutable in the human mind; that knowledge is the agreement
of the latter ideas with the former; and that the former are the models of
all created things and of human conduct. The Ockhamist tradition took
root among Franciscan, Dominican and Augustinian scholars. It took
over much of the philosophic enterprise at Oxford and Paris, while the
older tradition held fast mainly at Cologne (founded in 1389) and at the
newer University of Louvain, founded in 1425 in part as a reaction
against the *via moderna*. Gabriel Biel (1425–1495), an explicit nominalist, taught at Tübingen, and the Ockhamists at Erfurt and Wittenberg
called themselves the *Gabrielistae*.
    In the universities the anti-Platonist Ockhamism took on the title
"nominalism," a name drawn from its theory of knowledge. This said
that what can be predicated of an extra-mental object is only a *nomen*, a
name—a name, however, that can be predicated of many things because
of the close similarity in appearance of the many. The mind does form
concepts to go with the words (it does not have *a priori* ideas). But these
have no universal predicability because everything that exists is individual. Therefore concepts cannot serve as media of knowledge of the
world. They are the stuff of logical reasoning within the mind, where
they are ruled by the laws of logic. Only those propositions are true
which can be reduced to the principle of non-contradiction. Since no
extra-conceptual objects exist necessarily, no such true affirmations can
be made about them. The only proposition about extra-conceptual reality that is finally reducible to the principle of non-contradiction (as

Descartes was to urge later) is "I exist." This is so since the denial of it affirms the existence of the "I" who denies.

Of supposed causal relationships no more than empirical observation is possible. Hence causation is only a name given to the sequential movement of appearances. Therefore no proof of a first cause, a creator, is possible. Nor can one know that one creature as cause affects another. Certainty of God's existence can be had only by faith, as also faith alone brings certainty that he uses creatures in his intervention in human affairs—uses them sacramentally or otherwise.

John of Miracourt lectured on Lombard's Sentences at the Cistercian College of St. Bernard in Paris in 1344–1345. He agreed with Ockham that not physical things but God could be the cause of our sense perceptions. Therefore we cannot be sure of the existence of an external world unless God assures us of it, as he has through the scriptures. He agreed also that God's power and freedom extend to his dictating the law of nature, that transgressions of it are not sinful unless he decrees them to be so. He saw no compelling proof that God cannot obliterate past events, that he cannot cause them to have not occurred after they had in fact occurred. And since God is the universal cause, he can be the effective cause of sinful acts even in their sinfulness. Nicholas of Autrecourt, a student at the Sorbonne from 1320 to 1327, then canon of the cathedral of Metz in 1338, allowed that God could with moral goodness command a person to hate him.

When thought and language go on as free a holiday as this, specific consequences tend to follow. Since this volume cannot be a history of late medieval culture, only a few of these consequences can be pointed out, and only briefly at that. One of these is the creation in the dominant societies (in our case the Church) of a climate congenial to the juridical establishing of doctrine. The Platonist contribution to this works by legislating *a priori*. Instead of legislating after finding out, by examining real-life persons and their relationships, what are their natures and hence what are their good and their fulfillment, Church legislators do somewhat the converse. They first develop in the mind the ideal models of persons and their relationships, then by legislation impose these models on life. But in truth the developing of the models—and marriage is much in mind here—never has a "pure" beginning, as it cannot. The model is designed in order to resolve this or that difficulty, to survive this or that crisis. Here the hand of empiricism, the dominance of immediate and passing phenomena, reaches in. A mistreatment of the biblical models frequently has its part in resolving the problem. These models are made into criteria and are applied as though they came necessarily and immutably from the immutable and necessary divine ideas as from an exclusive source. But in fact they were in the time and place of their origin inducted from the problems and crises of the time and place.

To get to marriage in the Catholic Church as an example, whence comes the instituted idea, the doctrine, that "marriage is in its nature indissoluble"? Not from the common historical experience of marriage, since every society in history, including the Catholic Church, has dissolved marriages. Not from the scriptures. The Jewish scriptures teach in part that marriage ought to be permanent, but permit dissolution for certain causes, and even legislate that an infertile marriage must be dissolved after ten years, or that at least a second wife ought to be taken. The concept itself of the indissolubility of marriage never entered Jewish thought. Not from the Christian scriptures, because it is precisely a traditional reading of the divorce passages in the synoptic tradition and in 1 Corinthians 7, reinforced by Ephesians 5:21–33, that has kept open in Catholic teaching the possibility of dissolving marriages either not consummated or not sacraments, or neither. One may then suggest, from a Platonist point of view, that the indissolubility of real-life marriages is in them because of the necessary immutability of the ideal model, which has indissolubility as one of its traits. But this does not hold, because as a norm this model of marriage is used with a singular flexibility whereby Church authority executes or permits the dissolution of purportedly indissoluble marriages. It would not be accurate to call this an exact human analogue of divine voluntarism. Although canonical dissolution is called an exercise of the papal power of the keys to dispense inherently indissoluble marriages from their indissolubility, the warrant given for this is not the sovereignty of papal authority, but the limited indissolubility of a marriage either not a sacrament or not yet consummated. But the nominalism here is evident. The word "indissoluble" does not designate the nature of marriages in real life, but a juridical device in the mind of the authority.

The Refuge from Skepticism in Mysticism

A second consequence of philosophic skepticism's destroying the hope of knowing God by reasoned examination of evidence in the extramental world is that those who desire to know him then turn to religious intuition of him, to mysticism. Somewhat paradoxically the philosophic ground for the mysticism of the late fourteenth and fifteenth centuries had been prepared by the Augustinian-Platonist thinkers of the thirteenth, Bonaventure principal among them. His religious upbringing taught him that the world has been created as an image of and witness to the glory of God. Subhuman creatures do not know this, but human beings, having minds and loving wills, can know it and can bring all creation back to God by including them in their worship. The ultimate meaning of all human activity, of art, science and philosophy, is to image at the created level the divine knowledge and art. And the proper function of theology is to bring these human activities to this proper function. The goal of the sciences and philosophy is not to know things of nature themselves, but to find and know God through them.

Bonaventure held to Augustine's view of efficient causation in nature. Since in the moment of creation God created all things—things present and, in the *rationes seminales,* also things apparently future—all beings of nature develop from them by a set plan of divine providence, in the way that a rose develops from the bud. No new existence is produced by creature causation.

Truth too is God's preserve and his doing, because by definition it consists of affirmations that are necessary and unchangeable. It cannot be the yield of the contingent, changeable and impermanent human mind examining unnecessary, changeable and fleeting things. Affirmations about such things human beings can make by the natural light of intelligence. But this is not to attain truth. Truth is generated in human minds by God's illumining them and thus by their sharing his truth. If, as appears to be the case, this illumination is above human nature and undeserved, it is a grace. Therefore human beings have no natural certain knowledge even of their natures and the natures among which they live. Thus scientific knowledge itself is supernatural, and among its most effective instruments are prayer and contemplation. It follows too that what men and women deem the accomplishments of human effort and freedom should be attributed to their true source, who is God.

The history of such powerful visions of the universe as this shows that as they gather and expend their fullest energy, they both enhance authentic humanity and diminish it. This supernaturalism, or at least high pietism, led Catholicism in Europe back from the abyss to which nominalist skepticism was leading it. At the humble level of accomplishment it produced such groups as the Brethren of the Common Life, communities of men and women, simple of mind and heart, virtuous, devout, concerned for the poor. At the exalted level it produced the great mystics of the time between the crumbled medieval Church and the reformation, John Tauler, Jan Ruysbroek, Henry Suso.

An attitude that moves a person into contemplative and loving union with God and at the same time into working with compassion among the poor does enhance authentic humanity. This humanity is not locked within physical nature and cannot reach its completion there. For men and women to try to find it there is inauthentic. By fine paradox even the sensate dimension of human experience reveals the desire that reaches beyond sensate nature for fulfillment. So the mystics and the devout and caring Brethren did in their humility far more for human nature despite their not pondering it than did the philosophers and theologians of their age by their ceaseless speculation and dispute about it.

But this humility walks a narrow ledge. It can fall over into discouragement about human ability that comes near to despair. To confess that human inquiry can find little or nothing, and that what one needs to know is simple and can be provided by a loving God, does not enhance humanity but diminishes it. Let the reader consider whether a person is more fully human for agreeing with the following passage from *The*

Imitation of Christ, or less human. The *Imitation* is the arch-paradigm of the simple piety of the Lowlands in the middle of the fifteenth century. From there it spread around the Christian world, a masterpiece of its kind.

> All men naturally wish to have knowledge, but what does knowledge convey without the fear of God? The lowly rustic who serves God may do better than the proud philosopher who neglecting himself reflects on the course of the heavens. . . .
> Calm the excessive desire to know, for great distraction and delusion is found in that. The learned would gladly seem wise and be called so. Many things there are which when known do the soul little or no good.
> . . . The highest and most useful reading is this: genuine knowledge of and looking down on oneself.
> . . . Happy the one whom truth itself teaches, not by transient form and words but as self-revealed. Our opinion and our reason often fail us and seem so little. What use is great quibbling about hidden and unintelligible matters as to which we shall not be censured at the judgment because we were ignorant? It is a great folly that we reach out for the strange and the harmful while ignoring the good and necessary. Having eyes we see not: and why should we trouble about *genus* and *species?*
> He to whom the eternal word speaks is delivered from a multitude of conjectures. All things springs from the one word, and all utter the one, and this is the beginning which speaks also to us. No man understands or rightly decides without it.
> . . . Lowly understanding of self is a surer road to God than a profound seeking after knowledge. Science is not to be condemned, nor the simple knowing of anything which is considered good in itself, and divinely ordered: but a good conscience and a virtuous life are to be put first.[14]

Post-Medieval Humanism and Christian Marriage

The humanism that took root in certain segments of the European people beginning in the late fourteenth and early fifteenth centuries could not fail to have its effect on the common attitude toward marriage. Insofar as its main effect can be isolated and captured in one sentence, it was that those who thought and wrote about marriage tended to think and write about it as the married experience it rather than as celibate monks and friars imagine and think about it in its ideal model. But the humanist attitude comprehended vastly more than marriage. Therefore to understand how it affected attitudes toward and conduct in marriage it will help to review it in its comprehensiveness.

It affirmed the worthwhileness of life on earth. Without denying the reality of inherited original sin it discounted its significance. It affirmed and sought to enjoy the inherent goodness of the human person. It urged the spending of life not in preparation for death and the judgment beyond death, but in developing all the human capacities and enjoying their exercise—the capacities for artistic expression, for scientific learning and experimentation, for philosophizing, for soldiering, for governing, for rhetorical self-expression.

In some degree it must have been an equal and opposite reaction to the black death that carried off as much as one-third of Europe's population in the course of the fourteenth century. Sated with death the human spirit reasserted itself in a few energetic and adventuresome men to reaffirm life. We say "a few" because this humanism did not engage every segment of European society. The universities and their scholars mainly opposed it, and were in considerable degree the targets of humanist criticism. It throve first in academies such as that started up in Florence by Cosimo de Medici and led by Pico della Mirandola, and those in Rome, Venice and Naples. It moved into the palaces of the greater nobility and there found its wealthy patrons, the cardinals of the papal curia among the most enthusiastic. In central Europe it found favor especially among the newly affluent bourgeoisie, perhaps because as a social class they were the most obvious departure from and rebuff to medieval feudal society.

Because the humanist spirit took flesh most actively in men of letters such as Pico, Lorenzo Valla, John Colet, Thomas More and Erasmus, it is usual to identify humanism as a movement with the renaissance of classical literature and learning. The identification is in great measure accurate; the spirit helped to produce the renaissance while the renaissance channeled the spirit's energy and gave it a voice. Paradoxically the great men of the renaissance humanism broke with the immediate medieval past in order to create a different future order by going back into the distant past to recover the classical languages and literature—and there made their most damaging mistake by recovering Plato as their master.

But the long reach back to classical Greece and Rome brought humanism a trait that had the potential to affect Christian theology most thoroughly. This was a sense of history, of life as a developmental flow, a realization that things and institutions once thought unchangeable do change, that perceptions of experiences change—for example the experience of marriage—and that since the perception is part of the experience, the latter changes too. Since the humanist scholars were men of letters, they especially found out that the meanings of words and of formulas change, as do their uses. In short they found out that grammar and philology, not to mention history, anthropology and sociology, belong to the needed preparation for theology, along with philosophy.

This was a beginning break from the Augustinian assumption that all was created in the beginning according to the models in God's mind, and that life in time is the unfolding of what has been there from the beginning; that God's providential plan is a fixed scenario, and that persons' freedom, which is real, consists of decisions to live by that scenario or not. The humanists' study of history and of classical literature verified that men and women have truly innovated the shapes of their lives both privately and in society; that they have the freedom not merely to call social aberrations back to their pristine model, but to design society anew. More's *Utopia* is an example of this freedom. Compare it with Dionysius the Areopagite's *The Celestial Hierarchy* and *The Earthly Hierarchy* of the early sixth century and one sees what the humanists' appropriation of freedom to innovate means.

Where humanism could have most helped philosophy and theology was to repair the damage done by the exaggerated realism of the Platonic Augustinians in the universities and the reaction to it of Ockhamist nominalism. As we have seen, each worked in its own way to split human consciousness, to restrict contact with the physical world to the senses, and to lock intellect within itself to wrestle with ideas and propositions. Whether humanism could have healed this schism, given time and freedom, we cannot say. That it took Plato for its philosophic master hints that it may eventually have come to the same sundering of the mind against which it reacted.

The humanist attack on the scholastic philosophy and theology of the time had a special religious relevance. This attack was effective not for scientific reasons, since the humanists had neither a logic nor a physics to compete with those of the scholastics. But it was effective in the domain of value judgments. The scholastic theology was only minimally helpful to the people and even to the scholars themselves. It was too intricate; it tortured thought and language; it was alien to human nature, neglecting, as it did, sensate and emotional experience. Thomas More especially objected to traits of it that were its own technical virtue, its suppositional logic and other refinements that went far beyond Aristotle's humane and useful formal logic.

Erasmus and the Reform of Catholic Theology

The humanist reaction to the philosophy and theology of the medieval twilight, and the changes it sought to work in both, we find exemplified in Desiderius Erasmus, the scholar whose humanism has had the most lasting effect on Western Christianity.

In 1495, three years after his ordination to the priesthood as a canon of St. Augustine (in April of 1492), he went from his native Holland to Paris to take a degree in theology in the university, in the College of Montaigu. The scholastic theology he heard there earned his heartfelt disdain. In a letter to his erstwhile student, Thomas Grey, he satirized his experience of the Scotism dominant in the university. He likened himself to Epimenides, the Cretan philosopher of the seventh century B.C., who, according to legend, fell asleep as a lad in a cave and awoke fifty-seven years later to find that his soul, freed from the burden of the flesh, had studied philosophy and medicine and had made him a great scholar in the new world about him.

One day, out for a long walk, "making many discoveries about *instances* and *quiddities* and *formalities,* he was overcome with sleep." He slept for forty-seven years, dreaming all the while of the subtlest of subtleties. After this time he awoke and began to behave as if nothing had changed in the meantime. So also the Scotists. Then Erasmus continues:

"What if you saw Erasmus sit gaping among those blessed Scotists, while Gryllard is lecturing from his lofty chair? If you observed his contracted brow, his staring eyes, his anxious face, you would say he was another man. They assert that the mysteries of this science cannot be comprehended by one who has any commerce at all with the Muses or with the Graces. If you have touched good letters you must unlearn what you have learnt; if you have drunk of Helicon, you must get rid of the draught. I do my best to speak nothing in true Latin, nothing elegant or witty, and I seem to make some progress."[15]

Erasmus' complaint here against the abstract intricacies of the Paris Scotists is directed at their contempt for humane letters and for the elegant Latin of the literature he loved and had mastered. But his case against these "moderns" was aimed at more serious things than barbarous Latin. In his essay of 1518 on right method in doing theology, *Ratio verae theologiae,* he compared them disparagingly with the fathers of the Church.

. . . let him [the student] compare these ancient theologians, Origen, Basil, Chrysostom and Jerome, with these more recent ones. He will see a certain golden river flowing in the former, certain shallow streams echoing back, and these neither very pure nor flowing from their own source. The ancients thunder out oracles of eternal truth; in the moderns you have little fabrications of men whose examples vanish through insomnia the more closely you examine them. The ancients move you in a straight course toward the door of evangelical truth; the moderns struggle among the prolixity of human questions or smash into the Scylla of pontifical power or into the Syrtes of scholastic dogma or into the Symplegades of divine and human law, unless you prefer to make this Charybdis. The ancients, on the basis of the solid foundation of Scripture, raise a strong edifice into the heavens; the moderns, by the foolish arguments of men or even by flatteries not less foolish than monstrous, are raised to infinity by a huge superstructure. The ancient will satisfactorily carry you into the happiest gardens, in which you will be both delighted and satisfied; while the moderns will tear you to pieces and torment you among thorny hedges. The ancients have all the fullness of majesty, the moderns no splendor at all, saying many sordid things and few worthy of the dignity of theology, so that I abstain from a comparison of morals.[16]

The core of his complaint is that "the moderns" misuse or neglect the primary source of theology, the scriptures, and that their theologizing is constricted and falsified by the intricate but irrelevant disputes in the schools, by papal authority, by long-established law, and by the intransigence of the scholastics.

To assess accurately Erasmus' attack on the theology regnant in Paris at his time one must recall how faintly the philosophy and theology of Thomas Aquinas survived there. Erasmus knew of Aquinas and apparently read enough of him to make a careful distinction between him and the Scotists of the late fifteenth and the early sixteenth century. He admired Thomas and perhaps even exaggerated his estimation of his command of languages, since Thomas had learned little Greek, but depended on his protegé, William of Moerbecke, for reasonable command of this language. In his annotation on Paul's Letter to the Romans (Chapter 1, verse 5) Erasmus wrote:

It is remarkable to note how Thomas Aquinas agonizes over this passage, a man whose greatness has stood the test of time. For there is no recent theologian, at least in my opinion, who can outdo him in carefulness, in the sanity of his wisdom, and in the breadth of his learning; moreover he had a skill in language and had studied widely in literature, and he was worthy of such knowledge, for he skillfully put to use all the resources that were available to him in his day.[17]

Erasmus was too sincere a man, and too concerned, to settle for any self-indulgent brilliant criticism of the Scotist theologians. He meant every one of his harsh words against them. But when, fifteen or twenty years later, he had gained a mastery of Greek, had acquired some command of Hebrew, and had become aware of his influence throughout Europe as its master of classical literature, he also set out to work at the reform of theology in the Church. What this reform might have produced had the polemics of the reformation not intervened, one can only imagine.

The first step in his grand strategy for reform he borrowed from his experience with Latin literature. As a student among the Brethren of the Common Life and then in the Augustinian priory in Holland, he had conceived the desire to get back beyond the shrunken Latin of the schools to the classics at their source. To this purpose he dedicated about fifteen years to the search for manuscripts, to their translation and publishing. He soon enough came to see that to do the Latin classics he would have to go to their richest source, the Greek classics. He brought this idea over to his planned reform of theology. To do theology correctly is, first of all, to understand the scriptures accurately. But to do this one must go back, far beyond the Latin versions, as close to the Hebrew and Greek originals as possible.

He had a well-informed and severe judgment against the Latin versions used in the Church and in the schools of his time, with an especially severe eye cocked at Jerome's Vulgate. As early as 1440–1448 the humanist, Lorenzo Valla, had compared the Vulgate Latin New Testament with the Greek manuscripts in his *Annotationes in Novum Testamentum,* and had found in it errors and suspect translations. Erasmus found Valla's work in manuscript, still incomplete in 1448 when Pope Nicholas V appointed him apostolic secretary, and published it in 1505. It inspired him to do his own Latin version of the New Testament from the Greek texts and to publish it with commentary in 1516. To correct the Latin versions' flawed use of the scriptures he urged the following method and norms for their study.

First, the student must learn thoroughly the languages in which the scriptures were composed: Hebrew and Chaldaic (Aramaic) for the Hebrew scriptures, Greek for the Christian. Then he must read them in themselves, not in passages culled from their sources and used as proof-texts in scholastic theology, and not even in the homilies, exhortations and commentaries of the fathers.

Erasmus had a reply for those who claimed that the fathers had already interpreted the scripture sufficiently:

> First, I would prefer to see the original with my own eyes rather than through someone else's, and further, the ancient exegetes, granted that they have said a great deal, left much for later interpreters to explain. Is it not true that in order to understand their interpretations, at least an average knowledge of languages is required? And finally, when you come upon old texts in various languages that are corrupt (as indeed they are), what will you do?[18]

He went on to insist that the first sense of a passage that the student should labor to understand is the literal, according to the proper signification of words and phrases. To do this he must learn the history of the period about which he is reading, the literary devices common to its people, the social setting of the passage, the immediate concerns of the persons involved. He must resist the temptation to tangent off into more congenial and comfortable interpretations. Erasmus had once been especially insistent about this with John Colet during one of his sojourns in

England. The two of them had debated the cause of Jesus' agony in the garden of olives. Colet had insisted that Jesus agonized over the Jews and the guilt he knew they would incur for having murdered him. Erasmus argued that Jesus' agony was his human fear and revulsion in face of the torture and death he knew awaited him; that the passage (Lk 22:39–46) offered no evidence to support Colet's interpretation; that its literal sense supported only his own.

But while insisting that the first object of study is the literal sense of a biblical passage he claimed two other facts about the scriptures as a whole. Their over-arching sense is the tropologic, the intent to bring human beings to conversion. All the other senses—the literal, the allegoric, the anagogic (that which leads the reader into a mystical experience of the divine)—are at the service of the tropologic. The second fact is that the allegoric sense abounds in the Scriptures. He went through a period of devotion to allegoric interpretation, admiring its use by Ambrose, Jerome, Augustine and especially Origen. A reason for this was allegory's offer of resolution of passages wherein the literal sense is unacceptable because absurd, for example, in the sequence of creation of the universe according to Genesis 1. There light is created on the first day, but the sun and the moon, the sources of light, not until the fourth day. But interpretation according to allegoric sense had for Erasmus only a functional significance. He understood biblical allegory in a way both more restrictive and more inclusive than the forthright allegorizing of entire passages and books, such as Bede once did to the Song of Solomon. For him allegory was fundamentally any creaturely image used to express an otherwise inexpressible divine reality. The anthropomorphism of God's suppressing his wrath and changing his mind about punishing his people is allegory. The same is true of Jesus' promise, in John 2:19, that in three days he would raise up a temple. Erasmus claimed that Jesus' disciples knew he was referring (allegorically) to his body.

A final point about Erasmus' appreciation of the fathers of the early centuries will make even clearer how he prepared minds for the reformation. An added reason for his preferring the fathers to the scholastics was the heterodoxy of the former. He met criticism for helping to revive the study of the fathers, especially of Origen. It was urged upon him that their orthodoxy was not as firm as that of the scholastics, who taught only the faith of the Church. His reply was that a reason for their disagreement one with another is that there are many human versions of eternal truth. He insisted on this point as part of his strategy for the reform of theology, to pry minds loose from too easily and superficially taken dogmatic positions. The strain of pietism in him revealed itself in his remark in the *Vera ratio theologiae*, "Dogma certainly does not seem to me at all necessary for piety."[19]

The humanist scholars' main contribution to the coming Protestant reformation is evident there in Erasmus' attitude and advice. Whether it was on this advice that Luther acted or not, he took Erasmus' functional norm—"Go back past the theologians and the councils, back even past the fathers"—and made it into a norm of Christian faith, "Draw from the scriptures alone." Implicit in the humanist norm was a second contribution to the Protestant reformation, a spirit of critical challenge, an urgency to reexamine points of doctrine and find out how valid they are as interpretations of the scriptures or as conclusions drawn from them. An example of the latter offered by Erasmus himself involves the traditional interpretation of Paul's instruction in 1 Corinthians 7 regarding the permissibility of divorce for Christian spouses.

In his *Annotationes in Novum Testamentum* of 1515 Erasmus devoted twelve quarto pages to his study of the key divorce passage, verses 10 to 16. He said first of all that he intended no definitive judgment, although he felt justified in examining Paul's instruction anew. He questioned whether the words of Jesus that Paul passed on to his readers are really a command binding consciences. He suggested that these words no more than counsel an ideal that Christians should strive to realize in their marriages. He pointed to several practices in the Church that assumed to be counsel words of Jesus recorded in the gospels as commands. Apparently, Erasmus suggested, Paul understood Jesus' words as no more than counsel in his (Paul's) allowing "separation"—true divorce—to a Christian convert whose pagan spouse refused to live in peace. He pointed out the following instances of the Church's reducing to counsel words of Jesus that are read in the gospels as commands—and drew a conclusion from this.

> Because of the human weakness that the Church has in so many of her members no one is forbidden to defend his rights under the law; no one is forbidden to take oaths provided he does so seriously and does not perjure himself; no one is forced to be obligated to those who cannot be trusted. So why do we make of everyone and anyone this one demand in regard to divorce? If, because of their hardheartedness, the Jews were permitted to dismiss their wives for any cause lest they turn to more serious faults; and we see among Christian spouses crimes that go far beyond continual feuding—crimes such as murder, poisoning and the laying on of curses—if their ills are the same, why may we not use the same remedy? . . . When Christ recalled his followers to the original innocence of marriage he did not want divorce because he did not want hardness of heart. Yet Paul indulges human weakness by mitigating the command of the Lord in so many places. Why could not the Roman pontiff do the same?[20]

In his *Paraphrasis Novi Testamenti* (1517–1524) Erasmus apparently took a definitive stand on the effect of adultery on a marriage. He was of the opinion that the act of adultery itself dissolves a marriage.

When the faculty of theology at Paris, led by Noel Beda, issued a formal condemnation of a series of propositions drawn from the *Paraphrasis* and others of Erasmus' writings, the latter explained that he did not mean that with the act of adultery the bond of marriage is severed. He meant only that the guilty spouse has forfeited all claim to the rights of a husband or wife, even all claim to be regarded as such.

He added that while he considered it his prerogative to state the arguments favoring the conclusion that adultery dissolves a marriage, yet, since the meaning of the pertinent New Testament passages is not unambiguously clear, he was willing to submit to the authority of the Church in the matter. On just this point Luther was to take an opposite path. Because the instructions in the divorce passages were to him too not clear, he protested and finally rebelled against the Catholic authorities' coming down on a fixed and irreformable interpretation of them.

On the question of marriage's sacramentality Erasmus unleashed both his critical mind and his adventuring imagination. Taking his cue from the traditional marital analogy of the Church as bride of Christ, he moved on, in his *Christiani matrimonii institutio,* to a forthright allegoric interpretation of Jesus' conception.

> I think it would be no irreverent use of imagination to see, in this mystery, God the father as the bridegroom, the most holy Virgin as the bride, the angel as the paranymph, the Holy Spirit as the agent of conception, and the God-man as the one conceived.[21]

A theologian faithful to the Western Catholic tradition could not object seriously to this play of allegorical imagination, much as he might suspect that in it Erasmus' irrepressible irony may have been hinting at the extravagant possibilities of analogic constructions when used to interpret the scriptures.

But in his commentary on Ephesians 5:21–33 Erasmus returned to the same unambiguous criticism of Catholic teaching he had used in his *Paraphrasis in Novum Testamentum* when discussing the permissibility of divorce. Here in his commentary he got at the question of the sacrament in marriage. He pointed out the variations in Catholic teaching in the matter, that the fathers had never considered marriage one of the seven sacraments of the Church. He acknowledged that marriage is good and even sacred, but suggested that even some thing or person or event that is clearly not holy can be a type, or image, of a sacred reality—a *sacrae rei signum.* He cited as examples of these King David's taking Bathsheba from Uriah and to himself as wife, the prophet Hosea's marrying the prostitute, Gomer, and the story of Samson and Delilah.[22]

But he acknowledged that in the Catholic debate the opinion of the scholastics has gained status as the more probable: "But the judgment of some recent theologians has won out as the more probable, that in marriage rightly entered, as in the other sacraments, a special grace of the Holy Spirit is infused, by which the spouses are at one and the same time strengthened for maintaining lasting peace, strengthened too for bearing the burdens of this life, and made wiser for nurturing their children in good morals."[23]

Erasmus' intent here was the humanist enterprise brought to exact focus on marriage, namely to free the working model of it from the theologians and lawyers, and to enrich this model from multiple human sources—from classical literature, from the experience of the married, and from his own imagination.

The Changed Public Image of Marriage

The same European climate that helped to produce the scholarly humanists helped also to produce a new public comment on marriage. Perhaps it was the emerging mercantile middle class speaking with unprecedented freedom in its new position between the mute acquiescence of the feudal vassals at the lower end of a crumbling social hierarchy and the nobility at its upper end. Whatever the cause and the energy, the two older forms of European Catholic self-awareness about marriage now had to make way for a third. The medieval romances, such as Troilus and Cresyde, The Romance of the Rose, and Tristan and Isolde, had mirrored back to the nobility their dreams of the freely chosen lovers and sexual excitement their arranged marriages rarely allowed them. These romances had in an ironic way reinforced what centuries of fathers and theologians had taught about marriage, that wives are for children but not for sexual pleasure. But the troubadours went the next step and suggested that sexual pleasure—which will not be denied in any case—is what lovers and mistresses are for. The canonists and theologians on their part had devised a model of marriage that served the needs of Church and civil society by supplying children and providing a legitimate outlet for concupiscence.

But now the spokesmen for the new middle class offered a picture of marriage that was minimally a model and mainly a description of married life as the married experience it. A superb example of such a description is in Chaucer's prologue to the Wife of Bath's tale in his *Canterbury Tales*. Dame Alison, who like the Samaritan woman at the well of Shechem had been married five times, set out a shrewd, earthy and erudite analysis and appraisal of marriage that was of course Chaucer's own. A modern student can trace in it a précis of the major canonical and theological debates about marriage in the late fourteenth century. Chaucer's sojourns in France and in Italy would have brought him a far-reaching appreciation of the juridical vicissitudes of marriage at the same time he was learning Boccaccio's and Petrarch's language and reading their stories and their poems.

Chaucer's assessment of marriage through the mouth of Alison of

Bath is optimistic, and afterward in the Franklin's tale even exalted. But such was not the mood of all the commentators on marriage contemporary with him and after him. Some of these made wives the especial targets of their negative criticism. In 1513 Erasmus himself edited one of the milder attacks of a century earlier, Francesco Barbaro's *De re uxoria* (On Marriage Matters). In 1472 the German Albrecht von Eyb wrote his *Ob einem Mann sey zu nemen ein eheliches Weib* (Whether a Man Ought To Take a Wife). Again in 1513 the French jurist Turaqueau published his notoriously anti-feminist *De legibus connubialibus* (On Marital Laws). Jean Nezivan came to wives' defense in 1521 with his *Sylvae nuptialis libri sex* (Six Books on the Nuptial Forest). And in 1526 Amaury Bouchard did the same in his *L'Institution due mariage chrétien*.

All these tractates were partisan on one side or the other of a serious controversy about marriage. The question was about the goodness of marriage, the availability of happiness in it, whether it is possible for a man and a woman to live peacefully in prolonged intimacy—and who is most to blame for the endless failures at the attempt. The controversy occupied humanist writers mainly during the second quarter of the sixteenth century. Among them the devil's advocate par excellence was Francois Rabelais, in Book 3 of his *Pantagruel* (1533). Its defenders were the anonymous author of *La Parfaite Amye* (The Perfect Friend—feminine), and Cornelius Agrippa, who published in 1529 his Latin treatise, *De nobilitate et excellentia sexus feminei, de ejus praeeminentia supra alium sexum, et de sacramento matrimonii* (On the Nobility and Excellence of the Feminine Sex, on Its Superiority Over the Other Sex, and on The Sacrament of Marriage). Although a treatise ostensibly on the sacrament of marriage, it said nothing about grace; it allowed dissolution of marriage on the ground of adultery; it drew nothing from the scholastic tradition about marriage.

This last-named trait typified what I have already called the humanist enterprise as applied to marriage. This was to examine marriage as a human experience, setting aside assumptions about it drawn from the fathers, from Church legislation and from the scholastic theologians. Without doubt it called into question the structure of marriage conventional at the time, the lingering miniature of the feudal society that had passed away, in which the husband was lord and the wife his vassal.

There is no small irony in this humanist awakening's contribution to the Protestant reformation. By opening minds and arousing critical judgment on the past and its doctrinally fixed model, it helped to prepare for the reformers' reconsideration of Christian marriage. But one of the rules of the humanist awakening was redesign of the future by recovery of the past and its uncorrupted models of life. Since they were religious men, the past to which the reformers returned in order to recover truly Christian marriage was not that of the Greek and Roman classics, but the New Testament. They returned especially to St. Paul in his instruction to the Corinthians, to the Ephesians and to Timothy. These instructions in the hands of German, French and Swiss males put an early end to such budding feminism as Cornelius Agrippa's.

Disagreement Among the Catholic Authorities

The debilitated theology in the universities by itself left the Catholic authorities poorly prepared to meet the Protestant challenge to the received doctrine and discipline of marriage. But weakening the Catholic defense even further was the disagreement among orthodox Catholic theologians and jurists about certain matters of consequence. The most persistent dissent from the majority came from the Spanish Dominican, Melchior Cano (1509–1560). He attended the Council of Trent during 1551 and 1552 as theologian to Emperor Charles V. His *De locis theologicis* was published posthumously in 1563, the year during which the council dealt finally with marriage. Book 8, Chapter 5 of *De locis* is Cano's treatise on marriage.

The pivot of his disagreement was his insistence that a marriage of two Christians can be a sacrament only if it is created by mutual consent expressed in a verbal formula determined by the Church, and only if it is consecrated by a true minister of the Church. He denied that the spouses themselves can be such ministers. His demand for a determinate verbal formula of consent was a derivative of his assumption that each of the Church's sacraments must have such a formula. He added that because in different territories different formulas of consent are used, it cannot be that in every territory the Christian marriages contracted there are sacraments.

In his judgment the simple verbal consent accepted at the time as sufficient for creating a marriage—such as "I accept you as my husband/ wife"—is sufficient for creating only the contract. For such words can be pronounced even by a pagan, who is incapable of the Christian sacrament. With this it is evident that he held to the separability of contract and sacrament in marriage. He added as evidence of their separability that the Church had for centuries accepted the validity of marriages by proxy as well as of clandestine marriages, in neither of which was a sacramental formula pronounced over the bride and groom nor was a blessing bestowed on them by a priest. Furthermore, the Church has never held that in pronouncing marital consent an excommunicated Catholic or one in mortal sin commits sacrilege—which he or she would commit if every marriage of two Christians were a sacrament.

In summary, for Cano, the creating of a sacrament must find three elements functioning simultaneously. These are its matter, its form and its minister. The parties' consent is only the matter of the sacrament, but not its form. And it is the matter only if made in the Church's specified verbal formula. The priest is the minister of the sacrament; his declaration of the marriage and his blessing of the spouses are its form. Here too Cano clearly assumed the separability of the contract and the sacrament.[24]

He was not alone in this opinion. Cardinal Cajetan denied that a marriage contracted by proxies in the absence of the bride and groom is a sacrament. He allowed that it is no more than a civil contract. He insisted that the bride's and groom's vicarious participation through proxies is insufficient for their gaining grace, one of the essentials of sacramentality. And he thought it absurd to say that the absent spouses, perhaps asleep at the moment their proxies exchanged consent for them, could gain the grace of the sacrament.[25]

Domingo de Soto did not reject Cajetan's and Cano's opinion out of hand, but held as more probable that every marriage contracted by two Christians, even if by proxy, is a sacrament. He reasoned to this by a kind of forcing logic: The divine institution of the sacrament was simply an inclusive act. It made Christian marriage taken universally to be a sacrament, regardless of the way in which individual marriages are created. As for Cajetan's objection just above, he pointed out that even a sleeping infant can receive the grace of baptism, as can an adult imbecile.[26]

Estius sided with Cajetan, pointing out that in the twelfth century Pope Alexander III, in his canon *Cum ecclesia,* had called the priest's blessing the sacrament in marriage, and that Pope Nicholas V had done the same at the Council of Constance. He asked how simpleminded and ignorant spouses can be ministers of a sacrament about which they understand nothing and when they are ignorant of the Church's intent in conferring it.[27]

Catharinus held that the priest is minister of the sacrament; Maldonatus held that the priest is the ordinary minister, but that the spouses are extraordinary ministers. Etienne de Poncher, archbishop of Paris, reasoned that the priest cannot be the minister of the sacrament because he does not join its matter and form. Its form is the spouses' words or signs of consent. It is not the priest's blessing nor his words, "I join you in marriage." The latter are only a declaration that the spouses have created their marriage. The Church had acknowledged for centuries that without these words spouses had created their marriages clandestinely. The priest has three functions in a marriage: to hear the words of consent; to declare the joining of the spouses; to bless them in their newly created marriage.[28]

There was concomitant disagreement about the matter and form of the sacrament. For Soto, Bartolomeo de Ledesma and Covarrubias the spouses' persons are the matter, their words of consent its form. For others the spouses' consent as an act of will is the matter, the words in which they express this consent its form. The more common opinion, proposed by Bellarmine, Pedro de Ledesma, Sanchez and Suarez, was that the matter is the words of consent insofar as determinable, i.e. as expressing each spouse's giving his or her marital rights over to the other. The form is the same words as determining, as each spouse's accepting the other's giving over of these rights.

The Protestant Challenge to the Catholic Theology of Marriage

This mélange of opinions includes those theologians and canonists writing before the Protestant challenge, during it and the Council of Trent, and afterward. It is offered as evidence of the shaky Catholic readiness to take on this challenge, and of the indecisive reaction to it in what seem at first glance to be secondary issues in the theology of marriage. Even at the time they were regarded as secondary, over against four grievously felt and argued matters: whether marriage in the new law has been instituted by Christ as a sacrament (over against most Protestants); granted it is a sacrament in some sense, whether it is so in the true and proper sense of the word, i.e. as a grace-giving sign (against all Protestants); whether the Catholic authorities rightly hold jurisdiction over the marriages of all Christians (against the Protestants and some Catholics); whether the Church's authorities can make clandestine attempts at marriage null and void (disputed among the Catholics themselves). In the presence of these painful concerns disproportionately small worry was left over for the consequences of allowing that perhaps the priestly declaration and blessing create the sacrament. For if these words do create it, and since the Church had for centuries allowed that men and women themselves certainly create the contract, it follows that contract and sacrament are essentially separable. Since they are, what warrant has the Church for claiming exclusive juridical and judicial control of the contract? This question, lost and forgotten among the major matters of the Protestant challenge, was to bide its time for its own grievous challenge a century later.

As hinted above, this apparently peripheral issue was not the front on which the reformers mounted their attack. That the Catholics there presented no unified defense reinforced their judgment that the entire Catholic case for the sacrament in marriage was flawed. Yet the immediate target of at least Luther's attack on the Catholic doctrine and discipline of marriage was not the Church's theology of the sacrament. As we shall see in a moment he did deny that marriage is among the sacraments known from the New Testament to have been instituted by Christ. But this was apparently a change of mind even after his initial challenge to the Catholic teaching. For his declarations taken at face value in his Sermon on the State of Marriage delivered in May 1519, affirm the traditional substance of the Catholic teaching on Christian marriage's sacramentality. Then about fourteen months later, in his Prelude to the Babylonian Captivity of the Church, he had changed his mind on the subject.

The title of the Prelude suggests the exact object of his angry challenge. It was the popes' and the Catholic prelates' and jurists' taking the marriages of their Catholic people into "captivity." The philosophic ground of Luther's complaint was that marriage, even among Christians, is a natural institution, a thing of this world. It was created thus by God. Therefore it does not come under ecclesiastical jurisdiction but belongs under that of civil rulers. He therefore denied the sacrament partly in order to take away a major Catholic warrant for ecclesiastical jurisdiction over marriages.

His assessment of marriage as an institution in history was faithfully Augustinian except on one fine but significant point. He held that it was instituted by God with the first couple in the garden of Eden (whose story in Genesis he took for granted to be a factual account). But marriage's original goodness and innocence have been damaged by sinful concupiscence. This is one of the effects of the first couple's disobedience in the garden. The infestation of concupiscence in sexual intercourse is inescapable. But here is the point at which Luther differed from Augustine. The latter said that concupiscence's mere presence in sexual intercourse within marriage is not imputed as guilty and punishable sin (as *reatus*) provided a person does not capitulate to it and let it rule conduct. It is there only as a punishment (*supplicium*). But Luther said it is there as guilty sin. However just because its presence is inevitable and it is beyond the control of temperate will, it is not punishable but is excused by the mercy of Christ.

Luther's accounting for the original excellence of the first couple uses the image theology of the Augustinian Platonism in which he was nurtured. The same accounting also assumes the inferiority by nature of the woman, even though she is an integral part of the imaging in question.

And God created man according to his image, according to the image of God He created him.

Here Moses does not employ the word "similitude" but only "image". Perhaps he wanted to avoid an ambiguity of speech and for this reason repeated the noun "image". I see no other reason for the repetition unless we should understand it for the sake of emphasis as an indication of the Creator's rejoicing so that Moses intends to indicate that God was not so delighted at the other creatures as at man, whom he had created according to his own similitude. The rest of the animals are designated as footprints of God; but man alone is God's image.[29]

Male and female he created them.

In order not to give the impression that He was excluding the woman from all the glory of the future life, Moses includes each of the two sexes; for the woman appears to be a somewhat different being from the man, having different members and a much weaker nature. Although Eve was a most extraordinary creature—similar to Adam so far as the image of God is concerned, that is, in justice, wisdom and happiness—she was nevertheless a woman. For as the sun is more excellent than the moon (although the moon, too, is a very excellent body), so the woman, although she was a most beautiful work of God, nevertheless was not the equal of the male in glory and prestige.[30]

Luther regarded the creation poem in Genesis 1 as an introduction, as a kind of anticipatory sketch of what Moses was to elaborate more fully in the garden parable of Genesis 2 and 3. In the latter he takes up the verse, "The Lord God said, 'It is not good that man is alone; I shall make him a helpmate which shall be before him.' " Luther thereupon seems to forget what he had just written about the woman's natural inferiority.

Now also the household is set up. For God makes a husband of lonely Adam and joins him to a wife, who was needed to bring about the increase of the human race. Just as Adam was created in accordance with a well-considered counsel, so here, too, we perceive that Eve is being created according to a definite plan. Thus here once more Moses points out that man is a unique creature and that he is suited to be a partaker of divinity and immortality. . . .
But Moses wanted to point out in a special way that the other part of humanity, the woman, was created by a unique counsel of God in order to show that this sex too is suited for the kind of life which Adam was expecting and that this sex was to be useful for procreation. Hence it follows that if the woman had not been deceived by the serpent and had not sinned, she would have been the equal of Adam in all respects. For the punishment, that she is now subjected to the man, was imposed on her after sin and because of sin. . . . Therefore Eve was not like the woman of today; her state was far better and more excellent, and she was in no respect inferior to Adam, whether you count the qualities of the body or those of the mind.[31]

Luther's estimation of the role that inherited original sin has had in marriage came down undiluted from the early Christian fathers and from his medieval forebears.

Today, after our nature has been corrupted by sin, woman is needed not only to secure increase but also for companionship and for protection. The management of the household must have the ministration of the dear ladies. In addition—and this is lamentable—woman is also necessary as an antidote against sin. And so, in the case of the woman, we must think not only of managing of the household which she does, but also of the medicine which she is. In this respect Paul says (in 1 Cor. 7:2): "Because of fornication let each one have his own wife."[32]

And yet, in the presence of this antidote and in so wretched a state, the Lord fulfills his blessing; and people are begotten, although in sin and with sin. This would not have been the case in Paradise. The act of begetting would have been a most sacred one without any passion of lust such as there is now. . . .

. . . If Adam had persisted in the state of innocence, this intimate relationship of husband and wife would have been most delightful. The very work of procreation also would have been most sacred and would have been held in esteem. There would not have been that shame stemming from sin which there is now, when parents are compelled to hide in darkness to do this. . . .

Therefore was this fall not a terrible thing? For truly in all nature there was no activity more excellent and more admirable than procreation. . . . Although this activity, like the other wretched remnants of the first state, continues in nature until now, how horribly marred it has become! In honor husband and wife are joined in public before the congregation; but when they are alone, they come together with a feeling of the utmost shame. I am not (sic) speaking now about the hideousness inherent in our flesh, namely, the bestial desire and lust. All these are clear indications of original sin.[33]

I include these passages to point up a curious convergence of Luther's thinking with that of the medieval scholastics, whom he despised, at the same time that it diverged from theirs. In confessing emphatically the damage done to sexuality by inherited original sin, he named just the reason spouses need God's grace, albeit medicinal grace, as many scholastics called it. Luther acknowledged this need implicitly after admitting too that marriage was originally a divinely commissioned duty to procreate, and that both man and wife are images of the creator—although he here stopped short of saying that their union is an image of anything divine. But we will see his evidence for denying the sacrament in Christian marriage, drawn also from the scriptures, but rooted in his principle of *sola Scriptura,* that Christian doctrine is to be drawn only from what is explicit in the scriptures. He found no mention in them of marriage as a sacred sign installed by Christ in the Church.

In his commentary on 1 Corinthians 7 Luther pointed out a source of goodness and holiness in marriage different from its divine institution.[34] This is a source that produces its effect after the fact of human sin and misery. It also produces its effect contingently, depending on the faith and trust of the Christian spouses. The setting for the explanation of this source is Luther's attack on the centuries-old Catholic teaching that the life of consecrated virginity is inherently superior in holiness to that of marriage. This teaching had drawn on Paul's words in 1 Corinthians 7 which counsel marriage because of human weakness and the danger of sinning sexually (verses 2, 6, 9), and those words which prefer the unmarried state (verses 7, 8, 26, 28b, 32–35). Luther quite adroitly turned Paul's reasoning in the last of these one hundred and eighty degrees about—Paul's counsel, apparently drawn from life, that the cares of married life take husbands and wives away from the things of God. Luther insisted that, on the contrary, precisely these cares can drive spouses to God for help, can confirm them in faith and trust. He insisted, also on the contrary, that it is their being spared life's worries in the security of monastic life that keeps monks and nuns from turning to God in the same faith and trust. As vicar to the provincial superior of the Augustinians in Meissen and Thuringia—he who had to pay the bills— he may well have known personally whereof he spoke.

> . . . Now if any order is to be termed a religious one, then something more and different must be in it than such outward doings and life, namely, the faith of the heart, which is spirit and makes everything in man religious, both inwardly and outwardly.
>
> Now consider the religious orders so famous up to our time. The first thing you notice is that they are most securely provided with all the necessities of the body. A guaranteed income, food, clothing, shelter, and all sorts of other things they have in superfluity, earned by the work and care of others and given to them, so that they are not endangered in any way nor wish to be. Furthermore, no one enters the religious orders or wants to enter, unless he is assured that he will receive lifelong care for his body; and the majority in the monastic and clerical orders are on the lookout that their stomachs and bodies get their due.
>
> What else is this but to seek and have a position where one need not look to heaven and expect his daily bread from God or trust that God will provide? In short, in such estates faith has no place. . . .
>
> But if you take a wife and are married, this is the first shock: How are you going to support yourself, your wife, and child? And this will go on for your whole life. Therefore the state of marriage is by nature of a kind to teach and compel us to trust in God's hand and grace, and in the same way to force us to believe. For we can see that where there is no faith in marriage, there it is a most miserable institution, full of worry, fear and hard work. On the other hand, the less faith these famous religious orders have, the better they get along, for their stomachs are filled gratis, and they need not look to God's hand nor await his goodness.[35]

Consider this, then, as the first point, that marriage by nature is of such a kind that it drives, impels, and forces men to
the most inward, highest spiritual state, to faith. . . .[36]

Luther's talent for juxtaposing the earthy and the exquisite in his
reflections on marriage appears again in his sermons of 1532 on The
Sermon on the Mount.[37] Commenting on Jesus' judgment, in Matthew
5:27–30, on (married) men's gazing with lust at women other than their
wives, he pointed out that one of the utilities of a spouse is that he or she
makes such gazing redundant, since marriage provides the legitimate
outlet for the lust that inspires the gazing.

. . . Hence He [Jesus] says clearly, as we have heard: 'If you
look at a woman lustfully, you have committed adultery with
her in your heart.' He does not forbid looking at her; for He is
talking to people who have to live in human society in the
world, as the preaching in this chapter, both before and after,
amply demonstrates. But He does want us to distinguish between looking and lusting. You may look at any woman or
man, only be sure that you do not lust. That is why God ordained for every person to have his own wife or husband, to
control and channel his lust and his appetites.[38]

Shortly thereafter in the same passage comes the exquisite part,
with its evidence that Luther could abstract the ideal from the reality as
well as any scholastic monk or friar in order to make his case.

As I have pointed out in my other discussions of marriage and
married life, it would be a real art and a very strong safeguard
against all this if everyone learned to look at his spouse correctly, according to God's Word, which is the dearest treasure
and the loveliest ornament you can find in a man or a woman.
If he mirrored himself in this, then he would hold his wife in
love and honor as a divine gift and treasure. And if he saw
another woman, even one more beautiful than his own wife, he
would say: "Is she beautiful? As far as I am concerned, she is
not very beautiful. And even if she were the most beautiful
woman in the world, in my wife at home I have a lovelier
ornament, one that God has given me and has adorned with
His Word beyond the others, even though she may not have a
beautiful body or may have other failings. Though I may look
over all the women in the world, I cannot find any about whom
I can boast with a joyful conscience as I can about mine: 'This
is the one whom God has granted to me and put into my arms.'
I know that He and all the angels are heartily pleased if I cling
to her lovingly and faithfully. Then why should I despise this

precious gift of God and take up with someone else, where I can find no such treasure or adornment?"[39]

Ten years earlier than this sermon, in 1522, before he had learned to look at marriage through the eyes of a veteran husband, Luther had been even more lyric in his praise of it. In his revised Sermon on the State of Marriage (a revision and expansion of the original sermon of September 1519) he described married love and praised it as much as marriage itself. But while doing so he persisted in the caution that he had learned in his scholastic education but had not yet learned from his own experience. And amazingly he acknowledged that marriage among Christians is a sacrament, after having ridiculed this Catholic teaching in his Prelude to the Babylonian Captivity of the Church two years earlier, in the summer of 1520.

A woman is created to be a companionable helpmeet to the man in everything, particularly to bear children. And that still holds good, except that since the fall marriage has been adulterated with wicked lust. And now [after the fall] the desire of the man for the woman, and vice versa, is sought after not only for companionship and children, for which purpose alone marriage was instituted, but also for the pursuance of wicked lust, which is almost as strong a motive.[40]

Having just said that marriage's only purposes are children and companionship, he goes on to describe a love found in marriage that would be the glad claim of a medieval troubador, a renaissance sonnetist or a modern personalist.

God makes distinction between the different kinds of love, and shows that the love of a man and woman is (or should be) the greatest and purest of all loves. For he says, "A man shall leave father and mother and cleave to his wife" [Gen. 2:24], and the wife does the same, as we see happening around us every day. Now there are three kinds of love: false love, natural love, and married love. False love is that which seeks its own, as a man loves money, possessions, honor, and women taken outside of marriage and against God's command. Natural love is that between father and child, brother and sister, friend and relative, and similar relationships. But over and above all these is married love, that is, a bride's love, which glows like a fire and desires nothing but the husband. She says, "It is you I want, not what is yours: I want neither your silver nor your gold; I want neither. I want only you. I want you in your entirety or not at all." All other kinds of love seek something other than the beloved one: this kind of love wants only to have the beloved's own self completely. If Adam had not fallen, the love of bride and groom would have been the loveliest thing. Now this love is not pure either, for admittedly a married partner desires to have the other, yet each seeks to satisfy his desire with the other, and it is this desire which corrupts this kind of love. Therefore the married state is now no longer pure and free from sin. The temptation of the flesh has become so strong and consuming that marriage may be likened to a hospital for incurables which prevents inmates from falling into graver sin.[41]

It is perhaps this nearly blind fidelity to the Augustinian interpretation of both the nature and the real-life situation of marriage that lured Luther into acknowledging that marriage among Christians is one of the sacraments, and, even more than that, into explaining the sacrament in terms of the image offered in Ephesians 5:32, although he held that the sacred reality imaged there is the union of divine and human natures in Christ.

Thus the doctors have found three good and useful things about the married estate, by means of which the sin of lust, which flows beneath the surface, is counteracted and ceases to be a cause of damnation.

First, [the doctors say] that it is a sacrament. A sacrament is a sacred sign of something spiritual, holy, heavenly, and eternal, just as the water of baptism, when the priest pours it over the child, means that the holy, divine, eternal grace is poured into the soul and body of the child at the same time, and cleanses him from original sin. . . . In the same way, the estate of marriage is a sacrament. It is an outward and spiritual sign of the greatest, holiest, worthiest, and noblest thing that has existed or ever will exist: the union of the divine and human natures in Christ. The holy apostle Paul says that as man and wife united in the state of matrimony are two in one flesh, so God and man are united in the one person Christ, and so Christ and Christendom are one body. It is indeed a wonderful sacrament, as Paul says [Eph. 5:32], that the estate of marriage truly signifies such a great reality.[42]

How Luther could have written this, only a year after he had set out the reasonably careful arguments against the sacrament that we shall now see in his Prelude, can be understood only in the light of his impetuous mind's addressing every arguable issue during a harassed and busy life. It is no wonder that Philip Melancthon rather than Luther is acknowledged as the careful theologian of the first Lutheran generation.

First there is his unambiguous counter-thesis: "Not only is marriage regarded as a sacrament without the least warrant of Scripture, but the very ordinances which extol it as a sacrament have turned it into a farce. Let us look at this a little."[43]

The first sub-thesis is that the scriptures are empty of evidence for the essentials of a Christian sacrament as the scholastics understood these: Christ's institution of a sign of grace, his word of grace without which the sign would be inefficacious, the conferring of grace.

> We have said that in every sacrament there is a word of divine promise, to be believed by whoever receives the sign, and that the sign alone cannot be the sacrament [here is the Scotist argument that the sacrament of marriage must have for its *forma* a specific verbal formula]. Nowhere do we read that the man who marries a wife receives any grace of God. There is not even a divinely instituted sign in marriage, nor do we read anywhere that marriage was instituted by God to be a sign of anything.[44]

Secondly, marriage has existed from the beginning of creation, before the new law and its sacraments. Moreover it was just as holy among the Hebrew prophets and saints as it is now. So if marriage were a sacrament, why would it be a sacrament of the new law?

> Furthermore, since marriage has existed since the beginning of the world and is still found among unbelievers, there is no reason why it should be called a sacrament of the New Law and of the church alone. The marriages of the ancients were no less sacred than ours, nor are those of unbelievers less true marriages than those of believers, and yet they are not regarded as sacraments.[45]

But the most detailed challenge is aimed at the common Catholic interpretation at that time of Ephesians 5:32. Luther said then of the passage's meaning what a majority of Christian scholars say now.

> But they will say, "The Apostle says in Eph. 5 [31–32], 'The two shall become one. This is a great sacrament.' Surely you are not going to contradict so plain a statement of the Apostle!" I reply: This argument like the others betrays great shallowness and a careless and thoughtless reading of Scripture. Nowhere in all of the Holy Scriptures is this word *sacramentum* employed in the sense in which we use the term; it has an entirely different meaning. For wherever it occurs it denotes not the sign of a sacred thing, but the secret, hidden thing itself. Thus Paul writes in I Cor. 4 [:1]: "This is how one should regard us, as servants of Christ and stewards of the 'mysteries' of God," that is, the sacra-

ments. For where we have [in the Vulgate] the word *sacramentum* the Greek original has *mystérion,* which the translator sometimes translates and sometimes retains in its Greek form. Thus our verse in the Greek reads: "They two shall become one. This is a great mystery." This explains how they came to understand a sacrament of the New Law here, a thing they would never have done if they had read *mystérium,* as it is in the Greek.[46]

. . . Therefore, a sacrament is a mystery, a secret thing, which is set forth in words, but received by the faith of the heart. Such a sacrament is spoken of in the passage before us: "The two shall become one. This is a great sacrament" [Eph. 5:31–32], which they understood as spoken of marriage, whereas Paul himself wrote these words as applying to Christ and the church, and clearly explained them himself by saying: "I take it to mean Christ and the church" [Eph. 5:32].[47]

Christ and the church are, therefore, a mystery, that is, a great and secret thing which can and ought to be represented in terms of marriage as a kind of outward allegory. But marriage ought not for that reason to be called a sacrament. The heavens are a type of the apostles, as Ps. 19 declares; the sun is a type of Christ; the waters, of the peoples; but that does not make these things sacraments, for in every case there are lacking the divine institution and the divine promise, which constitute a sacrament. . . .

Granted that marriage is a figure of Christ and the church; yet it is not a divinely instituted sacrament, but invented by men in the church who are carried away by their ignorance of both the word and the thing.[48]

Evidence that Luther may have suspected that in conceding here to marriage's character as an "allegory" and "figure" of Christ and the Church, he had begun to undermine his case against the scholastics' interpretation of Ephesians 5:31–32 is this: In the end his clinching evidence that marriage is not a sacrament of the new law is that the gospels contain no record of Christ's having made it so. In short, his judgment is an inference drawn from his own principle of *sola scriptura.*

Melancthon

Philip Melancthon wrote the first edition of his *Loci Communes Theologici* (Major Issues in Theology) between April and September of 1521; he produced the last and expanded edition of it in 1543–44. It was an effort to put in *summa* form the major issues, as its title says, of the theology of the German reformers. Luther thought it a work of immortal significance. Of it he said, "You cannot find anywhere a book which treats the whole of theology so adequately. Next to Holy Scripture there is no better book." He went even the next step beyond that in praise: "Invictum libellum, meo iudicio, non solum immortalitate, sed canone quoque ecclesiastico digno [sic] ("An incomparable book, worthy not only of immortality but of inclusion in the Church's canon [of the Scriptures]. . . ."[49]

Melancthon was at any rate more orderly and incisive than Luther in his analysis of sacramental function. Starting from the premise of Protestant theology that grace is the reward of faith alone (one of his *loci communes*), he reasoned that even though the Christian life be replete with signs, and though the scriptures identify innumerable signs of God's gracing will, no sign can be the cause or medium of grace because, again, it is the faith of human beings alone which justifies them. The function of signs, including the sacraments, is to remind us of God's promise of grace and to testify or seal that his promise will be kept. And their witnessing these signs strengthens men and women to live out God's providence, as, for example, the sign that was circumcision strengthened Abraham.

> We have said that the Gospel is the promise of grace. This section on signs is very closely related to the promises. The Scriptures add these signs to the promises as seals which remind us of the promises, and definitely testify of the divine will toward us. They testify that we shall surely receive what God has promised. . . .[50]

> . . . So Baptism is nothing, and participation in the Lord's Supper is nothing, but they are testimonies and seals of the divine will toward you which give assurance to your conscience if it doubts grace or God's goodwill toward itself. . . .[51]

> . . . As for these signs, then, you ought to believe with as much certainty that God is merciful to you when you receive Baptism and participate in the Lord's Supper as you would if God himself were to speak with you or to show forth some other miracle that would pertain peculiarly to you. Signs are given for the purpose of stirring up faith. Those things which others call "sacraments" we call "signs" or, if you please, "sacramental signs". For Paul calls Christ himself a "sacrament" (Col. 1:27; I Tim. 3:16, Vulg.).[52]

Then Melancthon applies the Protestant criterion explicitly and even bluntly. He joins it to the theory of sacramental causation we have just noted, namely that those signs that are reported in the gospels as instituted by Christ relate to grace as no more than signs thereof, not as causes. The Protestant criterion is this: Only those signs in the traditional Christian repertory are sacraments that Christ is recorded in the gospels as having instituted as such.

> There are two signs, however, instituted by Christ in the Gospel: Baptism and participation in the Lord's Table. For we judge that sacramental signs are only those which have been divinely handed down as signs of the grace of God. For we men can neither institute a sign of the divine will toward us nor can we adapt those signs which Scripture has employed otherwise as signifying that will. Therefore, we marvel the more how it ever came into the minds of the Sophists to include among the sacraments things which the Scriptures do not mention by so much as a word, especially when they attributed justification to signs. From what source has their doctrine of ordination been fabricated? God did not institute marriage to be a special sign of grace. . . . This is the core of the matter: grace is not definitely and properly revealed except by those signs which have been handed down by God. Therefore, nothing can be called a sacramental sign except what has been added to the divine promises. For this reason, it was said by the ancients that sacraments consist of things and words. The thing is the sign and the words are the promise of grace.[53]

The definitive Lutheran position on the sacrament in marriage, on other marriage matters, and indeed on all capital points of Christian doctrine was set out in the Augsburg Confession of 1530. This document was prepared under the guidance of Philip Melancthon. It was prepared for an imperial diet summoned by the Catholic emperor, Charles V, in which he hoped to reconcile the two sides of the reformation dispute in order to unite the empire against the Turks.

The Wittenberg theologians of Saxony had already, in the summer of 1529, written up a kind of Lutheran credal statement titled the Schwabach Articles. To this they added a statement of the changes of religious practice which had been made in the churches of Saxony. Since the compilation had been done in Torgau, it was titled the Torgau Articles. These and other articles were taken to Augsburg. There it was decided to make a common Lutheran statement rather than merely a Saxon statement. This was presented to the emperor in both German and Latin on June 25, 1530; it bore by then the title by which it has since been known, the Augsburg Confession.

About the sacraments in general Article 13 said the following:

> It is taught among us that the sacraments were instituted not only to be signs by which people might be identified outwardly

as Christians, but that they are signs and testimonies of God's will toward us for the purpose of awakening and strengthening our faith. For this reason they require faith, and they are rightly used when they are received in faith and for the purpose of strengthening faith.[54]

The Confession itself contains no article reserved to the sacrament of marriage. But its mind on marriage and its sacrament is made clear in a document titled Apology of the Augsburg Confession, completed by Melancthon in May of 1531. Its genesis was this: After the Confession had been read at the diet a commission of Catholic theologians wrote and delivered, on August 3, the "Catholic Confutation." Since the emperor would not let the Protestants have a copy of this Catholic reply, Melancthon took until September 22 to prepare his own reply from notes taken during the reading of the Confutation. Even then the emperor would not let him read it to the diet. He took advantage of this refusal to revise his reply until the date of publication noted above. It became an official Lutheran confession of faith, published along with the Augsburg Confession, in Smalcald in 1537.

Melancthon's theology of the sacraments is summarized concisely in his commentary on Article 13 of the Confession. The pivot of his reasoning is his own definition of a sacrament. He makes his case by joining this, as we said earlier, with the Protestant principle of *sola scriptura.* And his understanding of the institution of a sacrament of the new law is combined from these two sources: it is a religious rite which has been put in the Church by God's express command through Christ, a rite to which God's promise of grace has been added. He understands the gracing that comes of the reception of the sacrament to be the augmenting in the recipient of faith, the ability to believe in and to trust God's mercy.

> In Article XIII our opponents approve the statement that the sacraments are no mere marks of profession among men, as some imagine, but are rather signs and testimonies of God's will toward us, through which he moves men's hearts to believe. But they insist that we enumerate seven sacraments. We believe we have the duty not to neglect any of the rites and ceremonies instituted in Scripture, whatever their number. We do not think it makes much difference if, for purposes of teaching, the enumeration varies, provided what is handed down in Scripture is preserved. For that matter, the Fathers did not always use the same enumeration.
>
> If we define sacraments as "rites which have the command of God and to which the promise of grace has been added," we can easily determine which are sacraments in the strict sense. By this definition, rites instituted by men are not sacraments in the strict sense since men do not have the authority to promise

grace. Hence signs instituted without God's command are not sure signs of grace, even though they may instruct or admonish the simple folk. The genuine sacraments, therefore, are Baptism, the Lord's Supper, and absolution (which is the sacrament of penitence), for these rites have the commandment of God and the promise of grace, which is the heart of the New Testament.[55]

The Apology does not accept that marriage qualifies as a sacrament of the new law because it fails to meet two interwoven criteria of such a sacrament: there is no evidence in the scriptures that God has made marriage a sign in the sense of a testimony, or promise, of grace and of the forgiveness of sins. Surely marriage was instituted by God and endowed with certain promises, but the latter have nothing to do with grace and forgiveness. At most marriage can be called a sacrament only in the extended sense in which any religious or semi-religious conduct has been commanded by God and favored with his promise.

Matrimony was first instituted not in the New Testament but in the very beginning, at the creation of the human race. It has the commandment of God and also certain promises, but these apply to physical life and not strictly to the New Testament. If anybody therefore wants to call it a sacrament, he should distinguish it from the preceding ones which are, in the strict sense, "signs of the New Testament," testimonies of grace and of the forgiveness of sins. If matrimony should be called a sacrament because it has God's command, then many other states or offices might also be called sacraments because they have God's command, as, for example, government.

Ultimately, if we should list as sacraments all the things that have God's command and a promise added to them, then why not prayer, which can most truly be called a sacrament? It has both the command of God and many promises. If it were placed among the sacraments and thus given, so to speak, a more exalted position, this would move men to pray. Alms could be listed here, as well as afflictions, which in themselves are signs to which God has added promises.[56]

John Calvin

For his refutation of the Catholic claim that Christ made marriage among Christians a sacrament Calvin reasoned in a way virtually synonymous with Luther's and Melancthon's. It started with the premise that was his and their assumption about the way in which Christ must have instituted his sacraments, namely as he did baptism and the Lord's supper. They joined to this a second assumption, that his instituting sacraments in this way must have been recorded in the canonical gospels. They reasoned that while "all men admit that it [marriage] was instituted by God," there is no evidence that Christ made it a sacrament.[57] "For it is required that a sacrament be not only a work of God [which farming, building, cobbling and barbering are] but an outward ceremony appointed by God to confirm a promise." Again, there is no evidence in the scriptures that God has done the last-named with marriage.[58]

He continues this first part of his refutation, turning it now against the presumed Catholic retort that in any case a Christian marriage is a sign; and a sign in Christian religious life is a sacrament. He uses against this another assumed definition of a sacrament of the new law, the same that Luther used. His logical tactic here is a *reductio ad absurdum*.

> But it is, they say, the sign of a sacred thing, that is, of the spiritual joining of Christ with the Church. If by the word "sign" they understood a symbol set before us by God to raise up the assurance of our faith, they are wandering far from the mark; if they simply understand [a sacrament to be a] "sign" as what is adduced for a comparison, I will show how keenly they reason. Paul says, "As star differs from star in brilliance, so will be the resurrection of the dead." [I Cor. 15:41–42.] There you have one sacrament. Christ says, "The Kingdom of Heaven is like a grain of mustard seed." [Matt. 13:31, Vg.] Here you have another. Again, "The Kingdom of Heaven is like a leaven." [Matt. 13:33, Vg] Behold a third. . . .[59]

Calvin then moves to correct the traditional Catholic interpretation of the passage that had stood for centuries as the clinching biblical text in support of the sacramentality of marriage. This is, of course, Ephesians 5:32. He argues against this interpretation, first, that Paul (whom he takes to be the author of Ephesians) did not intend in verses 28–32 to establish an analogy between the two relationships, Christ-Church and husband-wife, with the consequence that the latter can be seen as a sign of the former. He intended rather to offer the Christ-Church relationship as a model of the love with which Christian spouses ought to cherish one another. And Calvin claims that the model in turn that Paul drew from to describe the Christ-Church relationship was the real-life relationship (he took for granted) of Adam and Eve: She was drawn from his side and was proportionately dear to him; the Church was drawn from Christ's side and is equivalently dear to him.

> But they still press us with Paul's words, by which they say the term "sacrament" is applied to marriage . . . " 'For this reason a man shall leave his father and mother and be joined to his wife, and the two shall become one flesh.' This is a great sacrament. But I say, in Christ and in the Church." [Eph. 5:28–32,

Vg.] Yet so to handle the Scriptures is to mix earth with heaven. Paul, to show married men with what singular love they ought to embrace their wives, sets forth Christ to them as prototype. For as he poured out his compassion upon the church, which he had espoused to himself, thus he wishes every man to feel toward his own wife. Then the words follow: "He who loves his wife loves himself . . . as Christ loved the Church" [Eph. 5:28). Now, to teach how Christ loved the church as himself, nay, how he made himself one with his bride the church, Paul applies to him what Moses relates that Adam said of himself. For when Eve (who he knew was formed from his rib) was brought into his sight, he said, "She is bone of my bones and flesh of my flesh" [Gen. 2:23, Vg.]. Paul testifies that all this was spiritually fulfilled in Christ and in us, when he says that we are members of his body, of his flesh, and of his bones, and thus one flesh with him.[60]

Calvin closes his consideration of marriage by identifying exactly the referent, in his judgment, of the key Pauline declaration in verse 32.

Finally, he [Paul] adds this summation: "This is a great mystery." And that nobody may be deceived by an ambiguity, he explains that he is not speaking of carnal union of man and woman, but of the spiritual marriage of Christ and the church. Truly, indeed, this is a great mystery, that Christ allowed a rib to be removed from himself to form us; that is, when he was strong, he willed to be weak, in order that we might be strengthened by his strength; so that we ourselves should no longer live, but he should live in us [Gal. 2:20].[61]

The Council of Trent

The Catholic reaction to the Protestant reformers took two forms. The first was non-authoritative, in the writings of the major theologians after about 1530. The authoritative response came in the doctrine and decrees of the Council of Trent.

This is not the place to describe in detail the troubled history of that council. We recall only that shortly after Cardinal Alexander Farnese was elected to the papacy in 1534 and took the name Paul III, he announced a general council that was to convene in 1537. In 1536 he appointed a reform commission that a year later brought in its report on the needs of the Catholic Church that should be brought before the council-to-be. Because of war between France and Spain the bishops of these countries could not attend, so Paul postponed the council until May 1538. But this time the German emperor, Charles V, and the French king, Henry II, refused to allow the bishops to leave their respective countries. Accordingly Paul rescheduled the opening of the council for November 1543 at Trent in northernmost Italy. But still the two monarchs refused to let their bishops attend. Finally, on December 13, 1545, eight years later than Paul III had planned, the council was inaugurated at Trent with fewer than forty bishops present. Only thirty-seven were at the second session in January 1546. A year later the number reached seventy-two. The largest number to attend its second meeting was fifty-nine, while the third meeting numbered two hundred and fifty-five at its final session. But even these represented only a fraction of the Catholic Church.

The Protestant attack on the Catholic teaching concerning the sacrament was not the issue about marriage that most worried the bishops at Trent. In the degree that the attack reached only doctrine and not practice, the council's riposte called for little debate in its sessions. There was substantial agreement among the Catholic teachers and authorities about all points of doctrine except three. These were the identity of the matter and the form in the sacrament, the minister of the sacrament, and the separability of contract and sacrament in marriage. The consequences of divided judgments in the last-named issue lurked just outside the perimeter of attention, waiting to create turmoil a century later when governments in Catholic Europe were moving toward secularization. The first of the issues remained a subject of quiet debate among theologians.

It was the second issue, when taken over into the juridical domain under slight camouflage, that inspired the most prolonged and anxious debate in the council. In that domain the majority opinion by then among Catholic authorities that the ministers of the sacrament are the spouses themselves helped to exacerbate the problem of clandestine marriages, and helped also to prolong and confuse the search for a solution. For if the spouses are the ministers of the sacrament, and if they have the right to the sacrament from Christ himself, by what countervailing right could Catholic authorities restrain their exercise of this right? We shall see at the end of this brief examination of Trent what its bishops did to restrain the clandestine exercise of the right, and how they reasoned their way to justification for doing so.

The council first directed its attention to the Protestant attack in its seventh meeting, which was convened in January of 1547. This was in its *Decretum de sacramentis,*[62] which touched marriage only implicitly and virtually, since it declared concerning all seven of the Catholic sacraments collectively, but only concerning baptism and confirmation singly. The schema of the decree was proposed on February 26 and voted on March 3. The wording of the decree indicates how exactly the bishops had Luther's and Melancthon's writings in mind. The declaration of Catholic doctrine in the canons making up the decree takes the form that was conventional for councils of the time. It anathematized the contradictory opinion, in this case the Protestant.[63]

Canon 1: If anyone says that not all the sacraments of the New Law were instituted by Christ Our Lord; or that these are more or fewer than seven, namely baptism, confirmation, Eucharist, penance, last anointing, orders and marriage; or says that any of these seven is not truly and in the proper sense a sacrament, let him be anathema.

Canon 2: If anyone says that these sacraments of the New Law differ from those of the Old Law only in that they are different ceremonies and different external rites. . . .

Canon 3: If anyone says that these seven sacraments are equal, and that none is in any way more excellent than another. . . .

Canon 4: If anyone says that the sacraments of the New Law are not necessary for salvation, that they are unneeded [*superflua*], and that without them or without the intention to receive them, a person can through faith alone gain from God the grace of justification (granting that not all the sacraments are necessary for every person). . . .

Canon 5: If anyone says that these sacraments were instituted only in order to nourish faith. . . .

Canon 6: If anyone says that the sacraments of the New Law do not contain the grace that they signify, or that they do not confer grace on recipients who put no obstacle to it; but that they are only external signs of the grace or justification accepted through faith, and a kind of evidence of Christian profession by which the faithful can be distinguished from non-Christians. . . .

Canon 7: If anyone says that from God's side grace is not given always and to everyone through these sacraments even when received worthily, but that grace is given only sometimes and to certain persons. . . .

Canon 8: If anyone says that the power itself of the sacraments of the New Law is not active in the conferring of grace, but that faith alone in the divine promise suffices to gain the grace. . . .[64]

Five more canons follow to complete the decree. But these are about the ministers of the sacraments considered generally. None of them speaks to the question of identifying the ministers of the sacrament in marriage.

The council intended to examine the difficulties concerning marriage in 1552, but this examination was delayed by the Protestant representatives, who objected that this was a new item introduced in the council's agenda without their consultation. The examination then fell victim, along with the rest of the council's agenda, to the chaotic interference of German emperor, French king, Spanish king and Protestant armies, and the deaths meanwhile of four Popes, Paul III (in 1549),

Julius III (in office from 1550 to 1555), Marcellus II (in office only twenty-two days), and Paul IV (who reigned until 1559, and who never wanted the council, since he preferred reform in the Church by his monarchic fiat). Bowing to the conflicting demands coming from all quarters Julius III suspended the council on April 28, 1552. It did not reconvene until January 18, 1562, by then under the papacy of Pius IV (1559–1565).

The canons on marriage passed through four drafts. Without proposing to examine minutely each draft and the reasons for emendation from draft to draft, we will however note their significant changes.

The first draft was put before the bishops on July 20, 1563. It consisted of eleven canons, the first of which dealt with the sacrament as this was challenged by the Protestant reformers.

> If anyone says that marriage is not a true sacrament of the Law
> of the Gospel, that it is not divinely instituted but has been
> intruded (*invectum*) by men, let him be anathema.

The other canons in this first draft dealt with polygamy and clandestine marriages. All were debated in fourteen sessions from July 24 through July 31. But the first canon, on the sacrament, drew a dissatisfied response from the council, which wanted to declare not only against the Protestants that Christian marriage is a sacrament, but also against Durandus of Saint Pourçain that such marriage is *vere et proprie sacramentum*—truly and in the proper sense a sacrament, as truly a sacrament of the new law as baptism and the Eucharist and that it confers grace. The adverb *divinitus* also failed to satisfy. It said only that the sacrament was "divinely instituted," thus allowing that it was instituted by God the creator in the old law and carried forward to the new law. The council wished to say that it has been instituted by Christ in the new law. Some bishops wished also, but with lesser insistence, to identify the matter and form of the sacrament, and to declare the contract and the sacrament to be distinct, whether separable or not.

The theologians prepared a second draft of the decree. This was debated in twenty sessions from August 11 until August 23. Since there was little objection to the amendments to the canon on the sacrament proposed on July 20, these were written into it readily. We shall see its definitive formulation when reviewing the work of the final session of two months later. The multiple sessions within so few days were spent in debating a way of suppressing clandestine marriages. Since even the severest ecclesiastical penalty, excommunication, had been applied to the abuse for generations but had failed to stop it, the only effective block was to somehow render the attempt at clandestine marriage null and void.

But there was a serious resistance to any strategy for nullifying. As noted earlier, the sacrament is Christ's institution for all Christians, and he set no recorded conditions for its validity. Moreover, how could the Church put a nullifying block when the parties could bring to their marital consent all that is essentially necessary for creating the sacrament: its *materia* in their selves (or their bodies) offered for acceptance; its *forma,* in the accepting of this offer; the ministers of the sacrament, who are themselves; the expression of consent, for which no exact formula was specified?

A way past these obstacles was espied in the distinction between the contract and the sacrament in Christian marriages. The distinction was said to be all the more verifiable historically in Christ's institution of the sacrament. He did not invent a new human relationship; he simply "joined" the sacrament to the contract, or he "raised" the contract to the status of a sacrament. Could not one therefore block the couple's attempt to create the contract clandestinely without blocking their right to the sacrament, and do this by setting a condition for valid contracting?

But many of the bishops bridled at this tactic. It suggested that the contract and the sacrament are not only distinct but separable. Or, if they are only distinct, and if the sacrament is the contract itself raised to grace-giving capacity, can one set conditions for validly contracting without thereby setting the same conditions for creating the sacrament?

The third draft proposal was brought to the council on September 5 and was debated in seven general sessions from September 7 to September 10. This draft contained a new preface to the entire decree on marriage, twelve canons on the sacrament, twelve canons aimed at correcting abuses, and one proposing to annul attempts at clandestine marriage. This last canon embodied a suggestion made during the August sessions, that such attempts be made null and void not by presuming to block either sacrament or contract, but by inhabilitating the persons attempting such marriage—by decreeing them unqualified, incapable of creating the contract-sacrament. Already in Catholic law there were persons inhabilitated from marrying, such as those in their minority, and the mentally defective.

But this proposal drew the objection that such inhabilitations in the law are grounded in some real defect in the person rendering him incapable of the office or relationship in question. But in attempts at clandestine marriage there is no such defect in persons who could otherwise marry within the demands of the law.

The debates during the first week in September bore almost exclusively on the blocking of attempts at clandestine marriage. The French and German delegates argued passionately for such blocking; the Italians especially argued against the juridical tour de force they saw taking form. And the archbishop of the Latin church of Jerusalem reasoned that to block clandestine marriages by invalidating the attempt at them is to contravene divine law.

Sixty of the bishops remained opposed to such blocking, enough to create a stalemate in the council. At this point some recommended the move made so frequently by delegates weary of debate within a monarchy, namely to remand the problem to the monarch for resolution, in this case to Pope Pius IV. But fearing that the Italian pope's decision might go against them, the French and German delegates objected to this strenuously. The public and solemn session on September 13 ended in tumult. Debate was put over for a month.

The fourth proposal was brought before the council on October 13. The canons designed for correcting abuses were abandoned. There were twelve canons *De sacramento matrimonii,* on the sacrament itself, and ten canons *super reformatione,* of which the first was designed to render null and void attempts at clandestine marriage. Two general sessions, on October 26 and 27, debated these canons. Fifty-eight bishops voted *non placet,* to oppose the decree as a whole. Fifty-five rejected the canon against clandestinity, reasoning mainly that the Church has not the authority to require witnesses, not even the one witness of an authorized priest, as a condition for the valid creation of a marriage, and thereby change the *forma* of the sacrament. They argued also that in some places Catholics would meet grave difficulty in finding an authorized priest witness. But those who objected were a minority. So in this, the twenty-fourth session of Trent, on November 11, 1563, the decree on marriage was approved by majority vote.

The canons, which alone contain the council's promulgated doctrine, are preceded in the decree by a discursive statement which offers the justification for the doctrinal decree in sacred scripture and in the theology inferred from it. The statement had been discussed in the second and third drafts. In this final session it was accepted with little debate.

> The first parent of the human race, inspired by the divine Spirit, stated the permanent and indissoluble union [*nexus*] of marriage when he said, "This one at last is bone of my bones and flesh of my flesh. For this reason a man will leave his father and mother and will cling to his wife, and they shall be two in one flesh."[65]

This doctrinal explanation then turns to the words of the New Testament to verify Christ's strengthening the permanence of marriage, its *firmitas,* and his declaration of its monogamous nature.

> Christ the Lord taught expressly that no more than two persons are joined and united by this bond [*vinculum*] when, referring to the last words above, he said, "Therefore they are no longer two, but one flesh." Immediately he strengthened the permanence of this union that Adam had declared so much earlier, when he [Christ] said, "Therefore what God has joined man must not separate."[66]

The following paragraph asserts that the sacrament mediates grace to the spouses, and explains the effects of this gracing.

> Christ himself, the Holy One, who instituted the sacraments and brought them to completion, merited the grace which perfects natural love, which seals the indissoluble union and sanctifies the spouses. Paul the apostle hinted [*innuit*] at this when saying, "Husbands, love your wives as Christ loved the Church and gave himself up for her," and added shortly thereafter, "This is a great sacrament; I mean this in Christ and in the Church."[67]

The decree moves thence to countering the Protestant attack.

> Because through Christ's grace marriage in the law of the Gospel surpasses the marriages of antiquity, deservedly have our holy Fathers and councils, and the tradition of the universal Church, always taught that it is included among the seven sacraments of the New Law. Against this teaching faithless men of this world have raged. Not only have they interpreted this venerable sacrament falsely, but, as is their way, by claiming a freedom they pretend to draw from the Gospel, they have verbally and in writing asserted many things alien to the Catholic Church's understanding that has been sustained by tradition from apostolic times—and this to the great harm of the faithful. This holy and universal synod, seeking to repel this audacity, has determined to suppress the more notable heresies and errors of these schismatics lest they attract more followers by their pernicious contagion. And it pronounces anathema on the heretical among them as well as on their errors.[68]

Then follow the canons, which themselves declare the points of doctrine decreed by the council. Again, they do so by condemning the Protestant teaching that contradicts the doctrinal point in question.

> *Canon 1:* If anyone says that marriage is not truly and in the proper sense one of the seven sacraments of the Law of the Gospel instituted by Christ, but [says] that it has been instituted in the Church by men, and that it does not confer grace, let him be anathema.[69]

Canon 2 anathematizes those who claim the divine law does not forbid polygamy to Christians. Canon 3 defends the right of the Church to determine the degrees of consanguinity and of affinity within which these impede marriage. Canon 4 defends the right of the Church to create invalidating impediments to marriage and its accurate judgment in doing so. Canon 5 denies that a marriage can be dissolved because of a spouse's heresy or disrupting family life or deliberate absence. Canon 6 claims that a sacramental but unconsummated marriage can be dissolved by one of the spouses' solemn vows in religious life. Canon 7 defends the Catholic Church's interpretation of the New Testament passages that teach concerning remarriage after dissolution.[70]

Canon 8 defends the Church's permitting the separation of spouses for just cause but without divorce. Canon 9 condemns those who say clerics in sacred orders and persons solemnly professed in religious life can marry. Canon 10 asserts the superiority of the life of celibacy or sexual continence over marriage. Since the canon does not specify that the former way of life is superior provided it is consecrated to the work of the Church, it leaves one to infer that it deems it simply better not to marry. Canon 11 defends the Church's forbidding weddings during certain times of the liturgical year, and its custom of marriage blessing and other ceremonies. Canon 12 asserts the Church's jurisdiction over marriage cases, thus denying by implication the Protestant claim that such cases come under civil jurisdiction.

The same session decided finally in the matter of clandestine attempts at marriage in Chapter 1 of its decree on the reform of marriage practices. This decree, made up of twelve canons, is known as *Tametsi*, a title drawn from the first word in its formulation.[71] It did more than rule on clandestinity. It anathematized those Protestants and Catholics who hold marriages invalid if contracted by sons and daughters without parental consent, and who hold that parents have the authority to invalidate their children's marriage contracts.

The decree ruled on clandestinity by requiring that for the valid contracting of marriage Christians must make a marital consent that is witnessed by an authorized priest and two or three other witnesses. The priest must be the pastor of the parish of residence, or some other priest who witnesses the consent with the delegated authorization of the pastor or of the local ordinary. Persons who attempt to contract marriage without these witnesses are *ipso facto* inhabilitated for marriage by this decree, and their attempt is by it rendered null and void. The targets of the decree were Protestant Christians as well as Catholic. At the time the former were regarded by the Catholic authorities as heretical and dissident Catholics and therefore subject to Roman Catholic jurisdiction.

But a benign condition was put on the binding force of *Tametsi*. It was to become effective in a given place only thirty days after its promulgation in that place. Thus, if it were not promulgated, it would not bind, as it would not in territories ruled by Protestant civil authorities, who would hardly promulgate it. In this way was avoided the confusion of inhabilitating for marriage Protestants, who would not have their marriages witnessed by an authorized priest, and Catholics who could not have such witness in Protestant territories.

In requiring that the priest witness the decree in no way intended that he is the minister of the sacrament, but only that he witnesses the contracting of the marriage and can record its contracting. This was made clear by an interpretation coming from the Congregation of the Council, which was created by Pius IV in 1564 to interpret all of Trent's decrees and to supervise their implementation. It determined that the priest witness has no juridical role in the contracting, but serves only as a *testis spectabilis*, as a public witness. It added however that his mere physical presence does not constitute him such a witness. He must verify the parties' intent to marry as this is manifested in their words or other signs. The congregation ruled also that a priest acts as the required witness even if he observes the contracting against his will, and even if he is brought or kept there by physical violence. Thus was the possibility of the *matrimonium repentinum*, the surprise marriage, kept alive. To escape marrying a spouse chosen for them by their parents, young European Catholics could marry partners of their own choosing by, for example, breaking into the pastor's residence during the night and, while he rubbed the sleep from his eyes, pronouncing their wedding vows in his presence. For validity, of course, they must have brought two or three sympathetic friends along as the other required witnesses.

The Catholic Theology of Marriage After Trent

There is an epistemology of papal and conciliar teaching which says that the causes of the truth of such teaching decrees are two. The primary cause is God acting through his divine Spirit in the minds of teaching pope and other bishops. The second is the pope and bishops using their human teaching capacity as instruments guided by this Spirit, and guided at times inerrantly. This epistemology says that what the Spirit guides instrumentally is not the human capacity in these men for theological demonstration, but their formulation of the doctrine and their free submission to the divine impulse to decree the point of doctrine. In short, the doctrine in the formulation is true as doctrine not because it is the product of flawless theological reasoning but because God himself has caused its accuracy. This, to say it again, he has done not by guiding the pope and bishops to reason flawlessly, but to believe accurately and to formulate accurately.

This epistemology is urged even though the point of doctrine may have come into the agenda of a council as the child of theology, as the sacramentality of marriage came into Trent's agenda. The bishops of the council may themselves, and with the help of their theologian specialists, labor long and theologically at the reasons for the mooted points of doctrine, as also at the reasons against it. And their decree stating the doctrine may contain the theological reasoning to which it relates by the rules of logic as conclusion to premises. But still the principle stands: The truth of the doctrinal formulation is not the product of the reasoning. Why then is the reasoning almost always supplied in the decree, often painstakingly and at length? It is supplied for two interlocked reasons. The first is to show that the statement of doctrine is not absurd, that it involves no self-contradiction—to show the credibility of the statement by showing that it is not literally incredible. The second reason is to honor human intelligence's natural way of knowing and coming to judgments about truth and falsity, namely by examining evidence and drawing conclusions from it. Sometimes this reasoning is done before the promulgation of the decree in preparation for it, and, as said above, is often presented with the decree. Sometimes the reasoning is offered after the decree and as a kind of continuum with it, as a product of and apparently compelled by it.

Canon 1 of Trent's decree on the sacraments in general in its seventh session, and canons 1 and 7 of its decree on marriage in its twenty-fourth session, had just that effect. While they did not launch the Catholic intellectual enterprise that was neo-scholastic theology, they fueled it generously. This is nowhere more evident than in the post-Tridentine theology of marriage. It is only a slight exaggeration to say that for the ensuing four hundred years, until the Second Vatican Council, this theology was almost (but not quite) the following twin enterprise: to give and explain reasons undergirding the Tridentine decrees, and to provide a theological warrant for the Catholic law of marriage that was legislated during these centuries. This theology had also one other agendum that came ironically out of Trent's underestimating the seriousness of a familiar enough question that smoldered without definitive answer through and after the council. The question asked whether in Christian marriages the contract and sacrament are separable. Catholic civil rulers were to exploit the indecision by claiming jurisdiction over the contract while leaving to ecclesiastical jurisdiction only the sacrament, which they deemed anyway to be only the fleeting ceremonial blessing.

The problem that had clamored to Catholic parents and Church authorities for centuries before the council fell to only a whisper after it and gradually disappeared from theological writing. The decree *Tametsi* was decisive. Because it made clandestine marriages impossible wherever it was promulgated, sons and daughters could no longer present themselves to unforewarned parents as surprise spouses—except in the few instances of *matrimonium repentinum.* The Tridentine decrees left to the ensuing generations' theologians different preoccupations, much more fundamental than clandestine marriage. Canon 1 of the Decree on the Sacraments declared that marriage is truly and in the proper sense of the word a sacrament of the new law, instituted by Christ. This invited the theologians to explain (1) the nature of a sacrament of the new law, (2) that among Christians marriage contains this nature, and (3) that it was made so by Christ.

Canon 1 of the Decree on Marriage invited the theologians to demonstrate these same three points about marriage, and to show especially how it confers grace. Canon 7 bequeathed a twofold task. The explicit but paradoxically less important of the two was exegetical in nature, namely to explain the accuracy of the authoritative Catholic interpretation of the New Testament divorce passages, the interpretation saying that these passages do not allow remarriage for a person who dismisses his or her spouse because of adultery. The second task was one that Trent could be said to have kept out of its bequest, namely to sustain the doctrine of marriage's indissolubility. We recall that at the plea of the Venetian delegates the council skirted this issue. But everyone knew that this was what wanted proving. The need and the desire for proof are evident in the unfailing appearance of the effort at it in the post-Tridentine Catholic writers.

In examining their efforts one finds a predictable synonymity. For this there are two reasons. First, these theologians were heirs to the efforts of the centuries preceding Trent. Second, if there is in fact only one demonstration, however complex, of a theological conclusion, the versions of the demonstration cannot vary widely. Consequently our own method in this examination is to choose one of these writers and set forth his demonstrative argument as a kind of best sample. To quote other writers because of their agreement would be redundant. About quoting others because of their significant disagreement, one disputed issue has already been examined in this chapter, and this is in the argument of the champion of the minority opinion. This was Melchior Cano in his thesis that not every marriage of two Christians is a sacrament because not every one is contracted in a religious ceremony. The other disputed issue is sibling to that one. It is whether contract and sacrament in Christian marriages are separable. This was the heart of the conflict between the papacy and the Catholic rulers of Europe during the centuries after Trent. Consequently it will be examined in the chapter following this one.

Bellarmine's Theology of the Sacrament

The elected writer-theologian is Robert Bellarmine (1542–1621). He is elected because his defense of the Catholic teaching on the marital sacrament was at least as detailed and careful as any in his time. Moreover, to judge by the frequency with which he was quoted in the decades following his work, he was then taken as an exemplary proponent of the Catholic teaching.

His most thorough treatment of that teaching is in his *Twelfth General Disputation, On Last Anointing, Orders and Marriage.*[72] Our attention will center on his *Controversia Prima,* "Whether Marriage Is a Sacrament in the Proper Sense," Chapter 1, "On the State of the Question and the Errors of the Heretics"; on Chapter 2, "That Marriage Is a Sacrament Is Proved from the Holy Scriptures"; and on Chapter 4: "That Marriage Is a Sacrament in the Proper Sense Is Proved from Reason."

Bellarmine begins *Controversia Prima* by making clear the meaning of its interrogative title. He asks in it whether, in addition to being a man's and a woman's civil contract for propagating and nurturing children, a marriage is also a sign, an observable religious symbol to which has been joined by divine institution a promise of santifying grace.

After noting that both Luther and Calvin denied that marriage is a sacrament in any sense, he points out that the Lutheran theologians Melancthon (in his *Loci Communes Rerum Theologicarum*) and Martin Chemnitz (in his *Examen Concilii Tridentini*, 1565–1573) both acknowledged that in marriage there is a divine command and the promise of grace; but that they deny this is *gratia justificans*, the grace that reconciles human beings with God. That is, they accept that marriage is a sacrament in a limited sense, but deny that it is such *sensu proprio*, in the same way that baptism and the Eucharist are sacraments. Bellarmine adds that among Catholics Durandus of Saint Pourçain was the only theologian to agree with Melancthon and Chemnitz.

As he sets out, in Chapter 2, to prove from the scriptures that marriage is a sacrament, Bellarmine acknowledges that in order to do this he must find and verify in them three points of evidence.[73] The first is that marriage has been instituted by God; the second, that God has made it a sign of a sacred reality; the third, that marriage has joined to it the divine promise of justifying grace.

That marriage has been instituted by God, he says, can be understood in two ways. The first is that God has joined man and woman in order to propagate the human race; the second, that he has joined man and woman in order to image a sacred reality and in order to sanctify the persons thus joined.

The first of these, he claims, is verified by God's declaration recorded in Genesis 2, "It is not good that the man be alone. Let us make him a helpmate like himself." But in nothing else does a man need a woman as helpmate than in conceiving and rearing children. Here Bellarmine adds, and apparently subscribes to, Aristotle's opinion that in all other needs a man is better helped by a man—an opinion that reveals much about the sexual psychology of both the classic Athenian and the Tridentine Jesuit.

In the same chapter of Genesis Adam said of his union with Eve, "For this reason a man will leave his father and mother and cling to his wife." Bellarmine reasoned that these words contribute to the proof of marriage's divine institution, since Adam spoke them as an effect of God's inspiration. If this were not so, the declaration would not be in the scriptures. Finally there are Jesus' own words from the New Testament, in Matthew 19, "What God has joined man must not separate."

As for verifying the second point of fact, that God made marriage a sign, an image, of a sacred reality, Bellarmine says that it is useless to search in the scriptures for passages that say this explicitly. However, one can draw from certain passages a logic that verifies the point, a logic that applies the metaphysical principle of needed sufficient cause. Thus, if one finds in the scriptures that marriage is an image of a sacred reality, to which image has been joined the conferring of sanctifying grace, one can conclude that these things have been done by God, because only he can do them. They are simply beyond the power of any creature.

That marriage is a sign, or image, of a sacred reality, and is thus not merely a civil contract but also a kind of *mysterium,* a sacrament, is evident in Ephesians 5:32, where Paul wrote, "this is a great sacrament; I mean of Christ and the Church." About this verse Bellarmine says three points are to be noted. First, Luther's, Calvin's and Theodore Beza's charge that the Catholics have been deceived by the Vulgate New Testament's translation of Ephesians' *mystérion* into the Latin *sacramentum* is wide of the mark. It is so because the latter noun signifies exactly what *mystérion* signifies. Therefore its use affirms that marriage is what Paul meant by predicating *mystérion* of it. Bellarmine adds to his rejection of the charge by pointing out that elsewhere in the Latin Vulgate of the New Testament the noun *sacramentum* is used to translate the Greek *mystérion,* as in Colossians 1:27, in 1 Timothy 3:9, and in Revelation 1:20 and 17:5. But from none of these uses have the Catholics reasoned that they designate sacraments instituted by God. As for Ephesians 5:32, the Catholics have used it only to verify that marriage is not merely a civil or natural contract, but also a sign of a sacred reality.[74]

The next step in the proof is to determine whether Paul refers the words "This is a great sacrament" to the union of Christ and the Church or to the human marriage of husband and wife. Bellarmine knows that Luther, Calvin, Beza and Erasmus have insisted that they refer to the first of these two relationships, and that in this passage marriage is not called even a sign or a symbol, much less a *mysterium.* They added that there Paul designates as a *mysterium* no earthly sign or symbol of a sacred reality, but some sacred reality itself. And Erasmus pointed out that far from being a mystery, marriage is one of the most common and visible of human experiences.

Bellarmine replies that the text itself of Ephesians 5:32 refutes the Protestants' and Erasmus' interpretation of it and sustains the Catholics'. Thus, where Paul wrote "This is a great sacrament," the pronoun "this" necessarily refers to that which most closely precedes it. But this is the sentence, "For this reason a man will leave his father and mother and cling to his wife; and the two will be one flesh." Hence Paul's meaning is that this sacrament—namely that a man leaves his father and mother, etc.—is a great one because it images the marriage of Christ and his Church.

He adds that the message of the entire Chapter 5 of Ephesians supports his interpretation. Paul is exhorting the spouses to mutual love. Among the motives for this love, that on which Paul mainly insists is that their marriage is not a trivial thing, but contains a great mystery that refers to Christ and the Church. If, as his adversaries say, the entire mystery resided in Christ and the Church but pertained in no way to the spouses' union, Paul's entire argument would crumble. It would be difficult to find a reason for his including this reference to Christ and the Church there at the end of the chapter.[75]

Added to this is the fact that in the Greek original of the letter Paul wrote not "*in* Christ and in the Church" (*en Christô kai ekklesía*) but "*unto* Christ and the Church" (*eis Christòn kai ekklesían*). This shows clearly that he intended the union of Christ and the Church as the referent, or object, of the mystical image, that he therefore meant that the *mystérion* is in the spouses' marriage, and that this mystery's imaging has Christ and the Church as its object.

Bellarmine takes care to point out briefly that Paul hardly meant to say that only the marriage of Adam and Eve contained this mystery. The reference in Ephesians is rather to all spouses, since the words Paul quotes from Adam in Genesis are not "This is why *I* leave *my* father and mother and cling to *my* wife, etc." What is more, Christ himself, after quoting this passage (in Matthew 9:5–6), and adding his own judgment, "Therefore what God has joined man must not separate," could not have had Adam's and Eve's marriage in mind, since they were long dead.

That done, Bellarmine must set about verifying the third point of fact: that the scriptures reveal that as a sign of a sacred reality instituted by God, marriage has also, by his institution, justifying grace joined to it.[75]

He argues that this is found in the same Chapter 5 of Ephesians. For it tells not only that marriage is an image of the union of Christ and the Church grounded in the homogeneity of their human natures. It tells also of marriage's imaging their union that is grounded in the charity by which Christ loves the Church and governs it in holiness—the union by which reciprocally the Church adheres to Christ by faith, hope and charity, and submits to him in obedience.

That sanctifying grace is found in human marriage is borne out by this, that by homogeneity of natures Christ is united not only to the Church but to the entire human race. It is only to the Church that he is joined as spouse with spouse by spiritual love. It follows that as an image of the Christ-Church union human marriage must image this union of spiritual love—an imaging that certainly must contain grace. What is more, Paul urged just such spiritual union upon spouses when he said, "The Church is subject to Christ, while Christ loved the Church and gave himself up for her, in order to sanctify her, etc." But a human marriage cannot image such a union as this unless in addition to the civil contract between husband and wife there is in it also a spiritual union of souls. This is why Paul urged more than once that husbands love their wives just as Christ loved the Church, and that wives obey their husbands just as the Church obeys Christ. Thus the syllogistic reasoning concludes, since God joins a husband and wife so that by their spiritual union they may image the spiritual union of Christ and the Church, he surely gives them the grace without which they could not create and maintain such a union.

To bolster his case for the full sacramentality of Christian marriage Bellarmine added, in Chapter 4 of this *Controversia Prima,* a proof that he said is "from reason" [*ratione*], although it seems to draw its premises only slightly less from the New Testament than did his argumentation we have just seen. He begins this second proof with a tight syllogism, truncated by only an implicit inclusion of its major premise. Thus, "The marriage of two Christians is of one man and one woman and wholly indissoluble. Therefore it is a sacrament in the proper sense, one that confers grace."[77]

He verifies the antecedent in this syllogism from Christ's words in Mark 10, "A man who dismisses his wife and marries another commits adultery against her." The conclusion he verifies provisorily by this, that Christian marriage's being monogamous and indissoluble implies both that it is a sacred sign and that it confers grace. And these two traits make of Christian marriage a sacrament.

But now he must offer final verification by showing the truth of these two claims. It is in offering this verification that he makes clear why he calls all this ratiocination a "proof from reason."

That a Christian marriage is a sacred sign follows from the fact that the absolute indissolubility of this monogamous union must have as its primary, certain and necessary cause nothing less than its being an image of the union of Christ and the Church. (This is the claim that Augustine made repeatedly in *De bono conjugali.*) For if one considers marriage only as a dutiful vocation, an *officium* for producing offspring, it would be most difficult to explain why a man could not dismiss a sterile wife and marry another. Or if one considers marriage as a remedy against fornication, why cannot a wife suffering from an incurable disease be dismissed? Or why could the husband not take simultaneously a second wife? Thus it is evident that by the law of nature marriage has a certain degree of indissolubility [*quamdam indissolubilitatem*], but not a degree that puts it beyond the possibility of dissolution, and this especially if done by divine dispensation.

But that marriage be absolutely indissoluble has its principal and most effective cause from the divine institution which makes it to image the indissoluble union of Christ and the Church.

Finally it is evident from what Paul says in 1 Corinthians 7 that a merely civil marriage, even though consummated, can be dissolved, but that it cannot be if it is contracted following baptism. But no other cause of the latter marriage's indissolubility can be found than that it is a sacrament, a sign of the indissoluble union of Christ and the Church, whereas the former marriage was not. For apart from this sacrament the marriages of Christians and non-Christians do not differ.

Bellarmine goes on to add the human reasons for grace in a Christian marriage that we have already seen—that lifelong union with one spouse is so onerous as to need grace, but God does not fail to provide the help that his faithful need; that Christ said that his yoke is sweet and his burden light, but in the face of this marriage in the new law but without grace would be far more burdensome than in the old law, which allowed polygamy, divorce and remarriage; that the ends of marriage—offspring and the remedying of concupiscence—demand the help of grace, especially for Christian spouses, who must bring up their children in piety and virtue in the Church.[78]

Bellarmine knew well and was much concerned about Melchior Cano's opinion on the separability in Christian marriages of the contract and the sacrament. The opinion was, reductively, that not all civilly contracted marriages of Christian spouses are necessarily sacraments. Those that are not fall short of sacramentality because the ceremony, the sacrament in its moment of creation, has lacked its *forma*. This it has lacked because the marital consent was not exchanged in the presence of a priest witness, and no priest has blessed the new marriage. For Cano insisted that the priest who witnesses is the minister of the sacrament. He joins its matter and form. Cano had principally in mind clandestine marriages. He considered them civilly contracted but not sacraments. Implicit in his judgment was the claim of an historical event, that since Christ had instituted the sacrament, he must also have assigned a special form to it, in fact a verbal formula for its creation.

No doubt Bellarmine's worry was that Cano all but delivered the debate into the hands of the Protestants, since one of the favorite weapons of their challenge was that such a formula was nowhere to be found in the New Testament. He might have doubled his worry had he foreseen the day even in Catholic Europe when civil rulers would claim jurisdiction over the marriage contracts of their people, and leave to churchmen only the sacrament—separate from the contract and no more than the priest's blessing.

Bellarmine's reasoning in refutation of Cano is multi-faceted, and needs only a cursory review here.[79] He argued that if the ministers of the contract and the minister of the sacrament were not identical—if the former were the spouses but the latter the priest—both the sacred scriptures and the bishops at Florence and Trent ought to have made this clear. But none of them did so.

In fact, when the Council of Florence said that the efficient cause of a marriage is ordinarily the mutual consent expressed in the words *de praesenti,* it referred to the cause of the sacrament. And of course this consent is expressed by the spouses themselves. Trent implied that the essential difference between marriage in the old law and the sacrament in the new law lies not in the difference of formula of consent, but in the fact that the latter confers sanctifying grace while the former did not. Trent also anathematized those who say that before the decree *Tametsi* clandestine marriages were not true and ratified. But the Church has traditionally used the term "ratified" (*ratum*) to designate sacramental marriages.

After showing that Cano contradicted the overwhelming majority of theologians—or at least those who wrote on the subject—Bellarmine moved on to an argument drawn from logical consequences.[80] In it he fashioned a dilemma for Cano. Thus, marriages among Christians are either monogamous and indissoluble or they are not. If they are both these, they are sacraments, because their being sacraments is the only cause of their monogamy and indissolubility. If they are neither, then Cano can offer no conclusive reason why Christians who have not had a priest witness their vows and bless their marriage cannot dismiss their spouses or have polygamous marriages. But this inability to account for indissolubility is not the second horn of the dilemma. Bellarmine put it in place by pointing out that Cano must reductively contradict Catholic tradition and Trent itself, which have never allowed dissolution of Catholic marriages or polygamy just because the marital consent was not witnessed by a priest. On the contrary, the Church has always held clandestine marriages, provided they are consummated, to be as monogamous and indissoluble as any others. Therefore they must be sacraments even though their contracting had no priest witness and no priestly blessing.

Summary

By the eve of the Protestant reformation the scholastic theology of marriage, like scholastic theology as a whole, could make its case only feebly. It was a casualty of the philosophic skepticism endemic in the universities of Europe, a skepticism which communicated itself immediately to theology because philosophy, in its subset which is metaphysics, provides theology with its conceptual system and its vocabulary. This skepticism was born of the Augustinian Platonists' failure to account for human intelligence's gaining scientific knowledge via sense perception of creatures and their interactions. The failure showed itself in the exaggerated realism of Bonaventure and Scotus, and at the other extreme in Ockham's and the Ockhamists' empiricism.

Pietistic and voluntaristic affirmation of divine illumination as the source of human knowledge followed. In the domain of marriage skeptical pietism acknowledged that God can will that naturally indissoluble marriage be dissoluble where the latter is the better good. Especially damaging for the theology of the sacrament was the denial, or at least the doubt, that human intelligence can know with certainty the cause-effect relationships among physical creatures.

The greatest of the humanists, Erasmus, proposed a reform of theology that might have affected the Catholic understanding of the marital sacrament profoundly. He urged that the first step in studying the scriptures, the very source of theology, is to go back to the original biblical languages, Hebrew, Aramaic and Greek, to read the sacred books themselves in these languages—back beyond the frequent misinterpretation of them in scholastic theology and law. He insisted too that the first task of biblical interpretation is to find out passages' first and literal meaning—which demands in turn that students learn the history, the linguistics and the imagery of the age which produced them. Erasmus' richest contribution to the imminent Protestant reform was his insistence that many doctrinal conclusions were inconclusively drawn from their sources in the scriptures because these sources had been misinterpreted. He criticized the Catholic use of the New Testament divorce texts for just this reason. He criticized even more trenchantly the traditional interpretation of Ephesians 5:32 as a source of the doctrine of the marital sacrament.

Disagreement among Catholic teachers on significant doctrinal and canonical matters further weakened the Church's stance at the eve of the reformation. Melchior Cano made the strongest case against the teaching that every Christian marriage is a sacrament. Cardinal Cajetan too taught the separability of contract and sacrament, and Estius along with him. Disagreement reigned too about the minister(s) of the sacrament and about its matter and form.

Luther's attack on the Catholic doctrine and discipline of marriage was not at first directly at the sacrament. He aimed it rather at the Catholic authorities' "captivity" of marriage, against their claim to exclusive jurisdiction over it. He denied the sacrament partly as a strategy for taking marriage away from this jurisdiction. He rejected the sacrament of the new law in Christian marriage because, as he claimed, there is no record in the New Testament of Jesus' having instituted it as such, because it does not grace the spouses, and because "there is in it no divinely instituted sign. He especially insisted that the "great sacrament" of Ephesians 5:32 is not predicated of Christian marriage.

In his *Loci Communes Theologici* Melancthon added that the sacramental signs of the new law are only seals on God's promise to grace those who have faith. In fact God has given these signs in order to awaken faith. And only those signs are Christian sacraments that the gospels report Christ to have instituted as such.

Calvin's rejection of the Catholic teaching was in substance and justification substantially identical with the Lutheran. Along with it he insisted that the "great sacrament" of Ephesians 5:32 refers not to Christian marriage but to the spiritual marriage of Christ and the Church.

The bishops of Trent's main concern about marriage was to inhibit clandestine marriage, a concern exacerbated by the prevailing doctrine that the Christian spouses themselves are the ministers of their sacrament. In their twenty-fourth session, on November 11, 1563, the bishops issued their decree on marriage. It stated that God instituted marriage, and instituted it as indissoluble in the garden of Eden, and that Christ confirmed this indissolubility by his words "What God has joined man must not separate." They taught that he also merited the grace which confirms the natural love of Christian spouses and seals their indissoluble union, thus making it a sacrament. Paul implied the same in calling marriage a great sacrament. This session's decree, *Tametsi,* moved to end clandestine marriages by making invalid any Christians' exchange of marital consent without the witness of an authorized bishop, priest or deacon, and of two or three other witnesses.

The principal tasks that Trent bequeathed unfinished to later generations of theologians were to show again and more convincingly in what way Christian marriage is a grace-giving sacrament, and to show how Christ has made it such. The principal dispute it left unresolved was two-ply: whether in Christian marriages contract and sacrament are inseparable, and whether every marriage of two Christians must be and is a sacrament.

NOTES

1. Thus Albert, *In IV Sententiarum,* Distinctio 31, Articulus 17; Thomas, *In IV Sententiarum,* Distinctio 32, Quaestio 1, Articulus 3, ad 2m.

2. Denzinger-Schönmetzer, nn. 1300–1308, pp. 331–332.

3. *Op. cit.,* n. 1327, p. 336.

4. *Op. cit.,* nn. 1310–1311, pp. 332–333.

5. "Horum quinque prima ad spiritualem uniuscuiusque hominis in seipsum perfectionem, duo ultima ad totius Ecclesiae regimen multiplicationemque ordinata sunt." *Ibid.,* n. 1311, p. 333.

6. There is serious doubt about the immediate authenticity of the *Supplementum.* Scotus died at the age of forty-two, leaving much of his work unfinished. His pupils set about to finish it from his notes. Therefore what we read of this work may be Scotus' only at one remove. If this is so, we have an example of Scotist voluntarism perhaps a half-generation after the master's death.

7. In the *Editio Salustiana,* Romae, 1903, pp. 652–653.

8. *Op. cit.,* p. 653.

9. *Ibid.*

10. *Ibid.*

11. Distinctio 30, Quaestio 2, in *Opera Omnia, Quaestiones in Quartum Librum Sententiarum,* Vives edition, Vol. 19, p. 186.

12. *Opera Omnia,* p. 653.

13. *Ibid.*

14. *The Imitation of Christ,* by Thomas à Kempis. The full text of the Autograph Manuscript of A.D. 1441 translated into modern English by Edgar Daplyn, N.Y., 1950, pp. 20–22.

15. In Albert Rabil, Jr., *Erasmus and the New Testament: The Mind of a Christian Humanist,* San Antonio, 1972, p. 32.

16. In Rabil, *op. cit.,* p. 104.

17. *Op. cit.,* p. 107

18. From Erasmus' preface to Valla's *Annotationes in Novum Testamentum,* in Rabil, *op. cit.,* p. 61.

19. In Rabil, *op. cit.,* p. 108.

20. *Opera* (Basil, 1542), Tomus 6, p. 499 (quoted in G.H. Joyce, *op. cit.,* p. 391, note 1).
   21. *Opera* (Leyden, 1704), Tomus 5, Col. 615.
   22. *Op. cit.,* Tomus 6, Col. 692ff.
   23. *Op. cit.,* Tomus 5, Col. 623.
   24. Because Cano's disagreement touched so painfully a sensitive nerve in the theology of the sacrament, his fullest expression of it is worth reproducing here.

I know of course that baptism is a sacrament. But if it had neither a sacred form nor a minister, it would be a bathing but not a sacrament. I also accept the sacrament of last anointing. But it too, if it lacked a sacred form and a minister would indeed be an anointing. But it would not be a sacrament.

So also, even though marriage is a sacrament we are not obliged to consider every marital union to be such, but only those which have a sacred form and have been consecrated by a minister of the Church. Otherwise if any and every marriage of Christians is necessarily a sacrament, who will agree with Scotus, who denies that marriages contracted by mere signs are sacraments? And unless my understanding fails me, his denial is accurate.

What is more, not only the Master and St. Thomas but the Council of Florence teach that all the sacraments must have in them certain words; and that if these are missing, no sacrament is created.

If we once admit that the form of the sacrament can at times be gestures in place of words, we simply cannot avoid admitting too that a priest can grant absolution by a gesture and a bishop can ordain by a nod. Marriage itself is at times contracted by no other gesture than sexual intercourse. For all jurists and theologians admit that a true marriage is created when the betrothed have intercourse with marital intent subsequent to their betrothal. But to claim that sexual intercourse is a sacrament of the New Law is absurd. The Holy Spirit and the grace of the sacrament are not given through intercourse.

. . . sacraments in the true sense are sacred religious ceremonies. The exercise of sacred things belongs to religion, which is the cultus of God. A sacrament is an exercise of religion. And in the sacraments we are professing publicly our quest of salvation by God's mercy. But this profession, which is the exterior manifestation of interior faith, belongs to that virtue by which we give worship to God. . . . Augustine himself defined a sacrament as not just any sign of a sacred reality, but itself a sacred sign. . . .

. . . In this regard Augustine explained to Boniface (in his Epistle 23) that the physical things making up sacraments must themselves contain an image and likeness of the sanctification of which they are said to be both signs and causes. Thus by its exterior bathing baptism is the image and likeness of the spiritual bathing it effects. In the Eucharist the sensate nourishing by food and drink images an interior nourishing. In just this way in all the rest of the sacraments an interior sanctification is signified by a definite external action and imaging. But a merely civil and non-religious marriage neither images any sanctification nor does it pretend to sanctify under any exterior sign of sanctification. Therefore it is not a sacrament in the true sense. (Melchioris Cano, *Opera*, Patavii, 1734, pp. 242–243.)

25. In *Opuscula*, Tomus 1, Tractatus 12, Quaestio 1.

26. *In IV Sententiarum*, Distinctio 26, Quaestio 2, Articulus 3.

27. *In IV Sententiarum*, Distinctio 26, Quaestio 2, Articulus 3.

28. In Poncher's opusculum, *Septem Ecclesiae Sacramenta et Artem Audiendi Confessiones Declaramus* that he joined to Jean Gerson's *Opus Tripartitum* in 1507.

29. Lectures on Genesis in *Luther's Works*, Vol. 1, edited by Jaroslav Pelikan, St. Louis, 1958, p. 68.

30. *Ibid.*, pp. 68–69.

31. *Op. cit.*, p. 115.

32. *Ibid.*, p. 116.

33. *Ibid.*, pp. 117–118.

34. In *Luther's Works*, Vol. 28, edited by Hilton C. Oswald, St. Louis, 1973.

35. *Op. cit.*, p. 18.

36. *Ibid*, p. 19.

37. In *Luther's Works*, Vol. 21, edited by Jaroslav Pelikan, St. Louis, 1956.

38. *Op. cit.*, p. 86.

39. *Ibid.*, p. 87.

40. *Luther's Works*, Vol. 44, edited by James Atkinson, Philadelphia, 1966, p. 8.

41. *Ibid.*, p. 9.

42. *Ibid.*, pp. 9–10.

43. *Luther's Works*, Vol. 36, edited by Abdel Ross Wentz, St. Louis, 1959, p. 92.

44. *Ibid.*

45. *Ibid.*

46. *Ibid.*, p. 93.
The translator here is Erasmus. He edited the first published Greek New Testament in March 1516. Luther used it as soon as it came out.

47. *Ibid.*, p. 94.

48. *Ibid.*, pp. 95–96.

49. Quoted in *Melancthon and Bucer*, The Library of Christian Classics, Vol. 19, edited by Wilhelm Pauch, Phila., 1969, p. 17.
Melancthon's estimation of himself was less exalted. At the end of his brief discussion of "Mortal and Daily Sin" he wrote, "On these matters I prefer you consult Augustine or Luther rather than me" (*op. cit.*, p. 133).

50. *Op. cit.*, p. 132.

51. *Ibid.*, p. 134.

52. *Ibid.*, p. 135.

53. *Ibid.*, pp. 135–136.

54. In *The Book of Concord*, The Confessions of the Evangelical Lutheran Church. Translated and edited by Theodore Tappert, et al. Phila., 1959, pp. 35–36.

55. *Op. cit.*, pp. 211–212.

56. *Ibid.*

57. *Institutes of the Christian Religion*, Book 4, Chapter 19, "The Five Other

Ceremonies, Falsely Termed Sacraments, Although Commonly Considered Sacraments Hitherto, They Are Proved Not To Be Such, and Their Real Nature Is Shown," in *The Library of Christian Classics,* Vol. 21, edited by John T. McNeill, Phila, 1960, Vol. 2, pp. 1480–1481.

58. *Op. cit.,* p. 1481.
59. *Ibid.*
60. *Ibid.*
61. *Ibid.,* p. 1482.
62. Denzinger-Schönmetzer, nn. 1600–1630, pp. 381–384.
63. The eight canons recorded here are in Denzinger-Schönmetzer, nn. 1601–1608, p. 382. The translation of the canons is my own.
64. The Latin phrasing of this canon is "Si quis dixerit, per ipsa novae Legis sacramenta ex opere operato non conferri gratiam, sed solam fidem divinae promissionis ad gratiam consequendam sufficere. . . ." To translate this literally as "If anyone says that grace is not conferred through the sacraments of the new law by the working of the sacraments . . ." could imply that the sacraments produce grace "automatically"; at worst, that no faith, no trust, no love are needed in the participants in the sacrament.
65. Denzinger-Schönmetzer, n. 1797, p. 415.
66. *Ibid.,* n. 1798.
67. *Ibid.,* n. 1799.
68. *Ibid.,* n. 1800., pp. 415–416.
69. *Ibid.,* n. 1801. p. 416.
70. In their teaching on divorce and remarriage Luther and his followers repeated substantially the doctrine and the discipline of the Orthodox Catholic churches. They allowed divorce (by civil authority) because of proved adultery and equivalent crimes, immediate remarriage for the innocent spouse, and remarriage for the guilty spouse only after penance. However Luther recommended capital punishment for adulterous spouses who refuse to repent (cf. Sermon on the Estate of Marriage, in *Luther's Works,* Vol. 45, pp. 32–33), as he did for a wife who contumaciously refused to have intercourse with her husband (*ibid.,* p. 33).

The bishops at Trent initially planned a head-on anathema for the Protestants who contradicted Catholic doctrine on divorce and remarriage. But an unusual circumstance, and a most unusual plea born of it, led them to pronounce the anathema by a circuitous route and in softened form.

The Republic of Venice's delegates at the council pointed out that at that time the inhabitants of the islands of Crete, Cyprus, Cephalonia, Corfu and Ithaca were subjects of the Republic. They had for centuries lived under the Greek Orthodox discipline for divorce and remarriage. The bishops of these islands were appointed by Rome, but they had thus far chosen not to challenge this discipline. The Venetian delegates urged that with patience on the part of the Roman Church these Aegean and Ionian peoples might eventually be led to accept the Roman discipline. But if the tradition and practice permitting divorce because of adultery were anathematized by the council, they might rebel and break away permanently. The delegates proposed and even begged that the canon formulate a gentler and indirect condemnation.

They pointed out a tactical problem facing the bishops. It was how to not catch the Greek Catholics in the same target area with Luther, who had accused the Roman Catholic Church of teaching error. The Greek Catholics had never made this accusation. But at the same time the bishops had to assert the Roman Catholic discipline that allowed no more than dismissal and separation because of adultery, over against the Greeks, who permitted divorce because of it.

The adroitly and sinuously formulated Canon 7 was designed to resolve just this problem: "If anyone says that the Church errs when it has taught and still teaches, according to the doctrine of the gospels and of the apostles, that the bond of marriage cannot be dissolved because of the adultery of one or other of the spouses; when it teaches that neither of the spouses, not even the innocent one, who has given no cause for the adultery, can remarry as long as the other spouse still lives; when it says that the husband who remarries after dismissing an adulterous wife, and a wife who remarries after dismissing an adulterous husband, commits adultery; let him be anathema."

Thus worded the canon spared the Greeks, who had not accused the Catholic Church of error in teaching as the canon explains. But it anathematized Luther and the Lutherans, who had leveled just this accusation of error.

71. *Op. cit.*, nn. 1813–1816, pp. 417–418.

72. This is in *Disputationum Roberti Bellarmini . . . De Controversiis Christianae Fidei Adversus Hujus Temporis Haereticos.* Venetiis, apud Joannem Malachinum, 1721.

73. *Op. cit.*, p. 617.

74. Current, n. 74.

75. *Ibid.*, p. 618.

76. *Ibid.*, p. 619.

77. *Op. cit.*, p. 621.

78. *Ibid.*

79. This is in Chapter 7, "Every Legitimate Marriage Contracted Between Christians Is a Sacrament," *op. cit.*, pp. 630ff.

80. *Ibid.*, p. 631.

BIBLIOGRAPHY

Calvin, John: *Institutes of the Christian Religion*, Volume 2, Book Two, Chapter 19: "The Five Other Ceremonies, Falsely Termed Sacrament . . ." in *The Library of Christian Classics*, Volume XXI, edited by John T. McNeill, Philadelphia, Westminster Press, 1960.

Ehrlich, R.: "The Teaching of the Reformers on Marriage," in *Biblical Theology*, 1974, pp. 1–19.

Hillman, Eugene: "Polygamy and the Council of Trent," in *The Jurist*, Vol. 33 (1973) pp. 358–376.

Joyce, George H., *op. cit.*, Chapter 3, "The Formation of Marriage, ii": "The Institution of Obligatory Forms," Parts 2–5.

Kelly, H.A.: *Love and Marriage in the Age of Chaucer.* Ithaca, N.Y., Cornell University Press, 1975.

Luther, Martin: *The Babylonian Captivity of the Church*, in *Luther's Works*, Volume 36: Word and Sacrament, II, edited by Abdel Ross Wentz, Philadelphia, Muhlenberg Press, 1959.

————: *The Estate of Marriage*, in *Luther's Works*, Volume 45: The Christian in Society, II, edited by Walter I. Brandt, Philadelphia, Muhlenberg Press, 1962.

————: *A Sermon on the Estate of Marriage,* in *Luther's Works,* Volume 44: The Christian in Society, I, edited by James Atkinson, Philadelphia, Fortress Press, 1966.

Mackin, Theodore: *Marriage in the Catholic Church: Divorce and Remarriage.* Ramsey, Paulist Press, 1984, Chapter 14: "Secular Challenge, Protestant Reformers and Trent."

Melancthon, Philip: *Apology of the Confession of Augsburg,* in *Library of Christian Classics,* Volume 19: Melancthon and Bucer, Philadelphia, Fortress Press, 1969.

Purvis, Charles B.: *Marriage in Seventeenth Century Catholicism.* Paris, Desclée/ Montréal, Bellarmin, 1975.

11. THE SECULARIZATION OF MARRIAGE AND THE CATHOLIC REACTION

When the bishops in the twenty-fourth session of the Council of Trent defined about the marriage sacrament what they thought amenable to definition, they wisely determined only a minimum, as we have seen, although a serious minimum. (We have seen too that their most worrisome concern was not the Protestant denial of the sacrament, but clandestine marriages and the bitterness and grief they caused for parental families and for abandoned wives and children.) A study of the debate in the council leading to the decree on marriage would show the bishops and their theologians reaching unanimity about little more than what they did decree, namely that Christ raised marriage in his new law to the status of a sacrament, and that this is a sacrament in the full sense of the word—not only a sign of a sacred reality, but a sign that when applied, or administered, brings justifying grace to those to whom it is administered.

A cluster of other questions about the sacrament remained answered only in varying degrees of tentativity. The frequency of these questions' appearance in the treatises published by post-Tridentine theologians is not in direct proportion to the seriousness of doubt about their answers. But the variety of answers suggested in the various treatises is not without meaning. The following are the questions that were to be raised most frequently.

In which episode during his public ministry and by which words did Jesus make marriage in his new law a sacrament? No one claimed that he did so in words as explicit as his eucharistic mandate to the disciples at supper the night before his death, "Do this as a commemoration of me" (Lk 22:19), nor as explicit as in the liturgical addition to Matthew's gospel, "Go then and make disciples of all the nations; baptize them in the name of the Father and of the Son and of the Holy Spirit" (Mt

28:19). All admitted that Jesus' institution of the sacrament could be found only implicitly among his declarations about marriage. Since these were few and confined to his instruction about divorce and remarriage, his instituting the sacrament would have to be verified there, as long as all agreed that a record of the instituting would have to be found in the gospels themselves. The norm of verification for the search, the hypothetical model, was the definition of a sacrament inherited from the fathers and refined by the scholastic theologians. Could there be a fixed and final verification of some words of Jesus in which he made, or declared, marriage to be a grace-giving sign of an invisible sacred reality? That this could be done was pre-determined by the synergy of two premises. These were Trent's decree that Jesus had in fact made marriage to be a sacrament of the new law, and the definition of a sacrament just formulated. The task then was to identify once and for all the words and/or deeds in which Jesus did this.

That question about the episode and words of institution of the sacrament in marriage was a kind of scholion to Trent's decree about the fact of the sacrament. It was of concern mainly to theologians working within the Church to build a consensus in the explanation of doctrine, and to apologists defending the doctrine. A second question, in substance theoretical theology but trailing consequences both canonical and political as yet only faintly glimpsed, asked about the minister or ministers of the sacrament. In the eleventh and twelfth centuries a question ancestral to this had occupied scholars and authorities. It asked about the act or acts that create the marital union itself (the union later to be called a contract), and therefore about the agents of this creation. By the end of the fifteenth century its answer had been long accepted. These agents are the spouses themselves. And their act that creates the marriage is their reciprocal *consensus de praesenti*. That settled, the same question had to be asked about the sacrament in marriage. We have seen the answers to it proposed before, during and immediately after Trent. Despite a majority opinion that the spouses themselves are the ministers of their own sacrament, doubts remained. In every other of the Church's six sacraments the minister thereof and the recipients are distinct. If the officiating cleric is not the minister of the sacrament in marriage, his participation in the wedding—made by Trent's *Tametsi* a condition for the validity itself of the contract—is redundant.

But a third question, whose canonical and political consequences we have seen were already painfully visible, asked about the separability of the contract and the sacrament. Since all agreed that the sacrament in mind is that which Christ instituted in the new law, all agreed that the contract and sacrament are at least distinct. For even if one holds that marriage as instituted in the garden of paradise is a pre-Christian sacrament because a sign of God's purpose for marriage in the world, such marriages among pagans, or even among Jews and Muslims, cannot be

Christian sacraments. This third question asked therefore about the marriages of Christians. Even in their case the contract and the sacrament are admittedly distinct because the contract as contract is the same as that instituted by God centuries before Christ's coming, instituted for all the human race at the beginning of history. It is also the same contract as that created by a couple at first unbaptized, but that is held to become sacramental only later after both are baptized. Surely that which was at first not a sacrament remains distinct from it even when it is raised to the status of a sacrament.

But the question that bore such a weight of consequence was not about that distinction. This question asked whether contract and sacrament in the marriage of two Christians are separable, whether two Christians can create a marriage that is not a sacrament. Can they, though Christians, will effectively that their marriage not be a sacrament? This was not a question that engaged the Protestant theologians, since in denying that Christ had made marriage a sacrament in his new law they voided the question *a priori*. It was a question that vexed Catholics. And within its confines they were Catholics who vexed Catholics. As honored a theologian as Cardinal Charles Billuart wrote long after Trent, in 1750, "One who would exchange the consent of marriage without the intention to receive the sacrament could create a true and valid contract but would not create the sacrament, for intention is required for the validity of the sacrament. Even though God instituted the sacraments without taking account of the will of man, he did not will to impose their conferring the sacrament without the cooperation of their wills."[1]

The canonical and juridical issues hovering near because of this uncertainty and disagreement we have noticed already several times. If two Christians, indeed if two Catholics can create a marriage contract that is not a sacrament, there is no compelling reason for the Church's holding jurisdiction over them as married. Marriage returns to the place in society it had for at least the first eight hundred years of Christian history, to a family matter controlled by the families. If it needs governance by a more comprehensive authority, this is civil authority—as it was in the Christian Roman Empire.

What is more, the cause that Catholic authority has set for any marriage's indissolubility, the consummated sacrament, is missing from this union. This opens to civil jurisdiction the power to dissolve even the marriages of Catholics that are not sacraments.

The Catholic authorities after Trent knew from long experience that there are always civil rulers eager to claim such power. As early as the twelfth century the Italian communes that contested papal rule over central Italy—as well as that of the German emperor in the north and of the foreigner king of Sicily in the south—tried to end ecclesiastical control over marriage cases, especially over the setting of impediments and the dispensing from them. Lombard law was used to devise The Statutes of Pistoia, which sought to take away from Church courts the ruling on and dissolving of betrothals, the decreeing of nullity, the ordering of separations, the settling of property after annulment or separation, and the determining of legitimacy and of the liceity of relationships in marriage.

But the attempt to take control of Catholic marriages that stuck in memory most clearly was that of Emperor Ludwig IV of Bavaria in the middle of the fourteenth century, during the Avignon papacy of John XXII. Ludwig wished to marry his son to a wealthy noblewoman, Margrete Maultasch, in order to gain her considerable fortune. She was already married to Johann Heinrich of Bohemia. But Ludwig claimed that her marriage was unconsummated and therefore vulnerable to dissolution by papal authority. He demanded that John XXII dissolve it.

When the latter refused to do so, Ludwig in 1342 declared himself juridically competent in the matter and decreed the dissolution of Margrete's marriage. At John's protest two "publicists," two defenders of the authority of secular princes, set forth philosophic justifications for Ludwig's claiming and exercising authority as he did. One of these was William of Ockham, who had fled to Ludwig's refuge after having been excommunicated by John XXII in 1328. The other was Marsilius of Padua.

Obviously Ludwig's challenge to papal authority had as its target not marriage itself in the Catholic population but the jurisdiction over marriage in this population. In fact Ludwig claimed vulnerability to dissolution in Margrete's marriage on the same ground that Pope John might have claimed it. He did not say it was not a sacrament, nor that in it contract and sacrament were separable and under two different authorities, the civil and the ecclesiastic. He insisted, again, that even if a sacrament, it was not consummated as a sacrament. He was challenging nothing in the theology of marriage itself. What he challenged was a point of the theology of authority in the Church as this was incarnated in marriage law, namely the exclusivity of the papal jurisdiction over Catholic marriages.

The case that Ockham made for Ludwig's jurisdiction in his *Tractatus de Jurisdictione Imperatoris in Causis Matrimonialibus* (Treatise on the Emperor's Jurisdiction in Marriage Cases) depended on two points of fact. First, the Christian Roman emperors had exercised legislative and judicial authority over the marriages of their subjects, and the Church had acquiesced to this without complaint. But the Holy Roman Empire, over which Ludwig reigned, is the continuation of the Roman Empire and continues its authority. The second fact was that it is the office of the emperor to protect the public good in his realm. Therefore whenever obedience to Church law would injure this good, he can exempt himself from it and rule according to his wisdom.

Marsilius of Padua concurred in this theory. But he added a claim for civil authority in the execution of even divine law. Ecclesiastical authority can do no more than define the dispositions of divine law, can only say what they are. But coercive power in regard to this law belongs to the emperor alone. Since only he knows the facts of cases within his realm, he alone can decide the disposition of divine law in these cases.

Like Ockham he did not ground the emperor's authority over marriages in an alleged separability of sacrament and contract in them. But the Catholic Ludwig's maneuver, and these two Catholic publicists' rationalization of it, showed what was awaiting the juridical and judicial management of marriage from as early as three and four centuries before Europe's decisive secularization of it.

The Post-Tridentine Challenges

The earliest challenges after Trent to the Church's exclusive jurisdiction over Christian marriages came from the French monarchy. Fearful of antagonizing the Huguenots, the French kings held off even permitting the council's decrees to be ratified in their realm. Not until 1615 did the French bishops act on their own responsibility to accept these decrees and promise to comply with them. Meanwhile the monarchy deemed the entire French population, clergy included, to be exempt from their binding force. Insofar as it touched marriages in France this denial did not have as its assumed justification that Christian marriages are not sacraments. This was to come only two and a half centuries later in the revolution, when the Estates General would simply erase everything religious from French constitutional and juridical life. What the monarchy with its parliament alleged was that it had its share of jurisdiction over marriage in the realm, a share distinct from the Church's because within marriages themselves there is a distinct natural, civil, pre-religious element. This is the contract—the marriage itself—with its fundamental properties and conditions. To the Church belongs the religious element, namely the religious celebration which creates it.

We recall that in Canon 1 of its Decree on Marriage, the Council of Trent meant to declare implicitly that all marriages of two Christian spouses are sacraments by decreeing explicitly that Christ made marriage among his followers universally to be one of the sacraments of his Church. The apparent sense of the council, that which has been assumed by Catholic authorities subsequently, is that the abstract universal in the decree, "marriage," determines the concrete universal, "all (Christian) marriages."

The council decreed the Church's exclusive jurisdiction over Christian marriages also implicitly, but very nearly explicitly, in its Canon 12 wherein it anathematized those who deny that marriage cases do not come under the competence of ecclesiastical judges.[2] It approached this claim in its earlier Canons 3 and 4, which anathematized respectively those who deny that the Church can dispense from the invalidating degrees of consanguinity and affinity or can establish multiple degrees of the same, and those who deny that the Church can set invalidating impediments at all.[3] It was just this jurisdiction that the French kings claimed for themselves. We shall see in a little while the detailed rationalization for this claim.

It will help also to review briefly Melchior Cano's argument that the minister of the sacrament in marriage is the priest, not the spouses, and that the act which creates the sacrament cannot be the latters' consent, but must be some verifiable religious gesture by the priest—most probably his blessing. We do this because the early French challenge to exclusive Church jurisdiction drew its rationalization more from such patently orthodox theologians as Cano and Cajetan, however much it may have been inspired by the centuries-long and comprehensive resistance to papal authority exemplified in Philip the Fair's brutal rebuffs to Boniface VIII, and inspired too by the rebellion against papal authority on the part of France's old enemy, the Empire, in the person of Ludwig of Bavaria. Cano's disagreement nourished the French challenge because if he were accurate, if the sacrament in Christian marriages is administered by the priest, one could then argue that the spouses' consent effects something non-sacramental, even non-religious. This must be the marriage itself. And since it needs to be regulated by law, this regulation will not be religious but civil.

We recall that for Cano the spouses' marital consent, in the hylemorphic model of the sacrament, is only the latter's *materia*. Its form is the priest's blessing. In his favor he cited the disagreement and even confusion among his theologian predecessors and contemporaries concerning the constitution of the sacrament and concerning its minister(s). His intrinsic argument he drew from the axiom, *sacramenta significant id quod causant,* "the sacraments signify, or image, the effect they cause." But, he reasoned, the formula of consent that spouses used in his time, "I accept you as my own" (*Ego accipio te in meum/meam*), signifies no spiritual effect. It is religiously formless; it determines no religious meaning. Therefore it can have no more than a material, determinable function in the creating of a marriage. It must be determined by a different and formal element. Cano detailed his argument thus:

> It is unintelligible that a sacrament be formed without a sacred form. For just as the human form constitutes a man, and whiteness makes something white, so too must any sacrament exist by a sacred form. But in a marriage that is contracted in a merely civil and profane way there are no sacred words. So there is in it not even the appearance (*facies*) of a sacrament. . . . What is more, the form of a sacrament signifies that spiritual effect of which the sacrament is said to be the cause. For the sacraments, as the proverb in the schools has it, effect what they signify. . . . But the words, "I accept you as my own," are the sign of no spiritual effect.[4]

Add to Cano's logic here a marriage by proxy's obvious distance from any sacramental action. The proxies do nothing religious. Their execution of the principals' mandate has the character of a civil and contractual exchange. Not only is no love of the spouses for one another required, but they need not even know one another, and need not have ever met. How could such a relationship be the sign of a sacred reality? How indeed could two strangers who, let us say, meet one another not until a year after the marriage by proxy have imaged the love relationship of Christ and the Church during that year?

The Challenge from the French Royalists

The French monarchy opened its grand offensive against the Church's exclusive jurisdiction over the marriages of Christians at the beginning of the seventeenth century. It employed the talent of canonists to do so, all of them Catholics and otherwise orthodox, but imbued with the Gallican passion to free all significant parts of life from any regulation that was not French.

Their major thesis was that marriage is first and fundamentally a civil contract. The Royalist jurists developed variations of this thesis. The first we shall inspect was not one of their own, but borrowed from the *De republica Christiana* of Marcantonio de Dominis, erstwhile archbishop of Spalato in Lombardy. (De Dominis had abandoned the Catholic faith, migrated to England, and was there made the dean of Windsor. He wrote the *De Republica* there in 1620 and dedicated it to James I.)

De Dominis proposed two theses about the sacrament, one of them hypothetical and, in his judgment, contrary to the facts. This said that God instituted marriage at the beginning of history as a merely natural contract. In his time Jesus limited himself to reestablishing marriage's original monogamy and to making it indissoluble. But he did not touch the substance of marriage. He left it a natural contract, although amenable to civil regulation. Therefore its regulation belongs to civil authority. The Church can do no more than admonish this authority to obey the divine law.

Supposing there is a sacrament in a Christian marriage, its creation there is both temporally and logically subsequent to the forming of the contract. It is a spiritual and supernatural accessory to the contract. Therefore the Church has jurisdiction over nothing more than the supernatural effects of the sacrament. For example, it may require Catholic couples to receive the sacrament by accepting the priest's blessing. But it is understood that this blessing that creates the sacrament does not create the marriage. This already exists as the effect of the spouses' contractual exchange of consent under civil jurisdiction.

De Dominis' second thesis, which he proposed as the real state of things, was that there is no sacrament in any marriage. It is therefore inconsequential to argue that in Ephesians 5 Paul said that a devout Christian marriage is a symbol of Christ's union with the Church. In any case such a symbol would not make the marriage a sacrament in the new law, for if every symbol of a sacred reality in the new law were a sacrament, these sacraments would be absurdly numerous. But this consideration is void to begin with, since Paul did not say that a Christian marriage is a sign of a sacred reality. To say he did so is to misinterpret the passage. Nor does a marriage confer grace, if only because there is no record of a divine promise of grace attached to Christian marriage. In a word, de Dominis, having abandoned the Catholic faith, adopted a substantially Protestant theology of marriage.[5]

The Gallicans seized on and used de Dominis' first thesis as soon as an opportunity presented itself. This came in 1631 when Gaston of Orleans married Margaret, the sister of the Duke of Lorraine, the hated enemy of Gaston's brother, King Louis XIII—and did so obviously without Louis' consent. Louis feared losing his throne to the house of Lorraine. So at Richelieu's insistence he petitioned Pope Urban VIII to declare Gaston's marriage null on the ground that French law forbade the heir-apparent to marry without the king's consent. When Urban refused, Louis announced his intention to annul Gaston's wedding himself. The premise on which he claimed authority to do this is the by now familiar one, that all marriage contracts in France were formed under his authority as civil ruler because they are in essence civil contracts.

The Parliament of Paris acknowledged this authority on September 5, 1634, but Gaston denied it. Richelieu thereupon took the case to the Assembly of the French Clergy, which, after a year's deliberation, sided with Louis. Predictably it based its judgment on the distinction and even the separability in Christian marriages of contract and sacrament. But two years later, in 1637, Louis relented and recognized Gaston's marriage.[6]

The dispute between the two royal brothers inspired a number of treatises by French jurists during the ensuing decades, most of them written to reinforce Louis', Richelieu's, the parliament's and the assembly's judgments. All, with secondary variations, shared a common ground of agreement. All began with the assumption that the contract and the sacrament are distinct and separable. Hennequin, professor at the Sorbonne, reasoned that in instituting the sacrament Christ left marriage unchanged as a civil contract. He did no more than to "insert" the sacrament into the contract as into a needed foundation.

Hennequin explained the matter thus:

> Our Lord Jesus Christ, in elevating the civil contract, which is itself first grafted into the natural contract, to the dignity of a sacrament of the New Law, changed nothing in this contract as civil. He only imposed, attached, grafted the nature and dignity of a sacrament onto it as onto a trunk, as an accessory onto a principal element; in such a way that after this elevation the civil contract remains what it was before the elevation.[7]

This theory differed from that of the later secularists in accepting that there is a sacrament in Christian marriages, and that therefore the Church has a legitimate interest in these marriages.

In 1674 Jean Launoy wrote the *magna carta* of the Gallican claim to civil jurisdiction over marriage, his *De regia in matrimonium potestate* (On the Royal Authority Over Marriage). He began by citing the judgments of seventy theologians, medieval and contemporary, favoring the jurisdiction of the state over marriages. His substantive argument anticipated the philosophers of the Enlightenment and the theorists of the revolution. He urged that marriage is not a natural contract, and therefore not even as a contract is it divinely instituted by the author of nature. It is instead only a civil contract, a species of conveyance, devised by the state for the good of its citizens. Therefore civil authority regulates it according to the needs of public civil order. The sacrament is purely accessory to this contract. It is the nuptial blessing.

As for the history of ecclesiastical regulation of marriages, Launoy maintained that this has been a usurpation of authority from its beginning. The only authority held by the Church is for the regulation of the sacrament. He disposed of Canon 4 of Trent's decree on marriage (we recall that it asserts the Church's authority to establish impediments against marriage) by relegating it to the status of a merely disciplinary canon. He also reminded his readers that the council's decrees had never been promulgated in France. He added that in any case the term "Church" in the canon is to be understood to include princes and their authority therein.[8]

In 1690 Jean Gerbais published a treatise whose title tells of its peace-making intent and argument, an attempt to strike a compromise of conflicting claims: *Traité pacifique du Pouvoir de l'Église et des Princes sur l'Empêchements* (An Irenic Treatise on the Power of the Church and of the Princes over Impediments). He proposed that in Christian marriages there is both a civil and a religious element, a civil contract and a sacrament. He explained that marriage is fundamentally a natural contract, that the civil contract takes this and completes it, and that the natural-contract-become-civil is the matter of the sacrament. Therefore both Church and state have jurisdiction over such a marriage, but each over its proper element. The proper office of the state is to regulate the contract, which is the marriage itself, because marriage is the "seminary" of the state. The Church's office is to regulate the sacrament, which is accessory to the contract and therefore to the marriage. Both can set impediments and dispense from them without interference from the other. In regulating the contract the civil government does not touch the sacrament, Gerbais explained by analogy, any more than a surgeon in amputating a priest's arm touches his sacrament of orders.[9]

Gerbais' argument became the rationale of the Gallican bishops despite its gainsaying Canons 3, 4 and 12 of Trent's decree on marriage. Needless to say, its attempt at compromise was unacceptable to Catholic authorities for reasons we discern easily by now. The most basic of these was that it kept the substance of marriage, the contract, for civil jurisdiction, and of course not only distinguished contract from sacrament but separated them.

In 1753 the Parisian jurist, Pierre Léridant, ventured into theology in order to put the sacrament in this familiar tenuous relationship with the civil contract. In his *Examen de deux Questions Importantes sur le Mariage* he first insisted that in instituting the sacrament Christ did not "metamorphose" marriage. He maintained the contract and did not remove it from civil authority. For marriage existed centuries before Christ's coming, from the beginning of the human race. He simply added the sacrament to the integral contract in order to sanctify it and to confer grace on the spouses. And this sacrament is the priest's blessing. The Church's authority is limited to determining whether the parties are worthy of the sacrament, and to conferring it when they are. Any other rights the Church has at any time are given to it by the supreme civil authority, which can always revoke them.[10] (The *Code Napoléon* would adopt this last idea as a principle.)

Léridant's theological intervention was calculated to deny the compromise theory that the sacrament as the priest's blessing relates to the civil contract, in the hylemorphic model, as the form of the sacrament to its matter. He explained with some derision, and with the evident intent of keeping the sacrament as disjoined from the contract as possible while still allowing its existence:

> One must note first of all that the terms "matter" and "form," with which our Scholastic theologians have inundated their writings, are unheard of in antiquity. . . . However, if one insists on speaking of "matter and form," what shall we assign as matter and form in the sacrament of marriage? . . . To put it briefly, the oldest tradition tells us of nothing about marriage except the imposition of hands and the blessing—which are the same things. It asks "On whom does the priest impose hands?" "Whom does he bless?" So it is this imposition of hands, this blessing, that is the matter of the sacrament of marriage. The words which accompany it make up its form.[11]

That Léridant here was indulging not entirely in ironic jest is suggested by the similarity of his design for matter and form in marriage with that of baptism. Scholastic theology has regularly seen the matter of this sacrament to be also a physical gesture, the bathing with water, and its form to be also a fixed formula, "I baptize you," etc.

The Secularization of Marriage in Catholic Europe

The conflict we have just sketched between papacy and French crown concerning jurisdiction over marriages in that realm dealt not with an attempt at secularization in the radical sense. Richelieu, the

Bourbon kings, the parliament were professed and traditional Catholics. They shared the ancient world-view, inherited from the Hebrews, that life in the world is fundamentally religious. They believed in a God who is the creator of all, whose providence rules all, that life goes on under his gaze, and that men and women must finally account to him for their conduct. The target of their challenge to exclusive papal jurisdiction was its exclusivity. The premise of the challenge, in refined form, was that while all of life belongs to God and is in that sense religious, not all of it belongs to the Church. Elements of it come under civil rule, especially where the rulers are themselves Christian; and most especially do those elements ante-dating the coming of Christ and the Church not belong exclusively to the latter.

Secularization as a deliberate and sharply defined project began from a different premise and had a different target, even though in France it grew out of the Catholic royalist challenge in a semi-organic way. It divided the world of human affairs not into the ecclesiastical and the civil but into the religious and non-religious. Its progenitors were not atheists, as Francis Bacon, John Locke and David Hume in England certainly were not. But their concept of a creator God was not of an infinite intelligence active in a universe it is holding in existence by continuing creation. Insofar as his existence and nature can be known at all, he is the divine architect-artisan who has fashioned the universe as a closed, self-energizing system functioning according to its internal laws, and left to run its course on its own. His functional relevance to it, and its to him, ended with his act of creating it. Perhaps the secularist world-view is best exemplified in the assumption common to the modern Western mind (whether the assumption is parent to our religious toleration or child of it is hard to know). It is that a man's or woman's life can make sense apart from any relationship to a creator—as much sense in its own order as a life lived in relevance to a creator.

Consequently for the kind of secularist in question, even for a Christian, that in life which is non-religious is not merely non-ecclesiastic. It is out of God's purview; it is purely human. This was the destiny for marriage in the minds of the European secularists of the late eighteenth century: to understand it and to govern it as an exclusively human, this-world relationship—as a civil contract and nothing more. The effort came to fruition in the French revolution, thanks to the professedly atheist among its protagonists, the extremists among the Jacobins and Girondists, such as Chaumette, Hébert and Marat.

The secularization of marriage in France began obliquely and gently, confident of its doctrinal legitimacy thanks to the theorizing of Hennequin, Launoy, Gerbais and Léridant that we have reviewed. The *Code Matrimonial* edited by Léridant in 1770 in none of its articles touched the marriage bond directly. It preserved earlier penal legislation, for example an ordinance of 1579 that forbade a curé to witness marriage vows without the consent of the parties' parents. Like the later

Declaration Royale of 1639 it did not purport to annul marriages contracted without such consent, but deprived them of ordinary civil effects, such as the right of inheritance. The parliament more and more remanded to civil judges cases of marriages contracted by minors, or without publishing of the banns, or without witnesses, or without parental consent. To block *matrimonia repentina,* marriages contracted before a priest surprised and semi-coerced into witnessing the parties' consent, the parliament (not the pope nor even the Assembly of French Clergy) in 1698 legislated that the voluntary and active assistance of a priest is required for valid contracting.

We will see soon that the Gallican assumption of jurisdiction over marriages for the crown was the prelude and the path to the radical, non-Christian control of marriage in France during the revolution and permanently thereafter. There is irony in the fact that the Bourbon monarchs, their advisors and their pliant parliaments, who began the takeover of jurisdiction, were the most thorough casualties of the revolution that completed their project.

The Josephist and Febronian Challenges

Another set of monarchs in another sector of Catholic Europe followed closely after the French in invading the once exclusive Church jurisdiction. What the Hapsburg Joseph II intended in his legislation of 1780–1790 seemed to be a reduction of the Church in his empire to the functional status of a department of government. But he was not the one who innovated the effort. Gallicanism as an attitude had spread well beyond the borders of France. By the middle of the eighteenth century Wenzel von Kaunitz-Reitberg, chancellor to Empress Maria Theresa, was thoroughly imbued with it. He began the de-ecclesiasticizing process by removing priests and religious from teaching posts in the empire, including the removal of the Jesuits from the faculties of philosophy and theology at the University of Vienna.

In 1763 Johann Niklaus von Hontheim, under the pseudonym Justinus Febronius, published his *De Statu Ecclesiae et Legitima Potestate Romani Pontificis (On the Position of the Church and the Legitimate Authority of the Roman Pontiff).* It was a charter for the domestication of the Church in the empire. Hontheim's professed intent was to suggest a way of uniting dissident Christians to the Catholic Church. One of his strategies for this was to subdue the universal primacy of papal authority by recovering for Christian princes the authority over religion in their realms that he deemed had rightly been theirs before powerful medieval popes usurped its exercise. Indeed his Febronianism, as it came to be known, was a species of conciliarism, since his indictment of papal usurpation included the charge that it had taken over from the other Catholic bishops authority belonging to them individually and in regional council.

Hontheim's book and its ideas gained popularity in the antecedently sympathetic schools and clergy of the Empire. Since it was condemned by Rome it could not be made a manual of teaching. But its principles were reproduced in slightly mitigated form in 1772 by J. P. von Riegger's *Institutiones Jurisprudentiae Ecclesiasticae (Instruction in Ecclesiastical Jurisprudence)*. This was made the textbook of the universities and was imposed on all monastic and episcopal schools. Joseph II succeeded Maria Theresa at her death in 1780. His decrees asserting civil control over marriages in the Empire were clearly inspired by the Febronian theory and were a concrete application of it.

On September 4, 1781 he promulgated a law forbidding his subjects to seek marital dispensations from either the papal nuncio in the Empire or from Rome itself. Application for them was to be made to the bishop of one's diocese. But lest one think that the latter could dispense by their own authority as bishops, a different source of this authority was made clear to them in a letter of March 28, 1782 written to him by Joseph's minister, Philipp Cobenzl.

Marriage being a matter which is first and foremost civil, and in which the religious element is only accessory, the impediments to it are similar in character. Hence it is primarily for the civil tribunals to judge the necessity or utility of a dispensation. This being admitted, your Majesty held that the diocesan bishop and his Consistory are now as formerly more than competent to decide the cause in accordance with the sacred canons of the Roman Church.[12]

A year later, in 1783, Joseph took his campaign another and more drastic step. He issued a constitution withdrawing marriage cases from the Church courts all together. He claimed exclusive jurisdiction over them. He assumed that a marriage is a civil contract. Therefore it belongs to the state to decide the condition of its validity.

An even clearer indication of how far Joseph's plans for secularization reached came when Archbishop Migazzi of Vienna explained to his clergy in a pastoral letter that the new constitution touched only the civil aspects of their Catholic people's marriages, and that the Church's canon law remained otherwise in force. Joseph's reaction to this was to claim that the prescriptions of his constitution regarding marriage abrogated those of canon law, and that in the future his Catholic subjects were to be ruled in marriage matters by the former alone.

Compliance with this Febronian removal of marriage into the civil domain was almost universal among the people and clergy of the Empire. Few seemed to suspect in what direction and how far the removal was to lead. Like the Protestant reformers three centuries earlier comfortable in their vision of themselves as permanently Christian, they were comfortable in the vision of themselves as permanently Catholic. Their real concern was to loosen the tether of papal control over their lives generally. The regulation of marriage was merely the most opportune point at which to begin the loosening. A political-religious arrangement dating back to the early middle ages enhanced the desire for religious independence and simultaneously tranquilized any anxiety about a secular takeover. A number of the major bishoprics were held by prince-bishops. Among these were Cologne, Trier, Mainz and Salzburg. Their bishops were civil as well as ecclesiastical rulers of their dioceses. It was difficult for them not to think of themselves as vassals of the emperor. It was even more difficult for them to oppose his will to exclusive jurisdiction over marriages in the Empire because they knew they were to be the semi-independent instruments of his will, and could therefore guarantee the Catholic character of marriage regulation. They were sure that the anti-religious extreme to which civil regulation went in France during the revolutionary terror would never be reached in their territories.

They were accurate in this self-assurance. But their independence from Rome led to a different destiny than the one they anticipated. They did establish marital impediments at their own discretion, and dispensed from them in their dioceses. In 1788 they even asked Pope Pius VI to remove his nuncios from the dioceses in the interest of religious peace. They enjoyed their free exercise of jurisdiction, always against papal objection, for about two decades. But the Napoleonic wars and their aftermath tore up and redrew the political map of Europe. The ecclesiastical principalities of the Empire were abolished. At the Congress of Vienna, Cologne, Trier and Mainz were parceled out in pieces among Prussia, Nassau and Hesse. Salzburg was taken into the Austrian empire. And there marriages were regulated by secular princes far less Christian than the prince bishops.

A small but significant duplication of Joseph's strategy and tactics was brought off by his brother, Leopold the Grand Duke of Tuscany. He deemed himself so much the guardian of religion in his realm that he ordered its bishops to summon diocesan synods during which they were to install reforms designed by himself. Only three acceded to this demand, principal among them Scipione Ricci, bishop of Pistoia. He called his synod on July 31, 1786. It was thoroughly Gallican-Jansenist in character, so much so that preparation for it included a series of consultations with the Jansenist theologians and clergy of Paris. And Jansenist sympathizers from all parts of Europe attended the synod itself.

Leopold and Ricci envisioned a broad-ranging reform of Catholic life, including some in liturgical worship and pastoral conduct within parish life that merited adoption, anticipating as they did reforms that were to be installed in the nineteenth and twentieth centuries. But the synod brought papal condemnation down on itself because its fundamental intent was to break the authority of Rome over Catholic life and to shift it to regional bishops, and reductively to the Catholic civil rulers. This showed itself especially in the domain of marriage, where the synod repeated Emperor Joseph's claim to the civil ruler's exclusive right to set invalidating impediments against marriage and to dispense from them, and repeated too that churchmen can do the same only with the approval of the supreme civil authority.

Before surveying the papal reaction to these Gallican and Josephist campaigns to take Catholic marriage away from ecclesiastical authority, it will help to note again the different designs of the rationale for doing so. The most common premise within the diversity is one we have seen so frequently, that in the marriages of Christians the contract is the marriage in substance; that the sacrament is so distinct from it as to be separable; that the contract is a civil entity, and therefore comes by nature under civil jurisdiction. The sacrament, which is the priestly blessing, is administered by the authority of the Church. That the civil authority would be in the hands of Catholic princes was assumed as part of this design.

But even where the premise was not this alleged separability of contract and sacrament, a variant rationale urged that a Catholic prince too holds authority in the Church, and this authority has a legitimate claim on marriages where these affect the public good in the prince's domain. The legislating of impediments and the imposing and dispensing of them clearly affects this public good.

A subvariant of this we have seen in the strategies of both Joseph II in the Empire and Leopold in Tuscany. Without appealing to the assumed separability of contract and sacrament in marriage they claimed to so hold authority over the civilly relevant facets of marriage as to be able to delegate to the bishops within their realms the authority to impose impediments and to dispense from them.

What was common to all these was the conviction that the essentially civil character of marriage does not remove it from religious purview, but only from exclusive ecclesiastical jurisdiction within this purview. All these were assumptions, rationales and programs of reform devised by men who thought of themselves as naught but faithful Catholics.

The Catholic Reaction to Secularization

When one traces the reactions of the Catholic authorities to the campaign to secularize marriage in Europe one must take note of two kinds of reactions fitted diversely to the two kinds of campaigns. To that of the Catholic princes acting as Catholics convinced that they too held authority in the Church, and wanting only to regulate marriages they intended to leave Catholic (albeit with their sacramentality reduced to a minimum), there was one reaction. But to the attempts of anti-religious ministers and parliaments to make marriage a secular instrument of a secular state, the reaction was different and more severe. Examples of the latter are to be found in Pope Pius IX's *Syllabus of Errors* in 1864, and in Leo XIII's *Arcanum divinae sapientiae* of 1880.

The first reaction was a generic rebuff to the Gallican strategy of the

French crown. In 1681 and 1682 Louis XIV had ordered the General Assembly of the French clergy to approve four articles that asserted among other things his immunity from Church authority in temporal matters. These came to be known as the Gallican Articles. They claimed also that the pope's authority in religious matters is subject to that of an ecumenical council, and that his decrees gain their validity from the consent of the entire Church. But most to our point they claimed validity for the laws, customs and teachings of "the Gallican Church" apart from any external interference. Innocent XI condemned these articles on April 11, 1682. Alexander VIII repeated the condemnation in his constitution *Inter multiplices* of August 4, 1690.[13] Following the latter condemnation Louis himself wrote a letter retracting the articles' claims.

It was Pius VI (1775–1799) who resisted the most energetically the incursion on papal authority. In his brief *Super soliditate petrae* of November 28, 1786[14] he solemnly condemned the book *Was ist der Papst? (What Is the Pope?)* of the Viennese canonist Josef Eybel (1782), which embodied the principles of Febronianism as these had been laid out in Hontheim's *De statu Ecclesiae et legitima potestate Romani Pontificis.*

Two years later, on September 16, 1788, Pius aimed his counter-fire more exactly. In his letter *Deesemus nobis* to the bishop of Motola near Naples he laid down the correct interpretation of Canon 12 of Trent's decree on marriage.[15] The bishop had accepted delegation from the king of Naples as a civil judge to decide in a petition for nullity. He had justified doing so by interpreting the phrasing of that canon to not claim for the Church an authority in marriage cases that is exclusive. For its formulation is "If anyone says that marriage cases do not come under the competence of ecclesiastical judges, let him be anathema." The bishop saw there an opening for civil judges' sharing in this competence. Pius VI called this a cavil. He declared that the spirit and context of the entire Tridentine decree indicated exclusivity for ecclesiastical judges. He gave as the internal reason for this exclusivity the following familiar interpretation: "Since these cases belong to the judgment of the Church alone for the one reason that the marital contract is one of the seven sacraments of the new law, and since this status of sacrament is to be found in all marriage cases, it follows that all these cases belong exclusively to the ecclesiastical judges."[16] Pius' spare Latin could not have claimed the theological fact more firmly, nor set the fact more clearly as a principle in law: Where the marriage is of two Christians not only are the contract and sacrament inseparable, but the contract *is* the sacrament.

Six years later still, after delays brought on by the political turmoil in Europe, Pius published his response to the synod of Pistoia. In his constitution *Auctorem fidei,* addressed to the whole Church on August 28, 1794, he condemned eighty-five propositions culled from the synod and formulated in ways that here and there turned the synod's own meaning.[17] Condemned Proposition 59 contained the claim that authority to impose and to dispense from diriment impediments against marriage belongs originally to the civil authority, that authority in the Church to do the same comes to it from the civil ruler, and (Proposition 60) that the latter can take from the Church any authority to set impediments and to dispense from them.[18] But in this constitution Pius did not cite the sacramental nature of the marital contract between Christians as the reason for the Church's prior, legitimate and exclusive authority over these impediments.

The most inclusive reaction to the civil claims over Christian marriage made up a part of Pius IX's *Syllabus of Errors,* published along with his encyclical letter, *Quanta cura,* on December 8, 1864. But because the pertinent errors therein condemned include those derived from the thorough secularization of European marriages following the French revolution and the revolutions elsewhere in Europe in the first half of the century, a review of the Syllabus will follow a review of this secularization.

Thirteen years earlier Pius made his first entry into the dispute about marriage. This took the form of an apostolic letter, *Ad apostolicae sedis,* on August 22, 1851.[19] It condemned two books by John Nepomucene Nuytz, *Institutions de Droit Ecclésiastique* and *Traité de Droit Ecclésiastique* which, according to Pius, contained in concentrate all the errors of the civil authoritarians from the time of Trent and before. These were: the denial of the possibility of proving that Christ elevated marriage to the dignity of a sacrament; the assertion that the sacrament, invented by the Church, is no more than the nuptial blessing and therefore entirely separable from the contract; the denial that the bond is by natural law indissoluble; the denial that the Church has the right to establish invalidating impediments and contrarily the reservation of this right to civil authority, which alone has the authority to remove impediments and to adjudicate marriage cases; the assertion that the Church's prerogative of establishing impediments is something granted to her by civil authority, not something belonging to her by right; the denial that the form of marriage vows before a priest and other witnesses obliges under pain of nullity when civil authority prescribes a different form. Pius' summary judgment on Nuytz' thinking was that it sought to destroy the very nature of the Church by taking from her all authority in the external forum.

The Enlightenment

Students of this church-state tug-of-war over marriage know that within the secular challenge to papal authority a different spirit was by now at work, one not seen in Western history since the ancient cynics and epicureans.

In their own self-assessment the Gallicans and the Febronians may have wanted little more than to break the papacy's exclusive hold on marriage in their realms. But more searching reflection would have revealed to at least the later generations among them how much they were influenced by the minds of the Enlightenment. It would have revealed too how far beyond the freedom from ecclesiastical control they demanded these minds would take marriage in once-Catholic Europe.

The Enlightenment was a movement of mind and will that began among the educated elite in Europe about the middle of the seventeenth century. It was inaugurated by the thought and writings of René Descartes and John Locke, both of them sincere Christians. As the movement's name suggests, its intent was to free from ignorance, above all from scientific and religious ignorance—to use authentic science to free from this ignorance and its consequences.

Where the Renaissance was an effort to enliven the present by recovering a rich past, and the reformation an attempt to reform the present by reinstating a pure past, the Enlightenment sought to release Western man into a new future by breaking the grip of the past on the present.

We may take the following as a dominant four among the first principles of the Enlightenment. To begin with, human reason is the measure of all things. What cannot be understood by unaided reason is irrelevant to the human condition, and even loses its claim to acknowledged existence.

Second, reason and good will, rightly employed, are sufficient for gaining human well-being and happiness.

Third, as a derivation of the Ockhamist denial that intellect can penetrate to and understand the natures of physical beings, the meaning and goal of science shift from finding out these natures and their purposes in order to gain wisdom, to finding out their functions in order to use them for well-being.

Finally, in the hierarchy of values freedom resides immediately under the summit, second only to the continuity and peace of civil society. These, personal freedom and the peace and continuity, are reciprocally conditions for one another's existence.

It is worthwhile to account at least in part for the formally philosophic component of the Enlightenment, not as something peripheral to it but as something central and dominant. For vis-à-vis religion the Enlightenment was a philosophic reductionism. It accepted as much of, but no more of, the Christian religion than philosophy could accept.

The loss of confidence in deteriorated scholastic philosophy and conversely the impressive gains in mathematics, the natural sciences and engineering by the middle of the seventeenth century led philosophers to adopt as their own the principles and methods of mathematics and these sciences.

Descartes demanded the systematic doubt appropriate to the scientist: Accept from the past nothing in virtue of authority, nothing that has not been proved. Call all accepted theological, religious, philosophic and scientific affirmations into doubt. Go back to the beginning and start over, but this time with an invulnerable method of inquiry. Where the Ockhamists had urged that only those propositions be accepted as true which could be reduced to the logical principle of non-contradiction, Descartes urged that only those ideas be accepted as valid that, by mathematical criteria, are clear each in itself and distinct from all others. Only that knowledge is to be kept that can be formulated in certain propositions, with their certainty coming from clarity and distinctness. Thus the merely probable should be rejected from the treasure of knowledge, and with it all error—including the error of superstitious religious belief.

On their side Hobbes, Locke and Hume harvested the yield of the Scotist-Ockhamist sundering of intellect and sense. They insisted that all knowledge—at least all knowledge useful for carrying on life—comes through sense perception. But one cannot through this perception discover the natures of things; one cannot find an alleged human nature behind the phenomena of human presence and activity. Therefore one can discover no antecedent and given law of nature, no ultimate goal of human desire and striving, no fixed principles to guide conduct to this goal. What is left for guiding conduct is personal utility understood as the service of personal pleasure. Public morality can then be, and must be, the social contract: individual persons' negotiated agreement to limit their pursuit of private pleasure for the sake of one another's pursuit of the same pleasure. But it is taken for granted that no one can discern which pleasures, if any, are in themselves ultimately destructive or ultimately fulfilling.

The new method of cognition urged by Descartes and executed by the empiricists had this effect on religion: Where Scotus and Ockham split sense and intellect but kept a Christian faith that belied the split, the Cartesians on the one hand and the empiricists on the other appropriated the split and sought to carry on as Christians enlightened and animated by innate and antecedent moral will.

That much is a succinct positive statement of the Enlightenment agenda. A fuller understanding of its goal is available in a list of its principal targets for reform and even destruction.

It sought to purge the historical record of legend and fable. In religious matters this meant edifying legend and fable. It meant the centuries-long practice of seeking to preserve ancient popular faith by telling what could and should have happened and believing that it did happen, of rewriting the record to accommodate what the pious present wants to have happened. Anyone who has read the legend-filled hagiography of the times recognizes the target.

In philosophic matters this meant the neo-Platonic-Augustinian notion of knowledge as the discovery of ideal, abstract models—or, failing their discovery, the designing of them under the pretense of discovery—and, coming from this notion, the search for knowledge as a scrutiny of models designed by the alleged wise men of the past, in place of examination and testing of the concrete here-and-now.

It sought to end the intrusion of the so-called miraculous and super-natural into human affairs, the use of this intrusion to excuse from responsibility in managing these affairs, the turning to angels and demons to account for otherwise unaccountable happenings, and to religious magic and superstition in the effort to control them.

Linked with the foregoing was a rejection of the domination of Christian consciousness by belief in and a reach for a supernatural dimension of reality. This did not mean rejection of existence that transcends human perception, but rebellion against the belief that knowledge must remain incomplete without supernatural revelation, that the human will is impotent without supernatural grace, that human longing must remain unfulfilled unless rewarded by a beatitude beyond human reach—all this a denigration of humanity and a counsel for cowardice.

A most immediate target of the Enlightenment revolution was the claim of Church authorities over an unwarrantedly inclusive portion of life, their intrusion into private life and public territories of life that belong under civil authority or family authority, and simultaneously the whole panoply of clerical exemptions, especially those from taxation (of the vast Church-held estates) and from penal law.

The effects of the Enlightenment campaign against these objectives were bound to be severe for the traditional Christian religion. Granted the Enlightenment assumption that human intelligence cannot verify scientifically a domain that transcends the sensate, then its existence, including the existence of a Creator, can be held to only by voluntaristic faith. Out of this came the casting of God in a new role, that of respondent to emotionally felt human need. He was displaced from the center of religious concern, along with his providential plan and his governing will. Into that center came the freedom-seeking, perfection-capable human person. It was an anthropocentric Christianity replacing a theocentric.

There followed the rejection of the ancient penitential attitude, the sense of sin and guilt, of the constant need for repentance, forgiveness, redemption and justification. Most especially did the Enlightenment reject a pivot of the ancient Pauline-Augustinian Christianity, original sin—rejected it both as an historical event and as a permanent crippling and guilt endemic in the race. Into its place as the work of quasi-redemption came release from fear, the desire for education, for political liberation, for the freeing of the natural impulse for goodness.

Jesus himself was reinterpreted. He was no longer the pre-existing divine word come into the world to redeem and save. He was primarily a teacher of moral goodness, a character obscured in the gospels by miraculous narratives and other legends, all of which are irrelevant to his purpose. His teaching is to be judged by the norms of rationality. He is one of the several founders of worthwhile religions who have suffered at the hands—or more exactly at the mouths and pens—of his interpreters.

Not the Church but the state is the people's universal provider, especially in education and social well-being. The state is the most important social institution because it contains the richest representation of intelligence and civic virtue. It is by definition the collectivity of rational individual persons and their rights. It is created by these persons in their pursuit of happiness, by a social contract to not hinder one another unfairly in this pursuit. Therefore the will of the state is the united wills of all the persons comprising it. Therefore too this will is by definition supreme and unassailable. Its principal duty, as hinted above, is to guarantee freedom, including religious freedom, and to provide for the common well-being.

The champions of the Enlightenment—one thinks especially of Diderot, Voltaire, Rousseau, Grotius, Pufendorf—indicted the Catholic Church as the enemy of the people and of the state. It has been this enemy, they insisted, mainly because it has invaded the authority of the state and has claimed universal primatial authority in religious matters as well as in civil. The religious and ecclesiastic territory of life is only a fraction of what the Church has traditionally claimed. Indeed the Church rightly understood is a part of civil society. It is the agency within this society whose duty is to foster religion and morality. So the Enlightenment in its most respectable representatives did not seek to abolish religion and the Church, but to interpret their place accurately and to keep them there. As part of its duty to protect personal freedom the state must tolerate all religious groups and their conduct, except that conduct which is intolerant of other religious groups. The Catholic Church has for centuries shown such intolerance, and for this reason too needs to be tethered by the State. As the Gallican and Febronian theorists interpreted the Church-state relationship, the latter has general authority over the former (*jura majestatica circa sacra*). Within this it has the right of inspection (*jus inspiciendi*). The Church must have the state's approval for its governance (*jus cavendi*). And Christian citizens may appeal to the civil courts against the Church's jurisdiction (*recursus tamquam ab abusu*).

The School of the Law of Nature

The way marriage would be interpreted by the Enlightenment became clear in its earlier years in the School of the Law of Nature. This was a philosophic movement started up by the Dutch jurist, Hugo Grotius (1583–1645). (His name before being Latinized was Huig de Groot.) His 1625 masterwork, *De Jure Belli et Pacis* (On the Law of War and Peace), is regarded as the beginning of the scientific treatment of international law. But the school's moral and social philosophy was worked out most systematically by the German, Baron Samuel von Pufendorf (1632–1694), in his *De Jure Naturae et Gentium* (On the Law of Nature and of Nations, 1672) and in his *De Officio Hominis et Civis* (On the Duty of Man and of Citizen, 1673).

That this school of social morality and law is called Law of Nature instead of Natural Law is no casual variation of a traditional title. The difference of name bespeaks a significant difference of interpretation. For Aristotelian philosophy the finding and fixing of law is an inductive work within an accepted goal orientation. On the assumption that the good life in society is the well-ordered state, citizens experiment to find out which kinds of conduct tend to realize this goal, which do not. Aquinas' theory of natural law likewise demanded that human intelligence work inductively, since human beings act according to natural law when they search out which conduct leads to the end that is human well-being and happiness.[20] He differed of course from Aristotle in his identification of this happiness.

Grotius bridged from this scholastic understanding of natural law to a law of nature. Like the former he held to the existence of objective right understanding, to unchangeable moral principles, and to God as the highest source of law. But he differed from them in his thinking that such understanding, principles and law can be gained apart from a divine lawgiver. He was convinced that these could be found out deductively, that from an inclusive concept of the human essence one can infer via strict logic a full set of moral principles, and from these in turn men can develop a code of statutes satisfactory for regulating life in society. His debt to the conceptualism of the late scholastics seems clear, as does his anticipation of the a priorism of Descartes and Kant.

Pufendorf moved even further from the Aristotelian tradition and its scholastic adaptation. For him the law of nature was grounded in and sanctioned by God's will, not in and by his intelligence. What is fundamentally right in conduct is right not because it follows a divine plan but because it is willed by God. In this Pufendorf continued, whether knowingly or not, the voluntarism of Ockham. He held that law enters consideration only because of God's creating human nature as essentially sociable and because he wills human beings to live in society. Thus, from societal human nature considered abstractly one can deduce the fundamental principles of law, and these become binding when embodied in the positive law of the state. In effect, though Pufendorf may not have intended this, for the citizens civil law becomes natural law. The political philosophers become the mentors of law. And the Gallicans and Febronians have a theoretical warrant for the religious autonomy they want so dearly, and within it their civil control of marriage.

Pufendorf was Lutheran, and if he had reckoned the Christian religion's place in and hold on marriage according to the Book of Concord, he would have said that God instituted marriage immediately when joining the first couple in the garden of Eden. But consistency with his own theory of the law of nature called for him to relocate that institution on both the map and the calendar. He held that God's instituting marriage was mediated through the minds and wills of human legislators. This can be drawn by inference from his *De Jure Naturae et Gentium*. It opens with a long chapter on marriage. There marriage is said to exist not because God's kindness and wisdom provided a companion for the first man, but because human reason has found that the right ordering of society requires that the race be perpetuated within a stable heterosexual society. Men and women have an obligation to contribute to this propagation, but they may fulfill it in various ways determined by positive civil law.

Thus when men and women marry they contract to create a bond that is natural in the sense of needed for the good of civil society. For this reason there is a serious moral obligation to honor the contract, for the nurture of children to adulthood for this society. Neither spouse has the right to sever the bond at will. But either may sue for divorce if the other has violated the contract's essential terms—with which violation all obligation ceases. He saw three violations to be serious enough to warrant divorce: "Therefore by mere natural law one of the two will be freed from the marriage bond when the other is guilty of malicious desertion, as well as of obstinate and voluntary refusal to perform the due rights of marriage."[21]

Adultery violates the marital contract in the same way because a man has the right to gain marriage's end by procreating offspring he knows with certainty to be his own.[22]

There is nothing specifically secular and there is no denial of a religious claim in Pufendorf's defining the malice of adultery in this way. But such denial is explicit in his next words.

> It appears, then, that the reason why adultery and malicious desertion are recorded as a sufficient cause for divorce is not due to a special positive law of God, as though these were the two exceptions to the absolute stability of marriage, but to the fact that the common nature of pacts is such that when one party does not abide by the agreements, the other is no longer bound by them. So much so that not only is the injured party no longer required to cohabit with such a perfidious consort, but he or she may marry again. Whatever canon law urges to the contrary is nonsense.[23]

This German Lutheran scholar has left Martin Luther far behind. Canon law—obviously the Catholic variety—is nonsense now not because the theologians and canonists have misinterpreted the New Testament divorce passages, and not because the popes have foreclosed the centuries-long debate on the permissibility of remarriage after divorce by forcing their interpretation on the debaters. It is now nonsense because it contradicts natural law as conceived of by a mind more secular than the ancient Greeks—because it contradicts the nature of civil contracts.

In 1689 John Locke argued for the dissolubility of marriages, and for the reasonableness of it, in a way congruent with a theory of the natural demands on marriage coming from Aristotle's Nicomachean Ethics. In his "Essay Concerning the True Origin, Extent and End of Civil Government" (*Of Civil Government, Second Treatise*) he accepted that the natural end of marriage is the procreation and proper nurture of children.[24] To realize this end husband and wife must remain together until their children are duly educated, provided for, and able to live on their own. But once all this is accomplished, the reason demanding that they stay together lapses, and they may dissolve their marriage.

> But though these are Ties upon Mankind, which make the Conjugal Bonds more firm and lasting in Man, than the other Species of Animals; yet it would give one reason to enquire, why this Compact, where Procreation and Education are secured, and Inheritance taken care for, may not be made determinable, either by consent, or at a certain time, or upon certain Conditions, as well as any other voluntary Compacts, there being no necessity in the nature of the Thing, nor to the ends of it, that it should always be for Life; I mean, to such as are under no Restraint of any positive Law, which ordains all such Contracts to be perpetual.[25]

Voltaire was born the year Pufendorf died (1699), and took his thought about the origin and nature of marriage further along the path on which the latter had set it. Where Pufendorf insisted that marriage is intelligible by inference from nature and its law, prescinding from God as their author and sanction, Voltaire simply denied that marriage has come from the creator and his law. He insisted that it is the product of the law of nations, of the *jus gentium,* that it is a natural contract only in the derived sense that the law of nations has made it into a contract in the interest of civil harmony and stability. He went on to accuse the Church of attempting a kind of doctrinal and juridical abduction by making the marriages of Christians into sacraments.

> Marriage is a contract of the law of nations which the Roman Catholics have made into a sacrament. But the contract and the sacrament are two quite different things. To the former belong the civil effects, to the other the graces of the Church. Marriage can subsist with all its natural and civil effects independently of the religious ceremony.[26]

Voltaire did not deny the marital sacrament its place. But the place he allowed it was well outside the natural relationship and the civil contract. It was no more than the religious ceremony, and survived in existence only for the duration of the ceremony.

The French Revolution and the Secularizing of Marriage

A more careful study of history has long since gainsaid the popular notion of the French revolution as a violent proletarian insurrection. It has replaced this with the accurate understanding that it was mainly an effort by the French bourgeoisie to break the power of the Bourbon monarchy, and to install a constitutional republic modeled on the recently formed United States of America. It was because monarchy and Church in France were so intimately wedded that the revolution became also a spiritual and religious drama. For most of his reign (1610–1643) Louis XIII was completely under the influence of Cardinal Richelieu, who entered the Council of Ministers in 1624 and soon became chief advisor to the throne. Louis XIV was dominated by Cardinal Mazarin. Cardinal Fleury was Louis XV's teacher and then his prime minister from 1726 until 1743. Thus when the French looked at the monarchy they also saw the Church, and when they looked at the official Church they saw it as one department of monarchic government. Hence breaking the hold of the Bourbon dynasty on the nation demanded also the breaking of the Church's hold on the religious life of the people at least at those points where the religious and the civil converged. It meant also ending a clerical *modus vivendi* that had thrived for centuries in France. In its meeting of 1789 the Estates General presented its *Cahiers de Doléances*, its Bill of Grievances. Principal among these were the Church's ownership of ten percent of French land—un-taxed land at that; the exemption of the clergy themselves from any direct tax; the interference by the papacy in French political and religious life; the clergy's resistance, as part of the *ancien régime,* to needed social and political change.

The French middle class nursed a special dislike for the religious orders with their exemption from jurisdiction by the local bishops and their ultra-montane loyalty to the Pope (this animosity had got the Jesuits suppressed in France in 1764). The Gallican Jansenists were especially revengeful toward the papacy which had condemned their rigorism and their religious nationalism. The French Protestants demanded religious freedom and equality.

The original revolutionary reform had no intent to destroy the Church. What it wanted was precisely reform—reform of the whole of life in France, and the Church's cooperation in the effort. But the plan of reform held elements that churchmen would not accept. On August 4, 1789 the constituent assembly abolished clerical privileges. Bishops could no longer levy tithes, nor could they administer their own civil holdings. In November of the same year Church property was nationalized, the clergy were put on state salary, and the state took over the administration of hospitals and schools. At the same time the constituent assembly issued its Declaration of the Rights of Man, which included complete religious equality and freedom. To implement this freedom the assembly in the spring of 1790 declared all religious orders dissolved and actually suppressed those not engaged in nursing or teaching. In July of that year it promulgated its Civil Constitution of the Clergy, demanding of bishops and priests an oath to uphold the new constitution, a move that split the French clergy into the jurors loyal to the revolution, and the recusant nonjurors hostile to it and loyal to the papacy.

Pope Pius VI reacted within a year by solemnly condemning the Civil Constitution in March 1791, and by then condemning the principle of religious equality and freedom itself. He saw the revolution as nothing other than a Jacobin plot to destroy religion and the Church in France. When the French aristocratic families went to foreign monarchs for help in destroying the revolution and in restoring them to privilege, and Pius joined with them in this quest, the revolution was taken over by the most violent of its champions and moved into the first reign of terror in the summer of 1792.

The Revolution and Catholic Marriage

But the first and even pre-revolutionary move against Church control of marriage had been made five years earlier when, in 1787, an edict of the parliament granted Protestants the right to marry either before a royal judge or before a priest considered a civil magistrate. Until then French Protestants had either to compromise their religious loyalty and wed before a priest witness, or have their own ministers as witnesses despite their being unauthorized by the Catholic Church, and suffer the legal consequences of concubinage and the illegitimacy of their children. In failing to authorize Protestant ministers themselves to witness wedding vows the edict still fell far short of religious liberty and equality. But it did more than sanction this qualified religious freedom of Protestants. It implied that despite their Christian baptism their marriages were only natural contracts, or perhaps, according to Voltaire's mind, only civil contracts. In doing so the edict simply ignored the issue of these marriages' sacramental character.

The architects of the First Republic did not concern themselves with marriage until their final deliberation on the constitution of 1791. There under Title II, Article 7, the constitution named marriage a civil contract. This established a principle that was put in practice a year later, September 20, 1792 in two statutes: one under Title IV that established a system of purely civil legislation for marriage, a second that established the availability of divorce in consideration of personal freedom within the demands and prerogatives of the civil contract. Religious ceremonies at weddings were not forbidden, but they were denied any civil effects, which meant that they had no agency in creating the marriage.

What has been called the "de-Christianization of France" got seriously under way simultaneously with the aforementioned terror of the summer of 1792—the first and "little terror." It was a reaction to Pope

Pius VI's joining the deposed nobility in their alliance with the Empire and with Prussia to foil the revolution and regain their place. This reaction was first an assault by the legislative assembly, then by the national convention, on the Catholic Church and its religion, and then on all forms of Christianity, with their destruction as its goal. During the legislative assembly it was led by the Girondists, a small group of intellectuals bred and nurtured by the Enlightenment. Later the assault was taken over by the more violent Jacobins, the Mountain and the Commune during the period of the national convention. Robespierre, virtual prime minister of the Committee of Public Safety, and captain of the second and "great terror" from September 1793 to August 1794, was an odd counterpoint to the atheism of the others, Chaumette, Hébert, Marat, Fouché, et al. He was a Rousseauvian deist. He inaugurated worship of the supreme being in May and June of 1794, and sought to impose by law belief in him and in the immortality of the soul. But any mitigation of the thorough secularization of marriage he might have effected was blocked by his own execution in July of 1794.

But in the face of centuries-long French tradition the revolutionaries could not ignore the sacred character of marriage. The intellectuals and the religiously destitute proletariat of the newly industrial cities might have accepted the obliteration of that character. But the people of the provinces would not. So in a taunting and eventually self-defeating way the revolutionaries replaced Catholic ritual with a complete Republican ritual. The national convention established the annual Feast of Marital Love. A decree of 3rd Brumaire of the Year 4 of the revolution instituted a national Feast of the Spouses. The law of 13th Fructidor of Year 6 made obligatory the contracting of marriages on the 10th day of Decadaire.

An anciently Catholic French people's resistance halted the religious persecution temporarily. But in August of 1795 the Thermadorian convention voted permanent separation of Church and state and put an end to the short-lived constitutional church—a state church no longer of the monarch but of the Republic. Under threat of attack from its European neighbors who feared the infection of revolution in their own peoples the Directory regime sought reconciliation with the non-juring clergy and even with Rome. When this failed, persecution started up again and went on from September 1797 until November 1799. Meanwhile the Republican armies were victorious in fighting off the enemies of the revolution everywhere in Europe—and over-reached themselves fatally when General Berthier took Rome, deposed the papal court and brought Pius VI a captive to France, where he died on August 27, 1799.

The Napoleonic Era

One of the assembly's generals who had campaigned and conquered in Italy was Napoléon Bonaparte. He was shrewd enough to detect how deeply the French common people had been alienated by the excesses of the revolution, and knew that France could not survive against her massed enemies if torn internally by religious dissension. Indeed the persecution of the non-juring clergy and all things Catholic had had the counter-effect of spurring a religious revival in the country. After his victory at Marengo in June of 1800 Napoléon turned to the new pope, Pius VII, to work out a compromise whereby the Church could be revived in France and he through his chicanery could control it there and in the Europe he had set out to conquer.

This is not the place to sort out the details of Bonaparte's eventually defeated diplomatic warfare with Pius VII. But since he wanted a thoroughly tamed Church as a department of his empire, he kept that part of the legislation coming from the revolution that held marriages under civil jurisdiction. He included in his Code Civil the substance of the marriage legislation in the Constitution of 1791. It became Title 5 of his Code Napoléon, whose Articles 63–76 and 144–225 regulated marriage. Its Article 199 read as follows:

> Any marriage that has not been contracted publicly and has not been solemnized before a competent civil magistrate can be attacked by the spouses themselves, by the parents, by the ascendants, by all those who have a natural and current interest in it, as well as by the public minister.

In his Code Pénal, Articles 199 and 200, he ordered that the civil witnessing of marital consent always precede any religious ceremony. The assumption that even for Catholics the exchange of marital consent before a civil witness created a marriage had for its twin the assumption that the contract and the sacrament are separable. This was emphasized by the law's accepting as valid the marriages of Catholics who omitted any religious ceremony after contracting civilly. It goes without saying that this pre-empting of marriage under civil law presumed also civil authority to dissolve marriages. This it did on the ground of adultery, of *excés* (violence to the point of threatening death or great bodily harm), of cruelty, of a sentence of civil infamy passed against the spouse. But divorce for any cause was available only after two years of marriage and not after the marriage's twentieth year, nor (for her protection) after the wife's forty-fifth year. Apart from divorce a marriage could be ended by a spouse's condemnation under sentence of civil death.

The Code Napoléon with this legislation establishing marriage as a civil and dissoluble contract became law in the territories recently annexed by France, namely Belgium, Holland and the Rhine provinces. It proved attractive to other states as well, so that most of the other nations of Europe adopted it during the nineteenth century. And those holding colonies in Africa, Asia and the Americas installed it there. The newly formed Italian republic put it in its own civil code in 1866. Switzerland did the same in 1874, Germany in 1875. After gaining its independence Holland did so in 1833, as did Belgium after its separation from Holland in 1830. Spain did not adopt this legislation until the establishment of a republican government in 1931. This widespread adoption of the Code's legislation for marriage had not only the civil effect of making non-religious marriage available for non-confessing citizens in countries predominantly Catholic. It had also the religious effect of opening civil marriage to Catholics, of inviting them to it; and where it obligated them to the civil contracting apart from any religious ceremony, it split the contract and the sacrament even further apart in their religious perceptions.

The New Biblical Scholarship and Christian Marriage

The effects of the Enlightenment we have seen thus far on both the Christian west's understanding of marriage itself and on the theology of the sacrament were effects brought upon them from outside. For example, that the philosopher of law Samuel Pufendorf considered the institution of marriage a necessary inference from the law of nature, or that John Locke thought it a product of the law of nations, did not damage the ancient belief that marriage is from God. Nor did the two theories gainsay Christ's institution of marriage among Christians as a sacrament. About the first of these, granted that God is the author of nature, and that the law of nations rightly understood—and rightly designed—specifies and determines the law of nature, belief in the divine origin of marriage may be strengthened rather than weakened. About the institution of the Christian sacrament, Catholic authorities have taught from the beginning that this institution consisted of Christ's taking the extant human relationship and elevating it to the status of a grace-giving sign.

But from all the ancient and medieval sources we have inspected thus far it is clear that Christian belief in the divine institution of marriage was drawn from the logically prior conviction that the first two chapters of Genesis are an accurate account of God's bringing the human race into existence; and that this account presents the first generation of the race as a monogamous couple—that marriage was the primal human condition and is co-terminous with the history of the race.

One need not strain the imagination to picture the effect on this interpretation when scholars began to bring evidence that the taken-for-granted historical accounts of creation are not such accounts, that they came not from the mouth of Moses relaying to a scribe God's revelation to him of the primeval events, but that they are, respectively, a didactic poem composed in the sixth century B.C. by a priest-teacher among the Hebrew exiles in Babylon (this is Genesis 1), and a didactic parable coming from a religious teacher of the tenth century (this is Genesis 2 and 3).

One does not, of course, either credit or blame the Enlightenment thinkers for being the first to suggest that the "creation narratives" are in character and intent other than scientifically historical accounts. Augustine noted this at the beginning of the fifth century in his *De Genesi ad Litteram*.[27] But the modern critical study of the Bible that now takes for granted that the Genesis accounts are not factual began not with an Enlightenment philosopher, but with a French Catholic priest of the Oratory. He was Richard Simon (1638–1712), a convert from Protestantism. In 1678 he published his three-volume *Histoire Critique du Vieux Testament*. In undertaking this study of the Old Testament by literary and historical analysis he prescinded from doctrinal stances and authoritative interpretations in order to subject it to the same scientific scrutiny accorded any document of antiquity.

In the centuries since Simon's beginning, historical and literary criticism have been joined by astronomy, paleontology, anthropology, sociology and history to make clear that our planet and its environment, the solar system have existed not for the six thousand years suggested by Genesis but for years numbered in the billions, and that human beings have inhabited our planet not for the seventy-five generations counted from Adam to Christ in Chapter 3 of the gospel according to Luke, but for at least one hundred thousand years.

From its beginning the Christian claim about marriage's origin was inherited from the Jews. We have seen it repeated again and again in this study, that God invented it personally and explicitly either when (according to Genesis 1) he commanded the first man and woman to "increase and multiply, fill the earth and subdue it," or perhaps both then and in the second narrative (in Genesis 2) when the Lord God said, "It is not good for the man to be alone. I will make a suitable partner for him," and then took a rib from the man's side, built it up with flesh into a woman, presented her to him and evoked from him the comment, "This one at last is bone of my bones and flesh of my flesh."

In face of the discovery that in literary genre this is parabolic fiction in the service of religious teaching, how does one sustain the claim that marriage is God's invention? More than this, if one's claim for marriage's character as a religious relationship is inferred from its immediate invention by God that was also the invention of the human race in a moment of time, how can this claim be sustained if the invention is unprovable? Or what other meaning can the claimed religiousness of marriage have? One must also face the counter-claim of anthropologic history that marriage is an association invented by men (not women) for pragmatic reasons perhaps long after the appearance of human beings on this planet. Beyond this, if the latter claim is the accurate one, it follows that if marriage is a contract, it is so only where and when men deem it best for their purposes to give it this form. Marriage would not have come first as the primal cell of society and then have divided and multiplied to form the larger societal structures. But large, chaotic, undifferentiated, universal-family societies would have come first, then much later and by positive design blood-linked family groups within these societies would have appeared.

This was the interpretation produced by the newly-developed cultural anthropology of the nineteenth century. It almost certainly borrowed from the philosophy of Hegel and from the biological findings and theories of the naturalists of this century. J. Bachofen applied their premise, that living creatures currently on this planet are the latest stage in a process of genetic mutation joined with natural selection. In his *Das Mutterrecht* (Maternal Law) of 1861 Bachofen applied the evolutionary premise to the history of the family. L.H. Morgan did the same in his *Ancient Society* (1877), as did Giraud-Teulon in his *Les Origines du Mariage et de la Famille* (1884). This interpretation came to have decisive political importance when the socialists adopted and applied it. Friedrich Engels interwove it with Marx's economic theory in his *Der Ursprung der Familie und des Staats, des Privateigenthums* (The Origin of the Family and the State, of Private Property) (1884).

Taken ensemble the evolutionary theories came to this, that primitive human beings were dominated by sexual impulse, were incapable of the self-control and other-regard that make marriage possible. Hence the general promiscuity and uncertain parenthood among them. The first advance beyond this sexual chaos was the prohibition, spurred by the ruinous effects of in-breeding, of intercourse among blood relatives in the first degree. Next the prohibition was extended outward to include more degrees of consanguinity, while freedom of sexual activity was allowed between groups of males and groups of females (in group marriage). The most recent stages of development have been the patriarchal polygamous family, in which the women are reserved for one man, and finally the monogamous family.

This theory hardly went unchallenged. It was attacked by anthropologists and sociologists who had no religious reason to question it.[28] It was attacked also by Christian anthropologists, although their rejection was not developed from religious premises but as a challenge to the evolutionists' method of research and interpretation.[29] They criticized it for imposing the premise of an unswerving rectilinear development on the evidence of sexual relations among primitive peoples, and for assuming that sexually permissive conduct is by definition primitive in the chronological sense rather than possibly a later aberration.

In the first quarter of this century the most effective critic of the most dramatic conclusions of evolutionist anthropology was Emile Durkheim. He brought especially convincing evidence against Bachofen's and Morgan's theories of general promiscuity and group marriage among primitive peoples. But he brought little comfort to the traditional theology of marriage. His theory as much as the evolutionist rejected the biblical account of marriage's beginning in a single and therefore monogamous couple created immediately by God and joined by him immediately as husband and wife. Indeed he rejected the idea that the earliest form of family was marriage. In his view the first center-point and the residence of family life was the totem, the animal or natural object thought to be related by blood to a given family or clan and taken as its symbol. He held that it was the totem that accounted for the earliest exogamous marriage and marital relationship. He agreed with evolutionist theory that the monogamous patriarchal family is the later product of social development.

> The marital family is the terminus of evolution in the course of which the family shrank in numbers in inverse proportion as the social milieu with which each individual was in immediate relationship expanded. This evolution bred, as the first form of family, a large political-domestic grouping, the amorphous exogamous clan. It came to terminus in the contemporary marital family, whether uterine or masculine, through the undivided agnatic family in the Roman patriarchal model and the German paternal model.[30]

Thus the family is not the natural grouping of parents and children, but a societally established institution produced by social forces. In primitive peoples it was indistinguishable from the clan; in the life of the clan it was non-essential. It began only with the prohibiting of incest. These two forces in fact first produced the marriage that we recognize in our time: the organization within the clan of the family group centered still in the clan totem, and in heterosexual relations the prohibition of incest. Needless to say neither the authors of Genesis nor the fathers of the church would recognize this as the origin of marriage. Yet there is no compelling reason why monogamous marriage begun in this way could not be taken up into a sacrament of the Christian religion.

Kant on the Nature of Marriage

In his *Lectures on Ethics*[31] Immanuel Kant (1724–1804) designed for marriage a model wholly consistent with the immanentism of the Enlightenment. He did not draw the model, as the Greek academicians and peripatetics and the scholastics after them had drawn it, according to the needs of civil or of ecclesial society. At least in no evident way did he draw it from the didactic passages of the Old Testament. He seems rather to have inferred it from an a priori concept of the human person evaluated according to the distinction, so central to his ethics, between the subject and the object of moral acts. The apparently personalist assumptions and language of his interpretation in reality convey and apply a theory of natural law. The person in his moral reasoning is in fact a barely disguised essence.

His access to marriage is through an ethic of sexual conduct, and his first conception of sexuality is of a privately felt inclination. This is an impulse or appetite for enjoying another human being. This impulse is the only way in which one human being can make another an object of his indulgence.[32]

One must distinguish the sexual impulse from love, which is good will, affection, that seek the loved one's happiness and rejoice in it. The sexuality that is often confused with love makes the supposed loved one an object of appetite, uses him as a thing. But the inclination to do this is natural. It is the only case in which a human being is *designed by nature* as the object of another's enjoyment. Again the immanentism appears: what is natural is here found out by a private reflection on one's conscious impulses.

The narrowness of Kant's concept of sexuality is evident again in his calling it a principle of degradation in human beings. It is such because it is an inclination not toward another person as such, but only toward the other's sexuality. It seeks to dishonor the other person by dishonoring his or her sexuality. It does the latter by separating his sexuality from the entirety of the other person, taking it thus isolated to the animal level and using it for private satisfaction.

Kant's immanentism emerges yet again where he says that this self-serving inclination is natural to sexuality. Unlike Augustine and the other fathers he does not ascribe this egocentrism to inherited original sin. Therein lies a paradox: since the sexual inclination is natural, it is for human use. But its selfish exploitiveness is also natural.[33] So in what ways can a man use it without injury to his humanity?

He cannot sell his sexual acts, nor buy another's. While some philosophers have said this is morally wrong because it injures the self and the partner and society at large, it is wrong first for a reason intrinsic to human nature. There is something in the conduct itself of buying or selling sexual acts which is contrary to the dictates of morality.[34] This dictate is logically prior to and prescinds from any harm coming from the conduct. The dictate is the principle that a person cannot dispose of himself as saleable property because he is not such property to begin with. For property is a thing, but he is a person, a subject. He cannot be both proprietor (a person) and property (a thing). Nor is his body a thing and therefore disposable property. It is part of him as a person. Kant derives a moral conclusion from this: Since a person's body is not his property but an element of his self, he is not free to do with it what he wills.[35]

By the same moral logic one can conclude that concubinage too is immoral. Although the surrender of the two persons is reciprocal, it involves not their entire persons but only their sexuality. It excludes from the surrender all other elements of the persons. Because their desire is confined to the sexuality of one another, they use one another as things. They do not deal with one another as persons.[36]

Concubinage may be understood as a contract. But in real life it is one-sided because the man seeks to enjoy the whole person of his concubine. But in virtue of their contract he has no right over his concubine's whole person but over only the sexual part of her. Consequently he treats her as a thing and tries to make her into a thing.

> The sole condition on which we are free to make use of our sexual desire depends on the right to dispose over the person as a whole—over the welfare and happiness and generally over all the circumstances of that person. If I have a right over the whole person, I also have the right over the part and so I have the right to use that person's *organa sexualia* for the satisfaction of sexual desire. But how am I to obtain these rights over the whole person? Only by giving that person the same rights over the whole of myself. This happens only in marriage. Matrimony is an agreement between two persons by which they grant to each other equal reciprocal rights, each of them undertaking to surrender the whole of their persons to the other with a complete right of disposal over it.[37]

In marriage the self as person is not degraded. Because the self-giving is both reciprocal and equal the partners give themselves to one another as property and each gets the other in return as property, and thus gets the self back: "In this way the two persons become a unity of will. Whatever good or ill, joy or sorrow befalls either of them, the other will share it. Thus sexuality leads to a union of human beings, and in that union alone its exercise is possible."[38]

Kant's definition of marriage seems, again, *a priori*. He draws it not from experience but from the concept of human being as a person, as a subject possessing rights and the capacity to exchange rights with other persons. His concept of sexuality is *a priori* in the domain of sensation; he defines it as an internally felt impulse and desire. In this he is faithful to a long Christian tradition, since that is how the fathers and scholastics understood it.

While his idea of marital love is at least as congenial a matrix for the sacrament of marriage as is the patristic and early scholastic idea of it, he has no way in his theory of knowledge for believing that marriage may be a sacrament in the traditional Catholic sense. For one thing, a revelation from God via sensate perception—whether through the words of Christ or of Paul—is incapable of verification. The only possible guarantee of the truth of the revelation would be noumenal, beyond verification. Moreover there is no possible verification that a sensately grounded experience images an invisible sacred reality. Since for Kant it is mind that gives intelligibility to sense data, any sacramental reference in these data would have to be supplied by mind. This is so because sacramentality is fundamentally a relationship of causes and effects. Cause and effect were innate categories of thought for Kant. There is nothing in sensate phenomena that for Kant could bring him to verify in them a reference to God's entrance into human awareness through them.[39]

Hegel and the Nature of Marriage

The man whose theory of marriage broke with all of the European past except unwittingly with the vision of Hugh of St. Victor in the twelfth century was Georg Wilhelm Friedrich Hegel (1770–1831). And in the twentieth century the authoritative Catholic understanding of marriage that was to most nearly replicate his was that of Pope Paul VI in his encyclical letter of 1968, *Humanae vitae*. Hegel's understanding of marriage embodied his all-pervading assumption that the universe is a self-contained process of evolutionary development, that the latest and highest stage in this development is human consciousness, that this consciousness is itself in developmental movement toward the most perfect state of itself. He brought this assumption and this judgment to bear on marriage: in its most excellent form it is the fusing of two consciousnesses—for him these were two persons—into one.

On his way to explaining this fusing of two into one he accounted for earlier and inferior attempts at union that had been deemed marriage. He seemed to acknowledge that the more excellent union in consciousness may have the inferior union as its base, and that men and women may pass through the lesser union en route to the higher.

As an immediate and accessible kind of moral relationship marriage involves first of all the dimension that is physical life; and as a substantive relationship [it involves] life in its totality, namely the actuality of the race and its life-process. But beyond this marriage as this purely private, self-existent, external unity of the sexes is, in self-consciousness, transformed into a spiritual self-aware love.

Added reflection: Marriage is essentially a moral relationship. In the past it has been regarded, especially in the major theories of natural law, only from its physical aspect, only from what belongs to it from nature. It was dealt with as a sexual relationship. Consequently any path to a higher perception of it was closed off.

It is just as crude to conceive of it as a mere civil contract, a concept of it that even Kant harbored. This is a conception in which the parties commit themselves by reciprocal acts of will to a contract. Marriage is thus declared to be a reciprocal exchange and contractual use.

A third damaging conception of it saw marriage only as love. For a love that is only emotion delivers marriage over to passing caprice, to a character in which morality can find no place.[40]

Hegel has here broken open the traditional conception of marriage. He has rejected the minimalist version of it that makes it available to any men and women who can exchange the right to their sexual acts. He does not deny that this was and is marriage. But he deems it a form of marriage degrading of persons and inhibiting the development of the potentially excellent version of themselves. By implication he reverses the traditional concept of marriage: Instead of proposing that marriages serve the good of society and find their fulfillment there, he urged that society in its common and observable elements finds its fulfillment in men's and women's fusing in the exquisite union that is marriage. One may note in passing that there is no evident obstacle to this union's being homosexual, since Hegel envisions its rising above that stratum of sexuality at which gender difference is significant.

> From the subjective side marriage can have as its source the unique attraction of the two persons who enter the relationship. . . . But its objective source is the free consent of the persons—most especially in the will to make of themselves one person, to give over their natural and individual personhood into this oneness. From the conventional point of view this oneness seems a denigration of the self. But it is really a freeing of the selves because in it they rise to their definitive self-consciousness.[41]

Is marriage thus conceived amenable as the matrix of the Christian sacrament? The following elements of the conception seem to make it so. In a sacramental action and in a sacramental situation a supra-sensate agent "crosses over" into the sensate realm, reveals itself there and acts there. For Hegel the realm of materiality and sensation is the supra-phenomenal world-consciousness' self-manifestation in phenomena. This is self-disclosure in one stratum of consciousness.

In the developmental advance of the world-consciousness a prior state is abandoned, is left behind because imperfect. Since the evolving world-consciousness that transcends its earlier, imperfect states has reached the stage of human consciousness, it opens the perfectible human person to perfection, to full consciousness, a consciousness gained or at least abetted by the fusion (as in marriage) of two consciousnesses.

The *intentio,* the tendency of all reality is not centrifugal and dispersive, but is convergent and toward union—just as, according to the Christus hymn in Colossians 1:15–20 and the barely less poetic christology of Ephesians 1:10, 22–23; 4:13–16, all the created universe is said to strive toward union in Christ. For Hegel the divine condition will be attained when the multiple and dispersed manifestations of the world-consciousness are gathered into a single and perfect union.

But the amenability of Hegel's conception of marriage to the Christian sacrament is only apparent. The most serious difficulty in its way is that in the Christian sacramental vision not the least part of creation, not the humblest material entity is left out of its *economia* of salvation— salvation which is a rescue from aimlessness and futility. The failure of many of the fathers of the Church themselves to accept this fact blocked for centuries marriage's acceptance in full status among the Church's sacraments. For reasons not entirely different than Hegel's they could not see that the physical and emotional manifestations of sexual passion could disclose God's action and enhance men's and women's union with him. They condemned them as sinful, presuming that they hold the mind from contemplative union with God and the will from affective union with him. Hegel wanted them transcended because he thought they retard a process to perfect conscious union in pure spiritual fusion.

For Hegel the entry of the supra-sensate into sensate human experience, where sacramentality holds forth, was not literally gracious. It was not a personally unique and separate creator's entry into human affairs with the sole motive to heal and to rescue and bring into union with himself. As we have seen, for him it was essentially spiritual world-consciousness passing through that stage of development in which it manifests itself sensately. Therefore revelation in the traditional Judeo-Christian sense was for him impossible.

The traditional Christian notion of gracing has equally no place in Hegel's system. To be graced is not to be declared "just" in a juridical sense, i.e. forgiven and again in favor. Only in a secondary sense does it consist of being helped by God in avoiding evil conduct and doing good and thereby gaining strength in virtue. In its primary sense it is to be invited into communion with God and empowered to participate in this communion. It is called grace because the invitation and the empowering are literally gifts—*gratiae*. A human being has no claim on them in natural justice; by them he is capacitated beyond his humanness.

Grace in this sense cannot be in Hegel's system because grace postulates a creator who simply transcends human existence, who is a person existing distinctly from human personhood, who calls the human person into union with himself. For Hegel there are not creator, creation and creatures, but evolution of the cosmic mind through developmental stages to perfect consciousness.

The Catholic Authorities' Reaction

The highest Catholic authority's earliest response to the claim by civil rulers to jurisdiction over marriages in their domains was Pope Alexander VIII's apostolic constitution *Inter multiplices* of August 4, 1690.[42] This did not single out that claim and reject it explictly. The constitution denied the "Gallican articles" published by the royalist French clergy on March 19, 1682 at the behest of Louis XIV and his Estates General. The constitution rejected the claim that civil authorities are in no way subject to the authority of the Church in civil matters; that the decrees of general councils (with the Council of Constance named expressly) are equal in authority to those of the papacy; that the statutes of the Gallican church have independent validity, and the decrees of the papacy must be validated by this church to be effective in France; that papal decrees are not irreformable unless received and approved by the Church at large. The article most relevant to jurisdiction over marriage was the first. Alexander's rejecting it asserted implicitly that papal authority rules the marriages of Catholics everywhere even if they be considered civil contracts.

The inseparability of contract and sacrament in the marriages of Christians was reaffirmed implicitly in a reply of the Holy Office of the Inquisition of July 23, 1698 to Capuchin missioners working among Moslem peoples.[43] They had asked whether marriages attempted by persons originally baptized but then converts to the Moslem religion and married in its rite are true marriages and Christian sacraments. The reply of the Holy Office was that if the partners agreed antecedently on the dissolubility of their union, it is neither a sacrament nor a marriage. But in the absence of this agreement their union is both a marriage and a sacrament. The response implied, of course, that despite the partners' abandoning the Christian religion and conversion to the Moslem, the perdurance in their souls of the baptismal character made their marriages to be Christian sacraments.

We have already seen that on November 28, 1789, Pius VI, in his brief *Super soliditate Petri,* condemned the Febronian ecclesiology of Niklaus von Hontheim. We have seen also that two years later, on September 16, 1788, Pius directed his letter *Deessemus nobis* to the bishop of Motula in the kingdom of Naples, correcting the bishop's interpretation of Canon 12 of Trent's twenty-fourth session.

The Syllabus of Errors

The most comprehensive reply of Catholic authority to the accumulated philosophy, anthropology, jurisprudence, sociology, history and biblical criticism produced by the Enlightenment was the Syllabus of Errors published by Pius IX on December 8, 1864. This catalogue of condemned theses is well enough known among students of the history of religion in the West. Less well known is Pius' encyclical letter, *Quanta cura,* that he published with the Syllabus as its introduction. Apparently wanting to make emphatically clear his concern about marriage and family, he included a paragraph in this introduction that anticipated what he was to condemn in the subsequent list of errors.

His most evident target was the socialist adaptation of the theory that civil government holds the primacy of authority over marriages and families.

Not content with removing religion from civil society, they seek also to banish it from individual families. They teach the seriously evil error of socialism and communism that the domestic society, or family, derives the entire reason for its existence from civil law alone; and that consequently parents' authority over their children derives from and depends on civil law alone, which law has the prior right to nurture and educate these children.[44]

The origin of the Syllabus was the request put to Pius in 1849 by the provincial council of Spoleto to draw up a constitution condemning the philosophical and theological errors prevailing at the time among Christians, Catholics included. Three years later Pius commissioned Cardinal Fornari to draw up a list of such errors. But in 1860 Bishop P. Gerbet of Perpignan published in his diocese a pastoral instruction "on various errors of the present time." When this came to Pius' attention he formed a commission to formulate a syllabus of errors with Bishop Gerbet's instruction as its source and model. This commission drew up a list of sixty-one erroneous theses, along with their theological qualifications, i.e. the nature and seriousness of the error in each. This was presented to a group of three hundred bishops gathered in Rome for the canonization of the Japanese martyrs. A premature release of the list to the public raised a storm of protest throughout Europe (the anticlerical newspaper, *Il Mediatore,* of Turin got hold of it and published it). Pius thereupon appointed a new commission to formulate the syllabus independently of Gerbet's list. This group's revised list contained eighty theses, with the wording of each thesis drawn from Pius' earlier encyclicals, apostolic letters and public discourses. This was the syllabus sent to the Catholic bishops around the world, dated December 8, 1864—but strangely without Pius' signature. The valence of the condemnations of theses taken singly is that of the original papal document—encyclical, letter or discourse—from which its formulation was taken.

The theses were distributed in ten sections in the following way:

Theses   1–7: pantheism, naturalism, absolute rationalism.
Theses 8–14: moderate rationalism.
Theses 15–18: indifferentism and religious latitudinarianism. A paragraph condemning socialism, communism, secret societies, Bible societies, clerical-liberal societies.
Theses 19–38: errors concerning the Church and its rights.
Theses 39–55: errors concerning the state and its relations with the Church.
Theses 56–64: errors concerning natural and Christian ethics.
Theses 65–74: errors concerning Christian marriage.
Theses 75–76: errors concerning the temporal authority of the pope.
Theses 77–80: the errors of modern liberalism.

Even students sympathetic to the Syllabus must admit that it was a tactical error to have condemned intellectual and social, political and religious stances in the succinct and even truncated form of a syllabus— outside the nuancing context of the condemnations' documents of origin. For example, one could not expect the uninformed reader to know that condemned thesis 16—"Persons can find the way to eternal salvation in any religion at all, and can there gain salvation itself"—is later in sequence than and conditioned by Pius' encyclical letter, *Quanto conficiamur moerore,* of August 10, 1863, to the bishops of Italy.[45] There he wrote that salvation is indeed possible outside the Catholic Church for those who in good faith (he said "in invincible ignorance") do not accept this Church as the means for salvation established by Christ.

It is significant that the Syllabus' intention to reassert the Catholic authorities' jurisdiction over marriage in the Catholic population worldwide is carried out by its going first and directly to the sacrament. The condemned theses on this subject, although drawn immediately from Royalist and Febronian teachings, could trace their lineage as far back as the Protestant reformers, and even beyond them to Ockham and Durandus of St. Pourçain. Thus thesis 65: "In no way can it be proved that Christ raised marriage to the dignity of a sacrament."[46]

Condemned thesis 66 is this: "The sacrament of marriage is no more than an accessory to the contract and is separable from it, and is found exclusively in the nuptial blessing."[47] This condemnation supposes its immediate predecessor and builds upon it. It does not claim by implication that the contract in marriage is the sacrament. It claims no more than that when marriage is a sacrament (it supposes that all marriages of Christians are such), the contract and the sacrament are inseparable, and that the sacrament is something more than the nuptial blessing, although this may be included in the sacrament. Yet it does not hint at the relationship of contract to sacrament—a point of theology too exacting in any case for the formulation of a condemned thesis.

The third condemned thesis that bears on the sacrament is no. 73.[48] It determines more exactly what thesis 66 says about the inseparability of contract and sacrament in Christian marriages: "There can be a true marriage between Christians in virtue of a merely civil contract. It is also false to claim that the marriage contract between Christians is in every case a sacrament, or to say that there is no contract if the sacrament is excluded."

Read positively the condemnation insists that the only marriage two Christians can create is a sacrament. This implies that even marriages of non-Catholic Christians contracted validly before civil magistrates must be sacraments, although no explanation is hinted for how this is so. The last clause implies that it is possible for Christians to exclude the sacrament from their act of contracting. But if they do so, they create no marriage. But a finer point is implied in the verb "excluded." If the parties, Catholic or non-Catholic Christian, do not exclude the sacrament but simply ignore it or are unaware of it, they do create a marriage which is a sacrament nonetheless. Again one ought not expect that a formulation of this kind would explain how two Christians who are ignorant of or ignore their marital sacrament nevertheless create it and live in it.[49]

The Theological Response to the Enlightenment

A student examining the Catholic theologians' response to the Enlightenment secularization of marriage must be alert for double evidence. On one hand there is the continuing Catholic riposte to the Protestant reformers' denial that Christian marriages are sacraments of the new law. One could hardly expect this to end within a generation or two after the Council of Trent. The theology of marriage in Catholic seminaries until the 1950's was Trent's theology expanded and explicated, and it was aimed for the most part at the reformers. On the other hand there is the Catholic theologians' reply to the Enlightenment philosophers and scientists. In some measure it was synonymous with the reply to the reformers. Both had denied that the marriages of Christians are sacraments.

But their reasons for denying this were partly the same, partly different. The reformers' main reason, we recall, was the lack of evidence in the gospels that Jesus did with marriage what he did with baptism and the Eucharist, the two sacraments acknowledged commonly by all mainline Christians. A supporting reason was their contention that Catholic teachers had for centuries misinterpreted Ephesians 5:21–32, had read Paul to say that every Christian marriage is a *sacramentum magnum,* and that *sacramentum* meant to him what it means to Catholic sacramental theology. Consequently to refute the reformers' charge was, using the scholastic definition of a sacrament as the middle term, to demonstrate from evidence in the New Testament that Jesus did make marriage among the baptized a grace-giving sign of an invisible sacred reality.

The Enlightenment challenge was far more radical—literally radical. At its most evolved and sophisticated in Hegel it denied the very possibility of a grace-giving intervention of a transcendent creator, and the possibility that in turn physical persons and their actions could image the actions of a transcendent creator. Even the earlier and less developed Enlightenment criticism doubted the human mind's ability to get beyond appearances to substantial realities and actions in the physical world. In addition it cut away at any divine intervention in marriage at all by denying the historicity of the Genesis creation accounts.

Since these were not theological denials and disputes there could be no theological refutation of them. This may explain why the Catholic reaction to them was, in its most noticeable and emphatic form, such authoritative anathematizing as we have just seen in the Syllabus of

Errors—to not argue with the enemy but to destroy him, especially if he is an enemy within the walls. It may explain also why the theologians of this epoch seemed to prolong the debate with the reformers long after this ceased to be the crucial debate, and long after Catholics and Protestants might have been expected to form an alliance to protect traditional Christian belief. But for the theologians the Protestants were at least a foe within reach of theology's conventional weapons.

There is no profit in examining multiple samples of this era's Catholic theology of the marriage sacrament. From the generation after Trent until the early twentieth century this differed little from theologian to theologian, with the one exception of Mathias Scheeben in the middle of the nineteenth century. A better method is to single out one of the most representative thinkers, examine his theology, and interpolate from his contemporaries where these make significant additions. The theologian of choice here is Honoré Tournely, who published his *Cursus Theologicus-Dogmaticus* at Cologne in 1734. Volume 4 of this work is *De Sacramento Poenitentiae et Extremae Unctionis, De Sacramento Ordinis, De Sacramento Matrimonii.*

The *Secunda Conclusio* of Tournely's examination of the sacrament of marriage is "Marriage is a sacrament of the Law of the Gospel in the true and proper sense. This is asserted against the Lutherans and the Calvinists."[50] He gathers his proof first from the scriptures. He begins it in conventional deductive fashion by laying out the scholastic definition of a sacrament: "That [marriage] be a sacrament of the New Law in the true and proper sense, it must be a sensately observable sign of a sacred reality, must confer sanctifying grace, must be instituted by Christ, and [an addition to the usual definition] must be found continually and perpetually in the Christian religion."

His minor premise is that marriage meets all these requirements. (Surprisingly he claims this of marriage universally, not only of the marriages of Christians.) Thence his task is to verify point for point the claim in this premise.

He begins by pointing out the obvious, that the spouses' reciprocal consent is an exterior, sensately perceptible sign. Then he claims that as such it is a sign of a sacred reality. This is the sacred reality that is Christ's union with the Church. This in turn is either a union in human nature through the incarnation, or a spiritual union of charity. The evidence that marriage is a sign of this union, he continues, is in Matthew 19:6 ("They are no longer two, but one flesh. Therefore what God has joined man must not separate"), in 1 Corinthians 7:27 ("If you are joined to a wife do not seek to be freed. If you are free of a wife, do not seek for one"), in Hebrews 13:4 ("Marriage is to be honored by all, and marriages are to be kept undefiled"), in 1 Corinthians 7:3 ("A husband must give to his wife what is hers; so too a wife must give to her husband what is his"), and in John 1:14 ("The word was made flesh and dwelt among us").

But that marriage is a sign, Tournely continued, is especially evident in Ephesians 5. There Paul, exhorting spouses to a mutual love, gave them as an example Christ, who so loved his spouse the Church as to give his life for her. In light of this love he said of marriage at its institution and of the intimate union of marriage, "For this reason a man will leave his father and his mother and will cling to his wife, and they will become two in one flesh." And Paul added, "This is a great sacrament. I say this in regard to Christ and the Church"—as though he were to say, "Even though the marital union taken in itself may seem nothing great, yet in the domain of signs or images it is great because it signifies something great, namely Christ and the Church and their union." The man's leaving his parents, clinging to his wife and becoming one flesh with her signify *mystice* the Son of God's leaving the Father and coming to earth to join with the Church and become one body with her in the incarnation.

Vicenzo Gatti, a near-contemporary of Tournely, thought that Christ instituted marriage as a sacrament of the new law with his words in Matthew 19:6, "What God has joined man must not separate," because he thereby restored marriage to its initial ability, from the time of its first institution, to image the Christ-Church relationship.[51] This ability it had lost in the interim through human perversity and the permissive law of Moses.

Gatti accounted in the following way for the sacrament's conferring grace. In his relationship with the Church Christ sanctified her by giving his life for her. But since the Christian husband-wife relationship images that of Christ and the Church, it too sanctifies by the husband's loving his wife in the same way.[52] The grace of this sacrament produces various effects. It sanctifies the spouses so that they may love one another chastely and persevere together until death, so that they may bear and nurture children and educate them properly, so that they may restrain libido and persevere in right sexual conduct, both in regard to persons and in regard to method, so as to remedy concupiscence, and so as to support one another in weakness and correct one another gently when needed.[53]

As for whether any and every marriage of two baptized spouses is a sacrament, Gatti joined the minority of theologians who thought this not true. He considered that there can be a marriage valid and legitimate insofar as a covenant (*foedus*) and a permanent bond, which is nevertheless not a sacrament in the true and proper sense. His reason for saying this was that there is no compelling argument that proves the contrary. He noted the most frequently adduced reason for the sacramentality of every Christian marriage, that it is beyond men's power to separate from the marital contract the dignity that Christ gave to it in perpetuity when he instituted the sacrament. Gatti replied that this argues for no more than that where a marriage is created by the required religious ceremony, it is beyond human power to keep it from being a sacrament, and that Christians should marry only in the rite needed to create the sacrament. But it is one thing for Christians to be obligated to these, and another for them to fulfill the obligation. Very often Christians do not do this. (It is less likely that Gatti refers here to Catholics' failure to marry before the witnesses required by the decree *Tametsi*. More probably he has in mind Protestant Christians who are not bound by the decree.) Their marriages are valid as human and civil contracts creating the covenant (again the *foedus*) and the bond, just as vice versa their marriages could be valid as sacraments before God and the Church, but be null and void as civil contracts.[54]

It is obvious that Gatti did not hold that it is the fact itself of the spouses' having been baptized and having the baptismal character in their souls that makes the marriage to be a sacrament if it is in fact that—even though he quoted Innocent III's opinion in the *Liber Decretalium*, no. 1557, that "Although the unbaptized can marry validly, yet not in the sacrament, whereas the baptized do marry in the sacrament because they never lose the sacrament of faith [their baptism]; and this makes their marriages to be sacraments."

The Sacrament and Marriage's Indissolubility

Gatti agreed with the theology of marriage's indissolubility that was moving on into Catholic law, namely that because the marriage of two Christians is a sacrament, this *makes* their union's natural permanence more firm. His *Quaestio 5* is "De Proprietatibus Matrimonii" (On the Characteristics of Marriage); its *Articulus II* is "De firmitate seu indissolubilitate vinculi conjugalis" (The firmness, or indissolubility, of the marital bond"). Tournely's conclusion is that this bond is firm, permanent and indissoluble by reason of natural law and its primeval institution, by divine positive law, and by reason of the sacrament itself.[55]

He reasoned that because even the marriages of non-Christians have in them the sacrament understood in a more extended sense (*sensu latiore*) as signs of the union of Christ and the Church, they have a certain degree of indissolubility, but not the degree that is found in the marriages of Christians.

But if one takes the sacrament in the strict and proper sense, as it is found only in Christian marriages, this lends a certain firmness to these marriages' indissolubility because the permanent and indissoluble union of Christ and the Church is expressed more fully in Christians' baptisms and marriages—his union with it through his incarnation or through the flow of grace from him to the Church. It is consequential, although perhaps unnoticed at the time, that Gatti made the holding power of a marriage's permanence directly proportionate to the fidelity with which it images the union of Christ and the Church.

A century later J.-B. Bouvien set his consideration of the marital sacrament just barely within the context in which Scheeben was to develop it.[56] This is the sacrament as a relationship or institution of the Church and for the Church. He drew this from marriage's essential end that is the birth and nurture of children. Where marriage is a sacrament this end is the nurture of children in the Christian faith. Taken thus in its orientation to the good of the Church, marriage is the *materia* of the sacrament. It can thus be understood as a religious, or ecclesiastic, contract.[57]

Bouvien's demonstration that Ephesians 5:32 declares marriage a sacrament follows Bellarmine's of two and a half centuries earlier and Gatti's of the preceding century. He points out that in the Latin of the verse "sacramentum hoc magnum est" (which translates accurately the original Greek "to mystérion toûto mega estín") the relative pronoun "hoc" must refer to the substantive, whether word or phrase, most closely preceding it. But this is clearly marriage, he claims, because verse 31 is the quotation of Genesis 2:24 (and of Christ in Matthew 19:5), "For this reason a man will leave his father and his mother," etc.[58]

Bouvien continues that in verse 32, the "great sacrament" cannot refer to the union of Christ and the Church, as the Protestants insist, because this would demand the absurdity of saying that the union of Christ and the Church is a great sacrament in Christ and the Church. The only alternative is that "great sacrament" refers to the human marriage about which Genesis and Christ said "For this reason," etc.[59]

But Bouvien admits that in his time many New Testament scholars and theologians reject this interpretation of Ephesians 5:32. Therefore he falls back to the more modest claim that the Council of Trent had made in its doctrinal preface to the canons on marriage, namely that in this verse Paul only suggested (*innuit*) that Christ in his suffering and death merited the graces that meet the needs of the married.[60]

Bouvien's judgment on the nature of the graces conferred by this sacrament is the traditional one. It does not of its nature confer "primary sanctifying grace," that which brings a person from the state of sin to the state of friendship with God, but "secondary" sanctifying grace and sacramental grace. How thoroughly juridical his understanding of grace is appears in his definition of the sacramental grace of marriage. It is the right, grounded in sanctifying grace itself, to receive the actual graces that spouses need in order to realize the ends of this sacrament.[61]

The Changing Catholic Appreciation of Marriage

While the Catholic theology of marriage was being held in place almost without change during the three and a half centuries following Trent, two changes in the pre-theological appreciation of marriage were under way and were destined to affect this theology significantly. They came so slowly that even if noticed in themselves, few foresaw the effect they were bound to have. One of these changes was in the social setting of the marriages that the Catholic authorities and scholars observed, inspected and assessed. During the early and high medieval centuries these had been marriages among the sons and daughters of noble families, the *causes celèbres* whose adjudication established the precedents in Church law. Seldom were these marriages the products of the partners' love for one another. Frequently enough they were arranged through intermediaries and contracted through proxies, with the spouses meeting one another for the first time some weeks and even months after having become husband and wife. Even in the lower social ranks, where eventual spouses had earlier been acquaintances if not friends, the Germanic tradition giving fathers a decisive voice in their children's choice of partners kept love a peripheral consideration in this choice.

But as the feudal society of Europe and its rigid hierarchical structure began to break down at the end of the thirteenth century and the beginning of the fourteenth, while and because a mercantile middle class came into existence and grew rapidly, the social character of marriage changed—changed slowly but changed decisively. One comprehensive way of defining the change is to say that friendship and love began to have their chance as the motive for and the prelude to marriage.

At the same time the kinds of clerics who observed marriage and speculated and wrote about it also changed. In feudal society these had been monks or cathedral canons or bishops, not the sorts of churchmen who associate familiarly with married folk. Those clerics who did, the parish pastors and curates, were poorly educated and therefore without voice in the Church's interpretation of marriage and in its regulation. But at the end of the twelfth century and the beginning of the thirteenth a new kind of priest appeared in Europe, in the non-monastic, itinerant and vowed-to-poverty clerics called the *frères,* or friars—the Friars Minor of Francis of Assisi and the Friars Preacher of Dominic. Add to these the orders and congregations that sprang up during the Catholic counter-reformation—the Theatines, the Oratory of Divine Love (comprising both laymen and priests), the Jesuits, the French Oratory founded by Pierre de Berulle in 1613, the Eudistes, the Sulpicians, Vincent de Paul's Congregation of the Mission. Much of these groups' work was to educate students for ordination to the diocesan priesthood. Withal a new kind of cleric, coming from and living in reasonable proximity to middle class families and working with them, became the interpreters of marriage. Erasmus, the Augustinian monk who lived almost never in a monastery but almost always among or with layfolk, was the prime example of this at the end of the fifteenth century and the beginning of the sixteenth. Francis de Sales, the gentle instructor of souls who was made bishop of Geneva, the capital city of Calvinism, is the example who shone at the beginning of the seventeenth century. But be it noted that all these were clerics. There was still no married voice heard in the Church on the subject of marriage.

The second change was in nature far less visible and therefore is more difficult to identify. It was an effect of the first sociological change just noted. It is still very incomplete in the Church. It began and continues as an unarticulated and even half-aware method in defining marriage. For centuries those in the Church whose office it was to define it devised definitions as instruments for resolving difficulties. It should be obvious that defining marriage as a contract gave authorities a weapon for bringing clandestine marriages under control. For the valid creating of a contract demands a specified contractual good, and verification that the partners to the contract have both exchanged this good. Such defining is *a priori*. It does not draw from the people's experience in creating their marriages and living them, but imposes a model on this experience. What the definers in fact do is to design the model of marriage they find most amenable to juridical management.

But once those in the Church who pondered and taught about marriage came to be more and more the bishops and priests of the people described just above, their teaching too came slowly to reflect marriage as the married experience it. What seeds of change must have been sown in their minds the first time they heard and accepted the truth of a devout Christian spouse's declaration that his or her lovemaking, though ardent, was in no way sinful, and that its pleasure was not in the taking but in the giving. A philosophic estimation of what took place would say that the long overdue inductive defining of marriage had got under way. Its potential for a seismic shift in the Catholic understanding of marriage was eventually to be realized in the Second Vatican Council's "Pastoral Constitution on the Church in the Modern World." Its "intimate partnership of life and of married love," its "intimate joining of persons and actions," its "mutual self-giving of their persons," and especially its assertion that sexual intercourse in a singular way expresses and completes the spouses' love, inspires and acts out their self-giving (and is not inescapably selfish concupiscence asserting itself)—all these Origen, Clement of Alexandria and Tertullian would either not have recognized or would have rejected out of hand. This description of marriage and of married love can have come only from the experience of marriage, and even though written by celibate clerics, these must have listened to Christian spouses' narratives of their marriages.

Change, Reluctance to Change and Tension

The final part of this chapter will be a sampling of reflections on marriage showing the gradual softening of magisterial and scholarly judgment on its conduct. It will show the simultaneous tenacity of the ancient bias against marriage's sexual expression. And the tension between softening and tenacity will appear within the statements of individual writers. As we trace this change we do well to keep in mind that at their most significant level these writers are recreating the matrix of the sacrament, however hesitantly. There is a direct cause-effect relationship between the gradually gentled appraisal of lovemaking and the gradually enriched theology of marriage.

The major scholastics of the thirteenth century repeated the indictment of sexual intercourse as so easily sinful even within marriage because in it concupiscence overwhelms reason and will and thus inverts the right order of nature in men and women. But Aquinas later qualified this negative judgment. In his *Summa Theologica*, I, 98, 2 he rejected the ancient opinion (Gregory of Nyssa was its Christian champion) that if the first parents of the human race had not sinned, human beings would have been produced some other way than by sexual intercourse, since it is sinfully concupiscent desire for pleasure that drives them to intercourse.[62] In his reply to the third argument in favor of Gregory's thesis Thomas urged that even without the assault of concupiscence men and women would have found sensual pleasure in sexual union. In fact their pleasure would have been greater because the absence of concupiscence would have left them physically more sensitive (*corpus magis sensibile*). Indeed as far back as the middle of the twelfth century William of Auvergne had insisted that there is no sin in sexual pleasure if the higher appetite for pleasure is not debased. But this "higher appetite" is the desire to grant the spouse what is his or her due, or to keep oneself and one's spouse from sinning outside marriage.[63]

Thomas also challenged the opinion of Jerome and others who agreed with him that couples should refrain from receiving the Eucharist soon after having intercourse. He was too kind to Jerome in explaining the latter's judgment.

> Jerome's statement should be understood not of every married person without exception but only of those who are ministers of the Church, as in the Greek Church. . . . The rest of the faithful, as long as they are otherwise properly disposed, should not be kept from holy communion for having performed their married duty toward their partner. In this matter they are to be left to their own devotion and conscience.[64]

Thomas challenged also Origen's opinion passed on by Gratian: "Marriage when according to the law is indeed without sin; and yet during the time when marital relations take place, the presence of the Holy Spirit will not be given." Assuming that "the presence of the Holy Spirit" designates union with God in the love that is charity, Thomas made the obvious distinction.

> We are bound to God in two ways, by the habit of grace and by the act of contemplation and love. What breaks the first union is always a sin, but not what breaks the second.[65]

It appears that as early as the thirteenth century the sinfulness in sexual expression that the fathers thought virtually inevitable was located and in a sense confined to immoderation in this pleasure. How epidemic the sinfulness is depends then on how common immoderation is, and of course on the criterion of immoderation.

There was a yielding on another point at which the early fathers had been severe. We recall their conclusion drawn from the assumption that the natural inherent use of the sexual anatomy is for reproduction, namely that intercourse with a wife infertile for any reason is immoral because it cannot claim this natural use for its motive. Intercourse motivated only by the express intention to conceive was held to be its most virtuous use. Intercourse reserved to fertile periods in which the spouses are willing to accept a child was less virtuous.

But now another virtuous use is acknowledged. It is intercourse in order to save a spouse from sin. Abelard suggested this in the twelfth century, but without specifying the nature of the virtue: "They are clean of heart but not of body who do not crave this for pleasure, as we have said, but from need, to avoid offending God by illicit intercourse. These people will also be among the saved and will not lack the vision of God."[66]

Then along with others Duns Scotus saw this marital conduct as a sub-species of the virtue of justice.

> Justice requires that one grant the other what is his by right. And a person is bound to grant it, not only when there is question of a basic aim such as the good of having children, but also when a less basic aim is involved, protecting married chastity by keeping him from seeking illicit intercourse and acting against the good of fidelity.[67]

Once that exception to procreation as the sole sinless and virtuous motive for intercourse was admitted, questions were bound to be heard. One would expect that the first among them asked which other motives than conception and preservation from sin are sinless and virtuous. But it appears not to have been so. The first question was one that theologians used to painstaking scrutiny of moral habits would think of quickly. It asked how explicit in the spouses' intention conception must be if they are to avoid sinning in their intercourse.

The question is of more consequence than it may at first appear. For if the intention to conceive need not be primary nor always explicit, and if the alternative motive is not preservation from sin, the way is opened to some other virtuous motive. Perhaps these men may eventually allow love its chance—even the kind of love portrayed in The Song of Solomon.

Domingo Soto, another of the theologians at Trent, put the matter succinctly: "It is not required that the married actually have these aims in mind when they come together. It is enough if there is a virtual intention, in other words if they introduce no evil circumstance."[68] This is no more than permissive. It names no acceptable alternative motive.

Soto's contemporary and colleague at Trent, Alfonso Salmeron, went the obvious next step and found a place for pleasure in the motivation: "It would be wrong to consider enjoyment as the aim to which the act of procreation is related here or because of which it is desired. It is simply the cause which moves and impels them not to forgo having children."[69]

Tomás Sanchez opened the way even further for alternative motives by applying the moral maxim that an habitual and virtual intention to do good suffices to make an act good, and does so provided the person does not expressly exclude the inherent end of the conduct. He referred to the possible alternative motives as morally indifferent, i.e. not as inconsequential but as in themselves open to being either good or evil.

> Those who contract marriage for morally indifferent reasons extrinsic to marriage are usually excused from venial sin, because they usually choose them, not as their aims in marriage but as the reason for bethinking themselves of marriage, or of marriage to one particular person. The aim of their marriage is still the proper one even if they do not give it any thought. Unless they expressly exclude the proper aim, they intend it virtually and implicitly by the very fact that they intend to contract marriage.
>
> Nor in the marriage act itself is there any need to recall some one of the permissible aims. It is enough if the act is habitually related to them, just as, according to the common opinion of theologians, this is sufficient for merit. . . . Thus it is enough if in the beginning the couple enter upon marriage with them in mind and have no contrary aim in the act itself. . . . This is why Ledesma says that married people are excused from many venial sins. . . .[70]

Only a scholar abstracted from life and marriage and used to thinking abstractly could imagine, as Sanchez does later in this treatise, that a husband may have intercourse with his wife for no more reason than that she is his wife.

> From this we deduce that a husband making use of marriage and neither expressly intending nor excluding children but simply unmindful of them and intent solely on having relations with his wife because she is his wife, in no way sins. Granted that he does not intend children formally, he does intend them virtually, since that act, by its own very nature, is designed for the procreation of children, and the performer's intention is not directing it to any other aim.[71]

Other writers suggested that sexual pleasure is a useful good in that it is the hoped-for reward that leads men and women to marry. Early in the fifteenth century Denis the Carthusian put the idea in this form: "Pleasure cannot be avoided in sexual intercourse, and yet it is not a sin when it is not sought after and the act itself is performed as it should be. In the same way the pleasure in food and drink, natural as it is and related to a spiritual good, is not a fault."[72]

Denis took the thought further and asked the difficult question forthrightly.

The question is whether married people ought to love each other with a carnal love. And it appears that they should not, because carnal love is entirely unclean and tainted with sin, as the theologians say. Some theologians, however, say that married couples can love each other blamelessly with carnal love.

We must reply, then, that they should not love each other with carnal love as that means a love tainted with evil. But since a husband and wife can have relations without sin and virtuously, as has been said, there is a legitimate carnal love. They love each other because of the pleasure they have in and from each other to the extent that that pleasure is natural, joined to the marriage act by God's providence, and related to a proper aim.

As Aristotle says and St. Thomas repeats, our moral evaluation of an act and the pleasure joined to an act is the same. Therefore the pleasure from a good and virtuous act is good; and to the extent that it is good, it can be desired.[73]

Almost unnoticed Denis has here taken the judgment about sexual conduct's moral quality away from the presence or absence of "carnal pleasure" and located it elsewhere—apparently in the presence or absence of its proper aim. In this there is the implication that the pleasure need not be what Augustine insisted it must be in order to avoid sin, namely pleasure at the thought of conceiving a child for the kingdom of God.

Soto reasoned about the same matter with realistic sympathy for human nature.

Nature has wisely attached pleasure to that act because of the need to conserve the race. . . . Therefore just as taking one's food and drink with pleasure is no sin, neither is marital intercourse.

And certainly those who say the contrary, in other words that it is a sin unless a man abhors the pleasure involved, are trying to deprive men of their natural feelings. The mind is simply not able to elicit displeasure in that situation.[74]

Within this gradually relaxing severity an ancient, even pre-Christian worry about an effect of married life persisted. Aristotle was not the first to voice it, but he put it clearly in his succinct way: "The pleasures are a hindrance to thought, the more so the more a person delights in them. Take sexual pleasure for example. No one would be able to think of anything while absorbed in that."[75]

This is moral philosophy drawn from psychological experience. It apparently singles out the source of all the clerical worry of the centuries about sexual pleasure. It is presumed to cloud the higher mental operations, among them the prayer and contemplation wherein a human being joins with God. Continual absorption in pleasure hampers these severely and eventually makes them impossible. This may be a refined interpretation of the centuries-old rhetoric about the uncleanness, the shame, the sinful concupiscence of sexual conduct. It also assumes that the essential core of holiness is contemplative union with God. Or even if it does not assume this but sees love as this core, it finds any sensual pleasure taking the will and the emotions away from God and locking them on the object of the pleasure.

One could quote endlessly from the writers who, down to the twentieth century, caution the Catholic married against falling into this absorption. A few must suffice, and among them two most influential documents demand attention. They are of very diverse natures, the *Catechism of the Council of Trent* and St. Francis de Sales' *Introduction to the Devout Life*. The former was produced for pastors and catechists. It became the source-book of religious instruction in the Catholic Church for the centuries following Trent. The latter quickly became the preferred reading of the Catholic devout and even of many Protestants throughout Western Christendom.

It is significant that in its treatise on marriage, Chapter 7, *De Matrimonio*, the Catechism's first consideration is to reassert the superiority over marriage of the life of consecrated virginity. Indeed, to touch on a familiar theme, it proposes monastic life as the best Christian life because it is tranquil and there the mind can concentrate on and rest in God. But it assures that each person has his or her own gift from God of a way of life, and marriage is one of these gifts.[76]

The Catechism continues that by nature marriage is a pact, or covenant, in which the spouses grant to one another the right over their bodies for sexual intercourse. God is the inventor of marriage. By his will there are three honorable reasons for entering marriage. They are that men and women need one another's help; they need a legitimate outlet for concupiscence; and the principal reason, to produce and nurture children. These are the motives that one who wishes to marry religiously ought to have. Other motives, such as beauty and congeniality, do not conflict with these provided they are added to them.[77]

Christ himself made marriage a sacrament of his new covenant. He did so for two reasons: to provide a people trained for perfect worship (*cultus*) of the true God and savior, and in order to set before human beings a specific sign of his union with the Church, a union which is his love for human beings.[78] He put this sign especially in the union of husband and wife because no human relationship can be more intimate and binding, and none can have a greater love—the love that is charity. Because the model for and revelation of the potential of this union is in Ephesians 5:21–32, the husband should govern in the marriage and the wife should be subject to him.[79]

God confers his grace on spouses in this sacrament. The Catechism does not say that this intensifies their union with God. It does say that spouses joined in a bond of mutual love (*charitas*) are helped by the sacrament's grace to live happily with one another, to conduct themselves without sin in their own marriage, and to avoid illicit loves outside their marriage.[80]

The fundamental duties of a husband to his wife are to treat her as a companion (*socia*), generously and in a way that honors her, to support her, to create a family with her, to bring up their children in discipline. The duties of a wife to her husband are to be subject to him, to obey him in all that is not sinful, to bring up their children religiously, to manage their household well, and to not leave their home without his permission.[81]

The Catechism makes its case against sexual expression as an obstacle to piety in the following way; "Two rules apply to the use of marriage [a circumlocution for its sexual expression]":

> Because the spouses ought in their prayer to ask all goods [of marriage] from God, a second rule for pastors is that they teach the faithful to abstain from their marital duties now and then for the sake of this prayer. They ought especially to abstain for at least three days before receiving communion, and even more frequently during the solemn fast of Lent—as our Fathers have rightly commended. In this way they will experience the goods themselves of marriage increasing continually in their lives with the help of God's grace.[82]

The author of this passage has called the marriage of two Christians a sacrament. He has just called sexual intercourse the "use" of this sacrament. He seems not to notice the anomaly of advising that spouses gain in holiness by refraining from the use of their sacrament. Nor does he explain how this gain is secured by the non-use of something holy.

St. Francis de Sales

Of all the Catholic writers who turned their attention to marriage in the generations from the Council of Trent until well into the present century none was read so widely during that time as Francis de Sales. In the measure that the common husband-wife relationship in Roman Catholicism changed from that of pledged duty to tender affection, Francis was the ecclesiastical writer who more than all others inspired the change. Why this is so is evident in the circumstance in which he wrote his most universally read essay, *An Introduction to the Devout Life*. Though bishop of Geneva in the see of Annecy, he did not produce it as a seminary text, nor as a lecture-commentary on the scriptures or the fathers (although he quotes and borrows from them copiously), and not even as a formal treatise on asceticism and piety. He wrote it as a favor for an intelligent, devout woman who asked him to be her confessor and counselor. She was Marie du Chastel, who in 1600 married a relative of Francis, Claude de Charmoisy, ambassador of the duke of Savoy to the republic of Berne. Much of Francis' counsel to Madame de Charmoisy he communicated by letter. The *Introduction* is the collection and development, from its first edition in 1609 through its fifth revised edition in 1619, of this correspondence. In the collection a fictional counselee is adopted under the name, Philothea—"lover of God." The name is chosen with an obvious calculation that Francis revealed in Chapter 1 of Part 1: "True, living devotion . . . presupposes the love of God, and hence it is nothing else than the love of God."[83]

There is no need to dwell on Francis' doctrinal instructions included in his counseling on marriage. In that domain he was no innovator. What he had to say we have read in Augustine, Gregory of Nazianz, and the Catechism of the Council of Trent. Our interest is in his reflections on ordinary married life and especially on marital love. These were conditioned by a first principle he established in his preface to the *Introduction*.

> Almost all those who have hitherto treated of devotion have had in view the instruction of persons wholly withdrawn from the world, or they have taught a kind of devotion that leads to this absolute retirement. My intention is to instruct those who live in towns, in families, or at court. By their condition they are obliged to lead, as to outward appearances, an ordinary life. Frequently, under an imaginary pretense of impossibility, they will not so much as think of undertaking a devout life. . . . To such I will prove that . . . a vigorous soul may live in this world without being infected by any of its moods, may discover sweet springs of piety amidst its salt waters.[84]

Francis' counsel about marriage is traditional doctrine and morality applied to marriage as lived by the married. He holds it an honorable state of life. Its vocation is to provide citizens for the state and the Church, and thence for the eternal kingdom. It is God who brings devout spouses to one another and joins them.

The marital love required of Christian spouses includes but goes beyond natural affection and human love. Its model is the reciprocal love of Christ and the Church. It is precisely this love that both demands and produces fidelity and lifelong union. The natural fruit of marriage and of its love is children. Spouses co-work with God in producing them.[85]

When Francis embodies the Christ-Church model in real-life marriage he asks husbands to be constant and tenderly loving masters, and wives to be equally tender and obedient adult children.

> Preserve, O husbands, a tender, constant and heartfelt love for your wives. Woman was taken from that side of the first man which was nearest his heart, to the end that she might be loved by him cordially and tenderly. The weakness and infirmity of your wives, whether in body or in mind, ought never to provoke you to any kind of disdain, but rather to a mild and affectionate compassion. God has created them such, to the end that they should depend upon you and you should receive from them more honor and respect. It is also that you should have them for your companions in such manner that you should still be their heads and superiors. And you, O wives, love tenderly and cordially the husbands whom God has given you, but with a love respectful and full of reverence. . . . All Holy Scripture strictly recommends this submission to you. Yet the same Holy Scripture renders it agreeable as well, not only by prescribing that you should accommodate yourselves to it with love, but also by commanding your husbands to exercise it over you with a great charity, tenderness and mildness.[86]

Francis urged a point in the psychology of marital love.

> Love and fidelity joined together always produce familiarity and confidence. This is why the saints have used many reciprocal caresses in their married life, caresses truly affectionate, but chaste, tender and sincere. . . . The great St. Louis, equally vigorous to his own flesh and tender in the love of his wife, was almost blamed for the abundance of sweet caresses. Actually he rather deserved praise for being able to bring his martial and courageous spirit to stoop to these little duties so requisite for the preservation of conjugal love.[87]

Even if a woman's specifically marital love calls for her, in Francis' judgment, to be the deferential, obedient and tenderly cared for partner, yet he does not see her as a child in the rest of her marriage.

> St. Paul leaves to wives, as their portion, the care of the household. For this reason many think with truth that their devotion is more profitable to the family than that of the husband, who does not reside so much at home and cannot, as a consequence,

so easily care for it in virtue. Because of this consideration Solomon in his Proverbs makes the happiness of the whole family depend on the care and industry of the valiant woman whom he describes.[88]

About sexual expression in marriage Francis was approving, humane—and cautious. Surprisingly he approved not because he saw in it the tenderness, the affection and the constancy in love that he otherwise urged on spouses so strongly. Instead he approved of it as the rendering of a most seriously owed debt in justice.

But it is a debt so great that he [Paul] allows neither of the parties exemption from it without the free and voluntary consent of the other, not even for the exercise of devotion, . . . How much less, then, may either party be dispensed from it through a capricious pretense of virtue, or through anger or disdain?[89]

His caution is aimed at the always present temptation to excess of sensuality and carnality even in marriage. The excess he has in mind shows itself in preoccupation with bodily pleasure and in contraceptive intercourse. His indictment of absorption in bodily pleasure is that it captures and weighs down the mind so that it can no longer rise to God, loses sight of him, and leaves the person to live virtually an animal existence.

Married people are not to keep their affections fixed on those sensual pleasures in which, according to their vocation, they have indulged. When they are over, they ought to wash their hearts and affections and to purify themselves from them as soon as possible, so that afterward they may with undisturbed minds practice other purer and more elevated actions. . . .[90]

Francis closes down this consideration by enunciating a general ascetic-moral principle: "Let everyone use this world according to his calling but in such manner that he does not engage his affection in it and remains as free and ready to serve God as if he did not use it. . . . We should enjoy spiritual things but only use corporal. When their use is turned into enjoyment, our rational soul is also changed into a brutish and beastly soul."[91]

If this return to the early fathers' wariness of sensual pleasure is surprising, far more surprising ought to be the fact that in all his advice to Christian spouses who seek holiness in their marriages (and we have reviewed only a fraction of it here), Francis mentions the word "sacrament" only once. Even this is a passing remark: "The man who wishes to have a happy married life ought in his espousals to consider the sanctity and dignity of this sacrament."[92] He does not notice the sacrament when proposing the Christ-Church model of Ephesians 5 to husbands and wives. When reviewing the Augustinian goods of marriage and coming upon lifelong fidelity he does not identify this as the *sacramentum*. In fine, assuming that this passage mirrors Catholic spouses' perception of marriage in the first quarter of the seventeenth century, the sacrament was hardly in their awareness, which suggests that all the anxiety, debating and contesting about it that we have been reviewing were fairly isolated in the minds of scholars and authorities, both civil and ecclesiastic.

Despite this anxiety about sexual pleasure in marriage we find the writers of the post-Tridentine period repeating a theme as old as the book of Tobit. It is that when sincerely religious men and women come together in marriage, it is God who leads them there. It is difficult to detect when this statement is borrowed from the rhetoric of piety and when it is a formal assertion of belief. But its repetition is constant enough to demand the attention of the student of this history.

Assuming this strategy of divine providence, one must come necessarily to the conclusion that God can bring a man and woman together only by playing a consistently active role in their lives. For their part they can come together permanently in marriage only by free choice. It follows that their thus coming together results from their fairly constant response to God, from their accepting his gifts of wisdom, trust and courage. All this is to say that such coming together is growth in holiness. It remains to be seen whether the writers drew this conclusion from their claim that devout marriages are God's doing.

Luis de Granada, the best known Dominican spiritual writer of the immediate post-Tridentine period, explained thus:

> This love between married persons flows from the very will of God. The happiness they enjoy in that state, the actual benefits it produces, and the inclination of nature clearly display his will.[93]

> You who are not yet married and have the intention to be, put the Lord uppermost in your mind and the desire to please Him and save yourself. Then ask Him for the companion who can help you in this.[94]

Francis de Sales wrote to a widow, "It was God, my dear cousin, who gave you this husband. It was he who has taken him back to himself."[95] In other correspondence he was just as specific: ". . . since God has given each of you to the other, be always content in this arrangement."[96] And "Love your husband tenderly as one who has been given to you by the very hand of your Lord."[97]

In the late 1700's the Jesuit, Jean Grou, made an even more detailed claim for God's providential guiding of a man toward his marriage.

Beyond all doubt, a man's inclination, that indefinable something which touches his heart and determines it in favor of one
person rather than another, is something to be taken seriously.
This inclination, which has its source in nature . . . we can
regard as produced by God himself.[98]

God knows the one he has destined for you. Ask him for her
and wait for her with confidence from his hand.[99]

It was Francis de Sales who wrote most detailedly about the way to
holiness in married life. As we have seen, his *Introduction to the Devout
Life* had just this purpose, to convince the ninety-eight percent of the
Catholic population not in religious life that the highest Christian goodness is within their reach. But to make this case credible he and the
writers who agreed with him had to qualify the ancient Catholic assumption that the life of vowed chastity is the more perfect Christian vocation. They qualified it by transferring the question from the comparing
of abstract ideals to that of God's particular leading in particular life
circumstances of individual men and women.

It is certain fact that when God calls someone to a vocation, He
obliges himself as a consequence, in His divine providence, to
furnish him with the helps he needs to make himself perfect in
his vocation.[100]

I ask you, Philothea, is it fit that . . . married people should lay
up no greater store of goods than the Capuchin? . . . No . . .
true devotion . . . not only does no injury to any vocation or
employment, but on the contrary it adorns and beautifies
it. . . . It is an error, or rather a heresy, to try to banish the
devout life from . . . the home of married folk.[101]

Luis de la Puente, a near contemporary of de Sales, made the
qualification in the following way.

The state of perfection and the care of souls give more help to
acquiring great sanctity. Still the lack of these is often made up
for by the copious grace of God and the great diligence of the
man himself, aided by the same grace. The result is that,
though living in a less perfect state, he mounts to a more excellent sanctity than those in a state of great perfection.[102]

The state of marriage is the most imperfect of all the states of
the Gospel law, and yet the highest perfection of those who are
in the most perfect states can be obtained in it. For as has been

said above, the grace of God is not really bound to the different ways of life.[103]

Summary: The Ministers of the Sacrament

At the close of this chapter it is worth noting how a doctrinal declaration intended to end one dispute had, by logical consequence, the effect of answering a distinct question about the sacrament in marriage. The latter asked who are the ministers of the sacrament where a marriage of two Christians is in fact a sacrament. The question was kept alive by all those, beginning with Melchior Cano in the sixteenth century, who insisted that the marital contract and the sacrament are separable; that the spouses can contract marriage as a natural relationship without making this a sacrament; that where the marriage is a sacrament, the latter is only an accessory to the contract—is only the religious ceremony, perhaps only the priestly blessing. What is more, since two spouses at first unbaptized can contract a marriage that is not a sacrament, but if both are subsequently baptized, their marriage becomes a sacrament (as Catholic teaching holds) without their repeating the formula of marital commitment, it seems to follow that in no case are the spouses themselves the ministers of their sacrament. Who then? Only the priest who blesses them and declares them husband and wife.

The accepted Catholic answer to this question came, as hinted above, in the form of a logical consequence from the resolution of a more fundamental doctrinal dispute. From the Catholic authorities' insistence that two Christians can contract no other marriage than one that is sacramental, that the spouses themselves create the contract, and that for two Christians the contract is the sacrament elevated to a grace-giving instrument of God, it follows that the spouses create the sacrament as well. As conscious instruments of God they are the ministers of their own sacrament.

The late nineteenth-century theologian, Cardinal Louis Billot, explained why, unlike baptism and penance, the creating of marriage as a sacrament requires as minister no person in holy orders.[104] In those other sacraments the minister is preeminent over the recipient. But it is the ordained clergyman who is properly preeminent over the layperson. The difference in marriage is that those who confer and receive the sacrament are co-equal. Both the man and the woman present the *materia* of the sacrament. This they do not by first creating the contract and bringing it for a blessing. They do so by offering themselves each to the other contractually. And both determine this otherwise indeterminate *materia*—they supply the *forma* of the sacrament—by accepting one another contractually. In doing both to create the contract they administer the sacrament to one another.

The Protestant reformers' dispute about marriage that continued as the most serious practical concern after Trent was that of juridical rule and judicial control of Christian marriages. The attempt to break the churchmen's exclusive hold here had begun in the fourteenth century under Ludwig IV of Bavaria, with Ockham and Marsilius of Padua supplying his canonical rationale. After Trent the Gallicans in France and the Febronians and Josephists in the Empire continued the attack. Leopold, the grand duke of Tuscany and brother of Austria's Joseph II, concentrated it in the Synod of Pistoia in 1786. Scipione Ricci, the bishop of Istria, and a group of French Jansenists were the main figures in the synod.

These champions of secularization claimed civil control of Christian marriages on the ground of the separability in these marriages of contract and sacrament. They insisted that the state rightly holds jurisdiction over the former, which is a natural contract, while the Church holds it over the latter, which is nothing more than the religious element of the marriage ceremony—in *specie* the priest's blessing.

Secularization in a more radical sense was the target of the Enlightenment and of the architects of the French revolution. Their intent was not only to remove Christian marriages from ecclesiastic to civil control while leaving them presumably Christian, but to de-Christianize them entirely. This movement of elitist secular intelligence was embodied in the School of the Law of Nature, with Hugo Grotius and Samuel von Pufendorf the principal figures therein. These grounded the law of nature in God's will rather than in his intelligence, and insisted that the law that guides human conduct can be deduced from an ideal conception of the human essence. Because the philosopher and the civil legislator are the natural deducers of this law, they are also its natural monitors and executors. Natural law in the concrete thus becomes civil law.

The extremists of the French revolution denied to marriage any religious origin and character, and logically gave it over to the nonreligious state—in their circumstances to an anti-religious state. The First Republic's civil constitution of 1791 named marriage a civil contract. A year later Title IV of the constitution established a system of purely civil legislation and along with it the availability of civil divorce.

When Napoleon Bonaparte co-empted the revolution he ended its attack on the Church and sought peace with it—but peace on his own terms and with him in control of it in France and his growing empire. He kept for his Code Civil and his Code Pénal the marriage legislation of the Constitution of 1791. This authorized Catholics to exchange wedding vows before civil magistrates, thus implying the separation of contract and sacrament. It authorized divorce by civil authority as well, albeit on limited and strictly controlled grounds. This legislation became step by step the model of marriage law throughout most of nineteenth-century Europe.

Where the Enlightenment thinkers and those of the revolution attacked the religious character of marriage from outside it, the literary and historical criticism of the Bible during the eighteenth and nineteenth centuries undermined it from within. It did this by demonstrating that the creation narratives of Genesis 1 and 2 are not historical-factual narratives, but are didactic fictions. But for centuries Christian teachers had found in these fictions the presumed evidence for God's immediate invention of marriage and therefore of its essentially religious nature. In contrast, cultural anthropologists of the nineteenth and early twentieth centuries interpreted monogamous marriage as the latest stage in an evolutionary development in socio-sexual mores that had begun with promiscuity.

For Immanuel Kant, a son of the Enlightenment, the confinement and expression of sexuality is natural in the sense of a dictate of human nature as this is conceived in ideal essence and prior to experience. Because sexuality is part of a person, and a person is not saleable, he cannot sell his sexuality nor buy another's. Indeed, the only way to avoid using another person's sexuality as a thing, and hence the other person as a thing, is to make an equal commitment of one's whole person in exchange with the committed whole person of the other—in a word, in marriage.

Like Hugh of St. Victor eight centuries earlier, Hegel put the essence of marriage in the fusion of two souls—or rather, for Hegel, in the fusion of two consciousnesses. But marriage as thus conceived could not serve as the matrix of the sacrament of marriage, precisely because, as an exquisite state in the evolution of consciousness, it leaves behind bodiliness, passion, sensate expression of and union in love. And his self-contained, essentially monadic world soul could not acknowledge either revelation from a transcendent source nor the gracing of human beings from that source.

The magisterial Catholic reaction began in 1690 in Pope Alexander VIII's condemnation of the Gallican Articles. It continued through Pius II's condemnation of the Febronian ecclesiology of Niklaus von Hontheim. It climaxed in Pius IX's condemnation, in his Syllabus of Errors in 1864, of seven theses asserting the separability of marital contract and sacrament and denying the Church's exclusive jurisdiction over Christian marriages.

The theology of marriage that developed in the Catholic seminaries was an explanation and always in some degree a defense of Trent's decrees against Protestant dissent. This theology insisted especially that in virtue of the spouses' baptism every marriage of two Christians is a sacrament, and that the sacrament makes their natural indisssolubility "more firm" in these marriages.

The Catholic understanding of marriage began in the latter seventeenth century the slow change that continues today as the clerics who wrote and instructed about it came to be less frequently prelates and scholar-monks and more frequently priests of the people and pastors of the married. This conception of marriage began its elision from the ideal model to an appreciation of marriage as the married experience it. A gentling of the attitude toward sexual intercourse and its pleasure opened gradually a more receptive place for sexually expressed love in the theology of the sacrament.

NOTES

1. *Cursus Theologiae Universalis,* 1746–1750, p. 234.
2. Denzinger-Schönmetzer, n. 1812, p. 417.
3. Denzinger-Schönmetzer, nn. 1803 and 1804, p. 416.
4. *De Locis Theologicis,* Lib. 8, Cap. 5, Padova, 1762, p. 218.
5. Cf. *Dictionnaire de Théologie Catholique,* col. 2262.
6. *Op. cit.,* Col. 2263.
7. *Ibid.*
8. *Ibid.,* Col. 2264.
9. *Ibid.,* Col. 2265.
10. *Ibid.,* Cols. 2265–2266.
11. In Joyce, *op. cit.,* p. 202, note 3.
12. *Op. cit.,* p. 257.
13. Denzinger-Schönmetzer, nn. 2281–2285, pp. 478–479.
14. *Op. cit.,* nn. 2592–2597, pp. 516–517.
15. *Op. cit.,* n. 2598, p. 517.
16. *Ibid.*
17. *Op. cit.,* nn. 2600–2700, pp. 518–544.
18. *Loc. cit.,* n. 2659, p. 534.
19. Cf. *Dictionnaire de Théologie Catholique,* Col. 2278.
20. Aquinas' simplest and clearest presentation of his theory is in the *Summa Theologiae,* I-II, Question 91, Articles 1 and 2, and in Question 94.
21. *De Jure Naturae et Gentium,* in *The Classics of International Law,* edited by James Scott Brown . . . the translation of the 1688 edition by C.H. and W.A. Oldfather, N.Y., 1964. Book 1, Chapter 6, p. 877.
22. *Ibid.,* p. 878.
23. *Ibid.,* p. 879.
24. Second Treatise, Chapter 7, nn. 78 and 79, in John Locke: *Two Treatises of Government* . . . by Peter Laslett, Second Edition, Cambridge et al., 1967, "An Essay Concerning the True Origin, Extent and End of Civil Government."
25. *Loc. cit.,* n. 81, p. 339.
26. *Dictionnaire Philosophique,* "Mariage".
27. In Book 1, Chapter 1, no. 7 Augustine wrote, "In all the holy books one must take care to note which passages are disclosures of eternal truth, which are narratives of events, which are prophecies of things to come. In the narratives one must ask whether all things there are to be taken as figurative, or whether they are to be accepted and defended as actual events. But no Christian should simply presume to deny that they are to be taken figuratively. One must note that Paul said, 'All these things happened to them as a sign [*figura*]' (I Cor. 10:11); that he repeated the passage from Genesis, 'And they will become two in one flesh' (2:24); and that he proposed this is as a great sacrament in Christ and in the Church (Ephes. 5:32). . . .

"If therefore this passage is to be studied in both senses, we may ask in what other way than allegorically it says 'In the beginning God created heaven and earth' " (PL 34:247).

Augustine interpreted the creation poem's six days not as the length and division of time God gave to his work of creating, but as the sequence in which he created things. Indeed Augustine believed that God created all creatures of history simultaneously *in semine*—"not all things in their proper physical dimensions, but in causative strength and power" (Book 5, Chapter 5, PL 34:337). Yet, as Book 6 shows, he believed that God did create one man at the beginning of history (PL 34:347).

28. Among these were Starke, *Die Primitive Familie in ihrer Entstehung und Entwicklung* (1890), P.F. Sarasin, in *Die Weddas von Ceylan und die sie Umgebenden Völkerschaften,* and MacLennan, *The History of Human Marriage* (1891).

29. Thus the group of Catholic ethnologists: Graebner, *Die Methode der Ethnologie* (1911); A. Bros, *l'Ethnologie Religieuse* (1923); H. Pinard de Boulaye, *l'Etude Comparé des Religions* (1922–1925); and especially Wilhelm Schmidt's study of marriage among various pygmy tribes. His master work in twelve volumes is *Der Ursprung der Gottesidee* (The Origin of the Concept of God), 1912–1954.

30. G. Davy, "Vues sociologiques sur la famille et le parenté d'apres Durkheim," in *Revue Philosophique,* Jan.–Feb. 1921, p. 83 (in *Dictionnaire de Théologie Catholique,* Col. 2307–2308).

31. Translated by Louis Infield, London, 1930.

32. *Op. cit.,* p. 163.

33. *Ibid.,* p. 164.

34. *Ibid.,* p. 165.

35. *Ibid.,* p. 166.

36. *Ibid.*

37. *Ibid.,* pp. 166–167.

Kant passed severe judgment against adultery, and even more severe against homosexuality and other "sins of the flesh against nature": "Just as the engagement to marry is the most serious and most inviolable engagement between two persons and binds them for life, so also is adultery the greatest breach of faith there can be because it is disloyalty to an engagement than which there can be no more important" (*ibid.,* p. 169).

"[Homosexuality] too is contrary to the ends of humanity; for the end of humanity in respect to sexuality is to preserve the species without debasing the person . . . but the person is set aside, the self is degraded far below the level of animals, and humanity is dishonoured. . . . From the point of view of duties toward himself such conduct is the most disgraceful and most degrading of which man is capable. . . . It is the most abominable conduct of which man can be guilty" (*ibid.,* p. 170).

38. *Ibid.,* p. 167.

39. Kant devoted Part 1 of his Metaphysics of Morals to a study of the theory of rights. There he defined marriage nearly as Scotus had defined it in the fourteenth century, as the union of two persons of diverse sex who grant to one another reciprocal rights over their bodies for the duration of their lives. Each acquires a real and personal right over the other. Each possesses the other as a thing but must treat the other as a person—for a principle of freedom would be violated if they tried to possess a person as a person, or if one person treated the

other as a thing. ("The Metaphysical Elements of the Theory of Right, Part 1, Section 1: Private Right, Chapter 2, "On Acquiring Something External"; Section 3, "Rights *in rem* Over Persons"; Paragraphs 28 and 29, "Married Rights.")
40. *Grundlinien der Philosophie des Rechts,* in G.W.F. Hegel, *Sämtliche Werke,* Herausg. von Hermann Glockner, Stuttgart, 1938, 7er Band, p. 239.
41. *Op. cit.,* p. 290.
42. Denzinger-Schönmetzer, nn. 2281–2285, pp. 478–479.
43. *Op. cit.,* n. 2340, p. 464.
44. *Op. cit.,* n. 2892, p. 575.
45. *Op. cit.,* nn. 2865–2867, p. 571.
46. *Op. cit.,* n. 2965, p. 583.
47. *Ibid.,* n. 2966, p. 583.
48. *Ibid.,* n. 2973, p. 583.
49. The Syllabus condemned one thesis, no. 67, touching marriage's indissolubility: "That the bond of marriage is not indissoluble by the law of nature, and that in various cases it can be dissolved by civil authority" (*ibid.,* n. 2967, p. 583). The condemnation does not gainsay the Church's authority to dissolve marriages in certain cases. It claims to have authority to over-ride the law of nature in certain cases. It denies that civil authority can do the same.
   Three theses on the authority to establish and to remove impediments are condemned in nos. 68, 69 and 70 (*ibid.,* nn. 2968, 2969, 2970). One thesis, no. 74, bears on jurisdiction in general (*ibid.,* n. 2974). And one, no. 71, contradicts the requirements of Trent's decree, *Tametsi:* "That the Tridentine form is not required under the pain of nullity where civil law prescribes a different form and decides that a marriage is valid by use of this form" (*ibid.,* n. 2971). In this regard note that 145 years earlier Pope Benedict XIV had declared, in *Matrimonia quae in locis,* on November 4, 1741, that Protestant partners in the Netherlands (including Belgium) marry validly without the witnesses prescribed by *Tametsi,* as do Catholics who marry Protestants in the same territory (Denzinger-Schönmetzer, nn. 2515–2520, pp. 500–501).
50. "Matrimonium est verum ac proprie dictum Legis Evangelicae Sacramentum. Est contra Lutheranos et Calvinistas" (*op. cit.,* p. 378).
51. In *Theologia Scholastico-Dogmatica Juxta Mentem Divi Thomae Aquinatis,* Tomus III: In Tertiam Partem et Supplementum D. Thomae; Tractatus 13: "De Matrimonio." Venetiis, 1786, p. 473.
52. Quaestio 2: De Matrimonio ut Sacramentum Est; Dubium 1: "An Matrimonium sit Sacramentum," p. 473.
53. *Ibid.,* p. 474.
54. *Ibid.*
55. P. 419
   Gatti's formulation of the article shows that he conceived of marriage's permanence as its indissolubility, and that since this permanence can be made more firm, marriage can have degrees of indissolubility.
   If in formulating his conclusion he had kept in mind the Catholic tradition of dissolving unconsummated marriages, and by his time marriages that were not Christian sacraments, he might have said that in virtue of natural and divine positive law marriage is firm and permanent, but is indissoluble only in virtue of the Christian sacrament—and of the consummated sacrament at that.
56. In *Institutiones Theologicae ad Usum Seminariorum,* Editio 5a, Tomus Quartus, Parisiis, 1844.

57. *Op. cit.*, pp. 119–120.
58. *Op. cit.*, pp. 132–133.
59. *Ibid.*, p. 137.
60. *Ibid.*
61. *Ibid.*, p. 136.
62. *In IV Sententiarum*, Distinctio 26, Quaestio 1, Articulus 3, ad 3m.
63. *De Sacramento Matrimonii*, Caput 6.
64. *In IV Sententiarum*, Distinctio 33, Quaestio 1, Articulus 1.
65. *Op. cit.*, Distinctio 26, Quaestio 1, Articulus 3, ad 3m.
66. *Prob. Hel.*, n. 14., PL 178:701 (in Kerns, *op. cit.*, p. 67)
67. *Reportatio Parisiensis*, Distinctio 32 (in Kerns, *op. cit.*, p. 66)
68. *In IV Sententiarum*, Distinctio 26, Quaestio 1, Articulus 3 (in Kerns, *op. cit.*, p. 70).
69. *Commentaria in Evangelicam Historiam*, 8, Tractatus 51, p. 475 (in Kerns, *ibid.*).
70. *De Sacramento Matrimonii*, Liber 2, Disputatio 29, nn. 24–25 (in Kerns, *ibid.*, p. 71).
71. *Op. cit.*, Liber 9, Disputatio 4, nn. 3–4 (in Kerns, *op. cit.*, p. 71).
72. *Enarratio in Ecclesiasticos*, 18, a. 18 (in Kerns, *op. cit.*, p. 76).
73. *De Laude Vitae Conjugalis*, a. 8 (in Kerns, *ibid.*).
74. *In IV Sententiarum*, Distinctio 31, Quaestio 1, Articulus 3 (in Kerns, *op. cit.*, p. 77).
75. *Nicomachean Ethics*, Book 1, Chapter 11.
76. *Catechismus Concilii Tridentini*, Par. 1, pp. 278–279.
77. *Op. cit.*, Par. 7, p. 281.
78. *Op. cit.*, Par. 17, p. 285.
79. *Op. cit.*, Par. 18, p. 285.
80. *Op. cit.*, Par. 20–21, p. 286.
81. *Op. cit.*, Par. 31, p. 290.
82. *Ibid.*, p. 293.
83. *Introduction to the Devout Life . . .* translated and edited by John K. Ryan, Garden City, 1955, p. 36.
84. *Op. cit.*, p. 29.
85. Part 3, Chapter 38, *op. cit.*, pp. 214–215.
86. *Ibid.*, pp. 215–216.
87. *Op. cit.*, p. 217.
88. *Op. cit.*, p. 219.
The reference here is to "the ideal wife" portrayed in the Book of Proverbs, 31:10–31.
89. *Op. cit.*, p. 221.

Francis had a mixed judgment on the tradition of sexual abstinence in preparation for Holy Communion: "I must say a word to married people. In the Old Law God did not approve that creditors should exact their debts on festival days, but He never disapproved that debtors should pay what they owed to such as exacted it. It is an impropriety, though not a great sin, to solicit the payment of the marriage debt on the day of Communion; but it is not improper but rather meritorious to pay it. Wherefore, no one ought to be debarred from Communion for paying this debt, if otherwise their devotion incite them to desire it. It is certain that in the primitive Church, Christians communicated every day, although married and blessed with a generation of children. Hence, I have said that frequent Communion is by no means inconsistent with the state of a parent, husband or wife, provided the person that communicates be prudent and discreet" (Part 2, Chapter 20, pp. 112–113).

90. *Loc. cit.,* Chapter 39, p. 223.

91. *Ibid.,* p. 223.

The principle here is borrowed from Augustine: "It is the great evil of man to desire to enjoy the things which he should only use, and to desire to use those which he should only enjoy" (*De Octagintatribus Quaestionibus,* n. 30).

92. Part 3, Chapter 38, p. 214.

93. *Tractatus de Doctrina,* Liber 2, Caput 7 (in Kerns, *op. cit.,* p. 224).

94. *Op. cit.,* Liber 3, Caput 16 (in Kerns, *op. cit.,* p. 225).

95. Letter 250 (in Kerns, *op. cit.,* p. 226).

96. Letter 825 (in Kerns, *op. cit.,* p. 216).

97. Letter 1774 (in Kerns, *ibid.*).

98. *Livre du Jeune Homme,* p. 62 (in Kerns, *op. cit.,* p. 227).

99. *Ibid.,* p. 65 (in Kerns, *ibid.*).

100. *Entr. 17, Des Voix* (in Kerns, *op. cit.,* p. 241).

101. *Introduction to the Devout Life,* Part 1, Chapter 4, p. 40.

102. *De Christiani Hominis Perfectione* (1615), p. 63 (in Kerns, *op. cit.,* p. 240).

103. *Op. cit.,* p. 530 (in Kerns, *ibid.*).

104. In *De Ecclesiae Sacramentis. Commentarius in Tertiam Partem S. Thomae, Tomus Posterior, Secunda Editio.* Romae, 1897, pp. 350–351.

12. CATHOLIC TEACHING IN THE NINETEENTH AND TWENTIETH CENTURIES

It is reasonably accurate to see the beginning of the modern era of Roman Catholic teaching on marriage the sacrament in Pope Leo XIII's encyclical letter, *Arcanum divinae sapientiae,* of February 10, 1880. The intervening century has produced four long and formal authoritative statements on marriage. In addition to Leo's *Arcanum* there have been Pope Pius XI's encyclical letter, *Casti connubii,* of December 31, 1930; the Second Vatican Council's *Pastoral Constitution on the Church in the Modern World,* Part 2, Chapter 1, "Fostering the Nobility of Marriage and the Family" (the document's date of publication is December 7, 1965); and Pope John Paul II's apostolic exhortation, *Familiaris consortio,* of December 15, 1981. There are also Pope Pius XII's many short and informal statements, most of them made in discourses to newlyweds gathered in pilgrimage to the Vatican. Finally there are the statements coming from the international synod of bishops that convened in Rome on September 26, 1980, the synod whose one agendum was to examine "The Role of the Christian Family in the Modern World." The bishops of this synod, unlike those of Vatican II, produced no single document addressed to marriage, but (as indicated above) a collection of statements—which yielded the added benefit of reflecting the conditions of Christian marriages in various cultures throughout the world.

What of Pope Paul VI's encyclical letter, *Humanae vitae,* of July 25, 1968? It is only obliquely about marriage. Nevertheless it offers a descriptive definition of marital love which, in the degree it has been taken into Catholic thought, has enriched the matrix of the sacrament by grounding this more explicitly in the personalist psychology of men and women. This too calls for careful inspection.

We shall examine these statements, the long and formal as well as the brief and informal. But in order to find them in context, and therefore to appreciate them both in their continuity with what went before as well as in their departure from it, we shall look first at three brief papal statements that antedate Leo XIII's *Arcanum.* Two of these are Leo's own. The third we have already examined in some measure. It is Pius IX's *Syllabus Errorum* of December 8, 1864. A second consideration of it will glean more exactly its implications concerning the sacrament in Christian marriage.

Were it not for the awkward bulk it would afflict on a single chapter, it would be instructive to include here a few interpretations coming from the theologians of the period. (These must be put off until the following chapter.) Understandably it is among the theologians that the contrast in thinking from one end to the other of this period stands out most clearly. But what is not generally well known is that from one end to the other there is also a continuity with especially one man who thought and wrote at the beginning, in the 1840's and 1850's. This was the German, Mathias Josef Scheeben. About him it is no exaggeration to say that after two centuries during which the theology of the marital sacrament was treated mainly as a derivative of Catholic law, Scheeben set this theology free to develop from its own strength.

It would be instructive too to consider evidence that the authoritative statements coming from the popes of the era influenced the writing of the theologians, and conversely that their writings influenced the popes'. One could hardly doubt that the Germanophile Pius XII read Scheeben and admired what he read. One need only read Pius' encyclical letter, *Mystici corporis* of 1943, to come again upon the leitmotif and much of the substance of Scheeben's own thought, his theology of the mystical body of Christ.

We may notice too the growing humaneness of the later statements of both popes and theologians, their effort to consider marriage less in its ideal design and more as an in-the-flesh experience of men and women in the world. It is justifiable to wonder how much Vatican II's understanding of marriage comes from the fact that Pius XII thought about marriage during and just after being surrounded by newly married couples. It may be this ambience of both the pope in the Vatican's audience chambers, and of the theologians who taught in the universities of central Europe, that accounts for the intensified concern of both to understand the sacrament from its human underside, from men's and women's experience of marriage.

The Papal Statements

We recall that Pius IX published the *Syllabus errorum,* along with his encyclical letter, *Quanta cura,* as his response to the conclusions relevant to Christian belief that were derived from the new empirical sciences born in the Enlightenment. Of the eighty propositions he condemned because to his mind they formulated the errors among these conclusions, ten—numbers 65 through 74—he labeled "Errores de Matrimonio Christiano." Propositions 65, 66, and 73 are pertinent to our examination at this point.

> Proposition 65: "In no way can it be proved that Christ raised marriage to the dignity of a sacrament."[1]

> Proposition 66: "The sacrament of marriage is only something accessory to the contract and separable from it. The sacrament itself is found solely in the nuptial blessing."[2]

> Proposition 73: "By virtue of a merely civil contract there can exist a true marriage of Christian partners; and it is false to say that the marital contract among Christians is always a sacrament—as it is false to say that there is no sacrament where the contract is excluded."[3]

Despite our earlier consideration of these issues, in all their details, a second and a modest examination of them is worthwhile.

Condemned Proposition 65 denies the occurrence of an event in history that is the source and ground of a point of Catholic doctrine. But Pius' condemnation of the denial is not historically careful. Taken as written it implies that Christ made sacraments not only the marriages of Christians, but all marriages. Or, more exactly, Pius' abstract predication implies that Christ made not only Christian marriage but marriage universally to be a sacrament. There is no hint here that Pius refers to the "natural" sacramentality of any and all marriages since the beginning of the human race, because he speaks of something done by Christ. (We shall see that the 1917 Code of Canon Law formulated the claim more carefully to say only that Christ raised marriage among Christians to the dignity of a sacrament.)

The point of doctrine follows from the asserted fact of history: Since Christ made (Christian) marriage a sacrament, the marriage of any pair of Christian spouses has been, is, and will be a Christian sacrament. Note that this is implied of all Christians, not only of Roman Catholics.

The condemnation of Proposition 66 puts that of Proposition 65 in a more exact historical context. It gets at what Melchior Cano said in his *De locis theologicis,* and what was repeated by Royalists, Josephists and Febronians for almost two centuries preceding Pius. It was that where a marriage of two Christians is in fact a sacrament (the implication was that not every such marriage is), its sacramentality resides not in something done intrinsically to the contract, but that this sacramentality is something extrinsic and accessory to the contract, and separable from it. The condemned proposition then names what this is and repeats Cano in doing so: It is the nuptial blessing. We recall Cano's hylemorphic interpretation that in a sacramental marriage the natural contract is its *materia,* while its *forma* is the priest's blessing. It would follow not that the spouses administer the sacrament to one another, but that they co-work with the priest to create it for the brief span of his blessing, they supplying the *materia* of the sacrament, while he supplies the *forma*.

While the condemnation of Proposition 66 does not do so explicitly, nevertheless in combination with the condemnation of Proposition 65 it clearly implies the *locus* of the Christian marital sacrament. This is the marital contract itself—when Christians make it. The sacrament is the contract that has undergone the "elevating" of Christ's institution of the sacrament. Therefore between sacrament and contract there is— to repeat a precision made frequently in Catholic doctrinal statements—no more than a distinction of formalities within the one reality of the marriage.

The first clause in the condemnation of Proposition 73 denies a consequence of the claim that in Christian marriage the contract and the sacrament are separable. This consequence is the possibility that by doing no more than contracting civilly a Christian man and woman can create a marriage. The clause denies that they can do this. The second and third clauses make the same denial, but by condemning a proposition whose logic runs in the reverse direction. Construed positively these two clauses insist that if two Christians do in fact create the marital contract, this contract is the sacrament. The only kind of marriage they can create with one another is a sacramental marriage.

The last clause clinches the thought. If these Christian spouses exclude from their intent in creating the contract the creating of the sacrament as well, they fail to create even the contract. (Note the clear and mildly subtle difference here from saying what the condemnation has sometimes been falsely accused of saying, namely that whether they will to do so or not, even if they reject the sacramentality of their marriage, a Christian couple by pronouncing their wedding vows automatically create the marital sacrament. The condemnation here does not imply this. Again, it implies that if the couple try to create the contract while positively excluding the sacrament, they make impossible the creating of the contract itself. They themselves invalidate their attempt at even a civil marriage.)

Pope Leo XIII

As I have already noted, Pope Leo spoke to the question of marriage before publishing his major letter, *Arcanum divinae sapientiae,* on February 10, 1880. He did so on December 28, 1878 in his encyclical *Quod apostolici.* Within one paragraph he concentrated the principal points of Catholic teaching.

> The Church . . . teaches that matrimony—"to be held in honor by all"—instituted by God as indissoluble from the beginning of the world, to propagate and preserve the human race, took

on a more holy and permanent condition when Christ deigned
to elevate it to a sacrament, presenting it as the image of his
union with the Church.[4]

Five months later he returned to the subject in his letter of June 1,
1879 to the Italian bishops of the Piedmonte. Here he concentrated the
preceding two centuries' rebuffs of the Royalist, Josephist and Febronian
claims.

> The conjugal union is not the work or invention of men; God
> himself, the Supreme Author of nature, from the beginning of
> creation, ordained such union for the propagation of the hu-
> man race and the constitution of the family. In the order of
> grace, He willed that this union be further enriched by impos-
> ing on it the divine seal of a sacrament. Therefore, insofar as
> the substance and sanctity of the bond are concerned, marriage
> for Christian jurisprudence is an essentially sacred and reli-
> gious act, the regulation of which naturally belongs to the reli-
> gious power, not by a delegation of the State, nor by the con-
> sent of the Princes, but by the mandate of the Divine Founder
> of Christianity and Author of the sacraments.[5]

As we shall see, this much was a précis, almost a preliminary draft,
of what Leo was to say eight months later in his major encyclical letter.

Arcanum Divinae Sapientiae

Both the mood and the content of *Arcanum* reveal that Leo wrote it
from within his profound worry about the secularization of all things
human that had begun in the late fourteenth century in Europe; that had
been hastened by the partial amputation of Catholic authority in the
Protestant reform and the ambiguously settled political-religious conflicts
following it; that had continued with the Royalists' reclaiming of secular
jurisdiction over marriages; that had been accelerated mightily by the
Enlightenment and its offspring, the French revolution and its sowing of
the spirit of revolutionary liberalism throughout Europe; and that was
continuing apace as nation after ostensibly Christian nation (several
Catholic among them) made civil divorce constitutionally available to
their citizens.[6] Behind the move to secularization, of course, lay the assumption, both theological and political, that marriage is fundamentally a
natural institution, a contract by nature civil, and that therefore it is
rightly ruled not by ecclesiastical but by civil authority. Virtually everything Leo wrote in *Arcanum* worked at the gainsaying of this assumption
and of the consequences of it for marriage in Western society.

He begins the gainsaying by asserting a point from his theology of
history. The original and natural order of things is now a wounded one.

This order had begun with the first parents of the race in a graced and innocent relationship with the creator, but their sin of disobedience and the tide of sin down through the intervening millennia have crippled this order severely.

But Christ by his teaching, his death and his resurrection has rescued and healed this wounded nature in human beings. Now it is possible for them to be even humanly good. Now the human race belongs to Christ.

Within this theology of history Leo located the history of marriage's origin. Marriage is not the product of blind evolution, and it is not the invention of human authority. God himself invented it, at the dawn of history, in the garden of Eden. The first man and woman, Adam and Eve, were the first married couple. Without question Leo accepted the historical factuality of the first two chapters of Genesis as the source of this information. And he unembarrassedly combined the creation poem of Genesis 1, which tells of the Lord God's creating the man and woman together in a single creative act, with the garden narrative of Genesis 2 in such a way as to have Yahweh form the man alone from the earth on the sixth day of creation and afterward draw the woman from his body.

> We recall what everyone knows, and what no one can doubt, that after God had formed man from the mud of the earth on the sixth day of creation, and had breathed into his face the breath of life, he wished to give him a companion. In miraculous fashion he took her from his side while he slept. In his most providential care God thus intended that this married couple be the natural origin of all human beings.[7]

As the creator of marriage God himself designed into it its two principal traits, unity and permanence. Christ himself confirmed this, as his words of confirmation are recorded in Matthew 19:5 quoting Genesis 2:24: "That is why a man leaves his father and mother and clings to his wife, and the two of them become one flesh"; and in Matthew 19:6 adding his own radical evaluation, "They are no longer two, therefore, but one flesh. Therefore what God has joined no man must separate."

Between God's primordial institution of marriage, with its unity and permanence, and Christ's strengthening of both, there intervened four millennia of degradation of marriage, and with it of women. But Christ restored marriage to its original dignity. He began this restoration by working the first of his miracles at the wedding feast of Cana in Galilee. He completed the restoration with the words quoted above from the gospel according to Matthew. He ended the degradation of women by his condemnation, recorded in the same discourse (verse 9), of the divorce practice among his own people: "But I say to you, A man who dismisses his wife—except in the case of her unchastity—and marries another, commits adultery."[8]

When Leo gets explicitly at the sacramentality of marriage we note his going decisively to a kind of predication with which he only dallied earlier in the encyclical. It is a kind which he avoided when writing in detail about the innumerable degradations that marriages suffered during the four millennia between creation and the ministry of Christ. There he recorded the fate of marriages in their historical concreteness, in the misery of wives in real life. But here as he begins his reflections on the sacrament he recedes into abstraction; he writes about "marriage." And this leads into an at least *prima facie* inexactness, since he stays in his abstraction to say that Christ raised "marriage" to the dignity of a sacrament, not that he made the marriages of his Christian followers sacraments.

When naming the causes, the precise agency, of marriage's elevation to a sacrament Leo cites none of those suggested in the synoptic gospel tradition. He turns instead to the Pauline tradition, to the *loci classici* in 1 Corinthians 7 and in Ephesians 5:21–33.

> Therefore by virtue precisely of these causes [referring to those named in I Cor. 7 and Eph. 5] marriage has become a great sacrament, "to be honored by all" (Hebr. 13:4), holy, chaste, to be revered in its imaging and symbolizing of divine things.[9]

Using Ephesians 5 as his source, and the marital analogy in it as a model, Leo affirms that because of marriage's sacramentality emanating from this passage, the duties of the spouses are more clearly defined. Each must love the other deeply; each must care for the other; both must keep fidelity. More specifically for each spouse, the husband is ruler in the family and head of the wife. But because she is "bone of his bones and flesh of his flesh" she is subject to him not as a servant but as a companion. Finally and inclusively, since in virtue of this analogy the husband is the image of Christ while the wife is that of the Church, divine charity is the constant norm of their duties toward one another.

Leo refers the details and the meaning of the metaphor to the spouses in "marriage" not with deontological valence, but unhesitatingly with ontological. That is, he does not say that the husband *ought* to be guide to his wife as a head is to the body, but that the husband simply *is* head to the wife—husband in abstraction to wife in abstraction. The result is an ideal construct, and the metaphor has been turned into the reality.

He then replies to the claims of the first naturalists (Morgan, Durkheim, et al.) and of the Royalists concerning jurisdiction over marriage. To the first his riposte is that marriage is historically not the product of the semi-deliberate evolution of social structures, and certainly not, as the Marxists claim, capitalist society's economic arrangement of its tyranny over women. Marriage is, again, God's own invention from the beginning of the human race in the garden of Eden. Even from the beginning, and as a natural institution long before the coming of Christ, it has been in a certain way sacred and religious. This is so because from the beginning it has foreshadowed the becoming man of the Word of God.

Therefore marriage's sacredness is in it by nature, not as something accorded it accessorily by human beings. This is borne out by the multitude of ancient, pre-Christian customs that treated marriage as a religious state, and their joining of husband and wife as a religious event. Therefore too even by nature marriage transcends the jurisdiction of civil government. Its being made a Christian sacrament by Christ has only confirmed and sealed the Church's natural jurisdiction over it.[10]

His reply to the Royalists rehearses what had been said by his predecessors for more than a century.

> And let no one be taken in by the distinction that the Royalists intone. They split the marital contract from the sacrament, with this intent that they hand over the contract to the power and judgment of heads of state, while leaving to the Church only the sacramental aspects. For such a distinction—or more accurately a dismembering—cannot be justified, since it is certain that in Christian marriage the contract cannot be separated from the sacrament. Therefore there can be no true and legitimate contract without being at the same time the sacrament. For Christ has enhanced marriage with the dignity of a sacrament. And the marriage is the contract itself. . . .[11]

We note that here again, in the last clause of this passage, Leo claims sacramentality not only for the marriages of Christians concretely in history, but for marriage taken abstractly and therefore universally. The same abstract reference reigns in a brief statement saying exactly that in which marriage's sacramentality consists: Marriage is a sacrament because it is a sacred sign (*signum sacrum*) that produces grace by constituting it (marriage) an image of the mystical marriage of Christ and the Church. The form and figure of this image are produced by the bond of the marital union itself—which is nothing other than the marriage itself. Hence any marriage of two Christians is a sacrament. So it is ridiculous to say that the sacrament is something extrinsic to and separable from the contract. Leo feels no unease and suspects no anomaly in saying that "the form and figure" in a marriage's imaging the mystical marriage of Christ and the Church is a contract.[12]

Pius XI and *Casti Connubii*

When, fifty years later, on December 31, 1930, Pope Pius XI published his encyclical letter on marriage and family, the abuses that Leo XIII had deplored in *Arcanum* had grown in proportion to the half-century of opportunity that history had offered them. The growth had been accelerated mightily by the disillusionment with traditional forms of life and conduct bred by the horrors of World War I.[13] Pius spent the second part of his encyclical—twenty-one of the letter's forty-two pages—explaining the abuses, refuting them as fallacies and excoriating them as damaging to marriage and to society generally: companionate marriage, contraception, abortion, sterilization, infidelity, emancipation of women, religiously mixed marriages and divorce.

But they are the pages preceding these that contain Pius' reflections on marriage the sacrament, reflections both explicit and implicit. I choose to call implicit those that bear upon the nature itself of marriage, upon that which, in the phrasing long familiar in papal documents, has been elevated by Christ to the dignity of a sacrament.

Casti connubii is in substance a continuation of *Arcanum divinae sapientiae*. Pius says this expressly. But he explains the motive for his writing: He wishes to go into more inclusive and more exact detail than had his predecessor.

Where *Casti connubii* goes several valuable steps beyond *Arcanum* is in Pius' supplying detail in a particular territory of reflection. The reader may have noticed, in studying official Church statements on marriage thus far, how little concern the authorities have shown to work out an anthropology of marriage. We have seen their repeated insistence, grounded in the assumption that a marriage is created by the parties' contractual consent, that the contract is the marriage, and vice versa; that where two Christians contract marriage, this is a sacrament; that the sacrament is the contract elevated to grace-giving status.

Over the centuries canonists in the Church had refined the details of the contract. Since every contract is created by an exchange of either goods or services, they had determined that in contracting marriage a man and woman exchange a unique service, or more exactly each one's right to this service. This is the right to those sexual acts which are apt of their nature to produce offspring.

The raison dêtre of marriage, the reason for which it is designed, was said to be simply given by nature. From it the object itself of the consent was drawn. This is the conception and nurture of offspring. This was said to be marriage's primary end. Secondary ends were defined as the spouses' mutual help (*mutuum adiutorium*), and the remedying of concupiscence in them, the providing of a place for the sinless spending of sexual urgency. This profile of marriage the human relationship we shall see lodged in canons 1013 and 1081 of the 1917 Code of Canon Law.

Onto this juridical appreciation of marriage was imposed the conception of marriage the sacrament. Or rather, to stay with the formula used persistently in these authoritative statements, the juridical definition was raised to join with the sacramental conception. More precisely still, the juridical contract was said to become itself the sacrament. The joining of two separable realities is exactly what marriage's sacramentality was said not to consist of. Instead the lower, the human contractual element was said to become the higher, the divine sacramental reality.

The consequence of this interpretation was rarely laid out clearly. Since for centuries the sacramental character of the marriage sacrament had been said to consist of its imaging the love union of Christ and the Church, this interpretation found itself concluding that what images this union is a contractual exchange of sexual rights. The conclusion took on even more density for this, that the details of this union had been spelled out rather clearly in Ephesians 5:21–33. We have seen these details long since. It is enough to note here that the juridical-theological interpretation in place by the beginning of the twentieth century had Christian men's and women's exchange of their rights to sexual acts creating an earthly image of the self-giving, purifying, intimately caring, faithful-unto-death love of Christ and his people, the Church. More than this, their exercising this right was said, by implication, to be the replication on earth of such divine love as that.

It is clear that in writing *Casti connubii* Pius XI was aware of the need to build up the human matrix of marriage the sacrament, to describe in finer detail what it is that becomes the sacrament in Christian marriages. Apparently he understood that if the Church's teachers were to continue insisting that it is the marriage contract itself that becomes the sacrament, an opportune way to begin explaining the sacrament is to first explain the contract.

Through the first six paragraphs of the encyclical Pius recapitulated the major points of teaching on marriage that had been repeated by virtually all his predecessors of the two centuries before his. Christ established marriage as the principle and foundation of domestic society and therefore of all human intercourse. He raised it to the dignity of a sacrament of the new law. In doing this he restored it to the original purity of its institution by God at the beginning of history. He gave exclusive authority over it to the Church.[14]

Pius considered it crucial to insist that marriage has been instituted not by men but by God—crucial because from this it follows that marriage's natural indissolubility has a holding power greater than only the demands of marriage's nature. This greater power is the power, and the moral authority, of nature's creator. Therefore the ending of marriages does not fall under imagined human authority to dissolve them.[15]

Pius proposed his anthropology of marriage when he expounded the permanence of marriages over against a freedom claimed for the spouses to dissolve them. We find him here stepping over into historical concreteness and looking to the emotional needs of men and women.

Thus men and women are free in regard to their marriages, but free only in deciding whether to marry and whom to marry. They are not free to redesign marriage's laws set unchangeably by God. He has instituted marriage generally, with its inherent ends and laws. The place of men and women is to form marriages in particular, but to do so by co-working with God. What they do in this co-working Pius states in a humanistic way that will be remembered by the bishops of Vatican II: ". . . while man, with the generous surrender of his own person made to another for the whole span of life, becomes, with the help and cooperation of God, the author of each particular marriage. . . ."[16]

He goes to St. Augustine's *De genesi ad litteram* to verify what the *saramentum* in marriage is, or more exactly what the specific fruit of the *sacramentum* is.[17] There Augustine explained the three goods that make marriage good in its entirety.

> By fidelity the spouses take care not to have intercourse with partners outside the marriage. By the good of offspring the spouses take care to accept children lovingly. . . . By the *sacramentum* they take care not to separate the marriage, and if dismissed, not to remarry even for the sake of children.[18]

We saw in an earlier chapter Augustine's difficulty and indecision in fixing exactly the identity of the marriage *sacramentum:* it is either the irreversible commitment of the spouses to one another, or the commitment to remain in the marriage made by each spouse singly to God, or the spouses' joint commitment to God to remain in the marriage. Rather surprisingly Pius goes not to Ephesians 5:21–33 to find scriptural support for Augustine's reasoning, but to Christ in the synoptic tradition, "Therefore they are no longer two, but one flesh" (Mk 10:8).[19]

The manner of his drawing from Ephesians 5 and his reason for doing so mark another step in the anthropological enriching of his thought. The ground of possibility that a man and woman persevere in marriage through their entire lives is a specific kind of love they must bring to one another. He finds the model for this love in Paul's counsel to husbands in his letter: "Husbands, love your wives as Christ loved the Church" (verse 25).[20] Pius is quite specific about what this love demands and contains: constant mutual help in both the personal and domestic territories of life together; constant work together to mature in the interior life, both emotionally and intellectually; growth together in love for God and for others.

In Pius' next words this increasingly humane interpretation of marriage reaches its farthest advance in all the long centuries of papal declaration. Somewhat paradoxically Pius reaches back almost four hundred years in order to make this advance.

> This mutual inward molding of husband and wife, this determined effort to perfect each other, can in a very real sense, as the Roman Catechism teaches us, be said to be the chief reason and purpose of marriage, provided marriage be looked at not

in the restricted sense as instituted for the proper conception and education of the child, but more widely as the sharing of life as a whole and the mutual interchange and partnership thereof.

Having drawn the need for this marital love from Ephesians 5 Pius appropriates also the structure there of the love relationship. In the relationship the husband is as head and rules there. While the wife must live subject and obedient to this rule, the subjection and obedience are not those of a child but of a companion. Pius even insists that the subjection and obedience do not take away from the wife's freedom. She gains freedom because she holds the chief place in love—she is the heart of the marriage to the husband's head.

At the close of this first part of the encyclical Pius returns to the issue of marriage's permanence, even its indissolubility, its invulnerability to dissolution by human authority. He claims that its specific kind and degree of invulnerability has been in marriage since God's constitution of it at the beginning of history. Christ's injunction, "What God has joined man must not separate" (Mt 19:6), is really only a restoration of what had been attentuated by the law of Moses.[21]

Predictably Pius moves on to say that the only finally indissoluble marriage is the consummated sacramental marriage of two Christians. His reason for saying this is the traditional one: Only such a marriage images fully the union of Christ and the Church, a union which can never be dissolved.[22] Pius does not offer to explain the ontological link here, namely how it is that *because* the union of Christ and the Church in metaphoric marriage is indestructible, every marriage of two Christians is in fact indissoluble provided it is consummated. Nor does he explain how the consummation brings the imaging to its fullness.

With no evidence of concern Pius moves the issue of marriage's sacramental indissolubility from the ontological over into the moral when discoursing briefly on the grace of the sacrament. We note that he does this moving within one and the same statement. In raising Christian marriage to a sacrament Christ made it a sign and a cause of a specific grace by which the sacrament "perfects natural love, confirms an indissoluble union and sanctifies both man and wife." But he adds that to live and grow in the power of this grace the spouses must cooperate with it.[23]

At this point he seems to put the sacramental character and conduct, and the sacramentally rooted indissolubility of their marriage, within the power and choice of the spouses.

> [The spouses] should strive with all their might so that their marriage, not only through the power and symbolism of the sacrament, but also through their spirit and manner of life, may be and remain always the living image of that most fruitful union of Christ and the Church. . . .[24]

One leaves *Casti connubii* caught up a bit by its ambiguity. Pius simply repeats the tradition that the marriage of two Christians is a sacrament because it images the union of Christ and the Church. Apparently he means that it is such beneath and before any conduct flowing from and appropriate to this imaging, since he exhorts the spouses to just such conduct. Exhortation would be pointless if dereliction from that which is exhorted were not possible. So Pius implies clearly enough that even without their actually imaging, in their conduct, the union of Christ and the Church, the marriage of Christian spouses nevertheless does this imaging. One is left wondering how others might ever detect this imaging, and wondering too for whom the sacrament might be a sign of Christ's presence in the world. One does not expect an encyclical to untangle such a conundrum as this. But one's attention is caught when an encyclical creates it.

But withal Pius has brought the created and the uncreated components in marriage the sacrament significantly closer together than had any of his predecessors. He has hinted clearly at a place for love in the sacrament. He has hinted, although less clearly, that the spouses' freedom has a place in living the sacrament—that though the Christian wife lives in obedience she is somehow still free. Finally he has implied that both spouses are free—though they need exhorting—to work with the graces of the sacrament so that their conduct too may image what their marriage somehow already images.

The Sacrament in the Catholic Code of Law

Until 1917 the Roman Catholic Church had no code of law. What it had had since the twelfth century was a corpus of law gathered and arranged by jurists beginning with Gratian, the Camaldolese monk at the University of Bologna. The decrees of popes and councils added to the corpus continually. And despite attempts through the centuries to put order in the accumulation, by the beginning of the twentieth century it still contained duplications, obsolete legislation and even internal contradictions.

In 1901 Pope Leo XIII determined on an exact codification of the corpus and called the remarkably competent jurist, Pietro Gasparri, from Paris to Rome to supervise the work. Gasparri and the newly formed pontifical commission for the revision of the law began their work in 1904, under Leo's successor, Pius X. The codifying was expected to take twenty-five years, but Gasparri and the commission delivered the completed revision to Pius' successor, Benedict XV, twelve years later on December 4, 1916. The Code of Canon Law was promulgated on Pentecost Sunday, 1917. It went into effect exactly a year later.

The Code's marriage legislation is contained in its Book III, On Things (*De Rebus*), Title VII, "On Marriage," Canons 1012 through 1143.

Canon 1012 repeats and condenses what the popes of the preceding two centuries had been saying in reply to the Royalists and others who claimed jurisdiction over the marriages of Catholics on the ground that the marriage contract and the sacrament are separable. Its paragraph 1 does the unusual thing for a statute of law of asserting an historical event.

Christ Our Lord has elevated the contract itself of marriage between baptized persons to the dignity of a sacrament.

Being only a statute in a code of law and neither an historical essay nor a theological examination, the canon does not say where and when Christ brought it about that the marriages of all Christians be sacraments, nor does it explain the act by which Christ did this. The writer of the law was confident that these points of fact were verified elsewhere.

What the paragraph does do, and very carefully, is to admit the distinction between contract and sacrament while denying their separability. (If they were not distinct, the contract at first not a sacrament could not subsequently have been elevated to that status.) The paragraph all but expressly gainsays what the dissidents had been claiming since Melchior Cano and before, namely that even in the sacramental marriages of Christians the contract remains only that, a contract, while the sacrament is only a kind of garnishing added to it, such as the priest's blessing.

Paragraph 2 of this canon gainsays a conclusion that could be drawn from an admitted separability of contract and sacrament, and does so by denying the conclusion itself.

Therefore it is impossible for a valid contract of marriage between baptized persons to exist without being by that very fact a sacrament.

Since with two Christian spouses it is their marital contract itself that by Christ's elevating intervention becomes the sacrament, it is impossible that they not be married sacramentally if they contract validly. Said another way, the only marriage they can contract is a sacramental marriage. Therefore if they exclude the sacrament knowingly and willingly, their wedding vows do not create even the contract. (The Code exempted from this invalidation Christians who do not by a positive act of will exclude the sacrament, but only contract marriage in complete ignorance of the sacrament or in honest disbelief that their marriage contract is a sacrament. Their marriage is said to become a sacrament even without their knowing about marriage's sacramentality, or without their willing it despite knowing about it, or without either.)[25]

The sacramentality of Christian marriage emerges next in paragraph 2 of Canon 1013. There two effects of the sacramentality are affirmed.

The essential properties of marriage are unity and indissolubility, which acquire a unique firmness in Christian marriage by reason of its sacramental character.

The paragraph not only states two effects of a marriage's sacramentality but offers implicitly a novel meaning of the term "essential." It says that a marriage—any marriage, even the non-sacramental marriage of two pagans—is in essence unitary, that it can be of only two spouses, not of three or more in polygamous union. It says also that any marriage is indissoluble, meaning presumably that no human agency can end it, and that it can end in no way other than by the death of at least one of the spouses.

But the essentiality of these two properties is not really essential. The marriage of two non-Christians could lack either or both of these assertedly essential properties but yet be a marriage.

[For] here the law performs under historical duress. It wants not to deny that the holy men of old, the patriarchs of Israel, had polygamous marriages that were both polygamous and marriages. And it wants not to contradict and cancel what had been going on in the Catholic Church for four centuries, namely the dissolving by papal authority of marriages that are not sacraments. Nor does the canon want to touch an even older practice, the dissolving of sacramental but non-consummated marriages by entry into religious life and the pronouncing of the vows of this life. The canon saves a place for the radical possibility of polygamous marriage and of dissolution by adding that monogamy and indissolubility gain a unique firmness in the marriages of Christians by reason of their sacramental character. In other, merely natural marriages the monogamy is exceptionable and the indissolubility is dissoluble.[26]

Were the canon dealing with the reality itself of marriages instead of merely sifting juridical categories, it would have said that where marriages are unitary and indissoluble at all, these come of their being Christian sacraments. Again because it is only a statute in a code of law, it does not explain how a marriage's being a sacrament finally makes its unity proof against polygamy or its indissolubility indissoluble. This has been done in the theological treatises.

Canon 1016 adds a kind of period with exclamation to the long dispute between the Church and European Catholic civil authorities concerning jurisdiction over the marriages of the baptized.

The marriage of baptized parties is ruled not only by divine law but by canon law as well, with civil authority retaining competence over the merely civil effects of the same marriage.

The canon draws a conclusion from the principle asserted in Canon 1012, that Christ raised the marital contract of any two Christians to a sacrament, and that two Christians can together contract only a sacramental marriage. The conclusion is that because any marriage of two Christians is a sacrament, it comes under the competence of only that person authorized to rule the Christian sacraments. This is the Catholic Church in the person of its bishops, with the pope at their head. But the canon acknowledges that since the contracting of a sacramental marriage does produce effects that are merely civil in nature, civil authority has competence over these. Such effects are, for example, rights of inheritance, determination of parenthood, and determination of ownership.

Note that the canon claims jurisdiction over the marriages of all Christian couples, not only over those of Roman Catholics. But while claiming this jurisdiction in principle Catholic authorities do not attempt to exercise it over non-Catholic Christians unless the latter seek to marry Roman Catholics.

The effects of sacramental marriage appear in brief mention, and only implicitly, in two later canons. Canon 1110 says that a valid marriage creates a bond between the spouses that is by nature perpetual and exclusive, and that where the spouses are Christian and put no obstacle, the sacramental marriage also confers grace on them.

Canon 1118 repeats in its own way the claim of Canon 1013, but adds to it one specification. There the claim was that it is the sacrament that makes a marriage to be finally indissoluble. Here Canon 1118 says that a marriage that is ratified and is consummated can be dissolved by no human power and by no cause other than death. The adjective "ratified" (*ratum*) in the language of the law designates a sacramental marriage. The added specification is that not even such a ratified marriage is finally indissoluble unless it is consummated.

Pope Pius XII

Much earlier in this study I pointed out that the theology of marriage, as also the theology of any of the Christian sacraments, is a fusion of two elements. One of these consists of what has come by revelation from the divine source and has been passed down in Christian tradition. The other consists of what we learn from the conduct that is the sacramental action, such as the blessing, breaking, sharing and eating of bread in the Eucharist, and the blessing, pouring out, sharing and drinking of wine there. Again, the latter component is the human matrix of the sacrament. The former is the religious meaning of it.

During the nineteen years of his pontificate Pope Pius XII said much about both these components of the sacrament in marriage. Especially during his first three years, from 1939 through 1942, he discoursed frequently to newlyweds who had come to his audiences in the Vatican palace.[27]

What Pius said about the religious meaning of the sacrament of marriage brought no new understanding in that quarter. His assertions are familiar. Thus, for Christians their marriage is never a mere contract or only the ceremony. It is a religious act springing from and enriching the spouses' supernatural life.[28]

God himself raised marriage among Christian spouses to be an image of the indestructible union of Christ and the Church, the Church that Christ wills to be his spotless bride on earth so as to continue his work here. The apostle Paul proposed this marriage of Christ and the Church as the model for all Christian spouses. This model calls for purity and holiness in the spouses' marriage and is their source.

Christ raised marriage among Christian spouses to the dignity of a sacrament in order to bring enabling graces to them, graces that help them in parenting at two stages: in their bringing children into the world and in nurturing them in the Christian life.[29]

In the sacrament of marriage the spouses are participating causes in an indispensable role that the human minister has in none of the other sacraments. In regard to baptism, for example, God can bring to a person the grace of salvation without the actual conferring of the sacrament. (The traditionally understood "baptism of desire" is sufficient for this grace.) In regard to the sacrament of penance God can give the grace of repentance without the penitent's participation in the sacrament.

But in marriage the spouses are not only instrumental causes of this sacrament's gracing, but they are indispensable as such causes. The sacrament can be administered only by them, only by their vowed commitment to one another. Therefore they are indispensable as instrumental causes of its unique gracing. This is because its gracing is a kind of empowering; the spouses are empowered to live in permanent fidelity, to bring children into the world and nurture them in the Christian life. Since only they can produce that which is graced, their cooperation in the gracing is needed unexceptionably.[30]

Pius repeated what had by then become lodged in the Church as received doctrine: The marriages of Christians, once consummated, are in fact indissoluble. Not only must the spouses intend that their marriage be permanent and that they will remain together until death, but their marriage can end only with the death of at least one of them.

A Christian marriage is indissoluble, Pius explained, by virtue of its being an image on earth of the indestructible union of Christ and the Church. In some way that indestructible union affects the human but sacramental relationship to make it too indestructible except by death.[31] But even death, Pius insisted, does not put an end to the spouses' love, a love that is uniquely marital in that it includes the spouses' unreserved giving over of their persons to one another. (We shall examine this insight more carefully at the end of this chapter.)

In what we have seen thus far Pius spoke only with encouragement of marriage the sacrament. But as we shall see now, his encouragement was qualified. Like some theologians of his time (whose thinking we shall examine in the following chapter) he saw a limitation in the holiness available to men and women precisely from their participation in the sacrament. What prompted him to insist on and to explain this limitation more than once during the last four years of his papacy was a step forward in the theology of marriage developing here and there in Europe.

This development, in capsule form, was the following. The age-old Catholic teaching that a life of consecrated virginity is objectively a holier state of life than sacramental marriage must be brought back into abeyance and re-examined. For consecrated virginity is not a sacrament, while the marriage of two Christians is. There is no conduct specific to a life of consecrated virginity that is God's instrument for sanctification, whereas in marriage the spouses' specifically marital expression of love is such an instrument. Therefore at least objectively and generally the former life cannot be deemed a way of holiness superior to the latter.

Against this thesis Pius argued from two quarters. From magisterial authority he reminded all that the objective superiority of consecrated virginity is an element of Catholic doctrine, declared such by the Council of Trent in its twenty-fourth session.[32]

He also brought theological reason to bear on the question. He began with the assumption that holiness is in essence the union of the human person with God in the person of Christ. Here, Pius insisted, is where even a sacramental marriage comes up short, or at least shorter than consecrated virginity. The conduct belonging to the latter way of life brings the man or woman into an immediate love union with God. But marriage's specifically marital conduct, although it unites the spouses with God in love, interposes a medium between themselves and him. This medium is the person of the other spouse. Paradoxically the spouse, though a medium of access to God, is simultaneously a kind of obstacle to the fullness of this love union.

> To reach the heart of God, to love Him and be loved by Him, the virgin soul does not go through many other hearts, does not stop to treat with other creatures; nothing comes in between her and Jesus, no obstacle, no medium.
>
> It is a truth of faith . . . that virginity is superior to the married state because the virgin soul contracts bonds of absolute and indissoluble love directly with God, even more, with God incarnate, Jesus Christ.
>
> On the contrary, marriage, while it is a real sacrament, one of the seven sources of grace instituted by Christ himself; while it comprises the reciprocal offering of each of the parties to the

other; while it brings about a real fusion of life and destiny, nevertheless includes, in God's eyes, something which is held back, something which is not completely given.[33]

The last statement here, reformulated in combination with the first paragraph, reasons that the mediation of the spouse in a man's or woman's union with God keeps him or her from giving the self unreservedly to God. By implication Pius has said that what is given to the spouse in an act of marital love cannot be given to God.

Pius went on to explain the same limitation in terms of the grace of the sacrament of marriage. It is true, he admitted, that the conduct germane to this sacrament is gracing for the spouses. But this marital gracing does not have as its specific effect to unite the spouses with God. Rather, the first effect of this gracing is to strengthen their union with one another. A second effect is to enable the spouses to fulfill the obligations, and to live out the duties, of married life.

True it is that the sacrament gives husbands and wives the grace worthily to fulfill the duties of married life. True it is that it strengthens the bond of marital love. But the sacrament was not established precisely for the purposes of making the use of marriage an instrument of its nature better calculated directly to strengthen the bond of union in charity with God himself.[34]

Pius pointed to what he considered a further limitation in the capacity of the sacrament of marriage to sanctify. This limitation is found in the interlocked effects of bodiliness in the marital expression of love, and of inherited original sin in the spouses. That Pius cited the latter is not surprising. As a thesis in the Christian theology of marriage it is as old as Clement of Alexandria and Origen among the fathers of the third century.[35]

But Pius dealt his surprise when he said that bodiliness itself sets a limit on the holiness available in and by the sacrament. He claimed this not directly and explicitly, but obliquely and by implication, in his discourse to the Congress of Family Associations on September 15, 1957, within a year before his death.[36]

He began his explanation by acknowledging that a Christian marriage sanctifies sacramentally in that it images the love union of Christ and the Church. But this imaging must follow its model through its two historical stages. Christ during his life on earth formed the Christian community, the Church, as his bride. But now, though living in physical separation from his bride, he loves her more fully. This he does because he lives in glory with the Father. So too with the human spouses' love for one another. It is when they are separated by the death of one of them that their love images the more perfect love of the risen and glorified Christ and his Church—and thus images it more holily.

If the sacrament of matrimony, symbol of the redemptive love of Christ for his Church, already applies to husband and wife the reality of that love, transfigures them, makes them resemble the one Christ Who gives himself to save humanity, the other the redeemed Church, who accepts her share in the sacrifice of Christ, then widowhood becomes in some sort the goal and end of this mutual consecration; it is the figure of the present life of the militant Church deprived of the vision of her heavenly Spouse, but with whom she remains indefectibly united, journeying towards Him in faith and hope, living on that love which sustains her in all her trials, and waiting impatiently for the final accomplishment of the initial promises.[37]

To reinforce this conclusion Pius enlisted what he had written earlier about the limiting effect of bodiliness on marital love's power to sanctify. The death of one of the spouses frees this love—which need not end with death—from its native sensuality. Pius used this last term not as a synonym for sensateness, but derogatorily, to indicate an attitude, a habit of emotions that is self-seeking. He reasoned that death brings a violent cure to this self-seeking. It offers the surviving spouse purification of his or her love for the departed one—and to both of them even the possibility of a purer presence to one another.[38]

Implied in this theology, of course, is the exhortation that had been so frequently on the lips and the pens of the fathers of the third and fourth centuries (bitterly on the lips and pen of Tertullian), that holiness calls for Christian widows and widowers to remain in their widowhood. For them to remarry is to give in to weakness of the flesh—a surrender that is all the more flagrant when they remarry late in life and can no longer claim as their motive the bringing of children into the world. Only by remaining unmarried can they be faithful to their deceased spouses with the perfection of fidelity, because only thus can they image perfectly the love relationship of the Church with the now departed and risen Christ.

Pius XII on the Human Matrix of the Sacrament

But Pius' contribution to the developing theology of marriage was most helpful in the territory of the human matrix of the sacrament. I refer especially to his reflections on marital love.

It is barely necessary to explain how an enhanced understanding of marital love must enhance also the understanding of marriage the sacrament. I have already pointed out that each sacrament has its human matrix. In marriage this matrix is the human heterosexual relationship. The Catholic theology has said for centuries that this relationship *becomes* the sacrament. The sacrament is this relationship itself made a vehicle of grace in that it images the love relationship of Christ and the

Church. So, to explain the relationship's availability and aptitude for this imaging—to explain how the human heterosexual loving is ready in its own character to be put to this work of imaging the love of Christ and the Church—is to illumine the heart of the sacrament.

Pius' earliest statement on marital love, in a discourse to newlyweds on October 23, 1940, is so closely akin to what the bishops of Vatican II said twenty-five years later that one is compelled to think that they drew from Pius' words when formulating their own. In naming that which the sacrament graces in Christians who live the sacrament of marriage Pius singled out the ingredients of marital love.

> But what new and inexpressible beauty is added to this love of two human hearts, when there is harmonized the hymn of two souls vibrating with a supernatural life! Here, too, there is verified a mutual exchange of gifts; and then, with sensible tenderness and its healthy joys, with natural affection and its impulses, with a spiritual union and its delights, the two beings who love each other become one in all that is most intimate, from the unshaken profundity of their beliefs to the highest summit of their hopes. . . .[39]

Pius went beyond merely implying that this is the nature of marital love to saying that what he has just described is marriage itself.

> Such is Christian marriage, modelled, according to the famous expression of St. Paul, on the union of Christ and the Church. In the one as in the other, the gift of the self is total, exclusive, irrevocable. . . .[40]

From these passages we know what Pius believed lies at the heart of the sacrament, what he said one should expect to find in its imaging: a reciprocal giving of gifts, bodily tenderness (which is good and joyful), natural affection and impulses, spiritual union, an intimate union that involves a sharing of everything in the spouses' lives. This is very nearly the descriptive definition of marriage to be found in *Gaudium et spes*.

In a later address to newlyweds, on January 29, 1941, Pius probed further into marital love, and pointed out a paradox in this and in all human loves. God has designed into men and women the most powerful desire for union, for a perfect oneness. He wills that they gain this union. But left to itself marital love cannot create the union. It cannot even survive the vicissitudes of married life. To do both—to create the desired union and to merely survive—it must be energized and helped by the grace of Christ.

> A mutual affection, born solely in the inclination that attracts man towards woman, or even from the mere pleasure for the

human gifts which one sex discovers with such satisfaction in the other—such an affection, no matter how beautiful and deep-rooted it may prove to be and no matter how it echoes in the intimacy of the loving conversations of the newly married, would never of itself suffice, nor could it fully achieve that union of your souls which the loving Providence of God has intended and willed when leading you one towards the other. Only supernatural charity, a bond of friendship between God and man, can tie knots strong enough to resist all the shocks, all the vicissitudes, all the inevitable trials of a long life spent together. . . . And this charity and grace, is it not the strength and virtue which you went to ask of the great Sacrament you received?[41]

As Pius continued the thought he became more specific. The destroyer, or at least the inhibitor, of human love's perfection is jealousy, a form of selfishness. But only if they believe and trust can a man and woman ever heal this selfishness.

Is it not jealously, more often than not, perhaps a mitigated form of selfishness, that alters the nature of affection; of selfishness bereft of that true gift, that self-forgetfulness, that faith unfraught with maligning thoughts, but trusting and benevolent, which, even here below, thus becomes the most profound and inexhaustible fount, no less than the safest guardian and preserver of perfect love in a husband and wife?[42]

One of the most helpful of Pius' statements, because one of the most existentially attuned, is found in his address to newlyweds of October 21, 1942. Here he took up the problem of fidelity, probably because World War II had by then forced prolonged separation on tens of thousands of spouses. What is realistic was Pius' seeing the crisis in fidelity as a crisis in the history of love itself in a marriage. So often, he suggested, love begins between young men and women as a rapture and as admiration only lightly in touch with the painful reality of life and perhaps of the spouses themselves. Pius did not disdain this; he saw it as the nature of the love that leads to marriage. But then the objects of this love, the persons of the spouses, either begin to change or begin to emerge in their reality. Consequently the love too must change if it is to survive, and survive especially the spouses' temptation to recapture the thrill of youth in a romantic liaison outside the marriage. Then the challenge for love within the marriage is to accept the reality of one another and of the marriage as it is lived. It follows that only in this maturing, patient, tested love of spouses who accept and cherish the reality of one another does the matrix itself of the sacrament come to maturity.

Then, for true and faithful love, begins the struggle, and at the same time the challenge. No longer blind, it becomes perfectly aware of these failings, but accepts them with affectionate patience, conscious as it is of its own defects. . . . Love is ready to perceive what brings together and unites, and not what divides. . . . Far from showing off its own superiority, it tactfully asks advice of the partner, letting it be known that if it has something to give, it is also happy to receive. It is in this way, obviously, that a spiritual union is established in the wedded couple, an intellectual and practical cooperation which makes them both rise toward the truth in which there is unity, toward the supreme truth, toward God. What else is this fidelity but the mutual gift of their minds?[43]

A second examination of Pius' discourse of September 16, 1957 to the Congress of Family Associations brings to light a facet of Christian spouses' sacramental conduct that in Pius' judgment is among the most easily ignored, and even when observed is easily misunderstood. We recall that it was in this discourse that Pius exhorted widows to remain unmarried. We recall too his reasons in support of the exhortation. The death of one of the spouses opens the way, for the survivor, to the perfection of marital love, because it takes from him or her the possibility of loving selfishly. That is, since the deceased spouse has completed his or her sacrifice, the survivor can now detach himself or herself from the intense but fleeting joys of sensate and carnal affection.

Pius insisted that the spouses' sacramental vocation of imaging the love of Christ and the Church calls for such celibate widowhood. For marriage is a vocation to imitate and image a love that is sacrificial. Through his death and resurrection Christ has already completed his loving sacrifice. And during her terrestrial life within history the Church loves faithfully a spouse who has been taken from her physically—and therefore loves sacrificially. Pius' conclusion for the widowed spouse is obvious: To image this sacrificial love fully he or she must remain unmarried—while continuing to love the deceased spouse with a love more intense because now freed of self-seeking.

There is another conclusion latent in this reasoning that is somewhat less obvious. Pius has implied that the fullest degree of the sacrificial self-giving essential to this sacrament is not available within the sacramental marriage itself. Not only is the fullest degree not available there, but he suggests that the conduct in which marital self-giving can reach its fullness is not even specifically marital. To interpret him in this way I draw as a premise on something that the bishops of Vatican II said of marital love: "Such love, fusing the human and the divine, leads the spouses to make a free and reciprocal gift of themselves, a gift proven by both tender affection and by deed. . . . This love is expressed uniquely and perfectly through the marital act."[44]

If we do not wish to say that the bishops in 1965 contradicted what Pius had said in 1957, but if we agree with them that marital love comes to its fullest expression in intercourse, then we must conclude that in his reasoning Pius separated the gracing dynamic of the sacrament from its human matrix. He sundered the sacrament. For it is about the sacramental imaging that he said it can be perfected only after one spouse's death, only after the surviving spouse's love has been freed from the otherwise inescapable self-seeking of bodily expression. In short, marital love's sanctifying reenacting of the love relationship of Christ and the Church reaches its perfection after its expression is no longer marital.

This conclusion is a troubling one. We shall see in the following chapter how some quite competent theologians reflected on it before, during and after Pius' years in the papacy.

The Second Vatican Council

One of the most valuable accomplishments of the Second Vatican Council's statement on marriage in *Gaudium et spes*[45] was to gather into a single declaration the wealth of insight and interpretation that had grown up in the Church during the preceding three decades. The council's theological commission, chaired by Cardinal Alfredo Ottaviani, had prepared a document on marriage that in attitude and in form imitated Pius IX's *Syllabus Errorum*. It singled out and condemned the abuses of marriage that the commission deemed the most widespread and grievous, with divorce and contraceptive intercourse principal among them. In its positive parts it reaffirmed the contractual nature of marriage generally and repeated the juridicized theology of the sacrament. It proved so unsatisfactory to the cardinals of the council's preparatory commission that they rejected it in its entirety. The chapter on marriage in *Gaudium et spes* is the product of discussion, composition and argumentation that began only in the council's second year (1963) and came to a climax in its final session during October, November and December of 1965.

The bishops' interpretation of marriage in *Gaudium et spes* was their own. They did not seek to consolidate accepted teaching in detail by repeating earlier magisterial statements. They innovated at crucial points, even to the extent of putting in abeyance Catholic doctrine that had been taught for centuries. The non-doctrinal innovation was their refusal to consider marriage the human relationship as a contract. Nowhere in this declaration does the noun "contract" or the verb "to contract" appear. In view of the centuries-old, universal and taken-for-granted perception of marriage by Catholic authorities as a contract, this omission cannot have been accidental.

The point of doctrine that was called into question was that among the ends natural and inherent to marriage procreation is primary. When interpreting the place of procreation in marriage the bishops did not deny that it is a natural and inherent end thereof. Their exact phrasing of the matter was, in context, "Marriage and marital love are by nature oriented to the begetting and nurture of children. Children are the most valuable gift of marriage. . . . Hence, while not making the other ends of marriage of less value, the true conduct of marital love and the entire meaning of family life that comes from it have this goal, that the spouses be willing to co-work courageously with the love of the Creator and Savior. . . ."[46]

From Augustine's *De conjugiis adulterinis* at the beginning of the fifth century, in which he wrote, "Therefore the propagation of children is the first, the natural and the principal purpose of marriage," through its enshrinement in Canon 1013 of the 1917 Code of Canon Law, this primacy of procreation had been coming to the status of common Catholic doctrine. This status had been confirmed as recently as October 29, 1951 by Pius XII in his discourse to the Association of Italian Catholic Obstetricians. It is understandable that this calling back of the doctrine can have been done only after long and often impassioned debate in the council.[47]

It is important to note the contextual anxiety of the bishops' statement. By this I mean the real-life concerns that prompted their drafting it and in large measure guided their thinking and their formulation of it. Unlike Leo XIII's *Arcanum divinae sapientiae* and Pius XI's *Casti connubii,* the thematic worry of *Gaudium et spes* was not about any deliberate secularist denigration of the holiness of marriage nor about sins committed by the married. It was about the fragility of family life and of marital love under the duress of economic and political forces that attack stable society at every point. Modern warfare and its by-product of millions of poverty-stricken refugees and homeless children was only the most obvious such force. It would not be far wide of the mark to read the entire document as a plea for the survival of marriage in the sense of family, and counsel for a strategy of such survival.

So far from being even a précis of the theology of the sacrament, the declaration turns to the sacrament only in a kind of second intention. Probably because they addressed their words not only to Christians but to all persons concerned about the well-being of marriage, the bishops did not make the sacramentality of Christian marriage the theme and guide of their discourse. Nevertheless what they did say contributed richly to understanding the sacrament in the same way that Pius XII's discourses had done so. Again, a principle of sacramental theology makes clear why this is so. Every sacrament has as one of its two major components a creaturely, human matrix—as washing with water is the matrix of baptism. For the marital sacrament the human marital relationship is the matrix. Therefore the bishops' interpretation of marriage was by small indirection an interpretation of the sacrament.

It is helpful to distinguish their interpretation into discrete parts thereof and to examine them in sequence: the nature of marriage itself, the act by which a man and woman create their marriage, and the love that is native to marriage. Along the way we will take note of the place for the sacrament that the bishops saw in each of these.

Gaudium et Spes and the Nature of Marriage

The first designation of marriage is in the introductory paragraph of the chapter. It is that a marriage is a community of love (*communitas amoris*).[48] It is next called an intimate partnership of life and of marital love (*intima communitas vitae et amoris coniugalis*).[49] It is a sacred bond (*vinculum sacrum*), a marital covenant (*foedus coniugale*), the mutual gift of two persons (*mutua duarum personarum donatio*),[50] a Christian vocation (*vocatio christiana*), an unbreakable covenant (*foedus indissolubile*).[51]

The bishops identified the act by which a man and a woman create their marriage consistently with their refusal to continue designating marriage itself as a contract. They did not call this act a contractual exchange. They called it, as a human act, a personal consent by which the spouses give themselves over to and accept one another (*actus humanus quo coniuges sese mutuo tradunt atque accipiunt*).[52] The term "human act" is not included casually. In scholastic moral philosophy an *actus humanus*—in contradistinction to an *actus hominis*, "the act of a human being"—designates conduct which is the product of reason and will. It involves an informed and free decision. It negates any suggestion that persons can be put into marriage or lured into it in ways that override their freedom. The term "give over" translates the Latin verb *tradere*. Predicated of the self in this context it bespeaks a handing over of one's person. This interpretation is refined a few paragraphs later where the partners are said to create their marriage by making gifts to one another of their persons (*mutua duarum personarum donatio*).[53] The bishops add that this mutual giving over of the self need not end with the act that creates the marriage, and ought not. Where the spouses love one another with love that is genuinely marital, they continue to make gifts of their persons to one another freely and gladly, and with tender affection (*talis amor . . . coniuges ad liberum et mutuum sui ipsius donum, tenero affectu et opere probatum, conducit*).[54]

That tells something of the nature and role of the love that the bishops see as native to marriage. To begin with, its source is God's love for the spouses. It is covenantal love, one whose substance is reciprocal commitment. Its model is the love union of Christ and the Church. This double-linked love—of God for the spouses and of the spouses for one another—is both the point of entry of the sacrament into their marriage and its place of residence there: "For as in olden times God came to his people in a covenant of love and fidelity [this was the corporate sacrament in which the people Israel lived], so now the savior of men and the spouse of the Church comes to Christian spouses through the sacrament of marriage."[55] To make the historically resonating point that the sacrament is not limited to the religious wedding ceremony, the bishops add immediately, "What is more, Christ stays with the couple. And just as he loved the Church and gave his life for her, so also the spouses by their mutual self-giving may love one another with perpetual fidelity."[56] This means only secondarily that the Christ-Church love relationship is a model for the spouses. It means first that Christ's indwelling in their relationship lends them the strength to love with a love like this.

The insight continues: "The love natural to marriage [*germanus amor coniugalis*] is taken up into the divine love [is joined with it as its instrument] and is there enriched and ruled by the redeeming power of Christ and the saving action of the Church." The effect of this is to lead the husband and wife powerfully to God and to strengthen them in their vocation as parents.[57]

The familiarity of this theological language ought not hide a striking contrast in it with authoritative Catholic statements of past centuries. By the end of the high middle ages the Church's teachers, official and unofficial, were agreed that the sacrament in marriage makes it a means of gracing the spouses. But the gracing they acknowledged was an attenuated kind. It was not "primary grace," not the joining in personal union with God. It was secondary, helping, "actual" grace—the strength to resist temptation to adultery and to resist misuse of sexuality within one's marriage, the wisdom and strength to bring up one's children in Christian goodness.

Gaudium et spes here breaks out of that self-limitation. Clearly it implies that in and by the sacrament the spouses are brought into personal union with God in Christ, or their union there is intensified by it. The clauses that tell this are ". . . so now the savior . . . comes to Christian spouses through the sacrament of marriage"; "Christ stays with the couple"; "the love natural to marriage is taken up into the divine love and is there enriched"; "their love can lead them powerfully to God."

The helping function of the grace of the sacrament is affirmed, but it is presented as the effect of the spouses' union with God in Christ.

> Through this sacrament the spouses are penetrated with the spirit of Christ as they fulfill their marital and family obligations. This spirit suffuses their whole life with faith, hope and charity. Thus they grow continually each in his and her perfection as well as in mutual holiness.[58]

This sacramentality exists not only in the one-to-one union of the spouses but in their families as well. The family is the sacrament grown to fullness. Not until the bishops say this do they bring into play the traditional imaging role of the sacrament in marriage. Apparently their intent is to say that the marriage is this image—or is the image most effectively—when it becomes a family.

> Hence the family, because it arises from marriage, which is an image of the covenant of love of Christ and the Church, and a participation in this covenant, will disclose to all the living presence of the Savior in the world, as well as show also the authentic nature of the Church.[59]

Gaudium et spes devotes an entire section (no. 49) to a descriptive definition of this marital love, and labels the section appropriately: *De amore coniugali.* One may guess why it does so. It has already called marriage a covenant of love. But there are many kinds of love in human relationships, some of them constructive, some destructive. The bishops want to make clear the love they deem marital—marital, again, as the matrix of the sacrament.

They begin by pointing out that the Jewish and Christian scriptures urge the centrality of love in marriage. They also do what centuries of their forebears had refused or had feared to do: they named passages in the Song of Solomon as sources of this urging.[60] How radically they have freed themselves from the past is evident in their holding that the love described in these passages is marital love, and in implying thereby that it is this love that animates the matrix of the sacrament. The passages are 1:2–3 ("Let her kiss me with the kiss of her mouth! More delightful is your love than wine"); 1:16 ("Ah, you are beautiful, my lover.—Yes, you are lovely"); 4:16 ("Let my lover come to his garden and eat its choice fruits"); 5:1 ("I have come to my garden, my sister, my bride . . ."); 7:8–14 (these are the verses that describe in detail the girl's physical beauty).

The bishops describe marital love as fully and authentically (*eminenter*) human. It involves the entire person and seeks the good of the entire person. It is guided and directed to the partner by free decision, by an act of the will. Therefore it makes all bodily expressions of affection fully human—can make them manifestations of marital friendship. It is far from spontaneous, instinctive erotic response, which is by nature self-gratifying and temporary. This love leads to and expresses itself in the spouses' free and willing gifting of themselves to one another in tender and bodily expressions of affection. It suffuses all their selves; it grows continually. It is faithful, constant against all its enemies both inside the souls of the spouses and outside them. It wants to last for the spouses' lifetime together and does so.[61]

The bishops then make a point that is simultaneously psychological, moral and theological, and is a formal rebuff to eighteen centuries of Christian fear and suspicion of sexuality. They identify the conduct in which the exquisite marital love they have described is most typically and fully expressed. This is the spouses' lovemaking completed in sexual intercourse.

This love is expressed most clearly and comes to its fullness in the conduct that is proper to marriage. The acts by which spouses come together intimately and chastely are good and honorable. Expressed in a way that is authentically human they manifest the spouses' mutual self-giving and impel them to it— the self-giving by which they enrich one another with joyful and grateful wills.[62]

Finally, to return to an earlier element of marital love, by nature it is oriented to children and desires them. In this it strives to co-work with God in his love of creation—in his love to create. By loving in this way the spouses not only co-work with his love, which is essentially creative, but they also manifest this its nature to the world. By having children and nurturing them they interpret the nature of God's love correctly to the world.

Note what *Gaudium et spes* has done to a centuries-old thesis in the theology of the sacraments. That thesis said that God made marriage a sacrament at the beginning of history when he created the first human beings as an image—not as images—of himself; when for this imaging he made them man and woman; when he revealed the reason for and used their sexually correlated natures to extend his creation, "to increase and multiply and fill the earth"; when he gave the woman to the man and they joined and became one flesh. That was the primordial sacrament, even before the time of the law of Moses, and centuries before the coming of Christ. But now the bishops say that this essentially creative love of God is the love at work in the marital sacrament in the new law of Christ. Generations of fathers and theologians had insisted that God's love in the latter sacrament is medicinal for and controlling of men's and women's wounded sexuality. But here the bishops say that this love in the new sacrament is principally fertile and creative. In short, family is the filled-out sacrament of marriage—not widowhood, as Tertullian in the morning of Christian history and Pius XII a generation ago would have it.

Paul VI's Encyclical Letter *Humanae vitae*

It is commonly known that Pope Paul's encyclical letter, *Humanae vitae*, of July 25, 1968, was the completion of a task left over by the Second Vatican Council.[63] The council left it not unfinished, because the bishops never took it up, but left it untouched because Paul took it off the council's agenda. He reserved to himself the completion of the task. This was the reexamination of the Catholic Church's proscriptive moral judgment on artificial control of human fertility. Paul began action in the matter by announcing, on June 23, 1964, between the council's second and third sessions, his expansion of the Pontifical Study Commission on Population Control that his predecessor, John XXIII, had established. The commission was to study the matter and to report its recommendation to him. It did so, and recommended in the spring of 1966 a change toward mitigation of the proscription of artificial birth control. Paul's rejection of this recommendation is well known, as is his renewal of the proscription. This is set forth in *Humanae vitae.*[64]

Somewhat like his predecessors, Pius XI and Pius XII, Paul drew his condemnation of artificial limitation of birth from the nature of marriage. They had said that it contradicts marriage's primary end. But in the meantime, as we have seen, the bishops of Vatican II had voided the major premise of their moral logic that produces this conclusion, had done so by taking away the primacy of procreation among marriage's ends. Consequently Paul had to begin his moral logic with a different premise.

He found this premise in the same moral-anthropological territory in which many Catholic scholars had claimed reasons for the permissibility of contraceptive intercourse. They had drawn this permissibility from the demands of marital love and of responsible parenthood. In order to join issue with them Paul began *Humanae vitae* by setting out his own understanding of "these two great realities of married life." He drew explicitly from *Gaudium et spes* to do this.[65] As its bishop-authors had done, he claimed that for men and women the true source of their marital love is God's love. By this he did not mean primarily that God's love is the model for theirs. He meant something more practical.

> Conjugal love reveals its true nature and nobility when it is considered in its authentic origin, God, who is love. . . . Marriage is not, then, the effect of chance or the product of evolution or of unconscious forces; it is the wise institution of the Creator to realize in mankind his design of love.[66]

Unlike his predecessors over the centuries Paul does not draw on Genesis 1 and 2 as factual sources in order to explain how God's love has produced marriage and how it produces love in spouses. Nevertheless as the bishops of Vatican II did, he insists that God is the source of the spouses' marital love because he is active in their lives—active by his love that is essentially creative, essentially fruitful. This is a point essential to the teaching of *Gaudium et spes* and seems to be taken directly from it. But Paul draws a conclusion from it that the bishops did not. He says, or at least implies, that *because* God's love at work in the spouses' lives is essentially fruitful, their loves too must be fruitful. His love works to make theirs like his. If they keep it from being so, two consequences follow: Their love is not marital, but is something other and less—stunted, self-serving, private. And the spouses have contradicted God's action in their lives. This is in essence sinful.

This essentiality of fertility to marital love is the major premise of the moral logic Paul uses to warrant his condemnation of all artificial limiting of fertility. He expands the assertion of this essentiality into a complex principle. It is a principle about sexual intercourse within marriage. (Whether it is about intercourse prescinding from marriage is aside from Paul's point here.) He makes for it the claim he has made about marital love itself. It has two essential and inherent meanings—not ends, as had been said for centuries by the Catholic authorities, but meanings (not *fines* but *sensus*). These meanings are the procreative and the unitive. They are inseparable—inseparable in the sense that an act of intercourse in marriage cannot have one without the other. It either has both or it has neither.

To claim this is not to claim a moral principle. It is to assert a fact of human psychology. Set out fully it means that no matter the partners' intention and motivation, if they do not leave their act open to the possibility of conception, it is not unitive—it is not an act of love that is marital. Reciprocally, if the act is not unitive, neither is it truly procreative. It is only reproductive. The reason for this last conclusion is unstated at this point but hovers near: God's creation is in essence a loving act.

> That teaching [". . . that each and every marital act must remain open to the transmission of life"] . . . is founded upon the inseparable connection, willed by God and unable to be broken by man on his own initiative, between the two meanings of the conjugal act: the unitive meaning and the procreative meaning. Indeed, by its intimate structure, the conjugal act, while most closely uniting husband and wife, capacitates them for the generation of new lives, according to laws inscribed in the very being of man and of woman. By safeguarding both these essential aspects, the unitive and the procreative, the conjugal act preserves in its fullness the sense or meaning of true mutual love and its ordination toward man's most high calling to parenthood. . . .[67]

Because he has made this claim for sexual intercourse within marriage Paul has by implication made it for marriage itself. The two meanings, unitive and procreative, are essential to it and inseparable from it. If these two characteristics are not found within a relationship, at least in intention, it is not a marriage. How the procreative meaning or intention could be in the relationship of a couple marrying after the woman's menopause, or where either is sterile for any reason, is not clear.[68]

The encyclical is not about the sacramentality of Christian marriages since it is about marriage universally and a moral demand assumed to be in it universally. But Paul does not pass the sacrament by. His first mention of it is succinct but traditional: "For baptized persons, moreover, marriage invests the dignity of a sacramental sign of grace, inasmuch as it represents the union of Christ and the Church."[69] His second and slightly longer reference to it contains both doctrine and moral-ascetical counsel. It incorporates his assumption about the inseparability of the procreative and the unitive meanings of intercourse in marriage. It gives to the sacrament the work of manifesting this inseparability—gives it because this inseparability is a demand of God's love at work in the Christian spouses' union, and because this is the work of the sacrament, to manifest God's work in this union.

> Christian married couples . . . must remember that their Christian vocation, which began at baptism, is further specified and reinforced by the sacrament of matrimony.
> By it husband and wife are strengthened and, as it were, consecrated for the faithful accomplishment of their proper duties, for the carrying out of their proper vocation even to perfection, and the Christian witness which is proper to them before the whole world. To them the Lord entrusts the task of making visible to men the holiness and sweetness of the law which unites the mutual love of husband and wife with their cooperation with the love of God the author of human life.[70]

It goes without saying that the accuracy of this theology of the sacrament is in direct proportion to the accuracy of Paul's assumption that in marital intercourse the unitive and the procreative meanings are inseparable.

But *Humanae vitae*'s fullest contribution to the theology of the sacrament is of the same indirect kind as that of *Gaudium et spes*. This is by its enrichment of the sacrament's matrix. The encyclical does this by detailing the traits of marital love, and this it does to complete its explanation of the theological principle that because God has designed this love according to the model of his own love, and works in and through human marital love, it must have the same characteristics as his. The description of the first characteristic almost duplicates the thought of *Gaudium et spes*. It shares the latter's negative purpose, which is to gainsay the common persuasion in the Western world that the love germane to marriage is romantic infatuation or an emotional involvement closely akin to it.

> This love is first of all fully *human* [italics in the original], that is to say, of the senses and the spirit at the same time. It is not, then, a simple transport of instinct and sentiment, but also, and principally, an act of the free will, intended to endure and to grow by means of the joys and sorrows of daily life, in such a way that husband and wife become one only heart and one only soul, and together attain their human perfection.[71]

The second characteristic is almost equally a duplication of the descriptive definition in *Gaudium et spes*. It rejects in passing what the ancients, Aristotle among them, had said, that full and perfect friendship is less possible between a man and a woman because of the inferiority in her of the virtues needed for friendship, whereas full friendship calls for equality of persons.[72] *Humanae vitae* rejects this in saying that it is characteristic of marital love that husbands and wives share everything, that they make gifts of their persons to one another.

The third characteristic of marital love is the most briefly stated. "Again, this love is faithful and exclusive until death."[73] A supporting paragraph adds one of the few instances in the encyclical of fact that could be gathered only inductively: "The example of so many married persons down through the centuries shows not only that fidelity is according to the nature of marriage but also that it is a source of profound and lasting happiness."

The final characteristic that Paul finds in marital love belongs to the thesis of his letter and is the premise of its moral argument. It is that this love is fruitful. But here he adds presumably another point of psychological information, one that can be verified only by experience, namely that marital love cannot attain its full realization if confined within the husband-wife relationship.

> And finally this love is *fecund,* for it is not exhausted by the communion between husband and wife, but is destined to continue, raising up new lives. . . .[74]

This too must have consequences for the marital love in the marriages of the infertile—for whom, we recall, Paul has left the way to marriage entirely open.

In the preceding chapter I suggested that of all Pope Paul's predecessors (but now the bishops of Vatican II excepted) the German pantheistic idealist, Georg W.F. Hegel, came closest to understanding marriage as Paul would understand it a century and a half later. He said that as couples transcend the earlier and immature stages of their relationship that form only partial unions they approach a total communion of their beings. At least verbally Paul affirms the same:

> By means of the reciprocal personal gift of self, proper and exclusive to them, husband and wife tend toward the communion of their beings in a view of mutual personal perfection, to collaborate with God in the generation of new lives.[75]

But differences between Paul's understanding and Hegel's ought to be noted. For Hegel the communion of the partners was in consciousness alone. To attain this they must rise above the inferior phenomena of human interaction, including the bodily. For Paul the communion is of the spouses' entire beings, physical as well as spiritual.

For Hegel the communion was more perfect the more the distinct personal consciousnesses disappeared into the one consciousness. For Paul the communion, while diminishing the separateness of the partners, must maintain their distinction. This is so because they create the union by making gifts of themselves to one another, and sustain it by continuing to do so. This is possible only to distinct, free and volitionally self-possessed persons.

But both Hegel and Paul seem to agree in this, that the man and wife can reach the fullness, the perfection of their kind of love in this reciprocally self-giving union. In the degree that they try only to take from one another they destroy their union and also themselves.

A last reflection on *Humanae vitae* finds that probably without intending to do so, here in two combined subordinate clauses Paul may have pointed to the heart of his definition of marriage, and therein to the heart of the sacrament's matrix: "By means of the reciprocal and personal gift of self, proper and exclusive to them. . . ." "Proper to" in the traditional vocabulary of this document can mean "intrinsic to," "belonging to its essence," "of its nature." Its meaning here is fixed more accurately by the adjective "exclusive." It indicates a kind and an inclusiveness of self-giving that only a man and a woman can have. In it they can work toward the full realization of their persons—but only together and only by the self-giving. Here we are back beyond Hegel to Hugh of St. Victor in the twelfth century, who found marriage's finally distinguishing trait in the inclusiveness, the exclusiveness and the intensity of the love of the husband and wife for one another.

The 1980 Synod of Bishops and *Familiaris consortio*

It is better to examine simultaneously the statements coming from the international synod of Catholic bishops of September–October 1980 and Pope John Paul II's apostolic exhortation, *Familiaris consortio* of December 15, 1981. The reason for this is evident from John Paul's introduction to the exhortation.

> At the close of their assembly, the synod fathers presented me with a long list of proposals in which they had gathered the fruits of their reflections . . . and they asked me unanimously to be a spokesman before humanity of the church's lively care for the family and to give suitable indications for renewed pastoral effort in this fundamental sector of the life of man and of the church.
> As I fulfill that mission in this exhortation . . .[76]

Both sets of statements—that of the synod and John Paul's exhortation—are discourses, the former a collection thereof. If our own examination of these interpretations of marriage and the sacrament is not to wander through long incoherence, this examination must be a digest and a synthesis. Forming these is best done by singling out and analyzing the main themes in the discourses.

There are two themes logically prior to the discourses that suffuse them and condition all they say. The one carries over from *Gaudium et spes;* it is the formality under which marriage is considered in both the synod and in the pope's exhortation. This formality is not marriage the juridical institution, not the philosophic model, not the idealized religious conception. It is marriage the human society as it is lived in the world. It is the family. Even where the discourse is about spouses alone, they are dealt with as a family, as a mini-society meant by God to affect seriously the larger and ambient societies of which it is the irreducible component. To reflect on marriage under this formality is at least the intent of all the documents, even though one or the other in places leaves earth and existential description to ascend into idealized prescription.

Pope John Paul expressed his understanding of this first theme in the following way:

> Since God's plan for marriage and family touches men and women in the concreteness of their daily existence in specific social and cultural situations, the church ought to apply herself to understanding the situations within which marriage and the family are lived today, in order to fulfill her task of serving.
>
> This understanding is therefore an inescapable requirement of the work of evangelization. . . . The call and demands of the spirit resound in the . . . very events of history, and so the church can also be guided to a more profound understanding.[77]

The second prior and comprehensive theme is suggested by that first one. It was also made quite explicit by Pope John Paul and the other bishops. It is that this synod about the Christian family is a continuation of two earlier synods, in 1974 and 1977. Those dealt with evangelization and catechesis in and by the Church. Again John Paul's words—this time in his homily that opened the synod—explain this.

> Therefore we can say in all honesty that the theme of the present session of the synod is a continuation of the preceding two sessions. Both evangelization, the theme of the 1974 synod, and catechesis, the theme of the 1977 synod, not only look to the family but also receive their authentic vitality from the family. The family is the fundamental object of the church's evangelization and catechesis, but it is also the necessary subject for which nothing else can be substituted: the creative subject.
>
> As the subject, the family must be conscious of the mission of the church and of its participation in this mission, not only to persevere in the church and to draw from its spiritual re-

sources, but also to constitute the church in its fundamental dimension, like a "miniature church" (domestic church).

The present synod's job is to show all the families their particular role in the mission of the church. . . .[78]

Not by way of adopting a comprehensive and guiding theme of the synod, but to add an extraordinary participation to it, the bishops did something that had not been done by a group of prelates pondering marriage since the Pontifical Study Commission on Population Control established by Pope John XXIII and expanded by Paul VI. It invited married couples to attend the synod and to be heard there. The reason for this was not only pragmatic–prudential. It was doctrinal as well, as John Paul's words just above imply. Married couples participate, in their marital way, in the bishops' work. They share this work with them, each group *suo modo.*

Cardinal Basil Hume, archbishop of Westminster, gathered into one statement, on September 29, both the theological insight of married couples' participation in the ministry, and the need for bishops to consult them in order to learn about marriage—a matter no less theological, as he hints.

> . . . a notable passage in the synod's working document runs thus: "The prophetic mission of the family is related to the teaching office of the pastors in that the word of God forms the understanding of the faith of the people of God, which is expressed both in families and in pastors, in the way that is proper to each."
>
> This prophetic mission of the family, and so of husbands and wives, is based upon their experience as married persons and on an understanding of the sacrament of marriage of which they can speak with their own authority. This experience and this understanding constitute, I would suggest, an authentic *fons theologiae* from which we, the pastors, and indeed the whole church can draw.
>
> Married couples have, then, a twofold title to a special authority in matters concerning marriage. First, they are the ministers of the sacrament, and, second, they alone have experienced the effects of the sacrament, which enables them to participate in the love of Christ for his church sacramentally.[79]

The bishops expressed a dominant theme of the synod most clearly in their final and summary statement, "The Message to Christian Families." God's eternal plan is to bring all men and women to share in his divine life. (That he has a plan to unite all creation in Christ is the opening theme of Ephesians. That he intends for human beings to participate somehow in his own life is a Johannine theme expressed, for example, in 1 John 4:13: "We know we are living in him and he is living in us because he lets us share his Spirit." It is also a faith-theme of the sub-apostolic Church, as in 2 Peter 1:4: "In making these gifts [God] had given us the guarantee of something very great and wonderful to come; through them you will be able to share the divine nature . . ."). God the Father's calling all men and women to this participation in him and with one another, and their accepting this call—these create the people of God; these form the Church.

This plan of God informed and determined his creation. Both the synod in its concluding document and John Paul in *Familiaris consortio* developed in detail the thought of Genesis 1, that in creating human beings God created them "in his own image and likeness." And in order to create them in his image fully he formed both the man and the woman, the two different but correlated sexes. Indeed their sexuality—different but correlated—is essential to the imaging.

The reason for this is that in his nature God is not an ontological monad, not (metaphorically said) a solitary monarch. He is in essence an act of love, an act whose participants are within the one divine existence. Christians call this essentially loving existence the trinity of persons in God: the Father, the one who loves as origin of the love; the Son, or Word, as the beloved who returns his love to the Father; the Spirit, the reciprocal expression, the bond, of love between them. Because this is God's nature his intent to create human beings in his own "image and likeness" results in this, that love must be essential to human nature and the human condition. John Paul says this well in *Familiaris consortio*.

> God is love, and in himself he lives a mystery of personal loving communion. Creating the human race in his own image and continually keeping it in being, God inscribed in the humanity of man and woman the vocation, and thus the capacity and responsibility, of love and communion. Love is therefore the fundamental and innate vocation of every human being.[80]

Since God has made human beings to be bodily creatures—or more accurately said, embodied spirits, spiritual-physical composites—it is their nature to love in a combined physical-spiritual way. To be integral, total, human love must be both simultaneously—physical and spiritual.

> As an incarnate spirit, that is, a soul which expresses itself in a body and a body informed by an immortal spirit, man is called to love in his unified totality. Love includes the human body, and the body is made a sharer in spiritual love.[81]

To say this is to identify sexuality in human beings and to say what its role is in the divine plan. It is, to begin with, men's and women's bodily avenue and expression of love, the bodily domain in which they can join and commune in love. It is not an accessory or an attribute of their natures; it is of their essence.

Why, according to this interpretation, must human embodiment and thus sexuality be both male and female? Because the love in God that human beings are to image is simultaneously a love that is a communion of distinct persons, and a love that is creative, fruitful. Hence the human beings communing in love must be so designed as to be able to produce new life. They must be correlated in fertility.

When men and women respond to God's love by loving him in return, they do not abandon their bodiliness in doing so. They cannot reciprocate his love in a purely spiritual way. Their response is inescapably bodily. One of the bodily ways in which they may love him in return includes their sexuality, and their correlated sexualities joined in marriage. In this way the marital structure and expression of their love for one another can be at the same time a response of love to God. This is one of the ways in which their marriage can be a sacrament.

A Contemporary Catholic Interpretation of Sexuality

At this point in our examination it is opportune to include the main insights of two interventions in the synod by Cardinal (then Archbishop) Joseph Bernardin—the first on September 29, the other during the first week of October. The first intervention is about the nature of sexuality in men and women. The second outlines an asceticism of human intimacy, and in doing so offers an interpretation of this intimacy.[82] They are valuable among other reasons as evidence of how far some Catholic authorities have come in their understanding of sexuality from the quasi-Freudian estimation of it held by so many of the fathers and later authorities through the centuries.

Bernardin begins by acknowledging that if the Church is to gain people's—and its own priests'—attention when teaching about sexual morality, it must develop a realistic theology of sexuality. That he is convinced that acquiring such a theology depends on first acquiring a realistic psychology and anthropology of it is evident in the following elements of his interpretation.

His first point is scriptural: Sexuality is God's gift to human beings. Used as he intends, it is enriching and ennobling. It is not merely a capacity for performing certain acts. It is not limited to persons' genitality. It is a relational power and relational avenue. It is a God-given means for interacting with individual persons and with larger society. About the latter, a person's sexuality has a social dimension. As a constituent part of his or her nature it enters into all social actions and relationships. A person never functions simply as a human being, but always as either a woman or a man.

Sexuality needs the context of marriage if its expression is to be full and unreserved. It needs a stable, long-lasting relationship as its setting if it is not to be destructive—if its expression is not to disappoint, deceive and alienate.

This points to the need of intimacy in men's and women's lives. It has antecedently an essential place in their lives because of God's plan in creating them. He means for them to image his own life; but his is one of essential intimacy, of communion in existence. Of their nature human beings need intimacy also because without it they remain in isolation, incomplete.

Sexuality is one among the avenues of intimacy for men and women. Again it is more than genitality, but includes it. It has two reciprocal demands, that one be open, vulnerable, willing to make an honest disclosure of oneself; that one also let another into one's life, to influence it, make demands on it, become a care, diminish one's freedom.

To meet these demands one must first gain self-knowledge, self-acceptance; must rid oneself of masks and protections, must get out of narcissistic self-absorption. One must be willing to risk loss, to accept as well as to make demands for radical change. To carry on intimately with another also demands skill in communication, patience, sensitivity to the other, tenderness. Christ is a model of self-giving in intimacy. He loved so many men and women, entered their lives and welcomed them into his, and gave his life for them.

Genitally consummated intimacy of a man and woman—where it is truly an act of love—causes a unique bonding of the two. It makes their initial bonding explicitly and strongly male-female in character. This in turn impels them to want children and to be creative.

It is opportune to interpolate here John Paul's own interpretation of sexuality, now not from *Familiaris consortio* but from his homilies on the creation passages of Genesis 2 and 3, as Cardinal Bernardin drew from them for his own discourses. John Paul delivered the homilies in November 1979 and in January 1980. His contextual theme was "the nuptial meaning of the body."[83]

A person exists "in the image and likeness of God" not only as a single human being but also and mainly in interpersonal communion, especially in that of a man and a woman.

In its functioning sexuality manifests the unique person as male or female. It is not an attribute of the person but essentially constitutive of him or her. The human body in its male or female sexuality is not only a source of fruitfulness and procreation. It also possesses the nuptial element, i.e. the capacity to express love, specifically the love with which a person makes a gift of the self and in making this gift fulfills the meaning of his or her existence. Sexuality is a vivid and powerful way of making this gift. The awareness of this meaning of the body, especially of the nuptial meaning of its sexuality, is the fundamental element of human existence in the world. To say more exactly what this nuptial meaning is, a man and a woman, created each for his and her own sake, can discover their selves fully only in the sincere giving of themselves.[84]

In *Familiaris consortio* John Paul stated the conditions under which alone sexuality can be truly human (a quality, we recall, that *Gaudium et spes* demanded for sexual expression if it is to be not destructive but constructive). The fundamental conditions John Paul calls "totality."

> . . . sexuality, by means of which man and woman give them-selves to one another through acts which are proper and exclu-sive to spouses, is by no means something purely biological, but concerns the innermost being of the human person as such. It is realized in a truly human way only if it is an integral part of the love by which a man and a woman commit themselves totally to one another until death. The total physical self-giving would be a lie if it were not the sign and fruit of a total personal self-giving, in which the whole person, including the temporal dimension, is present. If the person were to withhold some-thing or reserve the possibility of deciding otherwise in the future, by this very fact he or she would not be giving totally.
>
> The totality which is required by conjugal love also corre-sponds to the demands of a responsible fertility. This fertility is directed to the generation of a human being, and so by its nature it surpasses the purely biological order and involves a whole series of personal values. For the harmonious growth of these values a persevering and unified contribution by both parents is necessary.[85]

Cardinal Bernardin traced the common history of marriages and interpreted it too as an image of God's work in the world—but now his creative work extended into the redemptive. It is in this extension that its imaging God's paternal creative love passes over into imaging his redemptive love carried on through Christ.

He says that it is common that a man's and woman's desire for intimacy, and their ability and willingness to sustain the demands of intimacy, run a rhythmic pattern. As pair-bonded persons they desire permanence in their intimacy. But as primates they long for freedom from entangling obligations.

A marriage often passes through four phases: from falling in love, to settling into a routine wherein the spouses become passive and cease their efforts to love, to communicate, to give their selves and to accept the other self; then rebellion against the restraints of marriage and its intimacy, and descent into crisis; then a beginning again.

This cycle may be repeated during a marriage, perhaps more than once. It can be destructive but at the same time healthy provided it does not come to an end in the crisis. Bernardin perceives that this cycle can be interpreted in analogy with the paschal mystery of Christ. The falling in love is the equivalent of the freshness of new life after God's creation. The settling into routine is the falling into the state of indeliberate sin, of fundamental sinfulness. The crisis is the explosion of this sinfulness into deliberate sin, into the calculated refusal to communicate, the destructive words and conduct, even the hatred. It is at this point that redemption can enter the marriage, with the sorrow, with the confession of malice, with the asking for forgiveness. In the sequence of the analogy, this is resurrection.

> It is precisely here, at the painful heart of the mystery and almost simultaneously with the accusations intended to wound and destroy, that the possibility exists for sorrow, born of acknowledgment of sin, to call forth forgiveness—a forgiveness so deep and purifying that the relationship is truly born anew. In short evil becomes sin, sin becomes murderous hatred, murderous hatred gives way to sorrow, and out of sorrow is born resurrection—all because the co-victims on the cross, the self and the other, are loved.
>
> For persons who have this experience, the Christ they crucify is not "out there" beyond their deepest feelings. Rather this Christ is as close as their very heart, the love of their life, enfleshed in their beloved, toward whom this sorrow in the face of truth and this forgiveness in the face of love are felt and savored, thereby generating powerful creative forces: in a word, resurrection.[86]

(One who has seen Edward Albee's play "Who's Afraid of Virginia Woolf?" has seen in the spouses there, George and Martha, an example of the death and resurrection to which Bernardin refers.)

It is at this juncture in a marriage that its sacramentality becomes most exactly Christian. Its nascent and primal sacramentality, as we have seen, is found in its imaging God's essentially self-communicating and creative love—in the spouses' unreserved self-giving in creating new life. But Christ's entry into the human race was needed on the massive scale for the reason we have just seen on the scale of the individual marriage. Sin surfaced very early in the race's history and killed in so many men and women the desire to give the self and to give new life, or to sustain life at all. In bringing to the entire race God the Father's restoration of life Christ acted as the primordial sacrament. A husband and wife, by passing through the death Bernardin has described, do multiple sacramental things provided their sorrow and forgiveness are the effects of Christ's spirit at work in them. They act as sacraments of Christ in that they bring resurrection to one another, manifest to one another God's saving effort. They serve as instruments of God's doing this. They manifest the same to the societies in which they live—to the Christian society that is the Church, to the society of their relatives, friends and acquaintances. They bring the possibility of and hope for resurrection to other spouses who are going through the same private and simultaneously mutual crucifixion.

In his discourse auxiliary bishop Francis Stafford of Baltimore (now archbishop of Denver) explained the Christic sacramentality of the spouses in slightly more traditional terms.[87] First are his preliminary and defining clauses. Two early elements of these are by now truisms in Catholic theology: A sacrament makes God's love for human beings sensately available through signs and symbols. The sacrament in marriage is not only the wedding ceremony but includes the entire marriage, especially whatever is specifically marital in it. A marriage is a sacrament in that it is a prophetic sign to the human race of God's covenantal love for it, and in that it makes real Christ's love for the Church in and through the spouses' love for one another.

There is this concatenation in God's sacramental action in the world: Christ is the most excellent sacrament because he is at once the most transparent sign of God's mercy and the most effective instrument of it. The Church in its men and women is a continuation of Christ the sacrament. And the spouses are a particular and specific realization of the Church as a sacrament. Stafford duplicated Archbishop Bernardin's description of the spouses' reenactment of Christ's sacramental scenario, in their forming the marriage covenant, then in the failures and sins in their relationship, their descent into a kind of death, and finally their resurrection through sorrow and forgiveness. This scenario can be enacted especially in their sexual communication with its desire and demand for self-surrender.

Archbishop Henri Legare of Grouard-McLennan, Alberta, in his address of September 30, echoed Pope John Paul's words about the demand for indissolubility in marriage, but with a difference.[88] He made the traditional point that the demand for indissolubility comes from multiple quarters in a marriage—from the need for unfailing fidelity inherent in human love, from the good of the children, from the good of society, from Christ's command, "What God has joined man must not divide." But he also pointed out what is so well known, that the final and definitive source of the doctrine of indissolubility is that a Christian marriage is to be an image of the indissoluble union of Christ and the Church. He adds that "this teaching, which is undeniably rich, leaves two questions unanswered."

> The first, which is theological, is linked to the experience of the people of God, a people saved in Jesus Christ but still a pilgrim people, who welcome salvation within a history where grace and sin are mixed. How does one speak of marriage as a privileged sign of the covenant between God and man? How express the difference between the relationship of Christ to the church and the relationship of the church to Christ? If the faithfulness of Christ to the church is absolute, we know very

well that the reality of the church's relationship to Christ is different. Can one then purely and simply equate Christ's relationship to the church and the church's relationship to Christ?

This essentialist philosophy within which the theology of the sacrament of marriage evolved can lead one to think that the church is already in a state of perfection, that it has in some sense arrived at its end. But that approach forgets that the church is truly in a pilgrim state, that it is constructed in history. Therefore should we rethink the theology of marriage in a more existentialist and personalist framework? Such an approach obliges us to take reality into account as it is historically presented to us, while still affirming (but in a different way) the indissolubility of marriage.[89]

The Marital Sacrament as Family

A most significant element of the synod's and of Pope John Paul's assessment of the marital sacrament was their identification of marriage as family, and the family as the sacrament. (This was pointed out at the beginning of our inspection of the bishops' and the pope's discourses.) Their shift of attention from marriage to family was no mere substitution of terms. Substantial meaning was involved. From their introductory remarks it is clear that they thought only an incomplete theology of marriage could be inducted from marriage pondered in conceptual abstraction, or even from marriage as the real-life relationship of husband and wife but out of its real-life context. Moreover their strategy of treating marriage as a component of Christian evangelization dictated that they examine it as a social relationship functioning among social relationships. In their conceptual vocabulary this made marriage to be family—made even the husband-wife relationship by itself, prescinding from parents, siblings and children, to be family.

A first and obvious way in which a family is sacramental is that along with other Christian families it makes up the Church, and the Church is Christ the sacrament continued in the world. As a constituent element of the Church the family participates essentially in its mission. Pope John Paul expressed it thus in his homily that opened the synod.

As the subject, the family must be conscious of the mission of the church and of its participation in this mission, not only to persons in the church, but also to constitute the church in its fundamental dimension, like a "miniature church" (domestic church).[90]

The conduct within families that constitutes the sacrament was pointed out by Cardinal Terrence Cooke of New York.

The family is the place where human life originates, where human love and human relationships are first experienced, where a knowledge and love of God are first learned, where values and attitudes are first found and shaped and passed on from one generation to the next.[91]

The same said in more detail urges that if Christians as adults are to be able to love with care both in their marriages and among their friends and colleagues, if they are to be able to bring forgiveness and reconciliation, to learn to be forgiven and reconciled—in a word, if they are to be able to live and function as sacraments of Christ—they must develop these abilities in their early years. These are the years ordinarily spent in the parental family.

Said in even finer detail, the members of a Christian family experience their sacrament in the following inter-related ways. Assuming the spouses are clearly intimate with God in their prayer and eucharistic participation, they are evidence for one another of God's action in their lives—and are instruments of his action—when they give themselves to one another in uninhibited lovemaking, when they are patient and sustaining of one another's weaknesses and faults, when they apologize, forgive and start over.

Their children experience the family sacrament when they experience the parents' love for one another and for them, when they are disciplined with love, when their parents teach them skills, when they open their minds to learning and wisdom.

The bishops referred to all this *ensemble* as "the family's response to God."[92] Their explanation of this response speaks for itself; it needs no explaining apart from itself. It is concrete, detailed, tightly stated. They addressed Christian couples in the following way.

Just as we are doing, you also are seeking to learn what your duties are in today's world. In looking at the world, we see facing you certain important tasks of education. You have the tasks of forming free persons with a keen moral sense and a discerning conscience, together with a perception of their duty to work for the betterment of the human condition and the sanctification of the world. Another task for the family is to form persons in love and also to practice love in all its relationships, so that it does not live closed in on itself but remains open to the community, moved by a sense of justice and concern for others as well as by a consciousness of its responsibility toward the whole of society. It is your duty to form persons in the faith—that is, in knowledge and love of God and eagerness to do his will in all things. It is also your task to hand on sound human and Christian values and to form persons in such a way that they can integrate new values into their lives. The more Christian the family becomes, the more human it becomes.

In fulfilling these tasks the family will be, as it were, a "domestic church," a community of faith living in hope and love, serving God and the entire human family. Shared prayer and the liturgy are sources of grace for families. In fulfilling its tasks the family must nourish itself on God's word and participate in the life of the sacraments, especially reconciliation and the eucharist.

Evangelization and catechesis begin in the family. Formation in faith, chastity and the other Christian virtues, as well as education in human sexuality, must start in the home. Yet the outlook of the Christian family should not be narrow and confined only to the parish; it should embrace the whole human family. Within the larger community it has a duty to give witness to Christian values. It should foster social justice and relief of the poor and oppressed. . . .

Out of a sense of fidelity to the Gospel, the family should be prepared to welcome new life, to share its goods and resources with the poor, to be open and hospitable to others. Today the family is sometimes obliged to choose a way of life that goes contrary to modern culture in such matters as sexuality, individual autonomy and material wealth. In the face of sin and failure, it gives witness to an authentically Christian spirit, sensitive in its life and in the lives of others there to the values of penance and forgiveness, reconciliation and hope. It gives evidence of the fruits of the Holy Spirit and the Beatitudes. It practices a simple style of life and pursues a truly evangelical apostolate toward others.[93]

The African Bishops in the Synod

A group of African bishops brought to the synod a concept of marriage of sufficient cultural difference that, if it were accepted by the Catholic authorities, would have eventually a substantial effect on the theology of the sacrament. The bishops offered their conception of marriage in the position paper they had drawn up in preparation for the synod. It reflected especially the marital traditions of the people of Zaire.[94]

Marriage among this people is a covenant. But as such it is as much a communitarian as it is a personal and private undertaking. It involves the continuation and the building up of the two families across multiple generations both preceding and succeeding the new marriage. To marry is to perform a sacred duty, an office in service of life oriented to the future of the race or tribe. The new marriage joins not only the spouses but the families of both, even their clans and their tribes. Consequently the bond continues to exist even after the separation or death of the spouses.[95]

In this tradition marriage is created not by a single event, such as the spouses' exchange of consents, that may occupy only a few minutes. It is created in stages that may need as many as two years. The families prepare for and execute each of these stages carefully and in succession. The final stage is the spouses' entry into their new household, or is even the birth of their first child.[96]

If one were to say that such a processual, multi-phase creation of marriage is erroneous, one could do so only on the assumption that the Roman tradition of the single exchange of consents is the sole valid way of creating a marriage. But from what principle could one draw this as a conclusion? One could say it is the tradition that best protects the spouses' freedom. But this is not to say that it is the only possible creation of a marriage. Indeed, the multi-step Jewish tradition was the accepted way of creating marriages during the first Christian generation, as was the multi-step Germanic tradition for seven centuries after the Christian religion had spread among the people of central Europe.

If, then, one may accept that the creation of a marriage in multiple steps is possible, so too must one accept the creation of the sacrament through steps. The consequences for the doctrine and discipline of divorce are obvious.

For the African peoples the creating of the "natural" marital relationship, the progressive building of the covenant, is a profoundly religious act. Reference to God occupies every step of the process. Ancestors too are included. It is inconceivable in this tradition that the faith commitment of the spouses could be contained implicitly in their merely willing to marry. Their community takes care that their religious intention be most explicit.[97]

The image of a fruitful God underlies and informs this understanding of marriage. It believes in God as father less as ruler of the universe, but more as the source of all life. In a way that suggests the Christian belief in the trinity of divine persons, God is conceived of as existing in essential polarity, in the attractive power of persons for one another. This is especially significant for marriage. It is this divine principle active in the universe that brings the man and woman together. Its purpose is the transmission of life. This principle of attractive polarity works itself out further in the forming of the new mini-family and in the drawing together of the ancestral families.[98]

Again, the effects of this cultural conception on the sacrament must be rich ones. More persons than the new bridal pair carry on the sacramental manifestation of God's work in the world. Both ancestral families take part in it. Keeping permanence as a crucial facet of this manifestation is the work of these families as well as of the couple. Indeed there remains a permanent bond between these families even if the couple's relationship ends by death or by dissolution. And the inability to produce a child brings on the dissolution of the spousal marriage. It is not so much that the marriage, integral in itself, has failed to realize its purpose. Rather the marriage has not reached completion, has not been consummated.

Here too a variation on the traditional theology of indissolubility is evident. In European Catholic tradition even a sacramental marriage is dissoluble if unconsummated, because the failure at intercourse leaves the imaging of the Christ-Church relationship incomplete. But in this African tradition the inability to produce a child calls for dissolution because of the failure to carry out God's work in the world, which is to give and preserve life.

The Zairian bishops sought to take this African conception of marriage into the traditional Catholic theology and fuse the two. They did so by drawing from the homily that Pope John Paul had delivered in Kinshasa on May 3, 1980. They undertook this fusion because they insisted on the principle that "It is where people live, in their own situation, that Christ is to be met and to take hold. . . . In the light of Christ, human experience and traditional religion can grow into a new relation. The African person can discover the great themes of the covenant, the mystical body, and the communion of saints in accordance with his own family experience."[99]

The bishops pointed to four parts of the Christian tradition which can be areas of fusion with the African. It is evident how the fusion enriches the elements of African marital tradition already outlined above.

> . . . First, the notion of God who is the source of the family. In the religious experience of the African people, God is the creating presence, the axis around which the entire universe turns. The "awakener" is experienced as the supporting force behind all that is. Secondly, this entails a notion of family which is wider and broader. The family of the Trinity is the foundation of the brotherhood of man and the model for family, society and the Church. Thirdly, there is the christian profession that God is married with His people. This is the spousal relationship par excellence and leads to the fourth element, namely that the covenant between persons is a sacrament of the Paschal Lamb. The marital relation formed between mortal persons becomes an efficient symbol of the spousal covenant between God and his people, between the Son and His Church, a new and everlasting covenant after the image of the trinitarian model. On the divine model one can ground a forceful marital spirituality. This would encompass the moral and spiritual fruitfulness of the spouses, the fulfillment of their wishes and a realization of the demands: an integrated fruitfulness and the missionary service of the family.[100]

But along with this possibility of enriching fusion goes the danger of a kind of religious colonial imperialism. This is the Western Catholic theology's threat of destroying what is humanly valuable, and therefore sacramentally valid, in African marriage.

All things considered, one could say that while marriage in Western tradition had moved toward the model of an interpersonal relationship between two individuals, African marriage had gone in the opposite direction, toward the notion that the vitality present within the community is entrusted to the persons marrying. Traditional African marriage is characterized by two aspects: it is solemnized in a purely communitarian context and style, and the drawn out process of solemnization can last for months or even years. In contrast to this stands christian marriage which comes into being through a short ritual exclusively involving the partners and a witness who is certainly not representative of the two families of lineage. Through this discrepancy between two different processes of institution and two different images of person and society it can easily be seen that christian marriage carries little weight in the perspective of the African people. As a result, at least according to the African episcopal representatives, it is necessary to be careful that customary African marriage is not looked upon as a form of concubinage but is correctly appreciated as a type of progressive marriage. Furthermore, the majority of African christians do not find Church marriage to be meaningful and many are uncomfortable with the idea of indissolubility of christian marriage because it does not take into account or in any way guarantee the fertility of the couple. The question with respect to this complex situation, therefore, touches upon the notion of the sacramentality of marriage in all its dogmatic, canonical and liturgical aspects. . . .

It can be summarized that in the minds of the majority of African bishops the first theological principle concerning the teaching of the Church is precisely the need for Africanization. According to bishop J.C. Bouchard (Pala, Chad), the center of gravity of christianity has shifted from Europe to Latin America and Africa. Evangelization in Africa should not contribute to the attack and destruction of the human values which already exist among these peoples; it should bring liberation and not threat.[101]

The Sacrament in the Revised Catholic Marriage Law

In the same homily, on January 25, 1959, in which he announced that he would convene the Second Vatican Council, Pope John XXIII ordered the revision of the church's code of law. This work of revision began early in 1966, after the council's adjournment on December 8, 1965. It had no Gasparri. The work was supervised at highest level by a *plenarium* of about thirty cardinals, presided over by Cardinal Pericle Felici. It was guided more closely by the Pontifical Commission for the Revision of the Code (chaired also by Cardinal Felici). The immediate formulating of the revised canons, or statutes, of the Code was done by several subcommissions, each with its own chairman. The revised Code was promulgated by Pope John Paul II on January 25, 1983, the twenty-fourth anniversary of John XXIII's announcement. It went into effect on the first Sunday of Advent of the same year.

The canons (statutes) on marriage needed revision for reasons peculiar to themselves. One of these reasons is suggested by the title under which they were published, along with the canons on the other sacraments. In the 1917 Code this had been in Book 3, *De Rebus* ("Concerning Things").

In the revised Code of 1983 they are in Book 4, "The Office of Sanctifying in the Church." This suggests that in the years since 1917 the Catholic authorities had ceased thinking of marriage—even of the marital sacrament—as a juridical category. Their change of mind was virtually mandated by Vatican II. Its bishops dealt with marriage as a man-woman partnership in love, as family, as a territory of goodness and holiness.

Although the statutes on marriage in the revised Code have tempered the enthusiastic humanism of *Gaudium et spes,* they do convey the bishops' mind in crucial places. They identify marriage as a partnership, not a covenant. They give love its place. They say spouses create their marriage by covenanting, not by exchanging rights.

Our attention to the role of the sacrament in the Code's canons on marriage will be relatively brief. Accounting for the historical context of this role has been the agenda of this examination almost from its beginning. True to the character of statutory law neither the original Code of 1917 nor its revision of 1983 contains in its canons explanations for their formulations—unless one wishes to say that the few canons that affirm either historical events or religious doctrine supply implicitly the reasons for being phrased as they are.

Old Canon 1012 in its paragraph 1 affirmed an historical event and in its paragraph 2 declared a religious fact which was drawn expressly from the event—known to be drawn from it because the second clause began with the Latin conjunction *quare*, "for this reason."

1. Christ Our Lord elevated the contract itself of marriage between baptized persons to the dignity of a sacrament.
2. For this reason it is impossible for a valid contract of marriage between baptized persons to exist without being by that very fact a sacrament.

We know by now the historical stimulus for formulating the two paragraphs of the canon in this way. The first had as its main target the Protestant reformers. The second had the Gallican, the Royalists, the Febronians, Josephists and *philosophes*—not to mention Melchior Cano and the generations of Catholic theologians and canonists who agreed with him that the contract and the sacrament in marriage are separable.

The cognate to this in the revised Code is Canon 1055. Its formulation too bespeaks a lively history, but one quite modern.

> 1. The matrimonial covenant, by which a man and a woman establish between themselves a *consortium* of the whole of life, is by its nature ordered to the good of the spouses and the procreation and education of offspring; this covenant between baptized persons has been raised by Christ the Lord to the dignity of a sacrament.
> 2. For this reason a matrimonial contract cannot validly exist between baptized persons unless it is also a sacrament by that fact.[102]

In 1975 the subcommission that drafted the revision of the Code's canons on marriage sent out to the appropriate persons and groups in the Church a preliminary version of its revision. It had left Canon 1012 unchanged. But during the months this version was in the hands of the national conferences of bishops around the world, of regional canon law societies, et al., it came under severe criticism. This bore mainly on two points. The first was the assumption that any and every marriage is a contract, and its ignoring that the bishops of Vatican II had abandoned this concept of marriage and replaced it with the biblical notion of marriage as a covenant. This was no mere matter of nomenclature. If one insists that the term "contract" is an essential predicate in the definition of marriage, one cannot also understand it under the biblical model. The latter is not a contract because in the strict sense a contract involves an exchange of goods or rights by the contractants, and their acceptance of reciprocal obligations. To insist that in the biblical model God and Israel literally exchanged rights and accepted obligations is absurd. God the creator cannot be obligated.

There is a Christian variant of the same religious anomaly. If the marriage of two Christians is a contract, and if the sacrament is the contract "elevated"—and if Christian marriage is a sacrament in that the husband-wife relationship images that of Christ and the Church—one must conclude that the latter relationship is contractual, that Christ is under obligation to the Church. This too is absurd. About the revising subcommission's referring to marriage as a contract, in this canon and elsewhere, the Canon Law Society of America had the following to say.

The draft repeatedly refers to the marriage as a "contract." This is contrary to Vatican II as well as to the traditional sources of faith. These have used such terms as "covenant," "communion," etc. In fact, Vatican II uses a variety of terms precisely because no one term adequately expresses the richness of the mystery of marriage. It might be better to use no category but simply refer to *matrimonium*. The issue is not simply a matter of terminology. The "contract" emphasis colors the draft's entire approach to marriage. The sacrament appears to be more of a juridical entity than a theological-pastoral one.[103]

The second part of the disagreement was an inference from the first, namely that if any and every marriage of two baptized persons is a sacrament, the sufficient cause of this must be that both of the spouses are baptized. In other words, no more is needed in the Christian spouses to make their marriage a sacrament than that they have been baptized. On this point the American group voiced one of its most trenchant criticisms.

An area of profound theological-canonical investigation today is the identity of the sacrament and every marriage relationship among the baptized. . . . This identity is a fundamental principle underlying the draft. Yet such automatic sacramentality of marriage among the baptized is questioned because of a renewed sense of the sacraments as actions of faith within the Church. . . . In Aquinas and other medieval theologians there was a strong sense of a real distinction between marriage as an *officium naturae* [a dutiful office of nature] and marriage as a *sacramentum novae legis* [a sacrament of the new law]. This issue of automatic sacramentality needs further study, wider consultation and authentic teaching by the College of Bishops before it is "frozen" into new law.[104]

Enough of the cardinal members of the supervising *plenarium* meeting in the last week of May 1977 shared the judgment of the American canonists to order the subcommission to rewrite this canon according to the mind of Vatican II and its *Gaudium et spes*. The latter group completed the rewriting, by early February 1978, of not only this canon but of all those treating of marriage.

The result was that the reformulation, both in its first form of 1978 as new Canon 242 and in its definitive form as Canon 1055, yielded on one point to the criticism coming from both the *plenarium* and the Canon Law Society of America, but resisted on the second point, which was criticized unanimously only by the Americans. The ground yielded is evident in the wording of Canon 1055 above. The noun *contractus* does not appear in paragraph 1, which intends an informal definition of marriage. But the biblical term "covenant" (*foedus*), which appears to have replaced it, does not function in the new canon as "contract" did in the old Canon 1012. There it referred to the marriage itself. In the new canon it refers not to that, but to the act by which the partners create the marriage. The new term replacing "contract" is "partnership" (*consortium*). This is what the covenant, the act, creates. This is the marriage. And it is a partnership in all of life (*totius vitae*).

But immediately an inconsistency appears within this first paragraph. Where its last clause designates what Christ has raised to the dignity of a sacrament, this is not the partnership but the covenant. Whether this means that the partnership and the covenant are one and the same is not clear. But either of these designates a human relationship far more available than a contract to be the matrix of the sacrament.

A second inconsistency appears in paragraph 2 of this Canon 1055 as the term "contract" reappears. This is the paragraph about which the American protest was futile. It remains unchanged from its formulation as old canon 1012, paragraph 2. After having called marriage both a partnership and a covenant in paragraph 1—and having done this as a mandated correction of originally calling it a contract—the subcommission here again calls the marriage a contract. It also says explicitly that this is what is the sacrament in all Christian marriages.

In this same Canon 1055 there is a most significant change from a doctrinal point of law that had been in old Canon 1013, paragraph 1. The latter named the two traditional ends of marriage, procreation and nurture, as primary, and the double secondary end, the mutual help of the spouses and the remedying of their concupiscence.

Canon 1055, paragraph 1 not only does not reassert this ranking of the two ends of marriage; it does not even mention ends. It says instead that marriage is oriented of its nature to both the good of the spouses and to procreation and nurture. Where mutual help was, in Canon 1013, a secondary end of marriage and unessential to it, now in Canon 1055 the two orientations are equal in value, are intimately associated and can even converge into one. What is implied by "the good of the spouses" is all that Pius XII, *Gaudium et spes* and *Humanae vitae* said about marriage as a man-woman relationship modeled on God's creative love and Christ's redemptive love.

Old Canon 1013, paragraph 2 is repeated in new Canon 1056 without change: "The essential properties of marriage are unity and indissolubility, which in Christian marriage obtain a special firmness in virtue of the sacrament."

The unity of marriage designates monogamy. These canons say explicitly that this is of the essence of marriage; they say implicitly that a marriage cannot be polygamous. But we recall that "essential" has had a qualified meaning among Catholic canonists and many theologians. For them it designates not the fixed and irreducible nature of a thing, in the way that "rational animal" designates the nature of a human being. It designates rather what God wills a thing to be—what God wills a marriage to be. In this sense of "essential" God could will the patriarchs of Israel to have polygamous marriages as a justifiable exception to the law of nature. That this essential unity of a marriage obtains "a special firmness" in virtue of the sacrament is a theological inference. Because Christ has and can have the Church as his only spouse, so the Christian marriage, which is an earthly image of the Christ-Church divine marriage, can have only one pair of spouses. The question whether the essential properties of marriage the sacrament are to be understood in the same way as those of marriage the human relationship, so that God can make an exception to its *special* firmness and permit a polygamous sacramental marriage, has never been addressed by the authorities.

Indissolubility as an essential property of marriage is understood in the same way. The term designates not a fixed characteristic of marriage the human relationship, but the will of God for marriage. And in the case of marriage it is the will of God interpreted by the supreme ecclesiastical authority. Thus, as we saw Duns Scotus say (in Chapter 9), God can will some marriages to be dissoluble, or all marriages to be such, since indissolubility is only a secondarily essential characteristic of marriage.

We know by now the ground for the claim that the sacrament gives a special firmness to this natural indissolubility, makes it really indissoluble. Because the relationship of Christ and the Church is indestructible, it *makes* the marriage of two Christians to be the same—except for death. As we have seen, it is not that the divine indissolubility merely imposes an obligation on Christian spouses not to dissolve their marriages. Its valence is not merely deontological. Rather, it makes the dissolution of such marriages impossible. Its valence is ontological.

We know also of the added qualification. The indissolubility becomes radical, it takes hold, only when the sacramental marriage is consummated by sexual intercourse. The explanation for this we saw in sources as early as the twelfth century: Although the marriage of two Christians in itself images the union of Christ and the Church, while still unconsummated it images only Christ's union with the members of the Church in grace, a union which can be dissolved by the latters' sins. But once consummated the Christian marriage images Christ's union in human nature with the Church, a union which is indestructible.

One more canon that mentions the sacrament explicitly deserves attention, as does one more that only implies it. New Canon 1134 states: "From a valid marriage arises a bond between the spouses which by its very nature is perpetual and exclusive; furthermore in a Christian marriage the spouses are strengthened and, as it were, consecrated for the duties and the dignity of their state by a special sacrament." This differs from old Canon 1110 in its second clause. There it was "a Christian marriage confers grace on spouses provided they place no obstacle to it."

Insofar as the second clause of Canon 1134 names the effects of the sacrament, it does so incompletely. The sacrament may indeed strengthen the spouses for their marital duties and consecrate them (perhaps "ordain" or "commission" would be a better term), provided they accept and work with God's action in the sacrament. But all we have read in this chapter and before suggests that the sacrament has effects deeper and more abiding than this. As Hugh of St. Victor urged in the twelfth century, a main effect of the sacrament is to join the spouses in an extraordinarily powerful self-giving love. Again, insofar as the clause tells what the sacramental gracing effects in the spouses, it seems to confine this within the ancient limitation that the marital sacrament brings only "secondary graces," those that a later terminology calls "actual graces."

It is paragraph 2 of Canon 1057 that implies something of consequence about the sacrament while not naming it explicitly. Its paragraph 1 names the kind of personal act that creates a marriage. This is the reciprocal consent of a man and a woman who are qualified to consent and do so legitimately, i.e. in the form required by law. This is synonymous with old Canon 1081, paragraph 2. New Canon 1057.2 tells more exactly the kind of consent that creates a marriage—tells by which of his or her faculties a person exercises immediate agency of consent, and what the object of this consent is.

> Matrimonial consent is an act of the will by which a man and a woman, through an irrevocable covenant, mutually give and accept each other in order to establish marriage.

The second clause in this paragraph contains one of the most significant changes in the Catholic teaching on marriage that has come from *Gaudium et spes.* Old Canon 1081 said that by their mutual consent the parties give and accept each other's "right to the body" (for sexual intercourse). This was the object of a consent and exchange assumed to be contractual. But here in Canon 1057.2—after having in Canon 1055.2 digressed momentarily to marriage as a contract—the law turns in formulation back to the covenant. It predicates the term "covenant" now not of the marriage itself, not of that which is created by the mutual consent. It refers the term rather to the parties' consent itself. Both covenant, or their consents together constitute a covenanting.

But what the paragraph names most significantly is what the parties exchange in their covenanting. This is their very persons. Not only does each give his or her person over to the other, but each accepts the other.

The relevance to the sacrament of such a covenantal exchange is obvious. First but less importantly, the new canon corrects a serious anomaly in the old law. It took for granted the traditional teaching that because for Christians the contract is the sacrament, the act of consent which creates the contract also creates the sacrament. And this consent was said to create the marriage by the parties' granting to one another the right over their capacity for sexual intercourse. The anomaly lay in the logical consequence that this juridical exchange of sexual rights must be all that is needed to create the sacrament, the human image of Christ's love.

But the more serious relevance of this paragraph to the sacrament is that it finally names in the law a kind of consent proportioned to and worthy of the sacrament, and capable of creating it. For Christian love that is sacramental, whether within marriage or outside it, must reenact in some way the kind of love Christ had and has for his people. This was and is wholly accepting of them, with all their weakness and meanness. It was and is wholly self-giving to them—not despite their weakness and meanness, but because being weak and mean they needed and still need his forgiveness and his strength to come back to life.

Summary

The main magisterial statements on marriage in the nineteenth century were still apologetic in intent however doctrinal in formulation. They were directed against the secularist claim that marriage is a mere human invention, that the sacrament in turn is no more than churchmen's invention, and that even Christians can, if they choose, create for themselves a non-sacramental, secular marriage. The fullest of these statements in the century was Pope Leo XIII's encyclical letter of 1880, *Arcanum divinae sapientiae.* In it Leo reclaimed all marriage for Christ. He insisted that the latter had restored it to its primeval dignity after four millennia of men's degrading it from the excellence it had had in the garden of Eden.

The first of the major twentieth-century documents was Pope Pius XI's encyclical letter of 1930, *Casti connubii.* The abuses of marriage it listed and excoriated were those that had been noted in *Arcanum,* but which had been multiplied and exacerbated by the massive moral disillusionment in Europe following World War I. Pius' most valuable contribution beyond that of *Arcanum* was to attempt in fuller detail an anthropology of marriage, and thus to begin to enrich the sacrament in its human matrix. In a crucial clause he claimed that men and women create their marriages by making to one another a self-donation of their persons. He also claimed a place for the spouses' love in their ministering the marital sacrament to one another. He brought the human and the divine elements in the sacrament closer together than any of his predecessors had ever done.

The Catholic Church's first codification of its law, in its canons on marriage, gathered in and systematized much of the centuries' legislation for marriage along with a small but significant element of its theology. The first canon on marriage (1012) claimed the historical fact that

Christ had made marriage for all time among all the baptized a sacrament of his new law.

In several discourses to newlyweds during the first three years of his pontificate Pope Pius XII continued Pius XI's work of enriching the matrix of the sacrament. More than ever before in papal teaching he sought to draw from the experience of marriage a portrait of authentic marital love. He insisted that Christian spouses can be for one another instruments of God's love, that reciprocally they can direct their love for God through their love for one another. But here Pius cautioned against thinking even sacramental marriage superior to consecrated virginity. He reasoned that marriage interposes another human being between a spouse and his or her love of God. This keeps the commitment to God short of the unhindered self-donation possible in consecrated virginity. He added that a main part of this limitation is the bodiliness of marital love and the residue in it of original sin. He reasoned that accordingly marital love can reach its perfection only with the death of one of the spouses, when the widowed spouse can love the deceased as the Church loves Christ who is departed and risen from death. Moreover, since Christian love is essentially sacrificial, marital love can reach its perfection only when death brings the spouses to sacrifice the physical immediacy of their love. Logically then Pius implied that the perfection of sacramental marital love can be gained only when the spouses are no longer capable of the specifically marital expression that the bishops of Vatican II were to call the fullness of this love's expression.

In their *Pastoral Constitution on the Church in the Modern World* the bishops of the Second Vatican Council enriched the theology of marriage by enriching further the matrix of the sacrament. They included the best of Pius XII's teaching. They also innovated. They refused to call marriage a contract or to say that it is created by the spouses' contractual exchange. They insisted on the model of the biblical covenant. The spouses create their marriage by covenanting, by exchanging gifts, by committing their persons to one another for a sharing in all of life and love. The bishops' most striking innovation was their refusal to continue the doctrinal claim that procreation and nurture are marriage's primary end.

The bishops relocated the place of the sacrament in Christian marriages. It is not precisely the taken-for-granted imaging of the Christ-Church relationship. It is rather the spouses' self-giving love for one another. The bishops also redefined the grace of the sacrament. It is not so much secondary or helping grace, that which enables the spouses to fulfill their duties and resist sin against their marriage. It is primary, sanctifying grace, that which joins them with God.

The place of children in marriage is that they are the natural fruit of its love. They too participate in the marital sacrament by disclosing the nature of God's love, which is essentially creative, a love of life.

Pope Paul VI wrote his encyclical letter, *Humanae vitae,* mainly to reassert the Church's proscription of artificial birth control. But in offering the demands of marital love as a new rationale for this proscription he contributed his own enrichment of the matrix of the sacrament. He insisted that this love is and must be essentially fruitful because God who awakens and animates it in the spouses does so with his own essentially fruitful love. Indeed the spouses' fruitful love is evidence, is a sacrament of the inseparability of love and fruitfulness in God's action in the world and in their marriage.

The 1980 synod of bishops on the family, and Pope John Paul II's exhortation in the following year, *Familiaris consortio,* are unique in acknowledging that the inclusion of married Christians' experience and understanding of their sacrament is essential for the theology of this sacrament. The synod's and Paul's central theme and thesis were that God has called all human beings into unity in the sharing of his divine life. Because God is essentially an act of love he is essentially generative of life in the divine Son and the Spirit. This same creative love has produced the human race and draws human beings together. Therefore their essential condition is by his intention one of love.

This condition is realized most vividly in marriage, because in order to be creative, human love, because it is embodied, must be sexual. And in marriage this condition is realized most especially in family. The marital sacrament in its fullest expression and in its primary meaning is life in family.

The exceptional value of the bishops' discourses and of John Paul's exhortation is their analysis, in the light of that comprehensive thesis, of the lived experience of marriage. And the value within this value lies in their understanding (explained by Cardinal Joseph Bernardin) that the pain and the crises of marital intimacy can constitute a sacrament of Christ's love that redeemed by his death and resurrection.

The African bishops' contribution to the synod, and potentially to the expanding and deepening theology of marriage, was to explain the forming of marriages among their peoples as a multi-step process involving the two extended parental families—a process that is completed, or consummated, only in the birth of the first child.

The revision of the Code of Canon Law in 1983—and within it the revision of the Catholic marriage law—incorporated some of Vatican II's teaching about marriage but rejected or was at least indecisive about parts of it. It first called marriage a covenant (*foedus*) instead of a contract, as did *Gaudium et spes,* but then claimed that it is the marital contract, not the covenant, that Christ made the sacrament. It said that what the spouses create by their consents is not a communion, a sharing (as *Gaudium et spes* said), but a *consortium,* a partnership.

The point of revision most relevant to the theology of the sacrament was the new Code's identification of that which the spouses exchange in the covenantal commitment by which they create their marriage. They give to one another the gifts of their entire persons. Each gives the entire self to the other; each accepts the self of the other.

NOTES

1. Denzinger-Schönmetzer, n. 2965, p. 583.
2. *Ibid.*, n. 2966.
3. *Ibid.*, n. 2973.
4. In M.J. Byrnes, *Papal Teaching: Matrimony*, p. 125.
5. In Byrnes, *op. cit.*, pp. 126–127.
6. The letter is published in *Acta Sanctae Sedis*, Vol. 12 (1879), pp. 385ff. The title of this official organ of the Apostolic See changed in 1909 to *Acta Apostolicae Sedis*. It is in English translation in Byrnes, *op. cit.*, pp. 132–165.
7. *Acta Sanctae Sedis*, p. 386.
8. *Loc. cit.*, p. 388.
9. *Loc. cit.*, p. 389.
10. *Loc. cit.*, p. 392.
11. *Ibid.*, pp. 393–394.
12. *Ibid.*, p. 394.
13. The letter is in *Acta Apostolicae Sedis*, Vol. 22 (1930), pp. 539–592. It is in English translation in Byrnes, *op. cit.*, pp. 219–291.
14. *Acta Apostolicae Sedis*, pp. 539–543.
15. *Op. cit.*, p. 541.
16. *Loc. cit.*, pp. 542–543.
17. Book 9, Chapter 7, Par. 12.
18. *Acta Apostolicae Sedis*, p. 543.
19. *Op. cit.*, p. 547.
20. *Ibid.*, p. 548.
21. *Op. cit.*, p. 551.
22. *Ibid.*, p. 552.
23. *Loc. cit.*, p. 554.
24. *Ibid.*, pp. 555–556.
25. Canon 1084 of the 1917 Code provides for this: "Simple error (*simplex error*) concerning marriage's unity or indissolubility, or concerning its sacramental dignity, does not invalidate the marital consent, even if the consent is made in consideration of the error."
26. From the author's *Marriage in the Catholic Church*, Volume 1, *What Is Marriage?*
27. M.J. Byrnes' *Papal Teachings: Matrimony* quotes from such discourses given on May 24, 1939; July 12, 1939; November 8, 1939; December 6, 1939; January 17, 1940; June 26, 1940; July 3, 1940; October 23, 1940; January 15, 1941; January 29, 1941; March 5, 1941; March 19, 1941; August 13, 1941; August 20, 1941; March 18, 1942; April 22, 1942; and April 29, 1942. After the last date here Pius' discourses were directed to various national and international associations and to such Catholic groups as the Roman Rota and the clergy of Rome.
28. Discourse to newlyweds, July 12, 1939 (in M.J. Byrnes, *op. cit.*, pp. 303–304).
29. Discourse to newlyweds, January 15, 1941 (in M.J. Byrnes, *op. cit.*, pp. 316–317).

30. Discourse to newlyweds, March 5, 1941 (in M.J. Byrnes, *op. cit.*, pp. 319–320). The same reasoning is in his discourse to parish priests and Lenten preachers of Rome, February 17, 1945 (*op. cit.*, pp. 359–360).

31. In discourses to newlyweds on August 13, 1941 (*op. cit.*, p. 330); on April 22, 1942 (*op. cit.*, pp. 342–343); on April 29, 1942 (*op. cit.*, pp. 346–347).

32. Canon 10 of this session reads as follows: "If anyone should say that the married state is to be held superior to that of virginity or of celibacy, and that it is not better and more holy to remain in virginity or celibacy than to marry, let him be anathema" (in Denzinger-Schönmetzer, n. 980, p. 1810).

33. Discourse to hospital nuns, April 24, 1957 (in Byrnes, *op. cit.*, p. 496). Pius had advanced the same thought three years earlier in his encyclical letter, *Sacra virginitas* (quoted in *op. cit.*, pp. 464–473).

24. Encyclical letter, *Sacra virginitas*, March 25, 1942 (*op. cit.*, p. 470).

35. For an explanation of this thesis see Volume 1, *What Is Marriage?*, Chapter 4, "The Fathers of the Church and the Defense of Marriage," and the development and fixing of the thesis, in Chapter 5, "Augustine on the Nature of Marriage."

36. In Byrnes, *op. cit.*, pp. 498–499.

37. *Op. cit.*, pp. 499–500.

38. *Ibid.*, pp. 498–499.

39. *Op. cit.*, p. 315.

40. *Ibid.*

41. *Op. cit.*, p. 319.

42. In Michael Chinigo, editor, *The Pope Speaks: The Teachings of Pope Pius XII*, N.Y., 1957, p. 24.

43. *Op. cit.*, p. 36.

44. In *Pastoral Constitution on the Church in the Modern World*, Part II, Chapter 1, no. 49. The Latin original of this passage is this: "Talis amor, humana simul et divina consocians, coniuges ad liberum et mutuum sui ipsius donum, tenero affectu et opere probatum, conducit totamque vitam eorum pervadit; immo ipse generosa sua operositate perficitur et crescit. . . . Haec dilectio proprio matrimonii opere singulariter exprimitur et efficitur."
It would be difficult to determine if there is important meaning in the replacing of *amor* at the beginning of this excerpt by *dilectio* as the subject of the last sentence. In classical vocabulary *amor* bespeaks self-seeking passion, while *dilectio* is generous seeking for the happiness of the beloved.
The adverb *singulariter* in the last sentence indicates not that marital love is expressed exclusively in intercourse, but that it is expressed there most typically and richly.

45. This is the title by which the *Pastoral Constitution on the Church in the Modern World* is popularly known. The constitution is in English translation in *The Documents of Vatican II*, Walter M. Abbott, S.J., General Editor, N.Y., 1966, pp. 199–308. The authorized publication of the constitution is in *Sacrosanctum Oecumenicum Concilium Vaticanum II, Constitutiones, Decreta, Declarationes*, Typis Polyglottis Vaticanis, 1966, pp. 681–835.

46. No. 50, *op. cit.*, p. 254.

47. The pertintent paragraphs of this discourse are in Byrnes, *op. cit.*, pp. 426–427.

48. No. 47, *op. cit.*, p. 249.

49. No. 48, *ibid.*, p. 250.

50. No. 49, *ibid.*, p. 253.
51. No. 50, *ibid.*, p. 255.
52. No. 48, *ibid.*, p. 250.
53. No. 48, *ibid.*, p. 251.
54. No. 49, *ibid.*, p. 253.
55. No. 48, *ibid.*, pp. 250–251.
56. *Ibid.*, p. 251.
57. *Ibid.*
58. No. 48, *ibid.*, p. 251.
59. *Ibid.*, p. 252.
60. These sources are listed in note 165, p. 252 of the English translation.
61. No. 49, *ibid.*, pp. 252–253.
62. *Ibid.*
63. A translation of the encyclical in English is *Encyclical of Pope Paul VI, Humanae Vitae, on the Regulation of Birth.* Glen Rock et al., 1968. The authorized Latin publication is in *Acta Apostolicae Sedis,* Vol. 60 (1968), pp. 481–503.
64. Paul never intended that *Humanae vitae* be a final statement about marriage, sexuality and procreation. About two weeks after publishing the encyclical he said that it does no more than clarify a fundamental chapter in the personal, married, family and social life of men and women; but it is not a complete treatise about men and women in this sphere of marriage, family and their moral probity. He added that this is an immense field to which the Church's *magisterium* could and perhaps should return with a fuller, more organic and more systematic exposition. This statement is recorded in *Origins,* Vol. 10, no. 17, p. 265.
65. Par. 7, *op. cit.*, p. 7.
66. Par. 8, *ibid.*, p. 8.
67. Par. 12, *op. cit.*, p. 10.
68. Paul did not skirt this difficulty: "These acts . . . do not cease to be lawful if, for causes independent of the will of the husband and wife, they are foreseen to be infertile, since they are always oriented to expressing and strengthening their union. In fact, as experience bears witness, not every marital act is followed by new life. God has wisely disposed natural laws and rhythms of fertility which of themselves bring about a spacing of births" (*ibid.,* par. 11, p. 9). But in one sense Paul does miss the point. The question here is not whether infertile intercourse is lawful but whether it is marital.

His solution creates more difficulties. How can a couple leave their intercourse open to conception when they know conception is impossible? Since, when conception is impossible, the strengthening of union by itself keeps intercourse morally good (as he insists), where is the inseparability of the two meanings? Since God and human nature intend the infertility of some and even most acts of intercourse, again where is the natural inseparability of their two meanings?
69. Par. 8, *op. cit.*, p. 7.
70. Par. 25, *op. cit.*, p. 18.
71. Par. 9, *op. cit.*, p. 7.
72. See Aristotle's *History of Animals,* Book 9, Chapter 1, and his *Nicomachean Ethics,* Book 8, Chapter 12.
73. Par. 9, *op. cit.*, p. 8.
74. *Ibid.*
75. Par 7, *op. cit.*, p. 8.

76. *On the Family,* Apostolic Exhortation, *Familiaris Consortio,* of His Holiness Pope John Paul II . . . Regarding the Role of the Christian Family in the Modern World, Washington, D.C., 1982, p. 2, par. 2.

77. *Op. cit.,* Part One, par. 4, p. 3.

78. In *Origins,* Vol. 10, no. 17, p. 259.

79. *Loc. cit.,* no. 18, p. 276.

80. *Op. cit.,* par. 11, p. 9.

81. *Ibid.*

82. The first discourse is in *Origins,* Vol. 10, no. 17, pp. 260–262; the second in Vol. 10, no. 18, pp. 286–288. It is titled "Toward a Spirituality of Marital Intimacy." The first discourse was delivered at the synod; the second was not, but was included in its *acta.*

83. They are published in *l'Osservatore Romano* of November 19, 1979, of November 26, 1979, and of January 7 and 21, 1980.

84. In *Origins,* Vol. 10, no. 17, p. 261.

85. *Op. cit.,* p. 9.

86. In *Origins, loc. cit.,* p. 287.

87. In *Origins,* Vol. 10, no. 20, pp. 317–318.

88. In *Origins,* Vol. 10, no. 18, pp. 280–282.

89. *Ibid.,* p. 281.

90. In *Origins,* Vol. 10, no. 17, p. 259.

91. This discourse, delivered on October 1, was titled "The Impact of Abortion"; in *Origins,* Vol. 10, no. 18, pp. 283–285.

92. This is an important part of the synod's summary closing "Message to Christian Families"; in *Origins,* Vol. 10, no. 21, pp. 321–323.

93. *Op. cit.,* p. 324.

94. This paper is studied in detail in Jan Grootaers' and Joseph Selling's volume, *The 1980 Synod of Bishops "On the Role of the Family,"* Bibliotheca Ephemeridum Theologicarum Lovaniensium LXIV, Leuven (Louvain), 1983, pp. 31–34.

95. *Op. cit.,* p. 31.

96. *Ibid.*

97. *Ibid.*

98. *Ibid.,* p. 32.

99. *Ibid.,* p. 33.

100. *Ibid.*

101. *Op. cit.,* pp. 90–91.

102. The English version of this and the other canons quoted from the 1983 revision are taken from *The Code of Canon Law, A Text and Commentary,* Commissioned by the Canon Law Society of America, N.Y./Mahwah, 1985.

103. In "Report of the Special Committee of the Task Force of the Canon Law Society of America on the Proposed *Schema Documenti Pontificii Qua Disciplina Canonica de Sacramentis Recognoscitur*" (unpublished document).

104. *Ibid.*

The subcommission that had drafted the revised marriage canons reacted to this criticism casually. How it proposed to deal with these and seven other comprehensive criticisms of its *schema* of revision is explained in this way:

> The consultors [in the subcommission] made some comment on each of the general issues touched [in the criticisms], but determined to make

no decisions of a general nature because of them, since these criticisms have come from only a very few of the groups reviewing the *schema,* while on the contrary the majority of them was pleased with it. The consultors will keep these general criticisms in mind so that when examining individual canons they may propose changes in them—if such proposals they have—which may take the criticisms into consideration. (In *Communicationes,* Vol. 9.1 1977, pp. 118–119)

BIBLIOGRAPHY

Pastoral Constitution on the Church in the Modern World (*Gaudium et Spes*), Part II, Some Problems of Special Urgency, Chapter 1, "Fostering the Nobility of Marriage and the Family," in *The Documents of Vatican II,* Walter M. Abbott, S.J., General Editor, N.Y., Herder and Herder/ Association Press, 1966.

Papal Teaching: Matrimony. Selected and Arranged by the Benedictine Monks of Solesmes, translated by Michael J. Byrnes. Boston, St. Paul Editions, 1963.

Pope Paul VI: *Encyclical of Pope Paul VI, Humanae Vitae, On the Regulation of Birth. . .* Glen Rock, N.J. et al., Paulist Press, 1968.

Pope John Paul II: *On the Family: Apostolic Exhortation, Familiaris Consortio, of His Holiness, Pope John Paul II.* Washington, D.C., United States Catholic Conference, 1982.

Dominian, Jack: "Vatican II and Marriage," in *Clergy Review,* Vol. 52 (1967), pp. 19–35.

Durkin, Mary G.: *Feast of Love: Pope John Paul on Human Intimacy.* Chicago, Loyola University Press, 1983.

Grootaers, Jan and Selling, Joseph: *The 1980 Synod of Bishops, On the Role of the Family: An Exposition of the Event and an Analysis of Its Texts.* Leuven, Leuven University Press, 1983.

Hogan, Richard and LeVoir, John M.: *Covenant of Love: Pope John Paul II on Sexuality, Marriage and the Family in the Modern World.* Garden City, Doubleday and Co., 1985.

Mackin, Theodore: "The Theology of Marriage in *Humanae Vitae,*" in *Thought,* Vol. 46 (1971), pp. 213–226.

———: "Conjugal Love and the Magisterium," in *The Jurist,* Volume 36 (1976), pp. 263–301.

McHugh, Joseph, editor: *Marriage in the Light of Vatican II,* Washington, D.C., United States Catholic Conference, 1968.

Coleman, Gerald: "Marriage: The Vision of Humanae Vitae," in *Thought,* Vol. 58 (1983), pp. 18–34.

Huizing, Peter: "Canonical Implications of the Conception of Marriage in the Conciliar Constitution, *Gaudium et Spes,*" in *Commitment to Partnership: Explorations of the Theology of Marriage,* edited by William P. Roberts, Mahwah, N.J., Paulist Press, 1987.

13. THEOLOGIANS AND THE SACRAMENT IN THE NINETEENTH AND TWENTIETH CENTURIES

When we turn to the theologians of this period—a period extending from just before the middle of the nineteenth century until the Second Vatican Council—it will help to remind ourselves yet again how history has compelled the theological enterprise.

In the sixteenth century the Protestant reformers denied that Christ has made marriage a sacrament in the new law—not, at least, a sacrament of the same kind as baptism and the Eucharist. So Bellarmine and the other theologians of the Catholic counter-reformation labored to demonstrate that Christ had indeed done so, and to this labor added the task of explaining what Christ had done to the natural marital relationship to make it his sacrament.

Less than a century later the Jansenists, and a century after them the Royalists, Febronians and Josephists, drove the Catholic theologians back to the same task—but via a different path. As we have seen at considerable length, they did not deny that in Christian marriage a sacrament is available. But in their zeal to take the marriages of Europe's and its colonies' Catholics under civil jurisdiction, they insisted that where the marriage of two Christians has the sacrament, it has it only very briefly, or only as a feebly attached adornment. They insisted that the sacrament is no more than the officiating priest's blessing, given within the wedding ceremony or outside it. Assuming the settled Catholic teaching that the marriage is the parties' contract, and that they themselves create the contract, it followed logically that they do not create the sacrament, and that the sacrament is separable from the contract—their marriage. Where, thanks to the priest's blessing, a Catholic marriage does have the sacrament, nothing is done internally to the contract to make it sacramental. It is not elevated to the status and power of a grace-giving sign or image. Again, the sacrament is the priest's blessing. And if this stays in the marriage in any way, it is only as an external adornment.

With contract and sacrament thus separated, it must follow that the contract, a civil agreement and bond, is rightly governed by civil authority even in the marriages of Catholics, while the ecclesiastical authorities may have custody of the blessing and whichever religious ceremonies provide its setting.

Thus it became the duty of the Catholic authorities to deny this separability and to assert the intrinsic unity of the marital contract and the sacrament. But to the theologians was delivered a vastly more complex and difficult task. In its several parts the task was the following. With Catholic doctrine set for them as their assumption, the theologians had to explain how it is that when not only Roman Catholics but all the baptized pronounce their wedding vows, they create not only their contract but their sacrament. They had to explain how it is that the contract and the sacrament are inseparable, so that creating the contract automatically creates the sacrament—to the point that either both are created or neither is created.

The theologians' task was not eased by the ancient inherited theology of the sacrament, but was troubled by it and made precarious. It is central to this theology that a sacrament is a sacred sign, a sensate manifestation of an invisible sacred reality. This reality was identified exactly. We have read again and again that it is the indestructible love relationship of Christ and his Church.

This being so, the theologians had to answer three sets of interlocked questions. First, what is there in the character of the natural marital contract that disposes it, that makes it available to become a sign of exactly this sacred reality? And presuming it can be shown that the contract has in itself this disposition, what is done to it, in this disposition, to make it the sacrament, to make it a manifestation of the love relationship of Christ and the Church?

The second set of questions came not from the inherited theology, but from its collision with a sad fact of Catholic history. By no means all Catholics have been aware that their marriages are meant to be sacraments. Of those who have been aware, millions have barely understood this or have cared little about it. And if this unconcern has ruled casually in the minds of millions of Catholics, whose Church teaches that their marriages are sacraments, it has been the product of a doctrinal stand for all Protestant Christians for four and a half centuries. Nevertheless the Catholic authorities have insisted that provided these unconcerned or disaffected or disagreeing Christians do not expressly reject their marriages' sacramentality, the marriages are sacraments in the rich sense of the traditional theology.

Hence the second set of questions: How is it that despite the unconcern of a Christian man and woman, despite the void in their lives of faith and love, their marriage is nevertheless a sacrament? And given the fact that in every sacrament there must be the essential component that is its matrix; given too that in the sacrament of marriage the matrix is the human relationship created by the spouses' consent, is there nothing that even unconcerned and disaffected Christians must contribute to the creating of their sacrament? Nothing in the domain of consent? Nothing sacred that may enter into the imaging of Christ's love relationship with his Church?

Lodged just as clearly and emphatically in the traditional theology is the claim that each sacrament is an instrument of God's gracing, a means of holiness for those who participate in it. This breeds the third set of questions, again about religiously unconcerned and disaffected Christian spouses. How can it be maintained that these spouses participate in the sacrament of marriage, a means to Christian holiness, while bringing to the participation an unconcern not only for the sacrament but for holiness in any form? The cutting edge of that question is sharpened by the Catholic doctrinal determination that the minister of the sacrament of marriage is not the officiating bishop, priest or deacon, but the spouses themselves. They do not "receive" this sacrament. They are its agents; they create it. (The clergyman no more than officiates and witnesses.) Therefore they are also in some sense the agents of the holiness that is gained in the sacrament. But how can Christian men and women be such agents who have at best no interest in holiness, or even an express disdain of it?

It will help our examination of the answers to these questions worked out by the Catholic theologians of the modern era if we take them up at about the midpoint of the nineteenth century or just before. Backing up to this point and then working forward to the 1960's will enable us to see development and enrichment. This will also turn up evidence of the ongoing influence of the official Catholic teaching on the theology, and even more, one may suspect, of the influence of the theology on the official teaching.

Traditional Theology in the Nineteenth Century

We begin with the French theologian, J. Martin (1792–1859), who published in 1844 his two-volume *De matrimonio et potestate ipsum dirimendi Ecclesiae soli exclusive subiecta* [On Marriage and the Power To Annul It Reserved Exclusively to the Church].

The thesis announced in this title is aimed, of course, at the claim by secular authorities in the Western world that they too, as well as ecclesiastical authorities, have the authority to declare presumed marriages to be null, and even to dissolve them. Martin denied this claim. He insisted, in refutation, that such authority belongs exclusively to the Catholic Church. He justified this claim by his way of interpreting the relationship between the natural marriage contract and the sacrament. And for this interpretation he alleged a fact that has been crucial in one strand of Christian thought since its earlier generations. It is that all marriages—not only all marriages of Christians, but all marriages in the history of the human race—have been taken up into the work of salvation begun by Christ. Christ himself declared this through the mouth of Adam (whom Martin considered the actual first human being). For Adam was a pre-figure, a type, of Christ. In Adam's declaring his union with his wife, Eve, to be indestructible, he was in effect Christ declaring his union with his bride the Church to be indestructible.

But all men and women in the Church are united with Christ. Their lives are lived in union with him; their marriages belong to him. This means the marriages themselves, the marital contracts. It is the Christian spouses' union with Christ that makes their marriages sacraments. Adam's words, spoken for Christ, brought it about that every rightly contracted marriage images, is related to, and continues the marriage of Christ and the Church.

> Therefore the words that Christ spoke through Adam, his type and image [*figura*], reveal and establish at one and the same time two marriages. One of these is the marriage of man and woman that is to be celebrated throughout history. The other is the marriage that is revealed in that first marriage as in its type, the divine marriage of Christ and the Church. This was to be created and lived out as one marriage in all of time. This marriage of Christ and the Church is to be imaged, signified and continued in every marriage that is rightly entered. . . .[1]

The Roman theologian, Giovanni Perrone (1794–1876) got at the issue by challenging Melchior Cano's old thesis that the minister of the sacrament of marriage is the witnessing priest. He pointed out that this interpretation allows the separation of marital contract and sacrament, since for centuries before the Council of Trent's decree, *Tametsi*, the Church had accepted as valid the marriages of Catholics contracted secretly, before no witnessing priest. Obviously if the priest were the minister of the sacrament, these marriages already for centuries accepted by the Church as valid would be only natural contracts.

Perrone denied this separability. He insisted, in scholastic terms, that the *materia* of the sacrament, its determinable element, is not the contract qua civil, but the natural contract. The sacrament, in turn, does not come to the natural contract as something subsequent and added. Rather the very act of the spouses creating the contract creates the sacrament, in a way analogously as the washing with water accomplishes the baptism in that sacrament. Contract and sacrament are distinct, but distinct not as two things, rather as two formalities of one thing, the marriage.[2]

Domenico Palmieri

During the last year of his tenure as professor of dogmatic theology at the Gregorian University the Jesuit, Domenico Palmieri, completed his *De Matrimonio Christiano*.[3] The volume is not a noteworthy contribution to the theology of the sacrament. But it holds in concentrate the teaching of the time. It also points unwittingly to a problem about the relationship of contract and sacrament that was not to fix attention until almost a century later. The problem arises from the Catholic authorities' insisting that in a sacramental marriage the sacrament is not a distinct and separable adjunct to the contract, but is the contract itself elevated to grace-giving capacity. But is a contract—is the marital contract as it was interpreted in 1880—itself amenable to being made a grace-giving image of Christ's love for his people? If one insists on the contractual nature of marriage, does one inescapably condition one's understanding of the sacrament? If so, is the conditioning compatible with the New Testament understanding of Christian marriage whence the sacramentality is drawn?

Palmieri repeated the commonplaces of his time. In Christian marriage the contract and the sacrament are inseparable, not as two distinct entities which need to exist together in order to exist at all, but as one and the same reality showing distinct formalities within itself.

Since among the baptized the marital contract is the sacrament, they marry necessarily in the sacrament or they do not marry at all.

The agency that creates the sacrament is identical with that which creates the contract. This is the spouses' consent. In creating the contract it creates simultaneously the sacrament.

That in which the sacrament consists internally (here is the hint of the lurking problem mentioned just above) is that in the marriage which images the union of Christ with his Church. This is the effect produced by the spouses' contracting, namely, the juridical marital bond. Thus by implication a man's and a woman's contracting to exchange certain goods produces an image of Christ' love-union with his Church. When, in a few years, Cardinal Gasparri will decide exactly that the goods exchanged contractually to create a marriage are the spouses' rights to sexual acts, and when he writes this specification into the 1917 Code of Canon Law, the problem will emerge clearly. The sacramentality of a Christian marriage consists of its imaging the love-union of Christ and the Church. And in the Christian marriage such a union is created by the contractual exchange of the rights to sexual acts.

Palmieri claimed a point of fact that illustrates again the epistemological frailty of much discourse about the sacrament in marriage. This claim is about the object of Christ's instituting will in regard to marriage's sacramentality. He raised to the dignity of a sacrament not marriages existing concretely in history. He raised "marriage as such" to this dignity. Palmieri's reason for saying this was to close the escape route of a recalcitrant Catholic who says that while Christ made the sacrament available to those who wish it, those who do not may create a marriage that is only a contract.

Cardinal Louis Billot

The possibility or impossibility of such an escape was a major consideration in the most inclusive and detailed exposition of the neo-scholastic theology of marriage in this era. This was in the two-volume treatise on the sacraments by Cardinal Louis Billot.[4] In his earlier years as a professor mainly at the Gregorian University in Rome at the turn of the twentieth century he had cooperated vigorously in Pope Leo XIII's project of restoring the philosophy and theology of Thomas Aquinas to Catholic seminaries. He had also had a considerable hand in the composition of Pius X's encyclical of September 8, 1907, *Pascendi dominici gregis,* written to condemn the Modernist movement in the Catholic Church. It is not surprising to find in his works a thorough distrust of positive theology. In our analyzing a very small part of his treatise on the sacrament of marriage we shall see a paragon of *a priori,* deductive theology. In it the inductive use of the scriptures is near an irreducible minimum. His fullest quotations or citations of them are oblique, where he finds them in passages from Augustine et al. that he summons to support his own conclusions arrived at by ratiocination from a premise that is frequently a definition.

Billot's Thesis 37 takes up a serious concern with which we are by now most familiar.[5] The thesis states that Christ has brought it about that any and every marriage of two Christians is a sacrament of the new law, so that there can be no natural bond of marriage between them that is not a sacrament. He makes the careful distinction that avoids identifying the bond and the sacrament absolutely. They differ as formal aspects, but aspects of one and the same entity that is the natural bond.

In constructing his proof for this thesis Billot makes a second distinction between a marriage contracted by partners already baptized, and one contracted by partners who are baptized only after having been married. Different argumentation is called for in the two cases. The one must demonstrate in the first case that to create the natural marriage bond is to simultaneously create the sacrament. The second must demonstrate that for married partners to be baptized Christians is to make their extant marriage a sacrament.

Billot begins his first demonstration with an interpretation of Ephesians 5:21–32 in which he moves easily from the universal, Christian marriage taken conceptually, to the particular. He repeats Bellarmine's interpretation that the demonstrative pronoun *hoc* (this) in *sacramentum hoc magnum est* must refer to the antecedent immediately preceding it. This is contained in verse 31, "That is why a man leaves his father and mother and clings to his wife, and the two of them become one flesh." Billot says this designates a marriage of two Christians because Christ referred these words from Genesis to the marriages of his followers, and that *sacramentum* in verse 32 designates a grace-giving sign of a sacred reality. Therefore his conclusion: This divinely inspired passage reveals that the sacrament is a new formality grafted inseparably in the marriages of all Christians. He concludes this initial argument by pointing out that since they are the spouses themselves who by their contractual consent create their marriage, they too are the agents, the ministers, who create the sacrament.

But that he understands more powerful causes than human mind and will to be at work in creating a sacramental marriage is evident in his reply to a common objection to his thesis.[6] This reply also exemplifies deductive theology at its purest. The objection claims that baptized Christians can and do contract marriage without the intention of creating the sacrament, without intending what the Church intends in contracting marriage. But the intention in the ministers of a sacrament of at least doing what the Church intends is essential for his or her creating the sacrament. Therefore Christians can create a valid marriage bond without creating the sacrament.

Billot's reply strikes in two directions that seem mutually contradictory. First, from the fact that Christ raised marriage itself to the existence of a sacrament it is impossible that Christian partners can ever intend to contract a marriage without by that very fact intending the sacrament, so that if they exclude the sacrament they do not create even the natural bond.

One may expect that this would close the case: If two Christians ignore the sacrament, which is identical with the marital bond, neither do they create the latter. But here Billot's reply takes its other direction. He insists again that from the fact that Christ has raised Christian marriage universally to the state of a sacrament, he has in anticipation made every marriage of two Christians a sacrament. Therefore two Christians' intention and will to create the natural bond is a sufficient will and intention to create the sacrament as well. The intention to create the bond always contains implicitly the intention to create the sacrament. This is so even if the partners go beyond ignoring the sacrament to positively rejecting it.[7]

Billot seems to say, in other words, that the oneness of contract and sacrament in Christian marriage taken universally can reach into the wills of men and women in the concrete. There it can over-ride their rejection of the sacrament to such an extent that their intention to create only the natural bond is nevertheless also an intention to create the sacrament.

The second thesis in this domain (Thesis 38 in Billot's treatise) envisions a man and a woman married before being baptized. It claims that when they are baptized their merely natural marriage bond becomes a sacrament automatically and instantaneously with their baptisms. His summoning more than merely human causation to account for this appears when he explains how this is done, especially when he explains that it is not the habitual perdurance of the spouses' contractual consent to the natural bond that causes it at their baptism to become the sacrament.

Again he begins with Ephesians 5:32. He insists that *sacramentum magnum* there is predicated of the marriage bond among Christians universally, irrespective of whether it is contracted before baptism or after it.

> . . . as soon as the marital bond begins to unite two persons who are sealed with the Christian baptismal character, by this very fact it unites persons who are members of the body of Christ; and through this character the membership their marital bond becomes a "great sacrament."[8]

Billot reinforces this argument by observing that the Ephesian Christians whose marriages the letter described as "great sacraments" were almost certainly converts who had been married before being baptized.

Clearly he has here introduced into his argument a new premise, the more than human cause I hinted at earlier. This is the baptismal character in the souls of the spouses. He adds a pregnant consideration that we shall shortly find Mathias Scheeben had already developed in the fullest, namely that a Christian's incorporation in the mystical body of Christ by this baptismal character is a cause of their marriage's being a sacrament. It is curious that Billot did not introduce this to explain, in the first case examined above, how it is that the marriages of Christians baptized before marrying are inescapably sacraments.

But here too in this second case he returns to the kind of deductive logic he used in the first. Since the cause producing the sacramental bond in the marriage of two Christians is their contractual consent, and since this same consent produces the natural marital bond, nothing more is needed to make the latter a sacrament than the spouses' baptism. Nothing more is needed to make it a sign of the union of Christ and the Church than the baptismal character in their souls. It follows therefore that the moment this character is fixed in their souls by the conferring of baptism the extant natural marital bond is made the Christian sacrament.

A distinction whose richness Billot may not have fully assessed appears in his reply to an objection drawn from the cause-effect relationship, accepted in scholastic theology as necessary in a sacrament, between that which in it is only a sign (the *sacramentum tantum*), and that which is both sign and effect (*sacramentum et res*). In a Christian marriage these are respectively the spouses' reciprocal consent and their marital bond. The objection is, accordingly, that in this sacrament the sign-effect can be caused only by a sign commensurate with its religious nature, namely a sacramental contracting. But the contracting before baptism was not this. Therefore it cannot be that the subsequent baptism alone can make the natural bond to be the sacrament.

Billot's reply to this objection appeals to the singular nature of marriage among the sacraments. He also brings into play a foundational element of Thomistic metaphysics. This is the distinction between the actual existence of an entity or quality, and the real potentiality for these in a pre-existing matrix. (A simple example of these is the actuality of a statue's figure and the distinct but real potentiality for these in the pre-existing marble—and of course the permanent real potentiality in the marble for always a different figure.)

Thus he argues that the singular nature of the sign-effect in marriage allows for its being produced also by a cause different from but equivalent to the usual sign. That is, since the sign-effect is fundamentally the natural marital bond, it can be brought into existence in successive stages. It can first be made only the bond by the pre-sacramental contractual consent, but later made into a sacrament by the baptismal character created in the spouses' souls by the religious rite of baptism. For the marital contract of the unbaptized is not alien to the sacrament, is not absolutely disjoined from it. There is in it the potentiality for being made a sacrament. This is so because in the unbaptized spouses themselves there is the potentiality for being made members of the body of which Christ is the head. Thus the baptism that makes them such Christian members in actuality brings the marital bond which joins them now as Christians to the actuality of the sacramental signification which it had only potentially.

In saying above that Billot may not have assessed fully the richness of this consideration, I meant that it probably did not occur to him that this same distinction between the potential sacramentality of a marriage and its actual sacramentality may explain the condition of Christians disaffected from their religion, ignorant of and indifferent to the sacrament available in their marriage. If he had accepted this, he might have found also that he must enlist more causes than he did to bring such Christians' marital sacrament to actuality.

Thirty-two years later Billot published the seventh revised edition of *De Ecclesiae Sacramentis.* This too is a commentary on Part III of Aquinas' *Summa Theologiae.*[9] Again because Thomas never reached marriage in his treatise on the sacraments in this *Tertia Pars,* Billot's commentary is on that part of the Supplement to the *Summa* that does treat of marriage, but was added by Thomas' student, Reynaldo of Piperno.

The changes in this seventh edition derive from Billot's taking the sacrament of marriage out of a methodological autonomous treatise on the sacraments and linking it with the theology of Christ's redemption. This setting the sacrament in a more comprehensive context we will see done most thoroughly by Scheeben. It will be done with increasing thoroughness during the years leading to Vatican II. Billot's way of approaching the sacrament here shows his concern for the larger setting. He points out that the incarnation of the eternal Word provides a crucial element of marriage's sacramentality. It not only provides the invisible sacred reality which can be imaged in marriage. In his incarnated life Christ did act out this imaging and continues to do so. He does this in his divine conduct carried out in human acts.[10]

Billot explains: Christ exists in two unions with human nature, and thus provides two unions to be signified by marriage. One of these is his physical union in the incarnation; the other is his spiritual union with the Church through grace. In itself the union of husband and wife contains images correlated to both Christ's physical union with human nature, and to his spiritual union.

First, in regard to Christ's physical union with human nature, marriage shows a similarity of ends to this union. These ends include procreation and nurture in order to provide human beings for the cultus of God. It also helps through grace to repair men and women for the worship of God and thus bring them to perfection. In the latter marriage images Christ's spiritual union.

Marriage's similarity of means to the physical union of Christ with human nature is in the former's indissolubility. This images the inseparability of Christ and the Church. It shares this similarity of means because the indissolubility of the spouses is needed as a means to attain the ends enumerated just above.[11]

Concerning the similarity not of images but of relationships, in marriage the husband is head of the wife, as Christ is head of the Church. Thus as Christ takes the initiative of love in the relationship with his spouse, so the husband takes the initiative of love with his, because he too is head to her as body.[12]

From this exceedingly intricate cross-correlation of images and relationships Billot draws the conclusion that marriage has from its beginning had a real potential and suitability (*idoneitas*) for being made an image of the eternal Word's union with human nature and of Christ's union with the Church. Here Billot adds the next step in the logic of this demonstration that Christ has raised marriage among his followers to a sacrament in his new law. Christ has in fact taken this potentiality and suitability and actually made marriage into such an image. Evidence for this is in Ephesians 5:32: "This (all this potentiality and suitability inherent in marriage) is a great sacrament."[13]

But since they were inherent in marriage before Christ and before Ephesians, why did the potentiality and suitability not make marriage a sacrament then? Because the Christ-Church relationship that was to be imaged did not yet exist. Hence marriage was then not an actual and effective image of that relationship. It was only a foreshadowing, a prototype of it.

What is more, baptized Christian spouses now participate in the good of the Christ-Church union because they are oriented to the same end as that of the incarnation. They exist in the same ontological order with it. For this end is to nurture children by grace for the beatific vision, and thus to perpetuate the Church.

To make these last points in another way, Billot explains that Christian marriage as a sign, or image, differs from the Old Testament analogic prototypes mainly in this, that the latter were only pre-figures of Christ's redemptive action because they were "empty." They were unable to accomplish what they prefigured. But Christian marriage as sacrament, like all such signs instituted by Christ, differs precisely in this, that it produces what it signs. This it can do because Christ's redemptive work has taken place and continues to take place. Christian marriage is thus a sacrament that graces because in this marriage the spouses are actually conformed to a union of Christ and the Church that is actual and continual.[14]

That this sacrament graces the spouses follows too from the fact that they need this gracing in order to nurture their children in faith unto salvation. In doing this they are conformed in a specific way to the Christ-Church union, a union which produces the Church community through baptism and nourishes it through the Eucharist.

The Sacrament of Marriage in the Theology of the Mystical Body

At about the midpoint of the nineteenth century a few theologians had begun to shift the epicenter of demonstration of Christian marriage's sacramentality. With gradually diminishing frequency did they seek to draw this verification deductively from Ephesians 5 by pointing to its verse 32, "This is a great sacrament," and concluding that it refers to the Christian spouses' imaging the relationship of Christ and the Church. They by no means abandoned this rich passage. But they shifted the examination of the sacrament into a more coherent context, as we have just seen that Billot did by beginning to make it a subset of Christology.

The reason for the diminishing appeal to the evidence of Ephesians on its lone merits is nowhere expressed by these theologians. One may guess reasonably that suspicion was growing that perhaps the author did not mean to say that it is the Christian spouses' marriage that is the great sacrament. Add to this the long-standing agreement that the word *sacramentum* as used by the fathers of Florence and Trent is not synonymous in reference with the Greek noun *mystérion* of Ephesians 5:32. But perhaps too the sad reality of so many Christian marriages affected the theologians' reasoning. Millions of northern European and American Protestant Christians did not acknowledge their marriages to be sacraments. Millions of Catholic marriages were plainly not, in their conduct, images of Christ's love relationship with the Church. And an uncounted number of these were either ignorant of the sacrament or cared little if it were.

But against this hard evidence stood the Catholic teaching that all these marriages, the millions of them, were indeed sacraments. To insist that they were by insisting in turn that they were images of a divine-human relationship was hardly convincing. Hence, presuming that one of the works of theology is to convince, the theologians had to relocate this work in the territory of better evidence.

One of the first to do this was the German, Mathias Joseph Scheeben. In his monumental *Mysterien des Christentums* he began his consideration of the sacrament as so many of his predecessors reaching back to patristic times had done.[15] He insisted that marriage has never been a merely secular relationship, but that from the marriage of the first man and woman in the garden of Eden it has been religious and even sacramental.[16] He claimed this on grounds that a Jew or a Muslim of any age could accept. All creation is God's work. It has its existence from him both initially and continually. The nature of things is his own design fixed in material creation as a whole, and in individual creatures and their significant relationships and institutions.

Marriage is a most significant institution. God has designed into it a primary goal, which is to bring children into the world and nurture them. But in their souls children are created by God, and his one final reason for creating them is to bring them to himself in eternal happiness beyond death. Thus their very existence is sacred on the two counts of their origin and their destiny. Therefore too the sexual union whose raison d'être is to produce them must be sacred.

Scheeben added that since it is only by acting as instruments of God the creator that men and women can bring children into the world, they enter marriage under his authority and live it under his power. He acts to realize his plan for the human race through them and their sexual joining. Therefore their marriages belong to him. So they are not free in the matter of realizing its purpose or in regard to ending it before death.

This multi-faceted causation that God carries on in marriage must certainly leave discernible traces in it, on the philosophical principle that an effect in some way manifests the nature of the cause that produces it. It is in this sense that marriage by its nature, as a thing of nature before being made a sacrament of the new law, is sacramental. It is inescapably an image of God's creation and design.

In the middle of the present century the French theologian, Gustav Martelet, saw an added and more existential element in the nature of marriage that makes it a sacrament in this pre-Christian sense.[17] Nature in human beings, he claimed, is not a secular reality. It belongs to Christ and has its meaning only in him. It is the human structure and human condition of a person in their entirety. This structure and condition are called "nature" because they are what is existentially given in a human being. But they belong to Christ because they are given by Christ. This is especially true of the human condition. A person is given both freedom by God yet radical dependence by Christ because only in union with Christ can a person's freedom gain its meaning by gaining its fulfillment. Hence human nature is sacramental without being a religious sacrament of the new law because it manifests to the person himself the paradox of his absolutely dependent freedom.

This paradox invests marriage. And its threat of damage to persons is more serious than ever precisely because of modern men's and women's intensified claim to freedom in their sexual relationships and conduct. This relationship and this conduct about which they demand to be free is by nature an instrument of the life-producing power that is God's alone. So it is really not free. Yet men and women claim this freedom precisely in order to gain from their sexuality a happiness which is paradoxically available to them only in eventual union with and submission to Christ.[18]

Scheeben's Response to the Secular Challenge

But Scheeben's interest was fixed on the marriages of Christians not as natural sacraments but as sacraments in Christ's new dispensation. He took up the secular challenge of his century, and in meeting it worked out his theology of the sacrament. He insisted in the most trenchant way that where a man and a woman are both baptized, they cannot marry one another in a merely natural, pre-sacramental union. His reasoning in support of this marks the shift of theological center that I hinted at above. He draws his reasoning from the theology of the mystical body of Christ, a pivotal metaphor in Pauline christology and ecclesiology.

Thus baptism joins a person to the body of Christ. It makes him a member of this body. It imprints the character of Christ on him. Because of baptism and the character it imprints, he belongs, body and soul, to Christ's mystical body. This incorporation raises him out of a merely natural order of existence. He is now oriented to a goal of life that is supernatural. He acts now in the strength of Christ's grace that is infused into him.

An inescapable effect on a Christian man and woman of this incorporation into Christ's mystical body is that they can marry only as members of that body. They are not free to return, because they cannot return, to a merely natural or secular order of marriage. By their baptism they are so thoroughly members of Christ's body that even their physical marital acts belong to Christ. For their bodies are no longer their own flesh but the flesh of Christ. In support of this assertion Scheeben quotes 1 Corinthians 6:15: "Surely you know that your bodies are members making up the body of Christ."[19]

Martelet approaches from a different quarter in urging this same thesis, that it is a man's and woman's baptism that makes impossible their marrying except in the Christian sacrament. He sets as a premise that Christ made marriage his sacrament when he restored its original indissolubility (according to Mark 10:9 and Matthew 19:6, "What God has joined man must not separate"), and thus enabled it to image the indissoluble union of Christ and the Church. Martelet then asks, "Why then is not every marriage a sacrament?" For Christ restored this indissolubility to all marriages, and the Catholic Church has subsequently defined indissolubility to be of the essence of marriage taken universally.[20]

Martelet's answer to his own question is that for their marriage to be a Christian sacrament the spouses must be baptized. A marriage's being a sacrament comes not from the spouses' moral disposition to remain with one another until death, but from their baptismal existence as such. Here Martelet's explanation repeats Scheeben's of a century earlier. In and through baptism the risen and glorified Christ exercises his universal lordship in a particular person. He establishes and exercises his power in him by virtue of his baptism. At this point Martelet inserts the theology of the mystical body of Christ. By his baptism a person is brought into this body, into the power of the risen Christ who is the head of this body. To live in this body is to live in the power of its head. It is to live as his member in his body.[21]

May one say that because Christ is the head of all humankind, every person belongs to Christ, and therefore every marriage is a sacrament? Yes, but original sin has obscured this belonging and weakened it. Precisely what baptism does is to recover and strengthen the relationship, to make effective again the radical dependence of the person on Christ. The baptized person is no longer of himself and for himself, but of Christ and for Christ. "You belong to Christ as Christ belongs to God" (1 Cor 3:23). "Your body, you know, is the temple of the Holy Spirit, who is in you since you received him from God. You are not your own possession; you have been bought and paid for" (1 Cor 6:19–20). "And for anyone who is in Christ there is a new creation; the old creation is gone, and now the new one is here" (2 Cor 5:17).[22]

This effect is worked in all the baptized even though it may not be empirically verifiable in all of them. All are brought into the power of Christ. This being assumed into him, into his body the Church, is the basis of the spiritual priesthood of all the baptized. That is, by their baptism they act in the power of Christ; they gain the power to manifest by their human existence what they become as Christians.

No matter how severe a baptized person's sin, or no matter how thorough his denial of Christ, he cannot destroy his incorporation in him, because he has not himself produced this incorporation in the body of Christ, but Christ has. This inescapable and ineradicable effect is, by use of another image, to be understood as the baptismal character. Put most simply, this character's effect in a person is to make him a Christian—once and for always.

For both Scheeben and Martelet—and for Henri Rondet too, a contemporary of the latter—the "imprinting" of a sacramental character in Christian spouses is not limited to that coming from baptism. The sacrament of marriage itself does this. It engages them in a kind of character or role in the Church. This it does, of course, first in virtue of their baptism. But analogously as the sacraments that produce a character in the soul lodge the person in a new state in the body of Christ (baptism, confirmation and sacred orders are said to do this), so marriage the sacrament also lodges men and women in a new state there. In Scheeben's words, "It puts them in a high place there." And grace, a special vital force, flows to them from Christ, the head of the body.[23]

Rondet adds that although it is traditional in Catholic theology to say that marriage as a sacrament does not produce a sacramental character in the soul, as do baptism, confirmation and orders, yet as a permanent bond created by an irrevocable commitment it sets the spouses in a specific function in the body of Christ. Indeed the entire family, Christian children as well as parents, live in and by the sacrament. They do this not by virtue of something coming to the marriage from outside it, but by the insertion of the spouses as spouses in the body of Christ."[24]

The Incorporation of Marriages in the Body of Christ

Let us take the hint contained there in Rondet's phrase, "insertion of the spouses as spouses in the body of Christ." He claims or at least suggests that the sacrament of marriage works in the spouses a second incorporation in Christ after baptism, or modifies baptism's first incorporation to a specifically marital place in Christ's mystical body.

It is evident that these theologians (and I add to them the Belgian, Emile Mersch) set as a first principle of their theology of marriage a pivotal element of St. Paul's christology. The point is this, that by his becoming man in Christ the eternal Son of God joined the human race to himself in an unending personal union. But how shall this union be understood? Do we have a human model to help in this understanding? To this Paul has offered an instant answer. We have a most useful model in the union of a husband and wife who love one another with a literally indefatigable love. Christ has "wedded" the human race to himself. Or said more precisely, he has wedded to himself the community of men and women who are willingly drawn into union with him.

Mersch explains this union as a kind of participation in the life of Christ.[25] But he sees it as only one level or fold in a structure of interlocked participations by various persons. The first of these is the participation of divine persons that is the life of the Trinity. Father, Son and Spirit each participates in his own way in the love that is the interior life of God: the Father speaking forth in love the person of the Son; the Son returning this fruitful love; this reciprocal love of Father and Son bringing forth the Holy Spirit.

At one level down, so to speak, this divine participation of persons replicates itself in Christ's incarnation. First of all the divine persons join the humanity of Christ to themselves at the point of the Son's personhood. Because this is a love union of spirit and flesh, it is aptly understood as marital. Then through Christ they join a human community, the Church, to themselves. This too is a reciprocal act of love, they for the men and women making up the community, and the latter for them. This union too of divine persons with human is understood to be marital, because it too unites spirit with flesh. The divine Spirit takes to himself the flesh of Christ; Christ, both spirit and flesh, takes to himself a community of men and women who are spirit and flesh. The power that takes them, that forms them into a community, the power to which they respond freely, is God's love.

Rondet has an even more inclusive vision of all this. He sees marriage—not Christian marriage alone, but all marriage—within a cosmic-historical plan that includes this interpretation of Paul's vision. But the more inclusive vision that he offers is also Paul's.

The movement that goes on in history, the ceaseless pilgrimage of the human race, is an effect in men and women of God's calling them— of his calling them back to himself through Christ to be rejoined with himself in Christ. The point of contact at which he seeks to rejoin them to himself is where Christ's humanity is joined to the divine personhood given to him by the Father. Since this union of Christ is one of flesh with divine spirit and is therefore marital, so too is God's call to men and women a call into a mystical marriage with himself.[26]

Martelet enters at this sensitive juncture to make a capital point, one to which he turns (as I shall return to it presently) when explaining why two Christians can marry only in a sacrament; why, if they try to commit themselves to one another outside the sacrament, in a merely natural marriage, they cannot join in even this marriage.

Martelet's point is that they are not the man and woman themselves who make their marriage a sacrament by committing themselves to one another. Rather it is Christ who makes their joining in marriage a sacrament. Even their most earnest and religiously sensitive love can no more than dispose themselves finally at the brink where Christ then takes their union into his union with the Father and the Spirit, and therefore into his own union with the Church. It is in doing this that Christ makes their marriage a sacrament. At the opposite extreme, even their being unaware that he does this does not keep him from doing it.

Barely hidden here too is the reason, the double reason, why only the marriages of the baptized can be fully sacramental, why only their marriages can be incorporated fully into the union of Christ and the Father. First of all, only they have been "seized," as it were, by Christ in baptism and joined to himself in the Church singly. For there, as in marriage, it is Christ who executes the sacrament and creates and fixes the sacramental character, not the person who is baptized. At most the latter can only dispose himself or herself to be incorporated.

Secondly, the incorporating even of a single person in Christ and the Church makes of this person—or rather of this person's union with Christ—a living sign of Christ's presence in the Church and therefore in the world. This is the empirical side of the sacrament, a visible, tangible, audible manifestation of Christ's presence and action among human beings. This is the essence of the Christian sacraments that human eyes and ears can detect, this signing forth of Christ's active presence. But only the baptized, when joining in marriage, can sign forth Christ's union with the Father and the Spirit, as also his union with the Church. This is because only they have been already drawn into and enlisted in this signing forth. Put more simply, only if they already live as single persons in Christ's body, in his love, can they also live there as a couple and manifest to others their living there.

Adaptation of Ephesians 5:21-33

It should be obvious to anyone who has studied Ephesians 5 how thoroughly these theologians draw on the marriage passage in verses 21–32. Certainly Scheeben does so. He says that when Paul wrote, in verse 32, that "this is a great mystery," the latter meant that this mystery is the union of Christian husband and wife.[27]

In explaining his meaning here Scheeben apparently makes of the Pauline metaphor the reality itself of the sacramental marriage. He says of the latter that its being a mystery consists of its imaging the marital union of Christ and the Church—but not only of its imaging thus. The marriage of a Christian man and woman could do this imaging even if left in its purely natural condition. But then it would be an image and no more, merely a symbol. It would not itself be a mystery, as Paul said it is, but only an image of a mystery, such as even the marriages of non-Christians are.

But the marriage of two Christians is the mystery that Paul said it is in that it "has a real, essential and intrinsic reference to the mystery of Christ's union with the Church. It is rooted in this mystery *and is organically connected with it* [italics added], and so partakes of its nature and mysterious character." The marriage of two Christians is a sacrament of the mysterious union of Christ and the Church because this mystery is active in the marriage.[28]

To explain this more exactly Scheeben turns to the effect of baptism that we have already noted, the incorporation of the person in the mystical body of Christ. According to St. Paul baptism makes the Christian man and woman individually members of Christ's body. In so doing it inserts them into Christ's union with the Church. So, as members already of the bride of Christ, the Church, they are already wedded individually to Christ. Consequently when they marry, the mystery of Christ's union with the Church is found in their union with one another. At this point Scheeben uses the analogy from Ephesians 5 in the most concrete application imaginable.

> They [the Christian spouses] can rightfully unite with each other in matrimony only for the end which Christ purposes in this union with the Church, that is, the further extension of the

mystical body of Christ. . . . They must unite with each other *as organs of Christ's body, as organs of the whole* that was brought into being by the union of Christ with the Church. Thus their union, their alliance, becomes an organic member in the grand and richly varied alliance between Christ and his Church. . . .[29]

In light of this reasoning it is clear why Scheeben would assert, in regard to the controversy over the separability of the contract and the sacrament in Christian marriage, that they are indeed inseparable. A Christian man and woman can unite with one another in marriage only within each one's union singly with Christ. The union of each in Christ singly is carried over into their union with one another. For the Christ in whom they unite, of whose body they are members, is a Christ united in a marital love union with his Church. When the man and woman join in committed marital love, they act as already joined to a Christ committed in marital love. Therefore they cannot not image this divine love commitment. They cannot not live in and by it.[30]

Decades later Mersch proposed the same thought but in the theological vocabulary of human participation in the divine. Marriage enriches and makes specific a Christian man's and woman's already established baptismal union with the Church. Their marriage joins them with the Church specifically as spouses. Consequently their consents creating the marriage, and thus too their marital acts, are made acts of the Church performed by the Church. The sacrament makes of their marriage a cell of the Church and a church in miniature. It gives to the spouses a participation in the mystical marriage by which the divine Son is incarnated in the humanity of Christ, the marriage by which the Church itself becomes reciprocally the body, the flesh of Christ.[31]

After first saying that in Ephesians 5:21–32 Paul made of heterosexual love a symbol of the love of Christ and the Church, and could therefore propose the latter love as a model of the former, Martelet joins Scheeben and Mersch in their theology of incorporation and participation.[32] He enters this obliquely as he says that all a Christian man and woman need do in order that their marriage be a sacrament is to intend to marry and commit themselves to one another by the wedding vows. The reason for this simplicity is that by their baptism their love is already under the power of Christ. Their baptism has already incorporated them in Christ, made them participants in his love. But it is their marriage that integrates them explicitly and sacramentally in Christ's relationship with the Church. This integration reproduces in the spouses' relationship the Christ-Church relationship. It makes their relationship an image of the latter.[33]

As Martelet continues he moves on into paradox. No one is more free in marrying than Christian spouses. Belonging to Christ, integrated in him by baptism, they are strengthened in their love and therefore made more free in it—more free to intend the reality of marriage and commit themselves to it. But at the same time their belonging to Christ by baptism takes their relationship beyond the limits of their own power and even of their own awareness. They are no longer masters of the meaning of their own love, nor of its signification.

To say this another way, because they marry as already integrated in Christ by baptism, and because this integration raises the existence itself of their relationship beyond its natural condition, it follows that their marital actions transcend the natural, whether they are aware of this or not.[34] For their marital existence is not only their own but is that of Christ as well. Therefore their marital actions—their decision to marry, their mutual commitment in the vows, their expressions of love in marriage—are simultaneously their own and those of Christ.

The spouses are, to be sure, the ministers of their sacrament by their reciprocal consent. But the making of their covenant to be sacramental is a work that surpasses their own wills and even their own subjective disposition. Again, it is Christ who makes their consent and their consequent union to be a sacrament. This is why even Christian spouses who do not positively intend that their marriage be a sacrament have their marriage made a sacrament nonetheless.

Here is the meaning of the term consecrated in the scholastic theology of the sacraments, that the sacraments produce their effects *ex opere operato*. This means not that they do so automatically, no matter the disposition of the recipients. It means rather that Christ is the principal agent in producing these effects. Their being produced does not depend primarily on the human participants, for Christ's action picks up theirs, empowers it beyond itself. So in marriage, by their own power the Christian spouses can commit and give themselves to one another. But they do so, because of their baptism, only and inescapably in the power of Christ. He takes their commitment up and makes it also a sacrament.

This does not deny the now accepted Catholic teaching that the spouses themselves are the ministers of their sacrament. But it insists that they are such only as instruments of Christ's action.[35]

In this regard Rondet is careful to point out that while it is true that it is the marital contract that Christ makes the sacrament, this is no mere civil contract. In itself it is a covenant, a covenant in the biblical sense, a profound commitment of person to person. It is for this reason that the marital contract can readily be made a sacrament. For Christ's commitment to the Church is itself covenantal, and it is into this transcendent covenant that the spouses' natural marital covenant is integrated, and by this integration made a sacrament.[36]

Marital Love and the Sacrament

Martelet states simply that the sacrament of marriage supposes the spouses' love for one another. What the sacrament does to this love is what it does to the marriage. It integrates it in the love of Christ for the Church, elevates it, empowers it beyond its natural capacity. He states his understanding of this love carefully. It is relational, in essence reciprocal. It is the spouses' total giving of themselves to one another and the correlative accepting of this gift. But as marital the giving and the receiving have a specific goal. This is to create and continue the marital community, which includes children.[37]

Martelet begins immediately to identify the territory and the function of physically expressed sexuality in the sacrament. His mind on the subject is also very much that of Rondet. Both acknowledge the excellent place of sexuality in the sacrament; they also perceive its limitations. Its major limitation is that because of inherited sinfulness in men and woman their sexuality is a weight dragging against the full conversion of marital love into charity, the full conversion of eros into agapé. Therefore it too readily retards the full integration of marital love into Christ's love for the Church, a love which is exclusively self-giving.[38]

It is true that the spouses' marital contract functions sacramentally in that it images the union of Christ and the Church. But what is unique in this imaging is that it goes on in a love union of the spouses that is physical as well as spiritual. Since the union is in part physical, the love is bound to a condition that diminishes the perfection of love. What is more, it is a condition which is transitory, which can pass away while the love goes on. Still more, while the spouses' marital love is personal, the physical element in it, which makes it marital, has for its specific purpose to increase the human race generically. This too as a function is transitory.[39]

Understanding that much makes clear both the positive contribution of sexuality to the sacrament and its limiting effect on it.

The sacrament makes possible the integration of sexuality into the sanctification that baptism begins and continues. It rescues it from remaining always a vagrant element. Marriage the sacrament gives eros a place in holiness. For one thing, the fidelity and permanence that Christ demands of the married, which are the most evident facets of the sacramental imaging, protect human fertility. So sexuality is an integral part of marriage's sacramental imaging.

But since the heart of this imaging is an imaging of the love of Christ and the Church, the heart of this imaging cannot be physical sexuality itself. It is rather that moment in their loving which is the conversion of love (eros) into charity (agapé). But this is done in the dispossessing of the self. Therefore that which is sanctifying in a specifically marital way in marriage, the physical-spiritual giving of the self in charity, paradoxically pulls away from one of the essential traits of sexuality, the assertion of the self in eros.

It is time to point out that what Martelet and Rondet write is in great part a reaction to an interpretation of sexuality in marriage that had gained powerful impetus for acceptance among Catholics thanks to the writing of a few German philosophers and theologians during the decades preceding them. Principal among these were Dietrich von Hildebrand and Heribert Doms. Their thesis was in one sense a counter-thesis to the accepted Catholic teaching about the natural end of marriage and of sexuality in marriage.[40]

We recall that this teaching claimed a primary goal, or end, for marriage and consequently for sexual intercourse in marriage. This is procreation and nurture. It also proposed a twofold secondary end, the mutual help of the spouses and their remedying of concupiscence in one another. In claiming that primary end the Catholic authorities implied that a marriage is an instrumental reality, that it exists in order to secure the good of persons or institutions outside itself—in this case to produce good citizens for the state and holy members for the Church.

Von Hildebrand and Doms challenged this accepted teaching. They did not counter-claim, as the Church's Congregation of the Holy Office protested when condemning their thesis in 1944, that procreation and nurture are not the primary end of marriage, but its secondary or even lesser end.[41] Indeed they accepted the traditional hierarchy of ends in marriage. What they did claim was that marriage is not to be understood primarily according to its ends, that its ends are not its first intelligible element. Marriage is not an instrumental reality, they insisted. It is not for anyone or anything outside itself.

They insisted rather that marriage is primarily understandable in its meaning. This meaning is the becoming-one, the being-one and the growing in oneness of the two sexually complementary human beings. Therefore too their sexuality is not instrumental. It is not meant to realize some goal outside itself. Rather it is the territory, the conduct, in which specifically and most richly the man and woman create their oneness and grow in it. As married persons they come to their chosen fullness of personhood mainly in their sexual lovemaking.

No rare insight is needed to see what effect this interpretation of marriage and sexuality, the natural relationship and the relationship's self-expression, must have on marriage the sacrament. Given the premise that the sacrament is simply the natural relationship made a grace-giving image of the relationship of Christ and the Church, a relationship of perfect, self-giving love, one must conclude that the imaging, the self-giving, the gracing are done most effectively in sexual lovemaking climaxing in intercourse. This seems to be the inference that Rondet and Martelet were unwilling to accept and against which they argue.

Rondet argues in terms simpler than those of Martelet, or at least in terms more familiarly and traditionally Catholic. He acknowledges that marital love does indeed impel a man and woman to make gifts of themselves to one another. But they can rise to a total and unreserved self-giving only by the strength of God. There are two reasons for this, one of which can be stated briefly, while the other needs fuller explanation.

It is God's love that impels and draws a man and woman to self-giving to begin with. And this is a call to himself. But human strength cannot by itself respond fully enough to give the self over as totally as this call demands. What is more, a man's or woman's love can be received fully only by God. Another human being's receiving of it always falls short. So marital love itself when released freely sends a person beyond all creatures on a trajectory to God.

The second reason is found in the effects of original sin on a man's and woman's ability to give themselves in love, especially on their ability to embody their love sexually. "Sexual union needs to be protected from itself," because original sin has damaged the relationship of the lower, sensate powers of the person to the higher rational powers.[42] While this disorder is experienced in all the sensate powers, it is felt with especial severity in the sexual power because it is already by nature so powerful, so imperious. To control this self-seeking sexual demand, so much stronger a love for the partner is needed in the higher powers, which are reason and will. Rondet singles out here as an example the selfless love a husband must have for his wife well along in her pregnancy.

Here is the place for the needed entry of the grace of the sacrament to reestablish the equilibrium between lower and higher powers set originally by God before its damaging by original sin.[43]

Marital love is understood accurately only when seen in the perspective of God's own creative love. His nature as a trinity of persons means that his love is essentially fruitful, essentially self-giving. The distinct persons in God are polarities of this self-giving. His work of creating imitates and embodies this, his existence. He gives existence to creatures so that he may draw them into the strength of his own love. But to draw them to himself God has designed the powerful desire, eros, into human beings, the desire to become "two in one flesh." But for a man and woman to become "one flesh" spirit must keep control of them. If their attempt to become one were only carnal, only sensate, their real oneness would be obliterated. It would be no more than the animal oneness which does only the sub-personal thing of preserving the species.

So intelligent and aware men and women come upon the paradox that in order to become two in one flesh as persons in the sense of fulfilling their desire, they must put self-denial into self-desire. They must make this desire sacrificial by sending it outside itself to seek the fulfillment of the other, the beloved. In order to accomplish this spirit must master flesh in them. Self-giving agapé must master self-seeking eros.

To the ancient and skeptical question, "How can a human institution whose native expression is so carnal be a Christian sacrament?" Rondet replies, first of all, that sexual intercourse can be a fully human act, not merely an animal reaction to stimulus. Marriage is not a union of two spirits who merely use their bodies in order to perpetuate a species. Human love is not animal instinct plus friendship. In itself sexual intercourse is not the use of another person as an object, but two persons in reciprocal and complete giving over of their selves.[44]

The old and conventional objection that in orgasmic intercourse a person loses control of his or her body and its demands is not in itself a difficulty against marriage's sacramentality. To give oneself over to eros, to nature's powerful desire, is not a degradation any more than is an artist's surrendering himself or herself to the creative daimon. For this desire is an élan fixed in men and women by God himself and energized by him in every case. Had sin not invaded it, sexual intercourse could have remained an act at once carnal and so spiritual that it could simultaneously produce new created life and the uncreated, supernatural life of grace.

But because of sin intercourse now brings death along with life. For the infant is conceived in alienation from God, without grace, with sense and reason soon to show their disorder. This is why the sacramentality of marriage is to be found primarily not in intercourse but in the marriage contract and in the marriage state.[45]

That Rondet's thinking on this point was quietly dominated by the traditional Catholic teaching that the primary end of marriage and of marital intercourse is procreation and nurture is evident in what follows in his essay. He reasons that once children have been born into the family marital chastity gets its chance to come to fulfillment. For this chastity now invites the parents to pass to a higher plane of the sexual intimacy that has been created by their sexual union itself—to a higher plane where this intimacy has a different raison d'être than procreation. Here self-giving love urges them to refrain from intercourse, for eros in them must now become agapé.

> . . . charity, which is never absent from legitimate desire, ought to transfigure this desire slowly to the point where it suppresses it, each spouse seeking only the good of the other, and both the good of the child; and the family as a whole opening itself to appeals from outside it in order to give there and not receive.[46]

Carnal union, though good in itself, remains always ambivalent. The only resolution of this ambivalence, Rondet seems to say, is to integrate it in the sacramentality of marriage, which demands exclusive self-giving. For this reason he denies what Doms affirmed, that it is intercourse which is "the privileged moment," the most effective conduct in the actualization of the sacrament.

Rondet confirms his judgment on the inability of sexual intimacy to be the fullest realization of the sacrament when he answers the question that asks, "If the sacraments have their efficacy only in relation to the mystery of Christ's death and resurrection, where is this relationship in the sacrament of marriage?" His answer is that because married life in family demands continual self-renunciation that fructifies in charity, it is a continual death and resurrection. Christ has loved the Church to the point of giving his life for it. Therefore such ought to be the love of spouses for one another.

The way is open here for Rondet to say that self-renunciation is at least possible and is often demanded in the self-surrender of complete sexual intercourse. Being celibate he probably did not suspect that this is so.

The Grace of the Sacrament

As one reads what these theologians say about the grace of the sacrament of marriage one comes upon the centuries-old habit of defining grace—or more precisely of describing it—in terms of its effects. Behind these effects one espies that they think of grace as simultaneously a relationship between the human person and God, and a kind of empowering of the person to carry on the conduct fitted to this relationship.

For Rondet the grace of the sacrament is produced by marriage's incorporation in the sacramental character of the Church as the mystical body of Christ. He goes far beyond the juridical notion of this grace that says one of the effects of the sacrament is to give the spouses the right to the actual graces needed to live married life well and holily—the notion that the grace of the sacrament is both the right to these actual graces and the graces themselves.

He sees the sacramental grace of marriage to be identical in substance with habitual or sanctifying grace. But it is habitual grace with two effects worked in it by the sacrament. These effects are the intensification of habitual grace already in the souls of the spouses, and the shaping of this grace to the needs and conduct of the man and woman specifically as spouses.[47]

Scheeben says of this that Christ graces the spouses precisely as members of his body so that they may do the work of his body. Martelet's way of putting it is that just as the spouses' marriage as contract is made a sacrament by reason of their baptism, so their sanctification in marriage is the working out of baptismal grace through their marital grace. The grace, the gift, of the sacrament of marriage is to live the life of baptized persons in the union of marriage. This is "to live their sacrament." And to live their sacrament is to image in their lives the love union of Christ and the Church. But the heart of this imaging is to turn their originally erotic love into charity, which is the dispossession of the self as the center and object of one's love.[48]

In any case, the gift to the spouses of marital sacramental grace works in them effectively only by their freely co-working with it. Their sexual intercourse is one kind of this co-working. What it does, said quite exactly, is to dispose the spouses for receiving this grace. It sets a context for this specific marital gracing. However—and here Rondet returns to a theme that runs through his entire theology of the sacrament—because sexual intercourse needs to be tempered and healed, it is more accurate to say that it is the entire ensemble of family life, all its joys, sorrows and sacrifices, that sets the context of and is the disposition for this gracing. This is so because it is the entire ensemble that is the lasting efficacious image of God's gracing. That is, every expression of self-giving love, not only the readily self-interested expression in sexual intercourse, is the spouses' expression of their will to receive grace and to communicate it to one another.[49]

Edward Schillebeeckx

The contemporary Dominican theologian, Edward Schillebeeckx, has published elements of his theology of marriage in three main sources. The earliest, in 1961, was "Le Mariage est un Sacrement."[50] It appears to be an outline, almost a précis, of an extended multi-volume treatment planned for later completion. Regrettably only two volumes of this later treatment have appeared thus far, both in 1963 (titled, in the English-language edition, *Marriage: Human Reality and Saving Mystery*).[51] These volumes contain that part of a theology of marriage that is its raw material, namely the historical development and the various understandings of marriage in the Jewish and Christian traditions. Volume 1 is "Marriage in the Old and New Testaments." Volume 2 is "Marriage in the History of the Church." That Schillebeeckx left this study of marriage unfinished is explicit in the last paragraph of Volume 2: "Later on in this work . . ." He intended to complete later a formal synthesis of the theology of marriage and to address "concrete problems which marriage raises."[52]

Schillebeeckx's third source is an essay of 1974 whose title translated into English is "Christian Marriage and the Human Reality of Complete Marital Disintegration."[53] He identified it as the preliminary draft of a chapter intended for his as yet unpublished third volume of *Marriage: Human Reality and Saving Mystery*.[54] As its title suggests the chapter is an analysis of the Catholic teaching and discipline concerning divorce and remarriage.

One who studies these essays would do well to first read Schillebeeckx's *Christ, the Sacrament of the Encounter with God*.[55] His basic theology of sacramentality is there laid out in detail. The later essays are understandable only as specific developments and applications of the larger theology.

On the threshold of examining these essays and offering a synthesis of their theology of marriage one faces two options. One can work up a single synthesis of all three, or one can trace through them one by one in the sequence of their composition. I have taken the latter option, first of all because our own study follows the sequence of development of the Catholic theology of marriage. The value in doing this has long since come clear. It helps us to understand our current theology as a literal point of arrival. It helps us to know whether we should stop here and for how long, by disclosing how we got here—by which use of which evidence, by which logic in coming to conclusions. We want to follow in sequence now the work—again regrettably unfinished—of the most penetrating, exact and inclusive theological analyst of marriage in Catholic history.

Running through all Schillebeeckx's theology in these essays is an assumption which is in fact a conclusion from the inclusive theology of sacramentality. It is an element of Pauline thought recovered most fruitfully for the consideration of the sacrament of marriage a century earlier by Mathias Scheeben. It is that a Christian is by baptism joined in action to the life and action of the risen Christ. A less exact way of phrasing this is "incorporated (even "inserted!") into the mystical body of Christ." This joining is maintained, from the side of the person on earth, first and fundamentally by the baptismal character in his or her soul. This is a seal of union with Christ; it is also a source of action with him. The joining is activated proximately by the person's faith, hope and love. As a consequence the person co-works with Christ in his work in the world. Add to this that Christ's work is his Father's work, and that their co-working is their Holy Spirit. Therefore—although Schillebeeckx develops this less than it deserves—when the Christian acts in faith, hope and love, he or she acts literally in-spired by the Spirit of God. What the Christian does is God's doing as well as his or her own. He or she acts in the power of God. One must understand this if one is to avoid attributing magical powers to human beings.

One of the values of examining Schillebeeckx's three essays in their own sequence is that one finds exemplified in them the methodological change that has been virtually a seismic shift in the theology of the sacrament—the change that made the 1980 International Synod of Bishops so extraordinarily helpful. In the first essay, "Le mariage est un Sacrement," he continues in the *a priori* reasoning of centuries of his predecessors. He writes about "marriage." Although he draws inductively from the passages on marriage in the Old Testament and the New Testament, his rich analysis then synthesis say what marriage is in the abstracted ideal. He deals with the sacrament not as it *is lived* in real-life marriages but as it *should be lived* there. Only intermittently and briefly does he cross over and write about Christian marriages in the concrete, about what they in fact are. Had he done this from the beginning and systematically, he would have explained what Christian marriages can be if spouses co-work with Christ's Spirit working in and through them. In a word, he would have shown how real-life marriages can approach the condition of the ideal model.

But this crossing over to the concrete is exactly what takes place in *Marriage: Human Reality and Saving Mystery* and in the essay of 1974. In them Schillebeeckx examines what I have called the matrix of the sacrament, its anthropological underside. He traces the Jewish and

Christian perceptions of marriage and their treatments of marriage through the centuries. He prepares the human evidence of marriage for its own marriage with divine revelation about it, a marriage that, if consummated in the unpublished third volume, would produce the integral theology of the sacrament.

An Anthology from Scripture and the Fathers

We move now through "Le Mariage est un Sacrement," setting out Schillebeeckx's detailed and even intricate anthology on the sacrament which he drew from the scriptures and from the fathers. We report its elements here topically, succinctly and in places almost epigrammatically.

A sacrament is a personal act of God in Christ, who lives now in triumph over death gained in his resurrection. This act enters the sensate conduct of men and women. It draws them into the mystery of his redemption and has them participate there. This mystery is his effort to rescue human beings, the entire human race, from their sinfulness and bring them into unending union with himself (p. 19).

Christ is God's primary sacrament. He is God making himself available to the sensate consciousness of human beings. His essential sacramental action is to carry out God's love relationship with human beings. This he does by his self-giving. He died for them. He rose from death, and now forgives and heals them (p. 19).

Christ's Church is a community of men and women engaged in the same self-giving in order to forgive and to heal.

The first way in which these men and women, and Christ through them, act sacramentally in the Church is in its ritual cultus. Christ takes the most active part in this. It invokes God the Father's gracious help from within the mystery of Christ's redemption. The father responds always by sending his Holy Spirit, and sending him in a sacramental way (p. 19).

As hinted earlier, reception of the sacrament of baptism is an absolute pre-condition for persons' participating in any of the other sacraments. Since marriage is "a sacrament of the living"—a sacrament of persons already drawn into union with the living and active Christ—it requires not only the objective condition of having been baptized. It calls also for a baptismal life in its existential fullness. This fullness includes the sacrament of confirmation (p. 20).

Since the Church lives in a marital relationship with Christ—it responds with sensate love to his initiative of sensate love—a person's baptism takes him or her into this marital relationship. Since a person through his or her baptism already participates in this marital relationship with Christ, his or her subsequent marriage becomes a specific manifestation and working out of this relationship.

To get his work done among human beings God has covenanted with them. He has entered into a lasting relationship with them of trust and love. He has therefore first designed marriage as a covenant in order to provide a plan or sketch of the greater covenant, and of the covenantal love he desires with the entire human race (p. 28).

In Christ God's covenant with the human race is already in a sense established integrally. This is because Christ is both divine and human. Therefore God and the human race are joined with him perfectly in the most personal of loves. The reciprocity of this love is perfect. It is perfect from Christ's human side because to evoke men's and women's love for the Father he has given up his life. This is the covenant of grace, "of sanctifying grace" (p. 29).

Because of their baptism men and women have been joined with Christ in his own relationship with the Father. Their marriages participate in the Father's love of all the human race by receiving it through Christ; they participate too in Christ's reciprocal love of the Father (p. 29).

By their marital sacrament spouses participate specifically as spouses in God's effort to love all human beings personally and covenantally. They are brought into the paschal mystery and the Pentecostal mystery specifically as husband and wife. It is therefore not as private persons that they are made holy by this sacrament. They are made holy in their marital union. The grace of the sacrament sanctifies the husband in his relationship with his wife, and her in her relationship with him. Indeed it is their marital relationship itself which is the sacrament (p. 21).

Thus the marriage of two Christians is the mystery of Christ's work of redemption realized in a human community. The community itself then participates in the mystery. And since it manifests God's love while carrying it on, it is a sacrament (p. 36).

As a sacrament marriage makes visible Christ's love for the Church and its love for him. The spouses create this visibility by their love for one another. They thus sanctify one another as Christ sanctifies the Church—a sanctification which he accomplishes through them. Eventually through them he sanctifies the entire human race (p. 37).

A marriage of two Christians does not manifest the union of Christ and the Church because it is a sacrament. Conversely, it is a sacrament because as the marriage of two Christians it is a specific realization of baptism. It is a manifestation of the Christ-Church relationship only if it is a celebration of their love, only if it is an effect of God's mission involving the spouses through their baptism (p. 36).

Only Christ can give a Christian man and woman to each other in marriage because only by their baptisms are they consecrated and joined to him radically. If their marriage is not an effect of Christ's mission of the spouses to one another, it is invalid (p. 36).

The Spouses' Participation in Christ's Passion and Death

Because the grace of marriage is the grace given by Christ's redeeming work, the spouses can co-work with him only sacrificially. The sacrament calls to the spouses to enter into the mystery of the cross, into Christ's self-giving death (p. 44).

As Christ was broken, so also their marriage can break a man and a woman, through grievous disappointment, infidelity, death. But Christ's love was so great that the infidelity of his friends did not destroy it. It led him to go to his death in the effort to forgive and heal this infidelity (p. 44).

A marriage that comes close to death but rises again in repentance and forgiveness reenacts in a real way Christ's passion, death and resurrection. Their sacrament takes all the spouses' suffering into Christ's suffering. St. Thomas explained that "The sacrament conforms the spouses to Christ's suffering not insofar as this is painful reparation for sin, but insofar as it is a work of love in which he suffered for the Church that he was to take as his spouse" (*In IV Sent.,* d. 26, q. 2, a. 1, ad 3m) (p. 45).

Thus the love that the sacrament demands of the spouses is an oblative love. (Their inability to express such love in a marital way— their inability to forgive and to accept forgiveness—often brings to ruin a marriage that began well.) The forgiveness that spouses can bring to one another is not only human. By it they can bring Christ's forgiveness too (p. 45).

The Ministers of the Sacrament

Understanding the minister of a sacrament as the person or persons who create it, Christ is the primary minister of the sacrament in marriage, as he is of all the sacraments (p. 41). The spouses are secondary and earthly ministers of their sacrament. They minister it to one another by giving themselves to one another. They give themselves to one another by the power of Christ gained in baptism. They grace one another and are in fact a grace for one another.

Because the spouses' reciprocal self-giving completes and manifests Christ's giving them to one another, it is an exercise of priesthood in the Church. It is an essentially ecclesial act; they execute it in the Church and for the Church. They carry out a mission given to the Church by God. This is the reason for the gesture in the wedding liturgy which is the priest's taking his stole and with it joining the right hands of the bride and groom. This signifies the Church's empowering them, with Christ's power, to give themselves to one another and thus create their sacrament in his power. It signifies too that they are carrying out the Church's mission in the world (p. 42).

This is also why the proper setting for the creation of a marriage is the Eucharist. Here the spouses can participate most intimately in Christ's self-giving by participating in his sacrament which does this par excellence. Each is nourished by the participation and can thus nourish and strengthen the other.

The Indissolubility of a Sacramental Marriage

The last element we record from this essay of 1961 is Schille-beeckx's understanding of the sacrament as the cause of a Christian marriage's indissolubility. It is both like and unlike the understanding accepted among Catholics by that time. It is like it in that the human marriage's indissolubility has its cause in the indestructible marital relationship of Christ and the Church. It is unlike it in that the indissolubility comes to the marriage not because it is an image of the divine marriage and must therefore imitate its indestructibility. Indissolubility comes to the human marriage because Christ, who is the first cause in creating it, creates in it a particular specification of the covenant he has created and does create with the Church. These are one and the same act on his part. Since he creates an indestructible covenant with the Church, the particularization of it in the human marriage is also indestructible.

> Since Christ gives the two persons to one another in marriage, effecting a specific realization of the covenant between him and his Church (the baptismal character is ineradicable), the sacramental marriage is likewise and equally indissoluble. The evident tendency toward absolute indissolubility that one can see in a "natural" marriage itself is fulfilled in the sacrament . . . (p. 43).

> However the sacramental marriage acquires its ultimate perfection when it is consummated in sexual union. This shows that this union constitutes an integrating element of the sacramental sign, of the religious "Yes" pronounced by the spouses. The fact that the indissolubility of a sacramental marriage before consummation is not complete . . . shows clearly that the sexual union has a special signification for the bond itself. Because of the incarnation of the human person, the "Yes" said to the absolute marital union is itself completed only by the incarnation of this "Yes" in the first sexual intercourse (p. 44).

One notices that here Schillebeeckx has simply ignored the role of the spouses themselves in bringing indissolubility to their marriage, aside from his adding that their sexual union (understood as no more than intercourse) completes the indissolubility. We shall see in his third essay how he there takes the spouses' conduct much more realistically into consideration when he looks to the causes of indissolubility.

Marriage: Human Reality and Saving Mystery

In *Marriage: Human Reality and Saving Mystery*, of 1963, the earlier essay's *a priori* portrait of the sacrament drawn from scriptural and patristic sources gives way to a different kind of study. This is of the historical development of the understanding of marriage in the Catholic churches, and of the consequent development of the understanding of the sacrament in marriage. Now the method is an examination not of what the Spirit has presumably voiced from above, but of what has grown out of the soil of human experience. Here we need only draw the essential elements from the conclusion of these two volumes. Our own chapters thus far have traced the same history that Schillebeeckx examined and have borrowed from him in places.

Schillebeeckx draws his first and most fundamental point from his theology of history. It is that God's plan for the human race has from its beginning been marital. He has intended and has sought to draw all human beings into an exchange of love with himself. This plan is marital because God has carried it out by taking the initiative in inviting human beings to a free response to himself, and because the human response must be natural, which is to say bodily.

He can call to human beings to respond freely because unlike the imagined pagan gods he transcends the human condition. He is not sexual and is not married to goddesses. Marriage is a creaturely relationship. But it is nevertheless transparent to his presence and action. It is malleable as an instrument of his action in the world. This is because it is where essential fellowship, personal union—which is his own nature as a trinity of persons—can be at its richest.

Marriage is amenable to manifesting and even imaging God's relationship to the human race also because both are dialectical relationships. Marriage is dialectical because it is the interaction of human wills and emotions. God's relationship with human beings is dialectical because God interacts freely with human beings to elicit their free response of belief and love (p. 385).

God has gone beyond this inclusion of marriage in his plan of creation and has included it in his work of redemption as well. Any marriage can be included in this work because it is therein that men and women learn dialectical self-giving love. There they bring children into the world and there they can nurture them to the same love. For this reason, again, every marriage is in some degree sacramental (p. 386).

In his gospel instructions Jesus pointed to the sacramental character of marriage by insisting, in the words of Genesis, that when they marry a man and woman consecrate themselves to one another for all of life. Paul's interpretation continued this by pointing out a model for this consecration and a source of strength for it. This is Christ's self-consecration for the Church. Jesus and Paul both made clear that marriage is for the kingdom of God. Its setting and purpose are both eschatological. Even as a union of husband and wife it is meant to take them beyond their union. It is meant to bring them to final happiness with God. Hence celibacy and sexual abstinence are not antithetical to marriage but are needed parts of its realistic context (p. 386).

The Church's awareness of the sacrament in marriage was at first centered in the liturgical celebration of the mystery of marriage. And at first it was the incorporation of Ephesians 5:21–32 into the liturgy together with Jesus' logion about the inviolable character of marriage which provided the norm for this development of the understanding of marriage as a sacrament in the early medieval Church. It was not the sacramental concept, which was in the meantime being formulated by the scholars, that provided it (p. 393).

The medieval scholars' richest contribution to the developing understanding was to put all of marriage—the social relationship, the spouses' juridical contract, the familial institution—into the sacrament. All this human and secular, and complex, reality came to be the sacrament because it was seen as a sign of the mystery of Christ's continuing union with the Church (p. 393). This means inevitably that there are many subtle gradations in the sacramental character of marriage. This character does not stand or fall with the liturgy of marriage. The liturgy is only a first culminating point in the creation of the sacrament (p. 396).

When one looks for the grace-giving power of the marital sacrament, one must therefore find it in the consent alone (whether there is a religious ceremony or not), not in the marital intercourse. It must be found also and principally in the marital bond itself.

Because of the medieval scholars' including the whole anthropological substance of marriage in the sacrament they differed from the fathers about the nature of the permanence in marriage and about the source of it. The latter said it is not *permissible* to dissolve a marriage because of the spouses' *obligatio,* their commitment to one another, and with one another to God. The medievals said rather that it is not *possible* to dissolve a marriage because the bond itself is the sacrament (p. 394).

In Schillebeeckx's judgment it is the spouses' consent itself which is the center of a marriage's permanence. This is so because the consent is irrevocable. It is their irrevocable promise to love one another. It *must* be irrevocable because it is essential for their marriage's making visible the unfailing love of Christ—in a word for their marriage's being a sacrament. This irrevocable commitment to love one another is also the soul of their marital sexual expression. It is what makes this expression to be marital. The expression thus becomes in turn the expression of the lasting love relationship. It participates in the sacrament. It is a sacramental expression (pp. 390–391).

A Study of Marital Indissolubility

Schillebeeckx's plan in the essay of 1974 was to write a critique of the Catholic doctrine and discipline of divorce and remarriage. A kind of thesis running through his critique is that the Catholic understanding of marriage's nature has changed with the passing centuries. At each change the Catholic authorities themselves have accepted that marriage as understood at that time can disintegrate. Given the conviction established by the medieval scholastics that the sacrament is the marriage itself, it follows that the understanding of the sacrament too has changed. It follows that the sacrament must have a role, active or passive, in the marriage's disintegration.

Schillebeeckx finds in the evidence not that the Catholic authorities and scholars have stood firmly in place and watched marriage change around them. Rather the concepts themselves, the images by which they have interpreted the marital relationship, have changed. They have changed along with men's and women's experience of marriage, and have in turn helped to change the experience. One commonly noted example is that from apostolic times until after the Enlightenment Christian marriage proceeded on a double stratum. One stratum held the patriarchal model, with the wife as child-property; the other held the New Testament model, with wife as sister, companion and partner in love. Since the Enlightenment, but more commonly since the Romantic era of the nineteenth century, Western men and women have come to experience marriage as a one-with-one quest for happiness within the marital union itself. Only since then have they come to see marriage the social phenomenon—not the bond of contracted persons nor the family concordat—as in essence a love relationship, reciprocal, personal and embodied in sexuality. For the first time in the West sexuality was emphasized as the bodily exchange of interpersonal love (p. 51).

Schillebeeckx developed his thesis in the following comprehensive way. In Jesus' time and afterward, until the center of the Christian population moved out of the Near East and the greater part of this population came to be Roman citizens, the patriarchal was the most common form of marriage among Christians. Since the wife was considered her husband's property, he owed her in justice no more than the care owed to a child. Adultery on his part was not infidelity to her. It was the violation of another man's exclusive right to his property—to his wife, his fiancée or his daughter.

Jesus' words recorded in Mark 10 changed this: "A man who dismisses his wife and marries another commits adultery against her [his wife]." Paul repeated the substance of this change in 1 Corinthians 7: Neither spouse may dismiss the other. But nowhere does the New Testament say exactly what a marriage is, despite both Jesus' and Paul's repeating Genesis' affirmation that a man leaves his father and mother and clings to his wife, and becomes one flesh with her, one person before the law (p. 41). What a marriage is (again this is Schillebeeckx's thesis) is an historically and culturally determined reality. What it is cannot be derived, a priori and fixed, from a given and fixed human nature. The Church's own successively varied understandings of marriage bear this out. The nature of marriage itself varies as human beings develop (p. 42).

Schillebeeckx gets at the successive interpretations of marriage's nature by following the successive interpretations of marriage's greater or lesser vulnerability to dissolution or to disintegration. Because marriage in Jewish society was a means for preserving and extending the family, it was considered complete only with the birth of a child. Therefore a sterile marriage was by definition a failed and disintegrated marriage (p. 43).

In Paul's time a pagan spouse's rejection of the other's conversion to Christianity was a cause of the marriage's disintegration. The Christian convert was not to prevent the pagan's departure from the marriage. He or she was not to play the slave (p. 44).

The exceptive clause in Matthew 19 shows that at least some Christian communities of his time accepted that under Jewish law a marriage could disintegrate because of the presence in it of *pornéia*, whatever the nature of this liability or delinquency may have been (p. 45).

In the twelfth century Pope Alexander III decided that Jesus' words forbidding the attempt at dissolution refer only to sacramental marriages, and among these only to those that have been consummated by sexual intercourse. Along with the installation of the Pauline privilege in the same century Alexander's determination finished undermining the position that marriage is of its nature indissoluble. But it also sharpened the question that asks: If it is not in its nature that marriage is indissoluble, where then does the indissolubility reside? And wherever it is, what causes it and sustains it? It cannot be the presence of the sacrament in a marriage, or the fact that a marriage is a sacrament, because from as early as the fourth century Catholic authorities have accepted that the marriage of two Christians (presumably a sacramental marriage) can be dissolved by one spouse's taking up monastic life, even if against the will of the other. And since the sixteenth century papal authority has dissolved the sacramental marriages of Christians provided that, even if consummated before baptism as natural unions, they have not been consummated as sacraments since the baptism of both spouses (p. 47).

The fact that marriage is now understood as a man's and a woman's relationship of self-giving love makes impossible the hold on indissolubility as a fixed and given characteristic of a marital institution. It is a condition-to-be-attained of the love relationship. If it is in a given marriage, it is there by the spouses' decision and by their effort to put it there.

A consequence of this historical development for our understanding is that the meaning, the requirements and the boundaries of the indissolubility of marriage are different in the different stages of historical development—in each according to the social value attributed to marriage in its own right, and according to its concrete function in the entirety of the given social system. Since in this sense a marriage ethos is the realization of a newer and higher form of humanity within an evolving social-economic milieu (which implies that no such higher form ought ever be abandoned), then in consideration of the type of marriage that has gained acceptance in the Western world in the last two centuries, we must draw the following conclusion. Since a marriage is admittedly an inclusive, reciprocal and permanent giving over of the selves to one another in love and care, then its indissolubility is not a property deriving with essential necessity from marriage *qua* institution. It is a vocation, a charge from within the marriage itself that must be brought to realization by the spouses. . . . Here indissolubility enters not as a characteristic belonging of itself to an institution; it is rather a characteristic deriving from and depending on a personal conviction, on the man's and the woman's decision that indissolubility will belong to what they mean to one another. If a marriage is conceived thus as an interpersonal marital relationship, then in the light of a humanity come to this point of development what we must conclude about the indissolubility of marriage is this: a monogamous and faithful marriage, in which two human beings give themselves over to care for one another for a lifetime, in fact "offers the richest possibility" for marriage conceived of specifically as an interpersonal relationship. However, not as though their private lives ruled all. Indeed precisely this love, because of the rich element of responsibility in it, turns and looks to an even richer future, namely to the child (pp. 51–52).

Schillebeeckx comes back to the same thought a few paragraphs later. As an anthropologic reality a marriage is a man-woman relationship created and sustained by interpersonal, self-giving, caring love. The marriage's indissolubility is a characteristic of this love.

Thus indissolubility depends on the personal conviction of two human beings who *will* to construct their marriage as an unbreakable covenant; which covenant existentially and from within itself excludes the very possibility of divorce, and this for precisely the reason that their interpersonal relationship has come to the point of union where existentially they can simply do nothing else than remain together in love.

Indissolubility is, again, a vocation, a commission to be realized despite and through a host of obstacles. It does not derive from an exterior "will of God", nor is it bound up with a preestablished and predesigned institution. It is not a command that simply comes and grips two persons as soon as they get married. At the same time this modern concept of marriage opens the door to a considerable tension. For what remains of this kind of marriage if the interpersonal relationship itself disintegrates completely?

But the interpersonal relationship is not the only nor the final ethical norm for the "anthropological validity" of a marriage. This relationship contains another element (pp. 52–53).

This element is the marriage's life and function within the larger societies, within the immediate family, the extended family, civil society, the Church. In one way the marriage exists for these larger societies. Therefore it must be ruled in some degree by these society's laws, which are themselves historically and culturally conditioned. Therefore although their indissolubility created by the spouses themselves is grounded in their interpersonal love, it is not grounded there exclusively. In order for their relationship to be a marriage at all, it must be acceptable to and accepted by the larger societies. If these demand indissolubility in marriage for their own good, a man and a woman must put it in their relationship if they wish it to be accepted as a marriage (pp. 53–54).

The Christian-Religious Dimension

It is the natural human relationship itself as just described that is the sacrament in a sacramental marriage. But a marriage is such only when the spouses enter deliberately into the working out of Christ's redeeming action in the Church. Taking up this work radicalizes their self-giving love to redemptive love. But reciprocally they can gain strength for this radicalization only if they do enter the sacramental action of God through Christ in the Church. Like indissolubility, the sacrament in a marriage is not there a priori and given. The spouses put it there by their decision and their work.

The sacramentality of marital love within a societal system does not consist of something simply given and automatic. It does not function as something beyond a person's consciousness and therefore as a kind of ontological modifier of this love. Neither does it consist, according to the ecclesial conception of it, in the mere awareness that it is an image of the bond of faithful love between God and man, between Christ and his Church. The sacramentality of marital love is the natural richness and authenticity of this human marital love itself to which a life of faith has developed it. This development of the human love is something the spouses have been committed to by their baptism. Such a union of persons brought to this degree of maturity, such a mutual gifting of the selves in every dimension of daily life, has at this point of marital love become two things.

It has become at once the definition of a humane marriage in the context of our modern world; and it has become the definition of Christian salvation—that is of a community of caring, creating, redeeming, healing and forgiving love. It is on these grounds that the Catholic Church calls marriage a sacrament. A marriage is indissoluble therefore not because it is a sacrament, a *sacramentum signum*. But it is a sacrament because and insofar as it bears within itself the will to develop an unbreakable covenantal love. Therefore it is not the mere historical fact of the spouses' having been baptized that makes their marriage a living sacrament. It is first of all the loving reality of the spouses' faith that makes it so (pp. 55–56).

The Christian character of a marriage shows itself in two forms. It does so first in the interpersonal relationship itself if this is born of faith and hope, and if its human love is radicalized to a total giving of the selves to one another in the model of Jesus' love. (In such a marriage the question of grounds of divorce is meaningless. No authority on earth can dissolve such a marriage.) The second form that the Christian marriage takes is social. This it does not only for the anthropologic reason that a marriage is in part a society for societies, as stated above, but also because the spouses' ability to believe, trust and love is given to them by these societies. And for Christians their marriages must participate in the mission of the Church itself, to bring God's redemption through Christ to the world.

Karl Rahner's Theology of the Sacrament

Karl Rahner's most valuable contribution to the theology of marriage is in Volume 10 of his *Theological Investigations*.[56] One finds there his reflections of 1965–1967, during the last session of Vatican II, which declared its mind on marriage in *Gaudium et spes,* and during the months thereafter. I include these reflections because they were not a prelude to *Gaudium et spes* but a kind of companion to and expansion of it.

Like Schillebeeckx Rahner had freed his theology of marriage from the tangential disputes that had trapped and held the official theology for generations. Also like Schillebeeckx he had drawn this theology in out of its methodological isolation as a quasi-autonomous treatise in the manuals. He lodged it where it belongs and where alone it is intelligible, within the theology of redemption and of the Church as Christ's instrument of redemption. And here in this volume he is again like Schillebeeckx in the latter's first essay. He develops a theology that designs Christian marriage abstractly and in the ideal, with the design drawn from the Church and its vocation in history as instrument of Christ's redemption. Noticeably absent from his reflections is any evidence that he drew from the experience of the married in developing them. Whether he thought so privately, he does not in this essay assume that that experience is a source of knowledge, and therefore of the theology, of marriage as a sacrament.

But he held clearly to two assumptions that run through the essay and determine its development. One of these is that nothing in creation escapes God's indwelling presence. Nothing is merely secular territory; no creature goes its own autonomous way. God is present to and active especially in every human being's life. Therefore all of creation is sacred. Every part of it can be sacramental in the sense that it can disclose God's presence.

His second assumption is twin to that one. Just as there is no purely secular domain in creation, there is not nor has there ever been a purely secular history of the human race collectively or of persons taken singly. This means not only that God has always intended a certain path for human beings. But he has been active in them, working to bring them along this intended path. Its end, its goal for all, is a union of love with Christ, a union in (understanding the term correctly and humbly) the eschatologically triumphant Church.

Rahner's first concern is to understand a sacrament correctly. It is never a private affair. It is something that takes place in the Church; it is something that the Church does. For the Church is itself the arch-sacrament of Christ's presence, since God acts through Christ and the Church to give himself to human beings and to call them to him. For the Church any of its sacraments is always its act of self-realization. It manifests itself there sensately, brings into the space-time dimension of the universe God's self-giving and calling. In its sacraments the Church also carries out the human response to God's call.

Precisely as an expression and a reaching of God's will to be with human beings and to bring them to himself in salvation, a sacrament is always efficacious, is always (in scholastic terms) *opus operatum,* a work carried out integrally. But the success of this work depends on men's and women's free cooperation with it (p. 201).

Marriage as Sacramental

Any marriage is ready to be a sacrament because any marriage is of its nature a sign, a manifestation. It is such independently of any Christian or theological consideration because it is a sign of the man's and woman's wills to be spouses to one another, to love one another. Their marriage is a sign because it exists in the sensate domain and in society. This sign is authentic when it really does contain and manifest the spouses' love for one another. But it can also be empty, inauthentic when it no longer contains and manifests their love (pp. 202–203).

The way in which a marriage manifests God's presence and action can best be understood by probing the nature of married love. It is through an examination of this love that Rahner in fact enters his consideration of the sacrament in marriage.

The dimension of their souls in which God is most active in human beings, in which they most immediately meet and interact with him, in which he can most evidently disclose his presence, is in their power to love and in their acts of love. Not only is the experience of loving needed for understanding God's love, but it is the means for loving God himself. Indeed it is impossible to love him without the experience of loving another human being, because, as just pointed out, one learns to love first in and by this human love.

> Only one who has encountered the world of personal relationships as a matter of concrete experience, has accepted it in love and has freely committed himself to it, can make real to himself and freely accept that transcendental orientation of the spirit in terms of knowledge and freedom, the ultimate basis and absolute goal of which is that mystery upholding and upheld by one which we call God (p. 204).

Two persons who truly love one another seek the depths of one another's being. There they may find their fundamental dependence on God and their orientation to God. Such a love must be sustained by God's grace. The self-surrender that is essential to love can be made only if its reason and its goal are God. For God always imbues such love with his own grace, his own salvific power. In doing so he raises this love and opens it to his own personal entry (pp. 204–205).

Rahner's ground for saying these daring things about marital love is the universal presence and action of God in human conduct and relationship that were pointed out earlier as one of the premises of his theology of marriage. The actual order of the human race is the order of salvation. Human beings' moral acts are never merely natural. God always enters them and orients them to himself. He does this by his self-bestowal to the human person; it is his self-bestowal that makes these acts truly moral. He takes the initiative in all this, and he does it all even though the person may be unconscious of it. He enters and acts in their actions especially when human beings love one another selflessly. Such love is always the *caritas* that God himself inspires and sustains. He enters this human conduct of love by his own self-giving to the persons and empowers them for the love by which they give themselves to one another (p. 206).

Although the persons' meeting God in this love seems private to them, it is not. Although it is their marital love, they do not form it and experience it in isolation from all others or against them. They form a new conjoined person, a we, in order to go out to others. The human cause of this is their already coming from a community wherein they first learned to love. And a further cause is the natural fruit of their love that is the child, who is oriented away from their private love toward the community. What is more, to truly love a spouse, a person must love *all* in his or her life. This demands a trusting acceptance of the unknown and unforeseen, including the other's ties to many persons. Any marriage carries a debt to the other persons who have made it possible (pp. 207–208).

Marital Grace

The societal dimension of seemingly private marital love is better understood in light of the grace that enables and sustains this love. This is God's covenantal grace. It is covenantal in that he enters the entire human race, he acts in it always in an effort to draw it to him in covenant and to draw it together in covenant. Consequently in gracing a man and woman, in capacitating them to live in a self-giving, marital way, he is drawing them into this covenant. From their side the man's and woman's accepting this grace takes them into God's act of loving all their brothers and sisters in the human race. When a person accepts and works with this grace, it frees from the limitations of merely human love and enables him or her to love all whom God loves and as he loves them— covenantally, in his effort to draw all together (pp. 208–209).

Thus a couple's marital love, and their marriage, are a sensate manifestation, even an embodiment of God's covenantal work in the world, and of his gracing the couple to take part in this work. This grace destroys egotism, even the egotism-for-two of a self-enclosed marriage.

Marriage and the Church

It is important to first understand something about the inner unity of the society that is the Church. Compare a marriage and the Church. The difference between them is not that of a couple from a crowd. Their difference is interwoven with their similarity. In both, the marriage and the Church, the bond that unites the persons is a love that is capacitated by God's covenantal self-giving and his calling, which are his grace. This is why the Church is a sign of interior love, as a marriage is a sign of such love.

But their difference is this, that whereas a marriage can be a false sign where it embodies neither the spouses' love nor God's love, the Church taken as a whole, as an integral community, cannot be such a false sign. In its belief, in its cultus, in its charitable work it is a sign of the redemption of the entire human race, even though this work may falter and even fail in times and places. But it is never false in regard to God's redemptive love at work in it. God is the cause of this authenticity. He is the one who makes the Church an indestructible sign in the world of his redemptive love of the human race. It is for this reason that even the perishable love of two human beings in marriage can be the sign of an imperishable love in the society of human beings that is the Church (pp. 210–211).

This union of love in the Church is the basis of and a model for the love union in marriage. From their side the spouses' love for one another is an actualization of the love that unifies the Church. Marriage taken as a whole is a manifestation of love which in turn helps to create the love that is the human reaction to God's self-giving. And this love unites human beings to one another as well as to God (p. 212).

To say this another way, when baptized partners bind themselves to one another in marriage, something happens in the Church and to the Church. For when married love produces this binding, it is not "a worldly affair" (it is not Luther's *weltliches Geschäft*). Their joining in love is an event of the love that unites God and man. Their marriage is a moment in the process in which the Church realizes its own nature and purpose. Their baptism empowers them to do this, to complete this moment of the Church's self-realization.

And this bonding is a sacrament, for in it the spouses make sensately evident this love at work in the Church. They express the love of God and man visibly. It is a sacrament because in the spouses the Church brings its own nature to reality (p. 213).

The Institution of the Sacrament

Almost as an aside Rahner insists that there is no need to search in the gospels or in extra-biblical tradition for Christ's words of institution of the sacrament. He adds that Christ probably never spoke such words. Rahner's own interpretation is that the "word of institution" consists of two factors. The first is that the religious relevance of marriage be acknowledged, and that this relevance be Jesus' doing. The second factor is that the Church has appropriated marriage as an eschatological sign of the salvation that God wills for all human beings for all time (p. 215).

There is likewise no need to look to Ephesians 5 to confirm the sacramental nature of marriage. Genesis 2:24 has raised marriage universally to a sign of the Christ-Church union. For any marriage, being a sign of mutual love, is thereby a sign of God's action in the world. A non-Christian marriage does not compare with a Christian marriage as a merely secular event with a sacrament. It compares with it rather as a human action that reaches for God (it is *opus operantis*) with this same action as taken up into a signing, an imaging in which God meets the person (*opus operatum*). The relationship is like that between an act of faith before baptism, an act (*opus operantis*) that justifies before it is taken into the sacrament, and the same act of faith taken into and participating, in baptism, in the sign of this justification (*opus operatum*) (p. 214). But one must understand that even a marriage that never reaches Christian sacramentality is wholly an event of grace. Again, a marriage does not become an event of grace only at the stage at which it acquires the status of a sacrament as the latter is commonly understood. The event of grace in every marriage becomes a *sacramental* event of grace (as *opus operatum*) in those cases in which it is completed between two persons baptized in the Church (p. 215).

It is commonly said that a marriage is a sacrament in that it is an image of the love relationship of Christ and the Church. A consequence of this is the persuasion that in his conduct the husband must reflect the headship of Christ, while the wife must reflect the submissive Church. If this were true, the love relationship itself of the husband and wife would be not the primary but the secondary referent and correlate of the Christ-Church relationship. But it is not true. The roles of husband and wife in the Pauline analogy are no more than devices in his catechetical instruction. The primary referent and corollary to the Christ-Church relationship is the two-in-one-flesh unity of husband and wife as this is reasserted in verses 29–32 from its source in Genesis 2:24 (p. 218).

The key question coming from Ephesians 5:21–32 as a source of knowledge about the marital sacrament asks where Christ fits into the dynamics of this sacrament (p. 219).

God's Covenant and Marriage

The relationship of God's creation to his covenant is that the former puts human beings in existence, while the covenant orients them, calls them back to him. Creation makes the covenant possible; covenant is the reason for creation. Christ is the point at which God and human beings meet in covenant. In this sense Christ is God's grace. The call to covenant in him is a call to grace, and the joining in covenanting is a gracing (p. 219).

Spouses are joined in a sacrament wherein their union is oriented to the end that God intends for all human beings. This orientation is toward a goal that is eternal. When spouses join in this union of love, they manifest God's gracing effort to bring all human beings into union. This is the effort that forms the Church; it seeks for the union of all human beings within the Church in union with Christ. Therefore there is not merely an outward similarity of the husband-wife relationship with that of Christ and the Church. The two unions are internally related; they condition one another. The specifically Christian relationship of husband and wife exists *because* the Christ-Church relationship exists. The former participates in the latter because this is the ultimate cause of the husband's and wife's unity. By reason of this cause-effect relationship of the two unions, the spouses' marital union achieves its full manifestation in the union of Christ and the Church (p. 220).

Summary

The most demanding task handed to the Catholic theologians of the second half of the nineteenth century was compelled by the secularization of marriage and of all else in Western society begun during the Enlightenment. This task was to explain how it is that every marriage of two Christians is a sacrament, even the marriages of Catholics inert in their faith, and of Protestants who do not hold their marriages to be sacraments.

The common core of the theologians' explanations was that not only all Christian marriages but all marriages have been taken up into God's work of salvation begun in Christ. Thus all are at least inchoately and potentially Christian sacraments. The marriages of Christians are actually such sacraments because their baptism joins them to Christ, and their marriages image the divine marriage of Christ and the Church and participate in it. Thus in Christian marriages the natural marital relationship and the sacrament are so inseparable that Christians can create no other than a sacramental marriage. Even if they wish to do so, they cannot create a merely natural, or secular, marriage.

A problem born of this insistence was to explain how a contract, the marital contract, can become this image of conjoined divine and human love. The problem was exacerbated by the added interpretation that the contractual good that the spouses exchange is their rights to sexual acts. It is indeed exacerbating to have to conclude that it is such an exchange as this that creates the earthly image of commingled divine and human loves of Christ and the Church.

A significant shift in the theology of the sacrament appeared during the second half of the nineteenth century. This was a change in strategy for verifying the inescapable sacramentality of Christian marriages. Less frequently did the theologians simply deduce this verification from Ephesians 5:32, "This is a great sacrament." They began to consider the marital sacrament as an element of Christology. Mathias Scheeben especially, and after him Louis Billot, repeated the ancient premise that from the beginning marriage has had in it the potentiality for being taken up into Christ's redemptive work, and taken up as a sign of Christ's redemptive work in and through the Church. For this reason marriage has never been merely secular. It has always been a "natural" sacrament and instrument of God's work, always in proximate potentiality for being made a Christian sacrament. But this potentiality has been actuated for Christian marriage universally by Christ's actually taking up his redemptive work. And the potentiality has been activated concretely in every Christian marriage because the spouses' baptism incorporates them in Christ's work.

This was the ruling vision of Scheeben's theology of marriage. Because Christian spouses are grafted into the mystical body of Christ by their baptism, so too is their marriage a condition and a function of this body. An inescapable effect of their baptism's incorporating a Christian man and woman into Christ's body is that they can marry only as members of this body.

They were the theologians of the two decades preceding Vatican II—Martelet, Rondet, Schillebeeckx principal among them—who worked at a formal, painstaking and inclusive interpretation of the place of marital love in the sacrament. It demands the spouses' total giving of themselves to one another, a judgment appropriated by the bishops of Vatican II. Because this is marital love's character, it can be taken up, along with the marriage, into Christ's love for the Church.

Although honoring the goodness of the sexual expression of this love, and according the expression a function in the sacrament, these theologians urged caution in its regard. Because it is so easily self-seeking it tends to diminish the selflessness of marital love. But the sacrament can purge sexual expression of this selfishness by strengthening the spouses to dedicate the expression to procreation, and to keep it within fidelity and permanence. And though the erotic sexual expression of love can be taken up into the sacrament, it is not this expression which most mirrors Christ's love for the Church. It is the transformation of eros' self-seeking into agapaic concern for the spouse that does so.

The concept of the grace of the marital sacrament is different in these theologians. It is no longer in the domain of actual, transitory graces—graces which are literally occasional divine helps for the spouses in fulfilling the demands of their state of life. It is rather in substance identical with habitual, sanctifying grace first received in baptism. It is this same grace now modified by the sacrament to help the spouses express their love sexually in a self-giving way, to help them bring children into the world and nurture them in goodness. The spouses' otherwise merely human expression of marital love disposes them for God's gracing.

Edward Schillebeeckx primarily, and Karl Rahner after him, were the two theologians whose interpretations of the sacrament have most influenced Catholic thought just before, during and after the Second Vatican Council. They finished what Martelet, Rondet, et al. had begun, the freeing of the theology of marriage from the four-century-old task of refuting the reformation Protestants, and from the more recent task of countering secularist claims on Christian marriages. They developed this theology in its rightful context, as an element of christology, the theology of God's rescue of the human race from its sinfulness, a rescue begun in Christ's death and resurrection and carried on in history through the Holy Spirit's action in the Church.

Schillebeeckx especially argued that God's fundamental relationship with human beings is itself marital, since it is a call to loving intimacy through the spiritual-sensate humanity of Christ. Christ first joins a man and a woman to himself, inducts them into his saving work, by their baptism. When they marry they continue this saving work specifically as married; their cooperation in this work, both physical and spiritual, becomes marital and thus sacramental. Because Christ began his saving work by literally embodying his love in a sacrificial death, so the spouses' love, to be sacramental, must be sacrificial, self-giving. And as Christ triumphed over death in his resurrection, so spouses can triumph over the many small deaths in their marriage by the forgiving love for which their sacrament capacitates them.

Schillebeeckx's argument for the indissolubility of sacramental marriages was not that because they are images of the indestructible Christ-Church relationship this indestructibility is simply put into them as indissolubility. Rather these marriages are indissoluble because they are particular specifications of Christ's indestructible covenant with the Church. He takes the marriages and, using the Christian spouses' ineradicable baptismal character, makes their marriages indissoluble.

But in his *Marriage: Human Reality and Saving Mystery,* Schillebeeckx staked the claim for sacramental marriages' indissolubility in a new and different place. It is not these marriages' imaging the indestructible Christ-Church relationship, nor even their being taken into Christ's redemptive covenant. It is rather the irrevocability of the spouses' consent that makes their marriage indissoluble. This consent springs from their baptismal faith. They make it in the power of Christ's own commitment; they make it as an effect of his gracing them. Indeed it is not the sacrament that makes their marriage indissoluble. On the contrary, it is their irrevocable commitment that makes their marriage a sacrament.

In his essay of 1974 Schillebeeckx carried this last thesis further. He insisted that indissolubility is in even a sacramental marriage not as a given and fixed trait. It is there as something to be attained—attained by the spouses' effort to love one another indefatigably. Thus he put the creating of the sacrament itself more thoroughly in the partners' own decision. Their human marital relationship is not made a sacrament by the *a priori* determination of even a divine cause. They must take their Christian faith to the point at which they freely will to cooperate with this cause to make their marriage a sacrament. They must join their wills actively to Christ's redeeming will to make their marriage a sacrament.

In his reflections on marriage as Christian sacrament in his *Theological Investigations* Rahner repeated Schillebeeckx's principal themes, but with emphasis in somewhat different places. He insisted that all of creation and all of history are divinely indwelt, divinely oriented from the beginning, and divinely drawn along one path toward one goal, namely union of all creation with God in Christ.

But while Schillebeeckx's concern was to understand the marital sacrament as an instrument of Christ's redeeming action, Rahner, while wholly accepting this, saw the marital sacrament more as an act of the Church. He emphasized even more firmly the role of the spouses' reciprocal love in creating and sustaining the sacrament. Self-giving love is that place, or moment, in human experience at which God can enter this experience most effectively because he himself is in essence an act of love. In fact all authentically self-giving love is empowered by God's own love, and is indeed possible only by this empowering.

As God's love for the human race through Christ is a covenantal love, and this covenant is realized most fully in that portion of the human race that is the Church, so too the spouses' love is covenantal. They help from the human side to sustain and enhance the covenantal relationship of God and the Church which was begun and is continued in Christ. In this the Christian spouses' marriage is a sacrament.

NOTES

1. Vol. 1, p. 56.
2. *Praelectiones Theologicae*, Vol. 7, 1838.
3. Romae, 1880.
4. *De Ecclesiae Sacramentis. Commentarius in Tertiam Partem S. Thomae* . . . Secunda Editio, Romae, 1897. Tomus Posterior, "De Matrimonio ut est Ecclesiae Sacramentum," pp. 322ff.
5. *Op. cit.*, p. 338.
6. *Op. cit.*, p. 344.
7. *Ibid.*, pp. 344–345.
8. *Op. cit.*, p. 353.
9. Romae, 1929.
10. *Op. cit.*, pp. 324–325.
11. *Ibid.*, p. 326.
12. *Ibid.*, p. 327.
13. *Ibid.*
14. *Op. cit.*, p. 347.
15. Scheeben completed the first edition of this work in 1865. He died in 1888, a few months before completing the first revision of it. The English translation of this work, titled *The Mysteries of Christianity*, is taken from the third German edition, a revision done by A. Rademacher. The treatise on marriage is in Part 4, "The Mystery of the Church and the Sacraments," Chapter 21, "Christian Marriage."
16. We are by now familiar with the claim that this first marriage was itself a sacrament, though literally pre-Christian because the marital union of Adam and Eve was a prototype, a foreshadowing of the union of Christ and the Church. Pierre Adnès repeated this claim in his *Le Mariage* (Tournai, 1963), insisting that the moment he instituted marriage in Eden God linked it to the later relationship of Christ and the Church. He added that where, in Ephesians 5, Paul asserted the husband:wife—Christ:Church analogy, he had in mind not only Christian marriages, but marriages generally in the history of the human race.
17. In his essay, "Mariage, amour et sacrement," in *Nouvelle Revue Théologique*, Vol. 85 (1953), pp. 577–597.
18. *Op. cit.*, p. 592.
19. *Op. cit.*, p. 599.
20. *Op. cit.*, pp. 579–580.

21. *Ibid.*, pp. 580–581.
22. *Ibid.*
23. *Ibid.*, p. 581.
24. *Introduction à l'Etude de la Théologie du Mariage.* Paris, 1960, pp. 154–155.
25. In *The Theology of the Mystical Body,* St. Louis, 1951 (published originally as *La Théologie du Corps Mystique,* 1944), Chapter 18, "The Sanctifying Office of the Church: The Sacraments. E: Matrimony," pp. 573–575.
26. *Op. cit.,* p. 16.
27. *Op. cit.,* p. 601.
28. *Ibid.*, pp. 601–602.
29. *Ibid.*, pp. 602–603. Italics added.
30. *Ibid.*
31. *Op. cit.,* p. 574.
32. *Op. cit.,* pp. 577–578.
33. *Op. cit.,* p. 583.
34. *Ibid.*
35. *Ibid.*, pp. 584–585.
36. *Op. cit.,* pp. 150–151.
37. *Op. cit.,* pp. 585–586.
38. *Op. cit.,* p. 580.
39. *Op. cit.,* p. 586.
40. Von Hildebrand's most influential works were two book-length essays, *Die Ehe* (1929), translated as *Marriage,* and *Reinheit und Jungfräulichkeit* (1927), published in English as *In Defense of Purity.* Doms' major work was *Vom Sinn und Zweck der Ehe* (1935), published in French (1937) as *Du Sens et de la Fin du Mariage,* and in English (1939) as *The Meaning of Marriage.*
41. This condemnation, dated March 29, 1944, is published in *Acta Apostolicae Sedis,* Vol. 36, p. 103.
42. Rondet, *op. cit.,* p. 132.
43. *Ibid.*, p. 133.
44. *Ibid.*
45. *Op. cit.,* pp. 146–147.
46. *Op. cit.,* p. 150.
47. *Op. cit.,* p. 154.
48. *Op. cit.,* p. 587.
49. *Op. cit.,* pp. 154–155.
50. In the journal, *La Pensée Catholique,* Brussels. It appeared earlier in Dutch in *De Bazuin.*
51. The English-language edition was published in 1965. The American edition (same date) was published as two volumes in one.
52. P. 397 in the American edition.
53. Its original Dutch version, "(On)ontbindbaarheid van der huwelijk," was published as Vol. 4 of *Annalen van het Thijmgenootschap* (Bilthoven). It was published in German translation in 1975 as one of four essays making up the volume, *Für eine neue Kirchliche Eheordnung* (Düsseldorf). It is from this German version that I have made use of the essay.
54. Cf p. 112, note 15 of the German translation indicated here in the preceding note.
55. The date of its publication in this English translation is 1963.
56. Translated by David Bourke, N.Y., 1973, pp. 199–221.

BIBLIOGRAPHY

Doms, Heribert: *The Meaning of Marriage.* Translated by G. Sayer. N.Y., Sheed and Ward, 1939.

Evdokimov, Paul: *The Sacrament of Love: The Nuptial Mystery in the Light of the Orthodox Tradition.* Translated from the French by Anthony P. Gythiel and Victoria Steadman. Crestwood, N.Y., St. Vladimir's Seminary Press, 1985.

Fuchs, Josef: "Theology of the Meaning of Marriage," in *De Matrimonio Coniectania.* Rome, Gregorian University Press, 1970, pp. 285–296.

Häring, Bernard: *Marriage in the Modern World.* Westminster, Md., Newman Press, 1966.

von Hildebrand, Dietrich: *Marriage.* London, Longmans, 1942.

Leclercq, Jacques: *Marriage, a Great Sacrament.* London, Burns and Oates, 1961.

Palmer, Paul: "Christian Marriage: Contract or Covenant," in *Theological Studies,* Vol. 33 (1972), pp. 617–665.

Rahner, Karl: "Marriage as a Sacrament," in *Theological Investigations, 10.* N.Y., Herder and Herder, 1973, pp. 199–221.

Schillebeeckx, Edward: *Marriage: Human Reality and Saving Mystery.* N.Y., Sheed and Ward, 1965.

van der Poel, C.: "Marriage and Family as Expressions of 'Communio' in the Church," in *The Jurist,* Vol. 36 (1976), pp. 59–88.

14. CURRENT CATHOLIC THEOLOGY OF THE SACRAMENT AND CRITICAL REFLECTIONS

From our examination of contemporary Catholic thinkers in the preceding chapter it is clear that significant changes have taken place in the Catholic theology of marriage, and that the impetus for change will continue. These changes appear partly in conclusions about marriage and the sacrament, at least where the conclusions are drawn by scholars working outside the official agencies of the Church. But they are to be found much more in the method of doing this theology, and found notably among the same non-official theologians. Schillebeeckx in the third of his essays, and Rahner at his best, exemplify these changes in method. I believe the main points of change are the following.

The sacrament is no longer studied proximately as a weapon in dispute with dissenters from Catholic teaching. If the two-century-long conflict with the Catholic governments of Europe about jurisdiction over marriages had carried on in ecclesiology, the theology of the Church, marriage's role in the conflict might have been that of a constituent of this theology. But the conflict was not theological. It was juridical. It was a contest of competing authorities. It is true that the theological thesis at the core of the Church authorities' argument had been proposed as early as the thirteenth century, namely that the marriage of two Christians is always a sacrament. But that this reserves the marriages of Catholics exclusively to ecclesiastical authority was not a conclusion drawn spontaneously from that thesis. The centuries of hesitation, before Trent's *Tametsi,* to end clandestine marriages by the full exercise of this authority, witness to that conclusion's fragile hold. Nevertheless the sacrament was asserted as the reason for the primacy of ecclesiastical authority over Catholic marriages, and the *a priori* sacramentality of every such marriage as the reason for the exclusivity of the authority.

Now the juridical captivity of the sacrament is coming to an end.

But not entirely. The current Catholic authorities' unbending insistence that for Christians the marriage as contract (or now as covenant) is inseparable from the sacrament is heir to the use of the sacrament in the juridical counter-attack against the Catholic dissenters of the seventeenth and eighteenth centuries. Nevertheless the change in method is under way. The sacrament in marriage is now under examination on its own merits, in its own character. This does not mean autonomously, in an unhistorical, supra-contextual atmosphere. As we shall see later in this chapter, such abstraction would itself falsify the sacrament. It has its proper place in Christian religion and the theology thereof. This is within the theology of Christ as savior and of the Church as instrument of his saving work. This first change in method is that the examination of the sacrament now goes on mainly in this place.

A second change is in the examination of the matrix of the sacrament, of marriage the human relationship. Virtually since the beginning of Christian theorizing about marriage this has gone on in dissociation from the experience of marriage. The theoreticians, all of them male and virtually all celibate monks or clerics, have designed models of marriage in the abstract. They have designed them tendentiously, in order to clamp them onto real-life marriages so as to make the latter amenable to regulation; in order to undergird a theory of marriages' indissolubility but at the same time to keep them available for authoritative dissolution; in order to provide *ex post facto* a human matrix for a sacrament equally *a priori* in design. Rarely was married Christians' experience of marriage consulted. Therefore the designers did not know in fact what a marriage is. They knew only what they wanted the definition of the conceptualized model to be. Moreover, because they ignored the changes in the marrieds' experience of marriage, their own changing of the conceptualized model was done not in order to reflect reality but in order to have a model ready to survive the theological or juridical crisis of the time.

But now the authorities, the theologians and the canonists are turning to the married to find out what marriage is—and therefore what the sacrament is. Better still, more and more the critical examination of marriage is being done by the Christian married themselves, by those who can write of their own experience. In telling of this experience they do what the bishops of the Second Vatican Council said must be done if the Church is to teach well. In their Dogmatic Constitution on Divine Revelation the bishops urged upon themselves the necessity of their going to those in the Church experienced in specific ways of life. In naming the persons in the Church who work to gradually clarify the meaning of traditions coming down from the apostles, they spoke of ". . . the meditation, the pondering carried on by the faithful who hold these things [this tradition] precious . . . through their personal, intimate understanding of the spiritual realities they experience."[1]

The image theology of the sacrament is disappearing, although more slowly from the thinking and writing of the official theologians. We have seen again and again that the marriages of Christians have for centuries been deemed sacraments because they are *sacrae rei signa,* signs of a sacred reality, and that they are such signs in that they are images of the marital relationship of Christ and the Church. One reason for holding to this interpretation is that it contains the most logical warrant for the indissolubility of sacramental marriage interpreted as a trait given and *a priori* in such marriage. Thus, the divine marriage of Christ and the Church is indestructible; therefore the earthly marriage is indissoluble—because the divine marriage makes it to be so. The imaged divine reality reproduces its indissolubility in the imaging human marriage.

But diffidence about this argument's validity has moved theologians to explain Christian marriages' sacramentality as the spouses' incorporation in the Church and their participation in Christ's saving work in the Church.[2] (A moment's thought will show that this interpretation does not contradict the earlier image theology, but leaves for it its valid function as the illustrative analogy that the author of Ephesians intended.) This interpretation honors the reality of the Church's historical experience. The Church is not, as a misunderstood version of that analogy has proposed, already a spotless bride of the savior Christ. This metaphor belongs to the family of conceptual models long inhabiting the theology of marriage. The real Church is a society of fallible, sinful human beings. But whereas they fit poorly in the image of a spotless bride, they can, with all their fallibility, take part in Christ's work in the world, and do so as husbands and wives.

A third change in this theology is really a change in the theology of grace. As one studies the centuries' explanations of any and all the sacraments' gracing function, one gets the impression of grace as a *tertium quid* passing from God to the human person, even passing from the sacrament as ritual (the *signum tantum*) to the person taking part in the ritual as "recipient." It is as though God passed a kind of gift (*gratia* in the literal sense) to the human person. Perhaps this image of gracing has intelligibility if one speaks of "actual graces," God's transitory capacitating a person for courageous conduct, for temperate restraint, for hope in the midst of reasons only for despair. Yet even here the image and the explanation are naive. Even in human relationships when one man evokes courageous action in another, he does not pass something to him. He evokes something from his spirit.

Part of the current correction here is that persons are less frequently said to "receive" sacraments and sacramental graces through them. They are understood to participate in the sacraments; they act out the sacramental ritual, live out the sacramental character of their lives. The gracing they experience is first of all their union with Christ—in marriage their union with him in and with the spouse. The gracing is also a capacitating, an empowering to sustain this union and to do Christ's work in the world in this union.

Accordingly a fourth change is a kind of non-linear heir to the question that so exercised the medieval canonists and theologians, and those of the reformation and Enlightenment eras. This asked about the minister or ministers of the sacrament—who this is or these are, and what is done to administer it. It has been long since and commonly accepted that the spouses themselves are the ministers. But now the question asks what the spouses must carry on in attitude and do in conduct to create their sacrament. Is a minimalist answer the accurate one? Is it sufficient that both have been baptized, carry the baptismal character in their souls, and intend in marrying to do what the Church does? Or is more required of them—a more observable manifestation of Christian faith and love? This question, along with that about the sacrament as the cause of marriages' radical indissolubility, holds the center of concern in the Catholic theology of marriage at this writing. In any case, the "sign" that is essential to any sacrament is now spoken of in marriage as a manifestation, as evidence of Christ's active presence in the union. Again, concern that this manifestation amounts to an imaging has all but disappeared from the contemporary theology.

A Critique of the Current Theology:
The Propositions of The International Theological Commission

Of the many possible ways of writing the critique announced in the title of this chapter I have chosen the following. In December of 1977 the Catholic Church's International Theological Commission conducted a symposium devoted to "the Catholic doctrine concerning Christian marriage."[3] One must trust that the statements coming from the commission, although not authoritative in themselves, nevertheless represent the current teaching of the Catholic authorities concerning crucial issues in the theology of marriage. More accurately, certain clearly identified statements among the many coming from the symposium represent this teaching. One must set this limitation because the members of the subcommission who edited the report distinguished three genera of statements. The entire commission accepted near-unanimous responsibility for only the first of these. These were five "propositions," or theses, concerning the doctrine of Christian marriage. Their formulation was the work of the entire subcommission. Given the identity and responsibility of the commission, one can assume that these propositions were meant to express received Catholic doctrine.

The second kind of statement was a "gloss," a brief explanation accompanying each proposition, and written by a single member of the subcommission. Because all these glosses were approved by the entire commission, they constitute an official commentary on the propositions.

The third kind was a "relation," a more detailed analysis and explanation of each proposition. These were written by single members of the subcommission; they are only their own interpretations of the propositions.

My own analysis and critique will select among the three kinds of statements, but mainly from the second and third.

Proposition 1:1. The marital union is grounded in preexistent and permanent structures that constitute the differences between men and women. Spouses themselves have "institutionalized" these structures, even though in concrete forms the institution is modified by historical and cultural changes as well as by personal differences in the spouses. In all this God himself has intended marriage to be an institution, for the sake of the help the spouses must bring to one another in love and fidelity, and for the sake of the children they are to nurture within the security of the family.[4]

The proposition intends a centrist position between two extremes, one that rejects anything *a priori* and given in heterosexual unions, any permanent structures, any antecedent norms, any juridical regulation, anything institutional; and the contrary extreme that would lock these unions into marriage as one adamant cultural form. The proposition acknowledges that on which Schillebeeckx insisted in his third essay, that marriage has changed and does change its character.[5] But it insists that this is always specific change within generic permanence, that marriage's institutionalization changes but is always there within specific cultural forms, moral obligations and societal authority.

It urges that the personal concerns themselves of husband and wife demand institutionalization. As soon as the sexually diverse individual "I's" create the heterosexual "I-Thou," the latter must take some form in order to realize two goals: to bring the spouses to their human fulfillment, and to provide for the children to whose birth and nurture the sexual union is inherently oriented. Moreover the marital pair is oriented to the larger community, as were the spouses as individual persons before their marriage. Hence the need for equipoise in the tension between the personal, private dimension of marriage and its societal dimension. Each gives meaning to the other; each sustains and energizes the other.

This understanding of marriage the human relationship is not pretheist, is not dissociated from the divine intention. For the Genesis creation poem tells that the two correlated sexes are God's design: "God created man in his image. . . . male and female he created them" (v. 27). It tells also that their heterosexual correlation is not only in his image, but that as the correlated pair the man and woman are to do his work on earth—are to be "societal": "God blessed them, saying 'Be fertile and multiply; fill the earth and subdue it' " (v. 28). The parable in Genesis 2 shows the societal and institutional character of marriage. To create his marriage a man departs from one clearly institutional society: "That is why a man leaves his father and mother. . . ." And he immediately constitutes another such society, becoming as one person with his wife before the people and the law: ". . . and clings to his wife, and the two of them become one flesh" (v. 24).

These passages in Genesis may indeed disclose God's intent for the man-woman relationship. In disclosing this intent they may also verify his will that in real life the relationship be institutionalized, that it be set within ethical, juridical and religious controls. But it is false to think of the passages themselves as literally primeval, as pre-dating all cultural determinations—as false as it is to think that they tell of marriage's golden age at the beginning of history before the sin of the first spouses damaged it. (The latter consideration will become especially important when we consider presently the commission's proposition that Christ restored marriage to its original integrity.)

The Genesis passages date from a relatively recent epoch in history, the garden parable from c. 1000–900 B.C., the creation poem from c. 450 B.C. They are almost certainly distillations of the authors' experiences of marriage, therefore of marriage in patriarchal societies. They certainly tell what the authors wanted marriage to be. Centuries later Jesus made clear his will that husbands and wives live according to the model drawn from the passages taken ensemble. But they do not void the possibility that either Marx or Durkheim may have traced accurately the *de facto* gradual institutionalization of the man-woman relationship. The Genesis passages may disclose, in poetic and parabolic form, what God wills marriages to be as the fruit of a long maturation, when man-woman relationships reach the maturity, if they ever do, that he has willed for them from the beginning. This does not challenge the traditional Jewish and Christian belief that it is God who brought marriage into existence. But there are two ways of bringing a relationship into stable existence. One is to design it beforehand, to mandate it and inaugurate it in its finished form. The other is to call it into existence via the long and developmental experience of partners in the relationship. When the relationship is created in this second way, the ancestors of its eventual matured form can have lived first the primitive, then the developing and provisional forms of the eventual optimum.

Is there any point in asking which is the optimum form, and by which criteria one may identify it? I can think of none that can be found in any one cultural form of marriage, even the most adroitly designed and sophisticated. What is certain is that if one begins with the assumption that God's original design was damaged early in its history but has been restored by Christ, one will be tempted to settle on some later form as the restoration most nearly replicating the original, while skirting the fact that the original proposed at least in Genesis 2 is one of the later forms. For there the man was created first, but the woman only afterward as a companion for him, a helpmate.

Professor Lisa Sowle Cahill has noted Pope John Paul's inclination to lock wives into the homemaker-mother role in his "Catechism on the

Book of Genesis" of 1979, and in his apostolic exhortation, "Familiaris Consortio." She acknowledges his affirmation that marriage demands of both spouses full reciprocity and communion of their persons; that they must be equal in self-giving, that indeed any human being discovers his or her identity only in a full giving of the self; that the duties and rewards of parenthood today can be shared more or less equally by both father and mother; that the wife has the right to a profession in the world. She observes that John Paul proposes all these as components of the ideal.[6]

But she also points out that when one begins to draw the implications for real married life from his statements accompanying the ideal or derivative from it, one espies the prior determinations that rule his thought. Thus his insistence that in order to maintain the *full* self-giving of their love, and a trust essential to marriage, spouses must leave each and every act of intercourse open to conception, has real-life consequences to which he does not advert. One of these is that the wife must, according to her essential place in the marriage, be ready to accept as many children as will be born, and must remain in the home as nurturer. Or as another option she and her husband must forego sexual intercourse, thus voiding their marriage of its native self-giving. Or as a third option they must practice periodic continence. This, as the experience of the married shows, can modify the *fullness* of their self-giving—ironically the same ground on which John Paul condemns contraceptive intercourse.

It seems to me that the criterion for judging any culture's and any epoch's optimum form of marriage must be found in marriage's situation in this epoch and its culture. Here a universal truth enters, a truth proposed in the Jewish-Christian tradition as essential. It is that human beings are always in need of God's rescuing entry into their lives. For Christians this means Christ's entry. Therefore in any epoch the optimum man-woman relationship is that which best keeps them open to God's healing and saving entry. The cultural form that does this at a given time is the optimum for that time. To suggest an extreme but not outlandish example: Which was the optimum form for a young man and woman, both members of the French underground, in the spring of 1942 when the German occupation seemed indefinite, and both knew they were targets of a hunt by the German SS?

The Propositions Concerning the Sacrament

The four propositions that follow this first about the institution of marriage all deal with marriage as sacrament. Proposition 2 states the sacramentality of Christian marriage and examines the link between baptism and the marital sacrament. Proposition 3 treats of the relationship between natural marriage (marriage of creation) and marriage the sacrament. Proposition 4 deals with the indissolubility of marriage. Finally, Proposition 5 deals with the divorced and remarried.

Proposition 2:1 Jesus Christ recovered the reality of marriage as God intended it from the beginning of the human race . . . and restored it through his death and resurrection. Therefore Christian marriage is lived "in the Lord", and is shaped and determined by the essentials of Christ's salvific work in the world.

Already in the Old Testament the marital union was an image [a figure] of the covenant of God with his people Israel (cf Hosea 2; Jeremiah 3:6–13; Ezekiel 16 and 23; Isaiah 54).

In the New Testament the marriage of Christians has been raised to even greater dignity, namely to a representation of the mystery that joins Christ and the Church (cf Ephesians 5:21–33). Theological interpretation illumines this analogy more clearly: Christ's supreme love and self-giving in his blood, *and* his faithful and even irrevocable adherence to his spouse, the Church, become the model and example for Christian marriage. The likeness of marriage to this model is a relationship whereby the spouses really participate in Christ's covenant of love with the Church. On its part Christian marriage presents the Church of Christ concretely to the world in the manner of a real symbol and a sacramental sign.[7]

2:2 In this way Christian marriage is configured to the mystery of the union between Christ and the Church. This assumption of Christian marriage into the economy of salvation can be called a sacrament in the broadest sense. But it is at the same time a real-life particularization and real actualization of this primordial sacrament [i.e. the union of Christ and the Church]. Therefore it is in itself truly and properly a sign of salvation that confers the grace of Christ. . . .[8]

It is clear even at this short distance into the propositions that Ephesians 5:21–33 is a main source of the conclusions that they will draw about the sacramentality of marriage. Already in Proposition 1.2, when explaining the meaning of "marriage in Christ," the commission's writers claimed to find in this passage a unique way in which Christian marriages are created "in Christ."

In the words of the Epistle to the Ephesians one reads not only an exhortation that urges the spouses to imitate, in their union, the union of Christ and the Church. In this text the Christian marital union itself is assumed, secured and sanctified by the union of Christ and the Church. . . . It [the Christian marriage] thus participates in the total and permanent donation that Christ made of himself to the Church.[9]

The reader may already have noticed that a mode of predication in these passages poses a special difficulty for their authors in drawing valid conclusions about Christian marriages. This mode predicates attributes not directly of Christian marriages as these are lived concretely by Christian spouses. It predicates them rather of "marriage" conceived abstractly in the mind, at most with concrete universal reference. Thus the claims made here for the marital sacrament are, taken literally, only about "marriage" thus abstractly conceived. The logic of these claims produces only the conclusion, for example, that the ideal model of Christian marriage has been assumed into the love relationship of Christ and the Church.

Here is the epicenter of much of the current Catholic debate about the marriage sacrament. However valid the conclusions about the ideal model of Christian marriage, on what conditions can these conclusions be drawn about and extended to real-life marriages? Can this missing link be supplied to the logic? If so, how? We will find the commission theologians providing this link in Proposition 2. They affirm that it is through their baptism and baptismal faith that real-life Christian spouses, and their marriages, are "inserted" in the mystery, the salvific love relationship of Christ and the Church. It is Christ himself who does this.

The Intent and Meaning of Ephesians 5

Because such crucial use as this is made of Ephesians 5 we must delay for a moment the examination of these propositions in order to find out more exactly the Pauline author's intent and meaning in this passage.[10]

Assuming for discussion's sake that Paul himself was the immediate author of Ephesians, we find that his inclusive intent in writing the letter was to enlighten his readers about God's *mystérion*, his plan of reconciliation established from all eternity. This plan is that through his death and resurrection Christ break down the barriers of hatred, and unite Jews and Gentiles in one great community, the Church. Since Christ has already died and been raised from death, the execution of the plan is already under way.

It is essential for understanding this passage that the Church as community is conceived of as dwelt in and quickened by the Spirit of God and Christ, and that it is the Spirit who moves the persons of the community to work out God's *mystérion*.

The presentation of this thesis—God's plan of reconciliation begun in Christ's death and resurrection—occupies chapters 1:3 through 3:21. Beginning in Chapter 4 Paul spells out gradually the consequences of this plan for the Christians' here-and-now conduct of life. He gives instruction about how to live in such a way as to manifest and realize the plan. In places the instruction elides into exhortation.

The first such instruction and exhortation are in Chapter 4:1–16.

There Paul urges his readers to acknowledge that different persons have received different gifts of the Spirit, some to be apostles, some to be prophets, others pastors, others teachers. But all these gifts are from the one same Spirit; all are given for the building up of Christ's body, which is the Church.

From 4:17 to 5:18 exhortation joins with instruction. Paul urges his newly Christian readers that as they have already abandoned an old and futile life, and have put on a new life and even a new self, they now resolutely give up the conduct of the old life. Here Paul begins his *Haustafeln*, the inventory of the kinds of conduct to be shunned, such as lying, foul talk, and drunkenness.

At 5:18 Paul turns to the kinds of conduct that *will* come from those who live by the Spirit, and exhorts his readers to them. He singles out for explicit instruction three kinds of personal relationships in the Ephesian community, and in every Christian community of his time: that of husband and wife, that of father and children, and that of master and slave. At every point in his exhortation to love, deference, obedience and care in these relationships, the motive he urges for such conduct is the love of Christ—Christ's love at work in the Christians, and reciprocally their loving fear of him.

Where he instructs husbands and wives how they are to love one another—the husband must love his wife as Christ loves the Church, even to the point of giving his life for her; the wife must love her husband as the Church loves Christ, in loving deference to him—Paul constructs the analogy with which we are by now so familiar. How he uses the analogy, what kind of effects he intends to produce from it, bears careful examination. And we shall get to this in a moment. But to account for all the richness of the analogy we must see how his devising and using it impels him to reach into the Jewish scriptures and there draw from Genesis something about the character of marriage. His verse 31 recites Genesis 24: "For this reason a man leaves his father and mother and clings to his wife, and the two of them become one flesh."

Genesis 24 in its Hebrew original, *le basar' ehad*, is literally "one body." Paul's quoting it in his Greek as "one flesh" (*mía sárx*) is most probably the consequence of his drawing the quotation from the Greek Septuagint version of Genesis where the term is exactly that, *mía sárx*. In the preceding verse in Genesis the Yahwist author had the first man say that the woman is his intimate and constant companion, the sharer of all his life, from his greatest strength ("bone of my bone") to his most abject weakness ("flesh of my flesh"). Verse 24 is the author's assessment of this union, of this sharing of all of life: In and by it the man and woman become "one body." They stand as one person before the people and the law.

Paul captures this thought aptly in his verses 28b and 29a: "In loving his wife a man is loving himself, for no man ever hated his own flesh. . . ." Not improbably he means to splice these two figurative assertions of the intimacy and strength of the marital union—his assertion in verses 23 and 28 that a husband and wife are united like a head and a body—with the Genesis assertion that they become one body. Indeed Paul may have found this anatomical image of marital unity in the Genesis passage to begin with.

Note that the symmetry of the two assertions is not exact. Paul's own metaphor makes the husband the head, the nobler and ruling member vis-à-vis the wife body. The Yahwist author evokes no such clear image and asserts no such subordination. On the contrary, we have seen that in calling the wife (through the mouth of the first husband) the sharer in all of her spouse's life, he rather asserts her equality. That Paul over-rides this is evidence that he is convinced that God's original plan has been affected by certain contingencies in the history of God's people and in marriages.

The referent of Paul's most remembered and repeated declaration, "This mystery is a rich one" (*to mystérion tôuto méga estín*) (verse 32), is itself a rich one. He understands the first covenant in his explanation, that of the first man and wife, to be a *týpos,* a foreshadowing or prototype of the second of the covenants, that of Christ and the Church. It is this typological relationship of the earlier covenant to the later that Paul calls the "rich mystery." The former discloses much about the nature of the latter: Christ and his bride the Church stand as one person before God and man; they are joined in a covenant of love; they share in all of life.

But the richness of disclosure Paul does not mean to end with these two relationships, because the reach of the mystery is not limited to them. The first couple's foreshadowing illumines also the marriages of Christian husbands and wives. By God's will these too are to be covenants. So they too have the characteristics of the primeval, foreshadowing covenant: one-personhood before the people and the law; companionship and sharing in all of life. They are also to have the characteristics of the second covenant, that of Christ and the Church—most notably its unfailing fidelity and the husband-Christ's self-giving love even unto death. And certainly Paul intends that the wife's deferential love be included in this covenant.

Paul's Metaphors and Analogies: Their Use and Its Limits

Paul's strategy for all this explaining to and exhorting of Christian spouses is to first construct the metaphors we have seen—a web of them—and then to build them into two analogies. One of these is explicit, the other only implicit.

The explicit analogy has the actual Christian husband as metaphoric head related to his Christian wife as metaphoric body analogically as Christ the metaphoric head relates to the Church, his metaphoric body. The implicit analogy has the actual Christian husband related to his actual wife as Christ the metaphoric husband relates to the Church, his metaphoric wife.

What effect does Paul intend to work by presenting these analogies? Whatever it is, it must at least be some new knowledge in the minds of his readers. This is the very nature of analogic predication, the intent that one's readers' prior knowledge of one facet of the analogy lead to their understanding the other facet by dint of one's pointing out the similarity of the relationships in each of the two facets—a similarity of which they were hitherto unaware.

Within this intent that one's readers gain new knowledge, the writer of the analogy can work for new knowledge of three main kinds. One is merely informative-illustrative. Thus when a biblical author calls King David the Lion of Judah, his intent is that David's hitherto underestimated courage in battle be known for what it is. For the author's assertion is that David as warrior relates to his foes as a lion to its prey. This first intent may elide into a second, namely that David be admired for his courage. Here illustration moves into exhortation.

In consort with this informative-illustrative intent, a second intent may be deontological. Thus, one may seek to both apprise his readers of a moral imperative bearing upon them, and also move them to act in accord with the imperative. And this acting can take place in two domains.

Let us assume that in his parable of the prodigal son, in Luke 15:11–32, Christ intended that the father represent God the creator, and that the wastrel and repentant son represent any and all sinful and repentant men and women. By offering this analogy-in-parable Christ most probably intended that his hearers come to know two things, and at the two levels mentioned above. The first is that God's forgiveness is given before men's and women's repentance and is held out to them unfailingly. The second is that the hearers *must,* as a moral imperative, understand God's forgiveness in this way, and not think that his attitude toward sinners is rejecting and vindictive.

The second domain of action targeted by such an analogy's deontological intent is the readers' own conduct. Such intent in Christ's parable touches its readers' conduct regarding sin and repentance. In their repenting they must accept God's antecedent and unfailing forgiveness—accept it as an indispensable condition for being forgiven as he forgives.

A third intent in analogical statement is rarer and more difficult to describe. Its nature is ontological. But its intent is not only to inform readers of an ontological state, but also to create one. There is an example of this in Christ's instituting the Eucharist in the community of his followers.

In their Passover supper Christ's people, the Jews, have established and acted out a metaphor. Their gathering and eating the bitter herbs; their breaking and sharing of unleavened bread; their blessing, pouring out and drinking of wine; their eating the Passover lamb, while reciting the narrative of their ancestors' exodus from Egyptian slavery into freedom; their praying to continue courageously in this liberation—all these constitute an annual metaphoric dramatization of the actual exodus circa 1290 B.C. It is most important to understand that this reenacting reestablishes, year by year, and ontologically continues, the Jewish people in their historical identity. If Jewish people ceased to celebrate Passover in this dramatic metaphor, the heart would be gone from their identity.

At supper the night before he died (according to the tradition holding that this was a Passover supper) Christ acted out this Jewish metaphor while inserting at its core a new substance of meaning. This new meaning is that the supper is made a metaphor of his own liberating action. This is his freeing men and women from a more ruinous slavery, the slavery of sin and its punishment in inescapable death. He made the acting out explicit in the blessing, breaking and sharing of the bread, and in the blessing, pouring out and sharing of the wine. The breaking and pouring out are death in metaphor; the sharing, the eating and drinking are a renewing of life in metaphor.

Thus the two facets of the analogy: on the one side the relationship of the Jewish people's Passover supper to their liberation from slavery; on the other the relationship of Christ's eucharistic supper to his liberating from the slavery of sin and death. The second facet's meaning is drawn from the first. Reciprocally, in the Christian point of view, the second completes the incomplete meaning of the first.

Just as crucial for understanding Christ's intent is to see his ontological-creative use of this analogy. His establishment of the dramatic analogy that is the Eucharist established *his* people. His people's continuing to act out this analogy continues their existence. Their ceasing to enact it would also be the loss of the heart of their identity as Christ's followers. In short, what Christ did in putting the Eucharist, the analogy of the Passover supper and experience, in the community of his followers was to say to them, "By doing this I establish you as my people." And he could say this to them because it was by establishing this analogy that he did in fact establish his people.

The relevance of all this to Paul's instruction about marriage in Ephesians 5 surfaces when we ask, again, in which of the ways just explained did Paul intend his analogies to work. Or more precisely, since he took for granted that God, in Christ, was the maker of the analogical relationship of Christian spouses to Christ and the Church, what effect did Paul think this had and still has on the marriages of Christ's followers?

To begin answering this question it is important to note that Paul's over-arching intent in Ephesians 5:21–33 is not to offer doctrinal instruction, not to set forth and explain significant points of belief. His intent is rather to instruct and exhort regarding conduct—conduct of Christian spouses that ought to flow from the doctrinally known facts of God's *mystérion,* of the Spirit's indwelling in and guiding the lives of sincere Christians, and of Christ's love for his people.

A second and more detailed caution is in order. When interpreting an analogy's metaphors one must not shove aside the reality of which they are a figure, and lodge the metaphors in its place. Metaphors and analogies are means for understanding the elements of reality. They are not the reality itself.

Thus Christ is in reality not a husband. The Church is not a bride, nor any individual person. It is a society of men, women and children. Christ is in reality not a human head, and the Church is not his physical body. Neither is a Christian husband a head whose body is his wife.

Fidelity to reality is at issue here. If one were to let the metaphors force the facts of the case, one might say that because a head and its body need one another absolutely in order to continue in existence, so too do a husband and wife. Or one might say that as the head (or more precisely the brain) naturally controls any movement of the limbs, so too should a husband control his wife.

One must note too the asymmetry in the balance of facets in Paul's metaphors. Christ is a physically real person; his "bride" the Church is not. This produces an asymmetry in the analogy that portrays the actual Christian husband as head relating to his wife-body analogically as Christ the head relates to the Church as his wife-body. Since "wife" in the first case here refers to a person collectively real, while the Church does not, the asymmetry has consequences—consequences that limit the Church as a model for the wife, and limit the wife's imaging of the Church. Similarly the fact that Christ is the risen Lord puts limits on his modeling for the actual Christian husband, and on the latter's imaging of Christ. To point out but one limitation, one can predicate an unquestionable holiness of Christ, and of the Church understood here in abstraction. But one cannot predicate the same unquestionable holiness of the actual husband and wife. The conduct of their relationship may image that of Christ and the Church or it may not. In real life they have a freedom to defect from the divine model that the Church in abstraction does not.

But even without going to the analogy, even while staying within the metaphor of the Church as body (or bride) of Christ, one stumbles over limitations. Because Paul metaphorizes into both a body and a bride for Christ a society of real-life men and women, he abstracts from the reality found in the society. Not all the men and women making it up let themselves be purified or ruled by Christ as the metaphoric Church-bride or Church-body does. If Paul did not abstract from the reality of the Church here, he would have to say that at times the Church is grievously unfaithful to its spouse (or unresponsive to its head) because men and women in the Church, singly and in groups, sometimes sin grievously.

To put this another way, note that for the dynamics of his analogical reasoning Paul posits three spousal couples at different moments in imagined history.

The first is a couple he believes once existed, the first in actual history, the presumed parents of the entire human race. But in fact they are fictitious characters in the Hebrew parable of the entry of sin and misery into this race. So their marriage too is a fiction in the parable.

Of the second couple the metaphoric husband is the risen Christ, an actual person now existing outside history, while the wife, the Church, is only metaphorically a person but is in reality a society of men and women existing in history.

The third couple consists of abstractly conceptualized ideals and/or concretely universalized conceptions of all the Christian spouses in history.

The homogeneous elements from couple to couple we have already pointed out. They are the commonplaces in the Catholic theology of marriage. The heterogeneous elements are not so frequently noted. In addition to the quite different ontological status of each of the couples and of the individual persons in the couples, there is in the third couple an element found in none of the others. This is a specific moral set, the moral contingency rooted in freedom of decision. The moral set of the other couples either is posited fictitiously and antecedently, or is what it is immutably. But while the moral set of the third couple could conceivably replicate that of the first two, and may do so in some of the couples making up its concrete universality, in no case and in no sense is the replication simply given or immutable. Each actual Christian married couple in the concrete universal either is free to never adopt the moral set of the first and second, or, having once freely adopted it, is free to later abandon it.

One consequence of this freedom is that one cannot reason with logically necessary consequence from a moral set in the first or second couple to the certain presence of the same set in the third couple. It does not have to be found in the third couple as a necessary effect of the causation in the first two.

The truth of this regarding Christians in the Church is borne out by Paul's assessment, in verses 26 and 27, of the Church-bride's treatment at the hands of her spouse, Christ.

> . . . 26. so that he might make her his by cleansing her in the bath of water joined to the word, 27. so that he might present the Church to himself in her splendor, having no stain or wrinkle or anything of this kind, but so that she might be holy and blameless.

Especially verse 27 tells of an accomplishment eschatological in nature and intent, and future in realization. Verse 26 says that Christ gave himself up for the Church, so that he might present her to himself as a bride, holy, without blemish, in her full beauty. But this does not tell of a work accomplished, a goal attained. It tells rather of an effort under way, of what is being accomplished progressively, of what will be realized fully only in a future climax of attainment.[11]

From both the structure of the analogy in Paul's exhortation, and from its individual elements, certain conclusions follow for the theology of the marital sacrament. First, and almost in passing, the predicate in verse 32, "This mystery is a rich one," does not refer to the actual marriages of Christian spouses, not even considered universally. One rarely finds contemporary theologians claiming that it does. So the verse taken in itself yields no knowledge of these marriages' sacramentality. But it is not without value. Given that its referent is the proto-marriage pictured in Genesis, specifically in its foreshadowing of the Christ-Church relationship, it helps to make clear that the kind of love in both these relationships is the kind God wants in actual marriages and will evoke in them—the one-flesh love of Genesis, the self-giving love of Ephesians. This is sacramental, this revealing the kind of love God wants and evokes.

It is equally improbable that one will find even traditional-minded theologians claiming that the passage as a whole but by itself is sufficient to demonstrate theologically that every actual marriage of two Christians is a sacrament. All seem aware that a link is missing from the logic needed for the demonstration. The core of this logic is that every Christian couple enters into the mystery of Christ's salvific work in the world (the traditional-minded phrasing says they are taken into it, or inserted in it), and thus participates in the sacramental manifestation of Christ. But one who reasons in this way must account for exactly *how* the spouses enter, or are taken, into this mystery. Their love, even if unitive and self-giving, cannot by itself accomplish this. If it could, any human couple sharing such love would be married in the Christian sacrament. (We recall Rahner's insistence that because of such love even an unbaptized couple live in a "pre-Christian" sacrament.) It is common, as we have seen many times in these pages, to complete the logic by saying that it is the spouses' baptism that takes them into this mystery. But this too leaves the explanation incomplete. Baptism is not enough to explain how the man and woman enter *specifically as married* into the mystery, into Christ's love for the Church, in the strength of which it does his work in the world. After all, Ephesians' conceptualized model is not the real Church. The spouses themselves are, along with millions of other men and women. Their baptism alone cannot make their marriages Christian sacraments. If it could, all the baptized would be married sacramentally. Something in the marriage itself must do so. What is this? Is it something required of the spouses themselves?

The Theological Commission's Proposition 2.3 gets at these questions immediately.

Like the other sacraments, marriage too communicates grace. The ultimate source of this grace is the work done by Christ, and not alone the faith of the recipients of the sacrament. But this does not mean that in the sacrament of marriage grace is given apart from faith or without faith. It follows, according to classical principles, that faith is presupposed as "a dispositive cause" of the fruitful effect of the sacrament. But on the other hand, the validity of the sacrament does not necessarily involve its fruitfulness.

The presence today of the "non-believing baptized" poses a new theological problem and a serious pastoral dilemma, especially if the absence of faith and even its rejection are obvious. The required intention—the intention "to do what Christ and the Church do"—is the minimal condition necessary for making the marital consent a true human act in the domain of sacrament. To be sure, one ought not confuse the question of intention with the question of the personal faith of the contractants. But neither can one separate them entirely. Authentic intention is ultimately both born from and is nourished by a living faith. Consequently where there is no trace of faith as such (in the sense of *Gläubigkeit, croyance,* readiness to believe), nor any desire for grace or salvation, there arises a doubt of fact—doubt whether the above-mentioned general intention, a truly sacramental intention, is present, and whether the marriage is truly contracted. The personal faith of the contractants does not in itself constitute the sacramentality of the marriage. But the absence of this personal faith compromises the validity of the sacrament.

This fact poses new questions that to date have not been resolved satisfactorily. It also imposes more serious pastoral duties in regard to marriage. "Above all, Pastors must stimulate and nourish the faith of those who are preparing to marry. For the sacrament of marriage supposes faith and requires it" [*le sacrement du mariage suppose et réclame la foi*]. (From Ordinances for the Celebration of Marriage, Prenote no. 7.)[12]

This proposition is a welcome confrontation of the question, unsettled and disquieting since Vatican II and earlier, that has been dubbed colloquially the question of "automatic sacramentality." Its source is the conduct of Catholics who request a religious wedding despite their being religiously inert, despite showing little or no interest in the Christian and specifically Catholic way of life. The commission acknowledges that this produces a dilemma. It does indeed. Its other horn is the Catholic doctrinal insistence that the only marriage that two Christians can create is sacramental. Thus, if their lack of religious faith incapacitates them for creating a sacramental marriage, they cannot marry at all. The Church's teachers do not accept a fall-back alternative for them, namely that they can create a sub-sacramental marriage.

The Theological Commission and the Faith Needed for the Sacrament

But the question within the dilemma—the question whose answer may either seal it in inextricably or break it open—asks, as I have hinted above: What more than the parties' baptism is needed as the faith sufficient to create the sacrament? What must the spouses manifest sincerely in religious attitude and conduct?

Before looking at the commission's own answers to these questions it is not beside the point to make clear the element of Catholic teaching that even a devout Catholic can create and live in a marriage that is not a sacrament. This is a Catholic who marries an unbaptized person. Because the latter is unbaptized, the marriage is not a sacrament. This raises a theological question far more serious than it seems at first glance. Suppose the unbaptized spouse mistakenly thinks he or she was baptized in infancy, now lives a most active and devout Christian life, together with the baptized spouse manifests a vigorous faith in and love of Christ, and thus provides superabundantly all the evidence of sacramentality that one could desire. Yet because of the lack of sacramental baptism the marriage is not a Christian sacrament. The empiric and the transempiric dimensions of sacramentality here contradict one another: a non-sacramental marriage is being lived sacramentally.

It is also pertinent to our examination to notice that by its formulation this proposition at least apparently intertwines two questions that are distinct. One of these asks what kind and manifestation of Christian faith is needed in order to create a sacramental marriage at all. The other asks what faith is needed if the sacrament is to be fruitful, if the spouses are to be graced in and by their sacramental marriage. The two questions can be asked separately, and justifiably so, as the proposition seems to ask them at one place. But they ought not be taken as variant formulations of the one same question. It is traditional Catholic teaching that a person can participate in the Church's sacraments validly but unfruitfully, that is, without being graced by the participation. For example a man ordained while in serious sin is said to become a priest thereby but not to receive the grace of the priesthood. Or a person in serious sin is said to be able to participate in the Eucharist without being graced by his participation.

Our question at hand, the more grievous of the two questions formulated above, asks about the faith needed to create the sacrament. How easy it is to slip from this to the other question about the sacrament's fruitfulness in gracing is evident in Msgr. Phillipe Delhaye's commentary on the proposition.

It simplifies the matter, but does not falsify it, to say that in reading Scripture in continuity with tradition, the Church's *magisterium* has always held that her *mysterique* and sacramental signs owe their efficacy to the action of Christ perpetuated through his ministers; but that on the other hand the graces offered by these signs must be received with faith by the persons who are to be beneficiaries of them. This is required as a primary condition for the sacraments' being efficacious and, even more clearly, for their being fruitful. If the subject's faith cannot be personal, as in the baptism of an infant, it at least has there a substitute in the faith of the Church, of the godparents and of the parents, before being taken up personally by a fundamental choice at the age of reason or by a ceremony of profession of faith.[13]

Vatican II sought to give witness to the traditional belief of the Catholic Church when it affirmed (in *Sacrosanctum Concilium,* no. 59) that the sacraments confer grace (this is homage rendered to the *ex opere operato*), but insisted at the same time that the sacraments presuppose faith, nourish it, strengthen it and express it.[14]

Thus far Msgr. Delhaye keeps the two questions distinct. But as he continues his commentary he makes the first question (about the possibility of creating the sacrament itself without faith) disappear into the second (whether without faith the recipients of the sacrament are graced).

This is what the International Theological Commission has for its part sought to explain (in Proposition 2.3). In Christian marriage grace is communicated in the power of Christ's acts. But on the other hand, to a baptized man and woman who seek to marry "in the Lord," no grace is given apart from faith and without faith (Proposition 2.3).[15]

After describing the ordinary path toward sacramental marriage of Christians who persevere in faith and grow in it, Delhaye turns to the case in question.

But what is to be done when this dynamism [of faith] is interrupted and even broken? The candidates for marriage have received baptism, the sacrament of faith. But they have not lived this faith or have even rejected it. It seems to the Commission . . . that this poses a double question. The first is lodged in the domain of fact: "When and how can one know if a young man and woman who seek a religious marriage really have faith or have lost it?" The second question is more doctrinal: "Can one say, with certain writers, 'No faith; no marriage'?" Or on the contrary can one let a certain automatism function: "They have been baptized. Therefore the only marriage possible for them is sacramental"?[16]

The automatism in the second question above is not identical with the oft-criticized "automatic sacramentality" at one time defended by conservative theologians and canonists. This is the opinion that because the parties to the wedding have been baptized, this automatically makes their marriage a sacrament, regardless of their lack of faith. Msgr. Delhaye seems to leave the way open to saying that since the only marriage possible for two baptized Christians is the sacrament, if they lack faith sufficient for the sacrament, they cannot marry at all.

He notes too the great difficulty of determining the point of fact, whether a man and a woman have Christian faith. He asks too the practical question about who has authority to determine its presence, and recommends that it is more prudent and more Christian to grant the benefit of the doubt to seemingly unbelieving Catholics. Then he suggests that most such cases can be subsumed into one or the other of two major options. First, there are those Catholics who seek a religious wedding for no more than external show or family convenience, while being personally indifferent or even hostile to Christ and the Church. Here is the point at which Delhaye combines psychology, philosophy and theology: *Ce bloquage de la foi entraîne celui de l'intention*—"This voiding of faith involves a voiding of intent [to marry]." To word it another way, the only intention by a baptized Christian that can create his marriage is the intention to create a sacramental marriage. Delhaye's doctrinal assumption here is quite visible and traditional: Where two Christians attempt marriage, the contract and the sacrament are inseparable. His practical counsel in such cases is to refuse a religious ceremony because it would be no more than a charade.

The other major option that Delhaye envisions is open to Catholics who are themselves open to a reviviscence of their hitherto functionally dead faith.

He closes his commentary with a reflection that invites its earnest prolongation:

> The key to the problem is in the intention—the intention to do that which the Church does in proposing a permanent sacrament which involves indissolubility, fidelity and fecundity. To have the possibility of a valid sacramental marriage there are needed baptism and an explicit faith, with both of these energizing the intention to insert one's conjugal love in Christ's paschal love. On the other hand, if the explicit rejection of faith despite baptism in infancy involves the refusal to do that which the Church does, it will be impossible to create a valid sacramental marriage.[17]

Delhaye closes with the question that his judgment inspires as a practical consequence: "Are such young persons for this reason excluded from all marriage, even a marriage at the psychological level?"[18]

His answer is a clear demand. To create a sacramental marriage—the only marriage possible for them—a Christian couple must bring more than the event of baptism in infancy, more than the baptismal "character" perduring in their souls, and more than the intention to marry in a general sense. In addition to baptism their faith must be explicit. And apparently this explicit faith must manifest itself over and above the intention in marrying to do what the Church does—although certainly it must manifest itself in this. Moreover, to have this intention the partners must intend indissolubility, fidelity and fecundity for their marriage, because these are what the Church intends for marriage. As for "inserting their love in Christ's paschal love," must the couple know and intend this explicitly? Do they accomplish it by intending the indissolubility, fidelity and fecundity that the Church intends? Or must they intend something more? Delhaye leaves this question unasked. But he does link his reflections with the next propositions by forewarning that these will take up the question that asks whether a Christian couple whose faith is lacking can as an alternative create a merely natural marriage, a marriage on no more than the psychological plane.

Further Theological Reflections

Before taking up the next proposition it will be instructive to examine briefly the reflections on Proposition 2 of Karl Lehmann, another of the commission's theologians. These reflections are in Part 2 of the commission's report, "Studies and Research."[19] Thus they are Lehmann's own. They do not represent the minds of all the commission members, although they obviously do not contradict them.

Early in his reflections Lehmann sets a thesis that determines all that follows. It is a familiar one, inherited from the patristic interpretation of the scriptures. We have seen it in Schillebeeckx and especially in Rahner. It is that God has never intended a merely secular, non-religious marriage. Marriage in the plan of his creation and as the product of his creation he has from the beginning included also in his plan of redemption. He has always intended for it to be taken into Christ's paschal mystery. Nature and grace, creation and covenant—these are not two dimensions of life and history merely juxtaposed. They interpenetrate.

This is the meaning of Paul's exhortation in 1 Corinthians 7:39 that his Corinthian converts marry "in the Lord." For Christians especially marriage cannot be a secular affair. Again, it is always taken into Christ's paschal work. And by this it is restored to God's original intention in instituting it. This is also what Ephesians 5:21–32 means to say. The "great mystery" is Christ's redemptive work in the Church. It has always been God's intention to take marriage, and especially marriage among his Christian faithful, into this mystery. This intention and its execution are the ground for saying that Christian marriage is an earthly image of the Christ-Church relationship.

It is at this point that Lehmann takes a crucial step in his reasoning:

> In its specific way marriage is a form of the presence in the world of God's eternal love realized in Christ. Between the union rooted in the love of two human beings and the union of Christ with the Church there is more than an extrinsic analogy. This is why the frequently used terms "image" and "comparison" bring ambiguity and difficulties. They can suggest no more than an extrinsic relationship.

> But what we see in the marital covenant is an actualization of the Christ-Church relationship in the history of salvation. Karl Rahner speaks of "a cause-effect relationship" between the two unions; the one exists *because* the other exists. The reciprocal analogical relationship between the two is not added to them from outside. This relationship is one of participation in the strict sense; the marital union takes its origin from the Christ-Church union. It is a participation in the fundamental sacrament that is the Christ-Church union. To use M.J. Scheeben's term, a marriage is an "articulation" of the great mystery of Christ and the Church. Thus God's love and fidelity, given once for always by Christ and actualized in the Church, are not only signified by the husband-wife union. This union is a real symbol of that love and fidelity which makes them present in the world. That which constitutes the essence of the mystery of the Church, i.e. the union of Jesus Christ with his people, is realized in the spouses' sharing of life.[20]

The same question that Delhaye's reflections inspired is inspired here by Lehmann's. What must be found in the human marital relationship—what must the spouses bring to it and sustain in it—if it is to be a realization, an "articulation," a making present in history of Christ's redemptive love in the Church? A variant form of this question arises from the claim for a cause-effect relationship between the Christ-Church marital union and the human marital union. Granted this relationship, must the human husband and wife contribute their own causation if Christ's causation is to create the sacrament? If they must, what is this? And from the divine side of this relationship, how does Christ's metaphoric marriage with a metaphorically conceived Church-bride cause an effect in an actual marriage? (To ask these questions is to ask, somewhat piquantly, how Lehmann may extend his explanation the one added crucial step, from Christ's action in Christian "marriage" to his action in real-life Christian marriages.)

Lehmann rejects any answer to these questions that would include an automatism, that would take the mere fact of the spouses' baptism and legal membership in the Church to suffice for their marriage's sacramentality.[21] He demands that the religious structure of the marriage be conditioned intrinsically by their baptism. He acknowledges that the question about the human contribution to the creation of the marital sacrament cannot be left in the abstract. The very concrete problem of baptized nonbelievers who seek a religious wedding demands a concrete answer. He acknowledges the difficulty in assuming that just because both partners have been baptized they have faith sufficient to create the sacrament. He is also aware that some theologians have proposed a non-sacramental religious wedding for such Catholics, and that others have recommended a progressive catechumenate of marriage, one that would involve a marriage in steps toward and into the sacrament.[22]

Without pretending to examine and resolve all the issues, Lehmann proposed the following essential ideas.

(1) A fundamental given for the sacramentality of marriage is the unity between the order of creation and that of redemption. It is from this unity as from its primary source that the inseparability of the contract and the sacrament in marriage derives. If one admits this unity, one must necessarily admit that the partners' consent that creates the marriage is at the same time a "sacramental sign" of the marital sacrament.

(2) While it is not the faith of the partners that produces the sacrament, yet the sacrament cannot be produced without their faith.

(3) One must distinguish carefully between the validity of a sacrament and its fruitfulness. Granted that a sacrament cannot be received fruitfully without faith, yet a sacrament can be received validly but not fruitfully.

(4) As for the axiom that the sacraments confer grace provided the recipient places no obstacle to this (*non ponens obicem*), a distinction must be made between two kinds of "obstacles." A person who carries on a deliberate fiction, who goes through an ostensibly gracing sacramental ceremony while positively disbelieving, is not graced by the sacrament. But one who is merely passive, who is *laissez-faire,* who does not positively disbelieve, does not clearly place an obstacle to grace. Lehmann calls this a "positive passivity" toward the faith which can include the formal will that God's action take place and have its effect in the sacrament.[23]

This interpretation of the way in which the sacrament can grace a recipient with only minimum faith on his part has taken Lehmann into the psychology of belief and of sacramental intention. He ventures even deeper into it when he explains what kind and degree of belief, and of intention, are needed for a person to cooperate in creating the sacrament itself.

He points out that in common Catholic doctrine a minimalist tendency prevails in answering this question. This doctrine, and the practice deriving from it, do not require that the spouses have an actual intention to create the sacrament. An habitual-implicit or a virtual-explicit intention is said to suffice. And according to the same teaching and practice the partners have either such intention if they do not positively exclude it.

But he acknowledges that precisely this minimalist, juridical, "technical" interpretation of the intention needed to create the sacrament opens the way to the automatism, to the caricatures of the sacrament by partners who come to marriage with little or no faith.

He acknowledges finally that the intention needed to create the sacrament must be at least the intention to do in contracting marriage "what Christ and the Church do." But he asks at this point how one can know whether in this global and general intention there is the faith needed to create the sacrament—a question that is most demanding when the partners are baptized non-believers.[24]

Here Lehmann takes his stand. For the valid reception itself of the sacrament of marriage, as well as for its fruitful reception, a trace of faith is needed. If the wedding rite is to produce the sacrament, the partners' intention must have at least some reference to eternal salvation, however slight and fleeting this reference. (But he adds that surely pastoral practice must take this shallow faith and by instruction deepen and solidify it. What is more, the partners should be accorded the benefit of the doubt. They have a natural right to marry. If they ask for a religious wedding, sufficient faith in them should be assumed, and the contrary judgment bears the burden of proof.)[25]

Lehmann undertakes finally to explain in the most complete and serious way the connection between the partners' faith, their baptism, and the sacrament in marriage. The explanation is familiar. We saw its explicit form for the first time in Scheeben's essay on the marital sacrament in his *Mysteries of Christianity*. And we have seen it laid out more fully and exactly in Schillebeeckx's first essay and by Rahner.

By his or her baptism a person is incorporated in the Church of Jesus Christ. This incorporation is not a simple moral obligation vis-à-vis Christ. Before all else it is an ontological and existential insertion in the body of Christ. Consequently it is not left solely to the baptized who marry to determine on their own the meaning and reality of their union. At the moment they join with Christ in taking up life together he himself intervenes in their marriage decisively.

This is intelligible only if one takes into account baptism's original structure, specifically at the juncture of act and cultus, of faith and incorporation in the Church. There is a kind of hierarchy among the Church's sacraments; each functions in its own way at its own level. For example baptism by itself cannot bring a person to belong to the body of Christ in a way that is full, alive and active. There are different degrees of incorporation in this body, and baptism is only a beginning degree. This incorporation is a gift, but it also brings a task to be done. Baptism and its task lead to marriage, as well as to and through other sacraments—confirmation, penance, and the Eucharist.

At this point Lehmann repeats a critical element of Rahner's interpretation of the marital sacrament. The difference between the marital situation of a baptized Christian without active faith and that of one with active faith is not like the difference between an impenitent sinner and one who confesses sacramentally in order to be forgiven. The difference is rather like that between one who has repented before and with the intention of sacramental confession, and one who has already repented and confessed. Lehmann suggests another comparison. Just as there are many degrees of belonging to the Church, so there are many degrees of being married sacramentally.[26]

He completes his reflections by repeating an element of his theology that he regards as essential but too often forgotten. It is Christ acting in and through the spouses who creates the sacrament. Therefore he, not they, determine its nature and its conditions.

> It is simply not accurate to say that the spouses confer the sacrament of marriage on one another. . . . The sacramental dimension of marriage is not at the spouses' disposition. What they do is to ask and admit Christ to sanctify their marital union. This is a consideration of special importance. For the sacramental marriage results not alone from the spouses' will nor from the human community. It is determined before all else by the sanctifying action of Christ. The wills of the spouses, who act not simply in their own name and as private persons, but who make their consent as members of Christ's body, are, in virtue of their baptism, determined intrinsically by Christ. For the spouses Christ is not as a lord who commands, but he acts in them and through them.[27]

As an answer, or as the core of an explanation, this stops again at the brink of the question we have seen repeatedly. Granted that Christ, not the spouses, is the primary cause in creating their sacrament, that his will rather than theirs determines the sacrament, but granted too that their wills are not inert and forced, what is their role in creating the sacrament? Since their nature is to will freely, what determining effect can their free wills have in creating the sacrament? And how do they carry on this determination? Until Lehmann answers these questions he leaves the way open for the automatism that he so clearly wishes to avoid.

Natural and Civil Marriage

Proposition 3 in all its subsets 1 through 7 deals with two interrelated issues, the natural, "sub-sacramental marriages" of unbaptized and non-believing spouses, and the possibility—or more exactly the impossibility—that baptized Christians can create this kind of marriage. Little comment on Propositions 3.1 through 3.3 is needed, since they do no more than lay down the theological premises we have already seen repeatedly.

Proposition 3.1. All things have been created in Christ, through Christ and for Christ. Therefore because it has been instituted by the God of this creation, marriage has been made an image (a *figure*) of the mystery of the union of Christ with his spouse the Church, and has been oriented in a certain way to this mystery. Where this marriage is celebrated by two baptized Christians, it is elevated to the dignity of a sacrament in the proper sense of the term, which is to signify and to participate in the spousal love of Christ and the Church.

Proposition 3.2. Where the spouses are both baptized their marriage as an institution willed by God the creator is inseparable from the marital sacrament. For the sacramentality of the union of baptized spouses is not something accessory to this marriage, so that it can be either present to it or not. The sacrament so adheres to the essence of their marriage as to be inseparable from it.

Proposition 3.3. As a consequence, for two baptized spouses no other real and authentic marriage can exist than that willed by Christ. In this sacrament the Christian man and woman, by giving and accepting their selves as spouses in a personal and free choice, are freed radically from "the hardness of heart" of which Jesus spoke (Mt. 19:8). For them it becomes really possible to live in perpetual charity, because by virtue of the sacrament they are truly assumed into the mystery of the marital union of Christ and the church. As a consequence the Church can in no way accept that two baptized persons are in a marital relationship conformed to their dignity and to their mode of being "new creatures in Christ" unless they are joined in the sacrament of marriage.[28]

These propositions follow logically from Proposition 2 in all its parts. As theses the latter claimed that Christ has made marriage among the baptized a sacrament. The comprehensive thesis here in Proposition 3 is that a sacramental marriage is the only marriage that two baptized Christians can create. It is directed against Catholic theologians who propose that non-believing Catholics can create religiously oriented marriages that are sub-sacramental, or such marriages that become progressively sacramental.

Msgr. Carlo Caffarra has written the commentary on these propositions. We have seen the pivotal principle of his reasoning again and again, in Schillebeeckx, in Rahner, in Lehmann's commentary on the preceding propositions. It is that the actual situation of all human beings is that God has created them for and has taken them into the plan of salvation carried out through Christ's death and resurrection. There is no other order in history. Therefore men and women are not free to live in another and purely secular order, because none exists.

A consequence of this fact-serving-as-principle is that all marriages from the beginning of history have been taken into this plan in a specific role, namely to manifest, to image the marital union of Christ with the Church. It is marriage in this plan of creation that is marriage raised to a sacrament.

Two corollaries flow from this: (1) It is impossible for persons who have been incorporated by their baptism in Christ and the Church to separate their marriage from the sacrament. It is not so much that they are forbidden to attempt the separation, but that the separation is impossible. (2) The Church simply cannot accept that two baptized spouses are married unless they are married sacramentally. This denial is not a product of canonical discipline. It is the acknowledgement of a religious-ecclesial impossibility.

The Marriages of the Unbaptized

That said, what of the marriages of the unbaptized? In light of the principle that God intends all marriages to participate in his redemptive plan for the human race, what does one say of the status and function in this plan of the marriages of the unbaptized? The next proposition in series contains the theological commission's answer to this question.

Proposition 3.4. Because of the universality of God's salvific will the strength and the presence of Christ's grace extends to all human beings, even beyond the boundaries of the Church. His grace informs every human marital love. It strengthens created nature and establishes marriage "as it was in the beginning." The man and woman who have not yet been reached by the Gospel join in the human covenant of a legitimate marriage. Such a marriage has in it authentic goods and values that assure its survival. Even if the spouses are unaware of the fact, these values come from God the Creator and are taken in an inchoative way into the spousal love of Christ and the Church.[29]

Caffarra's commentary draws, at its peril, from Genesis 2 as though it were historically factual. It is from verses 22–24 that he derives the conclusion explicit in the proposition above, that every marriage is taken into God's redemptive plan. He draws from Ephesians 5:31 the further conclusion that every marriage is drawn into—is inserted in—the explicitation and realization of this plan in the love relationship of Christ and the Church. But the insertion of the marriages of the unbaptized is only inchoative.

All this puts obligations and essential conditions on unbaptized spouses. They must become spouses according to God's design for marriage, not according to their own. Their growth in love will make them gradually aware of a need and then a desire for a purification and enrichment of their love that can come only from the sacrament. In this need and desire they will sense the gratuitous and supernatural orientation of their natural marriage to the sacrament. This growth in awareness is itself a grace coming from Christ acting imperceptibly in their souls. For Christ wills the holiness of all human beings and sends his Spirit into the souls of all.[30]

Before moving on to Proposition 3.5 it is pertinent to point out that the commission and Msgr. Caffarra have skirted a kind of marriage whose place in the "insertion" in Christ's paschal mystery is both significant and indecisively located in the theology that proposes this insertion. This is the marriage of a baptized and believing Christian, for example a devout Catholic, to an unbaptized spouse. The Catholic interpretation of this marriage is that it is not a Christian sacrament, and that it is not because the other spouse is unbaptized.

This marriage will be examined more closely after our examination of the propositions bearing on the indissolubility of sacramental marriage. But even now two reflections are in order. If the marriage of two unbaptized spouses is inchoately sacramental and a medium of grace for them, *a fortiori* is this marriage of a Catholic and an unbaptized person inchoately sacramental. But is it inchoately sacramental in the same way and in the same degree? Supposing that in the actual conduct of this marriage the Christian spouse loves with a religiously activated love and the other responds to this love, is the Christian spouse not drawing the non-Christian into the paschal mystery and deeper into the gracing experience of marriage? Are they not moving there together? If this is indeed what they are doing, it seems to call in question the denial that the specifically Christian sacrament can be created progressively.

Observation of the actual history of this marriage suggests another insight about what the "insertion" in the paschal mystery involves. Let us say that the unbaptized spouse is drawn gradually to conversion and Christian baptism. Granted that in the drawing and in the baptism it is Christ who is the principal cause of this incorporation. But this is hardly the abrupt seizing of an unconscious child. The hitherto unbaptized spouse has come to this moment as the fruit of long, persistent and strongly volitional cooperation with the divine attraction brought to bear on him by his Christian wife. And this cooperation he has brought freely. But can we believe that the freedom of his cooperation comes to an end at the moment of baptism? If it was essentially necessary for his incorporation that his response be free, is this freedom no longer needed once the incorporation is accomplished? Where in all the biblical sources whence this theology of insertion and incorporation is drawn is the evidence for exclusion and irrelevance of freely given love for maintaining the incorporation and therefore the sacrament once they are brought into existence?

On the Union of Christians
Ignorant of the Demands of Their Baptism

> *Proposition 3.5.* Thus it would be contradictory to say that there are Christians baptized in the Catholic Church who can reverse their path and return in fact to a non-sacramental marriage. This would be to think that they can be satisfied with the shadow when Christ offers them the reality of marital love.
>
> However one cannot ignore cases in which Christians so labor under consciences deformed by ignorance or invincible error that they believe sincerely that they can contract a true marriage while excluding the sacrament.
>
> In this condition they are incapable of contracting a valid marriage since they reject faith and lack the intention to do in marrying what the Church does. On the other hand, they still have the natural right to marry. Hence they are capable of giving and accepting their persons mutually as spouses by reason of their intention to form an irrevocable covenant. This mutual and irrevocable self-gift creates a psychological relationship whose internal structure differs from a purely transitory relationship.
>
> However the Church can in no way recognize this relationship as a non-sacramental marriage, even though it has the appearance of a marriage. For the Church there is no marriage of baptized partners separate from the sacrament, but only natural marriage raised to the dignity of a sacrament.[31]

The case envisioned in these propositions is that of two baptized Christians who have made themselves objectively incapable of creating a sacramental marriage because they have rejected the Christian faith and also the intention to do in marrying what the Church does. Yet they retain the natural right to contract marriage. This right is rooted in their nature itself as human persons. The demands of the Christian faith do not destroy this right.

Nevertheless, the proposition insists and Caffarra's commentary agrees that these spouses cannot create even a natural marriage, cannot so exercise their natural right as to create the marriage available to them by this right.

The reason offered for this denial is that the attempt to create a merely natural, sub-sacramental marriage would involve a contradiction. By their baptism both spouses have been taken out of the natural order into the order of Christ's paschal mystery. They have been taken into his mystical body. The assumption that they can nevertheless create a non-sacramental marriage contains in itself the assumption that the spouses can leave this order and return to the natural. But the proposition contends that not only would it be morally wrong for them to attempt this return, but the attempt is useless because the return is impossible.

Said more precisely, even though these spouses exercise their natural right to make the marital exchange of their persons in order to create a natural marriage, the exchange is invalid. It produces no marriage. The reason why it does not is that the consent by which they make the exchange has no object in reality. They would have it be a non-sacramental marriage. But for them no such marriage exists. Their natural right to create a marriage has itself been taken up, along with their persons and all their moral acts, into the paschal mystery. There their right to marry becomes the right to create a sacramental marriage.

What such partners do create by their marital commitment is a psychological union short of marriage but quite different from their prior relationship as fiancés. It is different in that they have created it (one may assume) by an irrevocable consent with the intent of forming an indissoluble relationship. (If they have not done this, their relationship does not differ from that in which they were fiancés.)[32]

This theology begs for criticism—criticism of its assumptions, its method and its conclusions. The target territory of the criticism has been hinted at above in the reflections on Proposition 3.4. But a full criticism is better delayed until after an examination of the commission's proposals concerning marriage's indissolubility.

The Indissolubility of Marriage

> *Proposition 4.1.* The tradition of the primitive Church, which is drawn from the teaching of Christ and the apostles, affirmed the indissolubility of marriage, even where a spouse has committed adultery.[33]

> *Proposition 4.2.* The Council of Trent declared that the Church has not erred when it has taught and still teaches that, according to the Gospel and apostolic teaching, the bond of marriage cannot be dissolved because of adultery. However the council anathematized only those who deny the authority of the Church in this question. The reasons for restricting this condemnation were certain hesitations manifested earlier (by the Ambrosiaster, by Catharinus and by Cajetan), and certain ecumenical considerations. Thus one cannot claim that the council intended to define indissolubility solemnly as a truth of faith. But one must take into account Pius XI's words in his encyclical, *Casti connubii* that refer to the Council of Trent:

"If the Church has not erred and does not err when it has taught and teaches this [about marriage], it is certain that marriage cannot be dissolved because of adultery. And it is obvious that the other and far weaker reasons alleged for divorce are even less valid as causes of dissolution, and are simply to be ignored."[34]

In his commentary on Proposition 4.1 Fr. Edouard Hamel explains that the Christian teachers of the first five centuries took Christ's synoptic instruction concerning divorce as a restoration of God's original intent that marriage be lifelong. He acknowledges that certain of the fathers of the first four centuries, and certain regional councils, were indecisive in their condemnation of divorce and subsequent remarriage. Such fathers were, for example, Origen, Lactantius, Hilary of Arles, Basil, and the Ambrosiaster. But Hamel urges a methodology that corrects and resolves these minority judgments in favor of the obvious majority position that simply interdicted divorce and remarriage.

But regrettably he neglects an important distinction in this matter between on the one hand an unexceptionable prohibition of divorce or of remarriage after divorce, and on the other marriage's indissolubility. These are not identical. Indissolubility—at least the intrinsic, "radical" indissolubility that is now Catholic doctrine—is understood as a quality in marriage itself. This is its invulnerability to dissolution by any cause other than the death of at least one of the spouses. Given this indissolubility, any attempt to dissolve a marriage is futile. And any attempt to create a second marriage is likewise futile (assuming the impossibility of polygamy) and involves adultery.

But one can claim marriage's dissolubility while still accepting that Christ has unexceptionably forbidden its dissolution and subsequent remarriage. One thus says that he has unconditionally forbidden to do that which is in itself possible.

Hamel claims that early Christian tradition "affirms the indissoluble character of the marital bond, even in instances of adultery." Sorry, but the tradition does not so affirm. As early as the fourth century Christian authorities acknowledged the dissolution of unconsummated marriages by at least one spouse's taking up monastic life.[35] And since the twelfth century the Church's own interpretation of "the Pauline privilege" in 1 Corinthians 7:12–16 has it that Paul accepted the dissolution of Christian converts' marriages where their spouses were pagans unwilling to live in peace.

A fundamental difficulty in sustaining any claim about the objective indissolubility of marriage as the substance of early Christian teaching is that the concept itself of indissolubility was unknown in the cultures in which Christianity grew up. In concrete circumstances, holding to the concept of indissolubility entails this, that the personal and social relationship making up the experienced substance of marriage ends irrecoverably; nevertheless the marriage continues in existence. This other entity that continues in existence can be only a legal bond existing apart from the persons' actual relationship. There is no evidence that the Christians of the first four centuries acknowledged such a bond as distinct from the relationship. The first suggestion of such a surviving entity is the *quiddam conjugale,* the "certain marital something" of Augustine's *De Bono Conjugali* and *De Adulterinis Conjugiis.* That this entity is the objective marital bond is an invention of later canon law.

The fact that the fathers of the Church called marriage after divorce adultery does not verify their acceptance of indissolubility as defined above. It may verify no more than that they regarded such remarriage as a serious sin against marital fidelity.

Hamel's own words expose best the sense of his commentary on Proposition 4.2.

> The extraordinarily cautious, convoluted and laborious formulation of this canon [Canon 24 of Trent] is no help in understanding it, and has led to divergent interpretations of it. Certainly it is not easy to decide exactly the theological note to give it.[36] The canon does not constitute a true definition of indissolubility even indirectly, as some have claimed. The doctrine is not presented explicitly as a revealed truth. From the character of the canon's third version at Trent its direct affirmation no longer bears upon indissolubility itself but upon the fact that the Church has not erred and does not err, and does not misuse its authority nor contradict the truth, when it sustains its teaching in conformity with the Gospel. It is more realistic to say—in any case as a minimum—that the indissolubility of sacramental marriage is "a Catholic truth."[37]

We note that the last sentence just above is discontinuous with what precedes it in Hamel's commentary and in the propositions themselves. It refers to the indissolubility of marriage that is sacramental. Trent's Canon 24 does not mention the sacrament. It declares concerning marriage taken simply. Neither do the propositions mention the sacrament. Hamel's bringing it into consideration at this point is almost certainly spurred by his awareness that incumbent Catholic doctrine holds only sacramental marriages to be in fact indissoluble, and among these only those that are consummated. It may be that Hamel is preparing for the next propositions, that do consider marital indissolubility as Catholic teaching locates it, namely in the Christian sacrament.

Proposition 4.3. The intrinsic indissolubility of marriage can be considered under different aspects and as grounded in various ways.
  From the side of the spouses one will say that the intimate

marital union, the mutual self-gift of the persons, the marital love itself, the good of the children—all these demand the indissoluble union of the spouses. From this there flows their moral obligation to protect the marital covenant, to preserve it and to nourish it.

From the divine perspective, the human act by which the spouses mutually give and accept their persons creates a bond rooted in God's will. This bond is appropriated into [*est inscrit in*] the creative act itself and transcends human will. It is not open to the spouses' volition, and as such it is intrinsically indissoluble.

In the Christologic perspective the indissolubility of Christian marriage has an even more profound basis. This consists of the fact that Christian marriage is an image, a sacrament and a witness to the indissoluble union of Christ and the Church. It is this that is called "the good that is the *sacramentum.*" In this perspective indissolubility becomes an event of grace.

Social perspectives too provide a reason for indissolubility. It is demanded by the institution itself of marriage. The personal decision of the spouses is taken into their society and is there nurtured and protected, especially by their ecclesial community. It is needed for the good of the children and for the common good (the latter is the juridical-ecclesial dimension of indissolubility).

These several aspects are intimately linked. The fidelity to which spouses are obligated must be protected by society itself, most especially by the society that is the Church. It is required by God the creator and likewise by Christ, who makes it possible by his grace.[38]

A hitherto unused term that first appears in the first line of Proposition 4.3 betrays the difficulty that the commission faced in formulating this proposition and the greater difficulty Fr. Hamel had in explaining it. This is the adjective "intrinsic" as a modifier of "indissolubility." The commission declared the indissolubility of marriage, and Fr. Hamel sought to explain its causes. But both knew that the only kind and degree of marriage the Catholic Church deems indissoluble in the sense of invulnerable to any human agent's dissolution is, as we have noted repeatedly, a sacramental marriage that is consummated. Hence their need to posit two categories, intrinsic indissolubility and extrinsic.

The meaning of extrinsic indissolubility is suggested in the next proposition in series.

Proposition 4.4. Concurrently with its *praxis* the Church has worked out a doctrine concerning its own power in the domain of marriage so that it may indicate clearly the extent and the limits of this power. The Church recognizes no power in itself to dissolve a sacramental marriage that is consummated. But for serious reasons, for the good of the faith and for the salvation of souls, other marriages can be dissolved by the competent ecclesiastical authority; or according to a different interpretation, this authority can declare such marriages dissolved.

This teaching is no more than a particular application of the theory, now generally accepted by Catholic theologians, of the way that Christian doctrine evolves in the Church. This theory includes the possibility that the Church can determine more exactly the meaning of the terms "sacramentality" and "consummation," and thus explain these realities more clearly. The entire doctrine concerning the indissolubility of marriage would thus be taught in a more profound and exact synthesis.[39]

How justified is the commission's honest admission here that the theology of indissolubility is incomplete (I would say also inconclusive) may emerge as we now examine its, and Hamel's, explanation of the nature and causes of marital indissolubility.

To begin with Hamel sets out more clearly the difference of extrinsic indissolubility from intrinsic. To do this he quotes the origin of the verbal distinction, Pope Pius XII's allocution of October 3, 1941. There intrinsic indissolubility designates the fact that the spouses themselves have no power to dissolve their marriage. Extrinsic indissolubility designates the reach but also the limit of the Church's power to dissolve. Thus despite the fact that the adjectives are used as modifiers of the noun "marriage," it is clear that indissolubility in fact is not a characteristic of marriage but is the power to dissolve, or lack thereof, residing in persons. Nevertheless the commission and Hamel find multiple identities for indissolubility and multiple causes of its presence in marriages.

First, the foundation [*le véritable fondement*] of indissolubility is in the nature of the marital bond that God wills to join the spouses. He has designed this bond as unbreakable and wills that it be so. Genesis 2:24–25 implies this: "That is why a man leaves his father and mother and clings to his wife, and the two of them become one flesh." It seems that with this, the ultimate cause of indissolubility is God's designing intention and will for marriage. And the first effect of this will is a characteristic of the marital bond itself: It is unbreakable. (But it is pertinent to keep in mind during this examination that it is just this bond that Church authorities break.)

Indissolubility is also in God's plan for the redemption of the human race through Christ. This is indicated in Matthew 19:6: "What God has joined man must not separate." We have seen the interpretation proposed by Lehmann and Caffarra, that through Christ God has taken marriage and its spouses up out of the ontological and moral order in which mere human wills can determine the character of the marital relationship. In fact such an order has never existed. From the beginning all marriages, indeed all human beings, have been taken into the order of redemption. There they are taken into God's dynamic that works out this redemption. In this dynamic it is God's will that determines the character of marriage.[40]

Next, the marital commitment itself is by nature irreversible. This is so because of its totality. In it the spouses give themselves to one another, and accept one another, in order to share all that they are and have for as long as they live. By definition such a commitment cannot be withdrawn, since it is made precisely to void the possibility of withdrawal. Moreover it puts into existence a bond which cannot be made not to exist. Another way to say this is that the love that impels the spouses' giving and accepting of their persons is in nature unchangeable. It is an act of will whose nature is unidirectional.

In the legal dimension indissolubility is the impossibility of violating the norm. This norm establishes the invalidity of any attempt to dissolve a marriage. Even if the spouses' love for one another vanishes and their relationship as an actual sharing in all of life ends irrecoverably, the moral obligation that this marital bond *ought not be broken* is protected and strengthened by the invalidating norm that this bond *cannot be broken.*[41] (Without saying so explicitly at this point the commission has identified the essential core of marriage as the juridical bond, since this is what continues to exist even when the love and the human partnership vanish.) We recall again that this unbreakable bond is what is broken by Church authority when it dissolves a marriage. It is the irreversible will mentioned above that is permitted to reverse itself in the same dissolution.

Next, in Hamel's explanation of indissolubility as an effect and a characteristic of the marital sacrament we see the meaning of the traditional assertion that marriage's natural indissolubility is made more firm by the sacrament. The assertion implies that this natural indissolubility left to itself is imperfect, that it leaves a marriage vulnerable to dissolution.

Hamel explains that every Christian community contains an actualization of the presence of Christ and thus of the Church and his relationship to the Church. Though the smallest of all, a marriage is such a community. That relationship of Christ and the Church is indestructible, and images and actualizes its indestructibility in the human communal relationship, and most perceptibly in marriage.

When spouses make the total gift of their persons to one another, God must be active through Christ in this giving and receiving. Only he can make them possible because they put the spouses at risk of the total loss of their persons. By his death and resurrection Christ has given and gives to men and women this power to give themselves. He thus frees them to do so. This empowering is his gracing of them; the power itself to give is his grace in them.[42]

Thus in Christian perspective the ground and source of marriage's indissolubility is the latter's character as an image of Christ's self-giving union with his people, who are the Church. His self-giving enters into and takes up their self-giving to one another. Reciprocally theirs participates in his giving of his self to the Church. His love commitment reaches them in and through their commitment to one another. By his gracing, his empowering them, he gives them the strength to love one another for life. Their "I ought to be faithful unto death" becomes "I can be faithful unto death."

To be most exact [*en définitive*] it is the grace of Christ acting at the heart of the spouses' personal commitment and union that assures the indestructibility of a Christian marriage. However this grace does not create the indestructibility. It perfects and assures it.[43]

The marital sacrament and indissolubility act in a kind of cause-effect circle. The sacrament demands indissolubility and makes it possible; marriage's indissolubility manifests the sacrament.[44]

Thus far in this explanation the traditional image-theology of the marital sacrament has appeared only faintly. Neither the commission nor Hamel has turned to it to verify that the marriage of two baptized Christians is a sacrament because it is a sign, an earthly image, of Christ's relationship with the Church.

But it is evident that they cannot escape a return to this theology. How else account for the centuries-old Catholic teaching and practice that even a sacramental marriage of baptized Christians can be dissolved if it is not consummated? The fundamental reason that the commission has offered for the "intrinsic indissolubility" of sacramental marriage no longer holds, namely that the spouses by their baptism have been taken into Christ's paschal mystery; that the unconquerable love with which Christ loves has taken up their love; that they have been "inserted" in his mystical body so that the unfailing marital love with which he as head loves his body the Church makes their love unfailing. All these can be done, yet their marriage can be dissolved if it has not been consummated.

It is this practice of dissolving unconsummated marriages, or of accepting their dissolution, that impelled Pope Pius XII in 1941 to distinguish the two kinds of indissolubility, intrinsic and extrinsic. The latter does two things: it sets the limit of the Church's power, vested in the pope, to dissolve marriages, and it claims his power to dissolve. Hamel points out the obvious history of this doctrine of the power to dissolve, namely that the practice has in large measure determined the doctrine. This practice is the use of the *potestas vicaria* (*vicaria* because delegated, and delegated to the vicar of Christ) to dissolve a marriage that is not a sacrament, or to dissolve a sacramental marriage that has not been consummated.[45] Or, as some theologians' alternative theory explains it, rather than dissolve such marriages, this power declares that they have by themselves dissolved; that they have died with the death of the spouses' love; or that as partnerships they have crumbled because the partnership is incompatible with one of the spouses' fidelity to Christ. In the face of a greater value these marriages have yielded and gone out of existence. Such a greater value is, for example, the possibility that one or both spouses may create a sacramental marriage after the dissolution of the first non-sacramental marriage, or the possibility of their creating a consummated sacramental marriage after the dissolution of one never consummated. In the face of the greater value of such second marriages, the interpretation continues, the value that is the indissolubility of either a non-sacramental marriage or of an unconsummated sacramental marriage is seen to be less than absolute. It loses its hold and yields.[46]

In either interpretation the comprehensive power to dissolve given by Christ to Peter and his successors in Matthew 16:19—"I will give you the keys of the kingdom of heaven: whatever you bind on earth shall be considered bound in heaven; whatever you loose on earth shall be considered loosed in heaven"—can be applied to the marriage and either act as the cause of its dissolution or verify the fact of its own internal dissolution.

But this power reaches its limit before a sacramental marriage that has been consummated. The reason for this is that the indissolubility that is natural to all marriages but incomplete in them, even when they are sacraments, reaches its completion where those that are sacraments are consummated as sacraments. This raises a familiar question with whose answer we are also familiar: Why is marriage's natural indissolubility incomplete even in sacramental marriages when these are unconsummated, but complete when they are consummated? It is the effort to answer this question that takes the commission and Fr. Hamel back to the ancient image-theology of the sacrament. They have recovered it and used it in the following way.

They reason that a marriage's natural indissolubility is brought toward completion by the sacrament. The latter does this by its character as a symbol, an image of Christ's marital love of the Church. A cause-effect link joins the imaged divine relationship and the imaging human relationship. The divine gives the human its essential characteristics. The divine, by being indissoluble, can and does reproduce its indissolubility in the human.

But this reproduction is conditioned by the completeness or incompleteness of the human relationship's imaging of the divine. Until the human relationship is consummated it images the divine incompletely. But with consummation the imaging is complete, perfect. Therefore the divine causation can produce its effect fully. It can and does bring the human marriage's natural indissolubility finally to completion—makes it, in the words of contemporary juridical theology, radically indissoluble.

The consummating act that produces this effect is the one claimed by Catholic law for centuries. It is sexual intercourse that is itself complete. The recent revision of Catholic marriage law has, in Canon 1061.1, added one characteristic of the intercourse as necessary for consummation. It must be *actus humanus,* a human act, intercourse willed and accepted freely by both spouses. No longer will mere physical penetration with semination, possible for a coerced and even semi-conscious partner, suffice to consummate. It is also most significant that according to this interpretation a single act of intercourse can consummate—can consummate the marriage not only as a human relationship but as a Christian sacrament. Which is to say that a single act of intercourse is held to bring to completion the marriage's imaging of the marital love relationship of Christ and the Church.

One is not surprised to find Fr. Hamel suggesting at this point that the interpretation of consummation's effecting radical indissolubility needs to be made more exact and profound. He suggests that the interpretation be taken out of the category of human images of the divine, and into the realm of Christ's gracing intervention in the spouses' relationship. He proposes that the spouses' first intercourse, as a sacramental act, functions in the power of Christ, *ex opere operato,* to produce radical indissolubility as an effect of grace. But he takes his proposal no further than this.[47]

A suggestion considerably more trenchant than Fr. Hamel's is also in order. It is that both Catholic law and Catholic theology give up predicating indissolubility of marriages. Since the term's primary signification is invulnerability to dissolution, but this law and theology accept that every marriage except that which is a consummated sacrament can be dissolved, to use the term is misleading. But to find a more accurate substitute is not easy because, as we have seen in the distinction between intrinsic and extrinsic dissolubility, the word "indissolubility" refers not only to a characteristic in marriages but more so to a limit in the papal power to dissolve them. A term that can also designate this limit is needed. For now I suggest "immunity" as a substitute. The use of this noun can admit of degrees, as indeed the Catholic practice of dissolving marriages presumes degrees of resistance to dissolution. A simple-minded analogy recommends the term. Thus, different persons' immunity as a condition of health can stand at different degrees. No one is misled if the various degrees are all referred to as immunity. The term also connotes the inability of foreign agents to invade and destroy health, while implying at the same time varying degrees in this inability.

A second suggestion is that the traditional attempt to demonstrate theologically the radical indissolubility of consummated sacramental marriages is inconclusive. Fr. Hamel admits as much where he recommends that the theology of sacrament and consummation be developed to greater depth and exactness. The attempt is inconclusive on two interrelated counts. One was pointed to earlier in this chapter. An indissoluble metaphoric marriage of the risen Christ with a metaphoric bride-Church cannot, in virtue of actual human marriages' imaging it when the spouses are baptized, *make* these marriages to be indissoluble. The only "ontological" conclusion that one can draw from the indissoluble character of the metaphoric divine marriage is that the conceptual model of human marriages intended to image it must also have indissolubility in its design. The one conclusion that can affect actual marriages is that since the inspired passage in Ephesians urges spouses to imitate the Christ-Church love relationship, they *ought* to commit themselves to and work for a lifelong relationship of faithful love. The link from the metaphoric divine marriage to actual marriages is not causative ontologically but deontologically.

The second count against the traditional attempt to demonstrate radical indissolubility is that the role of consummation in the demonstration leaves a fatal gap in its logic. We recall that even a sacramental marriage is not considered finally indissoluble until it is consummated—and consummated as a sacrament. Consummation is said to be accomplished by a single complete act of sexual intercourse. And it finally brings indestructible indissolubility because it finally completes the sacrament's imaging of the Christ-Church relationship. The key to this supposed completion is that by consummation the spouses become wholly "two in one flesh," and thus make perfect their imaging of Christ's two-in-one-flesh relationship with the Church. Or as an alternative explanation, it makes perfect the sacrament's imaging of the union of the divine nature with the human in Christ.

To begin with, "two in one flesh" in Genesis 2:24 refers not to the spouses' sexual intercourse but to their becoming as one person before the people and the law. Their sexual intercourse is but one component of this becoming one person. But the most serious weakness is the assumption that a single act of intercourse within the first hours or days of a new marriage can consummate it as a sacrament. To consummate is to complete. It is simply not believable that one act at its outset can complete the marriage's imaging of, or incorporation in, Christ's redemptive love for his people.

The Traditional Theology and Epistemological Difficulties

Again and again we have come upon an epistemological trait in the theology of marriage virtually from its beginning that has always weakened its probative capacity. This trait has shown itself in two ways. The first is the ease with which theologians, and canonists too, have moved from one to another of five different kinds of predication.

One of these involves reference to concrete singular reality, e.g. "This marriage is an image of Christ and the Church." A second refers to the concrete plural: "These marriages are images," etc. A third refers to the comprehensive concrete singular: "Each and every marriage is an image," etc. A fourth refers to the concrete universal: "Christian marriages are images," etc. The fifth refers to the abstract universal: "Christian marriage is an image," etc.

The following are ways in which the interchangeable use of these predications in theologizing about marriage undermines probative capability. For one, when a theologian says "Christian marriage is an image of Christ's union with the Church," he may without acknowledging the fact make a statement not about actual marriages but about a model conceptualized in his mind. It is fair to ask him for the origin of this model. If the origin is his own designing mind, his affirmation tells only of a trait of the model in his mind. It tells nothing about marriages in real life. If he claims its origin in actual marriages, one of whose traits he has found out inductively, we commend him. The only way of forming concepts in the mind that bring knowledge of real things is by induction from experience. But if he is to show the validity of his abstraction to universality, he must show how in this case his inductive search has found out that the claimed imaging is a property of all Christian marriages. He must show this if he intends his affirmation to be universal in reference. If he says that he found the model in the scriptures, then this same interrogation with the same questions moves over to the authors of the scriptures.

A second form of this debilitating trait has already been hinted at. It is to move by too easy deduction from affirmations with universal reference to those with particular reference. This has been done commonly by theologians, and more commonly by canonists, when they design certain traits into the conceptual model of marriage, then move deductively to affirm these traits of actual marriages. An example of this has been noted more than once in these chapters. Indissolubility as an essential element of marriage conceived as a juridical bond was unheard of for the first one thousand years of Christian history. But once canonists by their prescriptive defining had designed the conceptual model of marriage to be a juridical bond, the way was open to them to also design into it the traits they thought it needs. One of these they thought to be indissolubility because it seemed the most cogent way to embody in marriage itself Christ's will that spouses not dissolve their marriages. From that point the deductive impulse had its way. Since indissolubility is an essential trait of "marriage," then all actual marriages must be indissoluble—as Canon 1056 of the revised Catholic marriage law still implies. The way in which this natural indissolubility has been qualified into unintelligibility in consideration of the Church's tradition of dissolving naturally indissoluble marriage is one of the consequences of this epistemological carelessness.

The Theology's Need for the Experience of the Married

That the theology of marriage remains only an exercise in speculation unless it draws its principles and ultimately its conclusions from an inductive experience of lived marriages points to the role of the married in this theology. To say it simply, this theology needs the reported experience of the married as one of its essential elements. It is an element whose absence leaves an invalidating gap in the theology. That the theology of marriage from its beginning until about the end of the first generation of our century was, with the exception of Tertullian and of the widowed or divorced Paul, the product of celibate males' observation of others' marriages is one of the main reasons for its retarded condition still after nineteen centuries.

The reason for the essentiality of personal married experience to the theology is neither profound nor elusive. The theology's formal object is marriages as sacraments. On the assumption that what the sacrament is in substance is the marriage, no one can know what the sacrament is without first knowing what a marriage is. One does not find out the latter by imagining, and then, as a product of the imagining, designing an ideal model. Neither does one find out by determining which model of marriage is needed for resolving disputes and winning juridical battles. And one does not find out with universal and permanent accuracy by going to the biblical models and teachings, even though these may have been designed from their own experience by married Jewish males.

As Schillebeeckx made clear in the third of his essays examined in the preceding chapter, the specific nature of marriage changes from epoch to epoch, however generically it may continue always as a man-woman relationship.

Building on the premise in *Gaudium et spes* that a man and woman create their marriage by making gifts of their persons to one another, and that they sustain it by continuing their giving and by forgiving the failures in the giving and accepting, the bishops who offered this interpretation could draw from the example of Christ's love and say the self-giving is essential for making the marriage a sacrament. But this still leaves much unsaid. Christ gave his life; he loved even unto death. But though a love may not be sacramentally marital unless it is at least willing to give that much, in practice less is acceptable while much more is demanded. Christ never actually gave himself in marriage, never died the countless little deaths that are the compromises needed to sustain a marriage. Who knows what the continual and routine self-giving is except the married? Who knows the ability to give except the married? Who knows the conditions that make marital giving possible and those that destroy it?

Marriages are conative enterprises. If they are to last, the partners must strive to communicate more intimately, more openly, more satisfactorily. The kind of striving that develops such communication cannot be decided *a priori* except in the most general way. Only the married know what works.

The Need for Married Understanding of Sexuality

How essential for understanding the sacrament is Christian spouses' narratives of their experience is evident in the difficulty that the Catholic authorities and theologians, all unmarried, have had until well into our century in finding the role in the sacrament for sexuality.

To begin with, a man whose acquaintance with sexuality has been only in the confessional listening to guilty accounts of adultery, fornication, masturbation or contraception will be inclined to think of it as a mingled physical and emotional urgency that even Catholics who confess find great difficulty in controlling. If in addition he has his own struggle with continence, this perception of sexuality will be reinforced. It may be reduced to sexuality's brute minimum, an imperious energy as destructive as it is life-giving.

But which is the truer story about sexuality, that one or the one told by deeply happy spouses who are in love and frequently love-making? If the former is the truer, the truth of the fathers' and scholastics' indictment follows inescapably. The best that can be expected from sexual interaction even among devout spouses is that it will produce children, will stay within the marriage, will be rendered faithfully as a debt owed in justice to a genitally needy spouse, and (as Francis de Sales warned) neither spouse will become preoccupied with its pleasure.

But who is qualified to say which is the truer story? Hardly the men who can appraise them only from outside the experience. Only those experienced in sexual exchange within a context of total freedom and relaxation can report accurately on two issues: (1) which elements of life together can be included in the sexual exchange, which physical and which emotional elements; (2) which elements tend to bring happiness to the partners, to enrich their inclusive personal union as well as their relationships with their family, and thus create and sustain their sacrament.

We have seen repeatedly that a marriage is a sacrament because the spouses enter as spouses into Christ's work of redemption and thereby manifest his love for his people, the Church, and indeed for all people. The inescapable question asks how sexually expressed love takes part in this work, in this manifestation. One can be grateful that the Catholic answer to this question, while accepting as much truth as there is in the patristic and scholastic answer repeated just above, has moved beyond it. But in moving beyond it, it has moved into territory that is as yet barely explored by theologians and not at all by the Catholic authorities. It is territory that only the married can explore accurately.

Specifically it is the territory where passion and sin meet in a marriage. Passion in this case refers not to lust, not to genital urgency, not to romantic enthrallment. Its synonym is *eros* of classical Greek thought. It is, at bottom, the desire for life, the source of the struggle against death. It is a powerful desire for happiness in the experience of goodness and beauty. Augustine referred to it indirectly on the first page of his *Confessions:* "Thou hast made us for thyself, O Lord, and our hearts are restless until they rest in thee." For him it is the desire for God that leaves a person restless if it is settled on any creature, because only God can fulfill it. Only he can do this because he designed it into human beings as a desire for himself whereby he could draw them back to himself. Eros, passion, is the very soul of the Song of Solomon. The Song is meaningless without it. But the early Christian teachers feared and shunned it because the Greek tradition said that its best available satisfaction is in homosexual love. Perhaps Paul VI brought it back to life anonymously in Catholic teaching in the first part of his encyclical, *Humanae vitae.* There he set out his understanding of married love. He said it is a total love, one that involves all of a man and a woman; it draws them into a communion of their beings, leads to the fulfillment of themselves as persons.

This passion has in men and women many avenues it can use to express itself. It can do so in artistic activity, most especially, it seems, in great music and great drama. It can do so in physical combat. For some men it releases itself most fully when the combat is to death. When a man must kill lest he himself be killed, the passion to live can become a rage. It can be expressed in sexual intercourse, where it inspires our question.

How can this desire for union with God find him if it is expended in union with another human being, in physical and emotional union whose pleasure can be so self-enclosed, even solipsistic? For Christian spouses living the sacrament means engaging their marital love in Christ's redemptive work. How can they do this when this work took Christ to his death, then beyond death to resurrection; but their sexual expression first rebuffs death but then eventually gives in to it? It is difficult to imagine how any man or woman not thoroughly experienced in the sexual expression of passion could tell how this expression can be taken into Christ's redemptive work, as it must be if their marriage is to be a sacrament.

The Married in Christ's Redemptive Work

Spouses' joining in Christ's redemptive work, and doing so as spouses, is their joining in the task of taking sin out of the human race. I phrase it this way rather than "the task of forgiving sins" because this is the way the gospel states Christ's task: "Behold the lamb of God, the one who is *taking away the sin* of the world" (Jn 1:29). Because the noun is in the singular number (*hamartía*), the Baptist clearly refers to something other than the sins men and women commit, but which is yet sin.

The earliest Christian tradition—as early as the epistle to the Romans, Chapter 5—holds that this sin affects all human beings, and that it is in some way an effect and a replication of the primeval sin of the first man and woman in Eden. This is the rebellious will, the refusal to accept one's condition as God's creature, the demand for a false and disobedient freedom. Given that this interpretation of the sin is culturally conditioned, it may not dig deeply enough into the soul. Why else would

Jewish males in a patriarchal society have devised in Genesis a parable of rebellious wills unless they themselves had experienced rebellion against paternal authority in two forms—in their sons' and daughters', and wives', rebellion against them, and in their own remembered rebellion against their fathers?

Sin in its most fundamental and inclusive sense is that in human beings which most resists God's will for them. But since his will is to draw them into union with one another and with himself, rebellion is not the strongest and most lasting resistance to his drawing. Few men and women keep up rebellion all their lives. With most it lasts until they are convinced they have got their freedom from authority figures, or until they marry and find that this has neutered their careers as rebels, or until they have their own children and find themselves to be the authorities rebelled against. A deeper and longer-lasting resistance to trusting and loving union remains, and often grows even stronger with time and experience. This is fear, fear of the loss of self in some form.

Some men and women fear the loss of privacy—that they will have to tell their whole story to the one they want to love, the past along with the present. Some fear the loss of freedom, some the loss of a fragile pseudo-self. Some fear the loss at the core of love itself, that they will risk everything by fixing their passion on one person for a promised lifetime, but that the risk will prove fatal when passion is denied its fulfillment after too many years of futile trying, and it is too late to try again.

If this fear of the loss of self is what the sin of the world is at its core—is what most resists God's effort to draw human beings to himself, and resists human beings' efforts to draw one another into love—then Christ's redemptive work is to take away this fear of loss. Somehow he has to get men and women over this fear, has to get them to take the risk, to accept and act on the truth of his claim, "He who seeks his life will lose it. But he who loses his life for my sake, he will find it."

The question for Christian spouses asks how they can engage the sexual expression of their passion in this work of healing fear of loss in one another. Again the answer is the same question: Who else but men and women who have risked their passion in marriage, who have tried to take down protective barriers in their own souls and in their spouses', can say what sexual love may do to take away fear of the loss of privacy, of freedom, of self-regard, even fear of the loss of the one chance for happiness in intimate love?

Inclusion in Christ's Redemptive Work:
God's Initiative and Human Freedom

Certainly it is God who takes the initiative in drawing men and women into Christ's redemptive work. Taking it up supposes faith, which only he can give, as only he can inspire trust in the face of a most justified fear of failure.

God's formal and observable initiative in taking a person into this work is in baptism. This sacrament "takes away sin" by bringing the person to new birth in a community that seeks to take away fear of the loss of self by promising trust and caring friendship for the rest of the person's life. (To baptize but not provide this community is to contradict the meaning of baptism.) But baptism no more than brings the person into the community of Christ's work, and into no more demanding a status than that of a child who is to be given everything but of whom no more is expected than to accept what is given.

Confirmation is the observable step from this into adulthood in the Christian community. This sacrament is celebrated rightly when a Christian willingly accepts an active role in Christ's work, although in an as yet unspecified way. Here too the initiative is God's. He acts interiorly in the person's soul, and exteriorly through others in the community, to call the person to adult, caring work. But the call and the response in confirmation are significantly different from those in baptism. Here the one called cannot be passive, as a child can in baptism. He or she must respond with deliberation and decision.

To marry in the Christian sacrament is to take confirmation a step further, to make the response specific. The specificity here lies in a person's committing his or her sexuality to Christ's work. So the traditional theology is accurate to this point, that baptism must come first. A person must be taken into Christ's work in the Church. He or she must be empowered, strengthened by the Spirit in confirmation. But that theology stops too short. In its extreme form it stops far short in requiring for sacramental marriage no more than both spouses' baptism. This misunderstands both the marital component of the sacrament and the sacramental component of the marriage. It misunderstands the first because men and women cannot enter a marriage except by deliberate will. It misunderstands the second because they cannot take up Christ's work, and certainly cannot commit their sexuality to it, except by deliberate will.

There is a more nuanced form of this traditional theology. It says that in addition to their baptism the Christian spouses must first meet a negative requirement. They must not expressly reject the sacrament nor their Christian religion. The positive requirement is that in intending to marry they must intend what Christ and the Church intend for marriage. This names a minimal sufficient intention. With it the spouses enter a sacramental marriage even though they are religiously inactive and ignorant of or unconcerned about the sacrament.

This is a generous, sympathetic and faith-animated interpretation. It is generous and sympathetic because it wants to keep the sacrament in reach of as many Christians as possible. It is faith-animated because it insists on including in Christian religious function the invisible agency of God—the God who can do more in persons than human observation can detect. It rejects the reductionism one sometimes finds in contemporary

theology, the assumption that the only agency investigable and verifiable is the empiric, that human beings do it all in religious matters, or
that any other assumed agency is beyond knowing.

The weakness in this theology is its not giving their necessary places
to human will, freedom and action in the creating of the marital sacrament. To be most exact, it is doubtful that men's and women's understanding, intention and will act sufficiently to create the sacrament when
in marrying they intend and will in a general way no more than "what
Christ and the Church intend," while remaining religiously inactive and
ignorant of or unconcerned about the sacrament itself.

It seems to me that one reason for the traditional theologians' confidence that this intention to do what Christ and the Church do is enough
in addition to baptism to create a sacramental marriage is a too static
idea of incorporation into Christ's mystical body, of the spouses' being
taken into his redemptive mystery. The metaphor of the Church as the
body whose head is Christ lends itself to the static interpretation I have
in mind. In this metaphor the baptized are cells of this body, or even, in
Paul's expansion of it into an analogy in 1 Corinthians 12:12–30, the
various organs and limbs of the body. Let the analogy take over for the
reality in this theology and there is the temptation to conclude that the
body and all its organs and limbs act as one in unresisting and unthinking
obedience to the head. With this the body of Christ and its members
become the conceptual model that a theologian can design so readily,
and design to function according to his assumptions. In this model the
order that God has established in Christ consists of all parts integrated in
the body and functioning in obedient union with the head. Once a
person is taken into this "order" by baptism, he does what the head of
the body does even if he is unaware and unconcerned about it.

But there is an alternative vision of the order of participation in
Christ's redemptive work. It does not make the mistake of reifying the
analogy of head and body and substituting it for the reality. It cuts
through metaphors, through images, to existence and conditions of existence. It sees God as taking up the humanity of Christ as his instrument
to draw human beings to himself. He uses Christ's goodness and beauty
to draw them even as he acts interiorly in their souls to capacitate them
to respond. This is the sector of the order that is perfect because it is the
flawless union of a human will with God that is Christ's will. But there is
also a flawed and contingent sector of this order because it extends from
Christ to men and women. Like his their wills too are free. They can
resist and refuse to be drawn to God. Baptized Christians do this, those
already brought into beginning union with God. They can break off the
union or can refuse to let all of their persons and actions be drawn into
it. Or they can be ignorant of and unconcerned about God's different
ways of acting in them and drawing them within this order to himself.
One of these ways is through their marriage.

When Lehmann and Caffarra, in their commentaries on the theo-

logical commission's propositions, argue that the baptized can create
only a sacramental marriage because the only order in the human race is
that established by God in Christ, it seems to me that they reason in part
accurately, but in part inaccurately. They are accurate in their premise.
There is no other, no alternative order human beings can choose for
themselves, no order literally secular because God is not active in it,
because human beings have designed it and manage it independently of
him.

But their inaccuracy is to see this order as static, as a fixed structure
of categories. In this static order one of the categories is marriage—a
category available exclusively within this one divinely established order—
so that if a person chooses to enter marriage, he or she must enter this
category or forego marriage all together.

Even if they limit this structure of categories to the body of Christ,
and extend their claim no further than that the members of this body,
the baptized, can marry only within the body, only within a sacramental
marriage, their claim is undermined by the Church's own teaching and
practice. These acknowledge that if a baptized Catholic seeks to marry
an unbaptized person, he or she can do so, but their marriage is not a
sacrament because one of the spouses is unbaptized. (It is curious that
none of the commission's theologians in their commentaries and essays
take this kind of marriage into consideration.)

This theology's premise still holds in the man's case. He can marry
and has married only within the order of Christ's redemption. Even if he
could remove himself from it, he would not. He has married with Christian faith and love. He intends to do Christ's work in his marriage; he
hopes to bring his wife to the same faith and love. But this theology's
conclusion does not follow. He has created even within the order of
redemption a marriage that is not a Christian sacrament. Or more accurately, he has created a marriage that is inchoately a Christian sacrament
because it is the natural sacrament that the fathers, the medieval and
tridentine scholastics, and especially Schillebeeckx and Rahner have
insisted is found in every marriage created by genuine love—because
God lives and acts in all human beings and moves them to their love. If
this man's intention is realized, he and his wife will move gradually
toward and into the Christian sacrament. This will be made formal and
visible if his wife enters the Christian community by baptism.

As for baptized Christians, religiously inert, unaware of and unconcerned about the sacrament, because of this unawareness and unconcern
they cannot create a Christian sacramental marriage. They cannot create
it because, to say it again, this demands an aware commitment to
Christ's redemptive work. But they can still marry within this order, and
in something better than the merely psychological relationship to which
the Theological Commission limits them. They too can create the inchoate sacrament, the natural sacrament, if their love is truly marital. To
say that they can marry in less than the Christian sacrament one does not

have to postulate an alternative and secular order, provided one sees Christ's redemptive order not as a fixed structure of categories but as God acting in all human beings to draw them to himself. He acts in the religiously inert, keeps them in Christ's order. But they fail to respond because they are unaware of or are uninterested in him.

Forming Sacramental Indissolubility

If we understand the forming of the marital sacrament, and understand the sacrament itself, in this way, we can examine intelligibly the forming of a marriage's indissolubility (or, better said, its immunity to dissolution).

Just as not all spouses create the sacrament instantaneously by the same one act of consent that creates their marriage, and just as they do not consummate their sacramental marriage by a single intercourse, but *may* do the first gradually and *can* do the second only gradually, so they build immunity into their marriage only gradually.

The traditional Catholic doctrine itself holds to a gradual acquiring of indissolubility. Only when Christian spouses consummate their marriage as a sacrament does it acquire indissolubility. But the doctrine interprets this gradualness unrealistically. It sees the spouses passing through successive juridical categories until they enter finally the category that is the consummated sacramental marriage. Their minds and wills function to bring indissolubility into their marriage only by choosing to move from category to category. Indissolubility awaits in gradually "firmer" character in each succeeding category until they meet radically firm indissolubility in the last of them. (I obviously have in mind here spouses who would pass through the full succession of categories. They begin, because unbaptized, in a merely natural marriage. They consummate this marriage. Then, with the baptism of both of them, their marriage becomes a sacrament. Finally they consummate it again, but this time as a sacrament.)

The explanation of indissolubility's acquisition that is even older than that is only slightly more realistic, because a single act of intercourse that would complete the sacramental marriage as an image of Christ's relationship with the Church cannot be even a disposing cause of indissolubility. The reason why it cannot was made clear earlier in this chapter. An analogy consisting of Christ's metaphoric marriage with a metaphor of the Church cannot produce an ontological effect in an actual marriage. The sometimes alternative explanation that the single-act consummation finally disposes the marriage for God to make it indissoluble both begs the question and remains incomplete. It begs the question by assuming that only God is an immediate and positive cause of the indissolubility. It remains incomplete because we are searching not only for the causes of a marriage's indissolubility, but also for its nature and its locus in a marriage.

To consummate a marriage is not to enter a final marital category. It is to bring the marital relationship to its fullness. For two reasons this fullness is not a fixed and final point. First, the substance of a marital relationship is the spouses' caring love for one another. But such love has no fixed and final degree—unless perhaps it is the same degree to which Christ took his love by giving up his life. Second, for Christians the marital relationship is sacramental in that it participates in Christ's redemptive work. The only final form and degree conceivable for this work is also a replication of Christ's death. The move toward completion in both senses is always a process, a development that need end only with death.

What the spouses do if their marriage develops in this way is to move into gradually stronger union with God. There is a reciprocity in this: As they believe in and trust and love him more, he gradually strengthens their ability to do these. Thus a bond between him and them of faith, trust and love grows gradually stronger. But this reciprocity is not of the spouses singly with God. As their trust in and love of him grow, so do their trust and love of one another, and they come to believe in, trust and love him specifically as married to one another. He in turn acts within this, their marital union. In this way they can gradually form a union so strong that a conscious refusal on either spouse's part to believe in, trust and love one another and God becomes functionally impossible, however remotely possible it may remain in fact.

I use the term "conscious refusal" deliberately and carefully. One hears the plea to acknowledge that marriages can go out of existence by disintegrating. Assuming that this can happen, what may the negative dynamic of disintegration be? It is for psychology to find this out. But if we begin with the understanding that a marriage is a union of a man and a woman, a union whose roots are the abiding attitudes of trust and love in both, two dynamics of disintegration are imaginable. One is the conscious refusal mentioned just above. It is a deliberate refusal to trust and love any longer, a refusal whose repetition and prolongation eventually destroy the abiding attitude. That one or both spouses may be taken to the point of this refusal by external forces over which they have limited control does not take away the fact that the withdrawal of trust and love is deliberate. And the refusal need not be mutual. One spouse can decide for it and destroy the marriage. But there are spouses for whom such destroying is functionally impossible. Their marriages are indissoluble in the sense I intend here.

Indissolubility—or immunity to dissolution—is found realistically in a marriage wherein the spouses' union of trust and love has come to such strength that, as said above, functionally they could not deliberately destroy it. Final and absolute immunity to dissolution is a goal not attainable in this life. But it seems realistic to say that spouses can reach a point at which their faith is so clear that they could not judge any good attainable by rejecting their marriage and therefore Christ himself to be a more valuable good than their own union with the spouse and Christ. Therefore they could not choose that other good over this good. They would have consummated their marriage as a sacrament.

Can a sacramental marriage disintegrate indeliberately, against or at least apart from the wills of the spouses, for example as the casualty of mental or emotional deterioration? The key word in this question is "indeliberately." It keeps the distinction from disintegration in which emotional or mental deterioration in one spouse may bring the other to withdraw deliberately from the marriage. In the latter case there is justifiable suspicion that the other spouse's intention in marrying was from the beginning conditioned by the expectation of continued sound health. If this is true, the relationship has never been a sacramental marriage.

I do not think a sacramental marriage can deteriorate and go out of existence indeliberately. If it cannot, what can remain of it in a relationship wherein one spouse has sunk into psychosis, to cite a worst case? "A habit of the heart" can remain, aware and active in the healthy spouse, unaware and inactive in the ill spouse. Here the psychological evidence becomes intricate and elusive. But it seems realistic that where persons have developed habitual attitudes toward one another by repeated volitional acts, as spouses' love for one another must be developed if it is to be sacramental, the attitude can be destroyed only by repeated volitional acts that contradict this attitude. The habitual will for the other's well-being, which is the heart of marital love, can be destroyed only by the contradictory will to damage and even destroy the other's well-being. And this must be an informed will; it must be directed against the actual other spouse, not against a psychotic illusion of the other. The matter certainly needs psychological probing. The question asks: Behind the psychotic break-off from reality can an attitude of desire and will for the spouse's well-being, that had been years in the building and sustaining, still survive? I believe the burden of proof rests on those who claim it cannot.

Evidence of a Sacramental Marriage

Which traits must a marriage show in order to give evidence that it is a Christian sacrament? Two kinds of traits seem needed. The first of these are the formally religious; the others are the informally religious, those which earlier in this study were identified as the matrix of the sacrament. These traits fuse with the formally religious. At this point in our study none of them is unfamiliar. Those named here are intended as a minimum necessary.

Both spouses must love in a caring, self-giving way. Both must be capable of open and honest communication. Both must be reasonably adept at the bodily sexual manifestation of their love and must desire it. If they are fertile both must be accepting of children and capable of nurturing them. Their marriage must be helpful to those near to and touched by it. Both must be willing to work at sustaining their relationship, at defying the law of entropy in it. I add this perhaps curious trait because of the consequences for even a stable marriage wherein the partners fail to understand that it will not survive on its own, indeliberately, automatically—who fail to understand that boredom and disillusionment do not go away on their own, but have to be driven away constantly.

The formally religious traits are few but they are crucial. Both spouses must refer their persons and their marriage to God in some way that is both explicit and observable. They must pray in one or more of the several ways of prayer—in worship, in thanksgiving, in petition, in seeking for forgiveness.

This reference to God must be in and through Christ. He is God-among-us. For presumed Christians to ignore him is to ignore God's specific way of being present in their marriage. What is more, the union with Christ must be in Christian community, the Church, either in fact or in desire. Christian spouses cannot be religious in a wholly private way and have a sacramental marriage. This is true for a reason that has been made clear again and again in these chapters. A Christian sacrament is always in the Church, of the Church and for the Church as a community of believers. It is a participation in Christ's work in the world carried on by this community—the work that he wills it to carry on until the end of history. Christian husbands and wives participate sacramentally in this work when they make their sexually expressed love a visible part of this participation.

NOTES

1. Chapter 2, No. 8, in *The Documents of Vatican II,* p. 116.

2. I have already pointed out that this shift of argument began as long ago as Scheeben's *Mysterien des Christentums.* It is evident in Schillebeeckx's and Rahner's analyses of the sacrament we have just seen. In this chapter we will see how central it was to the Catholic Church's International Theological Commission in its study of marriage in 1977, as it was central to the 1980 Synod of Bishops and to Pope John Paul's *Familiaris consortio.*

3. The commission is not in itself an organ of the Church's teaching authority, its *magisterium,* as is the Congregation for the Doctrine of the Faith. It is a kind of subcommittee of the Congregation, an advisory group made up of specialists mainly in theology, but also in canon law and philosophy. The president of the commission in 1977, Cardinal Šeper, formed a subcommission to guide the work of the symposium and to prepare its results for publication. As the yield of its symposium the commission published, in 1979, the volume *Problèmes Doctrinaux du Mariage Chrétien,* as Number 4 in its series, *Lex Spiritus Vitae.*

4. *Problèmes Doctrinaux . . . ,* p. 28. The translation into English is my own.

5. Schillebeeckx notes four distinguishable variants in Judaeo-Christian tradition: (1) the parentally created marriage whose main goal was to continue and increase the family, but which must be dissolved if its sterility made this impossible; (2) the partnership in all of life defined by classic Roman law, from which the partners could withdraw by mutual consent; (3) the juridical bond created by the partners' contractual consent, a bond designed antecedently as indissoluble but nevertheless vulnerable to dissolution by Church authority; (4) finally the intimate partnership in life and love created by the partners' making gifts of their persons to one another—as described in *Gaudium et spes*, No. 48.

6. See her essay, "Community and Couple: Marital Commitment," in *Commitment to Partnership*, William P. Roberts, editor, Mahwah, 1987, pp. 86–89.

7. *Problèmes Doctrinaux* . . . , p. 65.

8. *Ibid.*, p. 66.

9. *Op. cit.*, pp. 32–33.

10. This analysis of Ephesians 5:21–33 is taken substantially, and in places bodily, from my essay.

11. Markus Barth makes this point in the following way in his exegesis of the Greek of verse 27: *hína parastésē autos heautô éndoxon tén ekklesían.* "The position of the adjective 'resplendent' (*éndoxon*) in the Greek text and the article before 'Church' (*tén ekklesían*) indicate that 'resplendent' has predicative force. That is, the Church as a bride is not always a virtuous and beautiful girl. But she is one who will be made wise and beautiful.

"In addition the change, in the same verse 27, from the participial construction describing the Church—*mē échousan spílon e hrutída*—to the finite subjunctive with *hína ē hagía kai ámomos* ('so that she may be holy and blameless') indicates that the Church is not already a bride spotless and unwrinkled, but one who will be made such. The reference here is to the eschatological future of the Church." (In *The Anchor Bible: Ephesians 4–6*. N.Y., 1974, p. 268)

12. *Problèmes Doctrinaux* . . . , p. 70.

13. *Ibid.*, p. 71.

14. *Ibid.*, p. 72.

15. *Ibid.*

16. *Ibid.*, p. 73.

17. *Ibid.*

18. *Ibid.*, p. 74.

19. *Op. cit.*, pp. 180–217.

20. *Loc. cit.*, pp. 183–184.

21. *Ibid.*, p. 191.

22. *Ibid.*, pp. 191–192.

23. *Ibid.*, pp. 192–194.

24. *Ibid.*, pp. 195–197.

25. *Ibid.*, pp. 197–198.

26. *Ibid.*, pp. 199–202.

27. *Ibid.*, pp. 204–205.

28. *Op. cit.*, pp. 77–78.

29. *Op. cit.*, p. 84.

30. *Ibid.*, pp. 85–86.

31. *Ibid.*, p. 88.

Proposition 3.6 reads as follows: "These considerations show the error and the danger of introducing certain practices. These consist of celebrating for the same couple several successive ceremonies in different degrees but linked internally. Furthermore, no priest or deacon is permitted to assist at such a non-sacramental marriage that baptized couples pretend to celebrate, or to offer their prayers at such a ceremony" (*ibid.*).

32. *Ibid.*, pp. 88–91.
33. *Op. cit.*, p. 100.
34. *Op. cit.*, p. 104.
35. Evidence of the doctrine and discipline of divorce during the first five Christian centuries is examined in such works as Henri Crouzel's *L'Église Primitive Face au Divorce;* Giovanni Cereti's *Divorzio, Nuove Nozze e Penitenza nella Chiesa Primitiva* (written in part as a challenge to some of Fr. Crouzel's interpretations of these centuries' evidence); and Volume 2 of this series, *Divorce and Remarriage,* Chapters 5, 6, 7, 8 and 9.
36. "Theological note" designates a proposition's doctrinal valence. Such notes are, for example, "solemnly defined *ex cathedra,*" "a truth of the Catholic faith," "common Catholic teaching." The kinds and degrees of assent required by the propositions are determined by their theological notes. The correlation of assents to those propositions whose theological notes are less valent than the first-named above is debated among Catholic theologians (as are the notes to be assigned to various propositions in Catholic teaching). But it seems self-evident that to propositions qualified to less valence than "solemnly defined *ex cathedra*" or "a truth of the Catholic faith," a correspondingly qualified assent is demanded.
37. *Op. cit.*, p. 107.
38. *Ibid.*, pp. 108–109.
39. *Op. cit.*, p. 113.
40. *Ibid.*, p. 109.
41. *Ibid.*, pp. 110–111.
42. *Op. cit.*, p. 186.
43. *Op. cit.*, p. 112.
44. *Op. cit.*, p. 190
45. *Op. cit.*, p. 113.
46. *Ibid.*, p. 115.
47. *Ibid.*, p. 116.

BIBLIOGRAPHY

Ashdowne, Michael: "The Sacramentality of Marriage: When Is Marriage Really Present? Future Dimensions," in *Studia Canonica*, Vol. 9 (1975), pp. 287–304.

Babos, Stephen: "Marriage as a Sacrament," in *Thought*, Vol. 58 (1983), pp. 5–17.

Cahill, Lisa Sowle: "Community and Couple: Parameters of Marital Commitment in Catholic Tradition," in *Commitment to Partnership: Explorations of the Theology of Marriage,* edited by William P. Roberts, Mahwah, N.J., Paulist Press, 1987.

Cooke, Bernard: "Indissolubility: Guiding Ideal or Existential Reality?" in *op. cit.*

Cuenin, W.: *The Marriage of Baptized Non-Believers*. Rome, Gregorian University Press, 1977.

Cunningham, Richard: "Marriage and the Nescient Catholic: Questions of Faith and Sacrament," in *Marriage Studies,* Volume II, edited by Thomas P. Doyle, O.P., Washington, D.C., Canon Law Society of America, 1982.

deNaurois, Louis: "Marriages of Baptized Persons Who Do Not Have the Faith," in *op. cit.*

Finn, Raymond C.: "Faith and the Sacrament of Marriage: General Conclusions from an Historical Study," in *Marriage Studies, op. cit.*

Kilmartin, Edward: "When Is Marriage a Sacrament?" in *Theological Studies,* Vol. 34 (1973), pp. 275–286.

LaDue, William: "Conjugal Love and the Juridical Structure of Christian Marriage," in *The Jurist,* Vol. 43 (1974), pp. 36–67.

Mackin, Theodore: "Ephesians 5:21–33 and Radical Indissolubility," in *Marriage Studies,* Volume III, edited by Thomas P. Doyle, O.P., pp. 1–45.

————: "How to Understand the Sacrament of Marriage," in *Commitment to Partnership: Explorations of the Theology of Marriage,* edited by William P. Roberts, Mahwah, N.J., Paulist Press, 1987.

Milhaven, John G.: "Conjugal Sexual Love and Contemporary Moral Theology," in *Theological Studies,* Vol. 35 (1974), pp. 692–710.

Malone, Richard and Connery, John R., editors: *Contemporary Perspectives on Christian Marriage:* Propositions and Papers from the International Theological Commission (translation of *Problèmes Doctrinaux du Mariage Chrétien*). Chicago, Loyola University Press, 1984.

Örsy, Ladislas: "Faith, Sacrament, Contract and Christian Marriage," in *Theological Studies,* Vol. 43 (1982), pp. 379–398.

————: "The Sacrament of Marriage in the New Code of Canon Law," in *Thought,* Vol. 58 (1983), pp. 35–44.

Wood, Susan: "The Marriage of Baptized Non-Believers: Faith, Contract and Sacrament," in *Theological Studies,* Vol. 48 (1987), pp. 279–301.

Index of Proper Names and Titles

Index of Titles [Published Works]

Scripture Index

700